"In his new translation of Bulgakov's *Lamb of God* Boris Jakim makes available to the English-language reader one of the most controversial works of Orthodox Christian theology ever written; he also makes a vital contribution to the creation of an Orthodox theological idiom in English. For both reasons this book will remain an irreplaceable resource for new work in theology."

— ROBERT BIRD
University of Chicago

THE LAMB OF GOD

Sergius Bulgakov

Translated by Boris Jakim

WILLIAM B. EERDMANS PUBLISHING COMPANY
GRAND RAPIDS, MICHIGAN / CAMBRIDGE, U.K.

Originally published 1933 under the title
Agnets Bozhyi by YMCA Press.

English Translation © 2008
Wm. B. Eerdmans Publishing Co.
All rights reserved

Published 2008 by
Wm. B. Eerdmans Publishing Co.
2140 Oak Industrial Drive N.E., Grand Rapids, Michigan 49505 /
P.O. Box 163, Cambridge CB3 9PU U.K.

Printed in the United States of America

14 13 12 11 10 09 08   7 6 5 4 3 2 1

Library of Congress Cataloging-in-Publication Data

Bulgakov, Sergei Nikolaevich, 1871-1944.
[Agnets Bozhyi. English]
The Lamb of God / Sergius Bulgakov; translated by Boris Jakim.
p.   cm.
ISBN 978-0-8028-2779-1 (pbk.: alk. paper)
1. Jesus Christ — Person and offices. 2. Incarnation. I. Title.

BT203.B8513 2008
232'.8 — dc22

2007032191

www.eerdmans.com

Contents

Translator's Acknowledgment	vii
Translator's Introduction	viii
Author's Preface	xiii
INTRODUCTION: The Dialectic of the Idea of Divine-Humanity in the Patristic Epoch	1
I. The Problem of Christology, with Particular Reference to Apollinarius of Laodicea	2
II. The Antinomy of Bi-unity in Christology	19
III. The Chalcedonian Synthesis	51
IV. The Dogma of Two Wills in Christ	74
1. The Divine Sophia	89
I. The Creaturely Spirit	89
II. The Divine Spirit	94
III. The Divine World	101
IV. The Divine Sophia	107
2. The Creaturely Sophia	119
I. The Creation of the World	119
II. Eternity and Time	131

	III. Man	136
	IV. Image and Likeness	140
3.	The Incarnation	157
	I. God and the World	157
	II. The Foundations of the Incarnation	168
	III. The Divine-Humanity	182
	IV. Two Natures in Christ: The Divine Sophia and the Creaturely Sophia	193
4.	Emmanuel, the God-Man	213
	I. The Humiliation of the Lord (the Kenosis)	213
	II. The Union of the Essences (the Communication of the Properties and the Theandric Action)	247
	III. Christ's Divine-Human Consciousness of Self	261
5.	The Work of Christ	321
	I. Christ's Prophetic Ministry	321
	II. The High-Priestly Ministry of Christ	333
	III. The Royal Ministry of Christ	410
	APPENDIX: The Lamb of God: On Divine-Humanity, Part I, *Summary prepared by Sergius Bulgakov*	443
	Index	449

Translator's Acknowledgment

I wish to express my heartfelt gratitude to my dear friend William B. Eerdmans Jr., the director of Eerdmans Publishers. It was his idea to publish a series of books of Russian theology in translation ("the Russian front," he calls it), and without his enthusiasm Bulgakov's great trilogy (completed with this volume) would never have achieved its English-language incarnation.

Translator's Introduction

I

The present volume[1] is one of the greatest twentieth-century works of Christology and, in my opinion, represents that century's crowning achievement in the theology of Divine-Humanity. The idea of Divine-Humanity had its origin in patristic times (Pseudo-Dionysius, Maximus, John of Damascus, et al.) and was rediscovered in the nineteenth century by Vladimir Solovyov.[2] This idea follows from the Definition of Chalcedon[3] and signifies that Christ has two natures (divine and human) in the case of one hypostasis; and this hypostasis is the Second Person of the Holy Trinity, the Logos: "In Christ's Divine-Humanity we have two distinct natures, united without separation in one hypostasis, but with each preserving its autonomous being."[4] This idea also signifies that all human beings participate, at least potentially, in the Divine-Humanity; that, individually, we are god-men, and that, collectively, we are the divine-humankind.

---

1. This volume on Christology completes the great trilogy *On Divine Humanity*. It is actually volume 1 of the trilogy; the other two volumes deal with Divine-Humanity in the domains of pneumatology and ecclesiology.

2. See Vladimir Solovyov, *Lectures on Divine Humanity*, revised and edited by Boris Jakim (Hudson, N.Y.: Lindisfarne, 1995).

3. Here is a key passage from the Creed of Chalcedon: "We ... teach men to confess one and the same Son, our Lord Jesus Christ, the same perfect in Divinity and also perfect in humanity; truly God and truly man ... ; consubstantial with the Father according to the Divinity, and consubstantial with us according to the Humanity...."

4. See p. 183 of the present volume.

According to Bulgakov, the precondition for the Incarnation is the original identity between the Divine "I" of the Logos and the human "I," an identity that does not exclude an essential difference between them. This identity consists in the relation of the image to the Proto-Image. The human hypostatic spirit has an uncreated divine origin from God's breath. Through his spirit, man communes with the divine essence and is capable of being deified. Man is not only man, but also — potentially — a god-man. Bulgakov writes that "man consists of an uncreated, divine spirit . . . and of a created soul and body. This humanity of his has, in its cosmic being, the image of the creaturely Sophia; and he himself therefore contains the creaturely Sophia, who is hypostatized in him. As a result, he is the sophianic hypostasis of the world."[5] Man is in a fallen state and needs to be restored. He is called to surpass himself in the God-Man: "Man bears within himself the coming Christ; and prior to Christ's coming man does not have the power to become himself (i.e., true man) or to realize in himself the new spiritual birth that is not of flesh and blood, but of God."[6]

The divine-humanity of every human being is guaranteed by the fact that Christ is Divine-Human. The Logos is the pre-eternal God-Man as the Proto-Image of creaturely man. "The Logos is the demiurgic hypostasis whose face is imprinted in the Divine world as in the Divine Sophia, by the self-revelation of Divinity through the Logos."[7] There is a mediating principle that serves as the foundation for the two natures, divine and human, in Christ; this principle is "the *sophianicity* of both the Divine world, that is, of Christ's divine nature, and of the creaturely world, that is, of His human nature."[8] Christ manifests the hypostatic image of the Divine Sophia; and "precisely as the hypostatic Sophia, He unites in the unity of His two natures the Divine Sophia, as His Divinity, and the creaturely Sophia, as His humanity."[9]

---

5. See pp. 186-87 of the present volume. Bulgakov's doctrine as developed in the trilogy *On Divine Humanity*, as well as elsewhere, is a sophiological one. In fact, the general title of the trilogy in the French translation (a title that was approved by Bulgakov) is *La Sagesse divine et la Théanthropie* (Divine Wisdom and Divine Humanity). The present volume, along with volume 3 of this trilogy, *The Bride of the Lamb* (Eerdmans, 2002), represents the culmination of Bulgakov's doctrine of the Divine and creaturely Sophia.

6. See p. 187 of the present volume.
7. See p. 187 of the present volume.
8. See p. 187 of the present volume.
9. See p. 203 of the present volume.

Translator's Introduction

2

Father Sergius Bulgakov (1871-1944) was the twentieth century's most profound Orthodox systematic theologian. Born into the family of a poor provincial priest, Bulgakov had a strict religious upbringing and entered the seminary at a young age. But owing to a spiritual crisis in the direction of materialism and atheism, he did not complete his seminary studies. He chose instead to follow a secular course of study, which led to his matriculation at the University of Moscow, where he specialized in political economics.

This marked the beginning of his relatively short-lived Marxist period. In 1901, after which he defended his master's thesis, "Capitalism and Agriculture" (1900), he was appointed professor of political economy at the Polytechnical Institute of Kiev. During his years there (1901-6), he underwent a second spiritual crisis, this time in the direction of idealist philosophy and the religion of his youth.

Influenced first by the philosophies of Kant and Vladimir Solovyov, and then by the great Orthodox theologian Pavel Florensky, Bulgakov gradually began to articulate his own original sophiological conception of philosophy. This conception was first elaborated in his *Philosophy of Economy*, for which he received his doctorate from the University of Moscow in 1912. Later, in *The Unfading Light* (1917), he gave his sophiological ideas definite philosophical shape. Following this, Bulgakov's intellectual output was, for the most part, theological in character. Indeed, his personal religious consciousness flowered in the following year, and he accepted the call to the priesthood, receiving ordination in 1918.

These years of internal crisis and growth in Bulgakov's personal life paralleled the tumultuous period in Russian political and social life that climaxed in the October Revolution of 1917 and the subsequent Bolshevik ascendancy. In 1918 Bulgakov left Moscow for the Crimea to assume a professorship at the University of Simferopol. But his tenure was short-lived, owing to Lenin's banishment in 1922 of more than 100 scholars and writers deemed incurably out of step with the official ideology.

Bulgakov left the Soviet Union on January 1, 1923, alighting first in Constantinople and then in Prague. Finally, having accepted Metropolitan Eulogius's invitation both to become the dean of the newly established Saint Sergius Theological Institute and to occupy the chair of dogmatic theology, he settled in Paris in 1925. Here, until his death in 1944, he would make his most fruitful and lasting contributions to Orthodox thought.

Translator's Introduction

During the theologically most productive period of his life, Bulgakov produced six books, grouped into two trilogies. The works of the so-called little trilogy — *The Friend of the Bridegroom* (1927),[10] *The Burning Bush* (1927), and *Jacob's Ladder* (1929) — are efforts to capture the glory, the uncreated light, streaming from John the Baptist, the Mother of God, and the holy angels. The great trilogy, *On Divine Humanity*, consists of volumes on Christology (*The Lamb of God*, 1933), pneumatology (*The Comforter*, 1936),[11] and ecclesiology and eschatology (*The Bride of the Lamb*, published posthumuously, 1945).[12]

3

In *The Lamb of God*, Bulgakov first reviews the patristic doctrines of Christology, with particular reference to early thought on Divine-Humanity; he then examines the achievements of the Chalcedonian dogmatic synthesis. He subsequently elaborates his own doctrine of the Divine-Humanity. In the middle sections he considers the roles of the Divine Sophia and the creaturely Sophia, examines the foundations of the Incarnation, and explores the nature of Christ's divine consciousness. The final chapter deals with Christ's ministries — prophetic, high-priestly, and royal.[13]

Especially profound and fruitful is Bulgakov's discussion of Christ's kenosis, which should serve as a model for every human being who is trying to realize his own divine-humanity. Of key importance for Bulgakov here is Philippians 2:6-8, where Christ is described as taking on the form of a servant and humbling Himself. Bulgakov writes that "this passage talks about not only an earthly event occurring within the limits of human life but also about a heavenly event occurring in the depths of Divinity itself: the kenosis of God the Word."[14] In the kenosis, God renounces Himself, empties Himself, and takes on the form of a servant. This path of kenosis culminated with His death on the cross, whereby He manifested

---

10. *The Friend of the Bridegroom* has been published by Eerdmans (2003) in Boris Jakim's translation.

11. *The Comforter* has been published by Eerdmans (2004) in Boris Jakim's translation.

12. *The Bride of the Lamb* has been published by Eerdmans (2002) in Boris Jakim's translation.

13. The appendix to the present volume contains a summary of the contents of *The Lamb of God*, provided by Bulgakov himself.

14. See p. 215 of the present volume.

Translator's Introduction

His complete obedience to the Father's will. Bulgakov writes that "in the Cross of the earthly path is realized the Cross of the heavenly kenosis."[15] But this passage concludes with testimony about the heavenly glorification of Christ (Phil. 2:9-10): kenosis leads to glory.

*   *   *

I have eliminated or shortened some of Bulgakov's notes, which tend to be over-detailed and sometimes arcane. Throughout the text Bulgakov refers to a number of his own works; I give the full bibliographic citation only the first time the work is mentioned. I have used the King James Version (KJV) of the Bible, since I consider it to be the English-language version that most closely approaches the beauty of the Russian Bible. I have sometimes modified the KJV to make it conform with the Russian Bible.

Here and there, in untwisting some difficult passages, I have relied on the excellent translation into French by Constatin Andronikof: *Du Verbe incarne: L'Agneau de Dieu*, 2nd ed. (Lausanne: Editions L'Age d'Homme, 1982).

---

15. See p. 217 of the present volume.

Author's Preface

And the Spirit and the bride say, Come. And let him that heareth say, Come.

Rev. 22:17

What can I say about the theme, aspiration, and heart of this book? What can I say about Christ's Divine-Humanity and about our divine-humanity? The salvation effected by Christ is accomplished in the individual soul, which is more precious than the world. And the path of the individual soul consists in the feat of the struggle against sin, against the tragic rupture in the soul of fallen man. Its path consists in subjugating the flesh to the spirit and in taking up Christ's cross. This indisputable truth abides at the center of Christian life, and we are clearly conscious of it.

But far from sufficiently understood is another aspect of the truth about salvation: salvation is not only personal and individual but also universal and omni-ecclesial. This is the truth about the reign of Christ in the world. The revolt of the kings and people of the earth against their Lord and Christ began long ago. In essence, this revolt dates from the very beginning of the Church; it did not immediately flare up into an open revolution, however, but by clever and sinuous wiles it tried to diminish, limit, usurp, and make impotent the coming of God in the flesh. This revolt tried to abolish the Divine-Humanity. Its aim was to enable the prince of this world to keep the world in his hands. Docetism and gnosticism, manicheanism and transcendentism, Hinduism and Jesuitism, and so on, a great multitude of conscious and half-conscious opponents of the Divine-Humanity — in the name of gnosis, piety, asceticism, moralism, spiritualism — have sought and still seek to abolish the power of the Divine-Humanity, to disincarnate the Logos. We can add to this the envious, theomachic, Antichrist-like divinization of man, which seeks to supplant the Divine-Humanity: the man-god seeks to supplant the God-Man. And this varied army of enemies that serves the Antichrist has succeeded in confounding and frightening humanity, in convincing it that Christ has abandoned the world and that His Kingdom, which is not of this world, will never be realized in this world. Compelled to adapt ourselves to this fact, our only recourse appears to be to diminish our goals, to accept signs as accomplishments, to resign ourselves to half-measures and incongruities, or simply to flee — in fact or in spirit, ascetically or theologically — from this world into the desert of nihilism, of indifference, and of contempt; for the world exists only to be rejected ascetically, to be relegated to fire.

A question slithers like a serpent over the earth: Whose world is it, the God-Man's or the man-god's, Christ's or the Antichrist's? Is it really true that Christ came to save the world and that the prince of this world has been expelled, that we are now witnessing the "last times" and the final convulsions of Satan, who is in an agony of frenzy, for he knows that the last times have arrived for him? This blasphemous question of semifaith receives the theomachic answer of rebellion against holiness: the war of the beast and the false prophet, Gog and Magog, surrounding the camp of the saints and stamping their mark on people by seduction and terror, the mark without which "no man might buy or sell" (Rev. 13:17), without which no man can find a place for himself on earth. And the entire power of evil, heresy, and unbelief is concentrated now around this lie, which serves as the stronghold of the rebels: the world is not Christ's, but our own!

In the hearts of those in whom the reigning lie has not completely destroyed the faith in Christ, who will come in glory and power, there resounds with unceasing pain the question: "Who shall roll us away the stone from the door of the sepulchre? . . . it was very great" (Mark 16:3-4). But "all things are possible to him that believeth" (9:23), and belief knows that the Divine-Humanity is God's Miracle in the world and that the angel will move the stone by God's power. And John, the Seer of Mysteries, to whom was revealed what was soon to happen, saw how in heaven the seven-horned Lamb, standing atop the mountain and as if slain, was worshipped, for He was "worthy . . . to receive power, and riches, and wisdom, and strength, and honour, and glory, and blessing" (Rev. 5:12), and "the kingdoms of this world are become the kingdoms of . . . Christ" (11:15), "the prince of the kings of the earth" (1:5), with His "kings and priests" (5:10).

In Christianity is born the new sense of life that one should not flee the world but that Christ is coming into the world for the marriage feast of the Lamb, the feast of Divine-Humanity — as the King and therefore as the Judge. In the battle for the Kingdom of Christ the faithful turn toward the coming Christ; their hearts are inclined toward Him in their expectation of Him, and one begins to hear the still timid refrain of the nearly forgotten ancient Christian prayer: "Even so, come." In the heresy concerning the world, in their disbelief in Christ's royal ministry, Christians have forgotten this prayer, for it had led them into fear, but fear is vanquished by love. This prayer remains the paschal hymn of Christ's humanity, however, for Christ is the King coming in the name of the Lord.

> Arise, O God, judge the earth: for thou shalt inherit all nations.
> God standeth in the congregation of the mighty: he judgeth among the gods.
> The foundations of the earth are out of course.
> I have said: Ye are gods; and all of you are children of the most High.
>
> hymns of Holy Saturday (cf. Ps. 82)

Paris, St. Sergius Theological Institute
30 September 1933

INTRODUCTION

The Dialectic of the Idea of Divine-Humanity in the Patristic Epoch

Christology is the main theme of patristic theology in the fourth to fifth centuries. The fruits of this theological thought were the christological definitions of the Third, Fourth, Fifth, and Sixth Ecumenical Councils. In schematic formulas obligatory for all Christians, these councils expressed the fundamental conclusions of this theological thought, although, to be sure, they did so in the language and concepts of the time. In order to understand their *dogmatic* content it is necessary to know the problematic and doctrines that these definitions had in view, as well as the meaning that was attached then to the dogmatic terms they employed. It is thus necessary to consider the *theology* of this epoch, which had numerous brilliant representatives. Their historical destinies differed: some are honored as doctors of the Church, while others are anathematized as heretics. The historian knows to what degree these characterizations represent a mixture of essential elements with accidental and even dubious ones. But one thing remains indisputable: all of these authors, irrespective of their destinies in the Church, were accomplishing a single common task, the task of creating the theology of the epoch; and their influence upon one another was so great that it is impossible to understand the theological doctrines or the council definitions without taking into account this unity and interconnectedness.

This simple idea has had the practical consequence that modern scholars (Bauer, Dorner, Harnack, Loofs, Seeberg, Schwane, Tixeront, Holl, et al.) have studied the theology of this epoch as a "history of dogmas," focusing on the immanent development of theological ideas irrespective of whether they were enunciated by heretics or by orthodox theologians. This historical research in the field of dogmatics deserves much credit for providing an understanding of the true development of the theology of the epoch. In its inquiry into the historical dialectic of ideas, this scholarship has prepared the ground for modern theology with its particular tasks. However, owing to its indifference to dogma and to its historical relativism, this scholarship is devoid of positive theological interest. Its direct influence on the dogmatic consciousness has been essentially negative: it led to the adogmatic skepticism that characterized Protestantism at the end of the nineteenth century. (Catholic scholarship does not play the leading role here.)

The time has now come for an *Orthodox* interpretation of the history of dogmas in the form of a dogmatic dialectic in which the Church truth is revealed for theological thought. And this is true, first of all, for Christology. To be sure, in examining this dialectic we will, above all, consider the authors of different doctrines as *theologians* who express a specific dogmatic idea. And only in the final analysis, in the light of the Church's supreme judgment, will we be able to decide whether these ideas are true or whether they are one-sided assertions *(hairesis),* which become erroneous when they are presented as certain and indisputable.

I. The Problem of Christology, with Particular Reference to Apollinarius of Laodicea

Despite the personal authority of Apollinarius as bishop and theologian, his doctrine was condemned by the Church at two local councils and at the Second Ecumenical Council, in 381 (it is true that it was condemned in a general way, being cited among a number of false doctrines). This is probably why no authentic complete works by this productive and learned writer have been preserved, and we must content ourselves with fragments or pseudonymous writings, painstakingly collected by modern scholars.[1] But even on the basis of these fragments one cannot deny that Apollinarius had a great theological gift, combined with literary talent.

---

1. Cf. J. Dräseke, *Apollinarios von Laodicea. Sein Leben und seine Schriften* (Leipzig, 1892; hereafter Dräseke); and the later, more precise investigation of H. Lietzmann, *Apollinarius von Laodicea und seine Schule,* vol. 1 (Tübingen, 1904; hereafter Lietzmann). Of the patristic works that contain fragments of Apollinarius, the most important are St. Gregory of Nyssa's *Antirrheticus contra Apollinarium* (PG 45), St. Gregory the Theologian's letter to Nectarius and Cledonius (PG 100, 102, 202), and Theodoret's *Eranistes* (PG 83). [In these notes, PG and PL refer to J.-Paul Migne's *Patrologia Graeca* and *Patrologia Latina.* — Trans.]

The Dialectic of the Idea of Divine-Humanity in the Patristic Epoch

He is indisputably one of the brightest stars in the brilliant theological constellation of the fourth century, and the magnitude of this star becomes even greater when he is compared with his critics. In the history of dogma, Apollinarius was the first to pose the problem of divine-humanity, or the so-called christological problem, and he put the stamp of his thought on the entire Christology of the Church. This defines his exclusive significance in the development of the dogmas: it was precisely he who identified the distinctive features of the *problematic* of Christology. It is therefore natural that his problematic should define the entire path followed by the theological thought of the epoch of the four ecumenical councils devoted to Christology. One could say that the theological thought of that epoch originates in his problematic.

The christological problem concerning the interrelation between the divine and the human in the God-Man naturally came to the fore as soon as the Arian disputes ended with the Nicene victory and the truth of the consubstantiality of the Father and the Son was affirmed. St. Athanasius the Great had prepared the path for his friend and ally Apollinarius. The theological thought of the early centuries of Christianity remained satisfied with the most general notion of the union of the Divine and the human in Christ.[2] For this thought, the essential element is the soteriological one: God assumed the whole man in order to save and deify him. This is the dominant theme of St. Irenaeus ("the Athanasius of the second century") and of St. Athanasius the Great himself. The union itself is usually characterized as the assumption of the flesh or the physical union of two different natures, and the question concerning the mode and meaning of this union is not yet posed.

Here one must take into account the total absence of an appropriate theological terminology, a circumstance that played such an enormous role in the history of the christological disputes. One can say that the terminology was created in the very process of the disputation, by means of constant misunderstandings. The trinitarian-homoousian debates introduced various nonbiblical terms into the theological language, such as *ousia, phusis, hupostasis,* and *prosōpon;* however, even in this domain an exact usage of these words was not established until the second half of the fourth century (it is sufficient to remember that, even in the anathemas of the Nicene Council, the terms *ousia* and *hypostasis* are still used synonymously). For want of anything better, this imprecise trinitarian terminology was transported into the domain of Christology,

---

2. Cf. R. Seeberg, *Lehrbuch der Dogmengeschichte,* vol. 2, 2d ed. (Leipzig, 1910).

Introduction

where its insufficiency became evident. One can say that christological theology functioned *without* a terminology, as if in semidarkness. Instead of being equipped with precise logical instruments, it operated, as it were, with clumsy stone blocks. For this reason the theologians had great difficulty in understanding one another, and if the Spirit of God enabled the Church to achieve its dogmatic definitions with even these means, this happened despite the imperfection of the logical instruments, which imperfection was reflected in the definitions themselves. This does not diminish the passionate and intense character of the theological thought itself. But the latter is expressed descriptively rather than in precise concepts, which led, of course, to an unnecessary expenditure of intellectual energy and to dogmatic misunderstandings.

Apollinarius was the first to consider a fundamental problem of Christology: What is the Divine-Humanity? Or, how is the Incarnation possible? What does it presuppose? Apollinarius went beyond the naive physical notions of his predecessors, who were satisfied with the soteriological postulates of the Incarnation and the affirmation of the fact of the latter. He began to analyze this fact, and from this analysis, Christology was born.

Apollinarius's doctrine already presupposes the rejection of the false doctrines that sought to abolish the very fact of the Incarnation. On the one hand, there was the doctrine of the Ebionites, revived by Paul of Samosata: Christ is considered a mere man, similar to the prophets, although the greatest of them — a man full of grace, whose sole virtue was that God's grace or wisdom reposed upon him. By contrast, Apollinarius firmly confesses that Christ is "the perfect Son of God."[3] On the other hand, the reality of the Incarnation was denied by docetism, which transformed the body of the Lord into a phantom and an appearance, even if of heavenly origin (in the case of the gnostics). Apollinarius confesses the reality of the Incarnation, that God truly received earthly human flesh from the Virgin Mary, whom he therefore calls the Theotokos, the God-bearer.[4]

Thus, according to the orthodox doctrine, in Christ we have the union of true divinity and true humanity. How are they interrelated? This funda-

---

3. *Detailed Profession of Faith to kata meros pistis;* Dräseke, 376.22.

4. "We confess that the Son of God truly became the son of man, not in name only but in truth, having received the flesh from the Virgin Mary" (ibid.); "The one hypostasis and the one person of God the Word, of Mary by the flesh, of God and of the woman" (*Ap. Encyclion*, Dräseke, 399.2-3).

mental christological question was crucial for Apollinarius's doctrine. His starting point here is the orthodox teaching that denies the duality of personal principles in the God-Man, a duality that was asserted in the school of Antioch, notably by Diodore and Theodore of Mopsuestia, and that later received its final expression in Nestorianism: "Not two sons: one Son — the Son of God, the true God and venerated.... We affirm that one Son of God and God, one and the same and not another one, was born of the Virgin Mary."[5] "I believe ... in the descent from heaven and the incarnation from the Virgin Mary and the appearance amongst people of God the Word and our Savior Jesus Christ, of the existent God and man Himself, not other as God and not other as man, but one hypostasis and one person of God the Word and of flesh from Mary — from God and the woman."[6] "God ... is not two persons, as if one were God and the other man."[7] How are *two* natures, divine and human, united in this *one* person of Christ?

Apollinarius's doctrine contains here a general premise that is, as it were, the initial axiom of the christological deduction. Let us add that this premise was later adopted (although in a different and more precise formulation) by orthodox Christology and, in particular, served as the basis of the Chalcedonian dogma. This is the axiom: *duo teleia hen genesthai ou dunatai* (two perfect [complete] principles cannot become one). Apollinarius also applies this abstract proposition to the Incarnation: "If the perfect man were united with the perfect God, there would be two: one, the Son of God by nature; the other, by adoption."[8] Apollinarius confirms this proposition by a particular argument based on the inequality of the two natures: the divine nature is unchangeable *(atreptos)*, whereas the human nature, as a result of the freedom proper to it, is changeable *(treptos)*. Therefore, the work of our salvation would not be certain if it were entrusted to the changeable human nature.[9] The latter must therefore be subjugated, made subordinate to the divine nature; it must become an instrument or receptacle for the divine nature, and therefore it cannot be perfect, that is, complete.[10]

---

5. The Epistle to Jovian (Dräseke, 341.27-29).

6. *Ap. Encyclion* (Dräseke, 398.24-399.3; Lietzmann, fr. 21).

7. *Antirrheticus contra Apollinarium* 56 (Dräseke, 392.5-6).

8. Ibid., 39 (Dräseke, 388.35-38).

9. "He received not a human mind, changeable and tempted by impure thoughts, but the divine mind, unchangeable and heavenly" (*Ad Diocaesar.* 2, Dräseke, 393.8-10). Cf. "The Epistle to Julian" (Dräseke, 400.14-18).

10. "The one essence would have been that of the Word and the instrument" (Dräseke, 363.23). Cf. Lietzmann, fr. 107.

Introduction

But this particular soteriological argument does not, of course, exhaust Apollinarius's general idea that the union of two perfect natures in Christ is impossible. In and of itself, this argument constitutes the weak side of his Christology, because it rejects human freedom. And the changeability of the creaturely nature, which in Adam led to the Fall, is transformed by Apollinarius into the inevitability and necessity of the Fall for man. Apollinarius thereby annuls and devalues the *human* feat of Christ, the feat of the obedience of the New Adam to the will of the Father; he thus opens the door to monophysitism with its mechanical conception of salvation by the Divine power acting as a *deus ex machina*.

However, Apollinarius's fundamental idea that the union of "two perfect" beings (i.e., of two beings self-sufficient in their fullness) is impossible has not only a soteriological significance but primarily an ontological one: union is *not* realized in the case of the duality of the natures in their fullness. "It is impossible for two principles with intelligence and volition to be united into one principle" (L., fr. 2). And "the true incorporeal God, who came in the flesh and is perfect with true and divine perfection, is not two persons and not two natures, for we do not teach men to venerate four: God and the Son of God, and man, and the Spirit."[11] If man in the fullness of his parts is united with God, this will be "not man, but a man-god."[12] Apollinarius rejects the union of two *(sunapheia)*, of "man united with God"; instead, he confesses "the incarnate God."[13] This union must be not a simple conjunction of two, but their true unity: "the mixing [*mixis*] of God and man,"[14] "mixing [*sunkrasis*] or unity."[15] "The essences of God and of man are not distinct from one another; rather, they have one essence in conformity with the union [*sunthesin*] of God with the human body."[16] Given the imprecision of the terminology of this epoch, the character of this union is expressed in the patristic writings by a number of descriptive terms: composition, mixing, union, and so on. And the body is sometimes defined as the instrument of the soul[17] or even as its temple.[18]

---

11. *Fidei expositio* (Dräseke, 377.7-10).
12. *Antirrheticus contra Apollinarium* (Dräseke, 390.32-33).
13. *Fidei expositio* (Dräseke, 377.1).
14. *Syllog.* (Dräseke, 352.11).
15. *In div. incarn. adv.* (Dräseke, 396.25-26).
16. *Ad Heracl.* (Dräseke, 363.22-23; Lietzmann, fr. 119).
17. "Having assumed the instrument [*organon*], God is God according to energy and man according to this instrument.... If one energy, then also one essence is proper to the Word and to the instrument" (Lietzmann, fr. 117).
18. Ibid., fr. 2.

The Dialectic of the Idea of Divine-Humanity in the Patristic Epoch

The fundamental difficulty of Christology and its central problem are clearly manifested here: How can one understand the *union* of the divine essence and the human essence in the God-Man without transforming this union into a duality, into nothing more than a certain harmonization (which is the conception of the school of Antioch)? In other words, how can one assure their real unification while preserving the authenticity and autonomy of each of the essences without the absorption of the one by the other (which is the conception of monophysitism)? Apollinarius's posing of this problem gives him his exceptional importance in Christian theology. Naturally, even his powerful intellect was not yet capable of solving this problem, but by formulating and analyzing it, he prepared the way for the future solution.

In attempting to answer the fundamental question of how the unity in Christ would be guaranteed, given the duality of the natures, Apollinarius affirmed that the God-Man is a unitary but *complex* being, a "complex hypostasis" (according to the later terminology of Leontius of Byzantium and St. John of Damascus). But how can one define this complexity? This serves as the starting point of Apollinarius's own doctrine, which provoked much misunderstanding among his contemporaries and, evidently, was not fully understood by his critics. In any case, Apollinarius's conception of the *unity* of the personality in the God-Man is a perfectly orthodox, Chalcedonian idea. However, one must not forget that Apollinarius expresses his thought with a totally different terminology, or even without any terminology. He expresses it descriptively, and he does so not in ontological concepts (hypostasis, ousia or nature) as in the Chalcedonian definition, but in anthropological concepts (which inevitably merge with psychological ones).

Apollinarius's question about the God-Man belongs not to the theological but to the anthropological domain: What is the human composition of the God-Man as man, since He is also truly man? Apollinarius arrives at the same conclusion as the Church: in the God-Man, man cannot be like every man, an individual among others. There is a certain complexity and a certain distinction in the God-Man's composition. The doctrine of the Church expresses this idea by the concept of the hypostatic union of the two natures in Christ *(unio hypostatica)*. To describe this, patristic theology developed the concept of *en-hypostasis*, the in-hypostatization of the human essence in the divine hypostasis (see pp. 64-74 below). According to this concept, the human nature is, in a certain sense, incompletely present in Christ; it is deprived of its proper human hypostasis. This is what constitutes the power of the dogma of the God-Man: the human nature is assumed fully. Lacking an appropriate terminology, Apollinarius expresses this general idea using unclear and imprecise anthropological notions, and the entire attention of his critics was therefore diverted from his central idea to its particular expression. As a result, Apollinarius was not understood by his contemporaries. In history his name is associated solely with a strange and obscure psychological theory of the human essence of Christ.

Let us try to expound this theory. The point of departure for Apollinarius (as it was earlier for St. Irenaeus and St. Athanasius and would be later for St. Cyril of Alexandria and the whole of monophysitism) is John 1:14: *kai o logos sarx egeneto*, "and the Word was made [or became] flesh." What meaning can we attach to this becoming (genesis) of the Word, who in Himself possesses divine unchangeability but who assumes flesh, "becomes incarnate and is in-humanized" (these two notions being equated according to the Nicene Creed)? The flesh denotes the body and thus refers to man's creaturely corporeality, which is opposed to the noncreaturely spirituality of Divinity. The in-humanization is thus defined, first of all, as the assumption of the *body*. We find this doctrine in particular in St. Athanasius:[19] to express the doctrine of the Incarnation (*sarkōsis*), he is content to use the notions of *sōma* (body) and *sarx* (flesh). Strictly speaking, there is no Christology here.

Apollinarius takes a first step in the direction of a Christology. According to his theory, the Logos *replaced*, in the human essence of the God-Man, the supreme principle in man, which Apollinarius calls (in the language of Hellenistic philosophy) *pneuma* or *nous* and which corresponds to the *hypostatic spirit* in man's nature. Because of the fragmentary character of the works of Apollinarius that have reached us and his terminological imprecision, it is not easy to reconstruct his thought. What meaning can we attach to the *nous* that is replaced in man by the Word? Is it one of the faculties of the soul, that is, intellect (which is its usual meaning, starting with St. Gregory of Nyssa); or is it truly *pneuma*, that is, the hypostatic spirit; or, using the language of the Chalcedonian dogma, is it the divine hypostasis and nature, with this hypostasis also uniting in

---

19. In his early work *De Incarnatione*, St. Athanasius understands the Incarnation simply as the reception of the body or flesh, which is the instrument of the Logos, a garment or temple (5.26). We encounter this idea in almost every paragraph of this work. The Word, which in general is present in the whole world and constitutes the image of God in man, is manifested in the body. "The universe is a body. And if it pleases the Word to be present in the world and to reveal Himself in the universe, it also pleases Him to manifest Himself in the human body" (7.41).

itself the human nature? It is precisely in this Chalcedonian sense that we interpret Apollinarius's thought.

Apollinarius's point of departure here is the notion of the man from heaven, as opposed to the man of earth. The Scripture texts that particularly draw his attention are 1 Corinthians 15:47 and John 3:13. "The man who came down from heaven is not a man of earth. Nevertheless, he is a man, even though he came down from heaven, for the Lord does not reject such a name in the Gospels.... If the Son of Man is from heaven and the Son of God is from a woman, then how are God and man not the same?... But He is God according to the spirit, being in the flesh, and man according to the flesh, received from God." "Even as man is one, consisting of two, soul and body... [so Christ too] would not be in the likeness of man if He were not an intellect clothed in flesh, as man." "He was thus man, for according to Paul, man is an incarnate intellect.... He was thus man and [also] from heaven."[20] "Man is composed of three parts.... And the Lord, called man, is likewise composed of spirit, soul, and body... but He is also the man from heaven and the quickening spirit.... If the man from heaven is composed of the same three parts as a man of earth, he, then, is not of heaven, but only a receptacle of the living God.... How does God become man without ceasing to be God if God does not take the place of intellect in man?"[21]

Thus, on the one hand, Apollinarius comes to the conclusion that the Incarnation cannot be the union of *two* integral persons, God and man, but is a certain concrete "synthesis" of two into one. And on the other hand, he establishes a distinction between Christ, as the man from heaven, and the first Adam, the man of earth, with respect to their human composition: in Adam there resides a creaturely human spirit, whereas in Christ the Divine Logos corresponds to it in the capacity of the spiritual principle, *nous* or *pneuma*.[22] Thus, we have the following parallel:

Adam: *pneuma (nous)*; soul *(psuchē)*; body *(sōma)*
Christ: Logos; soul *(psuchē)*; body *(sōma)*.

Although Adam and Christ have an identical psychophysical composition, an animal soul and body, they differ as far as the third and supe-

---

20. *Antirrheticus contra Apollinarium* 6, 7, 35, 37.
21. Ibid., 56.
22. "If the heavenly man is constituted by all those parts that we earthly men also have (so that he has the same spirit as earthly men), he then is not heavenly, but only the receptacle of the living God" (ibid., 48).

Introduction

rior part of the soul is concerned. In Adam this is the human hypostasis, since the spirit is, of course, hypostatic; in Christ this is the divine hypostasis of the Logos. We can see to what degree Apollinarius anticipates the fundamental scheme of the Chalcedonian dogma. To be sure, it can be pointed out that he speaks here not of hypostasis or person but of spirit or intellect (and this has indeed resulted in misunderstandings). However, if we recall that an appropriate terminology was absent in this epoch[23] and try to grasp Apollinarius's fundamental idea instead of nit-picking when it comes to particular expressions, we will understand that he had in mind precisely the supreme principle of spirit, the hypostatic center of the human personality.

The Chalcedonian definition, however, speaks also of two natures in Christ, divine and human; but this distinction is absent in Apollinarius, and he even appears to establish some new, composite nature (which led critics to compare his conception with various animal hybrids, including minotaurs, horse-deer, and goat-deer[24]). But this too is only a manner of exposition, which can be explained by the fact that the author directs his attention at clarifying the divine-human composition of Christ as the New Adam. For Apollinarius it is clear, first of all, that the assumption of the soul and body signifies the assimilation of the entire old Adam. This is the basis of his entire soteriology. For Apollinarius's conception, it is necessary for the salvation of the human race that the Savior be not a mere man, but that He differ from mere man by the Divine Spirit: "He

---

23. It is impossible not to agree with the following general characterization of the terminology of patristic theology: "All through the literature of the patristic age it is constantly evident how seriously its authors are handicapped by their lack of abstract terms and their habit of concrete and materialistic thinking. Instead of conceiving of God in terms of love, in terms appropriate to personality, they are concerned with substances, with images borrowed from the fusion of metals, the mixing of liquids or the hybridizing of animals, images too crude to do justice to the subtleties of living relationships and often making their whole treatment of the experience of religion seem artificial" (C. E. Raven, *Apollinarianism* [Cambridge, 1923], pp. 259-60). One can say that it was only by a kind of divine instinct, despite the imperfection of the terminology and the associated lack of conceptual clarity, that the patristic epoch was able to accomplish its gigantic dogmatic labor, crowned by the definitions of the ecumenical councils. The power of God is manifested in infirmity, and we bear the treasure of the faith in earthen vessels. However, in preserving this treasure, we must not try to hold on to the ages-old clay out of which the vessels are made; and truth be told, it is impossible to do so. For this reason, we must continue the theological work in the only way we can *at the present time,* that is, by using concepts of contemporary thought.

24. *Antirrheticus contra Apollinarium* 14.

who is a man and is subject to the corruption that is common to men cannot save the world." "We are not saved by God if He is not mixed with us. . . . He is mixed with us when He is made flesh, that is when he becomes man, as the Gospel says: 'the Word was made flesh, and made His abode in us' (John 1:14 [the King James Version has been modified to conform with the Russian Bible])."[25] Thus, for Apollinarius, that which is assumed by Christ, however this is defined, is man. That is, it fully conforms with the "human nature" of the Chalcedonian dogma: God assumes the entire fullness of the human nature into His hypostasis, with which He replaces man's proper spiritual essence, his hypostatic spirit *(unio hypostatica)*. Apollinarius asks: "How does God become man without ceasing to be God if God does not take the place of the intellect in man?"[26] "Having God in the place of the spirit, that is, the intellect, Christ with soul and body is justly called the man from heaven."[27] This differs from the Chalcedonian dogma in terminology, not in meaning, and historically this difference was perfectly inevitable. There is also another difference: Apollinarius does not say anything about the proper, divine nature of the Logos, which, according to the Chalcedonian definition, is united with the human nature. But in general, Apollinarius does not say anything about the Logos in terms of *hypostasis* and *nature*; borrowed from the trinitarian terminology, these terms were only later, at Chalcedon, applied to Christology. However, there is no doubt that he does not separate them in the general concept of the Logos.[28] Thus, if one were to unfold Apollinarius's conception of the union of God and man in the God-Man and give it an expanded expression, one would find that it contains the Chalcedonian dogma of the one hypostasis and the two natures.

Thus, in Apollinarius's Christology, *pneuma* or *nous* corresponds to the divine hypostasis, which is inseparably united with the divine nature.[29] But this aspect of his Christology was misunderstood, and it re-

---

25. Ibid., 51.
26. Ibid., 56.
27. Ibid., 9.
28. Ibid., 58.
29. In his work devoted to the Apollinarianists, Epiphanius puts into the mouth of Vitalius the following characteristic declaration: "We say that He is the perfect man if we take the divinity in place of the intellect, as well as the flesh and the soul, in such a way that the perfect man will be composed of flesh, soul, and divinity instead of intellect" (*Adv. Haeres., haer.* 77; *PG* 42.673). The British scholar Raven also comes to the conclusion "that *nous* signifies to Apollinarius what he calls *hupostasis*" (Raven, *Apollinarianism*, p. 238).

mains misunderstood even today, for various reasons, but mainly for reasons related to terminology. Let us attempt to get to the bottom of this misunderstanding.

Apollinarius's achievement is that he understood the christological problem also as an anthropological one and indissolubly linked these two problems. Apollinarius considers the man from heaven, the Second Adam, and the man of earth, the first Adam, as the two possibilities, so to speak, of one image of man. Thus, next on the agenda is the problem of *man,* in the limited sense, of course, in which this problem was accessible to the consciousness of that epoch. In particular, there arises the question of the composition of man, of whether this composition is bipartite or tripartite in character. There was no dominant opinion concerning this question in that epoch. The various scattered pronouncements on this problem are vague and accidental in character. Apollinarius was the first to examine this question in a substantive manner; he developed a particular anthropological as well as christological doctrine of the tripartite composition of man (spirit, soul, and body).

Vacillations have been ascribed to him in this matter, particularly in the early period, but we do not agree with this: trichotomism plays too central a role in his Christology.[30] Nevertheless, Apollinarius's doctrine has been stylized and vulgarized in the Church literature to such a degree that he is alleged to assert that Christ assumed only a body without a soul. However, even St. Gregory of Nyssa affirms that Apollinarius presents "a proof based on many writings that man is composed of three parts: of flesh, soul, and intellect [*nous*]. This is not far from our own opinion, for to say that man consists of a rational soul and a body, or specially considering intellect apart, is the same thing as to divide into three parts that which we conceive in man."[31] (To be sure, this difference is by no means only terminological.) Gregory adds that, based on this doctrine, Apollinarius makes of it the following christological application: "Having God in the place of spirit, that is, intellect, Christ with soul and body is justly called the man from heaven" (*Antirr.* 9).

It is usually not remarked that this trichotomic Christology agrees perfectly with the Chalcedonian doctrine, which in this respect is also confirmed by the Fifth and Sixth Ecumenical Councils: We confess "true God and true man, of a rational soul and body [*ek psychēs logikēs kai sōmatos*], consubstantial with the Father according to Divinity and

---

30. The opinion that he vacillated on is based on Rufinus, *Hist. Eccles.* 2.20.
31. *Antirrheticus contra Apollinarium* 8.

consubstantial with us according to humanity."[32] We confess "the union of God the Word with flesh, animated by a rational and intelligent soul [*logikei kai noera*], a union effected according to composition or according to hypostasis."[33] In other words, the anthropology serving as the basis of this Christology is trichotomic: body, rational soul, and hypostatic spirit, which in the God-Man is replaced by the Logos; or using Apollinarian terminology, "having God in the place of spirit, that is, intellect, Christ with soul and body."

Nevertheless, this fundamental christological idea was not understood by Apollinarius's contemporaries; the terminology he used to express his conception gave rise to a number of misunderstandings. First of all, as far as the divine nature of Christ is concerned, here, even though Apollinarius clearly has the Logos in mind, he refers to Him (perhaps not without the influence of Neoplatonic terminology) by the terms *pneuma* and *nous* — terms that are deficient in dogmatic precision. Since Apollinarius's intention is to reveal the composition of *man* in the God-Man, he considers neither the relation of hypostasis and divine nature in the God-Man nor the inseparable presence in Him of the two natures — that which is clearly expressed by the Chalcedonian dogma. Apollinarius does not deny this, but he also fails to develop it, although this idea perfectly conforms with his theory.

As far as the human nature in the God-Man is concerned, the fact that Apollinarius calls the divine principle both *pneuma* and *nous* leads one to think that *nous* replaces the rational faculty in man (i.e., it leads one to interpret *nous* not ontologically but psychologically). Apollinarius's conception is thus interpreted to mean that Christ assumed an *incomplete* human essence, namely body and soul, but without the human reason, which is replaced by the divine reason. That is precisely how Apollinarius's theory was interpreted by his contemporaries and his opponents, by St. Gregory the Theologian and in part even by St. Gregory of Nyssa.[34] Through this *reductio ad absurdum*, these opponents missed the essential and important elements of Apollinarius's Christology, elements that were discovered later in a new form in the history of dogma.

One must concede that, in the surviving fragments, Apollinarius's conception is imperfectly clear and somewhat ambiguous. On the one

---

32. H. Denzinger, *Enchiridion Symb.*, 13th ed., 148 (p. 66).

33. Decree of the Fifth Ecumenical Council, ibid., 216 (p. 91); Decree of the Sixth Ecumenical Council, ibid., 290 (p. 128).

34. *Antirrheticus contra Apollinarium* 35.

hand, there are propositions that apparently can be understood only in the Chalcedonian sense, where it is precisely the human soul that is the rational principle animating the body: "The flesh [of the Word] is not soulless [*apsuchos*], for it is said that it struggles against the spirit and fights against the law of the intellect" (*Antirr.* 7). "His flesh is rationally animated [*noeros psuchotheisa*]. . . . In the union of the Word with the animate and rational [*empsuchon kai logikēn*] flesh . . . the body and God are one and identical, and this body, without transformation of the flesh into the incorporeal, preserves as what is proper to it [*idion*] that which, from us, conforms with birth from the Virgin and that which, above us, conforms with the fusion [*sunkrasin*] or union with God the Word" (ibid. 396, 3-4, 24-26).

Here, Apollinarius insists on the fullness and authenticity of Christ's humanity, assumed from the Most Holy Virgin Mother of God: "We confess that the Son of God became the son of man not in name only but in truth when He received the flesh from the Virgin Mary; and that He is the unique Son of God and also the Son of Man."[35] Therefore, it is unjustified to oppose to Apollinarius's doctrine the affirmation that Christ assumed flesh and a rational soul (as even St. Cyril of Alexandria does), since that is Apollinarius's own opinion.

Alongside this definition of the trichotomic composition of man and of the God-Man, Apollinarius employs, in other fragments, the dichotomic language characteristic of his epoch; in those cases he speaks, as do St. Athanasius and others, only of the assumption of the flesh. Here, his main emphasis is on the inner unity of the God-Man, which unity is established by the fact that, in its unchangeability, Divinity is that which determines and moves the flesh, which is thus reduced to the level of an organ brought into motion by the Logos.[36] This Christology acquires a monoenergetic and monothelitic character,[37] and one can get the impression that the Logos takes the place of both the intellect and the soul, which are absent.

There is no doubt that, in this respect, Apollinarius is a representative of the monophysitic tendency in Christology, although here his direct predecessor is St. Athanasius and his successors are St. Cyril of Alexandria and the entire post-Chalcedonian monophysitism (following Severus), with all of its terminological imprecision. The task of Apollinarius's

---

35. *Expos. Fid.* (Dräseke, 376.20-23).
36. Lietzmann, fr. 108, 117, 150, 151.
37. Ibid., fr. 117.

The Dialectic of the Idea of Divine-Humanity in the Patristic Epoch

Christology (a task shared by his successors) was to understand and affirm the unity of the God-Man, given the authenticity of the Incarnation and the reality of the human flesh assumed by Him. Therefore in Apollinarius we sometimes encounter verbal expressions of this idea that are hard to accept, above all the well-known pseudo-Athanasian (later Cyrillian) formula: *mia phusis tou Theou Logou sesarkomenē* (one nature incarnate of God the Word). This formula acquires a fully orthodox meaning if we interpret the term *phusis* in the way that Apollinarius himself did: "Holy Scripture does not attest to any separation between the Word and His flesh; rather, He is one nature, one hypostasis, one energy, one person, integral God and integral man" (*Contra agoniz.*, Dr. 396, 15-18). (St. Cyril of Alexandria evidently understands this in the same way.) The subject of the discussion here is that which was later called *unio hypostatica*, whose consequence is the *deification* of the human essence of the God-Man. It is this deification that is attested to by Apollinarius, once again in a terminology that is not beyond reproach and that he shares with the whole epoch. He employs such terms as *sunthesis, krasis, mixis,* and so forth (all of which were commonly used in the patristic literature of the fourth and fifth centuries). He particularly insists on the deification of the Lord's *body*: "His flesh gives life to us through the divinity consubstantial with us: the life-giving [principle] is divine, but the flesh is divine, for it is united with God."[38] (Here the subject of the discussion appears to be that which was later called *communicatio idiomatum*.) But this idea is far from the monophysitism of Eutychian type, where the humanity is absorbed by or dissolved in Divinity. On the contrary, Apollinarius insists that "despite the difference between the natures [*allēs kai allēs ousias*], the veneration is one and the same, that is, of the Creator and the creature, of God and man, one veneration of Christ; and in conformity with this, God and man are thought in one name."[39] Here, Apollinarius's fundamental doctrine is fully within the mainstream of the Church.

With certain details of his doctrine, Apollinarius leaves his mark on the further development of Christology. But it should be noted that the weaker aspects of his argumentation had a greater influence than the stronger ones. Thus, he is the originator of those physical comparisons that were intended to clarify the interrelation of the two natures in Christ and that have seeped into the whole of the christological literature, irrespective of its tendency, from St. Cyril of Alexandria to St. John of Damas-

---

38. *Syllog.* (Dräseke, 353.14).
39. *Contra Heracl.* (Dräseke, 363.24-27). Cf. *Contra agoniz.* (Dräseke, 391.1-26).

cus. There is, first of all, the famous comparison involving fire that makes iron red-hot and permeates it without changing its nature (L., fr. 128), and then there is the comparison of the two natures united in Christ with the soul and body in an individual human being (L., fr. 129). These were helpless attempts to understand the unity of the God-Man.

There is yet another aspect of Apollinarius's doctrine that is hard to understand, in part because of the meagerness and obscurity of the surviving texts, and in part because of its substance. Apollinarius is the *sole* representative of Greek and Latin Christology (expect perhaps for Origen) who poses the question of the relation between the eternal Logos and man, or (which is the same thing) the question of the eternal Divine-Humanity as the foundation of the Incarnation. He arrives at this question, first of all, exegetically, when he interprets the texts concerning Christ as the man from heaven (see p. 9 above); and he also arrives at it theologically, when he seeks to understand the Incarnation not as a *deus ex machina* but as an act preestablished from the beginning. No aspect of Apollinarius's thought has been so grossly misunderstood as this one. The idea that the earthly flesh of the God-Man had descended from heaven was attributed to him, and to be sure, it was very easy to reduce this idea to the absurd. Modern scholarship has established that this accusation is without any merit.[40] However, the chief issue here is that this accusation is sufficiently excluded by Apollinarius's own numerous declarations to the effect that Christ had received real human flesh from the Virgin Mary, from the seed of Abraham.[41] And for this reason Apollinarius is usually accused of teaching that Christ has only a body, without an intellect and even without a soul.

What lies at the basis of this misunderstanding? Apollinarius repeatedly expresses the general idea that Christ is the man from heaven; this heavenly and eternal humanity is therefore the basis for His descent to earth. But he expresses this idea unclearly and imprecisely (at least in the surviving fragments): "How can one call a man of earth one about whom it is attested that He is the Man come down from heaven, who is called man and the son of man? . . . The Man come down from heaven is

---

40. Both the Catholic historian J. Tixeront (*Histoire des dogmes* [Paris, 1912], 2.101) and the Protestant historian Seeberg (*Lehrbuch der Dogmengeschichte*, 2.165-66) see a misunderstanding here.

41. "We do not say that the flesh of our Lord Jesus Christ is from heaven. Instead, we confess that God the Word was made incarnate from the holy Virgin Mary" (*Contra agoniz.*, Dräseke, 395.4-5).

not a man of earth. Nevertheless, He is a man, even though He came down from heaven, for the Lord does not deny such a name in the Gospels" (*Antirr.* 6). "And first of all [says Apollinarius] the man Christ exists not in such a way as if there were besides Him another spirit, that is, God, but in such a way as if the Lord, in the essence of God and man (of the God-Man?), were the divine spirit" (12). "The divine incarnation, according to Apollinarius, had its origin not from the Virgin, but preceded Abraham and all creatures" (15). "He [Apollinarius] says that man is a shining of God's glory ... and that the hypostasis of God is reflected in the God of flesh" (19). "To this extent he was man and (also) the man from heaven [*epouranios*]" (37). "He is both the man from heaven and the life-giving spirit" (48).

How can one interpret these propositions?[42] We fail to find here what Apollinarius's opponents accused him of. His thought is oriented toward the eternal humanity of the Logos, of that heavenly Man in whose image the earthly man was created. He approaches here the doctrine of the Divine-Humanity that is presupposed as the general foundation of all Christology: The union of the Divine and human essences in the God-Man is not an external, ontologically arbitrary act of the unification of two things that cannot be united, of two things that are totally different and alien to one another. Rather, it is the ontologically grounded and pre-established union of the Proto-Image and the image, of the heavenly Man and the earthly man. On the subject of this union, patristic theology did not know any other answer except a general reference to God's omnipotence. Apollinarius's achievement is that he perceived here a special problem that he expressed in the doctrine of the *interrelation* of the heavenly Man and the earthly man, that is, the doctrine of the Divine-Humanity. In this respect Apollinarius is a solitary and misunderstood figure in patristic theology; evidently, even he himself did not completely think through his highly significant idea.

Thus, Apollinarius's significance in Christology can be defined as follows: (1) He was the first to pose the problem of the unity of the God-Man as composed of two natures, although his solution to this problem was imprecise. (2) He understood this problem as an anthropological one, and with his doctrine of the composition of the God-Man he anticipated the Chalcedonian schema, although his own answer to this problem was imprecise owing to the imprecision of his terms and the insufficient clar-

---

42. Of the historians of dogma, only I. A. Dorner, *Entwicklungsgeschichte der Lehre von der Person Christi*, part 1, 2d ed. (Berlin, 1851) attentively examines this doctrine.

ity of his anthropological thought. (3) He was the first to pose the problem of the interrelation of the Divine and human essences as the basis of their union in the God-Man, although he himself did not go beyond ambiguous and obscure propositions on this subject; here, he had neither predecessors nor successors in patristics. With these elements, Apollinarius put the imprint of his thought on all of subsequent Christology, in which one can recognize the further development and refinement of his ideas or their polemical rejection. Although Apollinarius was condemned as a heretic, his actual influence in the Church remains significant, and more positive than negative.

His errors did not find adherents in dogmatics; on the contrary, it was the positive aspects of his doctrine that were adopted and endure in dogmatics. In this sense there is an essential difference between Apollinarius and Arius, with whom he is sometimes compared with reference to Christology: Although Arius did awaken the dogmatic consciousness, gave rise to the homoousian movement, and was indirectly responsible for the Nicene Creed (and one can only regret that *not all* of his questions were heard and answered at the council, in particular, the sophiological and cosmological ones), his proper doctrine represents a direct rejection of the truth, pure falsehood without any ambiguity. In contrast, in Apollinarius's doctrine everything has a double meaning; everything is a mixture of truth and error. In this respect he does not greatly differ from certain fathers who are honored as teachers of the Church, for they too are usually able to express the truth of the Church only antithetically, in a dialectical process, and thus one-sidedly. We can see this most clearly when we consider Apollinarius's direct successor, to whom he is extremely close, St. Cyril of Alexandria, and more broadly when we consider the entire opposition between the schools of Antioch and Alexandria.

After Apollinarius, and based on him, Christology evolves with full dialectical clarity in its antinomic character. On one side, we have the thesis, *the unity of the God-Man,* expressed by the theology of St. Cyril and later by monophysitism and monothelitism. On the other side, we have the antithesis, *the duality of the natures in the God-Man,* expressed by Antiochene theology, by Diodore of Tarsus, Theodore of Mopsuestia, Theodoret, Nestorius, the dithelites, and the adoptionists. The Church truth embraces both the thesis and the antithesis, the bi-unity of the God-Man and the unity of the hypostasis in the duality of the natures, proclaimed by the dogmas of the Fourth and Sixth Ecumenical Councils. But these dogmatic schemata become alive for us and full of content only when we perceive the entire dialectical antithetics of the patristic Christology in which the dogmatic thought lives. Therefore, neither of these theological doctrines taken by itself, irrespective of who its author is, whether he is honored by the Church as one of her fathers or teachers or whether he has been excluded as a heretic — neither of these doctrines, in its one-sidedness, expresses the truth of the Church if it is not included in the dialectical whole. The truth abides above personal opinions *(hairesis)*. But the *access* into historical dialectical Christology lies through Apollinarius's theological doctrine, and this constitutes his enduring historical significance and, of course, his great achievement in behalf of the Church.

II. The Antinomy of Bi-unity in Christology

A. *The Christology of Unity (Monism): St. Cyril of Alexandria*

The post-Apollinarian theology, which considered the christological problem in its distinctive elements, followed two different fundamental paths, which history represents as the opposition between the school of Alexandria and the school of Antioch. Christ is one, but He is also God and man. After Apollinarius's attempt to solve the problem of bi-unity, understood as the *mixing* of the two natures, theological thought confronts this problem in all its merciless severity: unity or duality? *Theologically,* it appeared that only "either/or" was possible here, where one principle suppresses or even excludes the other. There thus arises a "dialectical" Christology, which simultaneously develops in two directions that presuppose one another owing to their expressly antithetical character.

Representing the Christology of *unity,* or the monistic Christology, are St. Cyril of Alexandria, the soul of the Third Ecumenical Council, and his monophysitical allies, while the Christology of *duality* was represented by the school of Antioch. There are two striking features in St. Cyril's theological activity. The first is that, despite all the one-sidedness, imprecision, and sometimes outright helplessness of his *theology,* St. Cyril remains a pillar of orthodoxy during all the periods of his activity. He confesses the teaching of the Church in all its purity and without deviation, and guided by a certain higher reason, he correctly captains the ship of the Church during the dogmatic tempest. He possesses a certain instinct for the truth, even before it is understood, and precisely this defines his significance as a father of the Church.

The second striking feature of St. Cyril's theological activity is the general weakness and vulnerability of his theologizing. That is, if we examine St. Cyril not just as a teacher of the Church but also as a theologian, to the extent the one can be separated from the other, our evaluation of him will be mixed. Despite the exceptional dogmatic sensitivity thanks to which St. Cyril discovered the danger of diphysitism in its heretical deviation, in Nestorianism, the positive part of his theology is distinguished by a very great obscurity. First of all, he is not independent in his dogmatic creativity. Unlike Apollinarius and the representatives of the school of Antioch (Diodore of Tarsus, Theodore of Mopsuestia, Theodoret, and even Nestorius), who in their theology developed their own insights and dogmatic ideas, St. Cyril's thought was for the most part formed in polemical conflict. He develops not so much a Cyrillian as an anti-Nestorian or a general anti-Antiochene theology; he is ideologically dependent on his opponents in the most essential thing: the problematic. Therefore, in order to understand St. Cyril's ideas, it is necessary to take into account the ideas of his opponents.

To make things worse, St. Cyril's theology is marred by lack of clarity and by exceptional terminological imprecision. Here, to some extent, he shares the fate of his epoch, which did not have at its disposal a terminology suitable for Christology. (The precision of the terms it employed was not even comparable to that of the terms that had been developed for triadology.) But this problem is exacerbated by the peculiarities of St. Cyril's own style. His imprecision is so great that, in the absence of a special interpretation, it can lead one to understand his thought in a manner wholly other than he himself understood it. And for this reason his thought could serve to support the later monophysitism. He expresses his dogmatic ideas and even his doctrinal formulations not by means of precise terms but descriptively, "in his own words," as it were, with one notion merging into another. This is true even for the most fundamental concepts of Christology: for St. Cyril, person *(prosōpon)* is equivalent to hypostasis *(hupostasis)*, and hypostasis is equivalent to nature *(phusis)*; but at the same time he distinguishes between them and uses them differently in different cases, with his own thought thereby left in a sort of *clair-obscur*.

We must also mention that the teacher of the Church in St. Cyril is often in conflict with the theologian in him: the teacher puts forth postulates that, strictly speaking, not only do not derive from his theology but that even have no place in it. Thus, where others fall into heresy and end up at an impasse in striving to develop their dogmatic ideas consistently and responsibly, St. Cyril calmly links propositions that are not justified by his own theology but that conform with the teaching of the Church.

The Dialectic of the Idea of Divine-Humanity in the Patristic Epoch

He does this, however, not only in the name of subordinating the intellect to the unfathomable truth of the Church, but also because of a certain irresponsible character of his thought that lacks logical justification. We will encounter this feature a number of times in his fundamental christological definitions. All of these features of St. Cyril's theology are generally recognized in the history of dogma.[43] However, it is much more important to understand not the weak and one-sided aspects of his theology, but its positive significance, which is that it expresses a well-defined and dialectically justified stage in the antithetics of Christology, namely the thesis of the *unity* of the God-Man.

St. Cyril's polemical self-definition in relation to the past is expressed in the rejection of Arianism, which had ceased to be a pressing problem, and of Apollinarianism, which St. Cyril rejects on every appropriate and inappropriate occasion. This is in part explained by the tendency of his opponents (St. Theodoret and the Eastern fathers in general) to accuse him of Apollinarianism, which St. Cyril considers in a highly simplified and stylized form, a form in which Apollinarius himself, at least after the Council of Constantinople (381), did not express his doctrine. That is, the essence of this doctrine is perceived in the notion that Christ assumed only a body, without a soul. Therefore, when he speaks of the Incarnation, St. Cyril invariably adds that Christ assumed the flesh with a rational soul, or with a body, soul, and intellect.[44]

On other occasions, St. Cyril says (although without directly polemicizing with Apollinarius) that perfect God and perfect man were united in Christ. However, this rejection of Apollinarius, which is essentially based on a misunderstanding and provoked chiefly by the need for self-defense, does not abolish the real kinship that exists between the two theologians. Inwardly, this kinship is based on the fact that both of them express the postulate of *unity* in Christology, although they realize it in different ways. Therefore, it is not by chance that St. Cyril, accepting as Athanasian the Apollinarian formula of the unity of the God-Man ("one incarnate nature of God the Word"), made it his own christological banner, as it were. This borrowing is without doubt characteristic for St. Cyril's doctrine, but it in no way reduces its value.

---

43. See the works of Harnack, Seeberg, Loofs, Tixeront, Dornier, et al. Also see M. Jugie, *Nestorius et la controverse nestorienne* (Paris, 1912); and J. Lebon, *Le monophysisme sévérien* (Louvain, 1909).

44. *Quod Maria sit Deipara* (PG 76.265). Cf. *De recta fide ad Theodos. Imper.* 16-24 (PG 76.1156-68).

Introduction

To be sure, the unremarked influence of Apollinarius in what is essential is more important than divergence with him on points of secondary significance or on points of no significance whatsoever. When we compare the doctrine of St. Cyril with that of Apollinarius, we see that St. Cyril is completely free of the heretical tendencies of Apollinarius, but he is weaker as a theologian if only because he essentially returns to the pre-Apollinarian formulation of the christological problem. Apollinarius went beyond the imprecision in the doctrine of the God-Man and of the Incarnation that was common prior to him (even in St. Athanasius), and he asked not *what* but *how*, although he could not give a satisfactory answer to this question. In St. Cyril's theology this christological *how* (the answer to which was found in the Chalcedonian dogma, which presupposed Apollinarius's entire problematic) once again disappears, so to speak. In this formal sense, St. Cyril's problematic (although not his doctrine) is a step backward in the development of Christology, a reaction in the direction of simplification, a failure to distinguish the elements of the problem. Therefore, St. Cyril does not overly concern himself with tying together the separate elements of his doctrine, whereas a desire for coherence does characterize Apollinarius. In general, one must acknowledge that the rejection of Apollinarianism does not by any means characterize St. Cyril's theology per se; it is rather a means of self-defense against opponents who, in good faith or bad faith (the former evidently being much more common than the latter), identify St. Cyril's doctrine with the theory of Apollinarius that was condemned by the Church. St. Cyril's own theory does not inwardly overcome Apollinarianism, nor does it develop it further.

St. Cyril's Christology was formed in the polemic with Antiochene theology, taken in its shallowest and most popular aspect and therefore its most influential and dangerous aspect: Nestorianism. One can say that St. Cyril's Christology is an anti-Nestorianism developed into an entire doctrine. Therefore, the majority of the pertinent works of St. Cyril (*PG* 95-97) consist of anathematisms (the "Twelve Chapters") and their defense from different sides — in letters, proclamations, and a few treatises. The center and point of departure of St. Cyril's Christology are his twelve anathematisms against Nestorius, read and approved in Ephesus at the Cyrillian (Third Ecumenical) council and in turn contra-anathematized there at the *conciliabulum* of the Eastern theologians by Archbishop John of Antioch, Theodoret, and Nestorius himself.

Historically, the dispute between St. Cyril and Nestorius arose in connection with the name *Theotokos*. However, this apparently mariological disagreement actually reflects a fundamental christological divergence in the interpretation of the Divine-Humanity, a divergence in theo-anthropology. Against the Antiochene theo-anthropology, which interpreted the Divine-Humanity as the harmonization *(sunapheia)* of two persons into one, St. Cyril affirms in his "Twelve Chapters," or anathematisms, the unity of the Emmanuel. The distinctive features of his Christology are already apparent in the initial expression of this idea:[45] "The Word, who is from God the Father, was united with the flesh hypostatically, which is why Christ is one with His flesh, that is, God and man at the same time" (ch. 2). "He who in one Christ, after the union [*meta ten henōsin* (of the natures)], separates the persons, uniting them only by an alliance [*sunapheiai*] according to dignity, that is, in power and strength, and not by a natural union [*kath henōsin physikēn*], let him be anathema" (ch. 3). "He who refers the sayings of the Gospels and of the Apostolic books separately to two persons or hypostases . . . let him be anathema" (ch. 4).

This document, prepared with great care and a profound sense of responsibility, already contains the fundamental elements of St. Cyril's Christology, elements that are later repeated multiple times in his numerous works. First of all, there is the idea of the unity of the God-Man, though expressed in imprecise terms: This unity is defined as a union according to hypostasis; on the one hand, hypostasis is person, while on the other hand, it is nature.[46] This results in the formula *henosis kath hupostasin*[47] = *henōsis phusikē* (hypostatic union = natural union), a formula that Theodoret and all the Eastern fathers interpreted as a restoration of Apollinarianism. Furthermore, in different places St. Cyril uses these expressions with different nuances of meaning. It is thus clear that the fundamental distinction between nature and person (hypostasis) that was to serve as the basis of the Chalcedonian dogma is in general foreign to him. In the absence of this distinction, all his christological definitions remain vague, ambiguous, and unconvincing for his opponents. Nevertheless, as a guiding star there ceaselessly shines the dogmatic idea of the unity of the God-Man and of the reality of the Incarnation, an idea that St. Cyril

---

45. *PG* 77.120-21.

46. We can find examples of this usage in *Adv. Nest.* 3.6.161 (*PG* 76.65). Cf. *Epist.* 40 *ad Acac.* (*PG* 77.193).

47. St. Cyril interprets "natural or hypostatic unity" as "true unity," in opposition to "relative [*schetikē*] union," in the responses to Theodoret and Andrew of Samosata (*PG* 75.401, 332, 405).

Introduction

defended perhaps more by an act of will than by any dogmatic achievements during this tempestuous epoch. He sometimes admitted a modified — *adapted* or "economic" — expression of this fundamental idea. For example, the unional confession of 433 speaks not of "the one essence of the incarnate God the Word" or of "natural union," but of the unification of the "two essences" and of Christ as perfect God and "perfect man." Outside the official document, however, St. Cyril reverts to his preferred formulation, which shows that his fundamental point of view has not changed.[48]

The *religious* self-evidentness of the unity of Christ is an authentic unity, complete, essential, natural, and hypostatic, and contrasts with the Nestorian duality, which in the absence of such a union is overcome only by a certain alliance, *sunapheia*. This self-evidentness is soteriological in character for St. Cyril (as well as for St. Gregory the Theologian). The goal of the Incarnation is to restore man and to save him from sin; otherwise, God would not have become man.[49] "If Nestorius were right with his separation of God and man in Christ, the redemptive works would belong to man and they would not have salvific significance. We could not have been saved by the passion of a mere man; the blood of the Logos would not have been shed for us, and His body would not have been offered in sacrifice. He died for us not as a man, being one of us, but as God in the flesh, giving His own body as a ransom for the life of all."[50]

This religious self-evidentness, however, must be demonstrated and justified theologically, which St. Cyril attempts to do in his Christology. His fundamental idea is the integral, concrete union of the divine and human essences. But he considers this notion of *essence* without distinguishing between nature and hypostasis, and he interprets the union of the essences accordingly. Here, St. Cyril encounters difficulties and problems on all sides.

In the absence of a clear anthropology,[51] and with insufficient differentiation between hypostasis and nature in God and man (whence the

---

48. See for example *epist.* 14 *ad Succensum* (PG 77.232); *epist.* 42 *ad Succ.* 2 (ibid., 240); *epist.* 40 *ad Acac.* (ibid., 193).

49. PG 75.1369-412. Cf. *De recta fide ad Reginas* 1 (PG 76.1205).

50. *Ad Reginas* 1 (PG 76.1296, 1208); *Cont. Nest.* 5.1; *Quod unus Christus* (PG 75.1336); *Inc. unig.* (ibid., 1216).

51. St. Cyril uses his dichotomic formula, where the human essence consists of body with rational soul, only to defend himself against the suspicion of Apollinarianism. In the majority of cases when he cites this formula, he abandons it at once and passes simply to *sarx* (flesh) as a definition of humanity.

confusion of the terminology), the fundamental idea of St. Cyril's Christology remains unclear. This idea is not clarified by numerous repetitions, and without developing it, St. Cyril merely supplements it with the rejection of opinions attributed to him by his opponents. His opponents found it natural to understand his fundamental idea of the union of the divine nature and the human nature, of the uncreated and created principles, either as a transformation of Divinity into flesh (thus reducing his idea to the absurd) or as an absorption of the flesh by Divinity in a manner reminiscent of the later Eutychianism. Against the first position, St. Cyril had to proclaim the truth of the unchangeability of Divinity in the Incarnation: "The Word became man without experiencing transformation or change, for He is always the same and is incapable of experiencing even the shadow of change. We affirm that there did not occur any mixing, confusion, or intergrowth of His essence with the flesh; instead, we say that the Word was united with the flesh *unfathomably and ineffably and as only He knows how*,"[52] that is, "according to economy."[53] This idea of the unfathomability and ineffability of the union by which God becomes man without experiencing change is repeated in the course of the entire polemic of St. Cyril with his opponents.[54] His opponents, however, are unable to accept this antinomy clothed in apophatics; they continue to see here a mixing of the natures. It therefore becomes necessary for St. Cyril to deny such mixing, which he does by repeating almost identical declarations: He says that the Word was united with the flesh without confusion, without change, without mutation *(atreptōs, ametablētōs, asugchutōs)*;[55] and there was no dissolution, confusion, mixing, or transformation *(krasis ē sugchusis ē phurmos ē metabolē)*.[56]

Denying all change in Divinity, St. Cyril nevertheless confesses true hypostatic, natural union. Let us try, insofar as it is possible, to understand his thought more precisely. First of all, we must point out the role played in his thought by the Apollinarian comparison of the Incarnation with the union of soul and body in man. St. Cyril repeats this comparison constantly, sometimes several times in the same passage,[57] failing to recognize not only that it is inapplicable but that it is even false: the union of two in-

---

52. *Explanation of the Twelve Chapters* 1 (PG 83.31).
53. Ibid., 40.
54. Beginning with *Scholia de Incarn. Unig.* of the year 430 (PG 75.1373).
55. *Epist.* 45.1 *ad Succens.* (PG 77.232).
56. *Epist.* 40 *ad Acac.* (PG 77.193). Cf. *Quod unus sit Christus* (PG 76.1292).
57. *Scholia de Incarn. Unig.* (PG 75.1373-75, 1397); *Quod unus sit Christus* (ibid., 1292); *epist. ad Succens.* 2 (PG 77.241), etc.

Introduction

dependent and perfect natures is *not* similar to the unification of two principles that can exist only in union and that in this sense do not by any means represent two natures. Moreover, this comparison may be appropriate *only* for the doctrine of Apollinarius, although it was borrowed from him by all the orthodox fathers of the Church between the fifth and the eighth centuries. However, it had no influence on the fundamental christological doctrine, which affirms the union of the two essences, an integral union that is not partial and not only hypostatic (as in Nestorius), but also natural. "The essence of the Word or the hypostasis (which signifies the Word itself) was truly united with the human essence without any transformation or change ... and it is the true Christ-God and man."[58] In Theodoret this natural union evoked the following misunderstanding: "Nature is something moved by necessity and deprived of freedom. ... If the natural union took place in this manner ... then God the Word was compelled to be united by necessity, not by love of man."[59] Against this, St. Cyril offers the clarification that natural union, "the true, unmixed transformation and perfectly inconfusable mergence of hypostases ... is called [thus] so as to leave no place for untrue union, by inhabitation." But he does not deny that "the Only Begotten One depleted Himself not involuntarily, but became man voluntarily."[60] The term "hypostatic union" thus acquires a limited, polemical, anti-Nestorian sense.[61]

For St. Cyril's Christology it is essential to define precisely *how* one should understand the union of the two natures in Christ. There is a characteristic formula in his Christology: Christ is one of two natures, *heis ex amphoin* or *heis ek duo phuseōn*.[62] The two natures *before* Incarnation are opposed here to unity *after* Incarnation. However, this unity does not abolish the duality of the natures, which have been united without confusion and without mixing, so that "the difference of the natures is not abolished by their union."[63] However, St. Cyril insists that this duality is established only "by contemplation" *(theōriai monēi)*;[64] one cannot "discern it except by contemplation"[65] (contrary to the Nestorian distinction in reality it-

---

58. Theodoret, *Refutation of the Twelve Chapters*, Cyril's explanation (*Act. Concil.* 2.138).
59. Ibid., anath. 3, objection (ibid., 140-41).
60. Ibid., 144-45.
61. *Epist. 4 ad Nest.* (PG 77.45).
62. *Scholia de Incarn. Unig.* 30 (PG 75.1398); *epist. ad Acac.* (PG 77.193).
63. *Epist. 4 ad Nest.* (PG 77.45C).
64. *Quod unus sit Christus* (PG 75.1292B).
65. *Epist. 46 ad Succens.* 2 (PG 77.245).

The Dialectic of the Idea of Divine-Humanity in the Patristic Epoch

self, as two persons). This *ek*, in contrast to *on*, can also be interpreted in an Apollinarian sense, and it became highly significant in the history of monophysitism. What does St. Cyril really mean by *ek*? This question does not arise with reference to the divine nature of the Logos, who, existing in eternity, "remained what He was" even after the Incarnation.[66] But it does arise with reference to the human nature. Although full reality is attributed to the human nature, precisely *before* the Incarnation, it is indisputable that this nature, not existing then as Christ's individual humanity, can be understood only in an abstract Platonic sense, in the sense of the general before the particular, or of a combination of certain properties.[67] The human nature receives this reality only after Incarnation, precisely when St. Cyril forbids one from recognizing its existence otherwise than "by contemplation" *(theōriai monēi)* and insists on *mia phusis* (one nature), although as incarnate *(sesarkomenē)*.

St. Cyril is not aware of this aporia.[68] He rejects Apollinarius's mechanical union of the divine and the human, as well as their chemical mixing, which was later proposed by Eutyches. On the one hand, remaining unchanged in the Incarnation, the Logos does not appear to notice this fact, which does not exist for His eternity, while at the same time possessing the full power of reality. The humanity acquires the significance of not more than a garment or even of a temple,[69] but it remains a kind of accidental zero, although at the same time it is united inseparably with the Logos (the way soul and body are united in man). In the Incarnation, there is between God and man no bridge or foundation for their union such as Nestorius's *sunapheia*. For St. Cyril the Incarnation remains a kind of external act. He therefore reduces humanity to a combination of attributes that do not have a hypostatic substratum,[70] but are assimilated by the Logos; these are the "natural properties" *(idiotēs hē kata phusin* or *poiotēs phusikē, ho tou pōs einai Logos)*. Or he reduces humanity to flesh *(sarx)*, which, although it is provided with a rational soul, does not express the fullness of the human essence. However, St. Cyril affirms its fullness *(teleios)* against all docetism.

There is a certain lack of clarity in St. Cyril's Christology here, which

---

66. *Epist. 2 ad Succens.* (PG 77.240B).
67. Cf. F. Loofs's interpretation in *Leontius von Byzanz* (Leipzig, 1887), pp. 41-48, and the objections made to this interpretation by Lebon in *Le monophysisme sévérien*, pp. 305ff.
68. See Theodoret's objection to the third anathema (*Act. Concil.* 2.141).
69. *Virgo sancta peperit templum verbo unitum* (*Scholia de Incarn. Unig.*, PG 75.1374).
70. Cf. Dorner, *Entwicklungsgeschichte*, p. 77.

cannot be removed by interpretation and which is due to the deficiency of the basic premises of his anthropology and theo-anthropology. This lack of clarity, which is only magnified by imprecision, verbosity, and repetitions, is concealed under declarations that the mystery of the in-humanization of God is unfathomable. This explains St. Cyril's irrepressible tendency to monophysitism, which was restrained in him by his fidelity to the orthodox dogma, although somewhat against the logic of his own theology. But this tendency became manifest after him, in Eutyches and the monophysites. Strictly speaking, St. Cyril does not distinguish between the two natures in Christ; he recognizes only the divine nature, which has assumed the properties of flesh.

Nevertheless, St. Cyril seeks to draw consistent and definitive conclusions from the doctrine of the reality and fullness of the human nature and its union with the Logos. The question that arises before him now is the question not of the divine-humanity but that of the God-Man, whose image is given to us by the Gospels, and that of His life. The Gospel story and its interpretation in the light of one christological doctrine or another represent in general a verification and testing of the truth of the given doctrine; to be sure, the interpretation of the divine-human life in its concrete bi-unity will differ depending on the christological premises, dualistic or monistic. St. Cyril primarily expresses the idea of the *unity* of Christ. He thus continues the tradition of Apollinarius, from whom, however, he differs both in a positive and in a negative respect. His superiority to Apollinarius consists, of course, in his orthodoxy, which compels him to reject the idea that Christ is composed of different elements of the divine and the human nature. Apollinarius is superior to St. Cyril, however, in consistency and clarity of thought: the unity of the life of Christ and the resulting sanctification of the human essence *(communicatio idiomatum)* are, in their own way, sufficiently well grounded in Apollinarius's Christology, something one cannot say about St. Cyril's Christology.

According to St. Cyril's doctrine, the incarnate Logos is not divided but combines the two natures into one and mixes together, as it were, the properties of the natures (*PG* 75.1244). The "natures" are understood here as "properties."[71] The determining principle in this unity is the Logos. This leads to the crucial problem: How can one understand the life of the God-Man in the Gospel narratives on the basis precisely of this unity? In the doctrine of the school of Antioch, and in particular in that of Nestorius, this unity was replaced by the duality of the hypostases,

---

71. *On the Incarnation of God the Word* (*Act. Concil.* 2.196).

The Dialectic of the Idea of Divine-Humanity in the Patristic Epoch

united not by a natural union but only by a relative union of moral agreement. It is against this idea that St. Cyril directs his epistle to Nestorius[72] and, in particular, his fourth anathematism: "Anyone who applies separately to the two persons or hypostases the declarations of the Gospels and the Apostolic books, employed by the saints about Christ or by Christ about Himself, applying some of them to the man, whom he considers to be different from the Word of God, while applying others, as appropriate to God, only to the Word of God the Father — let him be anathema."

St. Cyril develops this general idea in his polemic with Theodoret, who poses the following questions in his objections to the fourth anathematism: "To whom should one attribute the agony at Gethsemane (Matt. 26:39), or the cry on the cross (27:46), or John 12:27 and Mark 13:32?" "To whom should one attribute hunger and thirst? To whom should one attribute wakefulness, sleep, ignorance, and fear? Who needed the help of angels? Who confessed ignorance (Matt. 24:36)?" Theodoret attributes all of this "not to God the Word but to the form of a servant."[73] The one who suffered was "not Christ, but man, assumed from us by the Word."[74] In response, St. Cyril affirms that "all belongs to Christ alone, both that which is proper to God and that which concerns humanity," the latter belonging not to another person but "to the measure of His humanity."[75] But St. Cyril further develops this general idea only at the cost of obvious contradictions and incoherent notions, which the Antiochene figures, who were more responsible as theologians, wanted to avoid.

Concerning Christ's human ignorance, St. Cyril says that if Christ is one by reason of true union, "it turns out that He possesses knowledge and a form of ignorance . . . [that He] possesses knowledge according to Divinity, as the Wisdom of the Father, but, being placed at the level of ignorant man, He economically accomplishes that which is proper to others as well,"[76] and "He assumes all human properties in order that we believe that He truly became man, that He truly assimilated the human."[77] But

72. *Act. Concil.* 1.442-43.
73. Ibid., 2.150-51.
74. Ibid., 191.
75. Ibid., 153.
76. Ibid., 151.
77. In general, the question of Christ's ignorance (of the day and hour of the Second Coming, as well as of such particular events as where Lazarus was laid) is resolved in the spirit of "economic" purposefulness and relativity. With reference to this economic docetism, one can agree with Bishop Gore that here St. Cyril displays "a tendency to al-

Introduction

this idea has a trace of docetism, which is intensified by the following general conclusion: "To attribute depletion to God the Word, who knows neither transformation nor suffering, is to conclude and say something about the man according to the economic union with the flesh. Although He became man, the essence of the mystery does not in any way harm His nature; He remains what He was, even in giving Himself to humanity for the salvation and life of the world.... We do not diminish His divine essence and glory because of His humanity, and we do not reject the economy, but we believe in the Incarnation of the Word Himself, which was accomplished for our sake."[78]

There is certainly no answer here to the objection of Theodoret, who did not doubt the divinity of God the Word. The theological, or more precisely the christological, question was as follows: How is it possible to conceive in one divine Person, together with His Divinity, also the reality of His humanity, which, because of its creaturely relativity, apparently had to dissolve, had to be annihilated, in the absolute self-sufficiency of Divinity? How is divine-humanity possible in one person, and how should one understand the life of this divine-humanity (its phenomenology, so to speak), which is described in the Gospels? To seek refuge in the idea that the union of the two essences surpasses the understanding is, of course, inappropriate for a theologian who made this the main subject of his investigation. Therefore, St. Cyril in effect vacillates between the two logical centers of his christological thought, which he would like to unify: between the unity of the incarnate Word and the duality of His natures, which remain without separation and without confusion.[79] For instance, in the epistle to Acacius, St. Cyril writes: "Certain expressions are more proper to the divinity, whereas others are more proper to the humanity, and finally there are intermediate expressions, as it were, which attest that the Son is God and man together and in one and the same,"[80] although "it

---

low its spiritual and intellectual reality to be merged in his emphasis on the Godhead" (C. Gore, *Dissertations on subjects connected with the Incarnation* [London, 1895], p. 152). For a list of St. Cyril's texts on Christ's "economic ignorance," see Alexander B. Bruce, *The Humiliation of Christ*, 5th ed. (Edinburgh, 1905).

78. *Act. Concil.* 2.57.

79. These expressions ("without separation and without confusion") of the future Chalcedonian dogma are commonly used by Cyril but did not originate with him. They were used by the Antiochenes, by Didymus and Amphilochius, and even by Apollinarius (Lietzmann, p. 294; cf. Seeberg, *Lehrbuch*, p. 217; Harnack, *Dogm. Ges.*, 4th ed., 1.353).

80. *Act. Concil.* 2.395.

is one thing to divide the essences themselves, but an entirely different thing to admit a difference in the expressions."[81]

To be sure, the most difficult question here is the question of to what in Christ one should refer the passion and the death on the cross. Can Divinity suffer and die? Precisely this question precipitated the most decisive collision between the Antiochene theologians and St. Cyril, whose twelfth anathematism proclaims: "Anyone who does not confess that God the Word suffered in the flesh, was crucified in the flesh, was subjected to death in the flesh, and finally became the firstfruits of the dead, since He is life and life-giving — let him be anathema." Theodoret strongly objects to this: "Suffering is proper to one who is subject to suffering. The impassible is above the capacity to suffer. Therefore, suffering was experienced by the form of a servant, that is, in union with the image of God . . . not by Christ, but by man, assumed from us by the Word."[82] St. Cyril responds to this only by referring to the union with the body, as if converging here with Apollinarius and temporarily simplifying the fundamental idea of the union of the essences: "All must confess that the Word of God is the Savior, who remained impassible in His divine essence but who suffered in His flesh, for by reason of true union the body that tasted death became His property."[83]

St. Cyril repeatedly and, as is his custom, verbosely describes the Incarnation as the voluntary impoverishment *(kenōsis)* of the Son of God, according to Philippians 2:6-8, in virtue of which "He diminished Himself not in an imaginary or illusory manner, but in fact." "The properties [of the two essences] were united in Him into one person." "He was God and also man."[84] However, St. Cyril does not go beyond the affirmation of this fact; his only response to his opponent is to seek refuge in the paradox of faith: "the One whom nothing can contain decides to confine Himself in the virginal womb. The limitless one is contained by flesh."[85] In the final analysis, St. Cyril ends the theological debate by an appeal to the authority of faith: "Do not inquire, I ask you, into this matter . . . such a union [of soul and body] is unexplainable. . . . Soul and body are inseparable from Divinity."[86] His argument is purely soteriological: From the reli-

---

81. Ibid., 397.
82. Ibid., 191.
83. Ibid., 193.
84. *On the Incarnation of God the Word* (Act. Concil. 2.196).
85. Ibid., 197.
86. Ibid., 199.

giously indisputable fact of the reality of our existence and our salvation, it follows that if the Word had not become flesh and had not suffered by trials and temptations, He would not be able to help those who are tried and tempted, and His sufferings would not do us any good. "Does a shadow suffer?"[87]

Anyone who is familiar with the works of St. Cyril of Alexandria knows how difficult it is to define and characterize his thought, given his numerous repetitions and the theological imprecision of his language and thought. St. Cyril's significance as a father of the Church is very great, but one should not exaggerate his significance as a theologian. One can even say that his theology is a failure, for it consists of vague assertions and contradictory expressions, and it is riddled with repetitions and verbosity. This is not just a personal peculiarity of style. It is also the chief theological means that he uses to defend the truth of the Church, but this means is deficient as far as both general concepts and premises are concerned. St. Cyril was a precursor of the Chalcedonian dogma and of Chalcedonian theology (to the extent that it existed at all).

All the same, St. Cyril's opponents, whose theology was more coherent, fell into heresies, whereas he kept the ship of the Church on a straight dogmatic course — not only because of the profundity of his ecclesial consciousness but also because of his insensitivity to his own obscurities and contradictions. One can say that at times he was saved by his theological weaknesses. In cases where he developed his thought consistently and thus one-sidedly, he too arrived at heresy in his conclusions. To be sure, Eutychianism and the later monophysitism (and even Apollinarianism) provide a much more coherent expression of the Cyrillian theology than St. Cyril himself did. And it can be said about him that in the most critical cases he knew how not to be his own follower.[88] Will and a kind of dog-

---

87. *De recta fide ad Theodos. Imper.*, chs. 8, 9 (PG 76.1144-45).

88. The question of the Theotokos is the element that has the least dogmatic significance in Cyril's theology. It was this question that Cyril used as a polemical weapon in his dispute with Nestorius and that determined the content of the first anathematism. For Nestorius the question of the Theotokos had an exclusively christological, not a mariological, significance; and in his first contra-anathematism he rejects this expression only in a specific christological interpretation (namely, that "the Word Himself was made flesh," *Act. Concil.* 1.461). In another, more precise sense, Nestorius accepts this term and "receives it into the liturgical usage" (V. Bolotov, *Lectures on the History of the Church*, 4.185); in general Nestorius was not guilty of an insufficient veneration of the Mother of God. In any case, the question of the Theotokos is only one of the particular aspects of the christological problem.

matic instinct, not intellect, are what guide his theology, which in Christology developed a single idea: the *unity* of Christ. But this thesis, as it is one-sidedly affirmed by St. Cyril, is dialectically conjoined with the antithesis of the duality of the natures, of the bi-unity of Christ. This antithesis was expressed in the school of Antioch.

B. The Christology of Bi-unity (Diophysitism)

The theology of the school of Antioch, represented by Diodore of Tarsus, Theodore of Mopsuestia, Nestorious, and Theodoret, was influential and brilliant in the fourth to fifth centuries. But it then began to wane, and after the Council of Chalcedon it left the stage, its place taken by monophysitism. Nevertheless, despite its historical fate, the Antiochene doctrine occupied an important place in the dialectics of Christology. It served as a necessary antithesis in relation to the Cyrillian (and the later Severian) theology; without it, the development of Christology would have been marked by a dangerous one-sidedness that was in fact manifested in monophysitism.

Antiochene Christology is characterized by its emphasis on the *humanity* of Christ. In the unity of the God-Man, Alexandrian theology puts the accent on the first part of this complex word and concept, while Antiochene theology stresses the second. In St. Cyril, all that remains of the humanity of Christ is a combination of attributes (*poiēsis*) deprived not only of a hypostatic character but also of a natural character. Therefore, this concept inevitably fluctuates between Apollinarianism and docetism, human autonomy being dissolved in the divine being-in-itself. In contrast, the school of Antioch seeks to preserve the full power of this autonomy even in the Incarnation, to defend the authenticity of the humanity in the God-Man. This was something the school of Alexandria had failed to accomplish: the union of the two essences was accompanied either by the absorption of the one by the other or by the illusoriness of the humanity.

Against such a unity, which was false in this sense, the school of Antioch sought to rescue the reality of the humanity in Christ; but on this path, it arrived not only at duality but even at the separation of the two natures. The dialectical relation of the two antagonistic tendencies led to a situation in which neither could be accepted without at the same time accepting the other. Taken in isolation, each of these tendencies is equally (although differently) false; each becomes dialectically true only when it is conjoined with the other. The truth resides not in the middle but in the antinomic unity of the two; and we have this truth in the Chalcedonian dogma, in which the Alexandrian and Antiochene theologies are joined together like Siamese twins and live inseparably in the Church's dogmatic consciousness.

It is natural that the doctrine of man, the anthropological element, should occupy an important place in Antiochene thought, whereas an anthropology is generally absent in St. Cyril's thought. In order to understand the divine Incarnation as the true union of the divine and human essences, the Antiochenes seek to show, first of all, that man is called to divine Incarnation by his nature and, second, that he must preserve his autonomous being in the Incarnation. As for the first element, it is necessary to note the significance that is attributed here to *the image of God* in man: at his creation man does not yet contain that to which he is called; he must yet ascend from the lower to the higher, which is accomplished in the divine Incarnation. To this is added the element of personal freedom and moral responsibility, which is inalienable from man (and which explains why the Antiochenes were so irreconcilably opposed to Apollinarius, who sacrificed human freedom for the sake of the divine Incarnation, and to some degree to St. Cyril, who in effect reduced humanity to a mere attribute).

The postulate of Antiochene Christology was the preservation of human freedom in Christ with all the reality of human life. This was closely linked with the emphasis the Antiochenes placed on the historical aspect of the Gospel narratives in their exegesis of these texts. Another self-evident postulate of the school of Antioch was the *fullness* of the perfect human nature, which this school did not conceive without hypostasis (which, however, it most commonly expressed by the term *prosōpon*). The inseparability of the nature and of the person is the axiom of anthropology here. Theodore of Mopsuestia declares: "When we distinguish the natures, we speak of the perfect nature of God the Word and of His perfect person, for hypostasis [that is, in this case, nature] is not impersonal; and we speak the same way about the human nature and person."[89] However, the presence of a *person* here signifies not so much individuality or personality as the real concreteness of nature.

This postulate of anthropology must be kept in mind if one is to ascertain the true meaning of the Antiochene christological theories. However, one must add that, despite the radical character of this axiom, the

---

89. Theodore of Mopsuestia, *De Incarnatione* 8 (PG 66.981).

The Dialectic of the Idea of Divine-Humanity in the Patristic Epoch

Antiochene theology, like the Alexandrian, did not articulate a coherent doctrine of man and of his composition. We must also mention the imprecision and sometimes even the hopeless obscurity of the terminology employed,[90] leading to a situation where the two disputing sides often did not understand each other and fought as if in the dark with a poorly seen opponent. Not only vehement mutual antagonism, but also profound mutual misunderstanding, marks the polemic between the adherents of the monistic and diophysitic Christologies. The chief misunderstanding occurs because when the Antiochenes speak of the *personal* character of the human nature in Christ, they mean, first of all, its concrete reality, whereas their opponents see only a *special* human individuality. But neither side has a coherent doctrine of the person in general or of the human person in particular, and both sides poorly distinguish and sometimes confuse the concept of nature as a general, generic property; the concept of individuality as concrete, unique, exemplary being; and finally the concept of person as spirit conscious of nature. All this is covered by the concept of *hypostasis,* which is sometimes taken to be synonymous with *nature* and sometimes with *person.* For this reason it so difficult to fully accept the position of either school; one can only show a preference for the general tendency of one school or the other.

It became necessary, in any case, for the school of Antioch to juxtapose the fullness of the humanity in Christ, which has the entire concreteness of the nature, that is, a person in all the indeterminacy of this term, with the fullness of the divine nature, which also has a person. This person is the Divine Logos Himself. However, one might think that when the divine person is spoken of, one should have in mind, first of all, not so much the *hypostasis* of the Logos as His *personal nature.* Therefore, in the doctrine of the union of two personal natures in Christ, it was primarily a question of *natures,* not of persons. But the imprecision of the terminology and the deficiency of the general theory of the person made this doctrine ambiguous and, what is worse, imparted to it an ever-changing meaning, which inevitably led to confusion. It is likely that the Antiochenes themselves did not fully understand their own theory of the division of the natures, which, against their will, appeared to lead to the doubling of Christ. A similar thing happened to their opponents with their natural unity of the incarnate Logos. This ambiguity gave rise to imaginary problems for both the adherents and the opponents of the diophysitic Christology, namely to imaginary problems concerning the relation between the two personal na-

---

90. Cf. the comparisons in Jugie, *Nestorius et la controverse nestorienne,* pp. 174ff.

Introduction

tures in Christ. The imaginary character of these problems was exposed by the Church in the Definition of Chalcedon, which did not solve them but simply annulled and abolished them (for the dogma, but not yet for the theology).

1. Diodore of Tarsus

Let us confirm the aforesaid by examining certain declarations of the Antiochenes themselves, declarations that were anticipated by certain ideas of Paul of Samosata (despite all the differences between the doctrines). The surviving writings of one of the founders of Antiochene Christology, Diodore of Tarsus, contain a characteristic statement of the problem together with the fundamental concepts: namely, he collides against the fundamental aporia of Antiochene Christology, that of the *two sons,* and attempts to overcome it.[91] But the true founder of the doctrine is Theodore of Mopsuestia, to the degree one can determine this from the few surviving writings of this productive author.[92]

2. Theodore of Mopsuestia

The theme of Theodore of Mopsuestia's christological doctrine is the same as that of Apollinarius and St. Cyril: "the Word was made flesh." However, he refuses to see in this an indication of any fusion, absorption, or transformation of the one principle into the other. The Word was made flesh only *kata to dokein*, in appearance, for the Word did not change into flesh. Theodore defines the relation between the perfect divinity and the perfect humanity by the word "inhabitation" (*enoikēsis,* which is also a biblical term); man is the *temple* of God. There had already been instances of the gracious inhabitation of God in righteous men of the Old and New Testaments, but in Christ we have a case of inhabitation that is unique and exclusive both with respect to its fullness (the Word had all His energy in Jesus, without separation [*achōriston*]) and with respect to the continuity of its presence (the Word is united with Jesus from the very beginning, from His conception in the womb).[93]

---

91. Diodore of Tarsus, *Fragmenta* (PG 33.1560).

92. In addition to general works on the history of dogma (see in particular Dorner, *Entwicklungsgeschichte,* vol. 2), see also P. Gur'ev, *Theodore of Mopsuestia* (in Russian) (Moscow, 1890); and L. Patterson, *Theodore of Mopsuestia* (London, 1926).

93. Theodore of Mopsuestia, *De Incarnatione* (PG 66.976).

The Dialectic of the Idea of Divine-Humanity in the Patristic Epoch

How can one define the character of this unification, which Theodore of Mopsuestia prefers to call not union *(henōsis)* but co-union *(sunapheia)*? He examines three possibilities: union according to essence, union according to energy, and union according to good will *(eudoxia)*. He rejects the first two possibilities inasmuch as neither the divine essence nor the divine energy is compatible with limited creaturely being. And so, only good will remains.[94] It is easy to see that this theory of Theodore of Mopsuestia is not successful: good will is a moral concept, not an ontological one, and therefore this concept is not in harmony with the fundamental ontological problem of the union and is also incompatible with the different types of the latter.[95] But Theodore considers good will to be the most intimate of unions, essentially an ontological one: "Having been united by good will with God the Word, He [Christ] became inseparable from Him, having in all things one and the same will and one and the same action with Him; and there is no connection that is stronger."[96] "What does *like the Son* signify? It signifies that the Word, inhabiting Jesus, united with Himself all that He received and prepared Jesus to enter into communion with all the dignity that He, the Son, by nature inhabiting Jesus, makes common for them. He makes Him one person with Himself by virtue of the unity to which He raises Him. He communicates to Him all primacy. He willed by good will to accomplish all things through Him: the judgment, the trial of the whole world, and His own coming."[97] Anticipating in part the Chalcedonian dogma, Theodore says: "We speak of the proper essence of God the Word and of the proper essence of man: the natures are distinguished, but the person resulting from the union is one." He clarifies this idea as follows: "When we attempt to distinguish the natures, we say that the person of man is perfect and that the divinity is perfect. When we consider the union, we attest that there is one person and that there are two natures."[98] To be sure, like all the authors of the ancient Church, Theodore compares the union of the natures in Christ with that of body and soul in man, but the meaning he ascribes to this comparison is opposite to that which we find in Apollinarius and St. Cyril: the union, which is not a confusion, does not abolish the difference of the na-

---

94. Ibid., 972.
95. This is indicated, among others, by Loofs in *Paul von Samosata* (Leipzig, 1924), pp. 248-49.
96. Theodore of Mopsuestia, *De Incarnatione* (PG 66.1013).
97. Ibid., 976.
98. Ibid. This text is characteristic of the confusion of person and nature, which are practically identified here.

tures.⁹⁹ But Theodore has his own comparison for the union of the natures: he compares it to marriage, in which two are united into one.¹⁰⁰

From the autonomous being of the human essence, preserved in the union of the natures, Theodore of Mopsuestia draws the very important conclusion that the God-Man possessed an authentic human life, manifesting a real human freedom and moral responsibility. Theodore thus establishes that evolution and works were proper to this life. The man in Christ accomplished deification in himself by a true feat of spiritual struggle. This idea is highly fruitful, for it abolishes the *deus ex machina*, divine coercion over human nature, but it does have a weakness, namely that, in postulating the union of the Logos with man from birth, Theodore is not able to link this with Jesus' human moral freedom, which could not be manifested in the fetal and infant states. He seeks a way out of this difficulty by postulating that, in virtue of His prevision, by a special privilege (which is analogous to the Catholic dogma of the Immaculate Conception), God united Himself with Jesus when He was still an infant.¹⁰¹ This assumption, which is evidently indispensable for Theodore, is indisputably a weak point of his doctrine. He also applies with a certain inconsistency the principle of moral freedom, in virtue of which Jesus followed the path to His glory: Theodore excessively asserts the objective power of the temptation of evil for the One who from His very birth had become the temple of God.

Theodore's fundamental idea concerning Jesus' earthly life is that He grew in holiness over the entire course of this life, and that He attained the crown of this holiness only after His death, when He became perfectly immaculate and unchangeable as far as His thoughts were concerned.¹⁰² The union of God the Word with the human essence is not only an initial fact but also a process that continues over the entire course of Jesus' earthly life, until His death and resurrection. The perfect union, accompanied by the deification of the human essence, is achieved only by the freely chosen feat of obedience to the Father's will, although the result of this process is the fullness of this union, a fullness expressed in the unity of the person in the case of the duality of the natures. In his own way Theodore of Mopsuestia anticipates the Chalcedonian formula.¹⁰³ He defines¹⁰⁴ this final

---

99. *Contra Apoll.* 4 (PG 66.1000).
100. Theodore of Mopsuestia, *De Incarnatione*, ex. 1, 4 (PG 66.981).
101. *Act. Concil.* 5.91.
102. See PG 66.976-78.
103. Ibid., 981.
104. Cf. *Expositio Symboli* (PG 66.1017).

The Dialectic of the Idea of Divine-Humanity in the Patristic Epoch

union as an *achōristos sunapheia* (inseparable co-union), in virtue of which he energetically rejects the duality of sons but affirms the unity of the Son of God, the incarnate Logos.[105]

The focus of Theodore's system is, without question, the affirmation of moral freedom, autonomy, and self-determination in the Lord's humanity. Owing to this focus, Theodore does not allow the humanity to be absorbed by the divine nature and transformed into an instrument (as in Apollinarius) or into an attribute (as in St. Cyril). This element of his doctrine, which characterizes the entire school of Antioch, leads Theodore to diophysitism, enables him to anticipate the future dithelitism, and becomes an integral part of the Christology of the Church. But his own Christology, like that of the entire school of Antioch, is undeniably dualistic. This is seen most clearly in his attitude toward the term "Theotokos" (bearer of God), which at that time had become current in the church literature. Like Nestorius, he does not by any means reject this term, but he interprets it in a certain limiting way by admitting "anthropotokos" (bearer of man) alongside "Theotokos," each in its own special sense.[106] But he considers it "madness to say that God was born of a Virgin," considering this to be a product of Apollinarianism.[107] Here, the christological problem for him consists in the preservation of the duality of the natures and the "perfect humanity."

Thus, that which for Apollinarius seemed a christological absurdity, that is, the union of two perfect natures, is for Theodore the initial axiom and fundamental postulate of Christology. But he expressed his doctrine with such a terminological imprecision (which corresponded to the obscurity of his thought) that it remained ambiguous. This explains why Theodore of Mopsuestia, who was considered an orthodox theologian during his life and departed this world at peace with the Church, was anathematized as a heretic after his death (at the Fifth Ecumenical Council).

The development of the christological doctrine put new dots over the i's and illuminated in a new manner the thought of Theodore of Mopsuestia with its obscurities and contradictions. Indeed, if one takes *prosōpon* to mean "person" in the sense of spiritual person, and not only in the sense of concrete nature, then Theodore's doctrine of two persons that are united into one person contains a contradiction. The moral unity of love, of good will, of obedience can establish the harmony of the life of

---

105. Ibid. Cf. *De Incarnatione* 20 (PG 66.985).
106. Theodore of Mopsuestia, *De Incarnatione* 15 (PG 66.862).
107. *Fragm. Contra Apoll.* 3 (PG 66.997).

two, but not their ontological unity; it is precisely the latter, however, that is required here. The union of the three hypostases in divine love establishes the unity of their life, but by no means does it fuse them into one hypostasis in the presence of the unity of nature or consubstantiality. In Christ we have, in addition to this, the distinction of the created and uncreated natures. Therefore, their fusion based on the model of adoptionism, or the identification of the human hypostasis with the divine, becomes incomprehensible.

Theodore's Christology is thus a failure, even though its postulates are correct. But his opponents, Apollinarius and St. Cyril, who also started from a correct postulate, the unity of Christ, were equally unsuccessful in their theology. In both cases the failure is dialectical, and both sides are right dialectically insofar as they mutually postulate each other in the movement of thought; both become wrong, however, when they transform this dialectic into a dogma. Dogma must transcend dialectic and overcome it in synthesis, but theologically this could not be accomplished at that time, or anytime during the entire patristic epoch.

3. Nestorius

The fate of Nestorius,[108] a disciple of Theodore of Mopsuestia, is a "tragedy" (as he himself titled his autobiography, which has not survived). It is a tragedy connected with his dispute with St. Cyril, a dispute that is an integral part of the history of the Church. This dispute polemically brought to the fore solely the essentially terminological question of the Theotokos, a question that for Nestorius had only a christological significance. Nestorius did not desire to diminish the veneration of the Most Holy Mother of God, nor did he unconditionally reject the term "Theotokos,"

---

108. Besides the fragments of Nestorius's works that are contained in the acts of the Council of Ephesus, in sermons, and so on (which are all collected in Loofs, *Nestoriana* [1905]), of primary significance for the understanding of Nestorius's doctrine is a book recently published in Syriac translation, *The Book of Heracleides of Damascus* (French translation by F. Nau, *Le livre de Héraclide de Damas* [Paris, 1910]). The Greek original has been lost; only the Syriac translation has been preserved, from which the French translation was made, as well as the English translation: L. Hodgson and G. R. Driver, *The Bazaar of Heracleides* (1925). Of the most recent literature on Nestorius that considers Heracleides, see Jugie, *Nestorius et la controverse nestorienne;* Tixeront, *Hist. des dogmes,* vol. 3; Bethune Baker, *Nestorius and His Teaching* (1908); Loofs, *Nestorius and His Place in the History of Christian Doctrine* (1914); the article "Nestorius" in *Dict. de théol. cath.;* A. d'Alès, *Le dogme d'Éphèse* (1931); Seeberg, *Lehrbuch,* et al.

he only insisted that it be defined more precisely. In a polemic against a particular christological doctrine, he proposed, as more precise, the term "Theodokos" (bearer of man and of God).[109]

The fundamental divergence between St. Cyril's monistic Christology and the school of Antioch, represented by Nestorius, can be reduced to different conceptions of the interrelation of the natures in Christ. For Nestorius, as well as for Theodore of Mopsuestia, there is no nature without hypostasis, or (as Nestorius usually says) without *prosōpon* (person). But terminologically, his notion of *person* is just as obscure as St. Cyril's notion of *hypostasis*.[110] The only thing that is indisputable here is that Nestorius does not conceive the true concrete nature without a *prosōpon*. Therefore, since the divine and human natures are concrete and real, they possess corresponding persons, which are in an interrelation of free harmony and union *(sunapheia)*. This union is such that it signifies a new person, namely *the person of the union*, Christ, who thus differs from the Logos outside of the Incarnation and from Jesus as a human person. But from the very birth of Christ there arises this hypostasis of union — Christ, the divine-human person. Nestorius accused St. Cyril of confusing the natures, while St. Cyril accused Nestorius of doubling the persons in Christ. They posed and solved in different ways the problem of the *divine-humanity* as the union of the divine and human natures. Nestorius did not have the slightest doubt that "for the two natures there exists one power ... and one person [*monadikon prosōpon; una persona unigeniti*]."[111] And his formula "I separate (distinguish) the natures, while uniting the adoration" expresses precisely this idea of unity *in* duality and *in the presence of* duality, in contradistinction to St. Cyril's unity *from* duality or *according to* duality.

Prior to the Council of Ephesus, Nestorius's thought in the polemic with St. Cyril was expressed in occasional statements. We are most famil-

---

109. Nestorius indicates (in *Heracleides*, pp. 91-92) that he did not provoke this dispute but entered it when it was already fully underway in order to extinguish it.

110. According to Jugie's opinion (*Nestorius et la controverse nestorienne*, p. 96), for Nestorius "les mots: essence *(henosis)*, nature, hypostase *(kath hupostasin)*, personne *(henōsis, physique)* sont en réalité synonymes. Ils designent la nature concrète, individuelle et douée de personalité, aucun ne signifie l'essence concrète ou abstraite par opposition a l'individu et à la personne." ["The words essence *(henosis)*, nature, hypostasis *(kath hupostasin)*, and person *(henōsis, physique)* are actually synonyms. They designate concrete nature, individual, and endowed with personality. None of them signifies the concrete or abstract essence in opposition to individual or person." — Trans.]

111. Loofs, *Nestoriana*, pp. 171, 176, 196, 224, 280, 281.

iar with it from the contra-anathematisms with which Nestorius responded to St. Cyril's "Twelve Chapters" of anathematisms. Much more interesting and substantive are the ideas Nestorius had arrived at during his long years of solitude, which are expressed in his posthumous work *The Bazaar of Heracleides*. This is his theological apologia before the Church, as if the voice of an exile from beyond the grave. This work is large and full of ideas, but it gives the impression of a collection of notes, with abundant repetitions and obscurities. Nevertheless, the freshness of thought that survived the arduous trials of exile is amazing. The fundamental points of the theological divergence with St. Cyril are exhibited here more clearly and substantively than in their direct polemic.

In conformity with the general tendency of the school of Antioch against the school of Alexandria, Nestorius attempts to dogmatically establish the true *humanity* in Christ. He accuses his opponent of inhumanity, of "not recognizing the perfect man in the nature and actions," and of thinking that "God ... was not human nature but in human nature and actions, so that God the Word was two natures."[112] For Nestorius, the postulate of true divine-humanity is the fullness of the two natures, whose condition is the presence in them of the concrete form of being – *prosōpon*.

What is *prosōpon*, this difficult notion of Nestorius's that appears to have many meanings? In the first place, "*prosōpon* does not exist without essence, but essence and *prosōpon* are not one and the same."[113] The most comprehensive definition of *prosōpon*, which we find in *The Bazaar of Heracleides* in connection with its frequent references to Philippians 2:6-7, is that it is the form *(morphē)* of existence of the one nature or the other, a modality (and in this sense it is a concept more general than "person," and in any case less determinate). Christ took "the form of a servant," being in the image of God, "not by essence, not by nature, but by resemblance and by *prosōpon*, in order to participate in the form of a servant and in order that the form of the servant participate in the image of God, so that there necessarily be one *prosōpon* with two natures, for the form is the *prosōpon*."[114] To be sure, such a definition is too abstract; it does not contain the concept of a living person but only the image of a person's being, an empty form. But this definition turns out to be fruitful for Nestorius when he develops his fundamental idea of the unity of the *prosōpon* of

---

112. *Le livre de Héraclide de Damas*, p. 165.
113. Ibid., p. 150.
114. Ibid., pp. 145, 147.

union (or the *prosōpon* of economy, as he often says) in the presence of the two *prosōpa* of the natures. The two are juxtaposed or included in one another, as it were; they become mutually transparent and, being different by nature, they are identified *in actu*. But they are identified not by natural necessity, but freely. They are identified by obedience, good will, and love.

In *The Bazaar of Heracleides*, Nestorius insistently and repeatedly develops the idea that the two natural *prosōpa* constitute one *prosōpon* of union, Christ. This unity must therefore be considered the initial postulate of his entire Christology: "The Word was made flesh, and dwelt among us. . . . He assumed flesh by assimilation into His own *prosōpon*, which exists for two: on the one hand, for the essence of God and, on the other, for union and assimilation of the flesh. Thus, the flesh itself, which is flesh by nature, is, as a result of the union and assimilation of the *prosōpon*, equally the Son. Although He is in the two, He is called one Son and one flesh. For this reason the one Son of God and Son of Man, one and the same of two, is called from two, because He assimilated the properties of both *prosōpa* into His *prosōpon* and is therefore designated as the one and the other as His own *prosōpon*. He speaks with men sometimes in the name of divinity, sometimes in the name of humanity, and sometimes in the name of both. . . . He is the Son of God and also the Son of Man and speaks [in the capacity of each]."[115]

"Union takes place not for the *prosōpon*, but for the nature. We speak not of the union of the *prosōpa*, but of the union of the natures. For in this union there exists only one *prosōpon*, whereas in the natures there exist both the one and the other, so that the *prosōpon* is known in their combination. It is precisely through His *prosōpon* that He assumed flesh, the form of a servant; it is in the name of the latter that He spoke when He taught, when He acted, when He accomplished His works. He gave His own form to the form of the servant, and of this form He spoke as of His own *prosōpon* and in the name of Divinity. The *prosōpon* truly is common, one and the same. The form of a servant belongs also to Divinity, and the form of Divinity to humanity. The *prosōpon* is one and the same, but not the essences, for the essence of the form of God and the essence of the form of the servant reside in their hypostases."[116] These obscure formulations come close to anticipating the Tome of Leo the Great and the

---

115. Ibid., p. 50; cf. pp. 53, 55, 66, 127, 129, 138-39, 140-41, 145, 146, 167, 169, 192-93, 194-95, 282. This enumeration (by no means exhaustive) shows the frequency with which Nestorius repeats this idea.

116. Ibid., p. 152.

Introduction

Chalcedonian formula. It is therefore not astonishing that Nestorius declared himself to be in full agreement with the Tome of Leo the Great,[117] just as he would have declared full agreement with the Council of Chalcedon, had he lived to see it. It is not by chance that Nestorius's friend and ally Theodoret participated in this council, although he was compelled to repudiate Nestorius.

In *The Bazaar of Heracleides,* Nestorius makes an attempt to *theologically* interpret this Chalcedonian idea of the unity of the hypostasis in the case of the duality of the natures by linking this idea with the initial thesis of the Antiochene doctrine of the duality of the *prosōpa* and the free and moral character of this union.[118] With this goal in mind, he advances the original, though confused, idea of the interpenetration or mutual encounter of the two *prosōpa* in the *prosōpon* of union. The natural *prosōpa* mutually use each other in that which is proper to them, just as in the vision of the Burning Bush, "the fire was in the Bush, and the Bush was fire, and the fire was the Bush, and each of them was the Bush and the fire, and there were not two bushes and two fires."[119] It should be noted that Nestorius decisively rejects the notion that the union with Divinity in Christ can be equated with the dwelling of the Spirit of God in the prophets or saints,[120] since this union is, so to speak, a prosoponic union. "In the *prosōpa* of union, one is found in the other, and this one is understood not as a diminution, mixing, or suppression, but as an action of receiving and giving, as an accomplishment of the union of one with the other; the *prosōpa,* not the essences, receive and give one and the other. We consider this as that and that as this, whereas both one and the other exist."[121] Thus, "the *prosōpon* of divinity is humanity and the *prosōpon* of humanity is divinity; it is other by nature and other by union."[122] And "incarnation is understood as the mutual use of the two [*prosōpa*] through its giving and receiving."[123]

Here, Nestorius approaches the idea of the interpenetration of the natures, which later is developed as *communicatio idiomatum* (see pp. 71-74 below). *Communicatio idiomatum* refers to the natures, but Nestorius applies this idea to the union of the natural *prosōpa* in an effort to solve the

117. Ibid., pp. 298, 303, 316, 327, 330.
118. Ibid., p. 34.
119. Ibid., p. 141.
120. Ibid., p. 49.
121. Ibid., p. 223.
122. Ibid., p. 268.
123. Ibid., p. 233.

The Dialectic of the Idea of Divine-Humanity in the Patristic Epoch

problem of the *prosōpon* of union, which arises before him in the framework of the school of Antioch's general premises.[124] It is an important theological achievement that Nestorius clearly recognized the problem of the *unity* of the hypostasis in the case of the *duality* of the natures, a clarity that we encounter nowhere else, either before Nestorius or after him, in the patristic epoch.

But at the same time it is obvious that, *theologically,* his thought was unable to master this problem, a problem that Alexandrian theology (in particular St. Cyril, with his obstinate monism) did not even notice. Nestorius's theory cannot explain how the divine and human *prosōpa,* that of the Creator and that of the creature, can interpenetrate each other if there lies between them an ontological chasm. Nestorius speaks of love, self-renunciation, and obedience as the conditions of the *prosōpon* of union, but this is insufficient to surmount the chasm. If one remains strictly within the logic of the duality of the natural *prosōpa* (the opponents of the school of Antioch were right in this respect), this duality remains insurmountable, and the harmony of the two, however far one extends it, does not become this *prosōpon* of union that Nestorius seeks without finding, going beyond the school of Antioch and approaching Chalcedon. In the history of thought, however, the seeking itself is sometimes a finding. Nestorius devalues the problem of the interpenetration of the natural *prosōpa* by a meager, purely formal interpretation of *prosōpon,* which approaches a simple modality. This interpretation, however, characterizes the whole of patristic theology: *temporis vitia, non hominis* (the fault lies with the epoch, not with the man). In any case, here Nestorius is a direct precursor of Leo the Great and knocks at the door of Chalcedon, not only historically but also dogmatically.

Nestorius employs the idea of *communicatio prosoporum* in an interesting way in his doctrine of kenosis, which represents a dogmatic exegesis of Philippians 2:7, to which he repeatedly returns. He interprets the idea of the taking on of the form of a servant by the One who has the form of God as the realization of the *prosōpon* of union, which is a divine condescension: the King becomes a servant and is obedient unto His death on the cross; man is clothed in God. Thanks to the good will of the conde-

---

124. It is curious that I. A. Dorner, a leading Protestant theologian of the last century, developed a theory of the origin of one person from two natures that is similar to Nestorius's theory (although he was of course not aware of the existence of *The Bazaar of Heracleides*). See Dorner's works *Entwicklungsgeschichte der Lehre von der Person Christi* (Berlin, 1856), 2/1.1260-61, and *System der christlichen Glaubenslehre* (Berlin, 1880), 2/1.436ff.

scension, Christ is "equally God and equally man: the form of God in condescension, in abasement and external appearance, and the form of the flesh as man. And man in his elevation is that which God is, thanks to the Name which is higher than all names. Thus, He was humbled in voluntary abasement even unto the death on the cross, using as His own *prosōpon* the *prosōpon* of the one who died and was crucified. And He served in His own *prosōpon* the one that belonged to the one who died, was crucified, and was glorified. Christ therefore has two natures, the form of God and the form of a servant, the one who is glorified and the one who glorifies."[125] "The King and Lord assumed the *prosōpon* of a servant as His own; He gave His *prosōpon* to the servant and revealed to him that He Himself is that one and that that one is He Himself; in the *prosōpon* of the servant He experiences infirmity, whereas in the *prosōpon* of the King and Lord the servant is deified."[126] With reference to the baptism of the Lord, Nestorius says: "Such is total obedience, not to demand anything for one's own *prosōpon* but [only] for the *prosōpon* of the one whose *prosōpon* He had and to accomplish His [the Word's] will, because the *prosōpon* of the Word was, strictly speaking, His, and He venerated His [the Word's] *prosōpon* as His [Christ's] own *prosōpon*; however, the *prosōpon* is one. It was for this reason that the Father indicated Him from heaven by the words: 'This is my beloved Son, in whom I am well pleased' (Matt. 3:17)."[127]

Nestorius's Christology thus exhibited a *dialectically* important aspect of the fundamental christological antinomy: he attempted to understand the bi-unity as a unity not of natures but of their personal centers. How is an authentic and full life of the natures possible without personal centers, and how is the union of the natures in the form of the union of these centers possible in the case of the full reality of each of them? This dialectical unfolding of the problem has a great theological importance, and anticipating our later discussion, we can indicate now that this question remained unanswered and even essentially unnoticed within the framework of patristic theology. Instead, it was simply prohibited by the anathematization of the whole of Antiochene theology at the Third and Fifth Ecumenical Councils after its relative and very limited triumph at Chalcedon (although this theology experienced a relative renaissance at the Fourth Ecumenical Council).

---

125. *Le livre de Héraclide de Damas,* pp. 54-55.
126. Ibid., p. 52.
127. Ibid., p. 61; cf. pp. 20, 58, 66, 76, 147, 189, 210.

The Dialectic of the Idea of Divine-Humanity in the Patristic Epoch

4. Theodoret

Theodoret played a major role in the Nestorian dispute as a friend, theological ally, and defender of Nestorius; however, for complicated reasons connected with church "economy," he was compelled to anathematize Nestorius at the Council of Chalcedon, although the anathematization applied more to the abstract theory of Nestorianism than to Nestorius the person. As for Theodoret's personal relations with St. Cyril, they were not at all friendly, but, again for reasons of "economy," he was compelled after St. Cyril's death to recognize him as a teacher of orthodoxy (in *Eranistes*). But these complex relations, in which personal convictions are complicated by "economy," belong to the domain of church history.

Despite his erudition and theological talent, Theodoret did not introduce any new themes in the development of dogma that had not already been considered by other representatives of the school of Antioch. In general, Theodoret supports Nestorius's conception of the duality of the natures in Christ, although he gives a much weaker expression than Nestorius to the idea of the duality of the natural *prosōpa*. He does much more decisively advance the doctrine of the unity of the divine-human hypostasis,[128] but we do not find in Theodoret a theological doctrine that would explain this union of the two natures in hypostatic unity (the sort of doctrine that Nestorius attempts to develop in *The Bazaar of Heracleides*). In Theodoret the school of Antioch is liberated from its extreme positions and joins the main current of the Church leading to Chalcedon.

This is a paradoxical historical fact: although St. Cyril was outwardly the victor at Ephesus, his council did not yield a dogmatic definition. (His "Twelve Chapters," with all their dogmatic inaccuracies, cannot be considered such a dogmatic definition, and it is even less warranted to consider the condemnations of Nestorius, with all their dogmatic imprecision, to be such a definition.) The sole dogmatic achievement of this council was the confession that united the Eastern and Western fathers who had been separated at Ephesus. This unional confession of 433 was sent by John of Antioch to St. Cyril, who accepted it. To be sure, this act is not a triumph of Cyrillian theology. It evidently was composed by Theodoret, and this formula, read at the Council of Chalcedon,[129] is Cyrillo-Theodoretian in char-

---

128. See the *Refutation of the Twelve Chapters* by St. Cyril of Alexandria (*Act. Concil.* 2.128-94).

129. It is remarkable that, after the reading of the epistle, the fathers of the council exclaimed: "We believe in the same way as Cyril. Eternal memory to Cyril!" As for Theodoret, he declared: "Anyone who speaks of two sons, let him be anathema" (*Act. Concil.* 3.277).

Introduction

acter (such was the judgment and synthesis of history, its *List der Vernunft*); and it of course anticipated the Chalcedonian formula. And, if in virtue of the same historical dialectic Theodoret's contra-anathematisms against St. Cyril were anathematized, once again for reasons of "economy," this did not augment the real influence of the Cyrillian theology, nor did it diminish Theodoret's real triumph, which was not his personal triumph but that of the entire school of Antioch; this triumph was accomplished at Chalcedon. Since their dogmatic conflict expressed the inner theological dialectic of the dogma itself, church history has justified each of the warring sides and even recognized that each was relatively right (and relatively wrong), although it cannot be denied that, in factual history, this dialectic appears to be accidental and even ambiguous in character, containing many random complications.

In Theodoret's *Eranistes*, written around 448 after the death of St. Cyril (444) and three years before Chalcedon, we hear echoes of this conflict, once again revealing the problematic of the school of Antioch and that of Theodoret himself. This work consists of three dialogues between an orthodox theologian (Theodoret himself, of course) and the "Eranistes," the questioner, a stylized figure of Alexandrianism.[130] The themes of these dialogues — (1) the Immutable, (2) the Inconfusable, (3) the Impassible — refer to the domain of Christology. The first dialogue considers the question of God's immutability, which appears to be contradicted by the idea of the Incarnation, in which change results from the union with the flesh. The Eranistes sees in this only a sign of God's omnipotence, which can transform change into nonchange. The inappropriateness of such an anti-ontological conception of the divine omnipotence is justly pointed out by the orthodox theologian, who understands the Incarnation as a "taking on" *(elaben)* of the flesh. Here God remains unchanged in His nature.

The thought here approaches the question of the very foundation of the Incarnation, but neither answer is adequate. The first amounts to a frank refusal to answer the question, whereas the second is an evasion of the question: to "take on" flesh is different, of course, from to "become" flesh, but it too is nonetheless a kind of change, not in the divine being itself, but in the mode of the divine being's relation to man. The question must be emancipated from formal verbal dialectic and raised to the higher principles of theo-anthropology: How is the divine-humanity possible? What are its general preconditions? But this question was posed neither by Antioch

130. *PG* 83.

The Dialectic of the Idea of Divine-Humanity in the Patristic Epoch

nor by Alexandria, even though only on the basis of this question could the two schools truly come to understand themselves and one another. Both schools remained in the plane in which Christology leads not to antinomy, which is inevitable, but to logical contradiction, which is unacceptable. In affirming God's immutability, the Alexandrianizing Eranistes is compelled to protect it against change by referring to God's omnipotence, which is understood as the ability to abolish contradictions. In contrast, the orthodox theologian, who differs from the Eranistes only in degree and not in substance, takes quantitative difference for qualitative, believing that he can thus overcome contradiction. Moreover, both equally affirm the reality of the Incarnation and reject the docetism that threatens them. In order to theologically admit the *divine-humanity*, both of them proceed not from the God-Man but from God *and* man; but in adding these components together, they get different results: On the one hand, the finite, creaturely quantity *man* becomes zero in the face of the infinite quantity of the absoluteness and thus the immutability of the Creator. On the other hand, being comparable and thus ontologically equatable with it, the finite quantity introduces a change in the absolute quantity — but this is a logical contradiction. The unanswerability of this question is shown in *Eranistes*.

The second dialogue, concerning inconfusability, considers from another angle the same question of the union of the natures. The Eranistes is found to confuse the natures, inasmuch as he recognizes two natures before the union and one after it. Ancitipating Eutyches, the Eranistes professes a true monophysitism where humanity is engulfed by divinity "in the same way that the sea swallows a drop of honey."[131] To this, the orthodox theologian opposes the union of the *two* natures, the perfect divinity and the perfect humanity, without confusion and therefore with their autonomy preserved.

But what does this union consist in? What is its power? To what extent is it a real unification and not a purely external juxtaposition? Astonishingly, we find here (at the opposite pole from Apollinarianism), instead of an answer, the Apollinarian (and also Cyrillian) comparison of the union between the essences in Christ with that between the soul and the body in man. In distinguishing the soul and the body, "we do not separate, but we call one and the same thing rational and mortal; and it is necessary to do the same thing with regard to Christ, attributing to Him both divine and human qualities."[132] Clearly, the comparison in this case

---

131. *Act. Concil.* 2 (PG 83.153).
132. PG 83.145.

is totally unsuitable because of its imprecision,[133] and it therefore turns out to be equally applicable to the most divergent doctrines (that of Apollinarius, St. Cyril, Theodoret, and others). It is especially unsuitable for the purpose considered here: to show the autonomy of the two natures in the case of the unity of Christ. But other comparisons borrowed from analogies with the physical world are even worse: light filling the air, iron made red-hot by fire, and so on.[134] Can any of this have any relevance for understanding the hypostatic unity of the two natures? And does this not show how far away even the theologian closest to the Chalcedonian doctrine remained, almost on the eve of Chalcedon, from a theological understanding of the fundamental christological problem: the problem of the unity of the personality and of the personal life in the case of two different natures and natural lives? In this sense, the joint labor of the schools of Alexandria and Antioch did not yield valuable theological results.

The final dialogue, on the Impassible One, does not have essential significance after the failure of the first two dialogues, although it concerns a very acute and popular question that was repeatedly posed in the theological polemics: the question of the passion of the Savior. To what degree and in what sense did His Divinity participate in the passion? The orthodox theologian answers this by referring to the unity of the person of Christ, in virtue of which He receives all things that are proper to the human nature, including suffering and the salvific death: "When we affirm that the body, the flesh, or the humanity suffered, we do not separate the divine essence from it." This point of view is already familiar to us from the polemic with Nestorius; it consists in a consistent application of the doctrine of the hypostatic union of the two natures, but it does not contain any new elements of the problem. Here, Theodoret is closer to St. Cyril than to the school of Antioch.

Present at the Council of Chalcedon, Theodoret attested how Antiochene theology, whose point of departure was not only the conception of two natures but also the conception of two natural persons, became an integral part of the Alexandrian-Antiochene (as well as non-Alexandrian and non-Antiochene) formula of one person and two natures. Was this acceptance due to a concession and to a rejection of the initial definitions, that is, of St. Cyril's unional creed, or was it the product of a theological worldview? But if that is the case, where and when was

---

133. Theodoret offers a painstaking refutation of Apollinarius's opinion on the trichotomic composition of the soul in favor of the dichotomic composition (ibid., 108).

134. Ibid., 156.

this step taken? When and how did Antiochene theology overcome its doctrine of two natural persons in the God-Man, a doctrine that so fatefully follows from the premises of this theology? There is no answer to this question, just as we do not know how to bridge the gap between the two natural persons and the one hypostasis of union. Nestorius, in the obscurity of his exile, tried to construct such a bridge in his then-unknown *The Bazaar of Heracleides,* but we do not see a similar attempt at a transition in Theodoret. He shared the fate of his opponent, St. Cyril; he bowed down before the truth of the Church by, in effect, repudiating his personal theological opinion. For both fathers the breath of the Spirit of God, guiding the Church, was stronger than their personal theological opinions. They both possessed a divine instinct for the truth of the Church that was stronger than, and could not even be contained by, their own consciousness.

The Chalcedonian dogma is a new birth (preceded by the unional definition of 433) that issues neither from Antiochene theology nor from Alexandrian theology *within their proper limits.* And it could not be otherwise, for each of these theologies was destined to manifest its own dogmatic dialectic, in which both the thesis and the antithesis are necessary and important in their polar tension but also erroneous and unnecessary in the one-sidedness of their self-assertion. A synthesis was necessary that could not be found on the pathways of Alexandrian-Antiochene theology, and therefore it was *not* found by this theology. But that which is impossible for men is possible for God, and that which was beyond the powers of theology was made manifest above the heads of the theologians — in anticipation of the future achievements of theology — to the divine instinct of truth, to the inspiration of the fathers of the Council of Chalcedon.

III. The Chalcedonian Synthesis

A. The Dogmatic Tome of Leo the Great

This divine instinct, or superconsciousness, that guides the Church was expressed in two dogmatic monuments: the Tome of Leo the Great, the epistle the great pope sent to Flavian, archbishop of Constantinople, in 449; and the Definition of the Council of Chalcedon.

The first document is associated with the condemnation of Eutychianism and the events at the "Robber Council" of Ephesus in 449. In his doctrine, the Archimandrite Eutyches exhibited the same tendency that led to monophysitism in the *theology* of St. Cyril (although not in St. Cyril's proper doctrine). The true theological meaning of the formulas *mia phusis, henōsis phusikē ē kath hupostasin* (one nature, natural and hypostatic union) and the union *ek duo phuseōn* (from two natures), which are distinguished according to union *theōria monon* (only in theory) — all of these *theological* foundations of the Cyrillian Christology can lead only to monophysitism of one type or another, even though St. Cyril himself was not a monophysite. He was capable of theological inconsistency and of including in his doctrine what his theology could not encompass (ending with the Antiochene formula of 433).

In contrast, although he apparently was not a theologian at all, Eutyches manifested a doctrinal consistency in the monistic tendency of the Cyrillian Christology. Eutyches' main assertion, to which he remained faithful even when he was judged by the tribunal of the Constantinopolitan council of Archbishop Flavian, was as follows: "Our Lord consisted of two natures before the union, and after the union I confess one nature [*mian phusin*]."[135] This later became the *communis opinio* of monophysitism and undeniably found favor at the Cyrillian Council of Ephesus, with its acceptance of St. Cyril's "Twelve Chapters." Thus, when the council demanded that Eutyches anathematize this opinion, he objected not without foundation that he was afraid of thus anathematizing certain holy fathers, including Athanasius and Cyril.[136] He was condemned for disagreeing with the "true dogmas." In expounding his doctrine, Eutyches exhibited much obscurity and confusion with reference to the Incarnation; in particular, he affirmed that, in Christ, perfect God was united with perfect man, while at the same time asserting that the body of the Lord, although consubstantial with the Virgin Mary, is not consubstantial with us ("the body of God is not the body of man, but is human"[137]). Does this not resemble the Cyrillian "assimilation" of human "properties," but without a special human "hypostasis"-nature?

Eutyches' doctrine was only a symptom that showed to what degree the arrow of the dogmatic compass had moved in the direction of St. Cyril, and even far beyond him. This doctrine needed to be corrected by a shift from thesis to antithesis, from monistic Alexandrianism to

---

135. *Act. Concil.* 3.287; Mansi 6.784.

136. "I have read the Blessed Cyril, the holy fathers, and St. Athanasius: they recognized two essences before the union, but after the union and incarnation they recognized not two, but one" (ibid., 289).

137. Ibid., 322.

diophysitism. Flavian's council had already taken this course in condemning Eutyches' doctrine, which provoked a violent reaction from militant monophysitic Alexandrianism in the person of Dioscorus and his "Robber Council." The response to this act was the Tome of Leo the Great, addressed to Archbishop Flavian.[138] Though it was not even read at Dioscorus's council, it played a determining role at the Council of Chalcedon.

This astonishing epistle, with its brilliant classical style, antithetical and lapidary, is the glory of the throne of Rome, occupied then by the great pope; it marks the turn in the development of dogma in the direction of Chalcedon. It presents the orthodox formula of the duality of the natures in the case of the unity of the hypostasis, which became the foundation of the Definition of Chalcedon. The Tome of Leo the Great does not demonstrate or even develop its dogmatic doctrine; instead, it decrees the doctrine as a development of the Roman creed. Anyone who expects to find here a synthetic way out of the christological dialectic, in the sense of overcoming its antithetics, will not find it, for Leo remains *outside* theology with its dialectic, at least outside theology of the Eastern type. And although the Tome reflects the influence of the Western tradition (Tertullian, Novatian, Augustine), it does not mark a decisive movement of theological thought with its problematic (as historians of different tendencies recognize[139]). The Tome does not contain a *theological* synthesis, and it only gropes toward a doctrinal definition by relying on *religious* evidence that has not yet been theologically substantiated. This is where the obscurities and imprecisions of the Tome come from.

As can be expected in such a situation, the central argument is soteriological in character: "It is not useful for salvation, as well as dangerous, to recognize the Lord Jesus Christ either only as God without man or only as man without God" (ch. 5); "from ours, He has a humanity that is less than the Father; from the Father He has a Divinity equal to that of the Father" (ch. 4). "To give our state its due, the impassible nature has united itself with the nature that is susceptible to suffering. And it was necessary for our salvation that one and the same mediator between God and man, the man Jesus Christ, could die in one [*ex uno*] and could not die in the other [*ex altero*]. Thus, in the integral and perfect nature of true man, God was born, all in His own [*totus in suo*], all in ours. . . . He took the

---

138. S. Leonis Magni ep. 28 *(Lectis dilectionis tuae)* (PL 54).

139. Protestant theologians (Dorner, Harnack, Loofs, Seeberg) and Catholic theologians (Tixeront, Battifol, Michel, et al.) are in agreement concerning this.

form of a servant without the foulness of sin, raising the human without diminishing the divine" (ch. 3). This union was accomplished "with the properties of each of the two natures and substances preserved"[140] (ch. 3), but with the "unity of the person [*personae*] conceived in each of the natures" (ch. 5), that is, "the person of God and of man [*Dei et hominis una persona*]" (ch. 4), and without the essences being confused: "the properties of the divine and human natures abide inseparably in Him."

The two natures often receive a characteristic designation in the Tome of Leo the Great: *forma-morphē*, a clear reference to Philippians 2:6-7: "Who, being in the form of God, thought it not robbery to be equal with God: but made himself of no reputation, and took upon him the form of a servant, and was made in the likeness of men." "He took the form of a servant without the foulness of sin, raising the human without diminishing the divine" (ch. 3). "Each of the forms acts in communion with the other in such a way as is proper to it [*agit (energei) utraque forma (morphē) cum alterius communione quod proprium est*]" (ch. 4). "The Word produces that which is proper to the Word, and the flesh realizes that which is proper to the flesh." "The one is brilliant with miracles, whereas the other is subject to humiliations . . . but each is the true Son of God" (ch. 4), "God because [*per id*] He is the Son of God by whom all things were made, and man because the Word became flesh, being born of it 'under the law' (Gal. 4:4)." "There is not the slightest falsehood in this union, since the humility of man and the magnificence of God exist conjointly [*invicem*]." "One thing in Him is the source of the humiliation that is common to the one and the other; and another thing is the source of the glory common to the one and the other" (ch. 4).

The Tome of Leo the Great does not define the basic concepts *persona* and *natura* (which, when translated into Greek as *prosōpon* and *phusis*, have a somewhat different ring than in the original Latin). The replacement or explanation of *natura* by *forma* does not by any means lead to clarity. The Apostle Paul's text about the humiliation of Christ, Philippians 2:6-8, does not, strictly speaking, contain a Christology; it speaks only of the *form* of this humiliation for Christ, "in fashion [*en schēmati*] as a man," as a form of obedience. Therefore, by using this concept to define the natures, Leo does not by any means clarify the situation (and he does not even eliminate the possibility of a docetic interpretation, despite all the assurances that this union is authentic). Leo the Great's doctrine of two forms in Christ can be compared with the analogous doctrine of Nestorius, which we find in *The*

---

140. *Utriusque naturae et substantiae;* apparently this is just a pleonasm.

Bazaar of Heracleides. It is thus not by chance that Nestorius declared himself to be in agreement with the Tome of Leo the Great. For Nestorius this idea was the key to understanding how from the two natures-forms there arises the *prosōpon* of union, which is both different from and identical to the *prosōpa* of the natures.

In general one must say that the school of Antioch, and *all* its representatives, never denied the unity of the person of Christ, the Son of God, and always rejected the duality of sons and persons in Christ. The conception of duality was attributed to the school of Antioch by its opponents as the necessary and only possible conclusion from their theology, even though the representatives of this school did not draw such a conclusion. The Antiochene theory of two hypostases proper to two true and concrete natures was only intended as an attempt to understand how the *two* natures could be united in *one* hypostasis, though these two natural hypostases were united to the point of total identification in the hypostasis of union. In the final analysis, this theory is not capable of showing and proving this identification of the two persons in one, and it therefore does not in fact overcome the duality of the persons. But that was not its intention. What it intended was to try to understand how one person can unite two natures, or how one person arises from two natures. In conformity with this intention, the Antiochene doctrine is a theory not of the duality of persons that are only components to be added, as it were, but a theory of their unity or sum. An analogous problem is absent in St. Cyril's Christology, which is its indisputable weakness, leading to the one-sidedness of monophysitism.

But what do we find in the Tome of Leo the Great, who with a brilliant antithetics powerfully reproduces the doctrine of the two natures in Christ, crowning them with one person? Do we find any sort of theological doctrine that could explain this unity of the person in the case of the duality of the natures and would be a religious consequence of Leo's soteriological considerations? Pope Leo stood outside the intense theological creativity in the domain of Christology that characterized the Greek East. Expounding his doctrine not without a certain theological naïveté in massive religious images, he cut the Gordian knot of Christology.

What does he mean by the unity of the person in the case of two natures? We can only draw indirect conclusions about this on the basis of an analysis of the Tome. We must first note the presence of definitions that have an Antiochene (and in particular a Heracleidean) ring to them. Then we have a series of juxtapositions of that which is proper to the divinity and that which is proper to the humanity in Christ, juxtapositions that reflect the Antiochene doctrine in its initial, not in its final, form. For the humanity it is proper to be born in the flesh, "to hunger, thirst, be fatigued, and sleep," "to weep from sorrow over a dead friend," "to hang on the cross," whereas for the divinity it is proper to work miracles.[141] Leo indicates two parallel series that are not conjoined in the unity of the life of the God-Man: "Although in the Lord Jesus Christ there is one person of God and man [*Dei et hominis*],[142] one thing [*aliud*] in Him is the source of the humiliation common to both and another thing the source of the glory common to both." Moreover, the distinction between the natures extends even into the domain of personal self-consciousness and, in the Antiochene fashion, doubles the one person: "It is not proper for one and the same nature to say 'I and my Father are one' [John 10:30] and 'My Father is greater than I' [14:28]" (ch. 4). It turns out that each nature speaks here from its own I, although the two I's are united in some manner in one I.

The following passage has a similar resonance: "from ours [from our essence in Him] He has a humanity that is less than the Father; while from the Father He has a divinity equal to that of the Father." What precisely does *una persona* signify, and how does it unite the two natures? The Tome of Leo the Great leaves this question unanswered. In any event, the Tome does not represent progress in *theological* thought, although it is an important step forward in church dogma. Like the Antiochene formula, which was even more imprecise, Leo's formula represented a compromise that was necessary and even inspired by grace, a compromise in which both sides, each interpreting this formula in its own way, could find refuge: the genuine diophysitism of classical Antiochianism and the monism of St. Cyril's followers. Nevertheless, this formula signified the triumph of the tendencies of Antiochene theology and therefore subsequently provoked the reaction of the zealots of monism, which led to monophysitism.

B. The Definition of Chalcedon

The Definition of Chalcedon is the *synthetic* resolution of the dialectical antithetics that we have in the Christology of the schools of Antioch and

---

141. This differentiation in miracles between that which belongs to God and that which belongs to man leads to some sort of alternation of the natures and thus to their confusion. This does not represent one of the finest pages in Leo's theology.

142. Bolotov translates this as "God-man" (*Lectures*, 269), but this is a theological interpretation. Leo does not have the concept of the God-man.

of Alexandria. In a certain sense, this definition says both "yes" and "no" to both schools, raising them to a higher unity. The dogmatic synthesis contained in the Chalcedonian formula was essentially prepared by the entire preceding development of Christology and represents the supreme achievement of the dogmatic consciousness in the domain of Christology. The Third and Fifth Ecumenical Councils can be considered the prolegomenon and epilegomenon of this formula, its historical foreword and afterword, as it were. These two councils should not be viewed independently but only in the same context as the definition. Indeed, the three councils can be considered a triune council.

But it is essential to keep in mind that, having all the force of a divinely inspired *dogmatic* definition, the Chalcedonian formula is, in its content, by no means a *theological* achievement. On the contrary, theologically ahead of its time (and to a certain degree even ahead of our time), this formula remained unclarified and unrealized in theological thought. It was more a schema than a doctrine. This is most clearly attested by the history of the Fourth Ecumenical Council. In this council we see the influence of external and accidental factors, of secular power and hierarchical rivalries (although this influence is perhaps less marked than at the Third and Fifth Ecumenical Councils). The Council of Chalcedon was conceived as a reaction against the early monophysitism, stylized in the form of Eutychianism. However, some of the participants of the council (including former participants of the council of Dioscorus, which just two years earlier had justified Eutyches) were adherents of Alexandrian Christology, defined according to St. Cyril, and they opposed not only "Nestorianism" (which perhaps had never existed in this stylized form) but also the whole of Antiochene theology, as well as the diophysitic Tome of Leo the Great. Meanwhile, the school of Antioch, which had gained an authoritative ally in the person of Leo the Great, also received the support of the secular authorities. The Definition of Chalcedon therefore turned out to be a compromise formula that somewhat unnaturally united St. Cyril's doctrine with the Antiochianizing Tome of Leo the Great.

Two epistles from St. Cyril were read at the council, one of which, to Nestorius (although *without* anathematisms), was typical for St. Cyril in the sense that he expounded his Alexandrian monism not in positive theses but in a series of negations that represented logical or at least possible conclusions from this monism. Therefore, despite its great theological imprecision, this epistle remains in the main stream of orthodox theology in virtue of its negative character. And in this respect it differs from the epistle with anathematisms, which was read triumphantly at the Council of Ephesus and revealed the distinctive features of the proper doctrine of St. Cyril. But at Chalcedon, instead of this epistle, the epistle to John of Antioch was read, which included the compromise formula of 433, by no means typical for St. Cyril. St. Cyril was thus represented at Chalcedon as having a strong tendency to Antiochianism, although the respect that surrounded his name also facilitated the approval of the Alexandrianizers. St. Cyril's fundamental dogmatic definition, "the natural union," was tacitly rejected at Chalcedon, whereas his formula of "hypostatic union" was interpreted in a sense diametrically opposed to his own: in the sense not of natural union, but of union in one person. The council also tacitly rejected St. Cyril's formula "two natures before union and one after," and even his "union *from* two natures," which was replaced by union *in* two natures.

But this victory of the Western and Antiochene theology did not result from agreement. On the contrary, opinions were divided, and if some stood beneath the banner of the Tome of Leo the Great, others attempted to seek refuge from the Tome behind the authority of St. Cyril; the balance was tipped only by the interference of representatives of the secular authority. The history of the council attests to this. First, despite its enormous authority, which was supported also by the secular authorities, the Tome of Leo the Great did not by any means remove all the dogmatic doubts and questions concerning its orthodoxy, even those of the Illyrian bishops, who depended on Rome, or those of the Palestinian bishops. In fact, it was these bishops who indicated what texts in the Tome were most vulnerable because of their ambiguity, notably the famous *agit utraque forma*.[143] But the wary archontes repulsed at the very outset this attempt at substantive dogmatic discussion, and no further attempts were made. It should also be remembered that the initiative of forming a *new* dogmatic definition came from the secular authorities, not from the fathers of the council. They initially resisted a new definition, preferring to retain the old ones based on St. Cyril's epistles and complemented by the Tome of Leo the Great in an appropriate interpretation. After the insistence of the archontes had triumphed, a special commission of bishops prepared a

143. "Both the one form and the other act in communion with the other, in the manner proper to it: the Word as is proper to the Word and the flesh as is proper to the flesh." The second text: "Our salvation requires that one and the same intermediary between God and man, the man Jesus Christ, could die on one side and not die on the other." Finally, the third text: "For although in the Lord Jesus Christ, there is one divine-human person, yet one thing serves in Him as the source of the humiliation common to the two, whereas another thing serves as the source of glory common to the two."

The Dialectic of the Idea of Divine-Humanity in the Patristic Epoch

draft definition (which has not survived) in which the Alexandrianizing tendency was expressed in the formula *ek duo phuseōn* (from two natures). A conflict thus arose in the council, which was resolved only by the Emperor Marcian's ultimatum that the council would be disbanded unless a consensus was reached by means of a commission of compromise. Only then did a commission of twenty-three, with the participation of the archontes, work out a new draft, which was then accepted as the dogmatic definition of the council.

This external history of the Definition of Chalcedon sufficiently attests that it was the product of practical necessity, not of theological thought (even though it was, of course, essentially rooted in the theology of the epoch). It was practical Rome together with the empire, not the philosophical East, that directly stimulated this new dogmatic birth. It was as if this birth occurred without the participants of the council willing it or being conscious of it *(List der Vernunft)*. This was truly a dogmatic miracle, surpassing the natural powers and possibilities of the dogmatic consciousness of the epoch; but precisely for this reason it was not embraced and assimilated by the epoch, as is evident from the history of the further dogmatic movements. In this sense the Chalcedonian *mia hupostasis — duo phuseis* (one hypostasis, two natures) resembles more than anything else the Nicene *homoousios*, which also was ahead of its time.

Was the Chalcedonian formula the theological response to the dialectical impasse of Alexandrian-Antiochene Christology? Was it the desired *theological synthesis?* Or was it only a dogmatic formula, schema, or theme for further theologizing? To be sure, these questions can be answered only on the basis of an analysis of the text.

The introduction indicates that, being guided by the two epistles of St. Cyril that were read at the council and by the Tome of Leo the Great, the council intended to eliminate the following errors: the division of one person into two sons, the assertion that Divinity is subject to suffering, the mixing or confusion of the natures, the opinion asserting a heavenly nature in Christ, and the opinion asserting two natures before the union and one after it (only the last of these opinions is anathematized). This is followed by an enumeration of the extreme positions possible for the various theological tendencies, although these extremes, except for the last, do not even exist; they amount to stylized Apollinarianism, Cyrillianism, and Nestorianism. The latter, which is anathematized, in fact contains St. Cyril's doctrine, which was later appropriated by the monophysites. Despite the dominant importance conferred upon his two moderate epistles, the text is also directed against St. Cyril's doctrine.

Introduction

The fundamental definition itself follows. In its most substantial expressions it is a paraphrase, in part, of the unional confession of 433 (from St. Cyril's epistle to the Eastern theologians) and, in part, of the Tome of Leo the Great (but without the characteristic *agit utraque forma*, etc.). In general, it has the character of a compromise formula between East and West, between Alexandria and Antioch, with the latter unquestionably dominant.[144] This is evident not only from the essential idea of one hypostasis in the case of two natures (with the formula *en duo phusein*), but also from the radical imprecision of Antiochene theology as to the meaning of this idea: Is the hypostasis simply one in the sense given it by St. Cyril, or is it composite, arising from the union of two natural hypostases? The possibility of such an interpretation is by no means excluded, for example, by the following definition from the Tome of Leo the Great: "The union does not in any way suppress the distinction between the two essences, but the property [*idiotes*] of each essence is preserved to an even greater degree and is united [*suntrechouses*] into one person and one hypostasis." What is especially remarkable is that this formula can also be interpreted in the sense of St. Cyril's *idiopoiēsis tōn poiotētōn* [appropriation of qualities], with the difference, of course, that *hupostasis*, which for St. Cyril is equivalent to *phusis*, is equivalent here to *prosōpon*. The concept of person or personality is generally not proper to antiquity, and here too it remains completely obscure.[145]

144. Here is the text of the definition: "We, then, following the holy Fathers, all with one consent, teach men to confess one and the same Son, our Lord Jesus Christ, the same perfect in Divinity and also perfect in humanity; truly God and truly man, of a reasonable [rational] soul and body; consubstantial with the Father according to the Divinity, and consubstantial with us according to the humanity; in all things like unto us, without sin; begotten before all ages of the Father according to the Divinity, and in these latter days, for us and for our salvation, born of the Virgin Mary, the Mother of God, according to the humanity; one and the same Christ, Son, Lord, Only-begotten, to be acknowledged in two natures, without confusion, without change, without division, without separation; the distinction of natures being by no means taken away by the union, but rather the property of each nature being preserved, and being united in one person and one hypostasis, not parted or divided into two persons, but one and the same Son, and only begotten, God the Word, the Lord Jesus Christ." [This translation, modified here to conform with the Russian text, has been taken from *The Creeds of Christendom, with a History and Critical Notes*, vol. 2, *The Greek and Latin Creeds*, ed. Philip Schaff, p. 62; revised edition, ed. David S. Schaff (Harper and Row, 1931). — Trans.]

145. Here is what Bolotov has to say about this: "It should be noted that the Fathers spoke in the language of their time; that the personal consciousness did not represent, in the psychology of this epoch, such an essential and determining factor for the

The Dialectic of the Idea of Divine-Humanity in the Patristic Epoch

From the religious point of view, the Chalcedonian dogma possesses a soteriological self-evidence, even though, from the theological point of view, it is the most complex of theologemes. The dogma can be divided into a series of postulates of soteriology: (1) for man's salvation by his participation in divine life (his deification), it is necessary that in Christ "Divinity abide bodily," that is, the Divine Person, *inseparable* from His divine nature; (2) it is also necessary that the "perfect" human essence be assumed fully, without any limitations; (3) it is therefore necessary that it not be some particular human individuality, which at the same time would be a limitation; (4) but at the same time, for the fullness of its humanity, it cannot remain without hypostasis; (5) and therefore the hypostasis of the Logos becomes also the human hypostasis. Thus, the duality of the natures in the case of the unity of the person, of the hypostasis, is postulated soteriologically.

The Chalcedonian dogma externally seems to be the desired synthesis of the thesis concerning the unity and the antithesis concerning the duality of Christ in the christological dialectic; this dogma says its "yes" to both of them. However, *theologically,* this dogmatic synthesis is only the juxtaposition of two ideas that remain in conflict, a conflict that manifested itself the day after the Council of Chalcedon. For those who continued to engage in theological thought, it was impossible to conscientiously execute the dogmatic decree of the council. The antinomy that is contained in the dogma is outwardly marked by four purely negative definitions at its core (*asugchetōs, atreptōs, adiairetōs, achōristōs* [inconfusedly, unchangeably, indivisibly, inseparably]), without any attempt at positive definition. This antinomy represents the sharp point from which thought slips off when it attempts to interpret the dogma. When we examine the natural origin of the dogmatic miracle of the Definition of Chalcedon (and it is undeniably a dogmatic miracle), this miracle turns out to con-

---

autonomy of spiritual being; that in the foreground of *hupostasis* one had the element of 'being by itself,' of 'being for itself,' and not the element of personal consciousness. It is natural that the Fathers did not foresee the points of view taken by modern thinkers. The Fathers only sketched out the principles which later polemicists and dogmatists successfully developed.... Consequently, without predeciding all the particulars, the Council of Chalcedon established the fundamental and universally obligatory point of view with regard to the person of the God-Man, excluding any dogmatic construction that would lead to the recognition of two sons, two hypostases. And if we understand 'hypostasis' in the sense of autonomous spiritual being as person, as self-conscious 'I,' it follows that the Chalcedonian definition obliges us to consider the person of the God-Man as one 'I' with one consciousness of self" (*History of the Ancient Church,* 4.293-94).

sist in a compromise, an external, mechanical union of two heterogeneous and mutually antagonistic conceptions that unexpectedly and miraculously yielded a chemical (instead of a mechanical) union, forming a dogmatic crystal. But one should not deceive oneself by thinking that, at the time of its formulation, the Chalcedonian dogma was theologically justified or even fully understood. Rather, it was externally and somewhat forcibly imposed on the council. This concatenation of events, however, manifested the work of the hand of God, the breath of the Holy Spirit, which "bloweth where it listeth" and no one can tell "whence it cometh" (John 3:8).

The Chalcedonian dogma is not only a doctrinal norm according to which the consciousness of the Church must measure itself. It was also given to human thought as a limit problem of the theological and philosophical understanding. It would be erroneous to think that the schools of Alexandria and Antioch, the theological schools of this epoch (which was distinguished by astonishing dogmatic talent but was also subject to inevitable historical limitations), had prepared and exhausted this dogma in their interpretation. It would be more correct to say that these schools expressed only the first presentiments concerning its significance in theology, anthropology, and theo-anthropology. Providence desired that this dogma should originate not from theology but somehow from *above* theology, although *for* theology as well. Providence desired that it should be a religious symbol (or a kind of dogmatic "myth") for all ages; and it belongs to our own epoch not less (and possibly more) than to the epoch in which it originated. One would like to think that it is precisely our epoch, in its striving for theological synthesis, that is called to be the Chalcedonian epoch, that is called to a new religious and theological disclosure and assimilation of this gift of the Church. For its own epoch the historical destiny of this dogma was distinctive in the sense that it marked the end of the epoch, while also advancing beyond it. The Council of Chalcedon marked the end of the blossoming of christological theology that was connected with the schools of Alexandria and Antioch in their opposition. The school of Alexandria continued its existence in the monophysitic epigonism, whereas the school of Antioch simply disappeared after the Chalcedonian victory.

But this victory, the *miracle* of the Chalcedonian dogma, was *theologically* so far ahead of its time that its reception brought not peace but a new tempest into the Church. What is most remarkable here is that the reaction against the Chalcedonian dogma (the various forms of monophysitism) was motivated not so much by the heretical rejection of it as by dog-

The Dialectic of the Idea of Divine-Humanity in the Patristic Epoch

matic and even terminological misunderstanding.[146] On the one hand, in the past (following the Cyrillian tradition) the monophysitic circles had identified the terms "nature," "hypostasis," and "person"; and from the purely terminological point of view, therefore, the Chalcedonian formula seemed to them a sort of abracadabra. On the other hand, as far as its substance was concerned, these circles considered the formula to be Nestorian in character and fought against it in the name of orthodoxy as expressed in the Cyrillian formulas. This tendency to protect the theological consciousness against possible Nestorian deviations was satisfied at the fifth council of Justinian by the symbolic condemnation of the "three chapters," with a somewhat altered exposition of the Chalcedonian doctrine in the direction of Cyrillian theology (without changing the substance of the dogma). The diverse spectrum of monophysitic theology abounds with subtle theological thoughts alongside crude heretical deviations, but it does not manifest new dialectical elements in the fundamental christological problematic. It does, however, contain much material that is interesting for the historian of dogma.

C. Leontius of Byzantium's Doctrine of Enhypostasia

In connection with the problematic of Christology we should not neglect a sixth-century writer who was perhaps less creative than the leaders of monophysitism but nevertheless clarified the theological problem of the Chalcedonian dogmatic synthesis, namely the problem of the *hypostatic union* of the two natures. We have in mind Leontius of Byzantium and Jerusalem, a polemicist about whom we have scant biographical information. He polemicizes against both deviations from the Chalcedonian dogma: Nestorianism (to which he was once close) and monophysitism. In his own exposition of the Chalcedonian dogma he exhibits a tendency to Cyrillian theology, and in this sense he is one of the precursors of the Fifth Council.[147] Leontius (together with Boethius in the West and St.

---

146. See in particular Lebon, *Le monophysisme sévérien;* M. Jugie, "Monophysisme," in *Dict. de théol. cath.* (Paris, 1929), pp. 87-88.

147. An inquiry into the authenticity of Leontius's works (*PG* 86.1-2) was carried out by Loofs, *Leontius von Byzanz*. Aside from the history of dogma (Harnack, Loofs, Seeberg, Tixeront, Schwane), see the following monographs: J. P. Junglas, *Leontius von Byzanz* (Paderborn, 1908); W. Rügamer, *Leontius von Byzanz* (Würzburg, 1894); V. Ermoni, *De Leont. Byz. et de eius doctrina christologica* (Paris, 1895); V. Sokolov, *Leontius of Byzantium: His Life and Literary Works* (in Russian) (Sergiev Posad, 1916).

Introduction

John of Damascus in the East) is one of the founders of scholastic theology, which seeks to overcome dogmatic difficulties by means of scholastic definitions. But at the same time the need for a coherent, self-examining thought (anticipating the later criticism) leads him to refine and analyze the problems. Here we breathe an air different from that which surrounds the initial elemental impulses of patristic theology. The continuity and dependence of theology on the philosophy of antiquity (primarily Aristotle) are manifested in Leontius's works more clearly than in the various representatives of patristic theology. Leontius's primary focus is on how to understand and express in concepts the union of the two natures in one hypostasis without falling into the natural unity of monophysitism or into the hypostatic duality of Nestorianism. His answer to this problem is the theory of enhypostasia, in-hypostatization, which, from the philosophical and theological standpoint, is generally designed to complete or refine the corresponding doctrine of categories and, with reference to Christology, to find a way to overcome the difficulties of the Definition of Chalcedon.

Leontius's point of departure is the Aristotelean distinction between *essence* and *hypostasis,* a distinction that had already been employed by the Cappodocians.[148] He defines essence *(ousia)* as the being of something;[149] and under it he subsumes everything to which the general name essence or its definition belongs, however numerous the differences of the essences might be. "We speak of the existence of the essence of God, of angels, of man, of animals, and of plants." (The abstractly formal and even physical – as opposed to metaphysical – character of this category is clearly demonstrated by the fact that he puts in one series the substances of God, angels, man, animals, etc.) Next in order of concreteness are genus *(genos)* and species *(eidos),* with their proper qualities.[150] Concrete being belongs to *hypostasis,* which also has its proper qualities. Following Aristotle, Leontius calls these qualities accidents *(sumbebēkota),* although he distinguishes between inseparable and separable accidents. In general, hypostasis is correlative with ousia or essence (or nature). "Nature [*phusis*] corresponds in its meaning to being, while hypostasis corresponds to a *particular* being (to an autonomous being [*kath' heauton*]). The former signifies a species, whereas the latter contains a specific quality [*idion*] of the

---

148. See the excursus to my essay "Chapters on Trinity: The Doctrine of Hypostasis and Essence in Eastern and Western Theology" (*Pravoslavnaya Mysl'*, no. 1).
149. Leontius, *Adversus argumenta Severi* (PG 86.1921C).
150. Ibid.

general. In brief, to *one* nature there properly refer unisubstantial (things), about which one speaks in general terms; whereas the definition of hypostasis contains that which is identical by nature but distinguished *by number* or which consists of different natures."[151]

For Leontius, characteristic synonyms for hypostasis are person *(prosōpon)* and individual *(atomon)* (PG 86.1305C). One can see from this that, for Leontius, the concept of hypostasis does not at all signify a spiritual being, a person, but is (as in Aristotle) the formally logical, abstract category of *individual* being in general, and in this sense it coincides with Aristotle's distinction between the first and second essences, that is, between concrete being, which possesses authentic existence, and abstract general being, of nature, existing not in itself but only in individuals.[152]

If for Leontius the concept of hypostasis coincides with a concrete being, that is, with a reality, it does not by any means signify a spiritual being or a personal principle: *to tinos* or *kath' heauton* (someone or something autonomous), in the general sense, does not at all contain this; "person" is only one of the *species* of hypostatic being, and for Leontius it remains just as indeterminate as it did for his predecessors. Thus, with reference to the question of the person and the personal spirit, Leontius remains faithful to antiquity, for which the absence of this problem was characteristic. And thus it becomes even more astonishing that the concept of hypostasis was central for his Christology.

From Aristotle's premise that only hypostatic being is real, Leontius draws a fundamental conclusion, which for him (as well as for the school of Antioch) is a kind of axiom: there is no nature without hypostasis, *ouk esti phusis anhupostatos* (1280A). Hypostatizedness becomes synonymous with reality (the anti-Platonic tendency of Aristotelianism is clearly visible here).[153] Leontius perceives, however, besides simple unihypostatic or unisubstantial being, also a special genus of *complex* being, produced by the union of natures. Here it is possible that two (or more) substances are united that exist neither self-hypostatically nor not *non*hypostatically, but precisely *in*-hypostatically, *enhupostasis*.[154] According to this conception, a

---

151. Leontius, *Contra Nest. et Eutych.* (PG 86.1280A).

152. Cf. Loofs, *Leontius von Byzanz,* p. 68.

153. The anti-Platonic sense of this ontological axiom of Leontius's is noted by S. Schlossmann in *Persona und prosōpon im Recht und im christlichen Dogma* (1906), p. 82. This shows how difficult it is to represent Leontius as a Platonist, which is sometimes done, despite his philosophical eclecticism.

154. An example of such in-hypostatization for Leontius is man, who has one common hypostasis (which one?) but consists of two substances: body and soul. See PG 86.1304BC.

combination of properties of a given nature, even if the latter is nonhypostatic, enters into an in-hypostatic union with another nature, no longer in the capacity of separate properties or accidents but preserving, so to speak, its proper natural person and existing not only by its properties but by nature. Leontius thus wishes to save the existence of this nonhypostatic nature by uniting it with another hypostasis. He attaches to it a foreign head, so to speak, while preserving its body. This is precisely what the in-hypostatization, *enhupostasia*, in another hypostasis means.

But this whole theory is based on a *petitio principii*, which consists in the arbitrary transformation of a combination of properties, without nature and without hypostasis, into a particular "nature." How can this be *logically* justified? Where is the criterion that establishes this? Not only does Leontius not have such a criterion at his disposal, but his entire theory is totally incompatible with Aristotle's clear and consistent (although, of course, insufficient) schema: There are things-hypostases that have being, or "first essences" (hypostases). And there is the nature of things, which is established by abstraction from concrete being — this is the "second essence." It is evident that the latter, according to Aristotle, cannot receive any kind of nonhypostatic recognition, on the basis of which it would enter *as nature* into another hypostatic being. Here Leontius is defeated by his own axiom: There is no nonhypostatic (or extrahypostatic) nature; in other words, a "nature" cannot exist as such, as a certain complex of properties, independently of its hypostatic incarnation. In this case one can therefore speak only about separate *properties, poiotētes*, not about their combination, that is, about a nature. From the point of view of Aristotle's categories, one can recognize a multi-unity in the composition of a complex hypostasis; for example, a multiplicity of separate human individuals constitutes a crowd or a regiment, but it would be absurd to suggest that these human individuals had a nonhypostatic nature prior to their unification, and that they were in-hypostatized into the hypostasis of the crowd or regiment.[155]

If such a doubt is legitimate even in relation to the general *physical* concept of hypostasis, the only concept of the latter that antiquity knew,

---

155. On this basis, those who remark this inconsistency wish to interpret the doctrine of in-hypostatization on the basis not of Aristotelian but of Neoplatonic philosophy. This is done by Junglas, for whom it is clear that Aristotle's doctrine (*Categ.* 8a.17) does not leave any place for a theory of in-hypostatization. It should be noted, however, that St. John of Damascus, philosophically an Aristotelian, accepts Leontius's doctrine of in-hypostatization and does not see anything doubtful about it (see St. John of Damascus, *Brief Exposition of the Orthodox Faith*, book 3).

then how much greater must our doubt be when it is a question of a hypostasis in the sense of a human person. It is clear that, within the limits of Aristotle's categories, there can be no man in general; human nature exists only in particular individuals (that is precisely why the heresy of tritheism grew out of the soil of Aristotelianism). The concept of humanity as *pan-human nature* clearly leads one beyond Aristotle's doctrine into the domain of Christian Platonism, in the light of which one can, in a certain sense, admit the logical primacy of humanity over particular individuals. But this leads us beyond Leontius's doctrine, within which the concept of *enhupostasis* represents a contradictory and arbitrary use of Aristotle's categories and, as such, serves no purpose, despite the influence it acquired in the later scholastic theology.[156]

But apart from these doubts of formal logic, one can also have doubts concerning the content or substance of the concept of in-hypostatization. According to Aristotle and also Leontius, what is a hypostasis? What is its *principium individuationis*? If one ignores Leontius's *kath' heauton*, which expresses nothing and which in any case is only a symptom or consequence of hypostatic being, not its foundation, then this *principium individuationis* is a particular attribute *(idikon)* or combination of attributes that must be *united* with the nature with its attributes of genus or species, concretizing them. For example: man (nature), African American (species), Uncle Tom (individual). Or: water (nature) + a temperature below zero = ice, and so forth. Such a combination of properties presupposes a certain relation among them but by no means presupposes their arbitrary union: for example, a man can be hypostatized as a person of a certain race or color, but he cannot be hypostatized as rice or as a gorilla. Different human individuals can form the composition of a collective or complex hypostasis, a crowd. However, cows cannot be part of this composition; they can only form a herd, which excludes man. In other words, the hypostatic attributes that compose a hypostasis are concrete and really individual; they do not lend themselves to the abstract in-hypostatization of anything at all: it is impossible to attach the head of a goat to a deer. Such a hybrid animal ex-

---

156. That is why one modern Catholic author, wishing to understand and accept Leontius's theory, is compelled to recognize that "c'est ne point Aristote mais plutôt de Plato qu'il depend. C'est à Platon qu'il emprunte son anthropologie sur la modelle de laquelle il construit sa christologie." ("It is not Aristotle but rather Plato upon whom he depends. It is from Plato that he takes his anthropology, basing his Christology on the latter.") (V. Grumel, *Dict. de la théol. cath.*, 9/1.425.)

ists only in the imagination, just as abstract in-hypostatization does not exist in reality.

But Leontius uses the concept of *enhupostasis* (the term is borrowed from various fathers of the preceding epoch) as a means to construct a Christology as a theory of the hypostatic union of the two natures. He also uses it as a polemical weapon to ward off the "Nestorian" doctrine of the duality of the hypostases and the monophysitic doctrine of the fusion of the natures. He finds in it an answer to a question that had remained unanswered, that is, he finds in it a theological interpretation of the Chalcedonian dogma, as well as the foundation for a kind of Chalcedonian theology.

Leontius applies the idea of in-hypostatizedness, as the middle or third state between hypostatizedness and nonhypostatizedness, to the interpretation of the Chalcedonian dogma of the two natures that have one, divine hypostasis, that of the Logos. The divine nature is pre-eternally hypostatized by the Logos; but although it is deprived of its proper human hypostasis, the human nature also has its hypostasis in the Logos: the human nature is in-hypostatized in this hypostasis. This in-hypostatization of humanity in the Logos yields the "complex" *(sunthetos)* hypostasis of *Christ* in the two natures, "both existing before the union in Christ" (1801B). The preexistence of Christ's human nature is one of the obscure and contradictory elements in Leontius's doctrine. On the one hand, Leontius denies the preexistence of Christ's humanity before His Incarnation, for His humanity never existed separately from His divinity. But on the other hand, he is compelled to acknowledge that Christ's humanity is not a particular case, *christotēs*, but the universal human nature, *anthrōpotēs*, because otherwise it would have no relation to us. At the same time, Christ's humanity must also be an individual nature, and not only the universal nature; otherwise, one would have to admit that "Judas and Pilate, Anna and Caiaphas, were made incarnate and were crucified for us not less than Christ" (1801A). Therefore, from our nature the Word assumed into His proper hypostasis a certain particular *(idikēn)* nature (1485C) through His birth from the Virgin.

Humanity thus acquires its own hypostasis by being in-hypostatized in Christ, and the postulate of Nestorianism is satisfied. But this hypostasis is not a human one, and instead of the duality of the hypostases there results one hypostasis, though a "complex" one. According to Leontius, Christ is nonetheless different from the Logos before the Incarnation, although He remains unchanged both before and after the Incarnation (1525A). "From the beginning the Savior's humanity existed not in its own particular hypostasis but in the hypostasis of the Word" (1568A). But this postulate is much easier to state than to apply. Using an abstract algebraic reasoning, it is easy to say that H *(Humanitas)*, which is usually hypostatized in the concrete human hypostases A, B, C, . . . , is this time hypostatized in X (Christ): H + A; H + B; H + X. The method of abstraction, however, serves here not to solve the problem but to draw us away from the essence of the problem. *How* is the formula H + X applicable, and is it applicable, if X is not a human hypostasis but a Divine one? And can one unite the natural and hypostatic properties in all manner of combinations? Or is there some specific foundation for this, and if there is, what is it? Leontius does not supply an answer to these questions, and we find here the same *petitio principii* that we noted above. Leontius's only answer is a sort of *testimonium paupertatis* of theology, namely an inappropriate reference to God's omnipotence: "If the cause of the nature and of the person is God alone, what then will prevent Him from transferring one nature into another hypostasis or one hypostasis into another nature? Here, all things are possible" (1593C). This is just a futile effort to suppress a problem that has already been posed.

Nevertheless, it is impossible to hide forever in an *asylum ignorantiae* (refuge of ignorance), because even such an application of the principle of *deus ex machina* will not do away with the doubts that appeared in the theological consciousness after Chalcedon. Leontius's theory does not dispel these doubts but only verbally conceals them. First, how can the hypostasis of the Logos, which according to Leontius is His personal property that hypostatizes in Him the nature of Divinity and is correlative to the personal properties of the other hypostases of the Holy Trinity, make itself conformable with the human nature in order to unite itself with it and thus become correlative to the personal properties of different human individuals? Does this not merely transfer the problem into another domain without solving it, a situation that weakens Leontius's polemic against both the monophysites and the Nestorians (since both had substantive relations in mind, not evasions based on formal logic)? But how is it possible ontologically for the divine hypostasis of the Logos to become also a human hypostasis, to become suitable for the hypostatization of the human nature? Or, to phrase it differently, how can the human nature encompass the divine hypostasis? Leontius evades a substantive treatment of this question by means of formal-logical abstraction. Even if one were to admit that different natures can be hypostatized by one hypostasis, it would not yet follow that all natures could be hypostatized by any hypostasis. An express conformity would be required, in virtue of which only certain particular hypostases could hypostatize only certain particular natures. In what does this conformity consist, and why is it that the divine hypostasis of the Logos can conform precisely with the human nature?

The *divine-human* problem is here posed in its essential content, but the polemicist Leontius, who is satisfied with his schemes, does not notice it. His conception also leads to another difficulty, which is just as inexorable: What is the basis of the autonomy of the human nature, which in itself is nonhypostatic and which is in-hypostatized only by the hypostasis of the Logos? We have already noted the difficulties and vacillations experienced by Leontius with regard to the question of the preexistence or nonpreexistence of the human nature in Christ: its preexistence results from the fact that, in His Incarnation, Christ assumes an already existent human nature, not one created anew; whereas its nonpreexistence results from the fact that this nature receives individual concrete being only after the Incarnation of the Word, being hypostatized in Him. But what does such a prehypostatic and as yet nonhypostatic human nature in Christ represent? Why is this a *nature*, which in general is correlative with a hypostasis and does not exist without it (Aristotle's "second essence"), while at the same time being the entire old Adam, and not only individual properties, which are attached to the divine essence as accidents in order to become mixed with the latter and dissolved in it in one way or another? This is also the teaching of the monophysites, who were impelled precisely by this difficulty to defend nevertheless the autonomy of the nonhypostatic and creaturely nature in its union with the divine nature (we have already seen this difficulty in the doctrine of St. Cyril of Alexandria). Certainly Leontius was guided here by the orthodox dogma of the two natures in Christ; however, he did not succeed in interpreting this dogma *theologically*, and he failed to demonstrate the existence of a human *nature* in Christ.

Thus, Leontius's attempt to construct an ontological Christology ended in failure, although formally he can be credited with expressing the dogma with greater precision. The principal reason for this failure (*temporis vitium, non hominis* [the fault is with the epoch, not the man]) is the absence of a doctrine of the *personal* spirit living in a hypostatic nature. The concepts of hypostasis and nature, applied here to spiritual being, are borrowed from the natural world; they are physical categories, which do not grasp and are incapable of grasping the problem of the relations between the spiritual and natural worlds. This represents the limitation of ancient theology, which is fatally insufficient for the theological interpretation of Christian dogmas. In Leontius, as in Boethius,[157] one can observe a certain shift toward personalism, a shift that is expressed in the definition of hypostasis not only as a particular distinguishing quality but also as an independent being *(kath' heauton to tinos einai)*. However, the magnitude of this shift should not be exaggerated: it is too indecisive and indeterminate.

Leontius's doctrine of enhypostasia was nevertheless adopted by patristic theology. St. John of Damascus in particular expounds it as an irrefutable theory.[158] This doctrine became a symbol of orthodoxy, even though it imperceptibly resurrected the principles of Apollinarianism, not in its imaginary and vulgarized form (the denial that Christ has a human soul), but in its true significance, in the idea that the human hypostasis in Christ is replaced by the Logos, and thus that the human essence is in a certain sense incomplete in Him. This is precisely what Leontius attests by his doctrine of in-hypostatization: his theory represents the humanity in Christ as a nature deprived of hypostasis, which is replaced by the divine hypostasis of the Logos. This constitutes a rehabilitation, though surely unintentional, of Apollinarius's Christology.[159]

The doctrine of enhypostasia poses a new and highly interesting problem, that of the interrelation of the natural properties in Christ, *koinōnia* and *antidosis, communicatio idiomatum;* this problem occupies an important place in dogmatics. All the difficulties that arise in connection with defining the interrelation of the two natures in Christ and that lead to monophysitism or Nestorianism are transferred here to the idea of hypostatic union. This makes it possible for Leontius to exploit the positive elements of both of these schools without sacrificing the dogma of the two natures, or at least not the letter of this dogma. "The proper qualities of each nature become the common qualities of the whole, whereas the common qualities of the whole belong to each nature separately because of the inconfusability of the qualities in the one and the other" (1941A). "That which is said in general about the hypostasis refers to the one nature and the other; everything that is said separately about the natures refers also to the whole hypostasis. Thus, He is visible and invisible, mortal and immortal, tangible and intangible in different aspects. Everything is said not about one and the same thing, but about different things in different ways, not as about one, simple nature, but according to differ-

---

157. See Boethius, *Liber de persona et duabus naturis Christi* (PL 64.1343-44).
158. See his *Brief Exposition of the Orthodox Faith,* book 3, ch. 9.
159. This was remarked by Seeberg, *Lehrbuch,* p. 259.

Introduction

ent natures, united and preserving in their union their natural property" (1945C). For Leontius this principle is also the key to understanding the events in the Gospels.[160]

We find a generalized expression of this idea in a brief passage from a writer of the same epoch, Pseudo-Dionysius: "He was neither human nor nonhuman; although humanly born He was far superior to man, and being above man He yet truly [remained] man. Furthermore, it was not by virtue of being God that He did divine things, and not by virtue of being a man that He did what was human, but rather, by the fact of being God-made-man He manifested to us a divine-human [*theandrikēn*] energy"[161] This idea of the theandric energy, so pleasing to the monophysites and indeed so close to their thought, was adopted by St. John of Damascus in his development of the general idea of the communion of the properties in Christ.[162] In this he sees a manifestation of divine-humanity,[163] which he understands as the hypostatic unification of two separate natures, despite their separateness interacting by virtue of the hypostatic union. "That which is proper to man, Jesus Christ accomplished not in the manner habitual to man, since He was not a mere man; just as that which is proper to God, He accomplished not as God only, for He was not just God, but God and man together"; "each essence acts with the participation of the other," and "the divine actions were accomplished by means of the body, as by means of an instrument" (is this not Apollinarianism?). "Thus, divine-human action signifies the fact that since God became man, that is, was in-humanized, his human action too was divine, that is, was divinized, and not deprived of participation in His divine action. Likewise, his divine action was not deprived of participation in His human action; rather, each of the two actions was contemplated together with the other."[164]

---

160. In particular instances, he applies this principle unsuccessfully, transforming the Gospel events into a confused mélange of the actions of the two natures. For example: "The walking on the sea was an action of the Divinity, whereas the fact that He died was a property of the human nature; remaining incorruptible, He manifested the power of His Divinity" (PG 86.1341C).

161. Pseudo-Dionysius, *Epist.* 4, *Caio monacho* (PG 3.1072). [The English translation has been adapted from that given in *Pseudo-Dionysius: The Complete Works* (New York: Paulist Press, 1987), p. 265. — Trans.]

162. *Brief Exposition of the Orthodox Faith*, book 3, ch. 4: "On the Intercommunion of the Properties"; ch. 19: "On Divine-Human Action."

163. Ibid., ch. 4, pp. 247-48.

164. Ibid., ch. 19, pp. 284-85.

The Dialectic of the Idea of Divine-Humanity in the Patristic Epoch

Although St. John of Damascus expounds the doctrine of the two wills and two energies in Christ in a corresponding manner, his interpretation of divine-human action, which he has in common with Leontius of Byzantium, is nevertheless a variant of monophysitism. And it cannot be otherwise, given the insufficient, physical conception of the hypostatic spirit that characterizes his interpretation. To be sure, there can be no argument with his thesis that the human essence is *deified* in Jesus, although he tends to understand this deification physically rather than spiritually (it is not by chance that we encounter here the famous comparison involving the red-hot sword, where "the action of burning belongs to the fire and the action of cutting belongs to the iron").[165] And as soon as he tries to define the mode and meaning of this deification more precisely, there arise — despite the dogma of the two wills and two energies — propositions of a monophysitic character, attesting to the absorption or suppression of the human essence by the divine essence. Particularly noteworthy is his interpretation of the miracles and other Gospel events, where we have either a form of monophysitism or a mechanical mixing or simple succession of the two natures (in this case, not only Leontius of Byzantium but also St. Cyril of Alexandria and Leo the Great are predecessors of St. John).

But if it is still possible to understand the meaning of the communication of properties in the case of the deification of the human essence, it is far more difficult to understand the converse: the influence of the creaturely, human essence on the divine essence. The only thing that St. John of Damascus says about this is that the human essence is "not deprived of participation" in the divine essence. And in general, in expounding the doctrine of the communication of properties, the dogmatic handbooks encounter insurmountable difficulties when they attempt to define how the human essence in Jesus can influence the divine essence. The only recourse the handbooks have is the kenotic theory, according to which Divinity becomes potential and humanity becomes actual. But we will discuss this elsewhere.

The question of the theandric, or divine-human, action in Christ is inevitable for Christology. It was correctly posed by Leontius of Byzantium and Pseudo-Dionysius and was later taken from them as a theme by St. John of Damascus. It is not just one of the particular questions of Christology; rather, it contains the most general and ultimate result of the christological problematic and is, as it were, the measure of the entire

---

165. Ibid., ch. 19, p. 285; cf. ch. 17, p. 281.

christological doctrine. This question is the starting point and end point of all Christology, and its true content or subject is the Gospel story, the appearance of the God-Man on earth, His life and His miracles. To be sure, in and of itself this question remains a *mystery* for man, a mystery that surpasses not only his consciousness but his very being (for man cannot have two natures, and he does not contain divinity). Nevertheless, this mystery is unveiled, at least in its outer layers, in the revelation of the dogma and in the theology that interprets this revelation by means of reason. And one must admit that, in general and in the final analysis, patristic theology could not master this problem of *communicatio idiomatum*: Neither Leontius of Byzantium nor St. John of Damascus, who clearly understood this problem, succeeded in solving it; just as, earlier, St. Cyril of Alexandria could not come up with a clear and coherent solution; nor could Theodoret and Nestorius. We find in these theologians a juxtaposition, confusion, or alternation of the natures in Christ instead of a doctrine of divine-humanity (or divine-human action). Instead of a theory of divine-humanity, their notions were only vehicles for monophysitism, Nestorian diophysitism, or even Apollinarianism.

IV. The Dogma of Two Wills in Christ

A. *Monothelitism and Dyothelitism*

The dogma of the two natures in Christ received a new expression and confirmation in the definition of the Sixth Ecumenical Council (680) concerning the two wills and the two energies. Leaving aside the external, ecclesiastical-political history of the monothelitic dispute, we will examine only its dogmatic results. Monothelitism was primarily a concealed monophysitism, and as such, it does not present any independent dogmatic interest. Besides this, however, it revealed a new and dialectically legitimate aspect of the christological problem: What relation should be established between the unity of the hypostasis and the duality of the natures in the one God-Man? This question was not posed in all its acuteness by Apollinarius, since he considered that the duality of the natures in the case of the unity of the person was absorbed by the unitary, although complex, composition of the God-Man, the humanity being only an instrument for the Logos. Nor was it posed by St. Cyril of Alexandria, because his tendency was to conceive a unity of the natures, which gave his thought a bias in the direction of monothelitism (as was pointed out by

The Dialectic of the Idea of Divine-Humanity in the Patristic Epoch

its adherents, for example by Pyrrho in his dispute with St. Maximus the Confessor[166]). Pseudo-Dionysius's doctrine of the new, divine-human energy in Christ was used in the same sense. Among those with an inclination toward practical monothelitism we unexpectedly see Nestorius, with his doctrine of the hypostasis of union, composed of two natural hypostases through their harmonization, *sunapheia*. This idea made it possible (only in appearance, of course) to overcome the duality of the hypostases. But this pre-Chalcedonian monothelitism lacked that conscious and acute character that monophysitism imparted to it. Monothelitism was a tactical means of counteracting the Chalcedonian dogma, just as, inversely, dyothelitism was a means of defending this dogma by developing it further.

The question was first posed with regard to the presence of two energies or actions *(operatio)*. In his synodal epistle, read at the Sixth Ecumenical Council, Sophronius, patriarch of Jerusalem and an early champion of orthodoxy in the epoch of the monothelitic disputes, spoke only of the two energies or actions in Christ. For Sophronius the notion of energy does not have any particular definition and does not even have the significance of a theological *terminus technicus* (either in the sense given it by Aristotle or in the sense in which it was later used in the Palamite disputes). Sophronius uses this notion as something self-evident; it was also considered self-evident when it was later introduced into the dogma at the Sixth Ecumenical Council. One can say that the notion of energy signifies, as it were, the active voice in relation to the notion of nature, which corresponds to the passive or middle voice. Energy is the action of nature, nature in action. Consequently, the problem of energy here consists only in determining whether the nature is active or passive, and in defining the operation of each nature. Thus, the duality of the actions follows self-evidently from the duality of the natures: "The distinction of essences is always determined on the basis of the distinction of actions. ... We also teach that any utterance or action, be it divine and heavenly or human and earthly, proceeds from one and the same Christ and Son and from His composite and unique hypostasis. Having become incarnate, He remained God the Word and, in a natural manner, manifests from Himself without separation and without confusion the one action and the other, in conformity with his essences: He manifests the divine and ineffable according to His divine essence, according to which He is consubstantial with the Father; He manifests the human

---

166. Maximus the Confessor, *Opuscula dogmatica et theologica* (PG 91.88, 101); *Disputatio cum Pyrrho* (ibid., 344).

Introduction

and earthly according to His human essence, according to which He became consubstantial to us, human beings."[167]

The further stage of the monothelitic dispute, where the theology of St. Maximus the Confessor plays a central role, is complicated by the introduction of the new notion of will, *thelēma* or *thelēsis*, alongside the earlier *energeia*; and one now speaks of two wills *and* energies, as this is expressed in the definition of the Sixth Ecumenical Council. It is futile to expect that the new notion of will or volition would have received a preliminary definition that could satisfy inquiring thought, a definition that could clarify whether will was being considered as a psychological faculty or as a spiritual (ontological) power. But the greatest difficulty here is that it is a question not only of human will but also of divine will; moreover, these two wills are clearly understood in the same sense, as two distinct but parallel wills. Comparatively imperceptible when one speaks vaguely of two actions, this anthropomorphism becomes perfectly obvious when one speaks of two wills. This parallelism of the two wills, divine and human, is advanced so decisively that one of Maximus's arguments consists in the following proposition: if will referred to the person, not to the nature, then there would be three wills in the Holy Trinity; but since there is one will in the Holy Trinity, it follows that will is correlated with nature.[168] This argument does not establish any distinction between the Divine subject and the creaturely subject with respect to will, as if it were a question of subjects belonging to the same genus, for example, different human beings. This one-sided anthropomorphism, which introduces psychologism into the depths of the Holy Trinity, constitutes the weak side of the formulation of the dogma, although it does not distort its fundamental idea, that is, the duality of the self-determination in the case of unity of life, this duality being expressed *descriptively:* as two wills and two energies, as the dual self-determination of the life of one subject. "Will" here is a particular expression of the general idea of this real duality of life in unity.

Maximus gives a series of scholastic definitions of will and volition. Will *(thelēma),* or volition *(thelēsis),* is called "the natural capacity to be excited in conformity with the natural essence.... What is called will is rational [*logikon*] or vital desire."[169] "Natural will is an essential [*susiodēs*] desire for that which conforms with nature."[170] This definition is applicable

---

167. *Act. Concil.* 4.319-20.
168. See *Disputatio cum Pyrrho* (PG 91.313).
169. *Opus. theol. et polem. ad Marinum presbyterum* (PG 91.13-14).
170. *Variae definitiones* (PG 91.193).

both to Divinity and to man. However, in relation to God is it appropriate to speak of the natural desire for something that, consequently, lies outside His possession? In practical terms, when one speaks of the *two* wills, the main interest is focused not on the Divine essence, which cannot be diminished, but on the human essence, which monophysitism and montheletism consider to be absorbed by the Divine essence.

The principal meaning and goal of the theology of dyothelitism is to expel monophysitism from its new refuge, to defend the human essence in the *fullness* of its life, that is, not only in its natural existence but also in its volitional self-definition. With reference to this goal, the particular arguments and controversies are only the historical and contingent means. These means include the scholastic controversy concerning whether will belongs to the hypostasis or to the nature. The Monothelites (in particular Pyrrho) considered that will belongs to the hypostasis, from which proposition they slyly derived the unity of the will in Christ (and then, of course, the unity of His nature) from the unity of His hypostasis. By contrast, the Orthodox, with Maximus at the head, related will to nature and derived the duality of the wills in Christ from the duality of natures.

From our present perspective this dispute appears to be academic. In essence, both sides are wrong. Both will and energy are manifestations of the life of the spirit, contained in itself and revealing itself for itself (or *ad extra*). But the spirit is the living and inseparable unity of person and nature, so that *in concreto* there is no impersonal nature or natureless personality; they can be separated and even opposed only in the abstract. It is evident that a movement of the will is impossible without a personal impulse, just as a personal impulse is unrealizable without a corresponding natural desire.[171] Having two natures, the one hypostasis of Christ lives a "composite" life ("without separation and without confusion"); and it thus realizes its life simultaneously and in parallel in the two essences in the case of the unity of the living hypostatic self-definition (it is in this sense that patristics calls it, although imprecisely, a "composite hypostasis"). But the center of gravity effectively lies in the recognition or nonrecognition of the two natures, that is, not only of the Divine but also of the human essence.

It was indicated in the course of this dispute that to conceive will as a function of the nature (and not as a function of the personality) involved a difficulty: freedom was negated, for it was absorbed by natural necessity. Maximus attributed volition to all natural being, and *a fortiori*

---

171. See Tixeront's discussion in *Hist. des dogmes*, 3.172-73.

to divine being. But he did not clarify this important element of the doctrine, and it can lead to misunderstandings. It is clear that one can attribute *different* meanings to volition and the freedom of volition, depending on whether one is speaking of the animate and rational world or of the inanimate and nonrational world. One can speak of will as the general proto-ground of being (which is reminiscent of the voluntaristic metaphysics of Leibniz or Schopenhauer), but it is clear that such an authentically *natural* will differs from the volition of free beings to such a degree that it cannot be united with this volition into a single general concept, as Maximus attempts to do. Furthermore, in the domain of free, conscious, self-defining will, we have, on the one hand, the self-sufficient freedom of Divinity, which nothing can limit either outwardly or inwardly and which therefore lies beyond the distinction or opposition between freedom and necessity, which remain here in a state of actual identity. On the other hand, we have creaturely freedom, which, being limited, is expressed in the opposition of freedom — as volition — to necessity, which is freedom's limit, condition, and object. This freedom is further expressed in voluntary, creative goal-setting and self-determination, corresponding to the state of *becoming* that is proper to creaturely being. Finally, on this path one encounters the possibilities of just and unjust becoming, sin and righteousness, good and evil, which result from creaturely limitedness as well as from free election; and freedom here turns out to be the knowledge of good and evil, the temptation of the ancient serpent. The question arises: Can this form of freedom be overcome by free choice? Can the creature place itself *beyond* good and evil?

Although Maximus identifies divine and creaturely will as *orexis phusikē* (natural passion), which makes it possible for him to speak of *two* wills, that is, to correlate divine will and creaturely will as homogeneous or at least as parallel quantities, he nevertheless also poses the question of how to more precisely define the *human* will in Christ in relation to its character. Being a manifestation of His perfect humanity, is the human will in Christ identical to human will in its changeableness and especially in its tendency to sin, which are associated with human limitedness, ignorance, and lust? Since changeableness and the tendency to sin are excluded in Christ, His human will differs from the will of ordinary men. The will of ordinary men makes a choice *(proairesis)* between different possibilities, being guided by judgments of the reason *(gnōmē)*, but this selective, gnomic will is not infallible. On this basis, Maximus denies that Christ possesses this *gnomic*, reasoning will, and he attributes to Christ's humanity only a natural, instinctively linear, and infallible will, affirming at the same time that it is free.[172] To this must be added that, as a result of the *unio hypostatica,* Christ possessed His human will not only in conformity with the nature but also above the nature *(huper phusin).*[173] (The imprecision of this addition nearly destroys the foundations of the doctrine of the human will in Christ.)

This scholastic and, of course, totally conventional distinction between natural and gnomic will, a distinction that corresponds to the philosophical capacities of the epoch and that dogmatically is not obligatory for us (it was not included in the dogmatic definition of the Sixth Council), expresses the general and indisputable idea that the human will of the New Adam, despite its natural unity with the will of the old Adam, differs from the latter in virtue of its sinlessness. This sinlessness has two aspects: It is natural in character, in virtue of the Lord's sinless birth, in virtue of the conception without seed, liberating Him from the chains of original sin. But it is also personal in character, in virtue of the perfect holiness of the God-Man, "the only one without sin." Rather than "sinless," Adam's condition before the Fall can more accurately be called "pre-sinful." It was sinless only in the negative sense of the absence of sin, not in the sense of the overcoming of sin. This condition of Adam is raised here to the positive holiness of the Man deified in the Incarnation, without this deification abolishing the authentic human nature as the monophysites understood it. In virtue of this, Christ's human will possesses absolute holiness, expressed both in the infallibility of His decisions and in His inaccessibility to the *power* of temptations, even when they presented themselves before Him (in the temptation in the desert, in Peter's opposition, in the appeals to descend from the cross on Golgotha). This holiness is united with perfect freedom, which is accompanied, however, not only by infallibility and thus the absence of choice, but also by the absence of changeableness. Changeableness, as the possibility of sin, is already partly overcome in creaturely being as well, depending on its spiritual maturity.

Such is the condition of the holy angels and of the saints (true, only in the world beyond the grave). The creaturely human nature cannot overcome changeableness, for it can be overcome only by spiritual maturity. This possibility becomes an absolute reality in Christ's humanity, without coercion over its nature, but as its true revelation. In order to accept this idea it is by no means necessary to deny or diminish the true properties of Christ's humanity, in particular the applicability to it of growth and the

---

172. See *Disputatio cum Pyrrho* (PG 91.368-69).
173. PG 91.1053B.

Introduction

natural limits of the creaturely essence. In the authenticity of His sinless and holy humanity, the Lord follows the path of the accomplishment of this humanity in its fullness, to the point where, in the name of His illuminated and transfigured humanity, He can say about Himself: "All power is given unto me in heaven and in earth" (Matt. 28:18).

This doctrine of the "two wills" (and "two energies") in Christ, or more precisely of the autonomy of the human will in Christ, leads Maximus to pose the question of the interrelation of these two wills (or the question of the "theandric energy," an expression that Maximus adopts from Pseudo-Dionysius).

However, in his theory of *how* precisely the two wills in Christ are not only distinguished but also united in the new "theandric" operation, Maximus does not go beyond the widespread interpretation of this unity in relation to miracle. According to this interpretation, the flesh is taken by Christ as a "kind of helpmate [*synergatēn*]." "He creates as God with His omnipotent command, quickening with His touch the flesh united with Him hypostatically, in order to show that it too is capable of being quickened by His essential energy, to which, properly speaking, touch, voice, and so on refer. And thus He showed the natural energies of Christ God, composed of two, *ex amphoin*, entirely united — His Divinity by all-accomplishing command, His humanity by touch; He showed them united by mutual union and permeation."[174] "The soul [accomplishes] that which is proper to it [by using] its own body as an organ as it were and the natural energy of the latter, and it thus manifests its natural energy, since extending a hand, touching, taking, preparing the mixture [of earth and saliva], breaking bread, and in general all that was accomplished by the hand or some other part of the body, all this referred to the natural energy of Christ's humanity, by which energy He Himself, by nature God, acted as man, accomplishing also the divine naturally."[175]

This interpretation has a practical tendency to Apollinarianism or monophysitism, the human nature receiving here only an *instrumental* significance. The common patristic argument, based on a physical analogy, is no better. It attempts to explain the harmonious operation of the two wills by referring to the example of red-hot iron, in which the energies of the fire and of the iron are united, "although they are inseparable in the red-hot cutting or in the cutting burning."[176] Analogously, "two opposite

---

174. *Opusc. theol. et polem.* (PG 91.88).
175. *Disputatio cum Pyrrho* (PG 91.345).
176. Ibid., 341.

or distinct [principles] cannot be united in one operation: thus, fire cannot both burn and cool, just as ice cannot both cool and warm. Similarly, having become man, the Logos does not accomplish miracles and [undergo] suffering, which are different in nature, by one and the same energy."[177] On the contrary, "just as burning unites in itself fire and that which is burned, and cooling unites in itself coolness and that which is cooled ... it is the same with deification and that which is deified."[178] It is almost superfluous to insist that neither the Apollinarian interpretation of miracles nor any of these analogies clarify in the slightest the union or harmony of the two natures in the unity of Christ's life.

Therefore, in giving an overall assessment of Maximus's theological contribution to the doctrine of the two wills, we must honor the energy with which he defends the thesis of the duality of the wills and energies in Christ. But at the same time we cannot affirm that he possesses an integral theological doctrine, especially on the most important questions, in particular the question of how the simultaneous operation of the two wills in Christ is possible. Although he affirms the future dogma, he does so without theological preparation, and he is far from being firm and consistent in applying it.

In general, St. John of Damascus expounds the doctrine of the two wills and two energies in Christ according to St. Maximus Confessor, but he does give certain clarifications regarding the conjoined operation of the two wills. If one ignores those clarifications that are reducible to abstract exposition or to the repetition in different words of the general formula of the two wills, the following idea draws our attention: "Since Christ is one, and the Willing One, according to each of the two essences, is one and the same, we must then say that the object of volition in Him is one and the same. And this is not because He willed only that which He willed according to His nature as God, for it is not proper to Divinity to will to eat and drink, and so on; but because He had such volitions as well that were related to the constituent attributes of the human nature, without contradicting freedom of choice, but as a result of the properties of the essences. For He naturally willed this when His divine will willed it also, and He permitted the flesh to suffer and to do what was proper to it."[179] Here the one object of the two wills is defined in such a manner that

---

177. Ibid., 344.
178. Ibid., 316.
179. John of Damascus, *Brief Exposition of the Orthodox Faith*, book 3, ch. 14 (*PG* 94.1036).

Introduction

God's will *permits* natural desires such as hunger or thirst, which, of course, cannot be called volition in the true sense.

In other passages, the *instrumental* character of the "flesh" takes center stage (in these cases, the "flesh" replaces, as in part in Maximus, human will properly speaking or, in general, humanity). "We speak of the divinization of the will, not in the sense that the natural impulse has changed, but in the sense that it has become united with His divine and omnipotent will and become the will of God made man."[180] "He naturally possessed the capacity of volition both as God and as man; however, His human volition followed and was subordinate to His (divine) volition, being set into motion not by His proper disposition, but desiring that which His divine will willed." "When the divine will permitted this, then [the human will] naturally experienced that which is proper to it."[181] Having clarified not so much the harmonious operation of the two wills as their interaction of subordination, St. John of Damascus repeats that both wills operated freely: "The Lord's soul willed, being freely set in motion, but it freely willed precisely that which His divine will desired that it will."[182] In the following chapter, "On Divine-Human Action," St. John of Damascus returns to the same idea: "The flesh participates in the operations of God the Word because the divine actions were accomplished by means of the body, as if by means of an instrument, and also because He who acted was One."[183] In general, even though this series of nearly incoherent and even divergent propositions was intended as a commentary on Maximus's doctrine, they cannot be considered a satisfactory commentary; and the fundamental question of the *union* of the two wills remains unclarified here and perhaps is obscured even further.

B. The Definition of the Sixth Ecumenical Council

On the basis of the aforesaid we are led to conclude that the patristic works against monothelitism were far from containing a finished positive theological doctrine of the two wills, human and divine, in the God-Man. Nor did these works give a sufficiently clear and precise definition of the concepts involved; in particular, they did not clarify the relation between

---

180. Ibid., ch. 22 (ibid., 1069).
181. Ibid., ch. 8 (ibid., 1037).
182. Ibid., 1076.
183. Ibid., 1080.

The Dialectic of the Idea of Divine-Humanity in the Patristic Epoch

the two wills, which therefore received an excessively anthropomorphic expression. It was only with this meager preparation that the question was submitted for definitive examination and dogmatic decision at the Sixth Ecumenical Council.

Were these difficulties removed to any extent by the acts of the council? One can scarcely give an affirmative answer to this question. In particular, Pope Agatho's epistle, which played a determining role in the council's decision, reproduces the current ideas of the dyothelitic theology without clarifying or deepening them.[184]

The extent to which the question of monothelitism or dyothelitism was *not* ready for *theological* resolution is demonstrated by the controversy with Macarius of Antioch, condemned as a heresiarch by the fathers of the council and, as such, expelled. When the council (in the eighth act) posed to Macarius the question of the wills in Christ, he answered by referring to the Areopagitic doctrine, accepted by the Orthodox, according to which "it was not by virtue of being God that He did divine things, and not by virtue of being a man that He did what was human, but rather, by the fact of being God-made-man He manifested to us a divine-human [*theandrikēn*] energy."[185] This energy, which the Orthodox dogmatics does not clarify in relation to the duality of the natures but tacitly accepts, is interpreted by Macarius in the sense of *one* volition, or rather is identified with it. It cannot be denied that the burden of proving the opposite thesis (and of course not by anathematization alone) lay here on his opponents. In Macarius's opinion, all the statements of Christ contained in the Gospels should be attributed to one person, to the one incarnate hypostasis

---

184. Having established the duality of the essences in the God-Man, Agatho concludes therefrom that "the Lord Jesus Christ has within Him two essences as well as two natural wills and actions, that is, divine and human: He has the divine volition from all eternity in common with the Father who is consubstantial with Him, whereas He received the human volition from us together with our essence in time" (*Act. Concil.* 6/4.66-67; cf. 75, 82, 85). In this manner, without any difficulty he puts the two wills, divine and human, in parallel, thus introducing an obvious anthropomorphism or at least "psychologism" into theology. Furthermore, he subordinates this particular notion of will and action to the more general and less definite notion of "properties," such that, in the Gospels, the Lord "sometimes manifests human and sometimes divine properties, or both at the same time" (ibid., 73). In general, the basic idea of the epistle is reducible to the proposition that it is impossible and against the order of nature for the essence not to have "properties and actions" (ibid., 99). In practice, Agatho, as was customary with his predecessors and contemporaries, applies this idea in the capacity of the alternation of the two wills (ibid., 77-81).

185. See n. 161 above. — Trans.

Introduction

of the Word, for "both the human and the divine [statements] were spoken by one person."[186] (For this reason one should not fail to remember the general conclusion of a modern Catholic historian, and one who is considered conservative, that "the heterodoxy of monothelitism" should be sought, above all, in the terminology used.[187])

A discussion of the fundamental dogmatic question of the two wills and their union in the "new theandric energy" did not materialize, being replaced instead by quotations from the patristic literature (together with disputes about the accuracy and completeness of the quotations) and a condemnation of the Monothelites as heretics. It was after this that the fathers prepared the council's dogmatic definition, which, starting with a confirmation of the five ecumenical councils and an exposition of the faith of the Nicene, Constantinopolitan, and Chalcedonian fathers, expounded the dogma in the following words: "We profess, in conformity with the doctrine of the holy fathers, that He possesses two natural [*phusikas*] volitions or wills and two natural operations without separation, without change, without division, without confusion; and the two natural wills are not opposed ... but His human volition follows and does not oppose or resist but rather is subordinate to His Divine and omnipotent volition. For, according to the teaching of the wise Athanasius, the will of the flesh had to be in action, but to submit itself to the divine will.... We affirm that, in the one and the same Lord Jesus Christ, our true God, two natural operations [*energeias*] exist without separation, without change, without division, without confusion, that is, there exist the divine operation and the human operation.... Each essence wills and produces that which is proper to it in communion with the other."

In analyzing this definition, we must first point out that it repeats a formula ("without separation ... without confusion") borrowed from the Chalcedonian dogma. It is used once with reference to the two wills and once with reference to the two energies, and the two definitions are externally conjoined without any attempt to establish their interrelationship or to define them more precisely. The most correct conclusion would be that will and energy are used synonymously as *hen dia duoin* (one by means

---

186. *Act. Concil.* 6.184-85. This idea is, to be sure, more correct (even though it is undeveloped) than the alternation or dichotomy (and sometimes even trichotomy) that patristics usually introduces into the Lord's words: according to divinity, according to humanity, and in the intermediate sense. Macarius correctly expresses here the postulate of the unity of the person.

187. M. Jugie, "Monothélisme," in *Dict. de théol. cath.*, fasc. 88, col. 2311.

of two), as descriptive terms that designate nature or essence.[188] Second, it should be pointed out that the four negative definitions ("without separation ... without confusion") are applied to the two wills and the two energies when defining their interrelation, as well as to the two natures. This underscores once more the fundamental idea of the dogma that the duality of the wills and energies is essentially identical with, or in any case proceeds from, the duality of the natures, as is implied by the insistent definition of the wills and natures as "natural" *(phusikai)*. The dogma of the Sixth Council thus represents a specification and amplification of the Chalcedonian dogma. (This is somewhat obscured by extensive clarifications with references to the holy fathers, references that, strictly speaking, do not have any direct dogmatic significance; and for this reason we do not cite them here.)

Thus, the most important idea contained in the definition of the Sixth Ecumenical Council is the *duality* of wills and energies, in conformity with the duality of the natures. This is thus a new and more emphatic expression of the idea that the *humanity* in Christ (not only as an essence but also as the activity of this essence in its freedom, that is, in its will and energy, or in its creative activity, so to speak) is preserved in its autonomy together with and in union with the Divinity. In a certain sense one can affirm that this also represented an unexpected triumph of the school of Antioch (buried at the Fifth Ecumenical Council but resurrected at the Sixth) and an even more decisive triumph than at Chalcedon. In the dialectic of the councils' thought, the Sixth Council was an antithesis to the Fifth, effectively correcting its one-sidedness. However, the Sixth Council did not go beyond the articulation of the general principle of *duality*, in other words, the preservation of the humanity in Christ in all its power from absorption by the Divinity (there could be no question of the opposite possibility, of the absorption of the Divinity by the humanity). And the council could not go beyond this without getting ahead of its theological epoch, with which it was linked. Both what was explicitly stated and what was left implicit express the divinely wise truth of the council's definition. It is a gigantic projector, illuminating the path of the past as well as the future. It affirms the fullness of the hu-

---

188. One's attention is drawn by the imprecision, bordering on negligence, in the definition of will, *thelēsis ētoi thelēmata,* volition or desire (the volitional impulse or its content). This confirms our general idea that here will (as well as energy) is spoken of not in the proper, precise (whether psychological or ontological) sense but only in the general sense of an *active* manifestation of nature.

manity of the Man in the Divine-Humanity, which is not diminished alongside the fullness of Divinity, dwelling corporeally.

But the definition of the council is not limited to the establishment of the duality of the wills; it also indicates their general relation. The Monothelites (Macarius of Antioch in particular) did not want to *count* the wills, since they justly feared that they would thereby, in a "Nestorian" manner, sunder the God-Man Himself into two; it was more important for them to see the harmony of the wills in the unity of Christ's life, in His "composite" hypostasis (as it was called then). The orthodox fathers also wished to retain this idea by means of Pseudo-Dionysius's doctrine of the theandric energy, "one from two," of Christ's living unity in His one hypostasis. However, there was no *theology* of this unihypostatic bi-unity (just as there is none today), and even the problematic of this bi-unity was insufficiently understood. The council's definition establishes the general *hierarchy of the wills,* while preserving the autonomy of each of them. Here it was a question, of course, of the *human will,* for the dogma concerns not so much two wills (one can speak of God's "will" or "energy" only metaphorically or anthropomorphically[189]), but rather one will in the precise sense, that is, human will that preserves its autonomous being in the union with Divinity. It was necessary to establish a hierarchy of the wills in order to dissipate the doubt raised by the Monothelites and formulated in the question whether the two wills can contradict each other or will different things. The response was that the human will (in Christ) does not contradict and oppose, but follows and "subordinates itself" to the divine will, so that "His human will, being deified, was not annihilated but preserved," and that "each of the two essences produces that which is proper to itself in communion with the other."

One surely cannot fail to see the imprecision and incompleteness of these definitions ("does not contradict," "follows," "is subordinate to"), especially if one remembers that the question is of the relation of the

---

189. The differentiation and opposition of the two natures and the two wills considered in this epoch were accomplished only according to the criterion of miracles and sufferings, as if the entire life of the Divinity in the God-Man were exhausted by the working of miracles, and as if the entire humanity were exhausted by infirmity and sufferings. This simplification, bordering on distortion, cannot be retained in the conception of the divine-humanity. Nevertheless, traces of this conception have been introduced into the text of the conciliar *horos,* or decree, not, to be sure, in the essential dogmatic part, but in accompanying discussions (although not directly). For example, "to the one and the same we attribute miracles and sufferings, in conformity with the one and the other essence," and so on.

The Dialectic of the Idea of Divine-Humanity in the Patristic Epoch

creaturely human will to the divine omni-wisdom and omnipotence. We know that the dyophysitic Definition of Chalcedon provoked a new tempest of monophysitism, which was motivated by the incompleteness and resulting imprecision of this definition. The same thing inevitably had to happen after the Sixth Ecumenical Council on the subject of the analogous question of the two wills and the two natures. In fact, it was far from easy for theological thought to conceive that creaturely human will must be "subordinate to and not contradict" divine will, while at the same time preserving its independence. The doors were here opened wide for a new monothelitism and dogmatic strife; and if this did not occur, it was largely because of the entire historical situation, and especially because of the impoverishment of the theological thought of the East after centuries of dogmatic intensity. It was now the epoch of reconciliatory scholastic compilations such as St. John of Damascus's *Brief Exposition of the Orthodox Faith*, in which the theological problems were not intensified but smoothed over and solved on the basis of the writings and definitions of the past.

After the Sixth Ecumenical Council the development of dogma thus breaks off, and for this reason alone the council's formulas are considered to have definitively resolved the question. This is true only to the extent that the council had erected firm signposts marking the way to the development of Christology as a theo-anthropology. But one cannot see such a development at the council itself. Rather, the question is only posed for further theological discussion, a discussion that should address the real relation of the two natures, the two wills, the two energies — in their fullness, freedom, hierarchical relationship, and bi-unity. The dogmatic definition here was even further ahead of the theology of the epoch than that at Chalcedon. The history of dogma handed this task over to a future that still has not arrived. But for this future the dogma of the Sixth Ecumenical Council remains a guiding star, lit by the council's divinely wise decision: not one will and one energy, but *two* wills and energies. To be sure, in and of itself, this arithmetical count is crude and does not accord with the true idea of the dogma (and in this sense, it would perhaps have been better not to *count*), but one cannot negate the importance of the idea itself that human will and energy preserve their autonomous being even when united with Divinity, which inspires and guides them. They are "divinely moved" *(theokinēta)*, as both parties at the council agreed.[190]

---

190. The imprecision that marks the understanding of the definition of the Sixth Ecumenical Council is well illustrated by the divergent ways in which two modern Catholic

Introduction

* * *

With the Sixth Ecumenical Council, the christological definitions of this epoch were concluded, or rather they were broken off by an expressive set of suspension points. The final "period" has not yet been placed here; the cycle of dogmatic development remains incomplete. The definition of the Seventh Ecumenical Council concerning the veneration of icons stands apart. Outwardly, this definition refers to questions of discipline and cult, but its inner or dogmatic meaning, which has been insufficiently clarified, also refers to Christology. Its dogmatic meaning refers not to the authenticity of the Incarnation, as the contemporaries of the council thought (here too the council's divinely inspired definition was ahead of the theology of the epoch), but to the unity of the Divine image and the human image, to the *person* of the God-Man, not to His two natures.[191] This raises a dogmatic cupola, as it were, over the preceding dogmatic definitions.

---

authors interpret it: Tixeront (*Hist. des dogmes*, 3.171-75) and Jugie ("Monothélisme," col. 2311). Jugie finds in Tixeront *"une saveur nestorienne"* (a trace of Nestorianism) in the fact that, for him, the falsehood of monotheletism consists in denying *"en Jesus-Christ homme toute spontaneité et tout acte de volonté libre"* (in Jesus Christ the man all spontaneity and any free act). Tixeront even speaks of *"deux séries parallèles"* (two parallel series) in *Hist. des dogmes*, p. 173, for the harmony of the two operations would have consisted of *"consentement libre et spontané de l'homme reglant ses actes et ses résolutions conformément au vouloir et aux actes divins"* (the free *and* spontaneous consent of the man regulating his acts and decisions in conformity with the divine will and acts). Jugie's objection to this is that *"un seul agent responsable des actes humains comme des operations divines"* (the sole responsible agent of the human acts as well as of the divine operations) is *"le moi divin"* (the divine I); and the human will and nature *"est vraiment subordonnée à son empire, à son enterprise tout-puissante"* (is truly subordinate to His omnipotent enterprise). This does not destroy the freedom of the human will, which acts *"librement et non automatiquement"* (freely and not automatically), although here, without doubt, one has *"le point mysterieux de la psychologie humaine"* (the mysterious point of the human psychology [sic!]) of the Savior. His nature remains "moved by Divinity," and one should not reproach the monothelites for this expression. However, do we not find here, in turn, *"une saveur monothélite"* (a trace of monotheletism)?

191. I have attempted to uncover the dogmatic meaning of the definition of the Seventh Ecumenical Council in *The Icon and the Veneration of Icons* (Paris, 1931); I will not return to this theme in the present work.

CHAPTER 1

The Divine Sophia

I. The Creaturely Spirit

Personal consciousness of self is proper to the nature of spirit: "I am that I am," Jehovah, says the Lord. Spirit is, above all, *personality* as personal consciousness of self, as "I." An impersonal ("unconscious") spirit is a contradiction. But this I is not an abstract self-consciousness that is not connected with anything and empty for itself (even the dreaming I of Hinduism at least has its dream and lives in it). It is a living I ("I am that I am"), the subject of a certain objectivity, the subject of a certain predicate, the receptacle of a certain content. The living I has its own life. It is the source of this life and its fullness, its beginning and end. The personal spirit thus has in itself its own *nature,* in which it lives, ceaselessly realizing itself for itself through this nature, defining itself and revealing itself to itself. This indissoluble unity of the personal self-consciousness, of I and its nature, grounding the life of the personal spirit, is the spirit's *limiting intuition* of itself and also the initial ontological axiom. This axiom is contained in Revelation, and it is attested by the Church in the fundamental dogmatic doctrine that God possesses personality and nature, *hupostasis, phusis,* or *ousia*. As a result, God is a hypostasis that has its own nature, and precisely in this sense He is a living personal spirit. Such a definition of personal spirit is applicable to *any* spirit, divine, angelic, or human. The distinctive property of the Divine Spirit is that this Spirit is not only a personal but also a trihypostatic spirit, a trihypostatic personality, which, however, has *one nature* and, accordingly, *one life* (not a life in common, but precisely one life), just as every unihypostatic spirit has one nature and one life.

The Lamb of God

One can view the nature of the spirit in two ways: The nature of the spirit is the *source* of every particular manifestation of life rising to self-consciousness; it is the dark depth nourishing the roots of being, a depth unilluminated by personal self-consciousness (it is the "subconscious" or the "superconscious," the extraconscious, the not-yet-conscious); it is in general the unconscious as well as the preconscious principle in the personal spirit. Without this source, without potentiality that can become and ceaselessly becomes actuality, *natura naturata*, entering the consciousness, the personal spirit would be empty, devoid of content. Without it the personal spirit would not be living, but only an abstractly "I-ing" self-consciousness (which is how Fichte considers it in his *Ich-Philosophie*). But the nature is the very life of the spirit, in the capacity of its accomplished self-revelation, *natura naturata*, in the capacity of the *content* of the life of the spirit and in this sense its authentic predicate. Between *natura naturans* and *natura naturata* there exists a *living* identity. However, a modal distinction in the life of the spirit is also manifested here, insofar as one and the same natural content exists for the spirit, on the one hand, as an *act* of its own life, a creative self-revelation, and, on the other hand, as a *fact* of a certain reality present before it — that is, the proper being of this reality according to itself and in itself. This content is not independent of the I, insofar as it is its proper act, creatively posited by the I in and for itself; however, in its reality, in its being according to itself, this content is also a fact independent of the I, and present before it. The living spirit reveals itself to itself in a certain objective actuality, which has its own reality. The spirit lives in this actuality, in this state of subject-object, as if in its own home.

For the moment, we are considering the concept of nature in an indeterminate sense: as the potency of the life of the spirit, which lies outside the spirit as personal consciousness but which belongs to the spirit and is revealed for and in it. In this sense, the nature of the personal spirit, as the predicate of all predicates, can be defined as the *world* of this spirit: the personality lives in the world as in its own nature, which it masters in proportion to the revelation or realization of this nature in the personal consciousness. The world is precisely the necessary "not-I" that Fichte postulated; in this case, however, it is understood, not in the negative sense as solely the limit of I (for the living I, the subject for all predicates, does not have a limit), but in the positive sense of an objective reality, which for I becomes a subjective experience, its personal life. We thus arrive at the conclusion that personality as the conscious center of being presupposes for itself the presence of the world as its nature, the presence of a being that is not yet personal, and not extrapersonal, but for the moment only impersonal. The personal spirit is not enclosed in itself (like Leibniz's monad) but open *for the world;* and the world thereby becomes the precondition of the personal spirit as living personality, for the spirit lives not by its "I-ness" but by the nature that is inherent to it. This nature must be understood here in the broadest sense as a not-I that enters into I and lives in it, including the psychological world, external nature, and (what is especially important) other living persons, other I's, as co-I's or we. Likewise, the life of the spirit, the entry of not-I into I, or the expansion of I into not-I, presupposes toward the world not only a passive and contemplative attitude. Such an attitude is, in general, not proper to the nature of the personal spirit with its actuality (as Fichte correctly pointed out, I itself is active self-affirmation, *Tathandlung*), and the life of the spirit is an active penetration into the world as one's own nature.

The personal spirit, which must find the foundation and fullness of its being in itself, thus turns out to be *conditioned* in its life by the *world,* or the nonspirit, although the world is able to enter into the life of the spirit and in this sense become its nature. As a result, the spirit is not free for itself, it is conditioned; it is not an absolute spirit but a correlative, *becoming* spirit. "It doth not yet appear what we shall be" (1 John 3:2), but before this limit is attained, the personal spirit, in its life, does not possess fullness and adequacy; on the contrary, it is enchained by relativity and limitation, which, however, are not capable of abolishing the indestructible seity of the spirit. This conditionedness is the mark of *creatureliness* that is stamped on every created spirit, whether human or angelic. In particular, the human spirit also is becoming. It has not yet become itself; it is only a part of itself, and even a small part. Nevertheless, this creaturely spirit possesses traits of the Absolute Spirit; it is the image of the Divine Proto-Image, and only on the basis of this fact can the creaturely spirit be understood in all the sublimity and absoluteness of its calling, as well as in all the relativity of its being, which is both becoming and unfinished. A particular creaturely eternity and even uncreatedness are proper to the creaturely spirit. Having created man's body out of "the dust of the ground," that is, having united him with creaturely nature as his proper world, God out of Himself "breathed into his nostrils the breath of life; and man became a living soul" (Gen. 2:7). The mystery of the createdness of the creaturely spirit consists in the fact that God gave hypostatic being to this "breathing into," to this outpouring of His essence. "For in him we live, and move, and have our being . . . we are also his offspring" (Acts 17:28). Spiritual being is rooted in Divine eternity; the creaturely spirit has an eternity that is analogous to the Divine, and it is uncreated. It bears the consciousness of this eternity and of this uncreatedness and, in general, of its divinity, which is why spiritual consciousness of self is essentially consciousness of God. Furthermore, the creaturely spirit is conscious of itself as self-grounding, self-affirming being. Here, it is I who start myself and affirm myself and belong to myself in my I-ness. I am not a thing, and no one can affirm my I except me myself; I myself create myself for myself. Hypostatic consciousness of self includes self-affirmation: in calling His breath to hypostatic being, in hypostatizing the rays of His own glory, God accomplishes self-affirmation by one eternal act *together* with the hypostasis itself. God's creative act asks, as it were, the creaturely I if it is I, if it has in itself a will to life. And God hears the answering *yes* of the creature.

But is the proper life of the spirit not extinguished in its natural condition, which is given to it from outside and even forced upon it in a certain sense? Is not spirituality lost to such a degree that man can become "flesh" (Gen. 6:3) and that even God Himself "repents" that He created him (Gen. 6:7)? "These be they who separate themselves, sensual, having not the Spirit" (Jude 1:19). Such a possibility exists for man as a consequence of the ontological complexity of his nature, which combines the eternal spirit and the created nature, the breath of God in the dust of the earth. This possibility does not exist, however, for the angelic (or demonic) spirits, because of their relative simplicity and spiritual self-evidentness for themselves, since they lack the "subconscious," that is, nature or "flesh." Even the fallen angels, who become demons and attach themselves to sinful human flesh, remain confined in their spirituality, and "spiritual life" is the only life that is possible for them.

In contrast, man by his composition is not only spiritual but also psycho-corporeal, or natural. In him there lives not only his spirit but also his nature, which also lives by its own life. Nature is not spiritual but only psycho-corporeal. It is alive and lives (the fact that the life-giving God "did not create death" is applicable to it); and this life has for itself its sensuality, its different degrees of consciousness, its "psychic" character. In nature we have all the degrees, from the absolute sleep and the imperceptible life of the minerals and in general of "inorganic" matter, to the life of the vegetative world, and finally to the infinite varieties of organic life with the faculty of consciousness. In its limitedness, this animal consciousness (which is not spiritual, although it is individual) remains inaccessible to us. However close the convergence between an animal with its "psychic" consciousness and man might be, there remains between them the insuperable limit of spiritual consciousness of self that is proper to man (just as man in his corporeality and complexity is transcendent for the fleshless angelic spirits, with whom he comes into contact only in his spirituality). But with the natural side of his being, man touches the animal world; he is an animal, although not only an animal. Man is capable of submerging himself in this animality to such a degree that it is as if the spiritual consciousness of self disappears in him and he is conscious of himself as only an animal, desiring to "descend from the apes." In such a state, man forgets about his heavenly homeland to such an extent that he is truly perplexed when he hears talk of spirituality.

Such a possibility results from a particular property of the creaturely spirit, namely from the fact that its proper nature is not exhausted by its proper spiritual world but potentially includes the entire created world, into which all the windows and doors are open for this spirit. The creaturely spirit can go out of itself through these doors to such an extent that the external nature in man can become for him the sole reality. Through this going out of himself, a man stops seeing himself as a spirit; he loses consciousness of his proper spirituality and sees only *psycho*-corporeality or simply "flesh" there where it is *pneumo*-corporeality that actually exists. Nonetheless, this state of "flesh" is for man a *spiritual* self-definition, a state of his spirit, although it is reduced to an exteriorized condition.

But man's spiritual essence, his "spiritual life," can become for him a fact of empirical self-evidence, of consciousness of self. A man sees himself and knows himself both in his eternity and in his creatureliness, both in his spirituality and in his natural condition. It is erroneous to think that "spiritual life," the spirit's consciousness of self, rips apart or abolishes the link between the spirit and nature, which lives in the former, and that it makes the spirit extranatural (illusory) or antinatural (self-disincarnating). It is just the opposite: spirituality heightens the sense of connection with the natural world, but it also gives an awareness of the proper depths of the spirit, not only of the nature of the world, but also of spiritual nature. For the spirit — every spirit, whether incarnate or unincarnate — necessarily has its proper *spiritual* nature, even if it is manifested in the spirit's life in the natural world. Without this proper spiritual nature the spirit would only be a dim candle of consciousness of self (Kant's "transcendental I"), illuminating the world's being but not living in it as an incarnate spirit.

Where does this spiritual nature come from, and what is it like? It is *divine* in its origin, inasmuch as the "sons of man" are also the "sons of God," born not of flesh and blood "but of God" (John 1:13), by a spiritual birth: "that which is born of the flesh is flesh; and that which is born of the Spirit is spirit" (3:6). And just as "God giveth not the spirit by measure" (3:34), so this spiritual life — that is, the life in God and by God, this deification of man — has many degrees, is an infinite ascent. This spiritual life of the sons of God does not remove them from participation in the natural life of the sons of man; on the contrary, the *duality of the natures* in man, his eternal divine-humanity, makes possible the deification of life, the inseparable and inconfusable communion of the two natures in man. If man were capable of freeing himself from his natural essence by the power of spiritual life, he would simply be God, and his life would be *fused* with divine life. However, although this is accessible to him (for "ye shall be as gods" [Gen. 3:5]), he can attain it only as a creaturely spirit. He can attain it precisely as a natural creaturely spirit, to whom the task of elevating all of creation to the image of spiritual being has been given. Thus, through the spiritual principle, the nature in man comes to belong to the spirit. It becomes spiritualized.

II. The Divine Spirit

God is Spirit. As such, He has a personal consciousness of self ("hypostasis") and a nature ("ousia"); and this inseparable union of nature and hypostasis is the life of Divinity in itself, a life that is both personally conscious and naturally concrete. This interrelation between hypostasis and nature, their inseparable union, is proper to both the divine spirit and the creaturely spirit. An essential difference, however, exists between the two.

In relation to the hypostasis of God as the Absolute Subject, there is the trihypostatic personality, which in one personal consciousness of self unites *all* the modes of the personal principle: I, thou, he, we, and you; whereas a unihypostatic personality has all these modes except I *outside* itself, in other personalities, and is thus limited and conditioned by them in its being. Fully manifested and actualized, the personal principle, the hypostasis, is a trihypostatic personality, in which the personal unity is revealed in the reality of three hypostatic centers, or hypostases, in triunity. Triunity is the divine number, not three and not one, but precisely triunity, Trinity. Such hypostatic being is realized not statically, as the unipersonal self-consciousness of the separate, isolated I in itself, reposing in its self-givenness (although this static and self-finished character is only apparent, for every I goes out into thou, we, you); rather it is realized dynamically, as the eternal act of trinitarian self-positing in another. This dynamic self-positing is *love:* the flames of the divine trihypostasis flare up in each of the hypostatic centers and are then united and identified with one another, each going out of itself into the others, in the ardor of self-renouncing personal love. *Statically*, the unihypostatic personality is the center of self-affirmation and of repulsion; it is egocentric. *Dynamically*, the personality actualizes itself as the initial principle of self-renouncing love, as the going out into another I. The Holy Trinity as a personality is precisely such a dynamic personal principle. In it, the static being of each personal center is the initial principle of the dynamic going out, where personal self-affirmation is removed and overcome, and the Person is realized as the ring of this trinitarian self-moving love. Therefore, the first thing one must say about the Divine Person is that, as trihypostatic, this Person is equally real in one hypostasis and in three hypostases, that this Person is the pre-eternally realized reciprocity of love that totally vanquishes personal isolation and identifies three in one, while itself existing by the real being of these personal centers.[1]

The trihypostatic Divinity is *one* Person, despite this trihypostatizedness, or rather in virtue of it. And in this unity of its personality (which nevertheless is not a monohypostatizedness) the Divine spirit does not formally differ from the creaturely spirit. And the Divine Person lives, actualizing His life in His nature. The one trihypostatic Divine Person has His divine nature — that is the fundamental definition of the Church. The trihypostatic God has His one nature, and He has this nature both as the Divine triunity in its unicity and as each hypostasis in its being: not only is the Son "consubstantial" with the Father (which was precisely the subject of dispute in the Arian epoch) but the Holy Spirit is "consubstantial" with the Father and with the Son. The three hypostases have their nature *not* in common, not in common possession (nor do they have it each one for Himself, which would be tritheism), but as *one* for all, homoousianly, not homoiousianly. In the domain of the theoretical reason, or rationality, this can be expressed only in equalities of the unequal: (1a) the Holy Trinity differs from each hypostasis, is not equal to it; (1b) the Holy Trinity is equidivine with respect to each hypostasis and consequently is equal to it; (2a) the Holy Trinity possesses one nature; (2b) each hypostasis also possesses one nature; consequently, the possession of one nature is equal and different for the Holy Trinity and the individual hypostasis. These rational contradictions, to which this idea is reduced, can be explained by the fact that rational thought deals with static quantities that are posited exter-

---

1. On this subject, as well as on the further considerations in the present chapter, see my work "Chapters on Trinity." I will not repeat the discussion in that work here.

nally in their finished facticity, whereas here it is faced with *acts* that are fluid in their dynamicity and continuity. These acts are therefore not subject to rational thought; they are not exhausted by its schemata.

In the relation of the Divine Personality to its nature, there exists a radical difference from what we know about the creaturely spirit. The proper nature of the creaturely spirit is an unexhausted and even inexhaustible *given*, a certain *mē on*, a possibility that is ceaselessly becoming an actuality, a darkness out of which new forms are emerging. In this sense, the creaturely spirit remains unrevealed and unknown for itself as well; it does not exhaust itself but is only in the process of *becoming* itself. Becoming is synonymous with creatureliness. Insofar as it is alive, the creaturely spirit always keeps accumulating for itself a new content of being, and therefore the proper nature of this spirit is, for it, both a given and a task that is proposed. Its proper nature is this not-I that belongs to its I only by ontological predestination, not yet in reality. Therefore, the I is not only revealed through this not-I but is also limited by it. The I cannot be realized by a self-affirmation (as Fichte attempted to do through *absolute Tathandlung*), by which in a certain sense the personal I posits itself. Not-I is the limit for I, potentially being I; that is, being destined to enter into the life of the I, into the possession of it, it remains *given* for the I. In his I, man also bears not-I; he is not transparent to himself and not fully knowable. In this sense, he is not self-positing; rather, he is a creature, although his personality is connected with his nature *on the model* of the self-positing spirit.

In the Divine Spirit the relation between person and nature is defined in another manner. In the Divine Spirit, there is nothing in a given or unrealized state. This Spirit is totally and thoroughly transparent to itself. For it, its nature is not not-I as a limit or an unactualized potential. God knows Himself with absolute, exhaustive knowledge: "the Spirit searcheth all things, yea, the deep things of God" (1 Cor. 2:10). Therefore, although nature is other than hypostasis in God as well, it is entirely hypostatized, rendered conscious in the personal life of Divinity, manifested and actualized. "God is light, and in him is no darkness at all" (1 John 1:5); in particular, there is in Him no meonal darkness, no nocturnal twilight of half-being. No opposition or even distinction between consciousness and nature in God can be admitted in this sense, for that would signify that the Divine life is limited. It would contradict the all-blessedness, unchangeability, and fullness of the Divine life. In this sense, in the life of Divinity there cannot be any place for a "subconscious," and especially not for a "superconscious." If personality in divinity has a nature, this nature is entirely personal; and one therefore cannot conceive in God a divine "nature" (analogous to Schelling's meonal "freedom"), which for Him would be a potentiality, a kind of *Urgrund* out of which the world would arise by its inner self-disclosure, God Himself being realized in this process (cf. Boehme, Schelling, and Hegel's dialectical self-disclosure of thought). The divine nature entirely and totally belongs to God; it is personally realized in Him as "His eternal power and Godhead" (Rom. 1:20). But in virtue of this realized state, even if the nature in God must be distinguished from His personality, one must not oppose to it, as another principle, a "fourth" in the Holy Trinity, a "Divinity" in God (such was the doctrine of Joachim of Fiore and Gilbert de la Porrée, a doctrine that was justly condemned in *this* sense by the Catholic Church[2]). The divine nature cannot "quaternize" the trine Divinity, for the nature cannot be categorically juxtaposed or "counted" with the hypostases: it is an autonomous principle and different from the hypostases. The divine nature is totally transparent for the Divine hypostases, and to that extent it is identified with them, while preserving its proper being. The nature is eternally hypostatized in God as the adequate life of the hypostases, whereas the hypostases are eternally connected in their life with the nature, while remaining distinct from it.[3]

This transparence of the nature for the hypostases and its total adequacy are realized in the unity of the trihypostatic life in conformity with the trihypostatizedness of the Divine Person. God has His nature by a *personal* self-positing, but one that is personally trihypostatic. God's nature is the *one* nature of the Father and of the Son and of the Holy Spirit, with each hypostasis having it *in its own way,* for itself and for the other

---

2. The Council of Reims (1148) against Gilbert affirms that *simplicem naturam divinitatis esse Deum* and *divinitas sit Deus, et Deus divinitas* ("only the divine nature is God, and divinity is God and God is divinity"). This was also established at the Fourth Lateran Council (1215) against Joachim of Fiore, who "quaternized" the Holy Trinity. (See Denzinger, 190, n. 431; cf. 191, n. 432.)

3. The proposition that the nature is hypostatized in God has a fundamental significance for sophiology. No one will dare deny the very being of the nature in God because of this hypostatizedness of the nature, and no one will see the quaternization of Divinity in this recognition of the reality of the nature. However, such a theological delirium is encountered every time it is a question of this very same nature as Sophia. Let those who are subject to this delirium reflect upon the fundamental relation between personality and nature in Divinity, for it contains the key to everything that follows. These delirious people speak insouciantly of the ousia in the Holy Trinity without fear of quaternizing it, but a panicked fear of this quaternization arises in them whenever this very same nature is considered as Sophia.

hypostases within the triune circle. The principle *(archē)* of the nature of Divinity, as of the entire Holy Trinity, is God the Father. He has His own nature, and His possession of it is a hypostatic, co-hypostatic, and interhypostatic act. The Father acquires Himself as His nature, not in Himself and for Himself, but in proceeding out of Himself and in begetting, as the Father, the Son. Fatherhood is precisely the form of love in which the loving one desires to have himself not in himself but outside himself, in order to give his own to this other I, but an I identified with him, in order to manifest his own in spiritual begetting: in the Son, who is the living image of the Father. The Father lives not in Himself but in His Son's life; the Father lives in begetting, that is, in proceeding out of Himself, in revealing Himself. The Father's love is ecstatic, fiery, causative, active. Unfathomable for the creaturely spirit is this *begetting* of the Son by the Father, of the Person by the Person. This begetting power is the ecstasy of a going out of oneself, of a kind of self-emptying, which at the same time is self-actualization through this begetting. The Father actualizes *His own*, His own hypostatically transparent nature, in the hypostasis of the Son, who is His Word, the "image of his person [*hupostasis*]" (Heb. 1:3). The Father has Himself in His nature as the *hypostatic* Word, His Word, and the Father is the one who speaks the Word. Thus, in the first place, God's hypostatic nature is the Father's hypostatic Word, which is uttered by the Father in the Son. "All things are delivered unto me of my Father: and no man knoweth the Son, but the Father; neither knoweth any man the Father, save the Son" (Matt. 11:27). For the Father, begetting is self-emptying, the giving of Himself and of His own to the Other; it is the sacrificial ecstasy of all-consuming, jealous love for the Other: "love is strong as death; jealousy is cruel as the grave: the coals thereof are coals of fire, which hath a most vehement flame" (Song of Songs 8:6).

The Father begets; the Son is begotten. These are two forms of generation: active and passive. To be sure, this should not be understood as the emergence from nonbeing of that which was not, for the Divine hypostases are equally eternal. The Father is the cause *(aitia)* of the Son not in the sense of His origination but only of eternal interrelation: that of begetter and begotten, the revealing one and the revealed one, the subject and the predicate. However, that which on the part of the Father is active begetting is, on the part of the Son, passive and obedient "begottenness." The Son, as the Son, has Himself and His own not as Himself and His own but as the Father's, in the image of the Father. Spiritual sonhood consists precisely in the Son's depleting Himself in the

The Divine Sophia

name of the Father. Sonhood is already *eternal kenosis*. The Son is not a flame of the Father's fire but the gentle Light of holy glory (as the vespers hymn says). The Son's love is the sacrificial, self-renouncing humility of the Lamb of God, "foreordained before the foundation of the world" (1 Pet. 1:20). And if the Father desires to have Himself outside Himself, in the Son, the Son too does not desire to have Himself for Himself: He offers His personal selfhood in sacrifice to the Father, and being the Word, He becomes mute for Himself, as it were, making Himself the *Father's* Word. Being rich, he makes Himself poor, becoming sacrificially silent in the bosom of the Father.

The sacrifice of the Father's love consists in self-renunciation and in self-emptying in the begetting of the Son. The sacrifice of the Son's love consists in self-depletion in the begottenness from the Father, in the acceptance of birth as begottenness. These are not only pre-eternal facts but also acts for both the one and the other. The *sacrifice* of love, in its reality, is pre-eternal suffering — not the suffering of limitation (which is incompatible with the absoluteness of divine life) but the suffering of the authenticity of sacrifice and of its immensity. This suffering of sacrifice not only does not contradict the Divine all-blessedness but, on the contrary, is its foundation, for this all-blessedness would be empty and unreal if it were not based on authentic sacrifice, on the reality of suffering. If God is love, He is also sacrifice, which manifests the victorious power of love and its joy only through suffering.[4]

This mutual sacrifice of generation, this self-emptying and self-depletion, would be a tragedy in God if it remained self-sufficient. But it is pre-eternally resolved in the bliss of the offered and mutually accepted sacrifice, of suffering overcome. This mutual sacrifice never exists unresolved, although it cannot be separated or excluded from this bliss, for it is its hidden foundation. Divine bliss cannot be understood as self-loving and empty self-admiration, analogous to egotistical human happiness; and the fullness of love demands real, not apparent, sacrifice. God is not the dyad of Father and Son, but the Trinity of Father, Son, and Holy Spirit, who is precisely the *joy* of sacrificial love, the bliss and actualization of this love. In begetting the Son and proceeding out of Himself in this begetting, the Father does not yet have the One who is being begotten as the already be-

---

4. One can also define this state of sacrifice as voluntary hypostatic dying, under the condition that the concept of death is liberated from the meaning it has in temporal creaturely life, a meaning that has nothing in common with spiritual dying as a manifestation of eternal divine life.

gotten One, as the object of His love and joy, just as the torments of human childbearing *lead* to joy but, in themselves, are not yet this joy. The relation of the Father to the Son therefore has two aspects: for the Father, the Son is not only being begotten, He is already begotten; He is "the only begotten, beloved Son." And the relation of the Son to the Father also has two aspects: for the Son, the Father is not only the Begetter but also the Father, in whom His own life is concealed: "he that hath seen me hath seen the Father" (John 14:9); "I am in the Father, and the Father in me" (14:10). I am Thou and Thou art I; I am We.

This identity of Father and Son, their self-identification in love, is realized by a hypostatic act: the procession of the Holy Spirit from the Father upon the Son (or "through" the Son). Insofar as the Father and the Son mutually know each other in self-renouncing love as an act being accomplished, their mutual being for each other has only an *ideal* character. It acquires reality only in the *accomplished* act, in begetting-begottenness. This reality of the divine nature, already revealing itself in an ideal manner in the fatherhood of the Father and the sonhood of the Son, is accomplished by the Holy Spirit, who proceeds from the Father, reposes upon the Son, and unites the two of them. This is the mutual love of the Father and the Son and the joy of this love; it is the accomplished self-revelation of Divinity in its nature, not only in Truth, but also in Beauty. This is no longer the sacrificial act; it is the triumphant testimony about itself of love and the self-knowledge of God's nature; it is not begetting but procession. The Holy Spirit proceeds from the Father and is received by the Son; He is the "third" person of the Holy Trinity, for He establishes the mutuality of the Father and the Son. God *ideally* defines His own nature in this begetting of His Pre-eternal Word by the Speaking Father. But the *reality* of this nature is experienced through the Holy Spirit. In God there is no self-definition that is not hypostatic. Therefore, the recognition of His own nature as *reality* is the hypostatic act of the procession of the Holy Spirit. This act determines not only the relation between the Father and the Holy Spirit but also the relation between the Father and the Son. This hypostatic relation is their mutual love. The Holy Spirit loves the Son, for He "reposes" upon Him; and together with Him, in an inseparable dyad with Him, the Holy Spirit reveals the Father and loves the Father as the source of love, the First Cause. The Holy Spirit Himself does not reveal the Son to the Father or the Father to the Son, but He unites Them in the reality of the divine nature. In this sense one can say concerning the "procession" of the Holy Spirit that it is not active but passive; the Holy Spirit issues, flows out. He does not reveal Himself, for He does not have

His own particular content; rather, He proclaims that which the Son says in the name of the Father. He is the Spirit of Truth, not Truth itself. In Him and through Him the depths of God become transparent as all-real Truth and Beauty. The trihypostatic God has His nature as the triune and unitrinitarian act of the love of the Father and of the Son and of the Holy Spirit, the *one* nature of the three hypostases.[5]

III. The Divine World

The spirit has personality and nature; the Divine Spirit also has its trihypostatic personality and its one nature, which, being totally transparent for the personality, is entirely personal, hypostatized. However, this does not diminish its special character as nature or Divinity *(theotēs)*.[6] This is the *Divine world* in God, who, as the living God, has His proper life and its source in the divine nature, or "depths of God." Sometimes Divinity, or the nature in God, is denied solely on the grounds that in God all is personal, and His entire essence is permeated with rays of consciousness of self, that is, it is hypostatized. This impoverishes His being, however, reducing it to *abstract* personal consciousness, that is, making it poorer than the creaturely spirit. But this being, which is transparent for the consciousness of self, nonetheless exists also *by itself,* the way our nature exists in us, not only insofar as it is still an unrealized given and an unilluminated depth, but also insofar as it enters into our conscious life.

God's nature is not diminished in its being by the fact that it is exhaustively realized in the divine consciousness. His nature exists not only for this consciousness of self but also *by itself,* as *ens realissimum,* as ousia. This ousia of God can be understood as God's life and God's power, that is, as something entirely simple and in this sense superqualitative, not only in the sense of its *transcendence* in relation to creation (the apophatic element), but also in the sense of the *fullness* of the absolute white light that cannot be decomposed into lines of the color spectrum but that contains them (the kataphatic element). However, this transcen-

---

5. The question of the character of the Third hypostasis is touched upon here only as far as necessary. A special study of the Third hypostasis can be found in the second part of the present trilogy, *The Comforter* [published by Eerdmans in 2004 in Boris Jakim's translation].

6. This distinction between God and Divinity plays a large role in the Palamite disputes and definitions.

The Lamb of God

dence for creation does not diminish Divinity and does not impoverish His nature in itself. The divine nature is not only the *power* of life but also its *content* — the absolute content of absolute life with all its "properties," the property of all properties. It is proper for this content to include All, for no limitations are applicable to Divinity; furthermore, this All should be understood not as an aggregate or series of an infinite number of elements of the All but as their organic inner integrity, as integral wisdom[7] in union. This is the All as unity and unity as All, *All-unity*. God's life is this positive All-unity, and the All-unity is God's nature. In this capacity God's nature as the absolute content of His life is that which Scripture calls the Divine Wisdom, Sophia (see Prov. 8:22 and parallel texts). Thus, the *Divine Sophia* is nothing other than *God's nature*, His ousia, not only in the sense of power and depth, but also in the sense of self-revealing content, in the sense of the All-unity.[8] When we speak of God's Divinity, we have in mind His nature both as the closed depths, the source of life, and as the open depths, life itself; and here the source of life is identical to life itself, even as Ousia and Sophia are identical.

Ousia is usually conceived as a Divine reality, whereas Sophia is usually conceived as only a property or combination of properties belonging to this reality, a property or properties that arise or manifest themselves only in the case of a definite relation, precisely to the creaturely world. There is no basis for such a distinction and separation. Divinity as Sophia is *ens realissimum* to the same degree as Ousia, insofar as the source of life cannot be separated from or opposed to its revelation. The Divine Ousia, like Sophia, is precisely the All-unity that is the life of God and that lives in God by the whole of Divine reality; having Ousia, God thereby also has it as Sophia. God is Ousia: *Deus est Divinitas, ho Theos theotēs estin*. The reverse, however, is not true: Ousia is not (the personal) God; Divinity is not the Divine Personality. Likewise, God is Sophia; Sophia is Divine. She is God in His self-revelation, *Deus revelatus*, although the reverse, again, is not true: Sophia is not *ho Theos* but only *theos* or *Theos*.[9] Sophia cannot be

---

7. The Russian word *tselomudrie*, here translated "integral wisdom," can also mean chastity. — Trans.

8. Wisdom in this sense is not only a "property" or one of the "properties" that are found in the appropriate scholastic rubrics of dogmatic theology. Rather, it is the "property of properties," in which all of them find their foundation. Wisdom is Divine being, the All-Unity, which is not only without qualities (since it surpasses qualities) but also possesses *all* qualities.

9. Sophia is not *the* God *(ho Theos)*. Rather, she is god *(theos)* or God *(Theos*, without the article *ho)*. — Trans.

The Divine Sophia

equated with the Divine Personality, and therefore particularly not with the Logos. The equality that here expresses concrete identity, life-identity, is *irreversible*, just as the subject and the predicate are irreversible. Only abstract, mathematical, and (in this sense) empty equalities are reversible: a = b and b = a.

Thus, God is Divinity, Ousia-Sophia. It follows that in God there is not only a Person (and Persons) but also Divinity, which is *not* a personality, although it belongs to a Person (and Persons) and is totally hypostatized. Divinity is therefore both personal and impersonal. Such is precisely the Church's dogma of the union of Hypostasis and Ousia in God: Ousia itself is not a personality, although in God it exists only personally. If we consider Ousia only in the aspect of *personal* being, we effectively abolish it. Ousia possesses both personal being (in relation to a Person) and impersonal being (by itself): at no moment of its being does it exist outside of and separately from personality, but also at no moment of its being does it merge with personality, for otherwise the personality too would lose itself, become deprived of nature, be transformed into an empty abstract I, and would not be a vital spirit, living in its own nature. The nature must therefore be considered not only as something existent in God, as Ousia-Sophia, but also as something independent, as Divinity or the Divine world in itself, existent not only in God but also for God. Thus, one can say not only that God *is* Divinity but also that He *has* Divinity, existent by itself, although not for itself (that is, not personally, not as a "fourth hypostasis").

What can one say about Ousia as Sophia? About nature as content? About Divinity as the Divine world? According to content, this is the All; according to mode of being, this is All-unity, Integral Wisdom; according to power of being, this is the living and eternally alive principle. Its reality is equal to the reality of God Himself (for it is precisely God in His self-revelation); its life is equal to the life of God Himself (for it is His proper life); its aseity is equal to the aseity of God Himself (for, apart from Divinity, the very idea of God becomes an abstract concept). Sophia is the Pleroma, the Divine world, existent in God and for God, eternal and uncreated, in which God lives in the Holy Trinity. And in itself this Divine world contains all that the Holy Trinity reveals about itself in itself; it is the Image of God in God Himself, the self-Icon of Divinity (according to the doctrine of St. John of Damascus). This world has in itself the life of Divinity. It is therefore not only a *thought* about the Divine world, not only an ideal, but unrealized and thus abstract thought (the Platonic *kosmos noētos*); it is not only the mute perception of this world, deprived of differentiatedness and transparence of being. It is the real and fully realized divine Idea, the idea of all ideas, actualized as Beauty in ideal images of beauty. The icon of Divinity is divine self-art, life in ideal images and in the reality of these images. Ousia-Sophia is a living principle, and it lives such a profound life that no creaturely life can be compared with it. Ousia-Sophia is the Life of life and the proto-ground of all creaturely life. She is the divine life in God, who is love. Therefore, divine life too is love, which is the power of this life: The *All* — multiform, multidiverse, but also one — is linked in the *All-unity* by the power of love as one in the many and the many in the one, as all in all. This is the *organic* image of the multi-unity, in which the unity is not established by the abstraction of concrete properties (as is the case with Aristotle's "one in many") and in which concreteness does not abolish the multi-unity. Love in God's life is an all-permeating, all-concrete multi-unity as a spiritual organism. This form of unity is not given to us in our rational logic, which corresponds to the corrupted state of the sinful world. The sinful world knows reality only as mutual repulsion, and it knows multiplicity only as extra-position or juxtaposition; its logic therefore has at its disposal only the *abstract* concept of the universal without any possibility of thinking the concretely universal. Therefore, the very idea of the divine all-concrete all-unity remains abstract for this logic. This all-unity is nevertheless a necessary ontological postulate for our thought and feeling in relation to life, not as this relation is given, but as it is proposed — the universal cosmic *sobornost*[10] of concrete all-unity in divine love.

Love is not only the linking or uniting force of the all-unity of the Divine world in this world itself, but it is also the link between this world and the hypostatic God. In our abstract logic of the world, the copula "is" represents the indifferent glue that formally links or unites the subject and the predicate. But in the statement *God is Ousia or Sophia, or the Divine world*, the copula "is" signifies not a relation of formal logic but the ontological link of love. *God is Sophia* signifies that God, hypostatic love, loves Sophia, and that she loves God with an answering, though not hypostatic, love.[11] Thus "is" signifies love. In Sophia, God loves Himself in His self-revelation; He loves His Own, existent by itself, objectified and reified. But

---

10. The concept of sobornost (derived from the Russian *sobirat'*, "to gather," and related to *sobor*, "council") is usually used to describe the divinely inspired fellowship of believers in the Church, their "catholicity." Here, Bulgakov extends this concept to the entire universe. — Trans.

11. See the chapter on Sophia in my book *The Unfading Light* (Moscow, 1917).

Sophia too, this self-revelation, loves the hypostatic God-Love by an answering love. She does not merely belong to God, she *is* God; that is, she *loves* the trihypostatic God.

This form of God's love for Sophia and, inversely, of Sophia's love for God requires special clarification, for the same term "love" is used to express three (or even four) different forms of one love. First of all, it is necessary to distinguish *hypostatic* love, love of person for person, which is love in the proper sense, the foundation of the trihypostatic unity of the Holy Trinity; it is in relation to this triunity that it is first of all said that *God is love*. We have an image of such love in the *personal* love between human beings, as well as in churchly love. Furthermore, one must distinguish hypostatic love for a nonhypostatic, although hypostatized, principle: this is God's love for Sophia, His self-revelation, God's love for the divine world. In the creaturely, sinful world, love for *one's own*, that is, in essence, love for oneself, acquires the character of self-love and prejudice, in virtue of which this "one's own" is prized not at its essential and true worth but precisely as one's own; this is the egotistical admiration of one's own image, "narcissism." Herein lies the principle of the fall of Satan, who fell in love with himself, who came to love *his own* with an egotistical, self-asserting love. But even in the sinful world there can exist a righteous love for one's own, a love based on an appreciation of the objective value of one's own, for the sake of which true self-renunciation with the forgetting of oneself is manifested. In this same way a creator loves his creation, and a doer loves his deed: he loves it for the sake of the deed itself, although he does not separate himself from it but in a certain sense identifies himself with it. Here the image of God's love for Sophia is imprinted in man.

The third form of love is Sophia's answering love for God, as the inner connection of the Divine trihypostatic Person with His nature. On the part of the nature, on the part of Ousia as Sophia, there is of course no place for personal love (the type of love exhibited in the first two forms of love), for there is no person here: Sophia is not a "fourth hypostasis," just as in general she is not a hypostasis at all. However, she too loves; otherwise we could not understand her relation to God, since the mere fact of belonging based on the right of property or possession does not, in itself, conform with God's essence: in the life of the spirit there is no place for thingness or facticity. Clearly, one must recognize a special form of *nonhypostatic love in relation to a hypostasis,* and this is precisely the relation of the Divine Sophia to the triune Divine Person. Sophia loves God without being a hypostasis. What can this mean? Sophia is not hypostatic being, but she is a living *entity*. The divine world is alive, for nothing nonliving can be conceived in God. This living entity is hypostatized in God as His personal nature and life, but in order to be hypostatized this entity must in itself be *ens realissimum;* it must live in itself by a supremely alive life, if one can use such an expression. The power of life — its fire — is love, and to live in God is to love. Nonhypostatic love cannot know the self-renouncing, sacrificial self-positing that expresses divine trihypostatic love, this circulation of personal depletion aimed at filling oneself in the other. The nature of nonhypostatic love is different: it can only *belong*, surrendering itself, loving and, in this self-surrendering, "feminine" love, realizing the power of life, the bliss of love. It is in this sense (but *only* in this sense) that Sophia's love is feminine. This is the original meaning of the biblical images of the wife and bride that are applied to the Church.

But it is precisely Sophia's self-surrender to God that signifies her hypostatization.[12] In order, however, to fully understand this idea of God's love for Sophia and of Sophia's answering love for God, without which God would inevitably be conceived of as without nature (which would constitute the most pernicious of heresies in the first and initial dogma of God), one must fully accept the reality of the divine world, without evading this acceptance under different pretexts and deviating into idealistic and spiritualistic mystification. Sophia, as the divine world, *exists* in God and, in a certain sense, is *present* before God and is *possessed* by Him in all her divine reality and authenticity. Any attempt to diminish this reality is an attempt to diminish the reality of the very essence of God.

But together with the reality of this divine world, we must not forget its *spirituality*, for God is Spirit and nothing nonspiritual can be attributed to Him. Consequently, the divine world in Sophia is a *spiritual reality*. In order to be real — in order to be supremely real — this world must be spiritual. In general, *reality* is by no means connected, as many think, with thingness and materiality (the angels are immaterial, but their reality is not thereby diminished). Reality, to the supreme degree, is proper to God Himself, who is in the Holy Trinity: we cannot speak of His nonreality if only because there can be no question here of any material and reified principle. Consequently, spiritual reality exists as the prototype of reality in general.

The reality of the divine world is that this world exists in God as the self-revelation of the entire Holy Trinity — of the Father, who reveals Him-

---

12. See my essay "Hypostasis and Hypostatizedness" in *Collection in Honor of P. B. Struve* (Prague, 1925). This essay has been translated as "Hypostasis and Hypostaticity" by A. B. Gallaher and I. Kutkova (*St. Vladimir's Theological Quarterly* 49:1-2 [2005]: 5-46).

self in the Word and shows the All in it; and in the Holy Spirit, who accomplishes this All for the Father and the Son. There cannot be another or greater reality, and the only matter for discussion is whether this self-revelation exists only for God, as His personal, "subjective" representation, or whether it is also real *by itself,* in order to be for God as well. Anyone who confesses that the Holy Trinity has one nature would hardly dare to affirm such subjectivism. Can one really allow that this one nature is not revealed in God and for God as His self-revelation or Sophia? To recognize the *reality* of the divine world, a reality that establishes the possibility of Sophia's answering love for the Divine Person, is to recognize in Sophia, as the divine world, her proper life in a certain sense. To be sure, this life is not hypostatic but natural; nevertheless, it has its *natural* (although by no means hypostatic) center or coherence. The entire life of this world, with its spiritual reality, is centered in love as an all-unity, as a pan-organism, and in this sense as a *spiritual body,* living one life, but a life that is all-one. This organizing principle of the spiritual body, this centering force of the spiritual pan-organism, is precisely *love,* as the inner life of this body. Here we encounter the idea of love in a new form, its fourth form. This love is completely devoid of the personal principle, for if Sophia is not a person, her inner life is not personal. Love is manifested here impersonally, as the connecting and organizing principle, as the universal mutual attraction and order of divine ideas existing in the divine world. This is not a mechanical attraction, which cannot exist in a spiritual organism; rather, it is the inner attraction and interpenetration of that which is kindred in multiformity and one in its nature. Love here is the natural order of the divine world.

IV. The Divine Sophia

The divine world is the objective principle of the life of God, of the being of the One who is. This world is this life itself, and through it no extradivine principle is introduced into Divinity. This life of God in His Divinity, or the divine world as an objective and living principle, is precisely what Scripture calls Sophia, or the Wisdom of God (see Job 28; Prov. 8-9; Wisdom of Solomon 7-11; Ecclesiasticus 1:24). In considering Sophia as Divinity in God, one can distinguish two aspects of Sophia, in conformity with Holy Scripture: She is, properly, Sophia (Hokhma), as the revelation of the Wisdom of God; and she is also Glory, as the revelation of God's Beauty and All-blessedness.

The Lamb of God

In Sophia is revealed the *content* of the divine nature, as All and All-unity. In this sense, she is the revelation of the Logos, the Word, saying All: "All things were made by him" (John 1:3). The Word-Logos is the principle of meaning, content, distinction, multiplicity, but also the principle of connection, correlation, all-unity. This is self-thinking Divine Thought, *noēsis tēs noēseōs*, whose object and content is itself. Thought is identical here with its object, the word with its content, and the all-permeating connection of thought is the connection of the all-unity,[13] the very wisdom of being. Multiformity and "logical" connectedness, differentiation and interpenetration in the dialectics of thought that posits and knows itself, the essential density of content of thought and its "logical" transparence, the clear and cloudless world of divine ideas — such is the Kingdom of the Logos. And so Wisdom, as wisdom, is proper to the entire Holy Trinity and each of its hypostases. And this Wisdom, as the content of all meanings, is also the consciousness of self of the trinitarian God. However, just as in the Holy Trinity the unity of life is established given a particular self-determination of each of the hypostases, so in this case Wisdom, as Logos, is the predominant self-revelation of the Second hypostasis as the Father's Word and the Father's Wisdom. The Father speaks His Word in the Son, and He also reveals His Wisdom in the Son. Sophia, as Wisdom, is the self-revelation of the Logos, through the self-determination of the Second hypostasis,[14] which is why the incarnate Logos, Christ, is called "the power of God and the wisdom of God" (1 Cor. 1:24).

However, Sophia as the Divine world, as the fullness of Divinity, *plērōma tēs theotētos* (Col. 2:9), is not only the Wisdom but also the *Glory* of God. The Glory of God, an expression frequently used in the Old and New Testaments to refer to God, must, first of all, not be understood in the subjective sense of a glorification of someone by someone else, in particular not in the sense of the glorification of God by creatures, for the Glory of God exists outside of any relation to creation, to the extradivine. The Glory is in God Himself and without reference to creation ("before the world was" [John 17:5]) as an intradivine principle. God glorifies Himself

---

13. That which Hegel attributed to thought as the sole principle of being is here completely applicable to the Divine Sophia in the capacity of the Logos. See my book *Die Tragödie der Philosophie* (1927).

14. There is a sophianic icon that expresses precisely this idea: the Pre-eternal Adolescent, the Word of the Father, the Vigilant Eye. This is not an icon of Christ in His adolescence but an icon of the Logos in the capacity of Wisdom.

The Divine Sophia

in Himself; glory belongs to God not only as praise of glory but also as the Glory proper to Him, about which Holy Scripture speaks. Scripture describes the Glory in massive religious images as the appearance of Divinity itself: to Moses on Sinai, to the people in the tabernacle and in the Temple of Solomon, to Isaiah and Ezekiel in their visions.[15] Its appearance to the prophet Ezekiel most fully expresses the essence of the Glory as Sophia. Glory, by its very concept, cannot be without object and content; by intention, it is glory about something — it has its object, which is given to it. And the Divine Glory is thus the Glory of God about His Divinity that is being revealed. This is God's joy about Himself. It is God admiring Himself, being comforted by Himself, seeing Himself in Beauty; and this relation should be taken in its essence, that is, apart from the self-love and narcissism proper to created beings.

God's Glory is about what is worthy of glory, about what is *glorious* in itself. In a unihypostatic created being, such self-glorification would inevitably be egocentric and even egotistic and prejudiced, insofar as love for *one's own* is inseparable here from love for *oneself* (nevertheless, here too, as we have indicated, it is possible to attain a certain self-renunciation in love for one's own, by recognizing it as a value). But in the trihypostatic God, in virtue of His trihypostatic character, all self-love or egocentric self-affirmation is excluded; and Glory here is just as inalienable and essential in the self-revelation of Divinity as Wisdom or the Word. In other words, that which is revealed in the Word as Wisdom is *glorious,* worthy of glory, and has Glory. This is the all-blessedness of God, the joy of Divine life as self-knowledge and self-revelation. The Glory of God expresses the divine self-relation of God to His Wisdom; the Glory has an object for itself. The Glory is therefore not the first but the second in the self-revelation of Divinity (to be sure, this is not a chronological but an ontological distinction). One can say that Glory in Divinity does not precede but rather follows the Wisdom of the Word. Glory is Glory *about* Wisdom; it reposes upon the accomplished revelation of the Word. Glory renders the Word palpable, valuable, desirable, joyous, full, adequate.

Thus, the revelation of the Glory is *inseparable* from the revelation of the Wisdom of the Word; the two are one and identical in the Divine Sophia herself, just as Sophia herself is one and indivisible. Here it becomes perfectly clear that, if Sophia, as the Wisdom of the Word, as the

---

15. For the texts on the Glory of God, see the excursus to my book *The Burning Bush: An Essay in the Dogmatic Interpretation of Certain Features in the Orthodox Veneration of the Mother of God* (Paris, 1927).

The Lamb of God

Logos, is the self-revelation of God in the Second hypostasis, then the Glory is the self-revelation of God in the Third hypostasis. In other words, *Sophia as Glory belongs to the Holy Spirit.* Also disclosed here is the relation between the Word and the Holy Spirit as the relation between the Second and Third hypostases: first the Word and then the Spirit. The Spirit reposes upon the Word; the Word and the Holy Spirit, their dyad and bi-unity, reveal, in the Divine Sophia, the Father. And therefore it is said about the trinitarian God: "thine is the kingdom [of the Father], and the power [of the Son], and the glory [of the Holy Spirit], for ever" (Matt. 6:13). In their *hypostatic* being the Word and the Holy Spirit are "distinctly personal," whereas in the Divine Sophia, as the self-revelation of the Holy Trinity, they are distinct but inseparable. They are distinct since the Son is a hypostasis other than the Holy Spirit, and the mode of His revelation is other than that of the Holy Spirit; but this *revelation* itself, as an objective principle, as the Divine world, the Wisdom of God, is *one*: in Sophia the Father reveals Himself through the Son and the Holy Spirit in His Divinity. Therefore, to say that the Logos in His *revelation* is the Divine Sophia is just as legitimate as to say that the Holy Spirit, the "Spirit of Wisdom," is the Divine Sophia in His *revelation* (although the converse is not true: one cannot say that the Divine Sophia is the Logos or that she is the Holy Spirit). But it would be just as legitimate to say that neither the Logos nor the Holy Spirit as such, as personally distinct, is the Divine Sophia, for Sophia is their self-revelation in *bi-unity*, in relation to the Father; that is, she is the self-revelation of the Holy Trinity as the Father in the Son and the Holy Spirit.

This definition of the relations of the Divine Sophia to the different hypostases of the Holy Trinity concretely manifests the fundamental position of the dogma of the Holy Trinity: the hypostases are *separate* and *distinct*, and at the same time their *equal dignity* and *equal divinity* are preserved. The Father and the Son and the Holy Spirit, and the entire Holy Trinity, Each equally is God, not more and not less. But in addition, the Holy Trinity is not identical to any of the hypostases, just as the hypostases are not identical to one another, although they are of equal dignity and divinity: they manifest equality with inequality and identity with distinction. But it is the same way in the Divine life and self-revelation, in the Divine Sophia,[16] as it is in hypostatic being. The Divine

---

16. This makes clear that, from the trinitarian and sophiological points of view, it is erroneous to fully equate Sophia with just one person, namely the Logos. If only the Logos were Wisdom, that would mean (contrary to churchly and patristic tradition) that

The Divine Sophia

Sophia can be defined both in relation to the entire Holy Trinity in its unity (which is without separation) and in relation to each of the hypostases (which are inconfusable and inseparable). However, here the particular character of each hypostasis is preserved in all its force, as is each one's interrelationship within the Holy Trinity.

The Second hypostasis is revealed in the Divine Sophia according to His hypostatic character not only as the Word and Wisdom but also *as the Son*. We recall that, in itself, the sonhood already represents a certain pre-eternal kenosis of the Son, His self-depletion in His love for the Father, the hypostatic sacrifice of the Lamb. This *sacrifice* of the Lamb is revealed also in the Divine Sophia — no longer as the *personal* self-definition of the Son in relation to the Father, but as His *natural* self-positing in the self-revelation of Divinity, in Sophia. The Son surrenders Himself as the *Word of All and about All* to the Divine world; He serves the self-revealing Divinity, and He posits Himself as the *content* of this self-revelation. He sacrifices *Himself* to the Father, and He sacrifices *His own* to the Divine world, sacrificially depleting Himself in all things and to the end. The *Divine world*, in its first state, is therefore the Word by whom all things were made. The imprint of the self-revealing hypostatic love of the begetting Father and of the begotten Son, of the Proto-Image and of the Image, lies also on the Divine world, in the Divine Sophia; the self-revelation of God is a work of sacrificial love, in which the Father is the loving priest and the Son is the loving sacrifice, revealing in Himself the Father. In its content, the Divine world bears the seal of the Lamb, of the Word of God. One can see in this a new confirmation of the fact that, in a *certain* sense, the Logos is Sophia. But the Divine world is not *only* the revelation of the Logos, for this revelation is accomplished by the Holy Spirit, who reposes upon the Logos, manifests Him, and answers the depletion of the Logos with *glorification* (the comfort of the Comforter). In this sense, if the Logos can be called the "demiurge" in the Divine world, then the Holy Spirit is its "cosmourge," its Comforter and Beautifier, the *Glory of the Word*.

There is one final definition of the Divine Sophia that follows from the aforementioned definitions of the Divine world, but that also is a re-

---

Wisdom is alien to the other Persons. If Wisdom belonged only to one Person, that would mean that the Divine triunity is sundered, and that it is replaced by a tritheism, with the gods on this pseudo-Christian Olympus divided, as in paganism, according to specialization. This also abolishes the one nature, life, and self-revelation of the Holy Trinity. Thus, to negate the Divine Sophia by reducing her to an attribute of the Logos constitutes first an antitrinitarian heresy and then (as we shall see) also a christological heresy.

flection of the creaturely world. By her *content,* Sophia, or the Divine world, is the pan-organism of ideas, the organism of the ideas of all, about all, and in all; she is Integral Wisdom. In herself, Sophia contains life, although it is not for herself, for she is hypostatized in God. How should one understand this divine organism, or this spiritual body, which is the revelation of the Glory of God? This organism is a certain living essence, a living, spiritual, although nonhypostatic entity, the Divinity of God, living by an integral but also differentiated and qualified life. What is this organism? Is it indefinable in concepts of the creaturely world (being entirely transcendent to this world) and expressible only in the *not* of apophatic theology (the *via negationis*)? Or is it accessible to the creaturely consciousness — to the human consciousness and to the angelic consciousness — also in a *positive* definition, so that it is possible to have a kataphatic theology with reference to it? A kataphatic theology is possible, not through human ascent into the Divine world (which is impossible for the creaturely consciousness), but only through the condescension of the Divine world to the creaturely world, that is, through a self-revelation of God that would be accessible to man. This accessibility is based, of course, solely on the divine being's also becoming a human being to a certain degree, enabling man — out of himself and through himself, through his knowledge of himself — to gain knowledge of God. A certain initial identity, which is the basis for human knowledge of God as a certain identification with Him (there can be no other path here), is the necessary condition for this. Without this identity, God would be absolutely transcendent for man, and we could think and say about Him only that which He is *not,* remaining silent about that which He *is.*

Such self-revelation can only be the proper work of God in the *creation of man.* This self-revelation is accomplished by God as the foundation of man's being and, in man, of the being of all creation. Man is created by God in "the image of God" (Gen. 1:27), and this image is the *ens realissimum* in man, who thereby becomes a creaturely god. This *ens realissimum* builds a bridge of ontological identification between the Creator and creation through the deification of the latter, and from the beginning it establishes a *positive* relation between the Image and the Proto-Image. This can be understood only in the sense of a relative, analogical identity that, although it has its particular path of development, its epochs or aeons, is already implanted in man and predetermined. This identity signifies not only the divinity of man but also a certain humanity of God — "we are . . . his offspring" (Acts 17:28). There is something in man that must be directly correlated with God's being, and this something is not some individual feature but man's very *humanity*, which is the image of God. Man, as a creaturely spirit, has personality (hypostasis) and his own nature, just as God has personality (trihypostatic) and His nature, Divinity, the Divine Sophia, the Divine world, the pan-organism of ideas of divine being. The divine nature must be understood in a *positive* relation to man's nature as it exists in the fullness of its powers, possibilities, and tasks, not yet manifested in the life of the integral old Adam but already manifested in the life of the New Adam. In ourselves, humanity is as yet an unrevealed essence, one that is only in the process of being revealed and that will be revealed only when "God will be all in all." The initial axiom of this revelation consists precisely in there being a conformity or *co-imagedness* between Divinity and humanity. In other words, the Divine Sophia, as the pan-organism of ideas, is *the pre-eternal Humanity in God*, as the divine proto-image and foundation for man's being.

The Divine Sophia as Humanity, or as its principle, is not yet Man. Man is a *hypostasis* living in its nature, which is precisely humanity. Thus Sophia by herself, as an essence that is nonhypostatic (but is only in the process of being hypostatized), does not yet express the full image of man, which necessarily requires a hypostasis. Man receives a hypostasis from God at his creation as "the in-breathing of the Divine spirit," and he thereby becomes "a living soul," a living man, I — in which, for which, and through which his humanity lives. But this humanity already possesses *the ability to be hypostatized*, and in this it already bears the imprint of its Proto-Image. Although the Divine Sophia is not a hypostasis, she is never nonhypostatic or extrahypostatic; she is eternally being hypostatized, and for her the direct hypostasis is not the Father (although He is revealed in the Divine Sophia) but the Logos, the demiurgic hypostasis who reveals the Father. It can be said about the Logos that He is the eternal Man, the human Proto-Image *before* the creation of the world, and that man is created in His image. In this sense, the apostles and the Gospels repeatedly call Him the Man from Heaven or simply Man, the Son of God and the Son of Man, in all the mysterious interrelation of these names.[17] And as the First Man, He is also the Lamb sacrificed before the creation of the world; that is, He is predestined to become also an earthly man. This idea is foundational for Christology, soteriology, and anthropology in their

---

17. Cf. the divinely inspired audacious words of the Apostle Paul: "the gift by grace ... [of] one man, Jesus Christ" (Rom. 5:15); "the first man is of the earth, earthy; the second man is the Lord from heaven" (1 Cor. 15:47). Also relevant here are the Lord's words from the Gospel of John: "he that came down from heaven, even the Son of man" (3:13).

unity: Sophia is the pre-eternal Humanity,[18] and the Logos is the Divine Man. The Divine-Humanity and the God-Man, that is, the humanity of Divinity and the divinity of humanity, are given pre-eternally in God. The Logos, the Second hypostasis, is the proper hypostasis of the Divine-Humanity in God.

However, we also know that the Holy Spirit reposes upon the Word, and He gives reality to the world of the Divine ideas of the Logos. The relation of the Third hypostasis to the eternal Divine-Humanity is therefore expressed, *not* in the fact that this hypostasis is the hypostatic center for the Divine-Humanity, but in the fact that it actualizes and reveals for the Son, and thereby for the Father as well, the Divine-Humanity as a divine reality, receiving and containing the Logos. In this sense, in the eternal Divine-Humanity, the Logos as the God-Man is distinguished from the Holy Spirit as the Divine-Humanity (the analogy to this in the life of the world is Christ as the God-Man and the Church as the Divine-Humanity). As a consequence, the following difference exists between the hypostatic relations of the Logos and of the Holy Spirit to the Divine-Humanity: The Logos, by its hypostasis, is immediately directed at the Divine-Humanity and is its "Head." In contrast, the Holy Spirit is directed at the Divine-Humanity that has already been revealed through the Logos; the Holy Spirit receives and quickens this Divine-Humanity not as His own hypostatic revelation but as the revelation of the Logos. The character of the Third hypostasis remains the same here as in the Holy Trinity: this hypostasis shows the Father not itself but the Son, and it shows the Son not itself but the Father, while becoming hypostatically transparent in this movement of love. And in the Divine-Humanity the Third hypostasis merges with it, as it were, in its being for the Son and thereby for the Father as well. In *this* sense, we can express the relation between the Second hypostasis and the Third hypostasis in the one Divine-Humanity by saying that their inseparable dyad is precisely the Divine-Humanity as the revelation of the Father in the Holy Trinity — in other words, as the Divine Sophia.

This character of the Second and Third hypostases in relation to the Divine-Humanity can also be expressed as the correlation of two spiritual principles in Divinity that, in the creaturely human world, are *reflected* as

---

18. This idea was expressed in a work of youthful genius, *Lectures on Divine Humanity*, by Vladimir Solovyov, who unfortunately never developed his insightful thoughts into a theological doctrine but instead obscured and distorted them with gnostic conceptions.

The Divine Sophia

the correlation of the male and female principles. The image of God in man is fully manifested precisely in the union of these two principles ("So God created man in his own image, in the image of God created he him; male and female created he them" [Gen. 1:27]). In the human world the fullness of this love is manifested as the love of mother, sister, bride, and wife in relation to son, brother, bridegroom, and husband, as well as the love of daughter for father. Precisely these images are applied to Christ and to the Mother of God and the Church: the Most Holy Mother of God is the Mother of Christ, but She is also honored as His Unwedded Bride (or, in the words of the Song of Songs, as "my sister, my spouse"). The Church, which has its personal center in the Mother of God, is "the bride, the Lamb's wife" (Rev. 21:9); at the same time, the most decisive comparison of the female principle in the human spirit with the Holy Spirit is found in the concluding part of Revelation: "and the Spirit and the bride say, Come" (22:17). This is said about the Church as the accomplished Divine-Humanity in its relation to the Lamb, the Logos-Christ. It follows that the hypostatic interrelation of the Logos and the Holy Spirit in Their common revelation in the Divine-Humanity contains a special, *personally* qualified form of love — a "qualification" that can be expressed in creaturely language by analogies of forms of love between the male principle and the female principle (and it is of course self-evident that anything having to do with sex or, in general, with sensuality must be excluded here). And just as the hypostasis of the Logos is the hypostasis of Christ, made incarnate in a male infant and reaching maturity as a "perfect male," so the hypostasis of the Spirit is most fully revealed for us in the Mother of God and becomes a reality for us in the Church, which is the "Spirit and Bride."

As far as the hypostasis of the Father is concerned, even though this hypostasis has a masculine name in human (or more precisely, in divine-human) language, nevertheless this usage can be chiefly explained by the absence of an appropriate term unrelated to the distinction between masculine and feminine. The masculine gender here is *masculinum majestatis*, which is used to magnify the fatherhood of God, not to define it. This is indirectly confirmed by the fact that the Father's fatherhood is "without maternity" in relation to the Son and is not exhausted by begetting (the masculine principle), but it also includes procession (the feminine principle), while remaining outside this distinction, which exists only in the juxtaposition of the two principles that are being distinguished. It follows that the Paternal hypostasis, as "omni-causative" and "initial," revealing itself in the Son and in the Holy Spirit, in the Divine-Humanity, remains transcendent in relation to the latter in a certain sense; that is, the Paternal hypostasis cannot be defined in terms of the Divine-Humanity. Unlike the Son, the Father is not the God-Man, and unlike the Holy Spirit, He is not the Divine-Humanity, although He is revealed in it: He has His proper image in the Divine-Humanity and is the universal Principle.[19] This explains why the Father, *although He sends* into the world the Son and then the Holy Spirit, does not appear personally in the divine-human world. He shows Himself only in the Son ("he that hath seen me hath seen the Father" [John 14:9]) through the Holy Spirit, who reveals the Son. The Father *is* the Divine-Humanity in the same sense that the subject is the predicate, but He *is not* the Divine-Humanity — in the very same sense. The subject is revealed in the predicate but is necessarily different from it, is not identified with it, transcends it.

We must add in conclusion that the definition of divine nature as preeternal Humanity or Divine-Humanity (which in this case is the same thing) is conceived as a reflection from the creaturely world, from creaturely humanity. In this sense this definition is only an *analogy,* but one that is understood *realistically:* that is, not only are all the distinctions of state preserved, but the identity of being is also preserved. We know man only as a creature, and therefore it may seem arduous to ascend from the creature to the understanding of God. However, we can also take the reverse path of "that which is above is also below"; that is, taking Divinity as the point of departure, we can understand man as the cryptogram of Divinity. And this path is directly imposed on us by revelation, which proclaims that man bears the Image of God, that is, that humanity in the world presupposes the Divine-Humanity. And one should not surrender this idea to militant atheism, which distorts it by understanding not man on the basis of Divinity but Divinity on the basis of man. But with reference to the Divine-Humanity one must exclude all the properties connected with the natural and material existence of creaturely humanity on the paths of its development, and it is necessary to conceive this creaturely humanity truly as an ousia, that is, as an intensive spiritual essence, containing in itself, in the capacity of noumenon, all the phenomena that manifest it. The Divine-Humanity in God possesses the whole of the absolute *spirituality* that is proper to Divinity. This is the "energy" of Divinity, which possesses an infinite multitude of radiations of the ousia (cf. St. Gregory Palamas's doctrine of energies, for which he was accused of polytheism).

---

19. It is in this sense that we understand the text of Ephesians 3:14-15: "the Father . . . of whom the whole family in heaven and earth is named."

However, this does not mean that, in God, the Divine-Humanity, as the revelation of Divinity, cannot also be understood as the *body* of Divinity, a body that is absolutely spiritual and in *this* sense incorporeal, but that also accomplishes what is proper to a body as such: to be the revelation of the spirit that lives in it and that even lives by it in a certain sense. Thus, we get a series of equalities in which one and the same quantity, God's nature, the ousia, receives its definitions as the Divine Sophia. Sophia is the Wisdom of God; she is the Glory of God; she is the humanity in God; she is the Divine-Humanity; she is the body of God (or the "garment" of Divinity); she is the Divine world, existing in God "before" the creation. All this contains "sufficient grounds" for creation in accordance with the principle "that which is above is also below." In other words, it contains "sufficient grounds" for the sophianicity of creation.

CHAPTER 2

The Creaturely Sophia

I. The Creation of the World

"God created the world out of nothing" *(ex ouk onton)*. What is the relation of this act of the creation of the world to the proper life of God or to His eternity? "God is a totally self-sufficient and all-blessed being." This means that God's eternity contains the entire fullness of His life, both through the disclosure of His hypostatic being (in trinitarity) and through the disclosure of His natural Divinity in the Divine Sophia. God is absolute in His proper, divine life, and He does not need the world for Himself. For Him, the creation or noncreation of the world is not a hypostatic or natural necessity of self-completion, for *tri*hypostatizedness fully exhausts the *hypostatic* self-definition and closes its circle, whereas God's nature is *fullness* that contains the All in itself. Thus, the necessity of creation does not follow from the proper life of Divinity and Divinity's self-positing; there is no place for creation in Divinity itself. And in this sense, the creation of the world can only be the proper *work* of Divinity, not in His hypostatic nature, but in His creative freedom. In relation to the life of Divinity *itself,* the world did not have to be.

However, this freedom in the sense of the absence of natural or hypostatic necessity does not at all signify the presence of randomness or arbitrariness in the being of the world. One should not think that the world was in fact created according to the whim of the omnipotence, without any reason and meaning for the Creator Himself but simply as a manifestation of His power. Such a notion is blasphemous and corresponds only to Schopenhauer's atheistic philosophy, according to which the Divine Will, at random or according to a meaningless whim, caused the world to appear. God's freedom in the creation of the world signifies only the absence of a determinate necessity for Him as a need for Him to develop or complete Himself (a notion that is not alien to the pantheism of Schelling or Hegel). But by no means does this mean that the world is not needed by God in some *other* sense (besides His own self-completion) or that He could have not created the world (a notion that diminishes the grandeur of God).

God *needs* the world, and it could not have remained uncreated. But God needs the world not for Himself but for the world itself. God is love, and it is proper for love to love and to expand in love. And for divine love it is proper not only to be realized within the confines of Divinity but also to expand beyond these confines. Otherwise, absoluteness itself becomes a *limit* for the Absolute, a limit of self-love or self-affirmation, and that would attest to the limitedness of the Absolute's omnipotence — to its impotence, as it were, beyond the limits of itself. It is proper for the ocean of Divine love to overflow its limits, and it is proper for the fullness of the life of Divinity to spread beyond its bounds. And if it is in general *possible* for God's omnipotence to create the world, it would be improper for God's love not to actualize this possibility, inasmuch as, for love, it is natural to love, exhausting to the end *all* the possibilities of love. We therefore have one of the following possibilities: Either the creation of the world is an impossibility for God, in which case the impossibility would constitute a limit for Him, would make Him limited; or in the case of such a possibility, God's love could not fail to actualize it by creating the world. Consequently, God-Love *needs* the creation of the world in order to *love,* no longer only in His own life, but also *outside* Himself, in creation. In the insatiability of His love, which is *divinely* satiated in Him Himself, in His own life, God goes out of Himself toward creation, in order to love, outside Himself, not-Himself. This extradivine being is precisely the world, or creation.

God created the world not for Himself but for the world. In creating it, He was moved by a love that was not limited even by Divinity but that poured forth outside of Him. And in *this* sense the world could not fail to be created. It is necessary for God; however, it is not necessary for God with a natural necessity, the necessity of His self-completion, nor is it necessary with a necessity imposed from outside, for there is no "outside" for God. Rather, it is necessary with *the necessity of love,* which cannot *not* love, and which manifests and realizes in itself *the identity* and *indistinguishability of freedom and necessity.* For love is *free* by its nature, but it is not arbitrary in its freedom. It is determined by an inner structure, a "law" of love.

The Creaturely Sophia

Therefore, the presence of creation and the relation to it are part of the fullness of the very concept of God. Creation cannot be eliminated from this concept as something accidental and inessential, as something that could exist or not exist. It is impossible for it not to exist. The Absolute, God in Himself, without any relation to creation (as He is understood in theology), is a conventional *abstraction,* in which one examines the essence of God. But concretely, the Absolute simply does not exist, for relation to the world and being for the world belong to the being of God and are inseparable from Him. *The Absolute is God.* It exists and can be understood only in relation to the world. God exists as the Creator, not as a self-enclosed, frigid Absolute. God is a relative concept that already includes a relation to the world.[1]

For the grandeur of God it is insufficient for Him to be the Absolute, self-enclosed and all-exclusive, if only in virtue of the absolute life in Himself. It is proper for Him to be God, that is, the *Absolute-relative,* a self-revealing Mystery that the language of logic can express only by an antinomy. The world is nothing, *ouk on,* as far as its autonomous being before the face of God is concerned; but this nothing is included in God's eternity, and God is inaccessible outside of His relation to the world. This inseparability of God and the world should not be understood pantheistically, as pan-divinity or the removal of the ontological boundaries between God and the world. The boundary between the Creator and creation must be preserved unconditionally, but the existence of this boundary does not abolish the *relation* or *link* between God and the world, outside of which God's life does not possess its fullness. The world cannot surmount the abyss that lies between the Creator and creation, but God Himself surmounts it. If God were without the world and remained in Himself, He would be the Absolute that does not exist for anything outside itself (given the absence of this "outside"), and thus He would not exist at all, insofar as to exist is to be for another. But God is not the Absolute — that is only His first self-definition. He is *God;* that is, He is the Absolute existing for another — precisely for the world.

To this degree this *other* of Divinity is included in the depths of the divine life. This is *panentheism,* where all is in God or for God, in contradistinction or opposition to *pantheism,* that is, pan-divinity and thus the absence of divinity. In diminishing the significance of the world for God, in reducing the world solely to an accident inwardly unconnected with God,

---

1. Cf. the chapter on apophatic and kataphatic theology (with the corresponding opinions of the holy fathers) in my book *The Unfading Light.*

we, desiring to magnify Divinity at the expense of the world, actually diminish Him, for we impoverish Divine love, transform it into an abstraction, and even blaspheme against it. For there is nothing inessential or accidental for love. If Divine love pours forth outside of Divinity, here too it possesses all the nature and power of this love. Love has many faces and many forms in God Himself, but all these faces and forms of divine love are *equidivine* at their source, and God loves the world with the same divine love with which He loves His Divinity. This is what makes possible this marvelous equation of Divine love: God so loved the world that He did not spare His own Son for its sake! What other confirmation of the inseparability of God and the world is needed after these words of revelation?

In Himself God is thus the Absolute, but for the world He is the Absolute-Relative, existing in Himself but also outside of Himself.[2] To go out of Himself into His other, to place Himself in extradivine being and to repeat Himself, as it were, to make an image of Himself outside Himself — this is the work of the Divine absoluteness as *omnipotence*. God's going outside of Himself into extradivinity is precisely the *creation* as God's pre-eternal creative act. It is no longer the self-revelation of God (which is the intradivine life) but is now the revelation of God outside Himself. For Him the act of creation is just as immanent as His Divinity. The absolute that is not trinitarian, that is not love (if it is at all possible to conceive such a product of mystical reveries and philosophical fantasy), can remain *alone*, enjoying itself in the boundlessness of its egotism (which is rather the image of Lucifer). It can — not for the sake of love, but in its omnipotence indulging its despotic capriciousness — create for itself playthings of creation if only for the purpose of destroying them. But this nightmarish image, full of contradictions, can arise only in the morbid imagination. The trinitarian God-Love, in His Wisdom, is therefore the Creator. And He did not begin to be the Creator at some determinate moment of time, when the creation of the world "began." *For God* and *in God*, His creative ac-

---

2. St. Gregory Palamas expresses this antinomy in his dogmatic language when he speaks of the distinction between the hidden and proper being of God, His *ousia*, which is inaccessible to the creature, and His *energeia*, which is accessible to the creature and reveals His essence. Leaving aside the issue of how apt these terms are, we see that it is a question here precisely of the relation of God to the world. In practice, God *exists* only as energy, whereas God in Himself, *Deus absconditus*, simply does not "exist." In Himself, He is the darkness of the Absolute, to which even being is inapplicable. But in God's energy, His ousia is known; His ousia begins to *exist* only in relation. Thus, Palamas's fundamental schema is the idea of God as the Absolute-Relative, the inclusion of relation (but of course *not* relativity) in the very definition of God.

tivity is just as *eternal* as His being, as the Holy Trinity itself in its Wisdom. The creation of the world begins *only for the world;* it does not begin for God. The creation of the world exists for God in His eternity, and in this sense it is equi-eternal with God. But that which in God is eternal is revealed for creation only in time, and here one truly needs a *translation* from one language into another. Even though creation, as God's creative activity, is temporal for itself, it is eternal for God. God in his eternity creates the world for time, and therefore in time. Here one has a genuine *transcensus* from the creative activity to creation, from act to fact, from eternity to time (and vice versa): *coincidentia oppositorum,* the identity of things that are distinct and opposite. The temporal world, the world that exists in time, as well as time itself, can be understood *only in connection with eternity,* which is their foundation; conversely, eternity has its image or reflection in time.

The temporal world is created by the eternal God; it is His creation. Such is the creature's initial and limiting intuition about itself and about the givenness of its being.[3] This givenness or creatureliness is a *metaphysical fact* that our consciousness and our being necessarily confront. This fact means that our being is posited in us and for us not by us ourselves. Knowing self-positing in our *personal* being, we are thus capable of knowing the boundaries of this being, beyond which *givenness* or *createdness* begins for us. In this sense of contradictoriness and limitedness, the creature has a metaphysical *memory* of its createdness by the One who can create — God. But beyond this, the very *act,* as well as the *fact,* of God's creation of the world is unfathomable for us; it is the boundary separating us from the Absolute. It exists for us only in its irreducible facticity, which is a limit concept *(Grenzbegriff)* for us. Creation is therefore known not by thought but by faith: "Through faith we understand that the worlds were framed by the word of God, so that things which are seen were not made of things which do appear" (Heb. 11:3). The very nature of creation is such that one can believe (or not believe) in its createdness with the same faith with which we believe in God, for the origin of the world, that is, of ourselves, *cannot in general be known.* The physical origin of the world in its different parts and epochs can be explained in a thousand different ways by knowledge and brought to a possible limit. But its metaphysical origin is beyond the limits of knowledge; it is closed off from thought by the fiery sword of "physical antinomy" (Kant), and we seek in vain to evade this antinomy by fleeing into bad infinity, that is, by pushing the causes further and further back into an imaginary eternity.

---

3. See the chapter on creation in my book *The Unfading Light.*

The Lamb of God

Nevertheless, bearing the image of God, we also know the creative act in our experience. Insofar as a ray of authentic creativity shines in this act for us as well, it is unexplainable and miraculous in the capacity of the creation of something new, of something that has not existed before. Such creation is unfathomable for us both as act and as fact, both in its *how* and in its *what*; and dealing only with the accomplished fact, we explain it causally, establishing a causal relation between the creation and its creator. But in themselves, creative acts are flashes of *another* light in the creaturely darkness. Even creaturely creative activity therefore attests that the creative act is unexplainable and miraculous. However, although creaturely creative activity bears the imprint of the divine Proto-Image, it is always limited by the given: it is the creative activity of *the creature in creation*. Being absolute according to its type, this creative activity is always relative in fact. In the absolute sense, it is not even creative activity — in the sense of creating what is new, not out of what is given, but out of nothing — that is, it is not the creation of what had been totally nonexistent. Creative activity is accomplished in, for, and *from* the world, which for this activity is the already created and present *mē on*, which contains *all* the possibilities of creative activity based on it. Human creative activity sculpts its treasures only out of the rock of this world. The very existence of this rock is not the object of creaturely creative activity but its condition. God's creation of the world is thus the Creator's proper *Work*, and in this sense it is an absolute Miracle, which we metaphysically postulate in its unfathomability but affirm only by faith. However, not being able to explore further this primordial and fundamental fact by our own powers, we can use revelation as a guide to attempt to understand its content, conditions, and consequences. Divine creative activity is absolute creative activity, which does not have anything for itself outside itself: in this sense, the world is created "out of nothing."

But does "nothing" itself exist?[4] One should not conceive of the relation between God and this nothing in such a way that the latter turns out to be the limit of the Absolute, of God Himself, as if a kind of void, a spatial receptacle for God's being. Such a conception is of course absurd (although it is often tacitly presupposed). "Nothing" does not exist for God as something totally extradivine. It is not even a void, since a void is conceived as a receptacle, that is, as a bounded, concrete being. There is only God, and outside of and apart from God there is nothing, just as there is

---

4. See the chapter on the "creaturely nothing" (especially the distinction between *ouk on* and *mē on*) in my book *The Unfading Light*.

not even any "outside of" or "apart from." Therefore, in order to *be,* "nothing" must arise, having been established by God, who, in the words of Pseudo-Dionysius, is the creator of nothing as well. In other words, *nothing* is a *relative* concept; it is correlative with *something,* that is, with already existing but, in itself, incomplete and nonabsolute being, in the pores of which *nothing* can find a place for itself. "Nothing" is thus not being but the *state* of being that corresponds to its incompleteness or becoming. "Nothing" finds a place for itself in *becoming* being; it is this very *becoming,* as Plato has attested for all time. By creating the world as *becoming* being, God thereby also established a place for the being of *nothing.* Creation out of nothing is nothing other than the calling to life of *becoming temporal* being. *Nothing* is therefore created by God as *temporality* and *becoming,* to which one can therefore apply the definitions of time: beginning, continuation, and end.

The "nothing" out of which "the world is created" is mythologically conceived as a kind of material of creation, analogous to Tiamat and to other religious and philosophical figures of the primordial matter. But the biblical idea of creation is precisely that there is no primordial matter:[5] God did not create the world out of something, for no such *something* exists (even if in the capacity of nothing). But out of what did God create the world? What constitutes the world's *something,* the foundation of its being? Here too, mythological thought tends to hold the view that, into the empty sack of "nothing," God poured different things, different forms of being, which were expressly conceived for this purpose by His "multiform wisdom"; and thus the world was formed. According to this mythological conception, which is close to that of Plato's *Timaeus,* the idea of this sack, which at the same time is the primordial matter for the realization of creatures, is just as impious and absurd as the idea of a God who realizes His inventions in this matter. According to this mythological conception, God is portrayed as sitting "before" nothing and thinking about what forms of being He can create from it. Such a conception of creation as a new and express invention, however unctuously it is expressed, must be rejected as blasphemous. This conception implies no more and no less than a denial of God's eternity, of the absoluteness and unchangeability of Divinity itself. According to this conception, it turns out that "before" the creation of the world, God did not

---

5. For this reason the biblical story of the creation of the world says nothing about primordial matter. (This feature of the story becomes more salient when we compare it with a story that is outwardly akin to it: the Babylonian epos, with its Tiamat, the primordial matter.)

The Lamb of God

have the idea of its content, which appeared for the first time not only for the world but also for God Himself only with the creation of the world. Thus, it is as if God as the Creator is different from God Himself, in the sense that some things exist for God from the beginning, whereas other things appear for Him together with the world. But neither biblical teaching nor Church tradition contains such impossibilities. The New Testament says that creation came into being through the Word: "All things were made by him; and without him was not any thing made that was made" (John 1:3); while the Old Testament says that it came into being through the Wisdom of God: "The LORD possessed me in the beginning of his way, before his works of old" (Prov. 8:22); "I was by his side, a master craftsman" (8:30; translation taken from *The Jerusalem Bible*). Likewise, the fathers of the Church speak of the eternal *prototypes* of creation in God,[6] confirming the idea that the content of the world is determined by God's own thought and that the same *All* is eternally spoken by the Logos in the depths of Divinity as well as in creation. In other words, the All in the Divine world, in the Divine Sophia, and the All in the creaturely world, in the creaturely Sophia, are one and are identical in content (although not in being). *One and the same Sophia is revealed in God and in creation.* Therefore, if the negative definition "God created the world out of nothing" eliminates the idea of any nondivine or extradivine principle of creation, its *positive* content can only be such that God created the world out of Himself, out of His essence. And the idea that the content of the world was invented ad hoc by God at the creation of the world must be fundamentally rejected. The *positive* content of the world's being is just as divine as its foundation in God, for there is no other principle for it. But that which exists pre-eternally in God, in His self-revelation, exists in the world only in becoming, as becoming divinity. And metaphysically the creation of the world consists in the fact that God established His proper divine world not as an eternally existent world but as a *becoming* world. In this sense, He mixed it with nothing, immersing it in becoming as *another form* of being of one and the same divine world. And this divine world is the foundation, content, entelechy, and meaning of the creaturely world. The Divine Sophia became also the creaturely Sophia. God repeated Himself in creation, so to speak; He reflected Himself in nonbeing. The cre-

---

6. Of the fathers of the Church, St. Maximus the Confessor has the most consistent doctrine of the divine "logoses" of creaturely being. His "logology" is essentially a sophiology. In the Russian literature, see S. L. Epifanovich, *St. Maximus the Confessor and Byzantine Theology* (Kiev, 1915); cf. G. Florovsky, *The Byzantine Fathers of the Fifth to Eighth Centuries* (Paris, 1933), ch. 7.

The Creaturely Sophia

ation is the Divine "ecstasy" of love, which is the creative "let there be" addressed outward, to the emerging extradivine being. In its appearance and becoming, the countenance of this being naturally received a multiple, multistage form; the All-unity became the All-multiplicity of differentiated being, and this was accomplished by the wisdom of the Creator during the Six Days, which established the hierarchy of being in its multiplicity and fullness. And only after having completely poured out the fullness of the divine world into the creaturely world, to the extent the creaturely world could encompass it, did God *rest* from His works.

But this implanting of the divine seeds into the world at its creation was, of course, only initial, incomplete, and nondefinitive. A seed is only a seed, not the plant. The becoming world must, in its becoming, follow the long path of cosmic being to the end before it can reflect in itself the countenance of the Divine Sophia, which, being the *foundation* and entelechy of the world's being, is only in a state of *potentiality*, which the world must actualize in itself. This potentialization by God of His proper Divine world into extradivine being is precisely *creation out of nothing*. Becoming is being that is submerged in and modified by nonbeing in all its cells, but it is also being that is liberating itself from nonbeing. The Integral Wisdom of the All-unity is realized in the All-multiplicity; this Wisdom binds and inwardly overcomes the All-multiplicity. "Nothing," understood as the potentiality of becoming, is in this sense truly the intelligible place of the world's being, Plato's *ekmageion*, the pre-ontic and extra-ontic darkness about which it is said: "And the light shineth in darkness; and the darkness comprehended it not" (John 1:5). This "nothing" is the cause of the multiplicity of the world and of its principles; in this sense it is even the "proto-matter" of the world *in* which (although not *out of* which) the world is created. The state of the initial and universal potentiality is the *earth*, created by God before the distinct acts ("days") of the creation: this is the potency of the world's being, which nevertheless already contains *all* the elements of the world. "The earth was without form, and void; and darkness was upon the face of the deep" (Gen. 1:2). But this formless and void proto-matter of the world, this initial alloy of the divine world with nothing, already has a plan manifested for it in the heavens and inscribed in the angelic world: "In the beginning God created the heaven and the earth" (Gen. 1:1). The holy angels are the hypostatic plan of creation; they are its ideas.[7]

---

7. I will not expound an angelology here but will instead send readers to my book *Jacob's Ladder: On the Angels* (Paris, 1929).

The Lamb of God

The creation of heaven and earth, as an act of God's love flowing beyond the limits of the proper divine life into the world, is, in relation to Divinity itself, a voluntary self-diminution, a metaphysical kenosis: Alongside His *absolute* being, God establishes a *relative* being with which He enters into an interrelation, being God and Creator for this being. The creative "let there be," which is the command of God's omnipotence, at the same time expresses the sacrifice of Divine love, of God's love for the world, the love of the Absolute for the relative, in virtue of which the Absolute becomes the Absolute-Relative. Being conscious of itself as relative-absolute, the creature reflects in itself the Absolute-Relative, the relation to which defines its being ("let there be"; "in him we live, and move, and have our being" [Acts 17:28]). God is not diminished by this in His Divine immanence, but He goes beyond its limits into the world. In God's self-definition this fact is not primary but secondary, in the sense that His love in the Holy Trinity, His being in Himself, is the foundation for His love outside Himself, for His creative kenosis. The creation of the world is therefore not an *inner self-positing* of Divinity, which is God in the Holy Trinity, but a certain *work* of God consisting of a series of works as creative acts, after the completion of which He "rested from all his work which [he] created and made" (Gen. 2:3). God's proper being belongs to eternity, where there is no beginning and no end, where the actuality of His self-positing is never exhausted, and thus the categories of time are totally inapplicable there. But the world, as a becoming world, belongs to time, which is precisely becoming. Therefore, even though the act of the creation of the world belongs to eternity insofar as it is God's self-definition, nevertheless when it is directed toward the world it takes upon itself the world's temporal aspect. It occurs in time, in the "Six Days" (however we interpret them); it has a beginning and an end, and it exhausts itself. In other words, what we see here is a transition from eternity to time, from the immobility of the Absolute to the becoming of the relative. This act, as an express work of God, contains the inspiration of love, God's self-inspiration, which in God is connected with the Third hypostasis and is the Holy Spirit: "And the Spirit of God moved upon the face of the waters" (Gen. 1:2) at the very beginning of the creation, even "before" the Six Days.

The world is created by God in the Holy Trinity, and each of the hypostases reveals itself in the creation of the world in conformity with its properties. Here too the Father is the principle, the first will. He creates the world according to His will. In conformity with the personal property of the Paternal Hypostasis, ecstatic love, He manifests it here not as the begetting Father but as the Creator of "heaven and earth, of all things visible and invisible." From Him proceeds the will to go out of Himself into creation through the creative "let there be." He is the Creator in the proper sense (as He is in fact called in the Creed). The Father's kenosis in creation consists in this going out of Himself, in which He becomes God for the world and enters into a relation with it as the Absolute-Relative. The *transcensus* toward the world is the sacrifice of the Father's love; analogous to it is the birth of the Son in the intratrinitarian life, when the Father, depleting Himself, begets the Son. The Father creates the world by the Word. "And God said, let there be" — that is how the Six Days of creation are accomplished, the six words of the Word spoken by the Father. For the Father, the Son is the content of creation, all its forms and aspects. The Son, as the Word of God, proceeds out of the Divine depths into creation in order to identify Himself with it in a certain sense and to become for it the Word about All and in All. And already here, in the creation of the world, the Son does the will of the Father, is sent by the Father into the world. However, He is not yet sent hypostatically, but only as the Word about the world, as the words of the Word in it. But this procession of the Word out of the Paternal depths, His entry into the world, is already the Son's particular kenosis, His eternal *exinanitio*, or humiliation, in the creation of the world. The Son, the Lamb of God, is pre-eternally "sacrificed" in the creation of the world, as the expressly cosmic hypostasis, the demiurge in Divinity. This image of the Son as the Lamb reveals a new aspect of the Father's sacrificial love, manifested in the creation of the world, for this love is not only the Father's own procession into the world but also the sending of the Son, the incipient *offering of the sacrifice*.

The participation of the Third hypostasis in the creation of the world is "decisive" or "definitive." This hypostasis gives *being* to the Father's "let there be"; it finishes "the heavens and the earth . . . and all the host of them" (Gen. 2:1). And His divine thought realized, His Word become reality, God the Father sees, in the beauty of the accomplishment, that "it is good." The Third hypostasis is the cosmourgic hypostasis, clothing in beauty the structure and order of creation. The object of God's creative activity, the world, is not only the universe but also a work of art, the *cosmos*, in which the Artist rejoices. The Holy Spirit, as the accomplishment of creation, is the Creator's *joy* in His creation: for the Father, it is joy in the manifested Word; for the Son, it is joy in the revelation of the Father in the world. The Holy Spirit is the inspiration of God's creative activity in the creation of the world. However, the Holy Spirit too has His kenosis in creation. Wholly reposing upon the Son in eternity, as the hypostatic love of the Father and the Son, here the Holy Spirit proceeds outward, as the Father's love for the Son in creation; and thus the Holy Spirit Himself proceeds into the becoming of creation. The Holy Spirit reposes upon the Son, who is the Logos of the world, to the extent that the world in its becoming can receive Him. The Holy Spirit Himself becomes, as it were, the becoming of the world, the realization of its content, just as the Son is the being of the world in its foundation. The Holy Spirit is sent, and also received, from measure to measure, from his first movement "upon the face of the waters" to the final culmination of "God will be all in all." The very life of the world is the Holy Spirit, the Giver of life; the very joy and beauty of the world are the Comforter. But the world, in the process of its becoming, can encompass neither the fullness of love nor the fullness of transfiguration, and this transition from unfullness to fullness is the work of the Holy Spirit, of His kenosis in the world.

Thus, the creation of the world is a *work* of God, a revelation of God's *fullness*, omnipotence, wisdom, and inspiration. But it is also a revelation of God's love, which seeks to spread also to the nonexistent, beyond the limits of the Absolute itself. And this is not a gratuitous, irresponsible love; love cannot be such by its very nature. Instead, it is an utterly serious and responsible love, a sacrificial love, a tragic love that, in its actualization, sacrifices all that it possesses. The Absolute descends from the throne of its absoluteness to the relative; God creates the world — by love. By understanding the act of creation in this manner, as a work and revelation of divine love, we eliminate all randomness from the being of the world, a randomness in virtue of which the world, being external for God, being not-God, could be or not be, or (which is the same thing) a randomness in virtue of which God Himself could be or not be the Creator of the world. On the contrary, we find that the Creator and the Absolute in God are united in the most intimate and indissoluble fashion. If God is the Creator as love, and therefore by virtue of love He cannot fail to be the Creator, then the object of His love, the world, exists for God precisely by the inner power of love. We therefore do not conceive God without the world, and the being of the world is thus included in the very concept of God. The idea of God as a being who is not only above the world but also without the world, a being who lives in Himself with all the fullness of His love, does not conform with the concept of God-Love. God is love, and therefore He is also the Creator. The light of God's eternity thus falls upon the world. And even though *in itself* it is creaturely and noneternal, the world, in its relation to the Creator, is coeternal with God. "All things were created by Him, and for Him: and He is before all things, and by Him all things consist" (Col. 1:16-17).

The Creaturely Sophia

II. Eternity and Time

Becoming is temporality that enters into and has its foundation in eternity. Temporality is opposed to eternity to the same degree that it is posited by eternity. Without eternity and outside eternity, temporality cannot exist as a continuous process; it will break up into separate atoms. In its flow, time is not only discontinuous and atomistic, such that each of its moments is replaced, expelled, destroyed by the next. It is also continuous, such that its separate moments belong to one general complex or content and mosaically reflect in themselves the countenance of eternity. Even though it is temporal, the world remains unified. It does not fall apart into an infinite number of temporal atoms of its being, and its unity is objectively established by the fact that it is a unity not only of temporal succession but also of causal cohesion. The rule of methodological investigation that is used to distinguish particular series of causality is *post hoc non propter hoc*. However, when it comes to the world's causality as a whole, the applicable principle, firm and inviolable, is *post hoc est propter hoc*. Time contains the lawful regularity of the logos of things; nothing can be included or occur in time that is not included in this logos. The world has a regular character in time based on a lawful regularity that determines time itself and that is therefore above it. The *unfullness* of the world's being belongs to real time in each of its atoms; each atom is expelled by another atom, but it is also included in the cohesive unity of the whole that reigns over time, defines it as a form of becoming, and exists prior to it. In other words, time is not only a flow but also a *becoming*, the realization of a certain content — as foundation and as task, or entelechy. Time has its plan and its synthesis within itself; it has content. (This idea is unconsciously expressed in the absurd notion of cosmic evolution out of a void, contrary to the axiom of cosmic being, *ex nihilo nil fit*: "evolution" precisely presupposes the appearance of a form of supratemporal being in temporal being.) Therefore, the world's causality is also purposiveness or entelechy in the world's being.

This content of the creaturely world, as well as its foundation, is the Divine world, the eternal Sophia. But the one, integral image of the All-unity in time is multiplied and atomized in the aspects of temporal being, which time gathers and unites by its lawful regularity. Thus, eternity is the depth, reality, foundation, and content of time. Time is correlative with eternity, does not exist without eternity; time is the image of the creaturely, becoming being of eternity. Time and eternity are the creaturely Sophia and the Divine Sophia. As a result, time is not empty; it is not the "vanity of vanities" of Ecclesiastes. Rather, time is full of eternity and asymptotically approaches it, more and more fully reproducing its image but without ever becoming identical to it *modally*, in mode of being. This appearance of the image of eternity in time is, in this sense, the *end* of time, which means that it also must have a beginning. Thus, the angel of Revelation swears, by the Creator of all things, who "liveth for ever and ever," that "there should be time no longer" (10:6), for "the mystery of God" (10:7) has been accomplished. Nevertheless, for this accomplished time as well, which manifests eternity, the "eternal" eternity that has its foundation in itself is distinguished from creaturely, temporal eternity that has its foundation in divine eternity and is the manifested image of the Proto-Image (this is the distinction between *aeternitas* and *aeviternitas*). It follows that the fluidity of time does not diminish its reality: time is real with the reality of its content, which is the Divine Sophia as its eternal entelechy, foundation, content, and limit. In creating the world, God created time and temporality; this is precisely contained in the concept "created." Time is the most general form of creaturely being as the becoming of eternal being. The multiplicity of all-unity in creation is manifested in temporal multiplicity as in a fragmented mirror that multiplies, repeats, and distorts the forms of true being, which in creaturely limitedness is united with nonbeing.[8]

A question arises that is essential for all of theology: What is the relation between time and eternity, not in creation, which is encompassed by time in virtue of its becoming, but in the eternal God Himself? Does

---

8. Analogous to time is space. Spatiality is a property of the world limited in the wholeness of its being by the fragmented multiplicity of its forms, whose reality is expressed in their outward positioning or mutual expulsion from a given place, which in general gives rise to spatiality. There is no place for spatiality in the integral Divine world, where all is permeated with all and filled with all in the integrity of being. By contrast, in its becoming, the creaturely world is characterized by fragmented multiplicity of being, that is, by spatiality, which is expressed in the reality of space. Space allows a place not only for the multiplicity of its points or atoms but also for their unity or connectedness. It not only separates but also unites; by virtue of this connectedness, space, static in its discontinuity, can be dynamically overcome and realized as unity. The spatial mode of being, like the temporal, has its foundation in supraspatial spiritual being, which is the true content of the spatial world. Space is not simply a sack for atoms. The spatial mode of the world is the static cross section of cosmic causality in the sense that all of spatial being is mutually conditioned or causally connected — not in sequentiality but in coexistence, attesting to the unity of the world. As a form of creaturely being, spatiality is less general than temporality, insofar as the former refers only to the natural, sensuous world, whereas the latter also encompasses phenomena of the spiritual world.

The Creaturely Sophia

time exist for eternity, and what is the character of this relation? The simplest and most widespread (although somewhat simplistic) opinion is that time simply does not exist for God, since His eternity makes time totally transparent and dissolves it. According to this view, time exists only for the creature, as a kind of illusion owing to the creature's limited condition; it does not exist for God, for whom there is only eternity. If thought through consistently, however, such a point of view leads to great difficulties. First of all, the entire Bible, as the divine tale about the relation of God to man, about God's economy, represents a total rejection of this point of view. The revelation of God to men and all of God's works in the world are portrayed in the Bible as occurring in time, both for God and for man. To consider this to be only an inevitable anthropomorphism, to deprive it of reality, is to undermine the entire content of our faith and to transform the living, merciful, salvific God, the Creator and All-Mighty, into the static absolute of Hinduism, in which all concrete being is extinguished and the whole world is transformed into an illusion. And to be sure, given such a point of view, the most difficult thing of all is to understand and accept the Incarnation, with all the associated events of the Savior's earthly life, such as His Resurrection and His Ascension. In order to be considered true, the whole of the Christian religion must presuppose the reality of time, not only for the world, but also for God, with the one reality conditioning the other.

Furthermore, in the biblical depiction and in the Christian belief that is based on it, God lives in the world and with the world, in an interrelationship. Not only does He act in the world, but He is also defined on the basis of the world: He "repents" (of the creation of the world), He is angry, joyful, and so on. To reduce all this to anthropomorphism is to close one's eyes to the Divine reality and to replace the fiery words of Holy Scripture with the scholasticism of seminarians.[9] In Himself, God is eternal with Divine eternity, which is the Divine Sophia, the fullness of His life, unchangeability and all-blessedness. In Himself, God is eternal with Divine eternity in His trihypostatizedness, which is the eternal act of the love of the Three in reciprocity. But God is also the Creator, who creates life *outside* Himself and lives in this life outside Himself. The reality of this world is established by God, and therefore the reality of the *time* of this world holds for God as well, for this reality is His proper work and also His proper self-positing. Proceeding out of God in the creation of the

---

9. N. A. Berdiaev gives due attention to this humanity of God in biblical representation (see his *Destiny of Man*, English translation, 1937).

world, His love in its kenosis establishes time for Him as well and makes Him live in time. In this sense, God participates in the becoming of the world: its history is the history of the Incarnation, and in 1 Corinthians 15:24-28 the Apostle Paul depicts nothing other than God's becoming all in all for the world.

The idea of God's becoming God not for Himself but for the world together with the becoming of the world — this idea necessarily follows if one fully accepts the Christian revelation. This is by no means a pantheistic doctrine that identifies God with the world as different states of one, immanently evolving absolute principle. That is, it is by no means the kind of doctrine we associate with the early Schelling (for whom God's complete evolution is identical with the end of the cosmic process), with Hegel (for whom "logic" is God *before* the "creation" of the world, being concretely revealed with it), or with Boehme (with his evolution of God from *Urgottheit*). The distinguishing trait of pantheism is that it considers God to be only the highest degree of the evolution of the world, while considering the world to be the initial principle of the evolution of God. Between God and the world there is no *transcensus,* no discontinuity in the evolution of being from the world to God; the world is only an incompletely evolved god, whereas God is the fully evolved and realized world. This theory abolishes the very idea of creation, which places a boundary between the Creator and the world.

All this is fundamentally different from Christian doctrine, which by the very act of creation places an ontological boundary between the Creator and the creature, between the Proto-Image and the image. For Christian doctrine the world is not the self-evolution of God but creation, a work of God that proceeds not from the metaphysical necessity of self-revelation but from the creative inspiration of love in its freedom. However, in considering this distinction and opposition between God and the world, fear of the phantoms of pantheism should not lead us to destroy the very reality of the world for God and transform it into an ontological illusion, thereby committing the error of docetic Hinduism. The world is real with God's reality, and it is thus real not only for itself but also for God, for whom it exists as an object of His love.

As a result, one must also acknowledge that the time of this world, without which there is no becoming, is real for God. It follows that, in the world and with the world, God Himself lives in time, even though He is timeless and eternal in Himself. This unity and thus identity of time and eternity are an eternal riddle for human thought, for it is a mystery of God that is just as unfathomable for creatures as their creation. However, being unable to understand this mystery, we nevertheless can and must delineate its external contours. The interrelation between God's eternity and temporality is rooted in the general relation of the Creator to the world. From the point of view of formal logic and static reasoning, so to speak, a mutually exclusive opposition exists between eternity and time: eternity extinguishes time, and time abolishes eternity. We have, as it were, both *yes* and *no*. Eternity belongs to the Absolute, whereas time is connected with the relativity of becoming, and the absolute cannot be equated with the relative. But this "planar" representation, so to speak, does not correspond to the real state of affairs if one considers this relation dynamically and ontologically, in which case eternity turns out to be not the negation but the foundation and depth of time. The fullness of eternity is actually disclosed in temporality, which has its power of being only from eternity. God, as the Creator who is correlated with time, does not stop being the eternal God; on the contrary, it is precisely His eternal Divinity that is the foundation for His creation. If He were not the Absolute in Himself, God would not be the Creator, just as, conversely, since He is the Absolute, He is revealed in the relative — that is, He creates the world.

Eternity and temporality are correlative, without intruding into each other or interfering with each other. In no wise and in no sense can temporality diminish or limit eternity, for it belongs to a *different* ontological plane. One can say that eternity is the noumenon of time and time is the phenomenon of eternity. They are linked by a relation of foundation and being, but there can be no mixture or confusion between them, and they cannot limit one another. The imprint of God's eternity therefore lies upon all of creation, for it is the revelation of His eternity. Time is the mobile aspect of eternity. But every aspect of time has its depth in eternity, is nourished by and permeated with eternity. Only by observing this principle of the continuity and correlativeness of eternity and time can one rationally accept the simultaneous affirmation of the unchangeable eternity of God and the temporality of all His works in the world, His multiple and multiform revelation, without falling into a series of obvious and insurmountable contradictions. Man too, as the image of God, bears in himself the mystery of this union of time and eternity. For man, eternity is not a specially qualified time that will arrive *after* temporal life, as an event in time itself; rather, it is the depth of his own being, a depth known in time and ceaselessly revealing itself. Eternity is man's rootedness in God, and this eternal life both begins and is accomplished in temporal life: "This is life eternal, that they might know thee the only true God, and Jesus Christ, whom thou hast sent" (John 17:3).

III. Man

Humanity participates in the Divine world. The Divine world is the heavenly Divine-Humanity of the heavenly God-Man, the Logos. Humanity signifies here the image and type of the being of multiple principles, ideas, or spiritual essences in unity, as the self-revelation of the Logos. And in *this* sense, humanity is His spiritual "body." The Holy Trinity is directed without mediation toward Sophia, or the Divine world, by the Logos, who in this sense is Sophia, her personal center, the demiurgic hypostasis, which nevertheless accomplishes itself through the Third, or cosmourgic, hypostasis. The creaturely world, as the creaturely Sophia, exists in conformity with its heavenly Proto-Image and is therefore also the *human* world, centered on and by man. Man is a "microcosm," and his imprint therefore lies upon the entire world, the macrocosm. The world has its fullness and pinnacle in man, who is the logos of the world; and speaking fundamentally, there is and can be nothing in the world in which humanity does not participate, nothing to which man's knowledge, feeling, and will cannot extend. Man is created to "subdue" the earth and to "have dominion over" all creatures (Gen. 1:28); the whole world is man's potential and peripheral body.[10] The world is made for man, and the "Six Days" represent the story of the preparation of the world for man, as well as the story of the gradual and step-by-step formation of the world. In general, they represent the story of the creation of the world as man's humanity.

Man's relation to nature essentially reproduces the relation of the Logos to Sophia, but it does so in a creaturely fashion, in the sense that the All, existing in Sophia in Integrity, appears here in multiplicity, creaturely hierarchy, and becoming. But the inorganic world, the vegetal world (in paradise), and the animal world are led to man at this initial hour of the world's being in order to become humanized from and in him and thus to realize their destiny. Creaturely humanity is expressed here in multiple degrees of the inorganic and then the vegetal and animal world, of the *prehuman* world in general, in contrast to its eternal Proto-Image, where All exists in the fullness and unity of Divine life without individualizing itself into particular centers of life, which are multiple and variable. The natural world is united with man through his body in all its fullness. First of all, the human body is formed of "the dust of the ground" (Gen. 2:7), that is, of the earth, the proto-matter that contains the creaturely *all*. Second, man is

---

10. See my book *Philosophy of Economy* (Moscow, 1910; English translation by Catherine Evtuhov, 2000).

created together with the whole vegetal and animal world as "all-vegetal" and "all-animal," according to the biological ladder; furthermore, he *inwardly* knows the animal world and names it. The corporeal unity of man with the world is reinforced by the eating of food (which is expressly instituted by God: Gen. 1:29-30; 9:3). Third, man is united with the whole creaturely world by the animal principle of life, by the animal soul, which is in the blood of both man and animals ("flesh with the soul thereof, which is the blood thereof, shall ye not eat" [Gen. 9:4]; "the soul of the flesh is in the blood" [Lev. 17:11; cf. Deut. 12:23][11]). The animal soul wholly belongs to the creaturely world and is its proper creaturely life. But the animal soul also forms the principle that provides the place and possibility for the awakening and development of spiritual life; moreover, as far as this particular feature is concerned, the animal soul must be obedient to the spirit. The animal soul, which is "in the blood" both of man and of animals, is multiform and has many degrees. It takes many forms within the diverse species of the animal world, where there is room for animal individuality. But being alien to the spiritual principle, the animal soul is spiritually blind and does not possess personality (although it knows individuality with its particular features). Even about man, when he submerges himself in the life of the flesh and forgets about the soul, God's wrath says: "he also is flesh" (Gen. 6:3). Like all creation, the animal soul is created, and it therefore does not possess *personal* immortality, for it is impersonal.

But man differs from the entire creaturely world, whose master he therefore is, by the fact that he (like the angels) has in himself the *uncreated* principle, a spark of the Divine spirit: "and the LORD God . . . breathed into his nostrils the breath of life" (Gen. 2:7). If we compare these words with God's creation of man "in our image, after our likeness" (Gen. 1:26), this clearly means that the human spirit (the "soul") has not a creaturely but a divine origin: man, according to this origin of his, is a created god. There is no need to examine here the question of the trichotomic or dichotomic structure of man, especially since this distinction is largely based on a misunderstanding.[12] What is important is that, ontologically, man is truly bipartite, that he has in himself an uncreated, divine principle, the spirit (the soul), and a created body, animated by the soul — the flesh. Man's ontological composition is therefore complex; it is more complex than that of the angels, who do not have flesh, and of the entire animal world, to which

---

11. In these two cases, the King James Version has been modified to conform with the Russian Bible. — Trans.

12. See my book *The Burning Bush*.

spirit is alien. All of created nature, the creaturely Sophia, belongs to the human spirit, which is her hypostatic center.

According to the *image* of his creation, in this complexity of his, man is already a god-man. The first Adam is created in the image of the Second Adam; he contains the image of Christ and is divine-human in his initial structure. He is formed in such a way that Christ can become incarnate in him, not only according to the body of Adam, in which (according to Tertullian) God foresaw the future body of Christ, but also according to his complex structure. Man in nature, as the spiritual hypostasis of the world, has the image of the heavenly God-Man, of Logos in Sophia. Despite the insurmountable distance between the Creator and creation, the Proto-Image and the Image are united by a certain identity that establishes between them a positive interrelation and announces the Incarnation to come. Despite its divine origin, the human hypostatic spirit does not belong to the trinitarian hypostasis of God, which exhausts and closes the divine hypostatizedness — in the Holy Trinity. This spirit is created; it is called to being by the act of God's creative love, which is unfathomable for creatures. God multiplied and repeated His hypostatic countenances in the angelic and human worlds; and by their very origin, these hypostases *participate* in the divine nature. This is the ontological foundation for the deification of man: "Ye are gods; and all of you are children of the most High" (Ps. 82:6; cf. John 10:34). This cannot mean that the children of God have God's nature in the same way that God has it, that is, by an eternal personal act; rather, it means that, by their very origin, they can *participate* in God's nature, that they contain in themselves the possibility of "being born of God," that is, of becoming true children of God who participate in the Divine life. "That which is born of the flesh is flesh; and that which is born of the Spirit is spirit" (John 3:6). For the holy angels this participation in God's nature is precisely life.[13] But man has his proper natural, creaturely life, which receives grace in virtue of its participation in God's nature. What is important here is that, by its divine origin, the human spirit is capable of participating in God's life, even if this is only a possibility; but this possibility is already an ontological reality. At the same time, the human spirit is immersed in the creaturely nature of man, who is therefore a god-man by design, since he has one hypostasis and participates in two natures, divine and creaturely. In other words, the first Adam, as god-man, is already an image of Christ that awaits its perfect revelation and accomplishment.

13. See my book *Jacob's Ladder: On the Angels*.

The Creaturely Sophia

Man is created in the image of God, but this means that he is created in the image of Christ; for man, Christ is the revelation and accomplishment of this image. The image of the coming Christ is imprinted in the first man not only in his body, which is an image of the sophianic world, and not only in his spirit, which in a certain sense is sent from heaven. It is also imprinted in the structure of man in the union of two natures (spiritual and psycho-corporeal) in one hypostasis. One can speak of the createdness of the human spirit only in relation to the Divine Pleroma, into which there is no entry for creaturely spirits that abide outside the divine being: they are created. However, in their nature, proceeding from and participating in Divinity, these spirits cannot be considered as only creaturely, for their divine nature is co-eternal with God. These spirits are also not created in time. (According to the creationist doctrine in its naive form, as soon as God sees a natural conception taking place, he immediately creates a new soul and sends it into the conception.) The human spirit is created, not in time, but in God's eternity, "before time,"[14] precisely at the very threshold of time, although this spirit is predestined for temporal being, which it in fact enters at the proper time. The *fullness* of the human race, as well as of the angelic assembly, exists from all eternity in Divinity, and this fullness is revealed in the simultaneous creation of the angels and in the gradual creation of human beings in the course of time. The entire fullness of humanity, however, which is actualized in reproduction, is already precontained and precreated in Adam. But this preeternal existence in God does not signify some other, preexistent life of the creaturely spirits, a life that is replaced by earthly life and represents a segment of it, as it were. The human world does not preexist "in heaven" as in another world, but it does find there a sufficient basis for itself: as far as its nature is concerned, the human world is based on the Proto-Images of the Divine world, and its hypostases are rooted in divine life. The creaturely hypostases are images of the noncreaturely Divine hypostases. These multihypostatic images, in their singularity, do not reflect God's trihypostatizedness; they can only reflect its individual hypostases. But can the Paternal Hypostasis be the Proto-Image for the creaturely hypostases when it itself is revealed in Sophia, the Divine world, not in its own countenance, but through the Son and the Holy Spirit?

---

14. By no means does this signify an Origenistic preexistence of souls within the limits of the world's time, before or after the creation of the earthly world. What we have here is not the opposition of two times, before and after, but the opposition between eternity and time. Cf. my book *The Burning Bush*, on original sin.

Even if one can admit the existence of holy angels corresponding to the Paternal Hypostasis, angels who are always submerged in Divinity as in Mystery and Silence, the image of the human hypostasis can only come from the hypostases that *reveal* the Father, both in His proper divine world and in the creaturely world.

The first of these hypostases is the hypostasis of the Logos; He is the Proto-Image of the creaturely human hypostases, and they are His rays: "That was the true Light, which lighteth every man that cometh into the world" (John 1:9). The human spiritual countenances are images of the Logos, the Man from Heaven. Insofar as the Logos as Christ gathers them into His body, into the Church, it is said about them that "there is neither male nor female" (Gal. 3:28).

Together with the Logos, the Third hypostasis is also the Proto-Image for the human hypostases, because the Third hypostasis reposes upon the Son and, together with Him, reveals the Father in the heavenly humanity. (In the Incarnation this hypostasis corresponds to the divine maternity, manifested by the Virgin Mary, the Spirit-bearer.) In other words, the human hypostases have a double Proto-Image, which belongs to the heavenly humanity in its two countenances: the Logos and the Holy Spirit. This also corresponds to the fact that man, created in the image of God, was created as both male and female, and the context of Genesis 1:26-27 compels one to see the fullness of the image of God precisely in this bi-unity. In man, a clear distinction is established between male and female, expressed in the fact that the female was made out of one of the male's ribs (not directly out of the dust of the earth) and, in general, in the fact that the male plays the dominant role, since he bears the image of the demiurgic hypostasis, the Logos. Male and female, differing as two distinct images of man, bear, in their unity, the fullness of humanity and, in this humanity, the fullness of the image of God: they bear the imprint of the dyad of the Son and the Holy Spirit, who reveal the Father. In their ability to reproduce, they contain the image of multi-unity that is inscribed in the human race as a whole. Thus, man is an uncreated-created, divine-cosmic being, divine-human in his structure by his very origin. He is the living image of the trihypostatic God in His Wisdom.

IV. Image and Likeness

The image of God is inscribed in man and is the ontological foundation of his being. This image is not limited to any particular aspect or property of man but permeates his entire life. He has the image of God in his spirit, as well as in his nature and in his relation to the world. The image is not the same thing as the Proto-Image, even though they share a certain identity. The image necessarily differs from the Proto-Image: it has the same thing but *in a different manner.*

Freedom is an inalienable property of the spirit. In general, all living things possess freedom as consciousness of self and as self-determination. Life is, in the first place, spontaneous movement as a certain initial self-positing, and this spontaneity has multiple degrees. This spontaneity is marked by a certain purposiveness, or "instinct," which can be considered the inner law of its being. It also has the capacity to feel its organic needs and to react to impressions. The animal consciousness can ascend to certain manifestations of understanding and intelligence, and the animal emotional faculty is marked by feelings and affects of maternity, anger, merriment and sadness, fear, self-defense, and, finally, attachment to man. Although this last trait, given the present state of affairs, is not universal, it nevertheless attests sufficiently clearly that man, according to his creation, is even now the master of the animal world.[15]

The "soul of animals" contains manifold possibilities of life, that is, of spontaneous reaction to the external world, which for this soul is a given, inexorable fact. The animal soul is limited by this given and does not have a creative relation to it, nor is there such a relation in the mutual relations of the animal world. One should not be surprised by extraordinary manifestations of purposiveness in the life of the animal world that represent something appearing to surpass even human reason — namely, the mysterious wisdom of instinct. This is a sophianic wisdom, implanted in animals as an internal law, but it is not the same thing as reason, something the animal soul does not possess. One should therefore also not be surprised by the extraordinary practical wisdom manifested in the work of bees, beavers, and ants, for this is the wisdom of the genus, of instinct, which does not develop but only unalterably repeats itself. Animals are given to themselves, and they are given to man, who with his reason understands this wisdom as the wisdom of the entire creation. Animals thus exist "after their kind" (Gen. 1:21, 25; see also v. 24), repeating themselves,

---

15. It should be mentioned that man's ability to domesticate animals is clear evidence of this primordial relationship. At the present time, man does not have the ability to domesticate all animals, for many have become "savage," but all of them possess the potential to be domesticated. We find examples of this, on the one hand, in the lives of saints and, on the other hand, in stories about animal trainers.

but they do not have a *history*. History is proper only to man's spiritual being. The spontaneity of the life created by God is, in itself, not yet a rational freedom, but this animal life in the broad sense of the word (i.e., the life of the soul) is included in human life, and it is united with man's spiritual freedom.

Freedom of the spirit is the capacity for *creative* self-determination, by which the spirit has its life from itself and for itself, as its self-positing. Such absolute freedom is proper only to the absolute, divine spirit, whose life does not have for itself any givenness whatsoever but is wholly its self-positing, which is its nature. Nature and freedom are identified here; nature is spiritual and therefore free. In the absolute spirit there is no place for the distinction or opposition between freedom as self-positing and the given as necessity (or nature). Freedom and necessity are adequately covered in the principle of the divine being (i.e., of the trihypostatic spirit), which is love. Love is free necessity, necessity as freedom. In His self-positing, God, who as Spirit is free, surpasses the interrelation between freedom and natural necessity. One can find freedom, however, not only in the life of the spirit, as the interrelation of personality and nature, of self-positing and the given, but also in personal consciousness of self as such, in pure I-ness. "I" contains the self-positing of I, and this is a pure act of freedom, realized prenaturally and extranaturally. The self-positing of I already includes freedom; it is a free act. Therefore, personal consciousness of self already contains the breath of freedom; it includes freedom as a fundamental theme of the life of the spirit. "I" as "I" is free; that is, it is spontaneous. This freedom can also be applied to the absolute, divine I as pure self-positing; it can be applied also to the creaturely I as the image of the divine I. It is clear, however, that one cannot attribute to the creaturely I the pure self-positing that is proper only to the absolute I. The creaturely I is nevertheless *created*; that is, it is awakened by God to being. This awakening, however, not only contains the divine act of creation, but also implies a divine question, as it were, for that which is created: Does it posit itself, since God cannot posit the personal I solely by His creative act without the contribution of "I" itself? This is not a limitation of God's omnipotence, which is fully manifested in this awakening of the creaturely consciousness to being (on the contrary, this act of the creation of the creaturely I is the most staggering of the works of the divine omnipotence manifested in the creation of the world); the omnipotence does not act arbitrarily in contradiction to the meaning of that which is created. Spirit is not a thing and cannot be created like a thing, that is, like the entire natural world, through the "let there be." I as I can only be a

The Creaturely Sophia

self-positing; and that is why, at the creation of I, the creative command "let there be" is addressed in an *interrogative* form to I that is self-positing, even though it is being created.

Therefore, even though the creaturely I is posited by God, nevertheless in this creation it is co-posited by itself as well. Strictly speaking, the creative act creates only the *possibility* of self-positing, which is actualized by I itself, saying its "yes."[16] This freedom of the self-positing I already contains the image of God in the creaturely spirit, human and angelic. The whole animal world, created as a "living soul," is created by a direct act of God's omnipotence; it is created *materially*, so to speak, precisely through God's command to the earth: "Let the earth bring forth the living creature after his kind" (Gen. 1:24) and "Let the waters bring forth abundantly the moving creature that hath life" (Gen. 1:20). The earth, the proto-matter, is also the mother of all earthly things. However, this direct creation does not apply to man; instead, God said: "Let us make man in our image. . . . So God created man in his own image" (Gen. 1:26-27). Creation in the image of God is other than that of the entire creaturely world; it includes creaturely self-positing for both the angelic I and the human I. This uncreatedness, so to speak, of the creaturely I already contains the possibility of deviation toward self-divinization. Insofar as man sees God as his Proto-Image, he is conscious of his own createdness, that is, of his metaphysical unoriginality; he knows himself as the reflection of the Divine sun in a drop of being. Furthermore, in man's voluntary recognition that he is only the *image* of the Other, of the Proto-Image, love for this Other is also manifested, that is, love for God, as an imprint of the Logos, as Divine-Sonhood: The Son loves the Father; and man, in loving God, sees himself only as an image of his Creator, from whom he has being. Man freely posits himself as an *image*; he accomplishes the act of the kenosis of love. But if he turns away from this Sun and rejects the kenosis, he remains alone with himself in the consciousness of his Luciferian self-positing. Self-divinized, he then considers himself to be his own source and proto-image; he transforms his creaturely I into a pseudo-divine I. This is the path of Satan, who extinguished love and fell into solitary I-ness; and it is the path of self-divinization in general, which is ontologically open for man as well, precisely in his character as a self-positing I.

Thus, in the personal consciousness of the creaturely I, the image of God (and specifically the image of the Son) consists in the fact that, by a free love, this image is conscious of itself as the image of the Proto-Image;

---

16. See the chapter on original sin in my book *The Burning Bush*.

that is, it has its personality as not its own, it surrenders its personality to God. Divine-Sonhood in this sense is immanent to the human I as an ontological task that is proposed as well as a given for the I's freedom. The Divine I, which for man is also the Divine Thou, is given to him in his human I, and he is called to understand it. And his creaturely I contemplates in prayer the absolute I.[17]

The image of God in man is also expressed in the relation of man to the natural world, which is also his own nature. *Man has nature;* it belongs to him as his proper *human world,* with which he is connected through the soul, which is akin to the whole animal world, and through the body, which makes him a citizen of the material world. This connection of man with the world contains the image of God in His nature, in the Divine Sophia. The world is the creaturely Sophia, creaturely humanity, whose foundation is the heavenly Sophia. This world is given to man in order that he might serve as its master and "dress" and "keep" the garden of God in it (see Gen. 2:15). Being potentially human, belonging to man, the world must be totally humanized by man; it must become transparent for man. The fact that man has dominion over the creaturely world makes the image of God more fully revealed in him than in the incorporeal angels, who do not have their own world, their own nature, but "serve" man and the human world. Man is the logos of the world; he is the "cosmourge," the artist who shapes the world.

However, the relation of man as a creaturely god to the world is only the *image* of God in Sophia, which has its foundation in the Proto-Image but substantially differs from it in its being. First of all, the Divine Sophia, as the self-revelation of the true God, is fully hypostatized and completely transparent as the proper life of God. There is therefore no givenness and potentiality in the Divine Sophia. She is the absolute life of God; she is God *(Theos).*[18] In contrast, the natural world in man and outside man is a given for him, a compulsory necessity that he does not dominate, but one that dominates him. This necessity can be compared to the chains of a prison for his spiritual freedom (not only in the sense of Plato's *Phaedo* but also in the sense of the Apostle Paul, who says: "O

---

17. This idea of the antinomy of the creaturely I (which is both a creature and a self-positing I, which is both an image of the Proto-Image and belongs to itself) can be considered to be parallel to (and to some degree associated with) the "second antinomy" of the personal self-consciousness, according to the theories of N. Hartmann *(Die Ethik)* and B. P. Vysheslavstev *(The Ethics of the Transfigured Eros* [Paris, 1931], ch. 7, sec. 2).

18. See p. 102, n. 9 above. — Trans.

The Creaturely Sophia

wretched man that I am! who shall deliver me from the body of this death?" [Rom. 7:24]). To be sure, this refers to the state of the fallen world, which finds itself under a curse for the sins of man. But even prior to the Fall, nature was a given and a compulsory necessity for man, from which, within certain limits, he was expressly liberated by the power of God: namely, "God planted a garden eastward in Eden; and there he put the man whom he had formed" (Gen. 2:8). Beyond the limits of Eden, however, the whole of the as-yet-unilluminated world remained, into which our progenitors were expelled for their sin. Man had not yet gained possession of the world, and the world, sophianic in its being, was not revealed in its sophianicity for man; on the contrary, its sophianicity was for the most part shut off from man after his expulsion from paradise, which for man was, as it were, the preliminary image of the world in its sophianicity. Another reason that Adam could not gain possession of the world in its sophianicity is that this world was not given to one man in his monohypostatizedness, not even to the forefather Adam; rather, it was given to the whole of humankind in its multihypostatizedness and in its *sobornost* in the image of the Holy Trinity.

Thus, the world that presented itself to man as a fact and a given was given to him as a task (a "project"), namely the task of achieving paradise, in order that he dwell in it and manifest in it his humanity. Furthermore, man's proper relation to nature was not stable for him as a creaturely spirit in his self-definition in relation to his nature. God's nature, the Divine Sophia, is spiritual with the spirituality of God. God is Spirit both in His hypostasis and in His nature, which is His life. In itself, however, the nature of the world is not spiritual but only psycho-corporeal; it is "flesh," that is, a living being, organized at its different levels. The nature of the world can (and must) become spiritual by participating in the commands of the spirit and by becoming spiritualized in the spirit, by losing its "fleshly" autonomy. But in its psychic character, nature penetrates into the life of the spirit insofar as man is an incarnate spirit; and a *stable* equilibrium between spirit and flesh can be found only by man himself, by his actuality. In relation to this self-definition, Adam was like a newborn who needed to test and exercise his spiritual powers (which is why God gave him a commandment symbolizing this call to his actuality).

Although at his creation man received the fullness of powers and the assistance of grace, it was still incumbent upon him to manifest his share of participation in his own creation by a free self-determination. Having in himself, as it were, two centers of being, spiritual and creaturely, man made his choice: deviating toward the flesh, he did not spiritually master its enticements but subordinated his spirit to them. This is the ontological event that is symbolized in the Bible as the violation of the commandment, or the Fall. As a potential god-man, Adam had in the depths of his spirit the possibility of participating in the divine life, of living by the divine nature, and of drawing from this nature the powers necessary to sophianize the world, to disclose the creaturely Sophia in the world. Instead, he closed off this path to divine life in himself, and he died spiritually; he stopped being a potential god-man and became a natural man. And nature turned to him not her sophianic but her creaturely face, the face of the "fallen" or "dark" Sophia, this image of nonbeing (i.e., of materiality) in an illegitimate, abnormal, distorted state, the state of the earth accursed because of man together with all creatures, groaning together with the one who subjected it (see Rom. 8:20-22).

And another life began for man in the land of exile. Christ was eclipsed in him, Christ who was pre-inscribed in the image of man — the image of God, the image of Christ. Man took an illegitimate step in the direction of the natural, animal world; namely, he placed the eating of that which is fleshly (the forbidden fruit) above the food that had been given to him: to do the will of the Father and to finish His work, which is taught by the example of the New Adam, Christ (see John 4:34). Instead of the food of the tree of life, which prefigured the heavenly food, the bread of life (6:48), man ate of the food of the earthly knowledge of good and evil, thereby entering onto the path of the magical, or natural — not spiritual or Christly — domination of the world. And man was thus possessed not by the innocent sensation of his body but by the evil sensuality of the flesh, which is antagonistic to the spirit but already bears within itself its own condemnation — shame. Before the Fall, our progenitors, being naked, were not ashamed of their nakedness, but after the Fall they saw it with lustful eyes and felt ashamed. Man, not being an animal, became part of the animal world, and he thereby fell below it, since the animal world retains its animal innocence, which corresponds to the animal soul. Animals do not know debauchery or sensual perversity. Only man knows such perversity: the higher the height, the greater the fall, and that which is natural for an animal, its norm, represents an abasement and fall for man. Instead of reigning over the animal world and leading it upward to the measure of spirituality that is accessible to it, instead of leading it to God and being the king, prophet, and priest of the animal world, man degraded himself by approaching this world; he thus diminished his spiritual force and his power over the world.

The image of God, given to man at his creation, is indissolubly linked

The Creaturely Sophia

with his *likeness:* "Let us make man in our image, after our likeness" (Gen. 1:26). The relation between image and likeness can be described in the following manner: The image is the given implanted by God, the sophianic image of man, whereas the likeness is the task proposed for man, his proper work, by which he is to realize his proper image in creative freedom, in the sophianization of himself and of all creation. The image of God is the inalienable ontological foundation; it is the initial *power* that is implanted in man for his life and creative activity. This power can increase in man or decrease, shine forth or become darkened as a function of his freedom. The likeness, in contrast, is the image of Divine creative activity and of the eternal actuality of the spirit. The likeness of God in man is man's free realization of his image. According to God's idea, man is created for creative *work* in himself and in the world, as is attested by the God-Man Himself, in whom the image and the likeness are identified: "My Father worketh hitherto, and I work" (John 5:17). The path of work, in the capacity of likening oneself to God, is an arduous path for man, full of temptations and requiring great exertions because of its unstable equilibrium. But it is also the royal, Godlike path, the path of freedom. Man belongs to himself, but he also finds himself in the world, which belongs to him, even as he belongs to the world. Furthermore, he does not fully know himself, and the world for him is still an unexplored terrain, as well as the width and depth of his own life. To what degree was there a place for temptation here? Temptation was *possible,* since it was immanently implanted in the very nature of creatureliness and in its freedom.

Creatureliness in its untested and un-overcome state is ontologically unstable; in this sense it bears within itself a certain risk of failure, which God's love takes upon itself in its sacrificial kenosis. First, the life of the creature begins with infancy and childhood, that is, with the state of inexperience and lack of knowledge about itself; and childhood, although innocent, is defenseless against temptations. God, protecting freedom, leaves man to his own resources (a condition that was utilized by the serpent for man's temptation). Second, creaturely freedom, with its limitations, is a domain of diverse possibilities and of the choice among them (such choice does not exist for divine freedom). Creaturely freedom must liberate itself from this bad freedom of immaturity before it can find stable ground for itself in the *sole* possibility that is natural for it, the possibility that conforms with the inner initial norm of being. Third, the metaphysical nature of the creature, based on nothing, the void, the abyss, contains in itself the danger that this nothing will be potentialized through human freedom and that the abyss will open up. "Nothing" is like a porous membrane; it is the inner limitation of being as becoming. And until the becoming attains its completion and the image is identified with the likeness, this limitation can be the source of illegitimate self-assertion, of creaturely egotism (which is already reflected in mutual spatial impenetrability) as the force of decay and "ever wakeful" chaos that "stirs" in it. Fourth and last (but ontologically first), the creaturely spirit conceals in itself the satanic temptation of its I-ness, which consists in its self-assertion as the proto-image.

The relation between image and likeness is thus like the relation between foundation and goal, between the given and the task proposed, between alpha and omega, beginning and end. The world, after the creation of which God could rest from His works, was therefore created only in its foundation; its creation can be completed only with the participation of man (just as the creation of the creaturely I consists not only in its positing by God but also in its self-positing). The creation of the world is completed by man; and this is the long, arduous path of freedom, which, *in abstracto*, conceals the danger that the world will not succeed and will fall apart into nothingness, or that at the very least it will be totally corrupted and become the kingdom of the prince of this world, who will reign together with his angels over a satanized humanity. However, the world will avoid the danger of being destroyed and annihilated, of reverting to nothingness, and the danger that creation will have failed totally, because it was created as the creaturely Sophia and thus contains the divine ideas of being and, over and above that, the uncreated sparks of Divinity, the angelic and human spirits. As a result, the world *cannot* revert to nothingness; it cannot be metaphysically destroyed. The world is indestructible in the form of its creation, as well as in its content. Furthermore, it is providentially contained and preserved in God's hand. This idea of the destruction of the world, this ontological paradox, must be totally rejected.[19] The suicide of the world (which, on the model of the Buddhist nirvana, is a delusion of the pessimist philosophers Schopenhauer and Hartmann and of the Kantian Renouvier) is ontologically impossible, because the world contains elements that are indestructible. Furthermore, a spiritually conscious, personal being is possible only in the case of a metaphysical will to life, which does not allow metaphysical suicide. Satan, as a bearer of the personal principle, is therefore also far from suicide; on the contrary, he

---

19. Cf. God's covenant with Noah (Gen. 8:21-22; 9:1-17): "While the earth remaineth, seedtime and harvest, and cold and heat, and summer and winter, and day and night shall not cease" (8:22).

strives to establish his kingdom in this world. The world is indestructible, and the ways of God are unfathomable in the accomplishment of His works. This long and arduous path of the continuing completion of the world by God together with man is called Divine Providence, "economy," and at the center of this path is the Incarnation.

Based on the above, a question naturally arises: Where is the final cause of man's fall? Does it lie in the temptation by the serpent, without which the Fall would not have taken place? Or does it lie in the very essence of Adam? It is obviously in the latter. It was to Adam himself, to his freedom, that God's commandment was addressed. The commandment contained a question to which *different* answers were possible: yes or no. And the answer depended on man himself. There are no grounds to assert that man — in one stage or another of his development, in Adam or in the Adamites — could not have fallen or turned away from God without the serpent's temptation, which only actualized this possibility in man. Adam's guilt, rooted in his freedom and thus in his responsibility, is confirmed by the fact that God first asks Adam himself if he has eaten of the forbidden fruit (Gen. 3:11); only then does He ask Eve, who is the one who had direct dealings with the serpent. He then condemns them as being fully responsible for their act. However, man continues to occupy the central position in the world despite his fall and his expulsion from paradise: If it is said that man was put into paradise in order "to dress it and to keep it" (Gen. 2:15), he is expelled from paradise in order to "till the ground from whence he was taken" (Gen. 3:23). What is meant here, of course, is not only the earth as a field of crops, the source of nourishment for man, but also the proto-earth, out of which God made man's body.

Nevertheless, the fall of man did in fact occur through a temptation emanating from the spiritual world, in which a fall had taken place earlier. This is, of course, not an accident for man, since his connection with the spiritual world is an element of the fullness of his humanity and derives from the co-humanity of the angels.[20] Therefore, to block man's access to the spiritual world in order to prevent satanic temptation would be to diminish his humanity, and it would contradict the fundamental structure of the world as "heaven and earth."

What was Satan's temptation directed at? He does not take the same direct satanic path by which he seduced his angels to rebel against and to oppose God in the name of their own self-godhood, through a direct refusal to realize the image of God in creaturely likeness. Although

---

20. See my book *Jacob's Ladder: On the Angels*.

man's spiritual being does contain the possibility of such a satanic seduction, Satan does not tempt man in this way, perhaps reserving this temptation for the future "man of sin" (2 Thess. 2:3) and for the "beast" with his false prophet (Rev. 13). The original sin is therefore not satanic but human in character, and man is drawn into this sin by *deception* (for Satan "is a liar" and "the father" of lies [John 8:44]). Satan's temptation takes as its starting point the determination of man's place in nature; it is directed at him as a *natural* being who has, as his immanent norm, his sophianicity as the foundation of his relation to the world. For man in his immaturity, this inner norm takes the form of God's commandment: man must define himself in relation to the world in the name of God and not by an act of self-willfulness, which subjugates him to the flesh. Satan deceived Eve's naïveté; and through her, he deceived Adam by darkening and confusing their consciousness. He suggested to them the idea that they were called to become gods in this world, not by obedience to God and thus by spiritual feat, but by the eating of the fruits of this world as a magical means to acquire power over the world. But this is actually a means by which the world acquires magical power over man. The "knowledge of good and evil" is not proper to God, for He does not "know" evil, which He did not create. But the knowledge of good and evil becomes proper to the creature man in his relativity and limitation insofar as he submerges himself in this relativity, in his selfhood or self-Godhood, and becomes not a God by grace but a "god who knows good and evil" in creaturely willfulness.

Even when they were tempted, however, our progenitors did not desire evil and did not rebel against God, although they turned away from Him by their disobedience. But having fallen into a misunderstanding about themselves and about their relation to the world, they, without desiring it, turned away from God toward the world; in this way the *impotence* of their creaturely essence precisely in relation to the world was immediately revealed. God's judgment over man, condemning him to *dependence* upon nature and to sicknesses, poverty, toil, and mortality, was only an outward manifestation of that which occurred in man when he violated the norm of his being, which thereby became abnormal.

The further unfolding of the power of sin in man goes in both directions: in the spiritual as well as in the fleshly direction. On the one hand, humanity becomes "flesh" in the sense that nature gains dominion over spirit in man. On the other hand, in practical atheism we see the development of the satanic ideology of opposition to God, even to the very idea of God. "Satanized" man desires to destroy the image of God in himself, to abolish the very idea of God. The image of God in man is indestructible, but it has been obscured and distorted, and it must be restored and revealed. This restoration is the task of God's economy, the task of the "salvation" of the world, about which God gives His promise when He expels our progenitors from paradise.

If man were not a generic being who realizes himself as the human race in time and who therefore has a *history*, his fall would be irreparable in humanity itself, just as, in a certain sense, Satan's fall turned out to be irreparable within the limits of the spiritual world. But man also had a *future*, and in a prophetic vision of this future, Adam called his wife Eve, that is, Life, immediately after the expulsion from Eden; and in God's sentence, which can be considered a proto-gospel, a promise had already been given concerning *the posterity of the Woman*. In the history of the human race, the sickness of sin was not only to spread and become more intense but also to be expunged through living experience, to the point where this new posterity — the Son of Man — would be born out of the Woman-Virgin.

The Fall had a determining significance not only for man but also for nature. Man is called to be nature's master, to humanize it, to become its *spiritual* center. For, in itself, nature ("the world soul") is not spiritual but only psychic in character, insofar as it is a living entity; by this life nature can, in and through man, participate in the life of the spirit, becoming a "spiritual" body (in contrast to the "natural" or "psychic" body that is inherent in it). Having in itself the seeds of the Heavenly Sophia as its natural foundation, reflecting and realizing the Heavenly Sophia in creaturely being, nature possesses in itself its own persuasiveness and authenticity, its own thought and beauty. Hierarchically, however, *psychic* being is a lower and deficient form of being that must be illuminated by the spirit and thus by no means abolished but raised to a higher state and purposiveness. Nature must be liberated from itself, from its psychic or natural condition; the one called to be its liberator is man, and nature must belong to him. But since man turned out to be unworthy of this high calling, and since he himself became subject to nature instead of becoming its conqueror and liberator, "the whole creation groaneth and travaileth in pain together until now" (Rom. 8:22). Creation has become an accursed land instead of being God's paradise, the body and dwelling of deified man. Creation nevertheless retains the hope of "apocatastasis," the hope that "the creature itself also shall be delivered from the bondage of corruption into the glorious liberty of the children of God" (Rom. 8:21), the hope that it will undergo a transfiguration to be accomplished at the end of the world, when there will be a "new heaven and a new earth." And this restoration of the dignity of nature is also the restoration of man, according to the words of the Apostle: "And not only [nature] but . . . even we ourselves groan within ourselves, waiting for the adoption, to wit, the redemption of our body" (Rom. 8:23).

"The creature was made subject to vanity" (Rom. 8:20); that is, the life of the creature became empty and was deprived of a higher purpose, remaining in the domain of becoming without limits and without content. The vanity of the life of the world was experienced in precisely this way by the divinely inspired witness, the ancient Ecclesiastes. Vanity is emptiness; and dehumanized nature, torn away from its higher meaning and deprived of spirit, is precisely emptiness, although this is an emptiness that is tormented by the desire to be filled, to be brought to spirit. Nature is protected, according to the thought of God, by angels of the natural world; but the holy angels act upon the natural world as if from outside, in the capacity of immaterial spirits that do not have inner access to it. Only man is the soul of the world, which unites him inwardly with the angelic world; conversely, by his fall, he has distanced nature from the angelic world. Nature is ontologically connected with man. It is predestined to be humanized by being made transparent to the spirit; but if the human spirit, weakened by sin, allows itself to be subjugated to nature and reduces itself as if to nonbeing, then nature too is made subject to vanity; that is, it is abandoned to its own emptiness: "The thing that hath been, it is that which shall be; and that which is done is that which shall be done" (Eccles. 1:9). This is "indifferent" nature, whose countenance sometimes fills the human soul with frigid cold. The fall of man involved an unnatural rupture between nature and man, after which he became the slave and prisoner of nature, which is accursed because of his sin. The natural relation between man and nature was perverted into its opposite: man is no longer nature's master and high priest; he no longer leads it to God. Instead, nature is now man's master and leads him away from God, terrifying him with its power, intoxicating him with its charms, subjugating him with its riches. Nature makes him "flesh." It enslaves him by making the maintenance of his life depend on it: Man is Prometheus bound; he is an Orpheus who has forgotten how to bring his Eurydice back to life. The fall of man was also the fall of nature. Nature lost its center and its meaning; it became a being by itself, a *fact* whose coherence depends on causal necessity. This multiform necessity is the law of the world, which has thus become not a cosmos but a mechanism.

In his fall, man did not destroy the image of God in himself but only obscured and weakened it. Likewise nature, when it was separated from

The Creaturely Sophia

man, did not lose its sophianic foundation or content, although its countenance was obscured. The world remains God's creation, and the eternal word about creation, "let there be," always resounds in the world. Thus, even after the fall of the world, the Divine Sophia shines in it as God's revelation. "The heavens declare the glory of God; and the firmament sheweth his handiwork. Day unto day uttereth speech, and night unto night sheweth knowledge. There is no speech nor language, where their voice is not heard" (Ps. 19:1-3). The divinely inspired poet bears witness here to "the glory of God," that is, to the Divine Sophia, who reveals herself even now in nature — and who among us does not hear this revelation! Not only believers, for whom nature is the unwritten book of Genesis, but also unbelievers, who in the blindness of their hearts do not know God, love "nature" in its magnificence and glory. The Apostle attests to this abiding sophianicity of the world: "the invisible things of Him from the creation of the world are clearly seen, being understood by the things that are made, even His eternal power and Godhead" (Rom. 1:20). "Godhead" *(theotēs)* is equivalent here to "glory" and signifies the Divine Sophia in her revelation in nature (cf. Job 12:7-9 and especially 28:23-27).

And this Wisdom of God, manifested in the world, is the inexhaustible source of the inspiration of life with the nature that elevates, purifies, strengthens, and saves the fallen man. This is the everyday experience of all of humankind. And this sophianicity of the world is the foundation of that which, in nature, is its proper, although impersonal life: "hypostaticity" that does not know its hypostasis but is capable of being hypostatized and of living its life for man, for angels, and for God. Man is only dimly conscious of this life of rocks, minerals, water, and plants, although he does have access to some extent to the life of the animal world. This life of nature, being the Glory of God in creation, sings this glory to the Creator, and the heavens truly confess this glory. (This is attested by the marvelous song of the three youths in the noncanonical third chapter of Daniel, in which they address all creation with the appeal to praise the Lord.) This is the radiant face of the creaturely Sophia, directed at heaven. However, nature also has a nocturnal, "dark face," the face of the fallen Sophia (to use V. V. Zenkovsky's expression).

Even though it is sophianic in its positive foundation and content, nature has received an illegitimate being in the fall of man. Being extradivine as a creation that originated out of nonbeing, nature was destined to be deified in and through man; but when man fell, nature was doomed to the illegitimate independence of extradivine being. It became the godless, self-sufficient world, the "great Pan," possessing the mighty

The Lamb of God

fullness of life. Having become the fallen Sophia, the world broke away from the Divine Sophia in the mode of its being, although of course not in its foundation. And in its disintegrated, chaotic being, nature preserves all its fullness as all-unity. But this multi-unity is only the external and mechanical coherence of natural law and is covered by it as by a crust, while the animal world, deprived of human government, is doomed in its life to the struggle for existence and mutual annihilation. The life of nature in its separate manifestations is subject to degeneration and decomposition. Parasitic forms of animals and plants emerge that represent, as it were, the creative activity of evil in the turbulence of nature. In its insubordination to man, nature acquires over him its own power as inhuman *magic*. In their elemental life, the forces of nature become the habitation of demons, who identify themselves with natural spirits.

The life of nature acquires a *mysticism* that captivates man's imagination and enslaves his will in the pagan religions and especially in the orgiastic cults. Nature appears before man as a goddess who demands divine worship from him. It is not that nature is humanized but, rather, that man is dehumanized and becomes a natural being. Nature turns out to be stronger than weakened man. Man, being its spiritual center, is called to be the "soul of nature." His task is to organize and spiritualize the life of nature. But in his fallen state, man is *actually* no longer the soul of nature, although he remains so potentially. Nature acquires its soul *outside* of man, as a false center, which nevertheless receives its reality because of the absence of the true center. Not belonging to man, this soul of nature, the living cohesion of the world, becomes demonic, a kind of pseudo- or anti-Sophia, an Achamoth. Although nature does not entirely belong to the demons either, because it is a sophianic creation, it becomes their habitation and instrument. Having lost its orbit and its spiritual center, the soul of the world becomes ambiguous and blind; it no longer knows good and evil; it becomes deceptive and a liar. It is dangerous for the human spirit to fully merge with nature, to entrust itself to her sovereign dominion. While loving nature, the human spirit must oppose her and ascetically assert its spirituality. For man is higher than nature; he is not a mollusk, a plant, or an animal, and if he lives only a natural life (i.e., only an animal life), this means that his state is a fallen one.

In a certain sense, therefore, man's relation to nature acquires a tragic character. For man, nature is a revelation of God's Glory, it is Wisdom and Beauty. But ceasing to be an other-being of the human spirit, nature becomes duplicitous and false: it entices man to become lower than he is, to renounce himself. This tragedy becomes most acute where contact with nature is most intimate: in beauty and in art, the creative servant of beauty. Nature as reason, as law, is revealed to man, the logos of the world; and knowledge in and of itself does not contain a hidden poison. Knowledge of nature acquires an illegitimate application only in relation to man's freedom, in relation to the sinfulness of his will. But beauty, which directly subjugates us, can contain a poison. Beauty can be deceptive, for the beauty of nature, or natural beauty, is independent of the Spirit; it is indifferent to good and evil, to which man cannot and must not be indifferent. The charms of Achamoth, the malign enchantments of the fallen Sophia, are most dangerous when they wear the mask of beauty. But beauty in nature is not only a mask.

Beauty in nature is the breath of the Holy Spirit over the world. Beauty is immanent to creation and clothes it. Beauty is paradise in nature, whose traces are preserved in nature's memory as a reflection of heaven, although in the fallen world beauty finds itself torn away from holiness. This natural beauty is revealed to man, who is called to receive its revelation not only naturally but also spiritually, in the entirety and fullness of his spiritual being, directed at God. For man, therefore, beauty is inseparable from holiness; it is not only natural but also "spiritual" beauty. Beauty has its own laws; it is free of morality in the capacity of norm or law, but inwardly it is not independent of the integral human spirit. Spiritual beauty is not a particular form of beauty or a place different from the world. On the contrary, spiritual beauty consists of spiritual eyes that perceive the spiritual content of beauty and judge it. There is no external criterion here, only an inner one. For spiritual beauty, beauty and sin are incompatible, and the sinful reception of beauty or the reception of sin clothed in natural beauty (and in general the kind of abstract aestheticism that has sometimes found a place for itself in Orthodoxy, e.g., in Leontiev[21]) is a contradiction. Evil that is clothed in natural beauty is not beautiful but grotesque, and not all things that appear to be beautiful are truly so.[22] For

---

21. Konstantin Leontiev (1831-91) was a major Russian philosopher who believed in the superiority of aesthetic values to moral and social values and applied this principle even to the domain of religious beliefs. — Trans.

22. If the "demon" of Vrubel' or Lermontov can enchant us with his beauty, this is a religious deception or delusion rooted in the spiritual limitations or even blindness of the artist. Or (and this is more likely) it could reflect a special type of gift that gives the artist the capacity to see beauty even in its fallenness, in a sort of chiaroscuro state. [Bulgakov is referring here to Mikhail Lermontov's poem "The Demon," whose romantic and seductive protagonist was painted by the great Russian artist Mikhail Vrubel' (1856-1910). — Trans.]

man, the most powerful and dangerous enchantments of nature are those that reside in beauty. To reject beauty, to blaspheme it, is to blaspheme the Holy Spirit, who is the source of beauty. To be blind to beauty is to close oneself off from the breath of the Holy Spirit in nature. To surrender oneself blindly to beauty, to abolish one's spirituality for its sake, is to chase a phantom, for true beauty is spiritual, although it is revealed in nature. Herein lies the tragedy, not of art, but of the artist, who in his creative activity is called to climb the mountainous path of ascent between two abysses — that of aestheticism and that of demonism.

Nature as the fallen Sophia thus terrifies man with its power, enchants him with its beauty, and impresses him with the mighty force of its life. This mighty force stuns, conquers, and captivates him; it makes him a *pagan,* that is, a natural, not a spiritual, being. Man lives in nature and is connected with it from his very creation, but his relation to it is also one of spiritual self-defense. Nature besieges man and defeats him. In the Old Testament the chosen nation was a small island in the midst of the pagan sea; it was chosen by God's grace for the battle against nature in the name of the supernatural, true God. With the coming of Christ, nature, the "great Pan," was abolished in its depths, because the New Adam defeated nature and made it subject to man. The Incarnation was an exorcism in relation to the natural spirits of the "great Pan." The great Pan is dead, and nature has turned out to consist of "empty and impotent elements." However, just as the demons that return to a purified place are more malicious than before, so, in Christian history, nature has turned out to be the place where Christ battles the Antichrist. The prince of this world has been expelled and his empire has been demolished, but his activity in the world continues. Nature, as a being that is a law unto itself, or Pan, has died, but man is now confronted by its dead mechanism, which he desires to conquer by turning himself into a mechanism (this can be called "rationalization"). What we see here is a new type of natural or "psychical" condition that opposes spirituality: man considers himself to be merely a phenomenon of nature, one of the links of its chain. In essence, this is the temptation of the natural, which has already been overcome by religion but which survives in virtue of inertia and religious vacuity. The new paganism is infinitely poorer than the ancient one, and the great Pan is attempting to find a refuge for himself in man. However, Christ dwells in man, and this attempt of Pan's to inhabit man is only the final convulsion of cosmism. Man has great cosmourgic tasks to accomplish in nature. The sundered connection between spirit and nature must be restored.

CHAPTER 3

The Incarnation

I. God and the World

God created the world by a single act (the "Six Days"), implanting in it the power of being forever. God's creative word resounds for all time. God "laid the foundations of the earth, that it should not be removed for ever" (Ps. 104:5). The world is real with the reality of God, for God's power sustains it. And the world is real not only for itself but also for God Himself. God does not repent of His works, "for he is not a man, that he should repent" (1 Sam. 15:29). But the reality of the world implies a real density of time, in which *becoming* occurs. Scripture represents God as living in time together with the world and with man and as acting in the *history* of the world.

God's self-positing in time, His going out from eternity into time, is an unfathomable mystery of His life; all we can do is accept this mystery reverently and with faith, as a given of our religious consciousness. Nourished by revelation, our religious thought arrives at this mystery and stops in awe before it. Our religious thought dares not doubt the eternity of God or the reality of time; it does not transform time into a subjective illusion. To recognize that God lives together with the world in time is to recognize that He is the Creator and God of the world, which is real in eternity and created for eternity, although it is becoming in time. Although at its end the spiral of time will be woven into a point, it will not thereby lose reality; the time that has passed will not become an illusion. God's life in eternity, in its fullness and unchangeability, in its nontemporality and supratemporality, transcends the world's being and time. But it is precisely out of the depths of this absolute life that the Absolute posits itself as God and turns its face to the world created by God while *simultaneously* (as man would like to say in his own language) remaining in its absoluteness. But there is no simultaneity here as a correlation in time, in its movement: the one moves while the other remains immobile. In its life, the Absolute is not conceived in time; it is not "simultaneous" with time but is deeper and higher than it. But the Absolute becomes correlative with time once time arises, because even if eternity does not intrinsically need time, time for its reality necessarily postulates eternity. It is "serious" time, not empty time, that thirsts for eternity; and this thirst is already possession. For God, *nothing new* occurs in time in relation to His eternity (which removes the chief difficulty that arises when one hypothesizes the existence of time for God). Even in time God lives by His proper eternity; He just has it a different way.

But as the Creator, God lives not only *in* Himself but also *outside* Himself; that is, He has a relation with the extradivine world, the reality of whose being is temporal becoming. This temporality becomes real for God too, insofar as He lives with the world. For the world each atom of time brings something new, something that has not existed before in the becoming of the world; but for God the flow of time does not and cannot bring anything new, anything that has not already existed in God, since God is "rich" with eternity, and time is totally transparent for eternity. For God in relation to the world, the only novelty time contains is its novelty for the world, insofar as God lives with the world. God is not alone in His absoluteness; rather, He exists together with the world, in *interbeing* and in *interaction* with it. Can the relation of God to the world be understood only as interbeing *without* interaction, in such a way that the world and God are mutually neutral? According to deism, the world resembles a mechanism that has been set in motion once and for all by an artful mechanic and no longer needs repair, so that the relation of God to the world is exhausted by the act of the creation of the world. Nothing contradicts both revelation and the rational understanding more than this theory. First and foremost, the comparison itself is faulty. The creation of the world is not a single act that exhausts itself in a moment of time; rather, it is an act continuing for all eternity. It is the continuing creative relation of God to the world, an *interrelation*. The conception that God-Love is only an artful mechanic who has forgotten about His creation is moral nonsense. God created the world, not to discard it the way a child discards a toy he is tired of, but to love it as His other, to have friends for Himself in the sons of the world (John 15:15), to live with them; for will God forget His creation? Deism is therefore a form of atheism; furthermore, it is an atheism of the worst and most blasphemous kind, for without denying the existence of the Supreme Being, it in fact blasphemes this Being. Nevertheless, deism does pose a legitimate theme or, rather, question: How is one to understand the autonomous being of the world alongside God? How is the autonomous being of the world preserved in the face of God's absoluteness?

An inequality exists in the relation of God with the world that makes the very possibility of this relation questionable. Can one really understand this relation as an interaction? And what is the nature of this possibility? If it is not the relation of a mechanic to a mechanism, is it not the relation of an absolute despot to a trembling creature? That is, is it not an attitude of arbitrariness that in relation to the creature appears to be predestination? Can this relation be expressed in another way? Are not all other attempts to moderate this radicalism of Calvinism or Islam only indecisive and inconsistent compromises? Can one really understand the interrelation of God and the world as interaction or, according to the Orthodox definition, as "synergism"? Catholic scholasticism attempts to avoid the iron logic of Calvinism (and Jansenism) by means of artificial constructions (the foremost of which is, of course, Molinism) in order to find a place for synergy and rescue the world from the all-engulfing power of the Absolute. But this scholasticism does not know any objective foundations within the world itself that could guarantee its autonomous being in relation to the Creator.

In its being, the world is a creation of God; it is posited by the creative "let there be." But in its content, the world is not an arbitrary invention, a caprice of the Absolute, as it is considered to be by systems of religious determinism or predestination. Instead, it has a divine foundation and a divine content; it contains a certain divine reality. This reality is the Divine Sophia, whose image is precisely the foundation of the world, the creaturely Sophia. In other words, the world contains something divine for God as well, as His self-revelation. The world is therefore not accidental or arbitrary in its existence but has in itself "sufficient grounds" for its being, grounds that, in their divinity, are indestructible even for the Creator. The interaction of God with the world is based on the interrelation of the Divine Sophia and the creaturely Sophia. The world is created, but it is not only created, for in its *proto-image*, in its idea, it is not created at all but exists from all eternity in God as His Divine world in the Divine Wisdom, as the word of His Word and as the breath of His Spirit.

However, if we thus elevate the world in its ontological foundation, does this not irrefutably confirm deism's conclusion that there is no interaction between God and world, since the world is not only a perfect mechanism but even more than a mechanism, namely the Divine Wisdom in a creaturely form? Is not such a world self-sufficient? Does it admit any action upon itself, and does it need such action? This doubt is easily dissipated if we direct our attention to the actual image of the world. Yes, the world is the creaturely Sophia, who has her foundation in the image of the Divine Sophia; but being creaturely, the world is still only in the process of becoming. As a result, in its being, the world is and is not the creaturely Sophia. In the world the nonbeing, or "nothing," out of which it is created has received the seeds of the Divine Sophia, but they have not yet sprouted. In the autonomous being of the world, a *process* is taking place in which the "nothing," raising its head after being fructified by the creative force and receiving being, does not easily or immediately assimilate its content but even resists it. Although the world was created in its fullness and perfection ("it was good"), in its present state it is not yet finished. It is called to assimilate and cultivate the seeds of being in itself, to become the image of the Divine Sophia. The world left the hands of the Creator not only as a finished given but also as an unfinished *task* that must be accomplished in the world process. The world was supposed to follow the path of its completion under the guidance of man — in and with man. But man stumbled in his vocation and fell, which made the world process infinitely more complicated and arduous. Thus, although the world cannot be destroyed in its sophianic foundation, in its unfinished state it needs divine assistance and government to become complete. The world, therefore, cannot be abandoned by God to its own fate but needs His assistance, which is usually called Divine Providence. The very being of the world includes becoming, and even *self*-becoming, for the world itself must realize its sophianicity in man.

But Divine Providence is not a new creation of the world, since the world is already created. Nor is it a transformation of the world on a new basis, necessitated by the supposed failure of the first creation. All fullness was placed into the world at its creation, and there can be no new foundations for it. Thus, in providentially governing the world, God leaves inviolate its autonomous being; He helps the world only in its becoming, in which it is not finished. The world is too unstable in itself to be able to dispense with this assistance. However, this assistance is not realized through outside interference in the life of the world, nor is it realized by virtue of the divine omnipotence or by cosmic miracles. It can be realized only from inside the world itself, by an action upon its laws through the freedom of created beings. God acts upon the natural world through angels, who protect it and direct it (as is clearly shown in Revela-

The Incarnation

tion), whereas upon the human world (and through it upon the natural world) God acts through the human soul, through its freedom, which contains diverse possibilities. In the most general sense, this action can be defined as *grace*, in which man is acted upon by divine thought and will, thereby bringing his will and activity into conformity with God's thought.

This interaction of God with the world, this unceasing communication of God's grace to the world, expresses God's love for creation as well as His condescension. In providentially governing the world, God really enters into its temporality; this intrusion of God into the life of the world is, in itself, an unceasing creative activity, although it is not a creation out of nothing but an *interaction*.

If the time of the world is real for God, what is its relation to God's omniscience? Does this not contradict His omniscience? But omniscience should not be understood anthropomorphically, as knowledge of all the parts of being in time and in space, that is, as knowledge of being as multiplicity. The world is present before God as all-unity, as the connection of all with all, not in the predeterminedness of events, but in the general connectedness or determination (and in this sense predeterminedness) of the *whole*. This "predeterminedness" of the world is its sophianicity: Established on the basis of Sophia, the world is to become Sophia. That is the ontological law of its being and, in this sense, its predetermined necessity. The world is created for the fullness of its being; there is no other being, and all its elements are given from the beginning. But this general predeterminedness, which comprises the given and the task to be accomplished, does not extend to becoming, in which creaturely freedom participates. Here, for time, there is no predeterminedness; God, in His providential government of the world, responds with His salvific action to all the questions of the world's being, questions represented by every act of creaturely freedom. Creaturely freedom is as real as the world, for this freedom is the image of the world's becoming; it is established by God as the condition for the realization of the world's sophianicity.

For this reason, the lawlike regularity of the world's being, despite the unity and predeterminedness of its foundation as entelechy, implies an infinite series of possibilities of realization. The Spinoza-Kant theory (according to which the lawlike regularity of the world is comparable to the motion of a flying arrow or a solar eclipse, or in general to an astronomical phenomenon) does not conform in any way to the concrete reality. Of course, when realized, all the self-determinations and acts of freedom become part of the chain of cosmic causality; they are immanent to this chain. But causality itself, through freedom, is a variable principle on the pathways of cosmic regularity. However negligibly small these variations might be, they do not allow it to be a purely mechanical regularity. It is precisely at the point of the freedom of the creaturely world — that is, in man — that God's grace, God's Providence, acts, straightening out and correcting the curve of the world by Divine wisdom without destroying or violating the life of this world. The world is never merely immanent to itself, or self-enclosed; it is always open to divine action, which is accomplished within the limits of the world and leads it to the good goal. The world cannot resist this action — not because of God's creative omnipotence, which He does not apply to the already created world, but because of His reason, which, in man, reveals to the world its proper path, its proper sophianic law. Divine Providence acts upon the world within the limits of the variations of its free creative causality, which contains an infinite series of possibilities, and Providence chooses the best possibility for each given case. God never leaves the world He created without providential government, but at the same time He observes the proper laws of the world. The relation of God to the world is therefore defined as an interaction. These actions are sometimes described in anthropomorphic images. (For example, in the story of the Deluge, God says of Himself: "I [will] bring a flood of waters upon the earth, to destroy all flesh.... I will cause it to rain upon the earth forty days and forty nights ... and God made a wind to pass over the earth" [Gen. 6:17; 7:4; 8:1].) These images must be understood, however, not in the sense of new creative acts of God, but in the sense of His providential action upon the elements obedient to Him, though within the limits of the life of the world. The idea expressed here is precisely that of the interaction between God and the world, on the basis of which Divine Providence acts in the world. For God knows His creation and all its paths; He established the law of its being. In virtue of this law, despite all the variations of creaturely freedom and of Divine providential government, the world is realizing its entelechic goal, its sophianic becoming, for which it was created by God in the image of the Divine world.[1]

---

1. This relationship between variations of the cosmic lawlike regularity and the fundamental path of this regularity can be likened (but not more than likened) to a statistical mean, expressing the regularity of a series, given all its variations. It is precisely in this manner (indeterministically, not deterministically) that the world's lawlike regularity must be conceived, and scientific thought is now arriving at such a conception. This results in prophecy's simultaneous unconditionality (with respect to the fundamental goal) and conditionality (with respect to the means of attaining it). See, for example, Jeremiah 18:7-10.

The Incarnation

The world therefore cannot contain in itself any being other than that which was predestined for it at its creation (just as man "by taking thought" cannot "add one cubit unto his stature" [Matt. 6:27]). But the world can and must contain the *entire* fullness of this being. We would erroneously understand the relation between God and the world, however, if we defined it only as the action of God in the natural world, assuming the natural world to be self-enclosed and self-sufficient (i.e., postulating total cosmic immanence). This would still be a form of deism. Such a self-enclosed cosmism is the aspiration of the false "prince of this world," who desires to ravish the world for himself and become its pseudo-god. But not only is the world not self-enclosed; it is predestined — given the absolute inviolability of its proper being as world and creature — to communion and union with God, to the point where "God will be all in all," that is, to the point of the total deification of the creature. God created the world, not only for His self-revelation in it, not only for the manifestation of the Divine Sophia in the creaturely Sophia, but also for personal spiritual communion with it through human beings and angels. The world has a composite structure, for in its created substance it contains divinely uncreated human and angelic spirits; God Himself descends into the world through them. In the human spirit, the world is open for divine grace, inspiration, and life. In this general sense, the world is already divine-human in its foundation. Divine life and creaturely life are united and identified at this point of the world's being, and rays of the deification of the world emanate from there. A personal meeting with God takes place in creation through the human soul; God's self-revelation is accomplished. The direct action of God takes place, and it is supramundane, supracreaturely, and free of the immanent laws of the world.

This action of God is *grace*. In the human monad, windows are open into eternity, into the heavens, for this monad is the image of God. There is therefore in man (and through him in the world) a double life, a double process. This deification of man is not an act of ontological coercion over him, for in his being he has the image of God and even is the image of God. It is natural for this image to identify itself, in an asymptotic approach, with the Proto-Image, without ever merging with it. This is the postulate of man's being and, in him, of all creaturely being, for man is the high priest of all creation. The divine-human foundation of creation is herein expressed. God created the entire world in its fullness and beauty, but only man did He create for communion with Himself. If we liken creation and the Creator to clay and the potter, we can say that both man and the last blade of grass in creation are separated from their Creator by the same abyss. From this point of view it might appear that, in virtue of His power in the world, God could as readily choose Balaam's ass for communion with Himself (or as the instrument of His will) as the prophet himself (see Numbers 22-24). However, even though man is immeasurably far from God, as all creatures are from their Creator, only man in the world (and only through him the world itself) is close to God as His image. Only man is predestined to be the son of God and the friend of God. It is through man that divine life enters into the world.

The history of humanity therefore *begins* with direct communion with God: In the figurative language of the Bible, God comes into the garden "in the cool of the day" (Gen. 3:8) in order to converse with man, and the judgment pronounced upon fallen man is depicted as a conversation with God. The memory of paradise, the rays of the initial divine revelation, is preserved even in fallen man in so-called natural revelation. Even though fallen man became a cosmic being by losing direct communion with God, the image of God in him nevertheless makes him a religious being; even in his natural state he is not deprived of a certain consciousness and knowledge of God. Even the frenzied atheism of our day bears negative witness to this: man desires to destroy in himself that which is indestructible.

After being expelled from paradise and deprived of direct communion with God, humanity *seeks* God — in itself and in the world. Humanity finds Him in a sophianic image, but the human spirit cannot be satisfied solely with the sophianicity of nature, which bears the imprint of the spirit, its revelation, but not the spirit itself. This is because nature lacks a soul. Man, condemned to the merely natural veneration of God, is therefore led by the force of things to pagan naturalism: the natural elements of the animal and material world are taken to be deities only because, in their sophianicity, they are revelations about God. Likewise man, as the image of God, in the fullness of his powers but also in his damaged fallen essence, becomes a god for man. On the one hand, therefore, fallen humanity has, in its sophianicity, a natural revelation about God; but on the other hand, it almost inevitably falls into religious aberrations, given its inability to distinguish the divine from the creaturely, and even from the sinfully creaturely. This desire of man to ascend above the world, to overcome cosmism, is touching; but his impotence to realize this desire is tragic.

If, however, paganism did not possess the *direct* revelation of God, God's word, does this mean that it was completely deprived of the breath of the Spirit of God, which "bloweth where it listeth"? There are neither biblical nor theological grounds for a negative answer to this question.

The Incarnation

The Apostle Paul says of the pagans, "That which may be known of God is manifest in them; for God hath shewed it unto them" (Rom. 1:19). These words attest to more than just the revelation of God through the examination of creation (Rom. 1:20). They also attest to a certain active manifestation that can be understood as a particular religious inspiration, the breath of the Holy Spirit. No dogmatic grounds can be adduced to deny this. On the contrary, it is impossible to admit such an exclusion of the whole of humanity from all grace, for, according to the Apostle Peter, "God is no respecter of persons: but in every nation he that feareth Him, and worketh righteousness, is accepted [by] Him" (Acts 10:34-35).[2] Nor does such an exclusion conform with the Church's recognition that there were pagan "Christians before Christ," that there was a "pagan" church, although it was "barren." Paganism is therefore not only a history of religious errors but also a positive religious process that has its revelations. But all these revelations belong to the realm of the Divine Sophia, who reveals herself in the world; they refer not to the hypostasis but to the hypostatizedness of God. They are cosmic and religiously immanent, for they contain neither the *personal* encounter between God and man nor God's *personal* revelation about Himself. Such revelation is already the action of God in man.

Revealed religion is conditioned by the *personal* action of God in man, as if in a return to that Edenic state where God conversed with man, and man was capable of hearing God and withstanding His burning proximity, the *pati Deum*. However great man's fall might have been in the sense of the weakening of his spirituality and the corresponding corruption of his nature, the image of God, as the foundation of communion with Him, was indestructibly preserved in him. And more than anything else, the very fact of revelation attests to this indestructibility. God reveals Himself to man "at sundry times and in divers manners" (Heb. 1:1), and this entire revelation is reducible to two forms: God *speaks* to man, and He *inspires* him. God is revealed to man as the word of God and the action of the Spirit. This refers to the content of revelation, which is clothed in humanly accessible forms of divine action: signs. On the pathways of God's

---

2. The pagans are guilty only of the fact that, having gained knowledge of God, they did not glorify Him as God but complicated this knowledge and "became vain in their imaginations" (Rom. 1:21) as a consequence of the delusions of their fallen essence. They sinned before the Divine Sophia, for they "changed the glory of the uncorruptible God into an image" (1:23) resembling man and animals. That is, they did not distinguish the Glory of God, the Divine Sophia, from the creaturely Sophia, fallen in man.

providential government, this revelation is not universal but limited. The chosen nation, the small island of salvation, is raised from out of the depths of the pagan sea, and in a land overgrown with weeds and tares the Lord establishes and protects His vineyard. He creates the Old Testament church in order to live in *personal* communion and revelation with it.

God speaks with man in the person of the patriarchs, who are pleasing to Him (Noah, Abraham, and others), as well as with the prophet Moses. God reveals Himself to man, shows him palpable signs of His presence in theophanies, gives him the law, and institutes divine worship. He directs the course of history of the chosen nation, making it the *sacred* history of the education of this nation, designed to serve the economy of salvation. We do not need to consider here the particular elements of this history, but we cannot escape the question: *Who* was the "God of Abraham, Isaac, and Jacob"? *Who* appeared to Moses in the Burning Bush and gave the law on Sinai with the assistance of the angels?[3] Providence, as well as the creation of the world, is the work of the entire Holy Trinity; each of the hypostases, however, acts in a particular and different way. The opinion that the God revealed in the Old Testament is the Logos acting in the world prior to His Incarnation is widespread in the patristic literature. (This opinion is clearly incompatible with the suspect schema according to which the Old Testament is the revelation of the Father, just as the New Testament is the revelation of the Son.) In the Holy Trinity, the Father is the revealed hypostasis, not a revealing hypostasis, and He is revealed in the Son. Even in the New Testament, the Father is revealed in the Son while remaining transcendent in relation to the world, not manifesting Himself in it. And this transcendental character of the Father in relation to creation is even more salient in the Old Testament. If the Father creates the world by His Word, He also provides for it and reveals Himself to it through this same Word. The direct divine subject of the Old Testament is therefore the same as that of the New Testament: the Second hypostasis, the Logos. He is the demiurgic hypostasis *par excellence,* and the economy of salvation belongs to Him. Furthermore, the Old Testament revelation of God to man, being divine in its source and content, was also human, because otherwise it could not have been received by man and would have remained transcendent for him. In other words, this revelation was already *divine-human:* the divine-humanity of the Word anticipates here the hypostatic manifestation of the Logos.

However, the revelation of the Word in the Holy Trinity is accom-

---

3. This question is considered by Augustine in *De Trinitate,* book 2.

The Incarnation

plished in bi-unity with the revelation of the Holy Spirit, who reposes upon the Word. Therefore, the Old Testament revelation could not remain only a revelation of the Word (i.e., only a doctrine). It had to be accompanied by the direct, accomplishing action of the Holy Spirit, by His inspiration. We know in fact that the Holy Spirit had manifested His action in various gifts and that He "spoke by the prophets" (according to the Creed) in the Old Testament. The revelation of the Word in man never was and never could be a mechanical communication from outside, as if it were a dictation. It could only be an inspiration. The Spirit therefore descended upon the prophets who spoke the Word of God, and in their inspiration they gave utterance to Him. One can even say that the inspiration of the Spirit preceded and was the condition for the revelation of the Word. This corresponds to the fact that, in the Holy Trinity, the Spirit reposes upon the Son and manifests the Son. However, this order is naturally reversed in creaturely revelation: first the Spirit for the reception of the Word, and then the Word. This is sometimes directly indicated in the prophetic books: "The spirit entered into me ... [and] I heard [the Lord] that spake unto me" (Ezek. 2:2). But even when this is not directly indicated, it is implied. If he is not overshadowed by the Spirit of God, man cannot see and hear God. The God of the Old Testament is thus the revelation of the Holy Trinity, of the Father *through* the Son and the Holy Spirit.[4] It is only through these hypostases that we have the mysterious revelation of the Father in a divine-human aspect, that is, in an aspect conforming with that of the Son. We see this in the prophet Daniel, in the vision of "the Ancient of days," to whom the Son of Man is brought (Dan. 7:13), as well as in the appearance of the three angels (which, however, certain fathers of the Church understand as the appearance of the Logos with two angels). The Holy Spirit is not revealed in the Old Testament as a hypostasis, as the Divine I; in the personal Yahweh the Holy Trinity manifests itself by the hypostasis of the Logos.

In the Old Testament we have not only the hypostatic revelation of the Logos and the grace-bestowing revelation of the Holy Spirit but also the revelation of the Divine Sophia. We see this in the appearance of the Glory of God to Moses, to Ezekiel, and to Isaiah, as well as in the direct revelation about Wisdom in Proverbs 8-9, Job 28, and the Wisdom of Solomon 7. The Glory of God is the Heavenly Wisdom in the image of which

---

4. Cf. 1 Peter 1:11-12, which speaks of the revelation in the prophets by the Spirit of Christ and the Holy Spirit. Also cf. 1 Cor. 2:10-13, 16, which speaks not only of the revelation by the Holy Spirit but also of "the mind of Christ" given to the Apostle.

the human world is created; the Glory is therefore human and can be encompassed in the revelation to man. (For this reason, the apostles could see the Glory in the Transfiguration of the Lord.) But Wisdom-Glory is not only human; it is also heavenly humanity itself, and it is in this human character that it is revealed in the Old Testament. The image of man participates precisely in the manifestation of the Glory in Ezekiel's vision (1:26): "Upon the likeness of the throne was the likeness as the appearance of a man above upon it." This manifestation of the humanity of the Glory is also that of the Heavenly Adam, the Son of God, the Son of Man, the God-Man, the coming Christ. This image is fully incorporated in the prophet Daniel's vision of the Son of Man being brought to the Ancient of days (Dan. 7:13). This is the Old Testament Gospel about the God-Man, although it does anticipate His New Testament name, the Son of Man, which Christ applied to Himself on earth. Here in Daniel He is seen in heaven: "one like the Son of man came with the clouds of heaven." And Christ Himself, in His conversation with Nicodemus, confirms this connection of heaven and earth in the Son of Man: "no man hath ascended up to heaven, but he that came down from heaven, even the Son of man which is in heaven" (John 3:13). Along with this direct revelation about man's divine-humanity, the Old Testament is also full of indirect revelations, in the form of prefigurings and prophecies that are explained only in the New Testament. Such, above all, is the tabernacle, with all its institutions (as explained in Hebrews 9); but there are also many other examples of persons, events, and symbols.

II. The Foundations of the Incarnation

According to the direct testimony of Scripture, the coming of Christ into the world, the Incarnation, is predetermined before the creation of the world. That is, it is included in God's pre-eternal plan for the world, in His counsel concerning the world. Christ is the "lamb without blemish and without spot: who verily was foreordained before the foundation of the world, but was made manifest in these last times for [us]" (1 Pet. 1:19-20). Thus was manifested "the wisdom of God in a mystery, even the hidden wisdom, which God ordained before the world unto our glory" (1 Cor. 2:7). In Christ, God "hath chosen us . . . before the foundation of the world" (Eph. 1:4); He "predestinated us unto the adoption . . . by Jesus Christ to himself, according to the good pleasure of his will, to the praise of the glory of his grace, wherein he hath made us accepted in the beloved" (1:5-

The Incarnation

6). God thus makes "known unto us the mystery of his will, according to his good pleasure which he hath purposed in himself: that in the dispensation of the fullness of times he might gather together in one all things in Christ, both which are in heaven, and which are on earth" (1:9-10). And this is "the fellowship of the mystery, which from the beginning of the world hath been hid in God, who created all things by Jesus Christ: to the intent that now unto the principalities and powers in heavenly places might be known by the church the manifold wisdom of God, according to the pre-eternal purpose which he purposed in Christ Jesus our Lord" (3:9-11). In this sense Revelation calls the Lord Jesus "Alpha and Omega, the beginning and the end, the first and the last" (22:13; see also 1:8, 11, 17; 2:8). God's pre-eternal design manifested His love for creation, which did not stop at the creation but went beyond it; as the act of the new creation of the world, it determined the descent into the world of God Himself, that is, the Incarnation. "God so loved the world, that he gave his only begotten Son . . . that the world through him might be saved" (John 3:16-17). "In this was manifested the love of God toward us, because that God sent his only begotten Son into the world, that we might live through him. . . . We love him [God], because he first loved us" (1 John 4:9, 19).

These texts make clear that the coming of the Son into the world is not only an act of God's *providential* government of the world, an act proceeding from God's interaction with the world. It is also God's primordial grace, existing before the creation of the world, that is, constituting the very foundation and goal of the world. One can even say that God created the world in order to become incarnate in it, that He created it for the sake of His Incarnation. The Incarnation is not only the means to the redemption; it is also the supreme crowning of the world, even in comparison with its creation. In the Incarnation, God showed His love for creation.

The most general and preliminary question that arises here is whether the Incarnation is only the means to the redemption and the reconciliation of God with man, that is, whether in this sense it is a consequence of the Fall ("O happy guilt of Adam!"), a soteriological act, or whether in a certain sense it is independent of soteriology and is an act predetermined in itself. That is how this question is usually posed in theology and in patristics, and it is answered in both ways, although the soteriological interpretation of the Incarnation predominates (especially in patristics).

Apart from the texts presented above, the Incarnation is also often represented in Holy Scripture as the salvation of man from sin by the Lamb of God's sacrificially taking upon Himself the sins of the world. This corresponds to the real and concrete accomplishment of the Incarnation "for us men and for our salvation." But the first half of this formula of the Nicene Creed, "for us men," has a more general meaning than its particular application in the second half, "for our salvation." Furthermore, the texts presented above indicate not the immediate, redemptive goal of the Incarnation but its final and universal goal: the goal of uniting all heavenly and earthly things under Christ. In the juxtaposition of these two goals, there is no either/or; there is only both/and. More precisely, the soteriological problem is included in the eschatological one, as the means in the goal: the redemption is the path to "our glory." Therefore, perhaps the best way to answer the question of whether the Incarnation could have occurred without the Fall is to reject the question itself as a *casus irrealis,* or as an inappropriate anthropomorphism in relation to the works of God.

The Incarnation was accomplished in all its significance as it was pre-eternally established in God's counsel, but it was accomplished for the sake of fallen humanity. As a result of the Fall, the Incarnation was, first of all, the means to salvation and redemption. It preserved the totality of its significance beyond the limits of redemption, however, for the Incarnation is not exhausted by redemption. The *casus irrealis* here consists in supposing that, if man had not sinned, God could have left Himself unincarnate. The Incarnation is thus made dependent on man, and in particular on his fall, on original sin, and, in the final analysis, even on the serpent. But the testimonies of Scripture cited above indicate that, to the contrary, the mystery of the Incarnation was decided "before the foundation of the world"; that is, it expresses the most fundamental and determining relation of God to the world and not only to a particular event in the life of the world, even if an event that is of capital importance for us. The world did not use man's fall to compel God to make Himself incarnate. (For how could the world compel God to do anything?) Rather, God created the world for the Incarnation. Concretely, however, the Incarnation was accomplished precisely as redemption, and it must also be understood as such. God's *foreknowledge* is often invoked in this connection: It is ascribed to Him that He knew in advance that man would fall, and He thus included the Incarnation in His plan for the world before its creation. Such a hypothesis is not ontological but anthropomorphic. And the anthropomorphic character of this theory is intensified by supposing that God could have saved man by means other than the Incarnation. This theory attributes to God a humanlike choice between different means and possibilities. The only thing indisputable is that, in its creatureliness, the creaturely world contained the possibility of the Fall.

The Incarnation

But God nevertheless decided to create the world, which in its freedom contained the *possibility* of falling away from Him. As a response to this possibility, God supra-eternally made His determination concerning the Lamb of God, sacrificed before the foundation of the world; consequently, He made this determination, to a certain degree, independently of whether this possibility would become a reality. God, so to speak, took upon Himself in advance the responsibility for the possible fall of man, who was subject to change because of his creatureliness. This would result only in the possibility of the Fall, however, not in its predeterminedness, which would shift to the Creator the responsibility for the fall of the creature. But if this possibility is not a necessity, which would be equivalent to the necessity of the Incarnation decided by Divine counsel, one must acknowledge that the Incarnation expresses a relation of God to the world more general than only redemption (although it does in fact also signify redemption).

It is therefore necessary, first of all, to examine the Incarnation with reference to its *general* ontological foundations. In what does the inexorable predeterminedness of the Incarnation consist? Its predeterminedness follows from the general relation of God to the world, which is the outward outpouring of His love for creation. This love, whose nature is sacrifice, renounces itself for the world, not only in that it posits the being of the world *alongside* God, making God correlative to the world, and not only in that God creates the world in man in His image (and that, in virtue of this conformity, the Divine Sophia is revealed in the world), but also in that God as Person enters into *personal* communion with man. God wants to communicate His divine life to the world and to make His abode in the world; He wants to become man in order to make man god. This surpasses the limits of all human imagination and audacity; this is the mystery of God's love, "which from the beginning of the world hath been hid in God" (Eph. 3:9), a mystery that even the angels do not know (see Eph. 3:10; 1 Pet. 1:12; 1 Tim. 3:16). There is no limit to God's love, and it cannot fail to reach its culmination in the fullness of God's self-renunciation for the world, that is, in the Incarnation. And if the very being of the world, in its creatureliness called out of nonbeing, is not an obstacle here, its *fallen* state is not an obstacle either. God comes even into the fallen world; God's love is repulsed neither by the infirmity of the creature nor by its fallen image. He is not repulsed by the sinfulness of the world but condescends to the point of taking upon Himself its sins: The Lamb of God, who takes upon Himself the sins of the world, comes into the world. God thus gives everything for the deification of the world and

The Lamb of God

its salvation; there is nothing that is not given. Such is God's love; such is love. Such is love in the intratrinitarian life, in the mutual giving of the three hypostases; such is love in the relation of God to the world.

If we understand the Incarnation in *this* way, which is how Christ teaches us to understand it (see John 3:17), then there is no reason to ask whether the Incarnation would have occurred if the Fall had not taken place. The greater includes the lesser; that which follows presupposes that which precedes; the concrete contains the general. God's love for *fallen* man, which is so great that He even assumes Adam's fallen essence, certainly already includes love for the uncorrupted man. This is expressed in the wisdom of the brief words of the Nicene Creed: "for us men and for our salvation." This "and," in all the diversity and generality of its meaning, contains the theology of the Incarnation. Precisely this "and" can be understood in the sense of identification (in the sense of "that is"). It is understood in this way by those who consider *salvation* to be the foundation of the Incarnation, and this is in fact what it concretely means for fallen man. But the "and" can also be understood as a differentiating element (as in the phrase "and in particular"), in which case it separates the general from the particular; that is, it does not limit the power of the Incarnation to redemption alone. "The Word was made flesh" (John 1:14) must be understood in the totality of its content: it must be understood theologically, cosmically, anthropologically, christologically, and soteriologically. Soteriology, being the most concrete of these, does not exclude but includes all the others; for this reason, it is erroneous to limit the theology of the Incarnation to soteriology. It is even impossible to so limit it, as the history of dogma attests.

The Incarnation presupposes the presence of "flesh," that is, of the creaturely world and of man in it, in all his indestructibility. In the Incarnation, God does not create the world out of nothing by His omnipotence but has before Himself the image of the world that He has called into being. Being the new Divine act in the world, the Incarnation does not represent an ontological coercion over the world, a coercion that God's love could not admit. The Incarnation is the revelation of the image of God in creation, which is ready to meet the descending Divinity. God cannot become incarnate in or be united with just any creature: Angels, animals, minerals, or things cannot encompass Divinity, despite all the limitlessness of God's omnipotence, which is silent here. The Incarnation is an act of God not *upon* the world but *in* the world. This act has not one but two aspects: The world, in the person of man, receives God; and God seeks this reception. The limitlessness of God's self-renunciation, His self-

The Incarnation

humiliation before the creature, reaches the point where the Incarnation itself depends, not only on God, who desires it in His love for the creature, but also on the creature itself, in its nature as well as in its freedom. The creature must be capable of and worthy of receiving God; it must desire Him by its will (the "two wills" in the divine-humanity, even prior to the Incarnation).

The Incarnation is the inner foundation of creation, its *entelechy*. God did not create the world to keep it from Himself at the insurmountable metaphysical distance that separates the Creator from creation. He created it in order to surmount this distance and to become perfectly united with the world, not only externally, as Creator and even Provider, but also inwardly: "the Word was made flesh." Therefore, the Incarnation is pre-inscribed in man.

The image of Divine-Humanity in man is imprinted in his entire psycho-corporeal organism. By his body man belongs to the creaturely world, which he, as microcosm, has in himself and unifies and generalizes. In his soul, animal man lives the life of this world, which also lives in him. The soul is the creaturely principle in man, which unites him with the entire animal world, that is, with the entire world that lives the life of this world. To be sure, the soul of man has reached the highest degree of the development of the world compared to the degrees of development attained by the souls of the various animals. The soul of man is "rational"; it possesses the faculties man needs in order to live in this world: the lower reason, which, in the wakeful human state, makes up for the absence of the instincts that are proper to animals and constitute their supra-animal wisdom. The fleshly, or "natural," man, in the capacity of a higher animal, possesses all the faculties needed for life in this world. There is a natural wisdom that "descendeth not from above, but is earthly, sensual, devilish" (James 3:15); and there are thus those who are "sensual, having not the Spirit" (Jude 19), about whom it is said that "the natural man receiveth not the things of the Spirit of God" (1 Cor. 2:14). However, if in its bad application this natural or sensual element represents hostile negation of and antagonism to the spirituality proper to man, in its normal relation it represents the foundation and possibility of spiritual life; in this sense it is said about man: "that [is] not first which is spiritual, but that which is natural; and afterward that which is spiritual" (1 Cor. 15:46). When this natural element in man occupies its legitimate, hierarchical relation to the spirit, for which it is the pedestal, it represents in him the life of the world. But just as the creaturely world is created in the image of the divine world and is thus the creaturely Sophia, so the sophianicity of man is revealed, in this sense, in man's psycho-corporeal organism, through which his life is identified with the life of the world. Of all the creaturely forms of sophianicity, only man represents its full realization: In his relation to the world, man, as a microcosm, is the creaturely Sophia, and as such, he bears the image of God; for just as God *has* the Divine Sophia or the Divine world, so man too has her in himself, as the image of the entire creaturely world.

The image of God in man, however, manifested in its relation to the world, would be imperfect and even totally distorted if this sophianicity were expressed only in man's natural animalness. For, having being in God *according to herself* as the Divine world, the Divine Sophia is eternally hypostatized in belonging to the trihypostatic Divine Spirit. Spirit is the *unity* of hypostasis and nature, and Sophia is the nature of the Divine Spirit. As such, she is inseparable from the Spirit and belongs to it: she is not self-sufficient. In man as the image of God there is a relation that corresponds to this relation of the Divine Sophia to the hypostatic spirit. According to his creation, which establishes the normal hierarchy of soul and spirit, man has in his soul a dwelling for his uncreated-created, originally divine, and therefore immortal hypostatic spirit; in this sense he himself is an incarnate spirit or spiritualized flesh. In the normal relation that is preestablished for man at his creation, the spirit is the governing principle, the master of the "flesh." Man deviated from this norm in his fall by first immersing himself in the psychical element and then in the corporeal element. This relation, which is normal for man, is restored by the Second Adam, Christ, the spiritual man. "There is a natural body, and there is a spiritual body. And so it is written, The first man Adam was made a living soul [see Gen. 2:7]; the last Adam was made a quickening spirit. Howbeit that was not first which is spiritual, but that which is natural; and afterward that which is spiritual" (1 Cor. 15:44-46). The Second Adam is also the first normal man, who has realized in Himself the ontological image of man and revealed the truth about him. And if man bears the image of the God-Man, the converse is also true, that is, it is true that the God-Man Christ Himself is man: "one man, Jesus Christ" (Rom. 5:15); "the first man is of the earth, earthy: the second man is the Lord from heaven" (1 Cor. 15:47). The Proto-Image of man in his sophianicity is the Divine-Humanity or the Heavenly Divine-Humanity of the Logos, Sophia, the Divine world reflected in the creaturely world. In the Holy Trinity, the Logos, the Second hypostasis, as the self-revelation of the Father, is Sophia par excellence, whereas the Proto-Image of man, of Adam, is the image of the *Logos in Sophia*.

The Incarnation

The foundations of the in-humanization of the Logos are thus already included in the very creation of man, who, as it were, awaits the reception of the Logos and calls Him. This is man's inner call to heaven, the task that is proposed for him. But this task cannot be realized by man himself; it can be realized *only* by God, for it surpasses the limits of the world and man. This alone is sufficient to prevent us from understanding the Incarnation solely from the soteriological point of view as a means for the restoration of fallen man, a means expressly found for this purpose by Divine Providence. After the fall of man, the Incarnation truly became, first of all, a means for his restoration; but this means is included, solely as a particular possibility, in the general relation of God and man. We have no data to judge how this relation might have unfolded if man had not fallen. But in the consciousness of the *fallen* Adam this striving for union with God was expressed in the waiting for the Redeemer (Job 19:25-27) and in the higher prophetic illuminations of the Incarnation. Such is Isaiah's prophecy about Emmanuel, "God with us," which the Evangelist interprets as a prophecy about the Incarnation (Matt. 1:23). The prophecy is, of course, inspired by the Holy Spirit, but He reveals what is precontained in man himself and thus can be encompassed by him. The entire Old Testament is full of foreknowledge of the mystery of the Incarnation and its prefigurings.

The aforesaid is sufficient to provide an answer to a question sometimes posed in patristics and dogmatics: Why was it precisely the Son of God who became incarnate and not another hypostasis of the Holy Trinity? To the extent that the human *why* is appropriate here (and it is appropriate insofar as man, as the image of God, bears within himself the living revelation of Divinity), here is the answer that is generally given: The Son becomes incarnate as the demiurgic hypostasis, the Logos of the world, by whom all things were made and who reveals in the Father this divine All. In this sense, the Logos is the hypostatic Wisdom of the Father, which reveals itself first in the Divine Sophia and then in the creaturely world. This predemonstrates the Incarnation precisely of the hypostasis of the Logos. In contrast, incarnation is absolutely excluded for the hypostasis of the Father because of the transcendental character of this hypostasis, both in the Holy Trinity and in creation. The Father is revealed through the Son in the Holy Spirit, while remaining closed in Himself. In the Holy Trinity, the Father pre-eternally begets the Son, proceeding upon Him in the Holy Spirit; in creation, the Father creates the world by His Word and completes the world by the Holy Spirit. In both cases the Paternal hypostasis is the *subject* of revelation, not the revelation itself. The Father contains the unuttered and unexperienceable Mystery of Divinity, which becomes manifest in the Son and the Holy Spirit. Therefore, the Father *begets* the Son and *sends* Him into the world. The Father is the first will; His is the power and the principle. But the world knows Him only in the Son, not only at the beginning of creation but also at its completion.

Nor does the Holy Spirit become *hypostatically* incarnate, although He is the cosmourgic hypostasis by which the creative Word is accomplished. Being inseparable from the Logos in the Divine Sophia, the hypostasis of the Spirit occupies the second place in this dyad of hypostases that reveal the Father (and the third place in the Holy Trinity as a whole). The action of this hypostasis presupposes the already accomplished revelation of the Word (and in the Holy Trinity His eternal begetting). The Third hypostasis *participates* in the Incarnation together with the Second; that is, the Incarnation itself is the proper work of the Third hypostasis through the sanctification of human flesh by descent upon the Virgin Mary, upon the Divine Infant, and then upon Christ, baptized in the waters of the Jordan. But the participation of the Holy Spirit in the work of the Incarnation has an accomplishing significance. Their interrelation in the work of the Incarnation can be defined as follows: the Son becomes incarnate as a person, whereas the Holy Spirit participates in the Incarnation through the "flesh" sanctified by Him, that is, through psycho-corporeal *humanity* (just as at the creation of the proto-earth, which was destined to become the matter-mother for the creation of man from "the dust of the ground," "the Spirit of God moved upon the face of the waters," anticipating His descent upon the Ever-Virgin). We can use a grammatical analogy to express the mystery of the Incarnation: the participation of the Holy Spirit is the copula ("is") linking the subject (the hypostasis of the Logos) with Him Himself in His Word, which is the universal *all.* In order that the hypostasis of the Logos, His Divine I, become the hypostasis for creaturely being, it is necessary that this creaturely being, the word of the Word in creation, be *united* with the Divine hypostasis, that it ascend to this union. This is what the Holy Spirit accomplishes as far as creation is concerned.

The Incarnation should thus not be understood as the work of the hypostasis of the Logos alone. It necessarily presupposes the participation of the Second hypostasis and the Third hypostasis: the Second hypostasis becomes incarnate, becomes the *subject* for creation, whereas the Third hypostasis, without becoming incarnate, descends upon the Virgin Mary for the sake of the Incarnation of the Logos and then in general is sent into the world by the Father through the Son in order to reveal and definitively accomplish the Incarnation.

The Incarnation

The inseparability of these two hypostases in the Incarnation is attested in the Creed by the words: "made incarnate from the Holy Spirit and the Virgin Mary." This expresses with great clarity the idea that the Incarnation is composed of two acts: the *introduction* of the divine hypostasis into man and man's *reception* of this hypostasis. The first of these acts is the proper work of the Logos, sent into the world by the Father, whereas the second is the work of the Holy Spirit, sent by the Father upon the Virgin Mary, in whose flesh the Incarnation is accomplished. Therefore, in no wise should this be understood to signify the paternity in some sense of the Holy Spirit, who supposedly takes the place of the husband. On the contrary, there is here a certain identification, as it were, of the Holy Spirit and the Virgin Mary in the conception of the Son: the Virgin Mary conceives the Son not by Her human powers but because the Holy Spirit reposes in Her and upon Her. But the fact that the Holy Spirit co-participates in the Incarnation (with this participation being a necessary condition for it) absolutely excludes the Third hypostasis's own incarnation. Hypostatic incarnation, which is perfectly appropriate for the Second hypostasis as hypostatic *sonhood*, is inappropriate for the Third hypostasis. Sonhood is hypostatic kenosis in the Holy Trinity, and the Son of God is the kenotic hypostasis, the eternal Lamb. And this eternal kenosis of sonhood is the general foundation for the kenosis of the Son that is the Incarnation: "great is the mystery of godliness: God was manifest in the flesh" (1 Tim. 3:16).

Regardless of how we might understand the general connection between the Incarnation and man's fall, the Fall, even though it is the concrete foundation for the Incarnation, is also an obstacle for it. The Logos could not assume a flesh stained by the Fall, burdened by original sin, just as the sinful flesh could not find in itself the will or the power to receive the Incarnation. If Adam's first impulse after the Fall was to hide from the face of the Lord (Gen. 3:8), this urge became a fixed one in his descendants, being transformed into a fearful consciousness: "We shall surely die, because we have seen God" (Judg. 13:22). In amazement Moses said about himself to the people: "we have seen this day that God doth talk with man, and he liveth" (Deut. 5:24), just as Isaiah cried out after the theophany that had been accomplished before him: "Woe is me! for I am undone . . . mine eyes have seen the King, the LORD of hosts" (Isa. 6:5). And the Lord Himself attests to this alienation of man from God that has replaced the Edenic possibility of direct conversation with God: "Thou canst not see my face: for there shall no man see me, and live" (Exod. 33:20). In order to enable the creature to receive the Incarnation, it was necessary to overcome the creaturely trepidation of "the children of wrath" (Eph. 2:3), of the "enemies" of God (Rom. 5:10), by love for the Lord, for only "perfect love casteth out fear" (1 John 4:18). But the only way to accomplish this was to overcome the sin that alienated man from the Lord. In order to liberate man from original sin and to reconcile him with God, a liberation and reconciliation that could only be accomplished through the Incarnation, it was necessary to weaken this sin to the point of rendering it inactive, although it retained its reality.

This was in fact accomplished in the Most Pure Virgin Mary, whose appearance in the world was the main *work* of the Old Testament church. A hereditary holiness, assisted by the grace of the Holy Spirit, had accumulated for centuries and millennia in the Old Testament church; this holiness, tried by fate and temptations and formed by the entire gracious life of the Church, had ascended higher and higher above the level of fallen humanity. In this way, in its creaturely and human aspect, the Incarnation was prepared from ancient times by the inspirations of the Holy Spirit, the action of the Third hypostasis. The peak of this holiness was attained in the Most Holy Virgin, whose purity was such that She was "full of grace," overshadowed even prior to the Incarnation by the constant illuminations of the Holy Spirit. In Her, original sin *lost its power* as an obstacle to the Incarnation. Being *personally* sinless, She was not subject to the power of original sin, although it lived in Her as the universal human destiny, as the hereditary illness of man's nature, which She bore in Herself. But in Her this sin was reduced to pure potentiality and did not exert any influence on Her will.[5] Her personal sinlessness opened a path to the unceasing action upon Her of the Holy Spirit. In the fallen, sinful world, She already manifested the original sophianic image of man, although She was united by fleshly and spiritual ties with fallen humanity and shared its sinful illness in Her love for it. Her holy soul, chosen from all eternity in the womb of the Lord, entered the world by God's will, having received flesh from the holy parents who carried in their loins the hereditary holiness of all Israel. Her coming into the world, preestablished from all eternity, was indeed the appearance of the "Woman" whose enmity for Satan was ordained by God (Gen. 3:15). And when She had attained such spiritual strength that She could withstand the direct overshadowing of the Holy Spirit, not in the separate gifts of grace with which

---

5. In reference to this, the Roman Catholic Church established its unexamined dogma of 1854 on the absolute exclusion of the Most Holy Mother of God from original sin. (For a critique of this dogma, see my book *The Burning Bush*.)

The Incarnation

She was abundantly adorned, but in the reception of the Holy Spirit Himself in all the fullness of His divine nature, it was then that the Incarnation took place. The archangel Gabriel was sent by God (of course, by God the Father, the Principle) to announce to Her the divine counsel: "The Holy Spirit shall come upon thee, and the power of the Highest shall overshadow thee" (Luke 1:35). The Holy Spirit, who in the Holy Trinity pre-eternally overshadows the Son, descends into the creaturely world and realizes this overshadowing of the Son in creation.

The Most Holy Virgin becomes heaven, and Her womb becomes the place of the overshadowing, which also contains the One who is overshadowed: the God-Word who is being begotten. And in response to God's question, asked through the archangel, whether she wants to serve the Incarnation, to receive God, the Virgin answers: "Behold the handmaid of the Lord; be it unto me according to thy word" (Luke 1:38). The "New Eve" does not seek to hide amid the trees from the face of God but obediently goes forth to receive the Lord. The answer of the Most Holy Mother of God manifested the very same creaturely human freedom that, in the person of Eve and then Adam, defined itself against God's will. But now, in the person of the Most Holy Mother of God, the creature realizes its freedom not in willfulness but in the obedience of love and self-renunciation. Divine Maternity is the human side of the Incarnation; it is the condition without which the Incarnation could not have been accomplished. Heaven could not have come down to the earth if the earth had not received heaven. The Most Holy Virgin Mary is therefore the eternally foreseen and preestablished center of the creaturely world.

One should remember, however, that, in general, no creaturely holiness is capable of encountering God — and *a fortiori* of supporting the birth of God — without being annihilated. Only God Himself can sanctify and deify a creature to the point where it becomes strong enough and worthy of the Incarnation. If the Son of God is made incarnate, it is the Holy Spirit, descending upon the Virgin and making Her the earthly heaven, who renders Him incarnate. In the Holy Trinity the Holy Spirit is the Third hypostasis; He follows the Second hypostasis and reposes upon it. But in the work of the Incarnation the Holy Spirit *anticipates* by His action the Son who is made incarnate. Just as in human birth the mother comes first and the child follows, so in the divine birth the Holy Spirit, descending upon the Mother of God, gives Her the power of Divine Maternity.

Through the Virgin Mary's reception of the archangel's annunciation, the Logos is born as Man, and the Son of God becomes the Son of Man. The Lord repeatedly applies to Himself the name "Son of Man" in all the multiplicity of its meanings. But in this case its most direct meaning is that the Incarnation is an *adoption* of the hypostasis of the Logos by the human race. Consequently, this is not a new creation but an inclusion into the already existing human race, an engendering from it. The Incarnation cannot be other than this, and thus the name "Son of Man" is, above all, an attestation of Christ's authentic humanity. When it is unfolded, so to speak, this name expresses the Gospel genealogies, which clearly show Jesus' human "parentage." The first of these genealogies, which is in Matthew 1, is in descending order and represents Christ as "the son of Abraham" (1:1) through "Joseph the husband of Mary" (1:16). The second genealogy, in Luke 3, is in ascending order and represents Him as "the son of Adam," "the Son of God," through Joseph, who was thought to be His father (3:23). Both genealogies are testimonies about Jesus, the Son of God, the Son of Man.

This testimony about the authenticity of Christ's humanity has, of course, a very great soteriological significance, according to the principle of "that which is not received is not redeemed." But here it has significance, first of all, in relation to the Incarnation itself: The Incarnation is not only the reception of men into the Divine race, making them into sons of God as a result of the redemption; before that, it is also the reception of the Son of God into the sons of men, His in-humanization through His birth from the Virgin. The Logos could truly become incarnate and human only by becoming the *Son* of man, that is, by entering into the already existing human race and not beginning it out of Himself. It is true that, as the New Adam, Christ *begins* the new race of the Sons of God, but this is only a *renewal* of the old, already created race and does not destroy the authenticity of His human genealogy. "The Word was made flesh" (John 1:14) signifies, above all, this human sonhood, and it eliminates all docetism in relation to the Lord's humanity, for an illusory shadow of humanity cannot be considered a human son.

A question can arise, however, concerning the "virginal conception" without a father and the birth "from the Holy Spirit and the Virgin Mary" (according to the Creed). Is this compatible with authentic human sonhood, and does it not abolish it? A *formal* answer to this question is given by the genealogies that include Jesus in the lineage of Joseph, although both of the Evangelists (Matt. 1:1-16; Luke 3:23-38) are certain that Joseph was not Jesus' father according to the flesh but that, as the husband of Mary, he was legally considered Jesus' father, even in the eyes of His Mother (see Luke 2:48). This inclusion in the lineage was not only a juridical act; it had a certain mystical reality, consisting in the *recognition* of son-

The Incarnation

hood or adoption for both the parents and the Son. By His fleshly birth from His Mother, Jesus became the Son of Man. The absence of an earthly father and of fleshly conception, which, *ontologically,* clearly does not exclude the possibility of virginal conception from the Mother through Her being overshadowed by the Holy Spirit, does not diminish the fact that the "flesh" Mary gave to the Infant is the common human flesh. If it is sometimes called the "likeness of . . . flesh" (Rom. 8:3; see also Phil. 2:7), this is not intended to diminish its authenticity but rather to indicate that sin, both original and personal, is absent from it. Begetting through fleshly union was only a consequence of original sin; it replaced *spiritual* begetting, which is unfathomable for us and which remained unrealized by man before the Fall. Hereditary sin, the envelopment of spirit by flesh, is transmitted through fleshly begetting, which corresponds to man's sinful state: "I was shapen in iniquity; and in sin did my mother conceive me" (Ps. 51:5). However, this did not come into man at the beginning, at his creation; it came into him only in the Fall. God did not create sin together with its consequences; they are not ontological in man. For him they are only a modality that can be removed without destroying humanity or diminishing its authenticity. On this basis, Jesus is the true Son of Man, even though He is begotten without a human father from His Mother; in relation to *sinful* flesh, however, His flesh, which is free of original sin, turns out to be only a "likeness of flesh." In a certain sense, this birth can be equated with a new creation in which God took the place of the father. But the first Adam was created by God directly from the "earth," and therefore he was not the son of man, but "the son of God" (Luke 3:38). However, the New Adam, as the Son of God but also the Son of Man, could now not be created directly from the earth. Rather, He was born from the Virgin Mary, who carried within Her the whole of human nature except sin, which does not belong to the essence of man.

The two names of Jesus that we find in the Gospels, "Son of God" and "Son of Man," express, when taken together, the mystery of the Divine-Humanity. What strikes one above all is that the two names designate the same thing but in different ways: *sonhood.*[6] Precisely the Son is the kenotic hypostasis in the Holy Trinity itself, as well as in the creation of the world and in the sending into the world. And in the fact that the in-

---

6. In scholastic dogmatics, one sometimes encounters the idea that it was precisely the Son of God who had to become incarnate because, in the Incarnation, He also had to become the Son, even if the Son of man. This idea, however, true in and of itself, has never been examined in depth.

carnate Logos becomes the Son of Man, one cannot fail to see the revealed kenosis of the sonhood — the divine obedience of the Word. He, the Creator of the world *par excellence* as the demiurgic hypostasis, comes into this world not as the Creator but as a creature, subject to the laws of this world and of this humanity that He Himself created. The Son of God, the New Adam, comes into the world in a different manner from Adam, the original man, who was the forefather of man, not the son of man (although he was "the son of God" [Luke 3:38]). And He becomes the Son of Man in order to be our co-human brother who has acquired knowledge in Himself of all things human and who has experienced all human experience, as the hymn of the Incarnation in Heb. 2:10-18 says: "For it became him, for whom are all things, and by whom are all things, in bringing many sons unto glory, to make the captain of their salvation perfect through sufferings. For both he that sanctifieth and they who are sanctified are all of one: for which cause he is not ashamed to call them brethren, saying, I will declare thy name unto my brethren, in the midst of the church will I sing praise unto thee [see Ps. 22:22]. And again, I will put my trust in him. And again, Behold I and the children which God hath given me [see Isa. 8:18]. Forasmuch then as the children are partakers of flesh and blood, he also himself likewise took part of the same; that through death he might destroy him that had the power of death, that is, the devil. . . . For verily he took not on him the nature of angels; but he took on him the seed of Abraham. Wherefore in all things it behoved him to be made like unto his brethren, that he might be a merciful and faithful high priest in things pertaining to God, to make reconciliation for the sins of the people. For in that he himself hath suffered being tempted, he is able to succour them that are tempted."

III. The Divine-Humanity

After a centuries-long dogmatic struggle, the Church established the fundamental christological dogma of the *God-Man* at the Fourth Ecumenical Council, at Chalcedon (although the expression "God-Man" is not used in the Definition of Chalcedon, which speaks simply of Christ). According to the Chalcedonian dogma, the structure of the God-Man Christ consists not in a simple relation (as in the case of Divinity or in the case of humanity as such) but in a *complex* relation, namely the unity of the hypostasis in the case of the duality of the natures. This hypostasis is the Second Person of the Holy Trinity, the Logos. The unity of the hypostasis

The Incarnation

guarantees the unity of the life, and the duality of the natures guarantees the complexity and duality of the life; but the union of the natures, headed by the one divine hypostasis, establishes a new and particular bi-unity, which exists neither in Divinity nor in humanity. For in Divinity we have unity of nature in the case of hypostatic triunity, with each hypostasis entirely possessing the nature; and in humanity we have unity of nature in the case of the multiplicity of hypostatic centers, each of which has the nature in its personal possession. But in Christ's Divine-Humanity we have two distinct natures, united without separation in one hypostasis, but with each preserving its autonomous being.

At first glance the Chalcedonian dogma looks like an ontological paradox that appears to negate all our initial definitions concerning the interrelation between nature and hypostasis. In fact, all spiritual being is an inseparable unity of hypostasis and nature, which can exist only in mutuality: the hypostasis in the nature and the nature in the hypostasis. Therefore, the hypostasis and the nature are by no means mutually independent principles or primordial elements of being that can be arranged and rearranged in different ways to form completely new combinations (in a kind of "in-hypostatization"). They are not at all flexible and do not allow themselves to be coerced in any way; the idea that they could be coerced is an ontological absurdity. And if it is impossible to attach the head of a dog to a man, it is even less possible to make the hypostasis of one entity the hypostasis of another entity. (When Apollinarius attempted such an unnatural unification, St. Gregory of Nyssa accused him of inventing minotaurs and other imaginary hybrid beasts.) The hypostasis and the nature do not exist separately but compose one *living* spirit; this unity of life is their inseparability, for separation here could only signify destruction.

In the Definition of Chalcedon, however, the divine hypostasis of the binatural Divine-Humanity — its subject, so to speak — is simultaneously the subject of both the divine nature and the human nature; and the two natures are united without separation in the unity of the life of this one hypostasis. The divine hypostasis of the Logos is also the human hypostasis, in the capacity of the subject of the human nature as well. The human nature, as the fathers of the Church explain, does not remain nonhypostatic, insofar as, in general, there cannot be any extrahypostatic natural being; rather, it is hypostatized by the divine hypostasis. If one insists in this case on the concept of "in-hypostatization," one must not give it an abstract, formal-logical definition without any relation to its ontological meaning; rather, one must show its concretely ontological significance. If we understand "in-hypostatization" to mean only a union of things different in essence and not unitable in life, this would be an empty logical abstraction based on the acceptance of what is ontologically impossible and erasing the boundaries of being in a universal mixing. However, beyond the limits of its formal application, the idea of in-hypostatization is *devoid of content*, and therefore it cannot help us to understand the Incarnation with the assumption of the human nature into the divine hypostasis.

The Chalcedonian definition concerning the unity of the hypostasis in the case of two natures is a theologically unclarified schema that still requires dogmatic clarification; without clarification it remains a "tinkling cymbal" (1 Cor. 13:1), even given the most sincere and zealous desire to uphold the Orthodox doctrine. To be sure, one can hide in *asylum ignorantiae* (the refuge of ignorance) and proclaim the Incarnation to be an unfathomable mystery, which in its essence it certainly is. However, reason can discover the dogmatic lineaments of this mystery — this is confirmed by the very existence of the dogmatic definition. Reason discerns in this definition the norm of the true doctrine, which our rational understanding can grasp, of course, only if there is the belief that it is true (for belief never establishes prohibitions for reason in its *proper* domain but, on the contrary, condemns lazy obscurantism). Moreover, it is now too late to prohibit the rational analysis of the dogma, after such an analysis has been attempted in the doctrine of in-hypostatization, a doctrine that not only has not been condemned as an illegitimate rationalization of the mystery but has even been approved by such ecclesiastical authorities as St. John of Damascus. Clarification of the Chalcedonian dogma by the analytic powers of reason, to the extent such clarification is possible, is therefore a pious duty for theology; the failure to fulfill this duty will be tantamount to burying the treasure of the dogma in the ground in the name of its illusory preservation, in the same way that the lazy servant buried the treasure entrusted to him.

What then does this "in-hypostatization" of the Logos in the human nature signify? Is it ontologically possible, and why is it possible? The question we pose concerns specifically *ontological* possibility, proceeding from the interrelation of the essences; we thus exclude the unanswerable reference to God's omnipotence as such, for which *all* things are assumed to be possible. Yes, all things are possible for God's omnipotence in creation, for God as the Creator. But after God had created the world and endowed it with indestructible being in its proper ontology, He accepted this ontology, and His relation to the world is now based not on omnipo-

The Incarnation

tence but on providential interaction. This also holds for the Incarnation. Although the Incarnation is, in a certain sense, a new creation, and one that is even more miraculous and unfathomable than the first, it is not a creation out of nothing and therefore cannot be understood solely as a manifestation of God's omnipotence. On the contrary, just as in relation to the world God posits its being as a condition and a boundary for Himself, so in the Incarnation He does not abolish the ontology proper to the world and, in particular, to man's nature. For his part, man co-participates in the Incarnation as such; he cannot be abolished or destroyed in his nature by God's omnipotence for the sake of the Incarnation, for if the Incarnation were realized at *such* a cost, it would not be the Incarnation. In the Incarnation the human essence is surpassed, not destroyed. Therefore, the Incarnation cannot include any act that would contradict man's nature, that would be ontologically impossible for man.

The first condition of the true Incarnation is that man remain himself, and that which is impossible for man cannot be included in the Incarnation. This ontological postulate of the Incarnation is recognized in the dogma by the attestation of the union in Christ of perfect God and *perfect* man, that is, man undiminished in his ontological fullness and with his humanity intact. This postulate possesses both christological and soteriological certainty. As far as Christology is concerned, it would be impossible to speak of the *in-humanization* of God if the human essence assumed by Him were substantially different from the human nature created by God; if it did so differ, the Incarnation would be impossible and would be a failure (but to assert this would, of course, be the greatest of blasphemies, the extreme of disbelief). As far as soteriology is concerned, the assumption by Christ of a nonhuman man would clearly not be salvific for man in his authentic essence. Thus, even in the Incarnation, man must not be diminished or surpassed, but remain himself, that is, "perfect" *(teleios)*.

If the human essence of the God-Man is thus "in-hypostatized" in the Logos in such a way that the hypostasis of the Logos has become the *proper* hypostasis also of His human nature, this is therefore ontologically possible and preestablished. But the question arises: How is this possible, and why could this have been preestablished? Could man's nature have received and encompassed within itself — *instead of* the human hypostasis or, rather, *in the capacity of* the human hypostasis — the hypostasis of the Logos? And how could such a descent have been possible for the Logos Himself? A general answer that refers to the image of God in man is insufficient here. It is necessary to show in what precisely the power of the image of God is manifested in the case of this "in-hypostatization," and what aspect of it is revealed here.

The human nature can live only in the human hypostasis, and it cannot receive even the angelic hypostasis (despite the proximity of this hypostasis to man), for the hypostasis of an immaterial spirit cannot encompass within itself the life of an incarnate spirit; it cannot truly receive human "flesh." It is thus necessary to conclude that, insofar as it hypostatizes the human nature, the hypostasis of the Logos *is*, in a special sense, a human hypostasis too, that it is proper not only to God but also to Man, that is, to the God-Man. In order to be a human hypostasis, the hypostasis of the Logos must be human or, more precisely, *co-human;* and for this reason the hypostatization of man's nature by this hypostasis does not destroy or coerce it but corresponds to a primordial interrelation between the two. On the other hand, man must also be capable of *receiving* and *encompassing* within himself, in the capacity of the human hypostasis, the divine hypostasis. In other words, by his initial essence man must already be divine-human in this sense; he must bear hypostatic divine-humanity within himself and represent, in this capacity, an ontological "site" for the hypostasis of the Logos.

Therefore, as far as the in-hypostatization of the Logos in man is concerned, the postulate of the Incarnation is a certain primordial identity between the Divine I of the Logos and the human I; this identity, however, does not exclude the essential difference between them. This is precisely the relation of the image to the Proto-Image, the relation that unites the identity existing generally between the image and the Proto-Image with the difference existing between eternity and temporality, between the Creator and creation. The human hypostatic spirit, which lives in man and which fundamentally distinguishes him from the animal world, has a divine, uncreated origin from "God's breath." This spirit is a spark of Divinity that is endowed by God with a creaturely-hypostatic face in the image of the Logos and, through Him, in the image of the entire Holy Trinity, insofar as the trihypostatic Face can be reflected in the creaturely consciousness of self. Through his spirit, man communes with the Divine essence and is capable of being "deified." Being united with and living by the divine nature, man is not only man but also potentially — by predestination, by his formal structure — a god-man. At the same time, in his nature, as the soul of the world, as "flesh" (i.e., through his animate body), man unites in himself the entire world, which in this sense is his humanity. Man consists of an uncreated, divine spirit, hypostatized by a creaturely I, and of a created soul and body. This humanity of his has, in its cosmic being, the image of the creaturely Sophia; and he himself therefore contains the creaturely Sophia, who is hypostatized in him. As a result, he is the sophianic hypostasis of the world.

To be sure, the state of sin obscures in man's consciousness his divine homeland and also deprives him of the fullness of sophianic being. This state makes him subject to the elements of the world, which appears before him not as Sophia but only as *natura* (which is to become itself, to engender itself) or as the elementally chaotic Achamoth. But this darkened state is not man's true state; it does not conform with his essence. Man needs to be restored, and this restoration consists in salvation from sin. He desires to become a son of God and to enter into the glory of creation, for he is predestined to this. Out of natural man he is called to become a god-man; he is called to surpass himself in the true God-Man. That is man's inner postulate. Man bears within himself the coming Christ; and prior to Christ's coming, man does not have the power to become himself (i.e., true man) or to realize in himself the new spiritual birth that is not of flesh and blood, but of God.

Not only is man the god-man by calling, but the Logos is the pre-eternal God-Man as the Proto-Image of creaturely man. The Logos is the demiurgic hypostasis whose face is imprinted in the Divine world, as in the Divine Sophia, by the self-revelation of Divinity through the Logos. The hypostasis of the Logos is *directly* connected with Sophia. In this sense the Logos *is* Sophia as the self-revelation of Divinity; He is her direct (although not sole) hypostasis. The Logos is Sophia in the sense that He *has* Sophia as His proper content and life, for in Divinity, Sophia is not only the totality of ideal and nonliving images but also the organism of living and intelligent essences that manifest in themselves the life of Divinity. Sophia is also the heavenly humanity as the proto-image of the creaturely humanity; inasmuch as she is eternally hypostatized in the Logos, she is His pre-eternal Divine-Humanity.

If we examine this series of propositions concerning the heavenly God-Man and the earthly, creaturely God-Man, we will understand and consider natural the Apostle Paul's fundamental anthropological doctrine that there is not one Adam, but two Adams; not one man, but two men: "The first man is of the earth, earthy: the second man is the Lord from heaven.... And as we have borne the image of the earthy, we shall also bear the image of the heavenly" (1 Cor. 15:47, 49). The anthropological meaning of what the Lord told Nicodemus is in conformity with this: "no man hath ascended up to heaven, but he that came down from heaven, even the Son of man which is in heaven" (John 3:13). And this duality of the images of the God-Man, the heavenly Man and the creaturely Man, is confirmed in the single image of the Man who unites in Himself the heavenly humanity and the creaturely humanity: "one man, Jesus Christ" (Rom. 5:15).

For this reason, the hypostasis of the Logos, of the heavenly Man, could become the hypostasis of the creaturely man and make him the true God-Man, realizing his original Divine-Humanity. The hypostasis of the Logos is human from all eternity and could therefore become the hypostasis for creaturely humanity as well, elevating but not abolishing it. One could say that the Logos simply and naturally replaced the creaturely hypostasis for Christ's human nature. But this turned out to be possible because this creaturely hypostasis itself was *supernatural*, representing the divine principle in man. In Christ, the uncreated-created, divine-human hypostasis of Adam was replaced by the divine hypostasis of the Logos. The significance of this is, of course, immense: in place of the creaturely hypostasis (although one that is of divine origin), man's nature receives the hypostasis of the Logos Himself. But this does not destroy man's general structure, which consists of two parts: his psycho-corporeal nature, created out of nothing and thus creaturely in the full sense of the word; and a hypostatic spirit of divine origin, which is created by God *not* out of nothing but has received life from God's own life.

Man's nature is united with the hypostatic spirit; and the hypostatic spirits that proceed from God are distinct and multiple, although they are interconnected in the multi-unity of humanity. The Logos includes Himself among these hypostatic spirits; in Christ's humanity He has replaced the personal human hypostasis. The human nature in Christ could receive this replacement and contain within itself the Divine Person in the capacity of its own person. We therefore confess Christ as the *perfect* man, in whom the human composition is fully preserved, for the inhabitation of the Logos in man has a sufficient ontological basis. The human spirit in man, which originates from God, is in Christ the Pre-eternal Logos, the Divine Spirit, the Second hypostasis of the Holy Trinity. The New Adam, Christ, who in His human essence is hypostatized by the Logos, is the perfect man; formally, in his composition, He does *not* differ from other men except by this particular hypostasis, which is proper to Him. The Logos receives man's psycho-corporeal essence *(sarx)* while preserving His Divinity, which is proper to Him in inseparable union with His hypostasis. In assuming "flesh" (i.e., the human essence), the Logos, in the capacity of divine hypostasis, is not separated from His divine nature; as a result, Christ has one hypostasis but two natures. In creaturely man, this "binaturality" is analogous to the fact that, being a creaturely hypostasis that hypostatizes the human nature, he is turned toward God according to the divine essence of his admittedly creaturely hypostasis, and he can commune by grace with the life of the divine essence. This possibility of communion with God, which in Christ is a reality, is in man the *formal potentiality* of binaturality or Divine-Humanity. Here too in Christ, therefore, no coercion is applied to the human essence; no incompatible element is introduced into His life. Rather, the true, pre-inscribed image of the old Adam is realized in the New Adam. For man is the ready form for true divine-humanity, for which he is created and to which he is called, though he is not able to realize it by his own powers. The Incarnation is not a catastrophe for the human essence, not a violence done to it. On the contrary, the Incarnation is the fulfillment of the human essence. Christ, being perfect God, is therefore also true man.[7]

The foundation of the Incarnation must be sought not only in the relation of the hypostatic principles in the Logos and in man but also in the relation of the divine and human natures. Clearly, the Logos could not have become a human hypostasis, could not have hypostatized the human nature, if in some sense He were not co-human with us, if the pre-eternal image of humanity were not imprinted in His proper life. Conversely, the human essence could not contain within itself the hypostasis of the Logos, could not be hypostatized in Him, if it did not bear His seal and contain His image. The interrelation of the divine and the human is ontologically revealed here: *humana natura capax divini* (the human nature received the divine nature). The world was therefore His own *(idios)* for the Logos, and when He came into the world, "He came unto His own [*ta idia*]," although "His own received Him not" (John 1:11). This "own-ness" of the world and of man's nature for the Logos constitutes the natural foundation of the Incarnation: not only the fact that man is co-hypostatic with the hypostatic God but also the fact that he is co-natural with Him (although he does not share one nature with Him), as is attested by the assumption of flesh by the Logos: "the Word was made flesh, and dwelt among us" (John 1:14).

A final question remains. The hypostasis of the God-Man is the Logos, the Second Person of the Holy Trinity, who bears in Himself His divine nature. We know from the general doctrine of the Holy Trinity that God is a trihypostatic hypostasis. The Divine Subject has three hypostatic

---

7. I omit here a two-and-a-half-page excursus in which Bulgakov tries to show that the theory he is developing is not a form of Apollinarianism. — Trans.

centers that coexist in Him, not destroying but revealing the autonomous being and uniqueness of the hypostatic Subject. These three centers in the Holy Trinity are equally real and equally subjects, so to speak. Each of them is a separate, equally divine I, but all three are one Divine I in its absoluteness — the consubstantial and indivisible Trinity. No difficulties regarding the unity of the Divine Subject and the trinitarity of the hypostatic centers arise insofar as we concern ourselves with the life of the Holy Trinity in itself (the life of the "immanent" Trinity, in the usual terminology of Western theology). Equilibrium is maintained between them, such that the unity exists in the union of three, and three are identified in one. Triunity is a particular absolute relation existing in the Holy Trinity, its sacred number, simultaneously 3 and 1. This number does not exist in human arithmetic, which is based on the rationalistic differentiation of things that are separate and similar in one way or another and on their placement in series or juxtaposition (i.e., on counting). In this sense, the Divine Three is not even a number, but a supernumber, obtained not through the rationalistic operation of counting but through an intuitive understanding of the absolute relation that the Holy Trinity presents, which is not subject to arithmetical definition.

However, it is not so simple to define the relation of the Holy Trinity to the world (the "economic" Trinity in contrast to the "immanent" Trinity) without introducing a certain differentiation, a new distinction, if not a separation. We know that the personal properties of the separate hypostases and their interrelations determine the character of the participation of each hypostasis in the creation and life of the world: The Father is the creator; the Son is the image of creation; the Holy Spirit is the life of creation, the giver of life. Creation, as becoming, exists in time; and therefore, as we have seen, it also draws God's being into time and, in particular, differentiates the action of the different hypostases not only according to their hypostatic character but also in a definite sequence. The Holy Trinity with its eternal *taxis* (the order of the hypostases) exists supratemporally, and in this sense the *taxis* is the determinate, concrete interrelation between the Father, the Son, and the Holy Spirit. Creation, drawing God's being into temporality, defines the *taxis* in its own way, differentiating the interrelation of the hypostases into a temporal sequence.

In the relation of God to the world there are unitary and collective acts of the entire Holy Trinity, defined by the concrete hypostatic action of all three hypostases: such, for example, is the creation of the world and of man by the Father through the Son in the Holy Spirit. But this is not the case with Divine Providence for the world, which God accomplishes

The Incarnation

not only in a trinitarian manner but also in separate hypostatic acts, by the action of the separate hypostases. In particular, the Logos is the hypostasis that acts and reveals itself in the Old Testament as God. At the beginning He comes into paradise to converse with the original man and woman, and He pronounces His sentence over our fallen progenitors. Over the course of the entire Old Testament He reveals Himself as Jehovah, Adonai, Sabaoth, and so on. He appears to man in various theophanies and doxophanies; and this does not include cases of divine manifestation specially marked by the trinitarian image: Genesis 18; Exodus 6; Daniel 7. Likewise, the Holy Spirit acts and reveals Himself in the Old Testament as the giver of gifts of grace for different ministries (that of kings, elders, high priests, prophets, military leaders, architects, artists, etc.).

In its relation to the world, the "immanent" Trinity thus assumes the aspect of the "economic" Trinity. What is the ontological relation between the two, and how should this distinction be understood? This question is usually not posed in such a general form either in cosmology or in Christology, except in certain particular cases. One must certainly exclude for dogmatic reasons any change in the Holy Trinity caused by the distinction between the immanent Trinity and the economic Trinity and, so to speak, by the transition from the one to the other. The Holy Trinity is one and identical to itself; and this distinction arises from the life of the creature and from its relation to Divinity, precisely to that image in which the creature receives the revelation of Divinity. The creature divides and multiplies this one revelation, which results in different modes of the participation of the separate hypostases in its life. However, it is precisely eternity that is the true foundation for revelation in time. It is necessary to postulate a direct connection between the immanent Trinity and the actions and revelations of the separate hypostases in the economic Trinity. Each hypostasis, as a concretely qualified subject, acts in conformity with its immanent hypostatic properties. Here we are not sundering the Holy Trinity into two; rather, we are distinguishing that which the Holy Trinity itself was pleased to distinguish in itself and thus to divide into two: life in itself and life in and with creation — God as the Absolute and God as the Creator. Ontologically, this distinction or division does not introduce anything new for the Holy Trinity itself, for in its positive content, temporality is adequate to eternity and, in the end, merges with it. In God, "Alpha and Omega," First and Last, beginning and end are identical. But looking out from the world, we receive for the world the revelation of Divinity as a reality that is revealed in time for us and that is *new* at each of its points, a reality that is in a state of becoming, that is being accomplished but has not yet been accomplished. In other words, from the point of view of the world, the world process with its accomplishments is reflected in the "economic" Holy Trinity itself. Eternity is identical to temporality; immobility is identical to becoming; the economic Trinity is identical to the immanent Trinity.

This general relation of God to the world in the economic Trinity is accompanied by the fact that the individual hypostases are separated out from this Trinity's unity and manifest their hypostatic action upon the world. In their being, the hypostases abide unchangeably in the bosom of the eternal interrelation of trinitarian, intrahypostatic love. But in their *action* in the world, they are, as it were, distinguished and isolated from each other; for these actions, differing in virtue of the properties of the individual hypostases, are manifested and differentiated for the world in its cosmic time and are incorporated in the history of the world. There is of course no trace of tritheism here; there is, however, undoubtedly not only a triune but also a trinitarian, separately hypostatic revelation of God to the world. In relation to the world, not only are the divine hypostases effectively united in *we* or *us* ("Let us make man in our image" [Gen. 1:26]), but they are also separated, as it were, so that that which the Father accomplishes is accomplished neither by the Son nor by the Holy Spirit, and *each* hypostasis has its particular mode of action in the world. The economic Trinity thus not only consists of "separate persons" but is also characterized by separate actions.

Based on these general considerations, it is possible to resolve a particular question of Christology, namely: In what manner could *one* of the hypostases of the Holy Trinity become incarnate and thus be separated, as it were, out of its triunity? Does this not introduce, in a hidden form, a real separation of the hypostases, a tritheism, a polytheism? And if it does not, how can the incarnation of only one of the hypostases be possible without the co-incarnation of the other two hypostases, with which the first is united without separation? This leads to further questions: How does the trinitarian divine life take place when one of the hypostases is absent from heaven (because it has "come down from heaven") and is made incarnate on earth? How is the participation of this hypostasis in the one consubstantial life of the Holy Trinity possible after it has left the unity of the latter? Furthermore, how is the Ascension to heaven of the Second hypostasis, which in contrast to the other hypostases bears human flesh, possible? And so on.

All these questions can be answered on the basis of the general principle of the interrelation of God and the world. As the Creator and Providence, God is revealed to the world, on the one hand, as consubstantial and indivisible and as manifesting His "properties" in the world; on the other hand, He is revealed as three divine hypostases, each of which reveals itself and acts in the world in its own manner. The Incarnation is the particular mode of relation to and action in the world that is proper precisely to the Second hypostasis. The ways of His general relation to the world include the Incarnation, and this Incarnation precisely of the Second hypostasis has its foundation in the pre-eternal sonhood of the Word. The Incarnation cannot be understood in the sense that, decided in the Divine counsel, it could be the work of any other hypostasis except the Second, since it follows precisely from the personal property of this hypostasis, sonhood, both in relation to the world and in relation to God. Imprinted in the world is the Face of the Logos, who in the fullness of time descends from heaven to earth in order to be "in-humanized" in it.[8]

However, the indivisibility of the Holy Trinity in the work of the Incarnation is manifested in the fact that it is accomplished with the participation of the entire Holy Trinity and of each of its Persons, in conformity with the personal property of each: The Father sends, and He sends not only the Son but also the Holy Spirit, who descends into the world upon the Virgin Mary, upon Jesus, and upon the apostles; the Son is made incarnate; and the Holy Spirit completes the work of the Incarnation. This does not diminish the personal Incarnation of the Logos, but His work on earth cannot be separated to any degree from the life of the entire Holy Trinity. Christianity is the religion of Christ, the incarnate God, the Second Person of the Holy Trinity; but precisely in virtue of this it is also the faith in the Holy Trinity, consubstantial and indivisible.

IV. Two Natures in Christ: The Divine Sophia and the Creaturely Sophia

The Incarnation is not only the assumption of man's nature by the hypostasis of the Logos, which thus becomes also a human hypostasis. It is also the union of two natures: of the divine nature, which is inseparable from the hypostasis of the Logos, with the creaturely human nature. How should this union be understood ontologically? We already know from the

---

8. It is not an accident that the two annunciations concerning the Logos, as cosmourgic and incarnate hypostasis, are placed next to each other in the prologue to the Gospel of John (1:3 and 1:14).

history of dogma that this union must not be viewed as the identification of the two natures or as the abolition of the difference between them; that is, it should not be understood monophysitically. The divine nature does not dissolve or abolish the human nature, for that would abolish their very union in their difference. Nor, of course, can the human nature abolish the divine nature. If the first notion was a great temptation not only for militant monophysites but in fact also for the orthodox (it is sufficient to remember the constantly fluctuating position of St. Cyril and his followers), the second notion could not have any adherents because of its evident absurdity, or it led beyond the bounds of Christianity, as in the case of the Ebionites, ancient and modern. At the same time, this union does not tolerate the kind of diminution that occurs in all types of Nestorianism (or adoptionism), where the union is effectively supplanted by the coexistence or juxtaposition of the two different natures. Finally, the union of the two natures should also not be understood as their *mixing*, as a kind of chemical synthesis resulting in a certain new nature that is neither divine nor human.[9] That, in a stylized form, would be "Apollinarianism."

The dogmatic efforts of the epoch of the ecumenical councils were in fact directed at preserving the equilibrium in the relation of the two natures, by suppressing deviations that would favor one or the other, or even their separation. Divine wisdom, guiding these efforts, maintained this equilibrium, and it was precisely the principle of the equilibrium of the two natures in their distinctive character and autonomy that the Council of Chalcedon proclaimed as a fundamental dogmatic definition. This principle of *equilibrium* is expressed, naturally, only in negative definitions, which prevent deviations in either direction: without separation, without confusion, without change, without division. Negative definitions are fully adequate for this goal. But it is just as natural to feel a certain dissatisfaction with these negative definitions, which, as we know from logic, cannot yield positive knowledge (the so-called infinite judgment in logic). To be sure, historical commentary renders instructive not only the negative meaning but also the concrete, positive meaning of this definition, since the negations eliminate here a certain type of christological judgment, which receives a negative assessment. But since these negations go in opposite directions, it is logically impossible, and dog-

---

9. In modern theology, we find a curious variant of this doctrine in Dorner, who conceives the Incarnation as a process of the temporal interpermeation of two independent natures. This process results in the appearance, in and from them, of the divine-human personality, uniting the two of them.

The Incarnation

matically difficult, to extract a *positive* definition from these opposite negations. These oppositely directed negations do not, however, constitute a logical contradiction, which would exclude their compatibility and reduce the judgment itself to the absurd. The oppositely directed negations in the Definition of Chalcedon involve not so much contradictory judgments (such as yes and no) as *different* judgments, although they go in opposite directions. They admit some middle or third — *synthetic* — judgment, although this judgment is *not expressed* in the definition. In fact, the expression "without separation and without confusion" eliminates both *total* separation and *total* fusion. But this expression still leaves a place both for differentiation of being (otherwise there could be no union) and for union, which is directly proclaimed in the dogma.

Thus, after having extracted the positive content from the negative definitions given in the Chalcedonian dogma, we arrive at the following conclusion: The *total* fusion of the natures being excluded, their *union* is proclaimed; that is, a certain *form* of fusion or identification is affirmed, but with the differences entirely preserved. And *total* separation being excluded, a certain *form* of differentiation is preserved, although with essential inseparability. In other words, what is sought and proclaimed here is a certain form of union in the case of inconfusability and a certain form of distinction in the case of inseparability; this form of union and this form of distinction do not produce a disequilibrium in one direction or the other.

The dogma is silent, however, on the *positive* interrelation of the two natures. What does this silence mean? Should it be dogmatically interpreted as a way of refusing to understand, of prohibiting definition? Or should it be understood only historically, as a de facto absence of definition? We have no doubt that only the second hypothesis provides the right answer. First of all, this second hypothesis is supported by the history of the Council, as well as by the entire set of circumstances in which this definition was worked out. We can even find among these circumstances an element of historical chance; for although the Spirit of God acts without regard to the chain of contingent causes, it is still necessary to take these into account. Second, the *unfinished* definition of the Fourth Council was effectively continued and completed by the definition of the Sixth Ecumenical Council concerning the two wills and energies, from which it follows that this question was by no means dogmatically resolved. Third, and most importantly, this question was subsequently subjected to continual dogmatic examination; in essence it was the only question being examined. Thus, the negative formula of the Council of

Chalcedon cannot be understood as a *prohibition* against positive definitions; it can be understood only as a *preliminary* definition, incomplete, inexhaustive, awaiting continuation. The apophatic position, which excludes the problem of the positive relation between the two natures, is therefore unfounded here.

In the dogma of the Incarnation we truly encounter something that is inaccessible to the creaturely understanding, but we must first explore everything that *is* accessible to us. Thus, the dogmatic question of the *positive* interrelation of the two natures in Christ is posed before us. Christ did not assume the human nature by an arbitrary act of abstract omnipotence, by an act that did not take into account the nature of things. He assumed it in conformity with the nature of things, for precisely the human nature was *appropriate* for this assumption, was ontologically capable of receiving it. Again, the Logos became the hypostasis for this nature not in virtue of abstract omnipotence but because precisely the human nature was called to be hypostatized by the hypostasis of the Logos. He could become a human hypostasis because it was the calling and predestination of the human nature to be united with the Logos. From the beginning, the Logos finds Himself in a positive relation with the human nature, just as, in its depths, the human nature bears His image and awaits His coming into the world. Therefore, the fact that "the Logos was made flesh" (i.e., the fact that He had assumed the human nature) was not, so to speak, something ontologically unexpected but, on the contrary, was the fulfillment of the predestination inscribed in heaven and on earth. But in becoming a human hypostasis, the Logos not only hypostatically united the human nature with Himself but also united it with Himself naturally, bringing into this union His proper divine life, or divine nature. Uniting His proper nature with the human essence, the Logos, as Christ, includes both of these natures in His life. Therefore, not only should one understand these two natures in their inseparability, inconfusability, and unchangeability (i.e., in their *autonomous being*), but one should just as forcefully affirm their union, which is accomplished no less than in the *unity of the life* of the God-Man, in virtue of the unity of the hypostatic center of this life. Christ is one; being in two natures, He lives one life, which attests to the very possibility of their union. The two natures, which are included in the one life of one hypostasis without dividing the personality, must in some way be kindred to one another, must be capable of this living identification. In the two natures, Divine and human, uncreated and created, there must be something mediating or common that serves as the unalterable foundation for their union.

The Incarnation

This common principle is the *sophianicity* of both the Divine world (i.e., of Christ's divine nature) and of the creaturely world (i.e., of His human nature). The creaturely world is created on the basis of the proto-images of the Divine world as the creaturely image of Divine Sophia in her becoming, but this Divine Sophia is the divine nature of the Logos. Thus, in their *foundation* and *content,* the Heavenly Sophia and the earthly, creaturely, and human Sophia are identified, differing only in the *mode* of their being: that which in heaven is the Majesty, Glory, Wisdom, and Beauty of the images of the Divine self-revelation finds itself in a state of *becoming* or process in the creaturely world, on earth, and it finds itself there in the capacity of eternal seeds of creaturely being submerged in nonbeing and sprouting on the basis of creaturely freedom. The Logos pre-eternally reveals the Father as the Word of all words, that is, of all the divine ideas and images in their all-unity; by the will of the Father He decrees that this All should have *creaturely* being: "All things were made by him; and without him was not any thing made that was made" (John 1:3). In other words, He repeats in a creaturely manner, as it were, that which is His own. The *relation of identity* between the Divine Sophia and the creaturely Sophia is for this reason just as natural and inevitable as the entire *difference* between eternal, uncreated being and creaturely, becoming being, which has not yet become itself but which will become itself, in order to then become identified with its Proto-Image and attain the fullness of its sophianization or deification. This makes it possible to understand how the Logos could assume the human essence without ontologically contradicting His own essence. The obstacle here would be not the incompatibility of the natures but only the difference between the two modes of natural being. Having the Divine Sophia as His nature, the Logos enters, through the Incarnation, into the process of her creaturely becoming and is thus diminished in the fullness of His proper being.

In essence, the Incarnation, considered as the condescension of God's eternity to becoming in time, is identical to God's creation of the world as Divinity's going out of itself into the extradivine domain of creaturely becoming. The only difference is that, in the creation of the world, the world remains outside of God, solely as the *object* of His salvific action, whereas, in the Incarnation, God receives creaturely becoming into His own life and thus becomes the *Subject* of this becoming, while preserving the eternal fullness of His proper natural-sophianic essence. That is what the dogma of the two natures with one hypostasis signifies. The eternal God becomes the becoming God and receives the becoming of the world into Himself and for Himself, into His proper life; He first of all introduces times and seasons into His life. The Logos becomes Jesus, who is born, lives, and dies in a particular place and at a particular time.

    This antithesis of eternity and time, of fullness of being and becoming, is the limiting concept with which human thought collides when it attempts to fathom the mystery of the Incarnation. The Incarnation truly does remain a mystery for the human understanding, insofar as, in it, the unchangeability of eternity inaccessible to man is united with temporal becoming, which is the only thing man knows. It is a mystery because, in itself, such a union surpasses the proper *measure* of man and thus remains ontologically transcendent for him. This mystery is also a source of revelation for him, however, insofar as it is directed toward man himself and his life. For man too, in the deepest depths of his temporality, under the veil of becoming, knows and touches eternity. Thus, having his homeland in heaven and not only on earth, man carries within himself the image of the two natures and manifests the noncreaturely Sophia in his creaturely essence. Such is the very foundation of his being, which is revealed even to natural man in mystical and philosophical contemplation (to which prophetic God-seeing mystics and philosophers of all epochs attest). But the authentic revelation concerning the compatibility of eternity and becoming, of the divine and the creaturely in man, is given by the Church. This life in Christ — where "not I, but Christ liveth in me" (Gal. 2:20); this gracious illumination by the Spirit, from which man is born spiritually; and generally, this *deification*, already begun in the militant Church — gives man the experience of his two united natures, of this union of divine eternity and creaturely becoming. But an immeasurable difference certainly exists between creaturely man, who knows the divine principle only as a gift and a task to be accomplished, and the God-Man, who has this divine life as His proper nature and human becoming as the work of salvific love and self-humiliation. That which in man is always an ascent is, in the God-Man, only a divine condescension. The union of the two natures in Christ is therefore not only an abstract dogmatic schema but also a truth of life that we receive on the pathways of our religious experience.

    Understood in this way, the dogma of the duality of the natures in Christ in the case of their unity of life in the one hypostasis of the Logos is also revealed to us by the four negative definitions. Their general meaning consists in establishing the inseparability and inconfusability of the two natures as uncreated principle and created principle. They are *inseparable* in the unity of Christ's life, for they do not differ but are identical in their content as noumenon and phenomenon, as foundation and consequence, as the principle and the revelation of the principle. This in-

The Incarnation

separability is not an external and arbitrary given — it is the immanent, inwardly motivated norm of the interrelation of the Divine Sophia and the creaturely Sophia, who are united in the unity of the life of the incarnate Logos. But the norm of *inconfusability* is no less immanent or inwardly motivated, for how can time and eternity, unchangeability and becoming, be confused (i.e, mixed or mechanically combined)? They therefore have their norm of interrelation, which permits neither their conjunction in the same ontological plane nor their mixing or alternation. An additional notion is implied by the four negative definitions: the unchangeability of the natures. This is only another way to express their inconfusability, for illegitimate fusion can change the natures. Unchangeability is already implied by inconfusability, and the union of the two natures, in virtue of which the Logos became Christ, is neither their change nor their confusion.

But at the same time it is impossible not to see that the two united natures do not possess an equal dignity, for one of them is uncreated, whereas the other is created, and this difference is reflected in the character of their interrelation. Although they are inseparable, they are not equal. The primacy of the divine nature is also manifested in the fact that the hypostasis of the Logos belongs precisely to it. The dogma of the Sixth Ecumenical Council concerning the two wills underscores this inequality of the natures by noting that human will, despite its autonomy, "follows" the divine will.

The assumption by the Logos of the human nature is associated with human nature's sophianicity. This sophianicity is precisely that *tertium comparationis* in which the image and the Proto-Image are identified with each other. However, we know that the human nature's sophianicity, which is ontologically indestructible, was damaged in its being by the power of original sin; and the world, sophianic in its foundation, became asophianic and even partly antisophianic in the mode of its being. Thus, can the "fallen Sophia," which is the human nature in the state of sin, be received into the hypostasis of the Logos? Is she worthy of being united with the divine nature, which possesses sophianic fullness and purity? Has the "fallen Sophia" not lost her dignity and the possibilities associated with it?

The preparation of the human race for the reception of the Incarnation was accomplished in the Old Testament church by God's providential government. This preparation was crowned by the appearance of the New Eve, the Most Pure Virgin Mary, in whom original sin was rendered impotent. The Most Pure Virgin was worthy of becoming the receptacle of the Holy Spirit and the Mother of the Lord. This fact should also be understood from the point of view of the sophiological doctrine of the two natures in Christ. The Virgin Mary was the adequate and worthy instrument of the Incarnation because the maximal sophianization of the human nature was realized in Her by the Holy Spirit's descent upon Her at the Annunciation and at Pentecost; then, after Her death, this sophianization was manifested by Her resurrection and Her assumption to heaven. She was thus placed above Adam and Eve in their condition *before* the Fall, for She overcame the temptation of disobedience that they had not overcome: "Behold the handmaid of the Lord" (Luke 1:38). As the Mother of the Lord, She fully manifested in Herself the image of the creaturely Sophia. Mary is precisely that human nature that was worthy of being united with the divine nature of the Logos through the reception of His hypostasis. In this sense, She is truly the Theotokos. Christ could receive the human nature only through birth. But the human nature does not exist extrahypostatically. Therefore, the New Adam could come into the world only through the New Eve.

The incomprehensible blindness and insensitivity that Protestantism manifests with regard to the Most Holy Mother of God prevent it from seeing this personal participation of the Virgin Mary in the Incarnation. Protestantism sees here only a natural act of birth without any everlasting significance and without any everlasting consequences either for the Mother or for the One born of Her. Protestantism does not understand that Mariology must necessarily be included in Christology as an inseparable part of it, for Christ, as the Son of Man, is the Son of Mary. Mary is His hypostatic humanity, the "second" nature that He assumed in the Incarnation. In this sense, the Incarnation is not only a binatural union in one hypostasis but also a bihypostatic union in one nature. Christ did not bring His human nature down from heaven, and He did not create it anew from the earth; rather, He took it from "the most pure flesh and blood of the Virgin Mary." And this "taking" is not an external and mechanical borrowing or coercion on the part of the Divine omnipotence; instead, it is a mutually hypostatic act: The Logos could *take* His flesh from the Virgin Mary only because She *gave* it, desiring to become the creaturely Sophia, the sophianic Mother of Christ's humanity, which must possess the fullness of sophianicity. That which was lacking for this even in the Virgin Mary's humanity (because She too was burdened by the weight of original sin) was provided by the Holy Spirit, who descended upon Her at the Annunciation. On the one hand, this descent of the Holy Spirit depended on Her spiritual openness to Him, on Her sophianic ma-

The Incarnation

turity, so to speak; on the other hand, His descent crowned Her sophianicity, so that the ontological postulate became a reality.

Taken in all its breadth and power, the Incarnation cannot be reduced solely to the birth of Christ, the incarnate Logos. It must also necessarily include the descent of the Holy Spirit upon the Virgin Mary. We see the full image of the Incarnation only in this bi-unity: the inhumanized Christ and Mary, His hypostatic humanity, the Virgin Mother of God, overshadowed by the Holy Spirit. The human nature assumed by the Logos exists not only *in* Him but also *outside* of Him, as Mary's hypostatic humanity. (His divine nature, on the contrary, does exist only in Him.) His human nature must somehow become fused or identified with this *hypostatic* humanity; otherwise, it will not be our true humanity. The creaturely Sophia, in the capacity of Christ's human nature, is destined to be hypostatized not only in the Logos, elevated to participation in the Divine life; she is also hypostatized into her proper and therefore creaturely hypostasis. Therefore, the two natures in the one hypostasis of Christ correspond to the two hypostases that hypostatize His human nature: alongside the hypostasis of the Logos, there is the proper, creaturely hypostasis of the creaturely Sophia, the Virgin Mary. The Mother of God therefore participates in the Incarnation not only by Her flesh, which would be a natural, instinctive, unfree, uncreative, and even blind act (which is Protestantism's de facto opinion concerning this act). She also participates in it by Her hypostasis; that is, She participates in it spiritually, consciously, in an inspired and sacrificial manner. This was a new birth from the Woman — independent of the flesh of the male because it was due to a virginal conception — that conformed with the original, divinely established norm of spiritual conception and birth for the virginal couple Adam and Eve *before* the Fall. Sophianic humanity in the person of the Virgin Mary gave to the Logos His human nature, and this birth was Her personal, spiritual-corporeal work. She received the strength for this work from the Holy Spirit, who pre-eternally reposes upon the Logos and who, in the temporal birth of the Logos, overshadowed the Mother of God and brought the Logos to Her.

The divine birth is therefore the spiritual meeting of the hypostatic creaturely Sophia with the Logos, and in this meeting the hypostatic creaturely Sophia manifests herself as the Soul of the world, the Queen of all creation, of heaven and earth. This dignity is not only the *recompense* given to Her for Her services; it is also the revelation of what is immanently contained in the virginal conception of the Son overshadowed by the Holy Spirit. What does it matter if the whole meaning of what was ac-

The Lamb of God

complished did not become immediately clear to the Virgin Mary, since, as the creaturely Sophia, She too was subject to temporality and becoming? It does not matter, because that which was contained in the divine birth was already manifested in the glorification of the Most Holy Mother of God. In the capacity of the One who *gave* to the Logos His human essence, the Virgin Mary is His Most Pure Mother, the Blessed Theotokos. In the capacity of the One who *received* Him into the perfect unity of life by the self-renouncing love of the "handmaid of the Lord," She is the Bride of the Logos or His Wife, who has made Herself ready for marriage (Rev. 19:7; 21:9). In the capacity of the bearer of the creaturely human essence in its intact state, restored by the Holy Spirit, She is the personification of the Church. She is also the Queen of Heaven, who cannot remain on earth after the ascension of Her Son to heaven, and She too is raised to heaven by Her Son.[10]

Thus — and this is the most important thing — the Incarnation of Christ is realized not in one Person but in two: in Christ and in the Virgin Mary. The icon of the Mother of God with Infant is therefore the true icon of the Incarnation (and thus of the Divine-Humanity). This duality corresponds not only to the duality of the natures of Christ in their union but also to the duality of the hypostases of these natures in their separateness; and the human nature, being in-hypostatized in the Logos, must have its fullness and autonomous being prerealized in its proper hypostasis, the Virgin Mary. Thus, Christ has His humanity in a double manner: in Himself, included in His proper hypostasis, and outside of Himself, hypostatized in the female hypostasis of Mary (for His humanity is not only flesh in the physical sense; it is also a *living* humanity in the totality of its spiritual-psychical-corporeal being). Connected with this is the revelation concerning the participation in the Incarnation not only of the Second hypostasis, the one made incarnate, but also of the Third hypostasis, the one that makes incarnate: The image of the Logos is the male Infant, maturing into the image of the perfect Male, whereas the image of the Spirit-bearer is the Virgin-Mother, who bears in Herself the One who is born of Her. This part of the dogma was not *directly* stated in the Definition of Chalcedon, which did not by any means pretend to be exhaustive, but it is precontained in the glorification of the "Theotokos" at the Third Ecumenical Council, as well as in the Church's entire veneration of the Mother of God, which veneration has not been adequately explored and clarified in its dogmatics.

---

10. Concerning all of this, see my book *The Burning Bush*.

The Incarnation

Christ — the incarnate Logos, who has His divine nature, Sophia, and who Himself reveals her ideal content — manifests the hypostatic image of the Heavenly Sophia in His earthly Incarnation. In this sense the Apostle calls Him "the power of God, and the wisdom of God" (1 Cor. 1:24). But precisely as the hypostatic Sophia, He unites in the unity of His two natures the Divine Sophia, as His Divinity, and the creaturely Sophia, as His humanity. For this reason He can be called the Wisdom of God in a double capacity: as the hypostasis of the Heavenly Sophia and of the creaturely Sophia. But the creaturely Sophia, whom He hypostatizes in His humanity, is also hypostatized in her autonomous being; this creaturely hypostasis of the creaturely Sophia is the Virgin Mary. Therefore, it is in no wise a contradiction to call both Christ and the Mother of God Sophia, although they are called Sophia in different senses. But in the Mother of God, as the Spirit-bearer, we venerate also the hypostatic revelation of the Holy Spirit (although not His incarnation). Thus, by confessing that the Mother of God is the creaturely Sophia, we attest that also the Holy Spirit — together with the Son, although differently from Him — is the hypostatic Wisdom of God.

In connection with the question of the Mother of God as the bearer of creaturely sophianicity, one can also resolve the controversial question of the Lord's *human individuality*. In entering into the world with its temporality and spatiality and in assuming the human essence, which is subject to history, the Lord also assumed an *empirical* form, became a historical individual. He was born in a particular place and at a particular time from particular parents; He belonged to a particular nation with its culture and spoke a particular language, and so on. In other words, He was a historical individual, and with respect to all empirical definition, the following principle is applicable: *omnis definitio est negatio* (all definition is negation [i.e., limitation]). He was not a Greek, Roman, or Slav, for example; and if He spoke Aramaic, this means that He did not speak other languages (perhaps not even Greek, in which language His words have come down to us). But this empirical individuality is only, so to speak, a mask of history or a formal empirical passport without which it is impossible to enter the empirical world.

In reality, Christ's individuality does not know any *ontological* limits. He was not a mere man, as one of a multitude of people. He was Man in the sense of Universal Man, and His personality contained all human forms; it was the All-Personality. There was nothing local, limited, or particular in Him. His empirical envelope was perfectly transparent and imperceptible. He was *equally* close and accessible to anyone who scrutinized

Him closely. In Jesus Christ there is truly neither Greek nor Scythian, neither slave nor free man, even neither man nor woman, since for each and for all He is the image that speaks directly to mind and heart, that penetrates into the hidden places. This is the basis of the universality of the Gospel, of its supreme all-humanity. In the person of Christ all people who come to Him will see themselves as they should be, as God desires them to be; and there is no one who will be nearer to us than He if only in our life we *meet* Christ, who is the *Neighbor* for every man. The testimony of religious experience affirms that, in Christ, we truly see the "perfect" man *(Ecce Homo)*, with the fullness of humanity and without any individual limitations. It affirms that nothing human except sin is alien to Him, and therefore no man whose authentic being is contained in His humanity is alien to Him. Dogmatically, this can be expressed as follows: Christ assumed the entire human nature without any limitation. Developing this idea further, one must say that in assuming the human nature, Christ also assumed all of cosmic being, insofar as man is the microcosm. Christ was the new, "last Adam" (1 Cor. 15:45). Although before the Fall our progenitor was a particular person, a concrete I, nevertheless he bore within himself the fullness of humanity: he was the universal man, and the entire human race with all its possible persons effectively lived in him. In this sense, even though he was a person, Adam did not have individuality in the negative, limiting sense of the word, in the sense of being a product of disintegrated all-unity, which has become the bad multiplicity of egocentrism. Our fallen humanity knows the personality as individuality, which we are proud of as the only form of personality accessible to us. But this was not the case at the beginning, when man was in his sophianic condition. Persons must be transparent for one another: all in all and everyone in all. That is the ontology of personality. With the Fall the image of all-humanity was obscured in Adam; he became an individual who could beget only individuals. And the firstborn of Adam was Cain, in whom egocentrism was manifested with maximal force, to the point of fratricide. Cain was the first individualist, with his descendants, the Cainites. Such an individuality is associated with the Fall, with humanity's loss of the sophianic image. But this image of sophianic humanity is realized in the New Adam; bad individuality is overcome in Him ("I came down from heaven, not to do mine own will, but the will of him [the Father] that sent me" [John 6:38]; "if any man will come after me, let him deny himself" [Matt. 16:24] — such are the principles of the new life in Christ).

    Empirically, Christ is one of many in historical mankind, but in reality He contains all of historical mankind in His humanity. That which is revealed in history in chronological succession is conjoined in Him in metaphysical unity: All humanity without any exception is contained in Him — the humanity of the past, of the present, and of the future. All of human nature is metaphysically integrated in His nature, and all the human persons called to being find themselves in their authenticity in the person of Christ. This metaphysical fact, this ontological relation, remains transcendent for the sinful, fragmented state of man; it is only a religious postulate. Nevertheless, this metaempirical fact is realized for us even in empirical reality, and this postulate is nothing other than the Church, the body of Christ, in which "Christ is all, and in all" (Col. 3:11).

In order to redeem the entire human essence and to transform the entire human race, the Lord had to assume human flesh. This flesh was Adam's, but He took it not from the fallen Adam but in another manner: "in the likeness [*homoiōmati*] of men" (Phil. 2:7). Christ did not assume the human essence in the manner that every man has it; His assumption of the human essence was not limited, truncated, or egocentric — in a word, it was not *individual* or atomistic. He assumed it in the manner in which it was possessed by the original Adam, who came out of the hands of the Lord. That is, He assumed it *integrally*, and this nature, this "flesh," was given to Christ by His Most Pure Mother. The negative condition for this was the absence of human conception "in sin," that is, conception without a father. Original sin is transmitted precisely through human conception, and with it are transmitted bad multiplicity, egocentrism, and limitation. The absence of natural conception was compensated for by the Holy Spirit, who inspired the Virgin Mary to spiritual conception, which consisted in the fact that self-renouncing love for the One who was to be born flamed up in the One who was giving birth. This love for the Son led to a total commonality of life, and even of corporeal life (i.e., conception without seed). However, a positive condition was necessary for this: The proper nature of the Most Holy Theotokos with Her personal and generic holiness was restored in its sophianicity and purified and integrated to a such a degree that the descent upon Her of the Holy Spirit could occur, communicating perfect sophianicity to Her. When the Most Holy Virgin Mary gave birth to the Lord, She bore within Herself the image of Sophia; She was the personification of the creaturely Sophia. The fruit of Her birth-giving was thus the sophianic man, the New Adam, who was distinguished from all men by the *form* of His humanity. This was true humanity, identical with the humanity of each of us (which is why we are Christ's "brethren" [Heb. 2:12]), but it differs from our humanity by the fact that it excludes no one and includes everyone, by the fact that it is not limited by anything but bears the image of chaste and wise Integrity. And it was the Virgin Mary who gave this to Her Son.

Protestant Christology allows that, in His human essence, Christ necessarily includes the whole Adam. Otherwise, the redemption of the whole human race would be totally incomprehensible: the individual man — the partial man, so to speak — cannot have such a significance. But because of its insensitivity to the Mother of God, Protestant Christology cannot understand *how* Christ could have assumed all of humanity. It has to attribute this to a miraculous coercion over man's nature, to a *deus ex machina*, but such a hypothesis inevitably leads to docetism: Christ assumed an essence that was different from the human essence, and as a result He was not a true man and therefore could not be the Redeemer. Catholic theology, in its 1854 dogma of the immaculate conception, introduces this element of divine coercion over the human nature into the very origin of the Virgin Mary, who is thus extracted from the human race. This shakes the whole edifice of the Incarnation. However, the universal veneration of the Mother of God in Catholicism is better testimony to Her significance in the work of our salvation than this unsuccessful dogma.[11] The Orthodox veneration of the Mother of God as the Queen of Heaven and the creaturely Sophia contains sufficient grounds for a dogmatic understanding of the idea that humanity as a whole could be assumed only from the One in whom it was restored in its sophianic image. However, Orthodox theology has yet to dogmatically clarify the treasure of revelation about the Mother of God that is contained in the Church's veneration of Her; this is partly because of antagonism to sophiology and partly because of tendentiousness in the polemic against Catholic one-sidedness. And so, we still await dogmatic clarification of the significance of the Mother of God as the creaturely Sophia, who in the capacity of Sophia was thus able to give the sophianic image of integral humanity to the One born of Her. Thus, the objective interrelation of the two natures in Christ and the foundation of their union consist in their *sophianicity*: the Divine Sophia is united with the creaturely Sophia, the Eternal Sophia with the becoming Sophia, the Proto-Image with the image.

Such is the *yes* implied by the four *no's* of the Chalcedonian dogma.

---

11. She is sometimes even called the co-redemptrix. This is an imprecise and ambiguous expression, although it could mean that the Most Holy Mother of God participates directly and positively in the Incarnation in the capacity of the reception of the integral Adam.

The Incarnation

There remains a final question about the two natures in Christ: the question of their union. The Chalcedonian dogma limits itself to establishing the fact of the presence of two natures in Christ in one person, but it does not touch upon the mode of their union. This question remains the subject of theological investigation. One must first summarize what had been done and — more importantly — what had not been done with regard to this question in the patristic period. Although it is customary to consider (or at least to give the impression) that all the christological questions have, in substance, been decided, this is in fact far from the truth, especially with regard to the most central point: the Gospel figure of Jesus Christ in the light of the dogmatic definitions established by the Church. It is still necessary to compare and to harmonize, so to speak, the christological dogmas and the Gospels with the aim of elucidating the biblical meaning of the dogmas. We find ourselves here in virtually unexplored territory, and the situation is made more acute by the fact that the "Bibleism" on which the modern Christian consciousness has been nurtured (an unparalleled investigation of biblical texts having been conducted in the modern period with all its exegetical capacities) makes us particularly sensitive to any lack of harmony and to any obscurity in this regard.

The Chalcedonian dogma does not touch upon the mode of the union of the two natures, but from this dogma there indisputably follows the fact of the *unity of the life* of Christ in two natures, but with one hypostasis living in both of them. How should one understand this composite life in relation to the participation of the two natures? In and of itself, this duality of the natures of one life presents unprecedented difficulties for thought, since the life of the natural world does not know such a duality. But the main difficulty here is that these two natures belong to different domains of being: divine and creaturely. How can they be harmonized? How can they act together and interact? How can the fire of Divinity engulf, without consuming, the "burning bush" of creaturely being, and how can this creaturely being ascend to a condition where it is harmonized with the life of the divine nature? Do we not have an incompatibility here that makes this very inquiry illusory, an exercise in myth-making similar to the numerous pagan myths concerning the descent of gods to earth and their union with mortals?

After the dogma of the two natures in one hypostasis was established, the center of gravity of Christology, the core of its problematic, was found precisely here, in the problem of divine-human life as it is revealed to us in the Gospels. We already know from the history of dogma what attempts were made to treat this problem of the mode of the union of the two natures. The first attempt that merits attention is, of course, Apollinarianism. Apollinarius resolved this question by effectively depriving the human essence of hypostasis. *Formally,* he did not do this to a greater degree than Alexandrianism and Chalcedonianism, insofar as he effectively understood the hypostasis of the Logos as a human hypostasis. However, the intention of his Christology was not to manifest the hypostasis of the Logos *also* as a human hypostasis, but to abolish with this hypostasis the human hypostasis and thus to diminish the fullness of Christ's humanity, so that one would no longer be able to recognize the presence of the "perfect man" in it.

Apollinarius's doctrine is the nodal point, as it were, from which the paths diverge in different directions: in the direction of Alexandrianism and various nuances of monophysitism and in the direction of the Chalcedonian theology (only not in the direction of Antiochianism). Alexandrian theology with St. Cyril at its head was full of a sincere striving to demonstrate the truth of the Incarnation as the authentic union of Divinity with authentic (not imaginary or docetic) humanity. In practical terms, however, the dogmatic equilibrium could be maintained here only by means of inconsistency or logical irresponsibility. Cyrillian theology was characterized by a tendency to monophysitism, which St. Cyril resisted but which, after him, became a type of Eutychianism that dissolved the humanity in the Divinity and understood the relation of the two natures in terms of a fire consuming brushwood.

The second approach to resolving the problem of the two natures of Christ can be found in the school of Antioch. It sought the solution to the problem of the bi-unity in an original duality — not only of the natures, but also of the hypostases, which, via moral union, harmony in love, form a new hypostasis: the hypostasis of union. This last idea constitutes, without doubt, the weak side of Antiochianism, attesting to a meager conception of personality.

According to the Antiochene conception, the christological problem involves the unification of two subjects that have not only different hypostases but also different natures, whereas in the doctrine of the Holy Trinity, as well as in the doctrine of the Church, we have a multihypostatic unification in the case of the unity and identity of nature and life, although the nature is hypostatized not by one but by many hypostases. This difference has a decisive significance, and it shows the Antiochene schema's inadequacy for understanding the union of the two natures in Christ. The union of different subjects with different natures, in particular the relation of man to God, is accomplished on the basis of a mutual

The Incarnation

penetration of the natures, or more precisely on the basis of the entering of one nature into the other (which is what we have in the *deification* of man), but with the absolute difference between the hypostases preserved. In relation to God, man does not in any sense lose his personal I; it is not extinguished in the light of God or drowned in His abyss. Even when there is perfect deification, man's relation to God is that of person to Person, of I to Thou. Nor does churchly love, uniting many hypostases in multi-unity, abolish personality; rather, it reveals it.

The Definition of Chalcedon gave a dogmatic schema, but it did not provide anything toward a dogmatic interpretation of this schema. It left such an interpretation for subsequent theology.[12] But the patristic thought of the epoch did little to clarify the Chalcedonian dogma of the two natures; specifically, it failed to elucidate the *mode* of the union of the natures in relation to one hypostasis. The patristic thought went in different directions and attempted to use different means to resolve the question. But failing to achieve any palpable success, it finally reached a point of exhaustion and even abandoned the domain of Christology.

On this subject, however, a highly significant word was pronounced that was capable of becoming the true banner of a future Christology. This was literally only a single word in a letter from Pseudo-Dionysius to Gaius: "theandric energy." "Theandric" means "divine-human," and so the word *divine-humanity* was pronounced as a certain key to the mystery. And this word, which expresses the initial concept of modern Christology (and which was already contained in a concealed manner in Apollinarius's doctrine), was heard at once. St. John of Damascus received it as an indisputable and self-evident doctrine (although it expresses only the beginning of the christological problematic), and he devoted a paragraph to it in book 3 of his *Critical Exposition of the Orthodox Faith*, where we find an extended commentary on this term. Through John of Damascus, the idea of "divine-human action" was received as a kind of *dogmatic testament* of the entire patristic epoch, but to this day it remains a capital that is yet to be exploited.

The idea did find partial application, however, in the doctrine of *metadosis tōn idiōmatōn* (*communicatio idiomatum*, or communication of properties). John of Damascus also devotes particular attention to this doctrine. He interprets the communication of properties, first of all, as

---

12. Alexander Bruce calls the image of Christ prevalent in this epoch "an anatomic figure in place of the Christ of the Gospel history." (See Bruce, *The Humiliation of Christ*, p. 66.)

the influence of the divine essence on the human essence as the result of the union of two unequal natures: the human nature receives certain properties of the divine essence, which is called deification *(theōsis).*

The general theme of deification can be treated from the christological or from the pneumatological point of view. John treats it only from the christological (and of course indisputable) point of view, in relation to the perfect sanctification of the human essence of the Lord Jesus, as a result of which He is venerated, without distinction, both in His divine essence and in His human essence. Here, it is of course necessary to distinguish between the Lord's abiding *in statu exinanitionis* and His abiding *in statu exaltationis,* between His humiliation and His glorification, which John does not do. However, when applied to deification, the principle of *communicatio idiomatum,* which in itself is indisputable, can receive a correct interpretation only when it is also considered from the point of view of the influence of the human essence upon the divine essence. But here the discussion becomes totally obscure. When St. John of Damascus (as well as the entire scholastic theology that is based on his ideas) considers the influence of the human nature on the Divine, he does not go beyond vague generalities. John is content to affirm that, alongside His divine nature, the Logos receives or assumes a human nature that is external and foreign to Him; this nature is a habitation or garment for Him, or a necessary means for the redemption of that which He has received. The two natures are *statically* juxtaposed, so to speak, without any internal interrelation. But the two natures are, in essence, unequal. Thus, the divine nature influences the human nature, deifying it (just as fire makes iron red-hot), but there is no reverse influence of the human nature, no dynamic interaction. In reality, therefore, we get neither "theandric" energy nor communication of properties here. The duality of the natures is not overcome, and the only practical conclusion here is a more or less veiled monophysitism.

Patristic theology thus did not find its way to a doctrine of the God-Man and Divine-Humanity. It knew only God and man, Divinity and humanity, outwardly conjoined but not inwardly united. It should also be noted that the state of affairs created by the Definition of Chalcedon was not altered by the definition of the Sixth Ecumenical Council concerning two energies and two wills. Promulgated in a period when christological thought was in decline and lacking sufficient theological preparation, this definition was only a new and triumphant confirmation of the Chalcedonian dogma and a certain concretization thereof. It did not introduce new elements of the problem, which is true to an even greater degree for the theology of the dogma of the Seventh Ecumenical Council. These two definitions proclaimed inspired truths, but they left them in the form of dogmatic schemata for future theological development.

The union of the divine and human essences, understood not statically but dynamically, inevitably leads us to ask *how* this union was accomplished and *what* it represented for Divinity and for humanity. To be sure, a certain general and preliminary answer to these questions was offered by patristic theology, in particular by St. Cyril. The reception of the lower essence by the higher, of the human essence by the divine, clearly represents a certain condescension on the part of Divinity, a humiliation, a kenosis. This is so clearly indicated by Holy Scripture that its testimony is impossible to miss. Patristic thought also developed a doctrine of the Incarnation as the kenosis of Divinity (we find this not only in St. Cyril but even prior to him, in the Western writings, particularly in St. Hilary). However, given the static understanding of the Incarnation and the general lack of clarity that reigned in Christology and that led to constant deviations toward docetism (particularly in Cyril and Hilary), the most that can be said about the idea of kenosis is that it was affirmed but not developed in the patristic theology. However, the entire christological problematic of the Chalcedonian dogma necessarily leads to the doctrine of the *kenosis* of Divinity in the Incarnation, which indeed is the foundation and premise of this problematic.

CHAPTER 4

Emmanuel, the God-Man

I. The Humiliation of the Lord (the Kenosis)

"The Word was made flesh" (John 1:14). These words of the Evangelist-Theologian, which express the mystery of the Incarnation, have been and will be the theme of theological speculations and theories, the object of disputes and divergences among theologians. But they will always remain the guiding star lit by the Word about the Word. They express an unfathomable mystery: God "was made [*egeneto*]" a creature, "flesh"; and however one interprets the word "flesh," it means that God became *not* God without ceasing to be God. This is the most evident and indisputable meaning of these lightning-bearing words in the Gospel of the son of thunder. One can understand the word "flesh" in different ways in this antithesis, narrowing or expanding its scope. But one meaning remains regardless of the interpretation: flesh is *not* God, and the indisputable content of the antinomy is therefore as follows: The Word-God (without ceasing to be the Word and God) became not-God;[1] *the Creator became a creature*. Furthermore, it is clear from the context that this "flesh" is man as the center and head of all creation, as creation in general.

Nondivine, human thought could not have been brazen enough to think and pronounce these words. It could not have found the grounds to think and say them. Only the word of God, moved by the Holy Spirit, who

---

1. Among the different usages of the word "flesh" in the Bible, broad and narrow, one of the most stable usages signifies creation in its relation to God: "Behold, I am the LORD, the God of all flesh" (Jer. 32:27); "I will pour out my spirit upon all flesh" (Joel 2:28); see also Ps. 65:2; Isa. 40:5.

penetrates "the deep things of God" (1 Cor. 2:10), could from God tell about God that He became His own creature. These words of the prologue to the Gospel of John express the content of the whole Gospel: "the Word was made flesh, and dwelt among us, (and we beheld his glory, the glory as of the only begotten of the Father)" (John 1:14). God left the supramundane absoluteness of His being and became the Creator; but the Creator, the Word, by whom all things were made (as this very same prologue forcefully points out in 1:3), Himself became a creature. From His absoluteness He descended into creatureliness. This Divine condescension, which Scripture describes as a humiliation or voluntary impoverishment, is expressed in the Nicene Creed as a "descent from heaven." The inhumanization for the sake of man and for his salvation follows from this descent and is realized in it: "For us men and for our salvation [He] came down from heaven, and was incarnate by the Holy Spirit of the Virgin Mary, and was made man." (One cannot fail to see in this crucial passage of the divinely inspired Creed a paraphrase of John 3:13: "he that came down from heaven, even the Son of man which is in heaven" and of John 6:38: "I came down from heaven").

"The descent from heaven" certainly does not have an empirical, geographic, or astronomical significance. That would be nonsense. Instead, it has a metaphysical or, more precisely, an ontological significance. The descent from heaven is completely parallel to the fact that God became the Creator, establishing outside Himself the world created by Him, a world with which He is interrelated and interacts as the Absolute with the relative, as the Creator with creation, while remaining "in heaven," outside and above the world. Here, God the Word *leaves* heaven with its unperturbed tranquility of blessed divine being and enters *inside* creaturely cosmic being, "becomes" a creature. This paradox of uncreated-created, divine-human being, with its antinomism, is what constitutes the meaning of the expression — so familiar to our ears but so difficult to understand — "descent from heaven." One thing is indisputable: the descent from heaven (i.e., the assumption of creaturely being) must be understood and received with all responsible realism, that is, without any docetic interpretations that remove everything but the name from the reality of the "descent from heaven." Above all, one must consider the full meaning of the biblical doctrine of the "descent from heaven" into the creaturely world as the self-humiliation of the Lord.

The biblical disclosure of "the descent from heaven" and of "God being made flesh" can be found in the fundamental text about the humiliation of the Lord, in Philippians 2:6-8. It is possible that part of an ancient hymn, *carmen Christi*, is preserved in this solemn confession.[2] This text has also been the subject of innumerable theological commentaries based on different christological premises. The Apostle exhorts the Philippians to be likeminded and of one accord, on the model of Christ's feelings. But suddenly, from this moral paraenesis he soars into the highest reaches of theology: "[Christ Jesus], being in the form of God [*en morphē Theou huparchōn*], thought it not robbery to be equal with God [*to einai isa Theōi*]: But made himself of no reputation [*ekenōsen*, i.e., humbled or emptied Himself], and took upon him the form of a servant [*morphēn doulou labōn*], and was made in the likeness of men [*en homoiōmati anthrōpōn*]: And being found in fashion as a man [*schēmati heuretheis hōs anthrōpos*], he humbled [*etapeinōsen*] himself, and became obedient unto death, even the death of the cross." (This is followed by a text concerning the glorification of the Lord, in 2:9-11.) Without going into a detailed philological and literary exegesis, let us extract the basic dogmatic ideas from this passage. First of all, this passage talks about the descent from heaven of the *supramundane* God; that is, it talks not only about the Incarnation itself but also about the act that preceded it in heaven: the decision or the will to enact the Incarnation. To apply the text concerning humiliation solely to Christ's earthly condition is to impoverish and weaken the most acute thought of this text, its most audacious antitheses between divine grandeur and voluntary self-humiliation, which results in the obedience unto death. Is it really possible to separate in Christ His earthly, human humiliation from His heavenly, divine kenosis, which the descent from heaven and the Incarnation itself represent?[3] One thing is realized in the other. In fact, this passage talks about the Lord's earthly humiliation and about His death on the cross, which was the fulfillment of the Father's will, the Son's obedience; but this earthly obedience is based on the Son's heavenly obedience.

In other words, this passage talks not only about an earthly event occurring within the limits of human life but also about a heavenly event occurring in the depths of Divinity itself: the kenosis of God the Word. The text thus reveals the character and power of this kenosis, which is expressed with lapidary succinctness by the same Apostle Paul in 2 Corinthians 8:9: "Our Lord Jesus Christ... though he was rich, yet for your sakes he became

---

2. Cf. E. Lohmeyer, *Kyrios Jesus. Eine Untersuchung zu Phil. 2:5-11* (Heidelberg, 1928).

3. "The Incarnation is the first stage of self-humiliation in the person of God, whom it pleased to conceal the glory of Divinity beneath the veil of humanity" (Bishop Feofan, *Commentary on Paul's Epistles to the Philippians and to the Thessalonians* [Moscow, 1883], p. 76).

poor." What does this kenosis or impoverishment consist in? According to Philippians 2:7, it consists in the change of the form *(morphē)* of God into "the form of a servant." What is *morphē*? Does this word differ from *ousia* and *phusis*? Although the dominant opinion of the patristic exegesis tended to identify these concepts with each other (not without a polemic against Arianism),[4] the dominant tendency of contemporary exegetes, based on philologico-historical and theological considerations, is to decisively reject such an identification. In the interpretation of Philippians 2:7, such an identification would inevitably lead to the extreme *kenotic* doctrine of Christ's total abandonment of His divine nature.[5] Bishop Feofan interprets *morphē* as the *norm of being*, corresponding to nature; this idea generally expresses the difference that exists between God's unchangeable *nature* and the *state* of life that proceeds from this nature as a general possibility and even property of being. The phrase "[He] thought it not robbery [*oux harpagmon hēgēsato*]" (Phil. 2:6) indicates precisely the opposition between greedy, egotisitical appropriation and possession based on natural right. This natural norm for the One who possesses the divine nature is expressed in the fact that He also possesses the divine form of being, thinking Himself "to be equal with God" (this expression referring not to the nature[6] but precisely to the form of being). And it is this form or norm of divine life that Christ voluntarily changed into the form of a servant; that is, He changed not the unchangeable nature but the changeable form. He did not make this form or norm of divine life the object of egotistical self-assertion, or "robbery," but because of His love for man He humbled Himself, taking on a form that did not conform with His natural norm: the form of a "servant." If one puts this passage in relation to the supramundane self-determination of Divinity "preceding" the decision about the descent from heaven and the Incarnation, the aorist *hēgēsato* expresses (not without an inevitable anthropomorphism) precisely this divine decision.[7] God volun-

---

4. See the discussion in M. Tareev, *Foundations of Christianity* (Moscow, 1901), p. 15 n. 5. The sole exception is Hilary (see Bruce, *The Humiliation of Christ*, pp. 18-19, also appendix, note A, pp. 357-59).

5. Cf. J. B. Lightfoot, *St. Paul's Epistle to the Philippians* (1908), excursus, pp. 127-33. "Though *morphē* is not the same as *phusis* or *ousia*, yet the possession of the *morphē* involves the participation in the *ousia*" (ibid., p. 110). Also see F. Prat, *La théologie de Saint Paul*, vol. 1 (Paris, 1908); and the discussion in Tareev, *Foundations*, pp. 14-18.

6. "The equality of the Son of God with the Father is designated in John 5:18 by another expression: *isos tōi Theōi*. By contrast, Phil. 2:6 has *isa* (an adverb, not an adjective, and *Theoi* is without the article)." (Tareev, *Foundations*, p. 18.)

7. Ibid., p. 25.

216

Emmanuel, the God-Man

tarily renounced His Divine glory. He removed it, bared Himself, emptied and impoverished Himself, took the form of a servant. The word "servant" here expresses not nature but relation:[8] the relation of the creaturely being to God. Being God by nature, when He came down from heaven into the creaturely world and became man, He put Himself in a *creaturely* relation to God. "The form of a servant" is synonymous with "the likeness of men" [*en homoiōmati anthrōpon*], that is, the image of the human race in the capacity of the New Adam, who differs from the fallen Adam by His sinlessness and in this sense bears only a likeness to him. Thus, the word "likeness" expresses both the identity and the difference between Christ's humanity and that of all men.

This idea is continued in the words: "and being found in fashion as a man [*kai schēmati heuretheis hōs anthrōpos*]" (2:8). *Schēma* expresses here *empirical* humanity, the human form of life that is expressed in movements of the soul and in the needs of the body: Christ lived like all other men. He had need of food, rest, and sleep. He moved about; He had sinless movements of the soul (emotions); He was subject to joy, sadness, indignation, and so on. In other words, we must eliminate here all docetism, for which all this was only an illusion, not an empirical reality. *Homoiōma* expresses here inner, ontological humanity, the human nature that the Logos united with the divine nature, whereas *schēma* expresses empirical reality, that is, the human form of life with its properties.

For the Creator, the taking on of the creaturely nature is already, in and of itself, the taking on "the form of a servant" (2:7). But as a human individual (although one who bears in Himself the nature of the integral Adam), Christ assumed the lowly form of humiliation and concluded His earthly path with the death on the cross; in this He fully manifested obedience to the Father's will: "He humbled himself, and became obedient unto death, even the death of the cross" (2:8). Thus, in the cross of the earthly path is realized the cross of the heavenly kenosis.

The passage concludes with testimony about the heavenly glorification of the Logos (2:9-10). The idea of the significance of Christ's earthly humiliation and of the obedience manifested in it is also expressed in Hebrews 2, which underscores the additional fact that this humiliation makes Christ kindred to men, makes Him their brother: "For it became him, for whom are all things, and by whom are all things, in bringing many sons unto glory, to make the captain of their salvation perfect through sufferings. For both he that sanctifieth and they who are sancti-

---

8. Ibid., p. 27.

fied are all of one: for which cause he is not ashamed to call them brethren, saying, I will declare thy name unto my brethren, in the midst of the church will I sing praise unto thee" (Heb. 2:10-12). "Wherefore in all things it behoved him to be made like unto his brethren . . . for in that he himself hath suffered being tempted, he is able to succour them that are tempted" (2:17-18). Further on, we encounter the strongest words about the Lord's earthly humiliation: "in the days of his flesh . . . he had offered up prayers and supplications with strong crying and tears unto him that was able to save him from death, and was heard in that he feared; though he were a Son, yet learned he obedience by the things which he suffered" (5:7-8). In the state of His kenosis, heavenly and earthly, metaphysical and empirical, the Lord *prayed* to the Father as God. This fact, expressed in the Gospels, should not be diminished or docetically reinterpreted for the sake of "appearance" or for the sake of "example," as is done in the patristic literature. Here it is not only a question of the significance of prayer for Christ Himself, as a "conversation with God"; the *efficacy* of this prayer is also attested: Through His prayer the Son received from the Father salvation from death — He, who Himself is the source of life, for "in Him was life" (John 1:4). Such is the depth of kenosis. Such is the degree to which God the Word stops being Himself and gives Himself wholly to the Father, although He "thought it not robbery to be equal with God" (Phil. 2:6).

The most general question of kenotic theology, the preliminary question we must ask, is as follows: Condescending to receive the flesh into His hypostasis and uniting with it the human nature and the divine nature (which are distinguished as the lower and the higher, the created and the uncreated), the Logos has these two natures in one life of one person, the Lord Jesus Christ. This life is lived not only in the duality and difference of the two natures but also in their inequality: the creaturely nature has a servile relation to the divine nature (having "the form of a servant"), and the very taking on of the creaturely nature is an "impoverishment." The union of the two *unequal* natures can be accomplished only in such a manner that one of the natures asserts its priority, thus establishing a certain asymmetry directed upward or downward: from humanity toward Divinity or from Divinity toward humanity, in an ascending or descending direction. But by no means can the lines be parallel, as the school of Antioch taught, for parallel lines cannot meet — they cannot be united in one hypostasis. The ascending direction is predominant in the patristic literature (which is exemplified by St. Cyril's doctrine, despite his acceptance of kenosis, not to mention various types of monophysitism).

Emmanuel, the God-Man

The opposite, descending direction is weakly represented in patristics (though we can mention Ebionism, the doctrine of Paul of Samosata, and, in general, the doctrines that replaced the Incarnation with the simple effect of grace; we can also mention Arianism). Doctrines that assert the ascending direction inevitably result either in a frank and conscious Docetism, leading to monophysitisim, or, in any case, in a diminution of the human essence so extreme that this essence is considered analogous to a curtain that veils or reveals Divinity as required, or to a screen onto which Divinity is projected. The true *union* of the divine and human natures in Christ must therefore be understood in another manner. We must be guided here not by the idea of the "taking on" of humanity by Divinity or the "inhabitation" of Divinity in human flesh but by the idea of the descent of Divinity down to man, the self-diminution of Divinity, His humiliation or kenosis.[9]

The Incarnation is, first of all, a kenotic act: "The Word was made flesh." For the human essence to be united with the Divine essence without being dissolved or annihilated, Divinity had to descend, to diminish itself to the human essence.[10] The Incarnation begins with the descent of the Son of God from heaven and ends with His ascension to heaven. The kenotic principle must be understood with an acuteness and clarity that did not by any means characterize the classical epoch of the christological disputes (if we ignore certain scattered statements of St. Cyril or St. Hilary[11]). "Kenotic theology" has done a great deal to advance this principle (first in Germany, then in England), although it has done so in a one-

---

9. The idea of Christ's kenosis is expressed with great clarity in the prayer of the preface of the Liturgy of St. Basil the Great: "[He] thought it not robbery to be equal with Thee, God and Father! But being pre-eternal God, He appeared on earth and lived with men; and He was made incarnate of the holy Virgin, and humbled Himself, having taken upon Himself the form of a servant, in conformity with the body of our humility, in order to make us conform with the image of His glory."

10. In the Epistle of the Eastern Patriarchs, art. 7, we read the following definition of the Incarnation: "We believe that the Son of God, our Lord Jesus Christ, humbled Himself, that is, took upon Himself, in His own hypostasis, human flesh, conceived in the womb of the Virgin Mary by the operation of the Holy Spirit, and was made man."

11. Strictly speaking, one can find a fairly specific idea of kenosis only in St. Hilary. However, one would seek a coherent and consistent doctrine of kenosis in his work in vain; on the contrary, his Christology consists in a combination of ideas belonging to two opposite orders of thought: kenotics and docetism. Hilary's achievement is that he stated the problem of kenosis, to which he gave the Latin name *exinanitio* or *evacuatio (formae Dei)*, based on Philippians 2.

The Lamb of God

sided manner. This theology thus represents the most important current of christological thought after the ecumenical councils.[12]

What does this kenosis really mean, and in what sense is it possible? What postulates must it satisfy to be more than just a monophysitic mixing of the natures by absorption? In becoming man, God does not stop being God; even after descending from heaven, He remains in heaven. Likewise, man does not stop being man after he receives God into himself. In voluntary self-humiliation, God renounces something, abandons something, in order to become accessible to man, in order to make possible the approach to man. And man, in opening himself up to receive God, transfigures himself, but this occurs without the human essence being abolished, without the possibilities implanted in this essence being destroyed. What is needed is a mediation, an ontological bridge to effect this union — a ladder on which this ascent-descent can be accomplished. The conventional opinion is that there can be no mediation between God and the creature: *tertium non datur* (this problem was the stumbling block for Arius). But in reality there *is* such a mediation between God and the creature: *tertium datur*, and this *tertium* is Sophia, the true Wisdom of God, eternal and creaturely. Creaturely sophianicity, however, is only the bridge

---

12. Our task does not include an exposition of the history of the so-called kenotic theology (one can find such surveys in Bruce, *The Humiliation of Christ;* and in J. O. Bensow, *Die Lehre von der Kenose* [1903]; as well as in the articles on kenosis in *Dict. cath. dogm.* and in *Dict. cath. apol.*). The most noteworthy representatives of kenotics are its founder, G. Thomasius, *Christi Person und Werk*, 3d ed. (1886), and other works; W. F. Gess, *Die Lehre von der Person Christi* (1856), and *Christi Person und Werk*, vols. 1-3 (1870-87) (this contains the most extreme view of Christ's self-humiliation); T. Liebner, *Die christl. Dogmatik* (1849); J. H. A. Ebrard, *Die chr. Dogmatik* (1852), and *Die chr. Glaubenslehre* (1861); F. Godet, *Comm. sur l'Évangile de St. Jean*, vol. 2 (1877); F. Bonifas, *Hist. des dogmes*, vol. 2 (1886); A. Gretillat, *Exposé de théol. systém.*, vol. 4, and *Dogmatique*, vol. 2 (1890); and J. Bovon, *Dogm. chrét.* Of the critics of kenotics, the most remarkable is Dorner, in various works: *Entwicklungsgeschichte der Lehre von der Person Christi*, 2/2; *System der christlichen Glaubenslehre*, vols. 1-2, and others. We find many twentieth-century representatives of kenotics in the Anglo-American world (unfortunately, not all of them have been accessible to me: Mackintosh, Sanday, Gifford, Forsyth, Mason, Powell, Forrest, A. Brown, Weston, Moorhouse, Hall, W. Bright, Rashdall, et al.). Here, kenotics to some extent loses the dogmatic profundity and seriousness that characterizes it in the German dogmatics; it takes on the traits of rationalism and liberalism, which are totally alien to the rather orthodox kenotic theology of Germany, which is why one usually lumps it together with "modernism" (see, for example, the polemical brochure of S. H. Scott, *Anglocatholicism and Reunion* [1923]). The history of kenotic theology indubitably deserves a special monographic investigation.

for, or the ontological possibility of, the movement of God and the creature toward one another. It is not the encounter between the two. The reality of this movement presupposes a series of christological postulates with their strange paradoxes. Without ceasing to be God, God ceases to be God (even though that is inconceivable and impossible), and He becomes man; that is, He enters human life in the most real sense, and He makes this life His own. Primarily, He adopts the fundamental feature of human life: temporality, becoming, gradual development, and, thus, limitation in each of its stages until fullness is attained. In other words, the eternal God becomes the *becoming* God in the God-Man. He removes from Himself His eternal Divinity in order to descend to human life and, in and through this life, to make man capable of receiving God, of living the life of God, of being the God-Man.

The initial dogmatic axiom of Christology is *the unity of life* of the God-Man in His Divine-human I and the manifestation of the two natures, which are joined but not combined: not only *two* natures but also *one* life. At first sight it appears that this axiom demands the impossible and leads to contradictions and absurdity: What does it mean for God to stop being Himself ("to come down from heaven") while remaining Himself? What does it mean for man to preserve his essence while allowing a place for God in it? Are these two equally indisputable postulates compatible? Can they be fulfilled? Scripture simply, directly, and decisively attests: "the Word was made flesh"; the Son of God became the Son of Man. Thus, these postulates are realizable, and by a reverse operation of thought, based on the indisputable testimony of Scripture, we must clarify precisely what occurred in the Incarnation.

Two aspects of the truth are necessarily united in the kenosis of Divinity: On the one hand, God in the Holy Trinity abides in trihypostatic interrelations and lives in one nature; and this ontological and substantial fullness of Divinity cannot be changed or diminished. On the other hand, the fullness of the *life* of Divinity, in living out its bliss, can in fact be limited — not by something from outside, but by Divinity's proper will. One can say that God, abiding in divine unchangeableness, can will to change and limit *for Himself* the fullness of His life. He can renounce the bliss of His life: "though he was rich, yet for your sakes he became poor" (2 Cor. 8:9).

A distinction thus enters into our idea of Divinity: the distinction between the life of God *according to* Himself, as He is in His unchangeable essence, and His life *for* Himself, as He lives out His essence for Himself in the living act. Here He has the power to change for Himself the *mode* of the living out of this essence. God's life is not a material fact, in the way that the being of created things is such a fact; rather, it is a living act, based on ontological reality and free for Divine self-determination. Even created beings who bear the image of God (angels and men) can live out their natural givens in *different* ways, and this constitutes their creaturely freedom in becoming. However, this freedom is connected with a fluctuating, indeterminate state, a state of choice, indecisiveness, limitation, creaturely impotence — although it also removes from the creature the stigma of "thingness," of enslavement to the fact. For God, self-limitation or, in general, distinction in the mode of the living out of the divine fullness is determined only by God Himself; it is the realization of His aseity and freedom. To attribute immobility and unchangeableness to God in the living out of the nature would be to diminish His absoluteness and aseity. It would be to assert that a law of necessity exists for God Himself, or that His Divinity exerts a power over Himself that is greater than He Himself (this is the impersonalistic conception of the Absolute, which is totally inadequate to the idea of the Personal God). Nothing can limit God's freedom in His proper life; and there is no principle that would necessarily define God's life in the fullness that is exclusively possible for it. Such ontological unchangeableness is possessed only by the very being of the trihypostatic unisubstantial God, in His three hypostases and in His one nature. There can be no "more or less" here, no "in this way or in another way": the *being-according-to-itself* is perfect in itself; in it, the freedom of the self-positing Spirit is perfectly identified with necessity. And the unisubstantial Trinity is equal to itself both in the eternal radiance of the life of the Absolute and in God the Creator, who is directed toward the world. There is no place for change, becoming, or process in the eternity of the unisubstantial Trinity. This eternity transcends not only the world with its becoming but also God Himself insofar as He defines Himself *in relation to the world* as the Creator and Providence. That is, it transcends the "economic" Trinity, as distinguished from the "immanent" Trinity. The "immanent" Trinity is invariably present in the "economic" Trinity. The "immanent" Trinity is itself in its proper depths and foundation, but it is also other than and *in this sense* transcendent to the life of the "economic" Trinity. This is the fundamental interrelation in the life of the Holy Trinity as the Absolute and God.

Being *in itself* in the Holy Trinity is necessarily conjoined with being *for itself*, that is, with divine life in its freedom. This is not the *abstract* and in this sense *negative* freedom of a void filled with limitless arbitrary possibilities. Instead, it is *ontological* freedom, which has its eternal and positive content. It is proper and "natural" for the freedom of the Divine life to live by the fullness of its nature. This manifests the entelechic character of Divinity, the identity between the given and that which is proposed, and the possible *variants* associated with this freedom can refer only to the *degree* of fullness or impoverishment of this being *for itself.* The basis for this possible variability in God's freedom, in the "economic" Trinity, is uniquely and exclusively God's love, which pours forth beyond the limits of Divinity itself into extradivine but divinely posited being-nonbeing (i.e., creation). In becoming the Creator of the world, God proceeds out of the fullness of *the being for Himself* proper to Him in His life (in the "immanent" Trinity) into the domain of becoming, the domain of the unfullness of creaturely being, with which He interacts by the voluntary self-limitation of the fullness of *His Divine being for Himself.* To be sure, this voluntary self-limitation of God in the *manifestation* of His Divinity (but not in the possession of it) occurs only with reference to specific ontological tasks and within specific limits. That is, becoming — which presupposes change, evolution, multiple degrees of development — leads to the goal established from the beginning: that God be all in all. In other words, it leads to the identification of that which is given with that which is proposed. There is no place here for anything ontologically new and unprecedented in God Himself, or therefore in the world that He brought into existence (for *all* is *all,* and there is nothing "new" beyond its limits). The only new thing here is becoming itself, the creaturely world as a work of the divine will.

Thus, God in His being *for Himself,* in the mode of the living out of His life and its fullness, is free to limit Himself. Such a possibility does not contradict God's absoluteness, aseity, and all-blessedness, for this self-limitation is not a consequence of limitedness and is not imposed from outside. Rather, it is a proper, voluntary self-definition of the Absolute, and the impossibility of such a self-definition would truly diminish Him. If God is love, for which it is proper to pour forth into extradivine being as well, then in becoming the Creator, God Himself and in His proper life accepts sacrificial self-limitation in the name of love for creation while preserving the entire fullness of His immanent being.

The kenosis thus expresses the general relation of God to the world. The creation of the world is a kenotic act of God, who posited outside Himself and alongside Himself the becoming of this world. But this kenosis is revealed in a wholly new way in the humiliation of the Word, who is united with creation, becomes man.

The character of the kenosis of the Word in the Incarnation can be considered from three points of view: that of nature, that of the hypostasis, and that of intratrinitarian life and the interrelations of the three hypostases. Let us begin with nature. The divine nature of the Logos, as the foundation of hypostatic being and the source of life, remains unchanged and undiminished in Christ. This is attested by the dogma of the Fourth Ecumenical Council concerning the two natures in Christ, and in particular concerning the presence of the divine nature in Him (it is also attested by the concretization of this dogma in the dogma of the Sixth Ecumenical Council concerning the two wills and two energies). Humiliation refers not to the nature (ousia) but to the *morphē*, to the divine form, which Christ removes from Himself in the Incarnation. It follows that, although the nature and the form are interrelated as foundation and consequence, they can be separated from one another.

It is appropriate to remember here the essential sophiological distinction between the nature and the *glory* in God. The "form" is precisely this glory, which the Son has as God but which He removes from Himself in His humiliation, although He will later once again put on this garment of glory (see John 17:5). The glory, in turn, is Sophia in the capacity of the divine nature manifested, revealed in itself. The glory is the love of the hypostatic God for His Divinity. It is the bliss and joy that proceed from this love. And it is precisely this joy that the Son of God deprives Himself of, empties Himself of: "[Instead of] the joy that was set before Him [He] endured the cross" (Heb. 12:2 [the King James Version has been modified to conform with the Russian Bible]).

Christ's removal of the glory from Himself is precisely His *descent from heaven*. The Son of God, eternally being God, "comes down from heaven" and abandons, as it were, the divine life. His divine nature retains only the potential of glory, which must be actualized anew, according to the high-priestly prayer: "And now, O Father, glorify thou me . . . with the glory which I had with thee before the world was" (John 17:5). In His kenosis, the Son of God, who in a special sense is Sophia, "comes down from heaven" into the domain of the *becoming* Sophia and abandons the manifested and glorified state of Divine life as Sophia. Glory and Divinity in Sophia pre-eternally shine in heaven for the Holy Trinity; but the Second hypostasis, in descending from heaven, abandons this shining. The Second hypostasis no longer has this shining for Himself; He assumes the form of a servant in the voluntary ascesis of kenosis. In this sense, the Man who is also the pre-eternal God stops having His divinity for Himself, as it were: He retains only the *nature* of Divinity, not its glory.

This unfathomable separation of the nature from the glory in Di-

Emmanuel, the God-Man

vinity is the proper work of the Second hypostasis. By this act the Second hypostasis removes from Himself His proper hypostatic will or energy while retaining His filial obedience but keeping inactive His proper hypostatic actuality. His Divine hypostatic power is "frozen" or "emptied," as it were; and His entire personal life is exhausted by obedience to the Father's commands, by fulfillment of the Father's will through the accomplishment of the works of the ministry by the Holy Spirit. His proper hypostatic act with respect to Himself, His personal self-definition, is entirely exhausted by this self-emptying or self-abolition, as it were. In virtue of this act, His life becomes not His own any longer but comes to belong to the Paternal hypostasis: the Father sends. The Father is revealed in the Son, who thus becomes perfectly transparent for the Paternal hypostasis: "he that hath seen me hath seen the Father" (John 14:9). That "depersonalizing" transparence of the revelation of the Father in the Son and of the Son in the Father, which is the hypostatic property of the Holy Spirit, also becomes a property of the Son in His kenosis. The Son is the hypostatic obedience to the commands of the Father, accomplished by virtue of the Holy Spirit reposing upon Him. Outside of and apart from this, the Son does not have Himself. *For Himself,* He stops being God *(Theos),* stops having Divinity *(Theotēs),* while naturally and hypostatically being the pre-eternal God *(ho Theos).* His Divine I dissolves itself into the Paternal hypostasis, and His proper hypostasis manifests itself as a human hypostasis that obeys God's will and acquires itself as the proper divine hypostasis of the Son only through this obedience.

While preserving His divine nature, the Second hypostasis thus abandons the divine life, which is restored in Him only together with the human life. Through the becoming Sophia, in the sophianization and deification of man, Christ returns to Himself and reacquires His abandoned glory and the divine life.

This separation of the nature and the life, which constitutes the kenosis of the Son, is not an empirical and human sacrifice but a metaphysical and divine one. It is a wholly unfathomable *miracle of God's love,* a mystery "which . . . the angels desire to look into" (1 Pet. 1:12). In the presence of this kenosis of Divinity, all creation can only remain astonished and prostrate itself for ages of ages.

We will now consider the significance of kenosis in relation to the hypostatic being of the Son. The Father pre-eternally begets the Son and pronounces in Him His unuttered Word, whereas the Son is pre-eternally begotten of the Father as the Logos. Both the begetting and begottenness are absolutely personal acts, so that in this sense the begetting of

The Lamb of God

the Son (together with the procession of the Spirit) is the very personality of the Father, just as the begottenness (together with the reception of the reposing of the Holy Spirit) is the personality of the Son. The kenosis of the Son therefore does not change anything in this personal relation of the Father and the Son, for even in the kenosis the Son remains the same Person, the Second hypostasis of the Holy Trinity, the divine filial "I." Likewise, the procession of the Holy Spirit from the Father to the Son and the reposing of the Spirit upon the Son, as well as the Son's reception in the Holy Spirit of the Father's love and of His own love for the Father, belong to the very being of the persons of the Father and the Son, together with the person of the Holy Spirit conjoined with them. One can say that the Father and the Holy Spirit together establish the person of the Son, that the Son through the Holy Spirit is correlated with the Father, and that the person of the Holy Spirit is established by the correlation of the Father and the Son.[13] Thus, neither the Holy Trinity nor the hypostasis of the Son in its relations to the other hypostases is affected by the kenosis. The kenosis does not extend to the very *being* of the hypostasis of the Son, which is rooted in the inner, interhypostatic relations of the Holy Trinity. The kenosis does not disrupt the being of the Holy Trinity (as certain kenotics in effect admit), and it does not even affect the Holy Trinity, for the unshakeable foundation of the kenosis is precisely the Divine Person of the Son, who, like the other hypostases, already bears within Himself the ensemble of interhypostatic intratrinitarian interrelations; in a certain sense, He Himself is such an interrelation in personal being.

Nor does the kenosis extend to the participation of the Logos in the natural consubstantial life of God and His self-revelation. The begotten Word reveals the thought of the Father, and the Holy Spirit accomplishes this thought with beauty. The Divine Sophia or the Divine world as the one self-revelation of the consubstantial Trinity abides in her eternal glory, and the participation of the Logos is neither abolished nor limited in this divine fullness of self-revelation. This participation is absolutely

---

13. Perhaps the weakest and strangest element of the kenotic theories (e.g., in Gess) is the supposition that, during the kenotic humiliation of the Son, the Holy Spirit stops proceeding "and from the Son," but proceeds from the Father alone. Without mentioning the false Latin dogma of the *filioque,* this idea of the exclusion of the Son from the Holy Trinity during the time of the kenosis is compromisingly absurd, since such a supposition would signify nothing other than the total self-abolition of the Second hypostasis (as well as of its kenosis). This idea contradicts the proper premises concerning the school of the divinity of the hypostasis of Jesus.

independent of the extent to which and the manner in which the hypostasis of the Logos has this glory *for Himself.* The fact that He is subjectively impoverished for Himself does not change His *objective* participation in the glory. The "immanent" Trinity does not know the kenosis of the Word, which exists only in the "economic" Trinity.

Furthermore, the kenosis does not affect the participation of the Logos in creation (as is powerfully shown in the prologue to the Gospel of John, where the doctrine of the Word, by whom all things were made, is juxtaposed with the testimony about the Incarnation of the Son). The Word created the world, and the words of the Word are the foundation of the world's multiplicity and "allness." The pre-eternal Word, uttered at the creation of the world, remains in it as the indestructible foundation of its reality. Here, we encounter in their full power the most audacious christological paradoxes: sleeping on the stern, the Lord contains the universe in His Word; hanging on the cross and tormented by the suffering unto death, the Lord is the Creator and the Initiator of life, who contains all created things in His Word; born in a manger and reposing in the grave, the Lord is the sovereign ruler of all creation; and so on. For this word about the world, resounding in the world, is His very personality, begotten of the Father and overshadowed by the Holy Spirit. The world is not shaken in this verbal foundation by the personal kenosis of the Word (which is attested by the Church when it sings: "When the creature sees Thee hanging on Golgotha, Thou who hast suspended the whole earth without support on the waters, it is shaken by a great horror").

A final problem arises: that of the participation of the Logos in His state of kenosis in the *providential government* of the world. The solution to this problem must show that this participation is not abolished or diminished by the descent of the Logos from heaven. The providential activity of the Holy Trinity in the world should not be understood as the action of three mechanics each of whom maintains a designated part of the machine in his own manner. The one trihypostatic Wisdom of God acts graciously in the world, and this action is the condition of the very being of the world. The world is determined in its being *from its very creation.* In particular, the most important thing is established in it then: the fullness of the human race, although its individual members come into the world over the course of time. It is upon this unshakeable foundation of humanity that the plan of the divine economy of salvation is accomplished. According to this plan, the Word of God in the Old Testament is revealed and acts as Jehovah, thus preparing His New Testament manifestation as the Lamb of God, which is followed by His glorification and ascension to heaven.[14] In conformity with this plan of economy, the providential activity of the Father and the Holy Spirit is defined in connection with the Incarnation of the Logos. As far as particular providential acts are concerned, they cannot be conceived anthropomorphically, as the direct action of the different hypostases of the Trinity on certain persons or events. The action of Divine Providence (which in its entirety is not subject to human understanding and which becomes transparent for us only in particular phenomena of our life) is, above all, the action of the inner sophianic laws governing creation, which is watched over by the holy angels, who realize God's plan. This inner law, the Divine Sophia, has as its content the revelation of the Logos. The creative word also acts in the world as the providential word, preserving and guiding the world.

Finally, as far as the direct participation of one or another of the hypostases in the providential government of the world is concerned, we must say that we have absolutely no knowledge of such participation — either outside the kenosis or in connection with it. Of course, only the Divine wisdom *knows* what the providential action of each hypostasis consists of. In the days of the Savior's earthly ministry, His hypostatic providential activity was revealed with perfect clarity in His personal effect upon people, in His works and in His work. It is sufficient to cite as an example the selection of the apostles for preaching and for "bearing witness," a form of action of Christ that was preestablished in the ages and for the ages. Consequently, it is absolutely incorrect to say that, because of His kenosis, the Logos does not participate in the providential activity. There are three reasons for this: First, the kenosis in itself is an act of providential government of the world, an act included in the pathways of the world from the beginning. Second, in its accomplishment, the kenosis includes a series of divinely purposive, directly providential actions upon souls. Third, the ways of Providence are in general unfathomable for us; we thus cannot permit ourselves to entertain the thought that, as a result of the kenosis, the hypostasis of the Logos could be temporarily excluded from these ways. This notion also includes a sundering of the Holy Trinity; that is, it undermines all the truths of the faith. However, parallel to this unitrinitarian life, each hypostasis is a particular per-

---

14. Certain adherents of the kenotic theories have doubts not only concerning the participation of the Logos in the procession of the Holy Spirit but also concerning the participation of the Logos in God's providential activity, which they even deny for the time of the Incarnation. They do not see here that the Incarnation itself must be considered a providential act.

sonal center that has its proper life: a life that, although it is one with the Holy Trinity, is its own and different from that of the other hypostases.

The Church expresses this general idea in the fundamental dogmatic doctrine that only the Son, and precisely the Son, came down from heaven and was made man, thus affirming His proper life, different from that of the Holy Trinity and that of the other hypostases. This specific character of the life of the Second hypostasis is, in this case, expressed in the descent from heaven. The Second hypostasis empties Himself of His Divinity. He abandons His Divinity — not as the source of intratrinitarian interhypostatic life, but as the source of His personal divine being: The Son stops being God *for Himself,* and therefore, in relation to Him, the Father is now not only an equidivine hypostasis ("I and my Father are one" [John 10:30]), but also *His God.* The consciousness of being the Son of the Father is eclipsed here, as it were, by the consciousness of being *sent by the Father,* of obeying His will and revealing Him. Similarly, the Holy Spirit is no longer only a co-divine hypostasis for the Son, revealing the Father together with Him. The Holy Spirit is now the force reposing upon the Son, the finger of God by which He accomplishes works.

For Himself, the Son leaves, as it were, the closed ring of the Triunity. He begins to exist for Himself in the third person, so to speak, as a being who, while one with the Holy Trinity, does not live in the unitrinitarian divine hypostasis but remains outside it as it were. The proper I of the Logos for Himself (although not according to Himself) descends, as it were, from the Holy Trinity into the creaturely sphere of being ("He comes down from heaven") and *is made man.* That is, the hypostasis of the Logos, ceasing to be a divine hypostasis for Himself while remaining such in His objective being, becomes a *human hypostasis:* His consciousness of self is realized through human consciousness. Thus, in becoming man, as having in Himself the divine hypostasis with the divine nature inseparably connected with it, He is the *God-Man* — God living a human life or Man containing the Divine life in His human life. "The Word was made flesh": the Word did not "put on" flesh like a garment (such a notion is incongruous and inapplicable). He did not inhabit it as if it were a dwelling (which would be Ebionism), nor was He Himself transformed into flesh (which is the most absurd and blasphemous of these notions). All of these statement say either too much or too little. The precise formulation is rather that the Word became a creature of flesh, man; that is, He *began to live* a creaturely, human life. The Creator became a creature: "He was in the world, and the world was made by Him" (John 1:10). That is the triumphant antinomy of the Evangelist Theologian.

The Lamb of God

But what does it mean that the *Word became man?* How can one come to a theological understanding of this truth? It presupposes, first of all, that, according to his creaturely essence, man is called to receive the Word and is worthy of receiving Him, that, as the image of God, man is the adequate form for this reception. Man is created as the god-man in the sense that, in his creaturely psycho-corporeal essence, he contains a spirit of divine origin. In the God-Man this spirit is the Logos Himself. And if the uncreated-created human spirit is open for the reception of divine life, for deification, for communion with the divine nature, then in the God-Man this divine nature exists, from the beginning, without separation from the hypostasis. The God-Man is thus a true man according to His *formal* structure; He is the "Man Christ Jesus," and in this sense the descent from heaven is naturally an in-humanization, for man is precisely the place in all creation that is prepared for the reception of the God descending from heaven. Therefore, in the God-Man, man for the first time realizes the entire fullness of his essence and attains the full stature of his calling: he realizes the truth about man. In his natural essence, man is the creaturely Sophia; it is precisely because of the sophianicity of his nature that he can be the receptacle for the Divine Sophia, who has diminished herself to the image of the creaturely Sophia, the form of a servant.

Man is an incarnate spirit, and this connection between spirit and natural, psycho-corporeal life is the most mysterious thing and also the most characteristic thing in man. In God, the divine nature is pre-eternally open in the immediate personal act of contemplation; there is no time or process here. By contrast, the spiritual being in man, his personality, is awakened, lives, and develops in the indissoluble unity of pneumo-psycho-corporeal experience in such a way that his spirit lives in a psycho-corporeal manner and the psycho-corporeality is qualified spiritually. This is the basis for the struggle between spirit and flesh, as well as for their inseparability and constant collaboration. And the desire to be made disincarnate, to become like a fleshless spirit under the pretext of asceticism, is ontological nonsense and a Manichaean heresy. The *whole* man, with not only his corporeal but also his spiritual being, finds himself in the process of becoming. His spirit *arises* in him, so to speak, and he therefore knows different ages, development, and growth. This represents one of the important features of man's being. Spirit as such is *actus purus,* and also an act that is absolutely personal. Spirit does not know development and is the intuition of itself: the personality sees itself in the image of its being, in its nature, and the nature is conscious of itself in the personality. This can be said about both the Divine Personality and the immaterial spirits. But in man it is otherwise. His spiritual personality with his personal consciousness of self is cast here into becoming. That which exists ontologically as the foundation of man's being, and as its limit, its entelechy, is realized in time as development, that is, as the becoming conscious of oneself and as self-knowledge in natural life. Man, who is a personal incarnate spirit, therefore has a *preconscious* life and different degrees of consciousness: the subconscious (or the superconscious), the unconscious (sleep, loss of consciousness), and, finally, perfect consciousness of self, which man will know in the future age when all that is in part will cease and we will know ourselves even as we are known (see 1 Cor. 13:12).[15]

It is a task of psychological investigation to study the relation between the conscious and the subconscious. Here we confront the empirical fact that our "I" is connected with and submerged in psycho-corporeal being, and that it is conscious of its spirituality in and through this being — a spirituality that it has possession of, but that in turn has possession of it. This is a domain of psychology that is capable of making a contribution to theology and is already beginning to make such a contribution in contemporary metapsychological and psychoanalytic studies. Spiritual consciousness of self, in particular the personal consciousness of self in man, is subject to becoming, that is, to growth and maturation. Being intrinsically intuitive and immediate, the spiritual consciousness of self becomes discursive and discontinuous; it becomes entangled in temporality, and it gazes into eternity only in and through time. It is awakened in man at a definite age, attains its apogee following an ascending curve, and gradually declines in old age until it finally fades in death — to be reawakened to new life. The temporality of the supratemporal I in man is a paradox of the human spirit in its becoming, but such is its unalterable foundation established by God, who created man for *temporal* (i.e., discursive) being, although as an image of eternity.

Within the limits of this aeon, humanity is temporality and becoming, to which the human I, the personal consciousness of self, is also subject. It is at this point that the idea of kenosis, of the self-humiliation of the Word, becomes maximally acute. The Son has not only "removed" His Divinity and abandoned His sophianic glory, and He has not only "become flesh" by "putting on" our gross essence; He has also become a *human hypostasis*. Here we have the unfathomable and astonishing self-diminution

---

15. Here, the Apostle powerfully confirms this fact of the development of the spirit and its ages: "When I was a child, I spake as a child, I understood as a child, I thought as a child: but when I became a man, I put away childish things" (1 Cor. 13:11).

of the eternal divine hypostasis of the Logos, who submerges Himself in temporality and discursivity — after disappearing, as it were, in the unconscious, "in the womb of the Mother" — in order to rise to the surface out of the waters of the Lethe as the dreamy consciousness of the Infant, who is to destined to grow (see Luke 2:40) and increase in "stature" (2:52), ascending "unto the measure of the stature of the fulness of Christ" (Eph. 4:13). This is the miracle of miracles of God's love for man, even compared with the miracle of the creation of the world. In-humanization thus means that the Logos did not assume flesh as something external and extraneous to Himself. Rather, He Himself *became* a human hypostasis and received human temporality into His proper *life;* He humanized Himself[16] not from outside but from within, entering into the creaturely life of temporality and becoming.

One must accept the kenosis of the Incarnation in all its terrifying seriousness: It is the *metaphysical* Golgotha of the self-crucifixion of the Logos in time. The *historical* Golgotha was only a *consequence* of the metaphysical one. The metaphysical Golgotha made the historical one possible and real. One must accept in all its force this voluntary, so to speak, dying of the Second hypostasis and His burial in time, as a result of which His birth in time was possible: "Christ is being born — glorify Him! Christ is coming down from heaven . . . Christ is on the earth. Come to meet him" (from the Canon of the Nativity). Then "God is placed into the grave" and reposes there with the three-day sleep of death. If this is not accepted, the entire Gospel story becomes merely a docetic "manifestation" of something that did not really take place; and if it did not take place, that means God did not want it to take place.

But is *such* a self-emptying, such a submergence of the light of eternity in the waters of temporality, possible? Is this not a self-annihilation, a self-extinction? This question is posed by impotent thought out of the depths of its perplexity.

Our human I is submerged in temporality. This I is constantly tossed about by time's waves, but it contains and knows eternity, despite

---

16. We find remarkably powerful words about the divine-humanity of the Word in Luther: "Gott ist Mensch, Mensch ist Gott in einer Person, Gottes Kind und Menschen Kind ist eins" (God is man and man is God in one person; God's child and man's child is one) ("Christmas Sermon," in Thomasius, *Christi Person und Werk,* p. 454). "Wo Gott ist, da ist auch der Mensch, was Gott thut, das thut auch der Mensch, und was der Mensch thut und leidet, das thut und leidet Gott" (Where God is, there also is man. What God does, that man does too; and what man does and suffers, that God too does and suffers) (ibid., p. 455).

this temporality of its being. The human I is the sun in the light of which temporality is perceived; it is the fixed point over which the waves of time have no power. In other words, the I that lives in time contains eternity as its foundation, and it contains spirituality as its inalienable treasure. This royalty and richness of the I are disclosed in temporal life as the self-revelation of the personal spirit that lives in time while belonging to eternity. In man one can see the cryptogram of the image of God, the mark of Divine-Humanity. If even the human I is capable of acquiring itself in its heavenly homeland, this is true to a superlatively greater degree for the Divine-Human hypostasis of Christ, the Son of God and the Son of Man. His *human* hypostasis, that of Jesus — "the son of Joseph and Mary," "the son of a carpenter," having an earthly parentage — is the *hypostasis of the Logos;* this is the profound mystery of His human consciousness, a mystery that is unceasingly and irresistibly revealed in Him as His Divine-consciousness and His Divine Sonhood (parallel to the growth of His temporal human consciousness). But this knowledge of the mystery of His Divine-consciousness, of His Divine Sonhood, does not abolish temporal human consciousness in Christ, *through* which and *in* which His Divine-consciousness shines in time, like an internal sun illuminating the moving clouds of the empirical consciousness. Even in the agony on the cross, just before death, His human consciousness and His Divine Sonhood are united in Him in the two cries: "My God, my God, why hast thou forsaken me?" (Matt. 27:46; Mark 15:34) and "Father, into thy hands I commend my spirit" (Luke 23:46). Christ is truly *Emmanuel* (God with us), who abides one and the same, in one and the same consciousness of self, although He reveals Himself for Himself at different depths of this consciousness: both as God and as Man — as the *God-Man.*

The self-consciousness of the God-Man's hypostasis, awakening from a preconscious state and gradually evolving and becoming focused, is essentially different, of course, from the normal human consciousness. *According to its type of development,* however, the divine-human hypostasis does not differ from the human hypostasis, and the God-Man is truly Man. In fact, the human hypostasis also possesses eternity — knowledge of itself not in becoming but in supratemporal being. This being is the foundation, depth, and mystery of the personality; and this mystery is revealed in the life of the personality, which is progressively synthesized here to become fully itself only beyond the limits of empirical temporal life. Similarly, during its life the human personality of Jesus becomes conscious of its hypostatic Divinity, of its hypostasis, which is inseparable from the Father and the Spirit and enters into the trihypostatic subject.

Jesus becomes conscious of Himself, of His hypostasis, as the Logos; but He is conscious of His hypostasis not only with an eternal knowledge but also humanly, discursively. Through this discursion the intuition of eternity is revealed, and the Sun of the eternal light shines: the Logos. This consciousness by which the Logos is conscious of Himself *through* the human prism and *in* human life (not outside or above it) is not only human and not only divine. It is the *divine-human* consciousness, in which the divine subject is the hypostasis for human life. The eternal hypostatic self-consciousness of the Logos is found below the horizon of the empirical human consciousness; it exists only as the "subconscious" or, more precisely, as the "superconscious," from which it passes into consciousness. In other words, Christ is the God-Man not only in the sense that the two natures (divine and human) are united in Him by one hypostasis but also in the sense that, in virtue of this union, this hypostasis also becomes *divine-human*: the union of the two natures penetrates into the proper depths of this hypostasis.

The Father sent and the Son went: the Son extinguished His proper divine life in Himself and thus His divine consciousness. He laid it at the Father's feet; He "gave Himself" to the Father in the same way that He commended His spirit into the hands of the Father when He was dying on the cross (see Luke 23:46) — and He was born in Bethlehem as the Infant Jesus. But the hypostatic spirit of this Infant is the Logos. By one supratemporal act, the totality of human spirits is created in God, and at the proper time God sends these spirits into the world for incarnation. Among the other spirits, the uncreated Spirit, the hypostatic Logos, was also sent into the world for incarnation in human flesh. And if created spirits know where they come from (and they at least *can* know this), the Logos who was made incarnate also knew who He was and where He came from. But having become incarnate in man and having been made man, He learned this in Himself and about Himself not only by eternal divine consciousness but also by temporal human consciousness, in such a way that the human consciousness was awakened, grew, and was strengthened in Him over the course of His temporal life, empirically attaining triumphant self-evidentness and perfect knowledge. This was, nevertheless, a progression from the lesser to the greater, from His appearance (which was certainly necessary, for without it there would not have been authentic temporality) to His total triumph. In Christ, the Son of Man, the genesis *(egeneto)* of the Word, the Son of God, was being accomplished and was accomplished. Thus, taking as our point of departure the analogy of human self-consciousness, we approach the divine-

Emmanuel, the God-Man

human self-consciousness, which in turn will become the destiny of the entire human race in glory when Christ will be imaged in all.

The Chalcedonian dogma expresses the general idea that Christ is "perfect" (*teleios*, i.e., possesses fullness) in His Divinity and in His humanity, that He is "begotten before all ages of the Father according to the Divinity, and in these latter days . . . born of the Virgin Mary . . . according to the humanity," and that He is "one and the same" *(hena kai ton auton)*. This formula is pronounced twice in the dogma, while *ton auton* appears four times: this repetition underscores the unity of the life of the God-Man in virtue of the unity of His personality, despite the duality of His natures. Furthermore, the dogma underscores the consubstantiality of Christ with God according to the Divinity and with us according to the humanity. Here, the humanity is defined as consisting of "a reasonable [*logikēs*] soul and body," which presupposes a tripartite structure of man where the third and supreme principle of the spirit is the Logos. It is important to establish that, according to the direct meaning of the dogma, only the human nature (the soul and the body) is present in the God-Man on the human side, *without* the hypostatic spirit, whose place is taken by the Logos. As a result, man is not complete here. Man in Christ is "perfect," but this does not by any means signify that he has a special hypostasis. Otherwise, Christ would be distinguished from other human beings not only by the duality of natures but also by the duality of hypostases, by a particular *complexity*, in virtue of which He would have, in addition to the human hypostasis, the hypostasis of the Logos, with the divine nature indissolubly connected with the human. No, Christ takes from humanity *only* the nature (i.e., soul and body, animated corporeality), which has a hypostatic spirit in the Logos. But this hypostatic spirit has its proper *spiritual* nature. In man this is the divine, eternal depth of his personality, the communion of the human spirit with Divinity. In Christ, on the other hand, the divine-human hypostasis of the Logos is united with its proper divine nature and is inseparable from it. Thus, the fact that Christ has one hypostasis and two natures does not *formally* prevent Him from being a true man at the same time.

What is the character of His one life in two natures, that is, of His life that is not only hypostatically but also naturally divine-human? *Inwardly*, to be sure, this union is an unfathomable mystery, but its external dogmatic lineaments are given to us. Outside of the kenosis, such a union is in general ontological nonsense, akin to adding infinity to a finite quantity, which necessarily becomes zero upon such addition. According to the direct requirement of the Chalcedonian dogma, however, the natures in

Christ are united without change and without confusion. The popular analogy of iron made red-hot in fire is not applicable here, since it is based on the supposition of a still bearable – although high – temperature, whereas the divine nature has such a high temperature compared to the human nature that even iron is immediately consumed by the fire. Therefore, if one does not recognize the *real kenosis* of Christ, the Chalcedonian dogma inevitably leads either to docetism or to monophysitism.

Christ's flesh is by no means only the "veil" of Divinity. This is another inadequate analogy from the natural world, for what creaturely and corporeal thing is capable of "veiling" the radiance of the Divine glory? It is not the flesh in itself that is the veil of Divinity but the *kenosis*, which extends both to the hypostasis and to the nature of the Logos in His Incarnation. The human I knows itself on the basis of life in its proper nature; and together with its personal self-consciousness, it also knows its natural essence. In man, the hypostasis of the Logos also knows itself in its human nature, which it knows in its personal life (it is to this *empirical* knowledge of the human nature that the words of the Apostle refer: "in that he himself hath suffered being tempted, he is able to succour them that are tempted" [Heb. 2:18]). But maturing in its naturally personal human self-consciousness, the personal I of Jesus is conscious of itself as the Logos, attains knowledge of its divinity; in this self-consciousness, His divine nature is revealed for Him *in actu*. The divine consciousness, which is unrestrainedly manifested in Jesus as His personal self-consciousness, is identical with this knowledge of His divine nature, of His eternal rootedness in Divinity.

This divine consciousness attains its fullness in the Savior's earthly life: He recognizes that He is the Son of the Father, existing from all eternity, "before Abraham was" (John 8:58). This divine consciousness, however, does not by any means abolish His humiliation (or His "descent from heaven"). His divine consciousness does not yet impart to the humiliated Christ the "properties" of Divinity: "Why callest thou me good? There is none good but one, that is, God" (Mark 10:18; see also Luke 18:19). In these controversial words of Christ to the rich youth, it is customary to see direct proof of the absence of divine consciousness in Him, or even an express denial that He possesses divine consciousness. In fact, however, it is an irrefutable testimony that the God-Man, having a divine personality and nature, *willed not to be God* during His earthly ministry; instead, He accepted humiliation and kenotically concealed His Divinity in *becoming*, having His Divinity, but not actualizing it. *How* could it in fact have been actualized? God and the world are so incommensurable that this relation

Emmanuel, the God-Man

cannot even be conceived of except on the basis of divine kenosis. This question has been completely obscured and distorted by the false formulation it has received in the doctrine of miracles. According to this doctrine, Christ accomplished *as God* certain works surpassing ordinary human powers: the miraculous feeding of the multitude, walking on water, raising from the dead. He accomplished His other works as man. For God, however, who created the universe by His omnipotence and governs the world while remaining above it, even the Gospel miracles (however astonishing they might be from the human point of view) are totally incommensurable with this Divine omnipotence and provide no basis for asserting that Christ accomplished them "as God," by the omnipotence by which "all things were made" (John 1:3). The miracles belong to Christ's life in humiliation.[17] Christ did not do anything "as God" or "as man." He did all things as *the God-Man,* in the inseparability and inconfusability of the two natures; this very distinction is already a monophysitic docetism or a "Nestorian" separation. The divinity of Christ was never manifested in the world as His glory and power, for the world — into which God had to "come down from heaven" in a state of humiliation — could never have withstood their manifestation. His divinity was revealed and apprehended only in inseparable connection with His humanity. For this reason, *prior to* the Resurrection He did not and could not say about Himself that "all power [i.e, divine power] is given unto me in heaven and in earth" (Matt. 28:18). After receiving this power, He ascended to heaven. The path of the Divine-Humanity in His life on earth is a *continuous* kenosis, not only an external, but also an inner kenosis.[18]

The divinity in Jesus inspired His divine-human person, and He was conscious of it *to the extent* His human essence could receive and contain it, but His human essence was not coerced here or bypassed. This expresses the unceasing, actual kenosis of the Divinity, which measures itself according to the humanity (according to the expression of St. Cyril).

17. On this subject, see my work *On the Gospel Miracles* (Paris, 1932).
18. Having clearly seen the complete authenticity of the kenosis, Thomasius interpreted it on the basis of the distinction of the "properties" of Divinity, immanent (absolute power or freedom, reason and bliss) and relative, manifested only in relation to the world (omnipresence, omniscience, omnipotence). Here, the Logos removes from Himself the relative properties while retaining the immanent ones. This application of the scholastic category of properties to the one Divinity in order to determine the measure of the kenosis is already a misunderstanding. The kenosis can be conceived only as one and universal. Kenotic theology is in general weakened by the absence in it of a sophiological foundation.

The Lamb of God

The humanity certainly has in itself the image of God, just as the Divine Sophia is the pre-eternal Humanity. However, the incommensurability and incompatibility between the infirm creaturely human essence and the divine essence are such that the latter restrained its manifestation in Christ by kenotic means of voluntary self-limitation until these limits were inwardly overcome by the glorification of Christ. Thus, the divine nature of the God-Man is not an external fact or given but a ceaselessly continuing process of the attainment of the divine in the human and of the human in the light of the divine. That is, it is a divine-human attainment. This *form* of divine life in the God-Man does not diminish the fact that Christ was "perfect" God, for this perfection refers to the authenticity of His divine nature, not to the form of its manifestation in Him, which is determined by the kenosis.

In the Chalcedonian dogma, the measure or form of the manifestation of Divinity in Christ is defined not only by the general postulate of the *unity* of the divine-human life (even though the expression "God-Man," which is unusual though not unknown in this epoch, is absent), but also by the four negative definitions of the form of the union of the natures: without confusion, without change, without division, and without separation. The general meaning of these definitions is as follows: First, neither nature absorbs or abolishes the other (which would of course be impossible for the human nature in relation to the divine nature, but its monophysitic dissolution in the divine nature is also excluded here). Second, the natures remain without separation; that is, there is a certain harmony, agreement, and conformity between them. By itself, the human nature is incapable of ascending to union with the divine nature, to a state where it is inseparable and coordinated with the divine nature; it is evident, therefore, that the divine nature kenotically renders itself commensurate with the human nature, so that God, in Christ, reveals Himself through man in a *divine-human manner*. This postulate excludes all theories that propose the *separate* action of the natures or their alternation.

At the same time, there are established the postulate of the unity and continuity of the life of the God-Man as well as, even more importantly, the possibility and necessity of the coexistence of the two natures, of their joint action. The *principle* that determines the content of this one divine-human life is, of course, the divine nature, but the *measure* of the manifestation of the divine nature in the God-Man is determined by the human essence: only that which the human essence is capable of receiving into itself can become a living acquisition for the Divine-Humanity. The

Emmanuel, the God-Man

Divine-Humanity is not an external juxtaposition of the two natures, divine and human, but their inner union. The God-Man is one living being, and all automatism is foreign to Him. In contrast, the widespread comparison of the two natures in Christ to the soul and body in man is marred precisely by such an automatism: divinity is compared here to the soul governing the life of the body, which is characterized not by independence but only by instrumentality and automatism. This comparison depicts a relation between the natures that is directly opposed to the Chalcedonian definition, which seeks to protect the natures against mutual diminution and absorption and to conjoin them in a unity of life by revealing the authenticity and fullness of each of them. This does not eliminate the *inequality* between them but affirms with greater insistence their *relative equality of rights*, which is guaranteed by an equalization according to the mode and measure not of what is higher but of what is lower, until a conformity between them is attained: "with the properties of each nature preserved" (according to Leo the Great). This is possible only in the case of the primacy in scale of the inferior essence, that of man (i.e., only in the case of the divine kenosis).

Kenosis is thus the fundamental idea tacitly implied by the Chalcedonian dogma. But the kenosis of Divinity is also the apotheosis of humanity. Christ is the God-bearing man and the in-humanized God. The impression He made on the people was that of a great prophet through whom God speaks. Wisdom, together with power and force, was given to Him. He Himself said that His teaching was not His own but of His Father, though He nevertheless preached in human language to men. The impression that He bore God within Himself sometimes attained such force and intensity that it compelled people first to recognize and then to confess His divinity: "Thou art the Christ, the Son of the living God" (Matt. 16:16). His humanity was never diminished or eclipsed by His divinity; on the contrary, it was illuminated and magnified: "God hath visited his people" (Luke 7:16). This was the glory and elevation precisely of the man, that God lived in him and was revealed through him. There was and could be no form of self-revelation of Divinity except in man and through man, if only because "no man hath seen God" (John 1:18), but He was revealed to people in human form by the only begotten Son of God. Indeed, man is incapable of receiving or encompassing the *non*human manifestation of God: God in His transcendence does not, in practical terms, exist for man; otherwise, His manifestation would totally destroy man ("there shall no man see me, and live" [Exod. 33:20]).

For men, therefore, the manifestation of Emmanuel was the manifestation of the "perfect man." Here, however, in His humiliation, in the accomplishment of His redemptive feat, this Man not only did not impress with external brilliance, but He was even diminished beneath the sons of men: He had neither "form nor comeliness" (Isa. 53:2). But divine grandeur does not require external brilliance, and spiritual power can appear without form or beauty. Christ's human countenance, which no man can know *entirely* in its divine-human grandeur, was seen (and is seen) by every man in virtue of a certain inner, spiritual revelation; but this Divine-Human countenance is also a human countenance, about which Pilate said (though without knowing what he was saying): "Behold the man!" (John 19:5). The Transfiguration of the Lord, in which Christ manifested His glory to His disciples, was also a *human* phenomenon, although a supernatural and gracious one. It was accessible to the human (even the "all too human") comprehension of His disciples. ("Let us make three tabernacles," said the Apostle Peter.) Nor did Christ's miracles represent manifestations of Divinity that were in contradistinction to or even in opposition to humanity. Rather, they were manifestations of God's power acting in and through man and were thus essentially *divine-human* works, which therefore could not be taken away or separated from His humanity.

Thus, *all* the works of the God-Man, His teaching and His manifestation, were an ineffable unity of that which was taking place in the interior of His human nature and that which He had in the depths of His divine consciousness of self. Least appropriate of all here is to think of this in terms of some divine oracle who imperiously dictates the pathways and achievements of humanity. The divine nature in its union with the human nature is not at all like this: It does not coerce; it inspires. Christ too — in the voluntary humiliation of His in-humanization — *sought* this inspiration, and He found it in the prayer to the Father. Through an intensity of spirit and a feat of prayer, He *sought* to know the Father's will, that is, to become conscious in Himself of the voice of His own divine nature. And this is attested by Christ's entire life of prayer, according to the Gospel, and more than anything else by the feat of prayer at Gethsemane, where with total clarity we perceive His struggle to hear the voice of His divine essence, the Father's will.

The Incarnation is accomplished from the very beginning, but the divine-humanity is realized and matures during the course of Jesus' earthly life: for the Divinity this is accomplished in virtue of the kenosis, while for the humanity it is accomplished in virtue of the general law of the human essence. Not one step of human development is realized in Him without a corresponding step in the growth of the divine self-

Emmanuel, the God-Man

consciousness, just as the latter never goes ahead of or coerces His human consciousness. The two are always commensurate and transparent for each other in the one God-Man and in His one divine-human life. The mystery and the power of the divine-humanity consist precisely in this conformity and agreement. This is a life in which the divine hypostasis, emptying itself to the level of the human hypostasis while at the same time remaining rooted in the Holy Trinity and the divine nature, inspires His perfect sinless human being. In its uniqueness, this life is inaccessible to the human understanding, even though it is a *human* life. Every man is given the power to approach this life, to seek and find in it his own life: "not I, but Christ liveth in me" (Gal. 2:20). Fundamentally *non-Chalcedonian,* and even anti-Chalcedonian, is the notion that the fullness of the divine life with its "properties" is not only present but is even actualized in Christ from the very beginning, and that the human essence is only added onto this life, with its path of development being marked on the part of the divine nature only by corresponding manifestations. This opinion was expressed both before and after Chalcedon, but always contrary to the direct testimony of the Gospel concerning the one divine-human life and its development: "the child grew, and waxed strong in spirit, filled with wisdom: and the grace of God was upon him" (Luke 2:40); "Jesus increased in wisdom and stature, and in favour with God and man" (2:52).

It would appear that there could be no clearer and more irrefutable expression of the idea that Jesus the God-Man passed through different stages of growth and was subject to progressive development. In His infancy Christ already potentially possessed the entire fullness of the Divine essence and the human essence; this fullness was not yet realized in His life-experience but remained the sacred mystery of His infancy. This mystery is swaddled in silence, as if in linens of body and soul, but beneath them the perfect man is already present with all that will be revealed (but not originated) in His development. Once born, an infant already exists for himself and for the world, for time and for eternity, in the entire fullness of humanity whether he lives or dies, whether his life is long or short. For this reason the Divine Infant is already, in the full sense, the one about whom it is said: "Behold the man!" This is not contradicted, however, by the fact that the manifestation *in actu* of this potentiality occurs in time, that it is a becoming; and the measure in which Jesus can contain the divine life, the measure of the self-revelation in the God-Man of His divine nature, corresponds to and is proportional to this becoming. This fundamental fact of the temporal *becoming,* or genesis, of the God-Man is attested not only by scattered texts (which could be considered accidental and whose significance could be denied by exegesis, correct or incorrect) but by the whole content of the Gospel, which gives a living, concrete picture of Christ's earthly life with its events and achievements, on the *way* to fullness and accomplishment: "I have a baptism to be baptized with; and how am I straitened till it be accomplished!" (Luke 12:50). Nowhere in the Gospel can one find the notion that there is such a separation and sundering of the divinity and the humanity in the one life of the God-Man that God, abiding in His divine absoluteness, would only *pretend* to be subject to human becoming and development (for the sake of appearance, adapting Himself to human needs), while in reality having nothing to do with it. Knowing all things, He would manifest ignorance; being God, He would pray; being unchangeable in His eternity, He would be subject to the principle of growth and maturation, and so on. To apply this doctrine consistently would be to abolish the Gospel image of Christ, both with regard to the Nativity and His years as a child and with regard to the days and hours of Gethsemane and Golgotha. Given such an interpretation, the sacred mystery of the Incarnation would become a kind of game. But that is impossible! The mystery, glorious and astonishing, consists precisely in the fact that God Himself lives an authentic human life in the God-Man, humbling Himself to the level of this life and maturing through it to the consciousness of the God-Man. The Divine-Humanity is a particular form of the Divinity's consciousness of itself *through* the humanity and of the humanity's consciousness of itself *through* the Divinity. It is the fusion of the Creator and creation, a fusion that is simultaneously the kenosis of the Divinity and the theosis of the humanity, and that concludes with the perfect glorification of the God-Man.

The assumption of the human nature by the Logos is ontologically based on the *pre-eternal Divine-Humanity,* in the image of which the creaturely divine-humanity (i.e., man) is created. By itself, however, this positive relation does not diminish or surmount the abyss that exists between the Creator and creation. The elevation of creation to communion with the Creator in hypostatic union represents, in any case, the proper work of the divine condescension (the kenosis) and the divine feat of love, which surmounts this abyss by its immeasurableness. In reality, however, there is here not only the ontological abyss between the Creator and creation but also a new abyss — the abyss between God and the *fallen* creation in man. The elevation of man to union with the Creator also signifies his *redemption* and his reconciliation with God, the victory over sin. The

Emmanuel, the God-Man

union of the two natures in the unity of the divine-human life — their harmonization without the coercion of the human nature by the divine nature — is the *cross* raised by the Son of God to save the world. Although the God-Man, the "only one without sin," received His flesh from the Virgin Mary by the Holy Spirit and was therefore free of original sin, nevertheless even this sinless flesh is not Adam's original essence, for it is weakened and burdened by the *consequences* of original sin. These consequences are not fully suppressed even in the human essence of the New Adam. Because of this state, in its weakness, this essence was less obedient to the commands of the spirit than is conformable with its primordial norm. "The spirit . . . is willing, but the flesh is weak" (Matt. 26:41), the Lord says during the night of Gethsemane, which itself attests to this weakness of the flesh and the resulting immeasurable intensity of the struggle with it. He "began to be sorrowful and very heavy" and said, "My soul is exceeding sorrowful, even unto death. . . . O my Father, if it be possible, let this cup pass from me: nevertheless not as I will, but as thou wilt" (26:37-39).

This shows the full reality of the God-Man's struggle against the weakness and heaviness of the flesh, as well as the full difficulty of subjecting it to the commands of the spirit. This particular weakness of the flesh is added to the natural infirmity of the creaturely human essence, which trembles in the face of death. One can say that if obedience to God's commandment was *natural* for the original Adam in Eden, then for the New Adam, because of His humanity, it required a victory over nature, an agony resulting in a sweat of blood. The union of the natures in the God-Man, therefore, does not signify their serene and harmonious coexistence and interpermeation but the intense and unceasing struggle in which this harmony is accomplished. In the God-Man, the fallen and infirm human essence, subjecting itself to the divine essence, becomes harmonious with and obedient to it. But this occurs not through the coercion of the human nature by the divine nature but by the spiritual overcoming of the "flesh" through its free subordination to the commands of the hypostatic spirit. In other words, this harmony and interpenetration of the two natures in the God-Man is *the feat and way of the cross*, which begins in the Bethlehem manger and ends at Golgotha. For the Son this is the path of *obedience* to the Father's will, the Son's accomplishment not of His own will but of His Father's will. In this submission to the Father's will the human nature, infirm in its creatureliness and weakened in its sinfulness, is overcome. The union of the two natures in Christ therefore cannot at any instant be understood statically as their mere juxtaposition; instead, it must be understood dynamically, as an ac-

The Lamb of God

tual interaction of energies. The nature is not only a given or a fact but also an actuality or a living and acting energy.

Such, precisely, is the energetic interpretation of the nature given in the dogma of the Sixth Ecumenical Council concerning the "two" wills or energies. This dogma interprets the hypostatic union of the two natures in Christ as *two streams of life,* to which all the general relations existing between the natures (without separation, without confusion, etc.) are applicable. Although the notion of "natural" will and energy remains indeterminate to some extent in this dogma, the novelty it introduces into Christology consists not only in an actual, energetic interpretation of the natures but also in a more concrete formulation of the problem of the relation between them. First of all, with a greater evidentness than can be found in the Definition of Chalcedon, this dogma demolishes the monothelitic doctrine of the absorption in Christ of the human will, which supposedly is subordinate to the divine will. In contrast, the *two* wills and *two* energies coexist as proceeding from the two natures. From this juxtaposition of two wills in correlation, the *kenotic* understanding of the divine will in Christ self-evidently follows; that is, the divine will is understood as being revealed in the temporal process, in becoming. When the dogma speaks of the divine will, it clearly does not mean the divine will of the Creator and Provider that possesses omnipotence in relation to all creation. Such a will cannot be correlated with the creaturely will, just as one cannot establish a relation between infinity and a finite quantity, for that would transform the finite quantity into zero. The divine will that can be correlated with the human will as *one of two* wills in Christ is clearly the divine will in the state of kenosis. This will is disclosed in Jesus in His divine consciousness in connection with the events of His divine-human life, in response to its calls and needs. In other words, the divine will is disclosed not as the absolute and omnipotent will of the Creator but as the consciousness of the divine truth and way in the God-Man's personal self-definition.

With this voluntaristic-energetic interpretation of the natures, however, a question inevitably arises, one that did not arise with such clarity in the Chalcedonian dogma's field of view: the question of the *hierarchical* relation of the two wills or the mode of their coordination. The dogma of the Sixth Ecumenical Council defines the relation of the wills negatively in the sense that they are *ouk hupenantia, non contrarias,* not opposite (which "only impious heretics assert"). Extracting the positive meaning from this negative definition, one finds that it indicates the relation between the natures that ontologically follows from the general foundations of the Incarnation. This *positive* relation of the wills is further expressed in the fact that the human will "follows" *(hēpomenon)* the divine will, that is, that its relation to the divine will is one of *free* obedience. This means that the human will is not broken or coerced but voluntarily and organically *grows into* the divine will. Furthermore, this "following" is once again clarified negatively: *mē antipipton ē antipalaion* (without contradicting or opposing). This indicates the *harmony* of the two wills, which is achieved by the effort of this "following." The definition concludes with a positive indication: "but it rather subordinates itself to His divine and omnipotent will." "Subordination" here — according to the meaning of the entire dogma of two autonomous wills as inseparable but inconfusable — signifies not the annihilation of the human will through its absorption by the divine will but the *hierarchical* relation of the two natural wills in one divine-human volition proper to the one hypostasis of the Logos. Any other interpretation of "subordination" would abolish the entire power of the Chalcedonian dogma of the duality and autonomous being of the natures, applied here to the particular case of the duality of the wills.

This duality exists in the unity of the divine-human will proper to the one God-Man; the will can be compared to a single thread woven of two separate threads. This unity is realized by the mutual transparence and identification of the two wills in volition. But the two wills, the two streams of volitions, harmonious and identified, must exist in a hierarchical coordination; the teleological primacy of the divine will, and of the supreme goal of the total deification of man, is natural and inevitable here. The divine will, recognized as supreme, offers the response to the movements and questionings of human will: "not as I will, but as thou wilt." This means that natural human will freely subjugates itself to that which is recognized as divine will. But this subjugation is not a passive subordination to a command or to an overwhelming force; rather, it involves the free choice and agreement of a will that accepts a superior content.

The divine will in the God-Man must be understood not as an immobile, eternal "predetermination" of the will of the omnipotent Divinity (to the extent it is legitimate to speak of a differentiated will with reference to the Absolute) but as a divine self-definition in accordance with the will of the Father that arises in the God-Man's consciousness at each moment of His life.[19] The Divine will and the human will in the God-Man

---

19. St. Maximus the Confessor (and following him, St. John of Damascus) denied the "gnomic" will, that is, the will that is free in the sense of the creative choice between different possibilities. Consequently, he conceived it as immutable divine necessity that

can be likened to two parallel streams flowing in the same direction and being united without mixing ("without separation and without confusion") in one flow of divine-human life. The unity of the hypostatic center, of the divine-human person, joins the two streams of the two wills into one volition. In the epoch of the monothelitic and dithelitic disputes, the connection between will and person (on which monothelitism was based) was generally rejected, and the "natural" character of the will was affirmed, with the resulting duality of wills a consequence of the presence of the two natures. Nevertheless, this by no means nullified the significance of the personal principle in natural volition: it is precisely the *person* that wills, even if *naturally* (i.e., on the basis of nature and through nature, which realizes its capability of volition only in and through the person). Person and nature exist everywhere inseparably; the one divine-human person wills by one act of volition, although it originates from a dual source — the divine essence and the human essence. Although this second part of the dogma of two wills, which refers to the unity of the God-Man Himself, was not an object of express examination at the Council, it nevertheless was the general, implicit foundation for the whole dogma (and the Chalcedonian definition is therefore woven like a scarlet thread into the dogma of the Sixth Ecumenical Council).

The hypostatic junction of the two essences, wills, and energies, implied by the unity of the person, is indirectly expressed in the definition of the Seventh Ecumenical Council concerning icons. According to the dogmatic meaning of this definition, Christ has *one* divine-human hypostatic Face, which the icon represents. The divine-human unity of the hypostasis, on both the divine and the human side, is dogmatically revealed here in the possibility of depicting the God-Man, so that the icon of Christ is, properly speaking, the image of the hypostatic Divine-Humanity.

The unity of the hypostasis that is simultaneously Divine and human (i.e., Divine-human) is also expressed in the unity of the Divine-Human name, *Jesus,* which is the name of both God and man. All the names of God are, in a certain sense, divine-human, insofar as God is revealed to man in the human word. The overwhelming majority of these

---

was *given* in the God-Man in the capacity of absolute guidance — both for volition and for action. But in general this denial of the "gnomic" will denies the divine will in the God-Man as *one of two* wills, which discursively defines itself in the life process of becoming and therefore is necessarily "gnomic." This denial can be interpreted only as the *infallibility* of the divine volition. But the will that manifests itself and realizes itself in temporal becoming with its freedom is necessarily conformable with time, or discursive; and therefore it must be gnomic.

names, however, are not so much proper names that refer to the hypostasis as descriptive names that refer to some "property" of Divinity (i.e., not the subject but the predicate). Only the expressly revealed names — Yahweh in the Old Testament and Jesus in the New Testament — refer directly to the hypostasis itself (i.e., not to the predicate but to the subject), and the name of the incarnate Word, *Jesus,* is a divine-human name representing a clear revelation concerning the divine-humanity (i.e., concerning the co-humanity of God and the Godlikeness of man, insofar as one and the same name is applicable to the hypostasis of God and to that of Man). On this basis, the naming of the God-Man Jesus, revealed by the Archangel in the Annunciation to Mary and then to Joseph in a dream before the birth of the Divine Infant, is such a testimony.[20]

II. The Union of the Essences (the Communication of the Properties and the Theandric Action)

From the christological dogma of the hypostatic union of the divine-human life, given the duality of the natures, wills, and energies, a series of questions follows concerning their interrelation. We already touched above upon the question of the progressive development of the God-Man, the question of His growth into a perfect man. If the divine nature in Christ is interpreted kenotically, the full reality of this development and growth must be accepted. Otherwise, the Incarnation loses its authenticity.[21]

---

20. In the present work, I leave unexamined the complex and difficult question of the naming and name of God, since I have already examined it in the unpublished work "Religio-philosophical Introduction to the Doctrine of the Name of God."

21. To be sure, the following argument is also put forth: If Divinity as such possesses omniscience and fullness, irreconcilable with any development and limitation, one can say that Divinity only takes on the *form* of ignorance and limitation, manifesting itself only to the extent that the human nature can receive it. Such a position is correct, but overly abstract. It must be understood as a real humiliation and self-limitation of Divinity, where Christ's divine self-consciousness grows and is deepened, instead of remaining in immobility, which is proper only to eternity. The kenosis consists precisely in the going out of eternity into temporality and becoming, such that eternity, being the foundation of temporality, is removed from its surface. This distinction is usually understood abstractly and statically; all becoming in the divine self-consciousness is then excluded in the name of the unchangeability of eternity, and the development itself acquires the significance of not more than a conventional mask.

But this particular question contains a more general one: What is the interrelation between the two essences in Christ in their hypostatic union, in the unity of Christ's life? Does the one exist in and for the other, or do they resemble liquids contained in vessels that are not in contact with each other and open only upward, in the direction of the one hypostasis? The possibility of such an answer is excluded by the christological definitions of the Fourth and Sixth Ecumenical Councils: Even though the natures are united without confusion, without loss of their autonomous being, they are also united without separation; as a result, they are in a relation of mutual influence and mutual penetration. This doctrine was generally accepted in the patristic writings as well, which established the "communication of properties" *(perichoresis, communicatio idiomatum)* of the two natures and the "theandric energy." The results of this doctrine are summed up by John of Damascus.[22] Ignoring the insufficiency of his definitions, one can accept his general goal, expressed in the following words: "We do not say that the actions [in Christ] are separate, nor that the essences act independently of one another. Rather [we affirm] that each of them accomplishes what is proper to it with the participation of the other one, together with the other one. For Jesus Christ did not accomplish what is proper to man in the way that man usually accomplishes it, since He was not just man. Likewise, He accomplished what is proper to God not in the same way as God, since He was not just God, but God and man together" (book 3, ch. 19, c. 1080). In what precisely is this "togetherness" expressed, the "togetherness" of the essences and their mutual "participation" in each other's life, that is, the participation of the divine essence in the human essence and the participation of the human essence in the divine essence? Where can the *possibility* of such participation, its *form* and *measure*, be seen? Such is the immensely difficult question that follows directly from the Chalcedonian definition and that has not been answered by patristics; the failure to answer it has given rise to all the deviations in the direction of monophysitism.[23]

---

22. See his *Brief Exposition of the Orthodox Faith*, book 3. The fundamental feature of his discussion, rooted in the absence of the kenotic point of view, consists in the fact that, although he shows the influence of the divine nature on the human nature in the deification of the latter, he fails to show the reverse influence of the human nature on the divine nature, although this is postulated by the "theandric" principle.

23. The main reason for this, here too, is the absence of an expressly established and consistently developed idea of kenosis. Here is the initial point of view of St. John of Damascus: "in order that the Word be made flesh, He did not leave the domain of Divine being and was not deprived of the perfections proper to Him and appropriate to God" (ibid., book 3, ch. 17, c. 1069). In effect, this excludes the descent from heaven and the humiliation.

The general principle of the interrelation of the two natures in the one life of Christ, according to the Chalcedonian definition concerning their inseparability and inconfusability, is as follows. It is not the case that the divine nature was always disclosed in unchangeable fullness and only adapted itself to the possibilities of manifestation in the human nature. Rather, both natures are disclosed in one life following the principle of *mutuality*, which necessarily involves not only interaction but also *mutual limitation*. We have here not only *pati Deum* for man but also *pati hominem* for God in the state of kenosis. The divine nature is present in Christ during His humiliation. It is present in the ontological fullness of its being but *not* in the fullness of self-revelation and consciousness of self, which are subject to the limitations of mutuality. One cannot imagine that the divine essence is initially present in Jesus in all the fullness and glory that are proper to Him as God in heaven, whereas the infirm human nature, with its changeability and different ages, transmits or does not transmit — as through a glass, darkly — the rays of the Divinity living in Him (as is usually understood). Such a notion would negate the whole force of the Chalcedonian definition, which establishes precisely the *mutuality* of the life of the two natures, their interaction and mutual reception.[24] This presupposes an activity of the two natures in which each reveals itself as such but the two mutually reveal themselves each in the other. This excludes the *passivity* of the human nature in relation to the divine nature, a passivity that would transform the human nature into a mere means or instrument.

As has been established in the patristic literature, the action of the divine nature on the human essence is *deification*. This principle is applied not only to Christ Himself but also to all of Christ's humanity. But deification does not consist in the external, physical action of one natural force on another (as one may be led to think by the common patristic analogies with fire and iron). Rather, it is a *spiritual penetration,* united with the inner *reception* of this action. The human essence of Jesus assimilated this deification progressively, from measure to measure. There were "times and seasons," degrees of growth, as even the partisans of the mechanical interpretation cannot deny. The *possibility* of deification is based on the fact that man bears the divine image in his human image and is

---

24. When the dogma speaks of Christ "as perfect in Divinity and also perfect in humanity," this refers to the ontological fullness and authenticity of the natures, not to their manifestation from the beginning. This is clearly not applicable to Christ's humanity, which undeniably underwent development. But in virtue of this, this is equally inapplicable to the Divinity in its kenosis.

The Lamb of God

therefore called to receive the divine life into his own life. In this sense, gracious and supernatural deification is normal for man; there is no coercion in it, nothing against nature. Deification does not necessarily signify the *empirical* manifestation of all the powers and capacities proper to man in the fullness of his humanity. In his human existence, Jesus did not by any means manifest all the human possibilities that can belong to human genius. He, the Word of God by whom all things were made, was limited by the historical context in which He was placed and did not differ in His empirical and historical aspect from a Jew of His epoch. It was as if world culture, whether past or present, did not exist for Him. He never revealed the mysteries of the world that only He knew and that human thought and knowledge were called to decipher — it was as if cosmic and historical being did not exist for Him, the Logos of the world. He had to accomplish the deification of the human essence in Himself and to regenerate fallen man by bestowing divine sonhood upon him, allowing the sons of men to become the sons of God and to discover their entire humanity themselves. He saved humanity in its metaphysical foundation. Nevertheless, although He limited His ministry exclusively to the religious domain, Jesus in His divine consciousness (which was manifested in His deified humanity) followed the path of unceasing exploit, by which He prepared His human essence for deification. In His holy and sinless humanity, which contained all the greatness given to mankind, the divine life was manifested in a manner that no man could encompass, not even the greatest of the prophets. However, this was human inspiration by the divine. In essence, this was prophetic inspiration, and when people who did not know that He was divine called Him teacher, rabbi, or prophet, He did not deny such names, but His acceptance of them was, of course, only in relation to His humanity.

The prophets, however, were not coerced by God either (they were only drawn by Him; see Jer. 20:7 [Russian Bible]). Nothing was given to them that was beyond their capacity to receive, and their human essence opened up to receive what it desired to receive. The prophets were not reduced to the level of a passive instrument or Balaam's ass. (Typologically, therefore, the Chalcedonian formula, "without separation and without confusion," is applicable to their deification.) In the prophet Jesus of Nazareth as well, insofar as He was a prophet and followed the "prophetic ministry," the divine was revealed in the human. In the God-Man there was no consciousness of anything divine *apart from* the human. The deification of the humanity is also the unceasing *identification* of the divine and the human, without separation and without confusion, without the

Emmanuel, the God-Man

mixing or abolition of the natures, in their living, organic unity: *natura humana capax divini* (the human nature receives the divine) just as *natura divina capax humani* (the divine nature receives the human). The patristic doctrine therefore justly affirms that Divinity is revealed in the human essence only in proportion to its capacity to receive this revelation; in this sense, Divinity adapts itself, so to speak, to the limitations and to the development of the human essence. However, applying the principle of relativity and mutuality to the relations between the divine nature and the human nature, the patristic doctrine effects a de facto abolition of this mutuality, affirming the fullness of the self-revelation of the divine nature in Christ apart from a real relation to the human nature (i.e., not "without separation"). This doctrine thus rejects the unitability of the absolute and the relative as inconceivable, transforming this unitability into nothing more than a manifestation.

But in order to be united with the relative, creaturely human nature and to be correlated with it in this union, the divine nature must in a certain sense remove the absoluteness from itself; it must become relative in its turn and correlative with the human nature. To use a physical analogy, liquids in two connected vessels must rise and fall simultaneously and proportionately, not in such a manner that one would be invariably full while the other would be empty and only gradually be filled from the other. The divine-humanity consists precisely in such a *correlativeness* of the divine and the human: the divine consciousness in Christ is commensurate with the human consciousness and does not exceed it. This relativity of the absolute, this becoming that occurs within the limits of the divine consciousness, is precisely *kenosis*. All of Christ's testimonies about His own Divinity are therefore *divine-human* revelations addressed to man: they are expressed in human language and are measured by a human measure.[25] As a *possibility*, therefore, the fullness of the divine consciousness, the "glory," was always ready to illuminate the God-Man to the extent His humanity was capable of receiving it. But this could be realized only after the Resurrection, when God gives to the God-Man the glory that was His before the founda-

---

25. Luther speaks of this with incredible power: "Gott ohne Fleisch ist nichts nütze. Ich habe keinen Gott, weder im Himmel, noch auf Erden, ich weise auch sonst von keinem ausser dem Fleische, welches in dem Schosse der Jungfrau Maria liegt. Denn Gott ist sonst auf alle Weise unbegreiflich, aber allein in dem Fleische Jesu ist Er begreiflich" (God without flesh is of no use. I have no God, whether in heaven or on earth, and I know no God except the God in the flesh who lay in the womb of the Virgin Mary. For God is always unknowable, and is known only in the flesh of Jesus.) (Thomasius, *Christi Person und Werk*, 1.453).

tion of the world. The life of the God-Man is one and inseparable in the union of the two natures, and all that is divine in Jesus is also human, just as all that is human in Him contains the revelation and life of Divinity. In the God-Man there is nothing that is only Divine or only human; the one in and through the other is Divine-human. The two natures are united not only without separation but also without confusion.

The deification of the human essence in the God-Man, therefore, does not by any means signify the dissolution, absorption, or depersonalization of this essence. In general, it does not signify the loss by the human essence of its natural human properties; on the contrary, *salva proprietate utriusque naturae* (the properties of each nature are preserved). The deification of the human essence in Christ during the days of His earthly ministry made Him *Christ*, the anointed of God. He was sent in order to manifest God in the human image as the Son of God and the Son of Man (by word and deed, by prophetic preaching and miracle working). But as a consequence of the union of the divine and human natures in Christ, He was not liberated from the properties of the human flesh: He thirsted, hungered, became fatigued, slept, journeyed — in short, He lived like a man. He also knew the impulses of the soul: love, anger, sorrow, joy, and so on. The features of human corporeal spatiality, with its limitations, were proper to Him: He sends His disciples to prepare a room for the celebration of Passover; He looks for fruit on a fig-tree; He asks who touched Him, where Lazarus was laid, and so on. All these properties of human psycho-corporeal limitation remain compatible with the ongoing deification of His human essence, just as they were compatible with the deification of the prophets when they were illuminated by the Holy Spirit, for the natures are united *without confusion*. Only that which in the human nature is *not* compatible with deification has no place in the God-Man. But this refers only to sin, and no one will ever find sin in the only one who is without sin.

One is therefore astonished by the number of apologetic inventions in the patristic and later writings that attempt to negate the direct and irrefutable meaning of the Gospel narratives that indicate the true humanity of the God-Man. Christ wept before He raised Lazarus, and He asked where Lazarus had been laid. The pseudo-apologists conclude that He did this only to "demonstrate" His humanity, even though, as God, He knew all things. Basing their argumentation on a false idea, these apologists sunder the inseparable union. But God's "omniscience" and "omnipotence," and in general His "properties" in relation to the world *in abstracto*, are totally inapplicable here *in concreto* to the life of the God-Man. Is it not simpler to humble oneself before the testimony of the Gospel and accept

Emmanuel, the God-Man

that the God-Man truly did not know where Lazarus had been laid, that He truly sought fruit on the fig-tree, and so on? For His divine gifts were in no wise directed at freeing Him from his human properties, and His Divinity inspired Him not to know the things of the natural world supernaturally, but to know and do the will of the Father, to abide in union with Him.

The falsity of this interpretation of deification, which forgets about the inseparability and inconfusability of the natures in Christ, becomes most clear with reference to three particular questions: the question of miracles (which we will not consider here[26]), the question of Jesus' ignorance, and the question of His prayer. In the Gospels we encounter not only cases where the Lord is ignorant of various particularities (though the ignorance is, of course, accompanied by His prescience) but also His direct testimony that He does not know the day of the Second Coming. Patristics, for the sake of doctrinal considerations, used various ploys to evade the direct and irrefutable meaning of the Lord's words; a new heresy even arose: that of the Agnoetae.[27] But why not simply admit that, during His earthly ministry, the God-Man could have been ignorant of the day of the Second Coming, since knowledge of it was not a direct necessity for Him? A *kenotic* interpretation of this text becomes inevitable here: In descending from heaven and becoming incarnate, the Son of God Himself confined His divine essence (together with the power of His omniscience) *within the limits of the divine-humanity;* He potentialized His divine essence and made it correspond to the measure of man. The Son of Man did not know the day and hour of the Second Coming (Mark 13:32) because the measure of His divine-humanity had not yet reached its fullness, and the divine nature had not yet attained the fullness of its revelation in the human nature. But one can no longer say this about Him in His glorification, when the God-Man testifies about Himself: "All power is given unto me in heaven and in earth" (Matt. 28:18); and of course that day and hour are already known by the Lamb of the visions of the Apocalypse, who attests: "Surely I come quickly. Amen" (Rev. 22:20).

This limitation is even more applicable to the childish state of ignorance and maturation of the Divine Infant. To be sure, childhood has its own power and depth, its own human wisdom, for the child contains the man in a hidden manner for himself and for other people; he contains

---

26. See my work *On the Gospel Miracles.*

27. The Agnoetae were a monophysite sect founded in the sixth century whose members attributed ignorance to the human soul of Christ. — Trans.

the man with his destiny in the present age and the future age. But the immediate state of childhood is spiritual potentiality. In the holiness of the Divine Infant this potentiality embraces not only the perfect sinless humanity of the New Adam but also — united with this humanity without separation and without confusion — the Divinity of the Logos together with the Logos Himself. In conformity with the law of the development of the human essence, however, the divine-humanity too was manifested and consciously recognized only gradually, with the growth of the man ("the child grew and waxed strong" [Luke 2:40]). There is a widespread notion that the Divinity in Jesus only *accommodated itself*, in its revelation, to His human ages and possibilities, but this notion destroys the divine-human unity by abolishing the becoming, the temporal process that is proper to the authentic Divine-Incarnation. Only the inconfusability of the natures remains here; their inseparability disappears. Only the kenotic idea of the Incarnation, which extends becoming to the *entire* God-Man with both of His natures, accords with the Gospel testimony that, in His earthly life, Christ was subject to temporal development. Divine knowledge entered into Him; it was realized in Him together with human knowledge.

A similar difficulty arises with regard to Jesus' prayer. According to the testimony of the Gospel, the Lord accomplished a continuous feat of prayer from the beginning of His ministry to the end. Was this prayer necessary for Him? Was it possible? To whom did He pray as God? Was His prayer addressed to Himself? In answering such questions, certain patristic commentaries attempt to weaken one of the most important and startling facts of the Gospel narrative. According to such commentaries, the Lord prayed only for the sake of example;[28] that is, He prayed without praying — in His "prayer" before the baptism, before the election of the apostles, before the Transfiguration, before the raising of Lazarus, in His "high-priestly prayer," at Gethsemane, on Golgotha, and so on. This is one of the numerous and striking consequences of the docetism that becomes inevitable when the kenosis is denied, when the Lord's self-humiliation is insufficiently understood. But in humiliating Himself to the point of becoming man, the God-Man established for His earthly life not the supreme measure of the fullness of His Divinity but only the relative measure of humanity, with which He united Himself without separation.

If worship of God and prayer are proper to the human essence, for

---

28. See St. John of Damascus, *Brief Exposition of the Orthodox Faith*, book 3, ch. 24, c. 1092.

the God-Man prayer is life and breath. He does not do anything without prayer. The Father who sent Him into the world and whose will He is called to work in the world is His Father and God (see John 20:17). Therefore, the divine nature, which is united in a state of humiliation with the human nature, not only does not hinder prayer, not only does not make it superfluous for Him, but on the contrary, it inspires His human essence to unceasing prayer, for prayer is also divine inspiration: "God hath sent forth the Spirit of his Son into your hearts, crying, Abba, Father" (Gal. 4:6). There was never a time in the life of the Lord when He did not pray: He prayed before the people and in isolation, in a solitary room and in the temple, on a mountain and in a vineyard. Prayer even accompanies Him beyond the limits of the Ascension: "I will pray the Father, and he shall give you another Comforter" (John 14:16), He says in the Last Discourse, although it marks the transition to the glorified state, where the God-Man enters into the glory of God: "whatsoever ye shall ask in my name, that will I do, that the Father may be glorified in the Son" (14:13). After the Resurrection, the disciples "worshipped Him" (Matt. 28:9) as God, and Thomas cried: "my Lord and my God" (John 20:28). According to a widespread doctrine, Christ was God who only used the flesh as a veil. If this doctrine were correct, He would not be our brother, praying with us and for us, just as He would not be the Intercessor and the Redeemer, the High Priest according to the order of Melchisedec, offering Himself as a redemptive sacrifice. All this would then be only an appearance and a kind of demonstration. But the Logos became the God-Man, Emmanuel, Christ; and Christ cannot be understood only as a manifestation of the Logos beneath a veil of flesh, who is like us only in appearance but in essence is totally unlike us, who in fact is only God, not the God-Man. Christ has the hypostasis of the Logos with His divine nature, but He is not the Logos in His eternal being. Rather, He is the God-Man. The Logos lives in Christ, but He lives in Him not as in a temple or behind a veil. The Logos lives in Christ in the kenosis of Divinity and in the fullness of divine-human life. In other words, in the God-Man there are no manifestations of the divine life that are not human, just as there is nothing human in Him that is not deified, full of grace, permeated with divine light, even if not yet glorified. In the God-Man all things are divine-human. "When the fulness of the time was come, God sent forth his [only begotten] Son, made of a woman, made under the law . . . that we might receive the adoption of sons" (Gal. 4:4-5).

Thus, in the hypostatic union of the two natures the God-Man reveals Himself in His divine nature in His unitary life only to the extent that this nature can be contained by His humanity, to the extent of the deification of His humanity. *Theōsis* in the God-Man's earthly life must therefore be understood not in relation only to the one human essence but also in relation to the *two* essences, in relation to the one God-Man. Being God by hypostasis and nature, but humbling Himself to the point of union with man and emptying Himself, He actualizes His Divinity for Himself only in inseparable union with the human nature, as a function of its receptivity. Therefore, the perichoresis, the communication of the properties of the two natures in the God-Man, goes in both directions: not only from the divine to the human but also from the human to the divine.

This idea is accepted as a postulate by St. John of Damascus, although he gives only a negative definition for the latter relation: "His divine action was not deprived of participation in the human action." He does not go beyond this in developing his thought. This side of the perichoresis, the movement from the human nature to the divine nature, is in effect denied, since the idea of the *divine-human* union of the natures in Christ is insufficiently developed. Although the human flesh is received into the hypostatic union for the sake of its redemption, in itself it remains, as it were, outside the life of the God-Man. It remains an instrument (St. John of Damascus), a veil, or a kind of annex or accident in the theophany; it is not a nature or ousia existing for the Divinity itself. It is remarkable that all the mutually antagonistic christological schools (with the possible exception of Apollinarius) converged in this de facto denial that the flesh participated in the proper life of the God-Man. This included St. Cyril with his unintentional docetism, the school of Antioch with its radical separation of the natures, and monophysitism with its de facto abolition of the human nature, considered to be absorbed by the divine nature. But against all these theological subtleties that tended to diminish or to deny the reality of the Incarnation and the authentic divine-humanity of Emmanuel, and that subjected to doubt the very possibility of the union of God with the creature, there thundered the divinely inspired words of the son of thunder: "And the Word was made flesh, and dwelt among us" (John 1:14). "Was made [*egeneto*]" must be understood in all the power of the reality that the Creator gave to His creation, and the union of the two natures in the Incarnation is the meeting of a reality with a reality. To be sure, the first reality is uncreated, whereas the second is created, but this difference in ontological rank does not by any means make the created reality illusory or only instrumental in its union with the Divine proto-reality. These two realities are similarly real, so to speak, and therefore their meeting takes place on the plane of reality, not on the plane of illusoriness. A similar relation — also on the plane of reality — exists between God and the world as far as Divine Providence is concerned; but although it is based on interaction and presupposes the autonomous being of the world, this relation nevertheless remains *external* in a certain sense: God governs the world while remaining above or outside it. But here, by the kenotic act of humiliation, the Son approaches the world, comes down from heaven, becomes flesh, which thus becomes for Him not only an external fact but also an inner fact of His proper divine-human life.

In His divine-human life the God-Man lives an authentic human life, and as a result, His divine nature is subject to the influence of this human life, is determined by it "without separation" and is conditioned by it "without confusion." The humanity exists in the God-Man *together with* His Divinity, as a certain autonomous force that does not oppose His Divinity but rather "follows" it. But by the very fact of its existence it complicates His life: "two natures, two wills, two energies," and consequently, as the resultant of this interaction, one "complex" life (the fathers imprecisely speak here of a "complex hypostasis"). And this inevitably gives rise to a further thought: Does God suffer with human suffering, or does the Divinity remain in the God-Man outside or above this suffering? To simply reject all participation of the Divinity in the human suffering as "theopaschism" would be to reject the Incarnation itself and to reduce it to a mere appearance. From the early days of Christianity, there was a tendency for human thought, paralyzed by the scandal of the cross, to flee the mystery of the Incarnation: we see this in the Ebionites, the gnostics, and all sorts of docetics. As a theological postulate, their thought succumbed to the satanic temptation articulated by the Jews at the foot of the cross: "If thou be the Son of God, come down from the cross . . . and we will believe [thee]" (Matt. 27:40, 42). The passion of the Son of God on the cross appeared to be a stumbling block for human thought: "the doctrine of the cross is a folly for those who perish" (see 1 Cor. 1:18). And the crucified God's only response to this was a new and final confession of His Divine Sonhood: "Father, into thy hands I commend my spirit" (Luke 23:46). The incarnate God was crucified and suffered on the cross. It is thus impossible to speak of the impassibility of the Divinity in the God-Man. Having appropriated the human nature in His humiliation and with His hypostasis living in it as well as in the divine nature, Christ also appropriated the sinless character of the divine nature. But just as one cannot separate His hypostasis from His divine nature, so one cannot limit the appropriation of the human nature to the hypostasis alone: the human nature is united with the divine nature in the unity of the divine-human life without separation and without confusion, and consequently it puts its imprint on the divine nature in this nature's kenotic self-diminution. In other words, a real perichoresis occurs also in the passion on the cross. The human nature makes the divine nature a coparticipant in its destiny and in its passion. This relation, clear in its principle, cannot be elucidated in its details, for it surpasses human understanding.

Nevertheless, St. John of Damascus examines certain particular features of this interrelation. First of all, he speaks of Christ appropriating "all the natural passions [*pathē*] of man" except sin; these "passions" (i.e., corporeal states and emotional impulses, and in general the entire psycho-corporeal life of man) are "not in our power; they are those which have entered human life as a consequence of the condemnation of man for his crime, such as hunger, thirst, fatigue, toil, tears, corruption, horror of death, sickness, the agony before death, from which come sweat, drops of blood, assistance from the angels on account of the infirmity of the nature, and suchlike which is proper to human beings by nature."[29]

But in what follows John abstains from a consistent application of this principle.[30] That is, although he acknowledges that the Word appropriates the sufferings of the body, John excludes His "impassible" nature from this appropriation.[31] "We say that God suffered in the flesh, but in no wise do we say that Divinity suffered in the flesh or that God suffered through the flesh. When the sun illuminates a tree and an axe chops down this tree, one can be certain that the sun is not chopped down and is not subject to suffering;[32] but how much greater is the certainty that the impassible Divinity of the Word, hypostatically united with the flesh, remained unaffected by suffering when the flesh suffered" (book 3, ch. 27, c. 1096).

Thus, while acknowledging that the Word had accepted the sufferings of the flesh, St. John of Damascus denies that these sufferings had any relation to the divine nature, which is "impassible." However, can one separate the hypostasis from the nature in this manner (as John in effect does) and consider that which is proper to the hypostasis (the suffering of the flesh) to be totally alien to the divine nature? Does this not contradict

---

29. Ibid., ch. 20, c. 1082.
30. Ibid., ch. 22.
31. Ibid., ch. 26, c. 1094.
32. The clarification of divine things by physical analogies, characteristic for ancient thought, appears strange here and explains nothing.

both the letter and the meaning of the Chalcedonian definition, according to which the natures are united *without separation* (which serves as the basis of the principle of perichoresis, proclaimed by John himself)? Can that which occurs with one of the natures have no effect on and no relation to the other nature? Does this not separate the inseparable natures in the divine-humanity? Does this not introduce into the life of the divine hypostasis itself a certain duality in virtue of which the God-Man's life is no longer one life but a dual life? Can it be the case that, being impassible in one life, He suffers in the other? Here too, the chief foundation for such a conclusion is the absence of the kenotic principle in Christology. According to St. John of Damascus, the divine nature united itself with the human nature in all its pre-eternal fullness, power, and glory; this "inconfusable" union therefore appears to be incomprehensible — this union which, although it is, properly speaking, impossible for Divinity, turns out to be possible for the hypostasis of the Word. If we accept Christ's self-humiliation as the foundation of the union of the natures, the main difficulty in understanding this union is then removed. Christ's divinity is revealed in Him together with and without separation from His humanity; that is, it is revealed divine-humanly. Contrary to St. John of Damascus, it is not revealed in separation from, and especially not in opposition to, His humanity. In virtue of the perichoresis, the human nature puts its imprint on the life of the divine nature, in a manner unfathomable for us. To be sure, it is not possible to say that the divine nature in Christ could suffer together with the flesh, *as* flesh. But the soul too, after all, even the human soul, while suffering with the flesh suffers not in a fleshly manner but in a spiritual manner. We human beings have been given the capacity to spiritually co-suffer when it comes to the fleshly sufferings of another person; this is especially true when we are called to co-suffer in relation to the wounds of our Lord Jesus Christ ("I bear in my body the marks of the Lord Jesus" [Gal. 6:17]). Even though the flesh is, of course, foreign to it, the Divinity of the Lord Jesus Christ spiritually co-suffers in relation to the fleshly passion of the hypostatic Word, for the nature cannot fail to suffer if its hypostasis suffers. This is an authentic perichoresis or *circumsessio,* a reversible and reciprocal movement. This idea possesses a kind of ontological self-evidentness, which follows from the inseparability of hypostasis and nature. We cannot and should not attempt to find a more precise expression for this spiritual co-suffering of Christ's Divine essence in relation to His human essence. In this co-suffering, one can see one of the manifestations of that general kenosis or "humiliation" to which Divinity subjected itself in Christ.

The Lamb of God

Furthermore, one cannot admit an "impassible" or indifferent relation to Christ's passion on the part of the hypostases that are not made incarnate, and first of all on the part of the Father, who sent His only begotten Son into the world and determined according to His will that His Son should drink to the bottom the cup of death. One can and should emancipate oneself from false Patripassianism or Theopaschism (associated with the name Peter Gnapheus, who in this sense distorted the Trisagion, insofar as he had the First hypostasis participate in the Incarnation and even in the Crucifixion together with the Second). But this does not abolish that connection of love in the Holy Trinity in virtue of which the Golgotha mystery is accomplished in its special sense in heaven as well, in the Father's heart, which is the Holy Spirit. This is sometimes attested iconographically by representations of the sorrowing and suffering Father leaning from on high over the crucified Son, with the sun darkened and the earth trembling.[33] The wisdom of the iconographer's vision is more profound here than scholastic theology. To be sure, human language does not have the means to express this sorrow of the Father, who *sends* His only begotten Son to His passion on the cross; but this is the *sacrifice* of the Father, precisely the sacrifice of love, for it is thus that God the Father *loved* the world, and there is no love without sacrifice. The very *sending* of the Son into the world is not an act of power on the part of the Father (as if a caprice) but the act of sacrificial love that contains the initial principle of the Incarnation. And the Son more than once indicates, implicitly, this property of the Father: "shew us the Father"; "he that hath seen me hath seen the Father" (John 14:8, 9). And if the Son is the sacrifice of love, what is the Father? Isaac is led to the sacrifice, but who leads him if not his father? Whose heart is torn apart if not that of Abraham, the father of the faithful, the earthly forefather of Jesus, "the son of Abraham" (Matt. 1:1)?

It is inappropriate here to seek a confirmation of God's "impassibility" in His unchangeability. In general, this very notion is the product of an abstraction and, to tell the truth, does not correspond to anything. It does not refer to the intratrinitarian life of Divinity in itself, to the "immanent" Trinity, for "impassibility" is a notion that is relative and negative at the same time: without a relation to "passion," whose presence in it must be denied, it is deprived of content and does not signify anything. If this notion is used to define the relation of the Absolute as God to the world, it is totally erroneous, for in creating the world and providing for

---

33. For example, on V. M. Vasnetsov's frescoes in the Cathedral of St. Vladimir in Kiev. Sometimes emblems of the Holy Spirit are added to this image.

it, God interacts with the world and enters into a relation with the world process and with human freedom. And God is referring not to His impassibility or indifference but to something wholly other, i.e., about the fire of love, when He says about Himself: "the LORD thy God is a consuming fire, even a jealous God" (Deut. 4:24; cf. Heb. 12:29); and "I the LORD thy God am a jealous God" (Exod. 20:5; cf. 34:14). This does not at all correspond to impassibility or indifference, especially when the most earthshaking and significant event in creation occurs: the death of the Son of God in torment on the cross. If it is not possible to admit impassible indifference even in heaven, it is less possible to admit it in the crucified Son, whose divine essence, in its impassibility, supposedly did not participate in the passion on the cross and supposedly did not even notice it. No! Contrary to the antikenotic static character of such a notion, we must affirm, on the basis of the Chalcedonian dogma and the resulting doctrine of perichoresis and theandric action, that in its own manner (spiritually, of course) the divine essence also participated in the sufferings of Christ. The God-Man, with His one hypostasis, suffered in the inseparable and inconfusable union of His two natures, in His *entire* being, that is, in His hypostasis as well as in His two natures. Although the ontological "site" of the suffering, its origin and its accomplishment, refers only to His human nature, the divine nature too, in its humiliation, "cosuffers" with the human nature. To be sure, the divine nature is not subject to necessary or compulsory suffering, since the very participation of this nature in human life is a work of love; love is free and a law unto itself, and the passion of the God-Man is voluntary.[34] But according to the dogma of the two wills, the divine will participates in all human volitions, and it does so not by an abstract assent but by an actual co-experiencing.

III. Christ's Divine-Human Consciousness of Self

A. *The Son of God and the Son of Man*

As a result of the union of the two natures, even given their mutual transparence in the perichoresis, Christ's natural life is "complex" in a cer-

---

34. St. John of Damascus writes: "In Him, we do not see anything compulsory; everything is voluntary. For by His own will, He hungered; by His own will, He thirsted; He was afraid voluntarily; He died voluntarily" (*Brief Exposition of the Orthodox Faith,* book 3, ch. 20, c. 1084). But this "proper will" to die voluntarily, the Divinity's consent to this, is no longer the impassibility of nonparticipation.

tain sense. But one cannot say this about the one hypostasis that unites the two natures in its one life. This hypostasis is *simple* in its unity, like all personal consciousness of self; *in this sense* Jesus Christ's consciousness of self is similar to the human consciousness of self. In virtue of the kenosis of the Logos — who by a voluntary sacrificial act extinguishes His divine glory, abandons the fullness of the Divine life, and "comes down from heaven" — He receives His personal consciousness of self in the image of the human consciousness of self, *schēmati hōs anthrōpos*. Temporally, the human consciousness of self, the eternal human I, does not shine forth all at once in man. At first it remains submerged in the night of the unconscious, or rather the preconscious, in the night of infancy, but then it is ignited and illuminates life with the light of personal consciousness of self. This consciousness of self develops and is clarified for itself as the man grows and matures, passing through different ages and developing into the "perfect man." Jesus was born of the woman in the human image as an Infant. Having assumed true humanity, the Lord received and sanctified all the ages of man, from infancy to the age of the perfect man, thus manifesting the fullness of humanity.

The Divine Infant Jesus reaches the age of the child; He is strengthened and develops in this age. The Gospel conceals this period of His earthly life behind the veil of silence, and we will not make fruitless attempts to uncover this mystery, which is wholly expressed in three words of the Gospel of Luke: "the child *grew*, and *waxed strong* in spirit, filled with wisdom: and the grace of God was upon him" (2:40). In this silence, His personal consciousness of self was awakening and was awakened in Him as the consciousness that He was God — as his divine consciousness. This veil of silence is lifted for a brief moment to show us this divine consciousness already awakened in the twelve-year-old adolescent Jesus. We find this in the narrative of His journey to Jerusalem and His conversation with the doctors in the temple. To the timid reproach of His parents who were seeking Him, He responded: "wist ye not that I must be about my Father's business?" (2:49). The lightning of divine consciousness flashed out in these words of the Divine Adolescent, but even His parents did not understand the meaning of His words (2:50). And further it is said: "He went down with them, and came to Nazareth, and was subject unto them . . . [and He] increased in wisdom and stature, and in favour with God and man" (2:51-52). However, for people He remained only a "carpenter" (Mark 6:3) and a "carpenter's son" (Matt. 13:55), all of whose family was known to them; but Mary alone "kept all these sayings in her heart" (Luke 2:51). And thus it was until the time when, having attained maturity ("about thirty years of age" (Luke 3:23]), He left home and went to seek the baptism of John. It was then that the voice from heaven testified about Him: "Thou art my beloved Son; in thee I am well pleased" (Luke 3:22; see also Matt. 3:17; Mark 1:11); together with the testimony from heaven, He also received on earth the testimony of John: "Behold the Lamb of God, which taketh away the sin of the world" (John 1:29, 36).

With this, the self-revelation and revelation from above of the Divine Personality of Jesus have already been accomplished and completed. But what is the character of His consciousness of self? Is it the consciousness that He is God? Is Jesus conscious of Himself as God, to whom worship is due? Does this consciousness separate Him from the sons of men? What is the character of this divine consciousness in Him? First of all, it is necessary to say that, despite His divine consciousness, Christ did not manifest Himself as God to people; otherwise, it would have been impossible to say about the glorified Jesus "that God hath made that same Jesus, whom ye have crucified, both Lord and Christ" (Acts 2:36). The divinity in Jesus was concealed behind humiliation, and calling His Father His God and praying to Him as God on an equal footing with men and together with men, He Himself never taught men to pray to Him or to worship Him as God. On the contrary, He testified that He "came not to be ministered unto, but to minister" (Matt. 20:28). Jesus' consciousness of self was not directly identified with His Divinity, which, in virtue of His humiliation and impoverishment, He had left in "heaven," from which He descended. But at the same time it could not fail to be, and in fact it was, His personal divine consciousness. By His hypostasis, Christ was God. His Person was divine. And if His Divinity was concealed in kenosis, and if in virtue of the Incarnation His "naturality" was defined by the union of the two essences, divine and human, then in His *personal* consciousness of self there was no place for anything mediatory or complex. From the moment it was awakened in Him, Jesus' personal I could only be, and was, the direct divine consciousness. Kenosis did not and could not extend to this divine consciousness. God the Word had removed from Himself His Divinity but not His divine hypostasis. This *personal* consciousness of self, however, separated from the consciousness of Divinity or rather diminished in it, remains wholly and exclusively the *personal* self-revelation of the divine I. And we human beings are conscious of our uncreated-created I not abstractly, but as qualified in a certain way: First of all, in our I we contain a deeply implanted, hidden knowledge of our heavenly homeland, of the divine sources of our personality; second, we contain in it a generic consciousness of our connectedness with the human race, together with a consciousness of our particular and unique place in the human race (i.e., of our individuality).

But what is the character of Jesus' personal I? What defines it, and what qualifies it? Rooted in the Holy Trinity and the intratrinitarian life, this personal I is defined in itself by its begottenness from the Father, by *sonhood,* and is itself this hypostatic sonhood. Jesus' personal consciousness of self as divine consciousness is therefore the consciousness of the *Son* of the Heavenly Father; this filial consciousness of self is, in its fullness and exclusivity, not the consciousness of sonhood in general or simply of a son, as one among many, but the consciousness of the unique and *only begotten* Son, begotten of the Father. The Divine Sonhood is precisely Jesus' Divine I, His self-consciousness as Divine consciousness. We first encounter this perfect awakening of the personal divine consciousness in Jesus as Sonhood in His answer to His parents in the temple: "I must be about my Father's business" (Luke 2:49). Only the Son calls His Father "My Father" and knows Him as such. He taught people to pray to Him: to *our Father.* But He never taught anyone to address Him as "my Father," for this was proper only to Himself, to Him alone.[35] Sonhood also has a secondary definition, which follows from the relation to the Holy Spirit, who pre-eternally reposes upon the Son. This is revealed to us in the solemn attestation of the truth and fullness of His divine consciousness at His baptism, when together with the voice from above, the Holy Spirit descends in the form of a dove upon the One being baptized and reposes upon Him as the Spirit of "adoption." But even before the baptism, "the grace of God [i.e., the Holy Spirit] was upon Him" (Luke 2:40).

Thus, Jesus' hypostatic I is the Son of God, the Son of the Heavenly Father. During the days of His earthly ministry, Jesus' divine consciousness is manifested exclusively as Divine Sonhood; moreover, in conformity with His state of kenosis, it is expressed in complete obedience to the will of the Father, who sent Him into the world. One can say that the personality of the Son is entirely this obedience. It is as if this personality itself — with its will, its action, its divinity — does not exist; it is entirely exhausted by the will of the Father. Although the Son's being, in its fullness in the pre-eternal life of the Holy Trinity, is Divine Sonhood, it nevertheless possesses its own divinity: God is the Father, and God is the Son, just as God is also the Holy Spirit. The pre-eternal Word, which was with God,

---

35. Even when He unites Himself with people in relation to the Father, He nevertheless tacitly separates Himself from them: "I ascend unto my Father, and your Father; and to my God, and your God" (John 20:17).

was also God Himself in His all-enacting omnipotence, manifested in the creation of the all. But the Divine Sonhood of Jesus, being kenotically detached from its own divinity, appears as personal self-renunciation in the surrender of Himself and of His own to the Father; it is, as it were, a voluntary depersonalization in the name of filial obedience.

Numerous texts (especially in the Gospel of John) reveal to us this Divine Sonhood of the Son come down from heaven precisely as the fulfillment of the Father's will,[36] given all the fullness of their essential unity as Father and Son. This perfect communion with the Father expresses the very essence of Jesus' divine personality, the character of His divine consciousness: The Son is like the Father; He is the image of His hypostasis (see Heb. 1:3). The Gospel testimonies do not indicate any "more or less" in this consciousness of self, any development or change of this consciousness. The very task of the Evangelists consists in showing Jesus Christ precisely as the Son of God (Mark 1:1; Luke 3:38; John 20:31: "these are written, that ye might believe that Jesus is the Christ, the Son of God"). Indeed, can one seek any development or gradualness in that which is absolutely not subject to such development? The Evangelists never intended to show the development of the divine consciousness in Jesus; in fact such a task would be meaningless, for it would exceed the bounds of that which is accessible to man. Once it becomes the acquisition of Jesus' personal consciousness of self, once it is ignited in this consciousness, the Divine Sonhood, like the sun, illuminates the entire life of the God-Man, in parallel with His human consciousness of self, except that it emanates from the depths and the heights of the divine consciousness of self. The stages of its development are indistinguishable and inaccessible, and therefore they simply do not exist for us. The only thing we can say is that the God-Man's entire path of life, the entire experience of His earthly life, from the beginning of His ministry to Golgotha, corresponds to this consciousness of self as the affirmation of the will of the Divine Sonhood and presents Him with growing possibilities for the self-renunciation that constitutes the very essence of the Divine love for the world, as well as of the Divine Sonhood. Finally, "not as I will, but as thou wilt" (Matt. 26:39) and "Father, into thy hands I commend my spirit" (Luke 23:46) — these words contain the fullness of the sum of this experience, the entire power and energy of the Divine Sonhood. During His entire ministry (i.e., in the conscious and definitive surrender of Himself to the Father's will), He was conscious of Himself, of His I, as the Son, as the

---

36. See John 7:16; 8:28; 12:49-50; 14:10, 24; 5:19-20; 10:30; 10:38; 10:36. Cf. Matt. 11:27.

The Lamb of God

hypostatic sonhood, which was the source of the divine light pouring forth in the God-Man Himself and from Him. This divine I, the fixed sun of the divine consciousness, is not the static given of some fact but the living dynamics of personality, the feat of self-renunciation, hypostatic love.

It is noteworthy that when Jesus attests to His Divine Sonhood, He generally does so descriptively, so to speak; that is, He affirms Himself in the Divine Sonhood by acts, while rarely calling Himself the Son of God. Others call Him the Son of God and attest that He is the Son of God, but He Himself does not. First of all, the Father Himself, at the baptism and at the Transfiguration, attests that He is the beloved, only begotten Son. Then comes the Forerunner's testimony (John 1:34). We also find such testimony in the words of the archangel Gabriel (Luke 1:32, 35), in Peter's confession (Matt. 16:13-16), in the words of the apostles after Jesus had walked on the sea (Matt. 14:33), in the words of the Apostle Nathanael (John 1:49), in the words of Martha (11:27), in the words of the man born blind (9:35-37), and finally in the words of the centurion and of them that were with him (Matt. 27:54; Mark 15:39). But none of these testimonies, except the Annunciation and Peter's confession (which was specially confirmed by the Lord as proceeding from the Father), are distinguished by accuracy; they rather attest to the power of the impression produced on the witnesses by the person of the Master.[37] A special place in this series is occupied by the high priest's question and the Savior's answer: "I adjure thee by the living God, that thou tell us whether thou be the Christ, the Son of God. Jesus saith unto him, Thou hast said" (Matt. 26:63-64; cf. Mark 14:61-62). The Lord *confirmed* it, but without calling Himself the Son of God. We find a similar case in the Gospel of John (but not in the Synoptic Gospels), where once again the testimony is indirect, in the third person, as it were. This is more a teaching about the Son than His naming: "For God so loved the world, that he gave his only begotten Son. . . . God sent not his Son into the world to condemn the world; but that the world through him might be saved. He that believeth on him is not condemned: but he that believeth not is condemned already, because he hath not believed in the name of the only begotten Son of God" (John 3:16-18). Indirectly related to this is the doctrine of the Son in relation to the Father (in the fifth chapter) and finally the question posed to the man born blind (9:35). In all these cases, however, we

---

37. Numerous are the testimonies of demons, provoked evidently by fear and envy (conditionally, of Satan himself in the temptations in the wilderness: Matt. 4:3, 6 and Luke 4:3, 9; and positively, of demons through the possessed: Matt. 8:29; cf. Mark 5:7; Luke 8:28; Mark 3:11-12; Luke 4:41).

Emmanuel, the God-Man

have more a *teaching* about the Son than His naming of Himself with this name. The Lord teaches about His Divine Sonhood; He preaches it and confesses it. But He does not give Himself the name *Son of God* as His proper and unique name. Why? Because He has another name in the capacity of His *proper name*, equivalent (as is every proper name) to the first-person pronoun. This second, as if synonymous, name of the Son of God is the *Son of Man*.[38] This expression is a biblical one; it signifies, first of all, simply *a man* (as in the entire book of Ezekiel, as well as in Daniel), but it also has an apocalyptic and eschatological meaning, under the influence of the prophecy of Daniel 7:13 (as well as in the apocalypse of Enoch).

In the Gospel, the expression "Son of Man" sometimes primarily means "man" and approaches the significance of a personal pronoun. We find this in Matt. 8:20 and Luke 9:58: "the Son of man hath not where to lay his head." This meaning of the expression becomes particularly evident when we compare the parallel texts of the Sermon on the Mount from Matthew and Luke: "[men] shall say all manner of evil against you falsely, for my sake" (Matt. 5:11) and "[men] shall reproach you, and cast out your name as evil, for the Son of man's sake" (Luke 6:22). In a number of other cases the expression tends to signify messianic election: "the Son of man hath power on earth to forgive sins" (Matt. 9:6; Mark 2:10; Luke 5:24); "the Son of man came eating and drinking" (Matt. 11:19; Luke 7:34); "the Son of man is Lord even of the sabbath day" (Matt. 12:8; Mark 2:28; Luke 6:5); "He that soweth the good seed is the Son of man" (Matt. 13:37), and so forth.

Other groups of texts, finally, contain the idea that the Son of Man is one who, preexistent, has been sent from heaven, has come into the world, and is destined to come into it again. The following texts are pertinent here: "Whosoever speaketh a word against the Son of man, it shall be forgiven him" (Matt. 12:32; Luke 12:10); "ye shall not have gone over the cities of Israel, till the Son of man be come" (Matt. 10:23); "so shall the Son of man be three days and three nights in the heart of the earth" (Matt. 12:40); "the Son of man shall send forth his angels, and they shall gather out of his kingdom all things that offend, and them which do iniquity" (Matt. 13:41); "until the Son of man be risen again from the dead" (Matt. 17:9; Mark 9:9); "so shall also the coming of the Son of man be" (Matt. 24:27);

---

38. It is encountered seventeen times in the Gospel of Matthew, fourteen times in Mark, eight times in Luke, and twelve times in John (in spite of the predominantly theological character of this Gospel). It is also encountered in Acts 7:56 and Revelation 1:13 and 14:14.

"then shall appear the sign of the Son of man in heaven . . . and they shall see the Son of man coming in the clouds of heaven with power and great glory" (Matt. 24:30); "the Son of man must suffer many things, and be rejected" (Luke 9:22), and so forth. To this cycle one can add the following passages: "ye shall see . . . the angels of God ascending and descending upon the Son of man" (John 1:51); "the hour is come, that the Son of man should be glorified" (John 12:23); "now is the Son of man glorified" (John 13:31); "how sayest thou, The Son of man must be lifted up? who is this Son of man?" (John 12:34); "behold, I see the heavens opened, and the Son of man standing on the right hand of God" (Acts 7:56); "[I saw] one like unto the Son of man, clothed with a garment down to the foot" (Rev. 1:13); "upon the cloud one sat like unto the Son of man" (Rev. 14:14).

All these cases of the use of the name "Son of Man" contain the doctrine of the Man who, while being a man, is at the same time the "Messiah," the *super*man, God. In this connection, two synoptic texts are particularly noteworthy, where this equivalence of the "Son of Man" and the "Son of God" is attested with perfect clarity. The first text involves Peter's confession. Jesus asks: "Whom do men say that I the Son of man am?" (Matt. 16:13). Peter answers: "Thou art the Christ, the Son of the living God" (16:16). The Son of Man is the Son of God. And blessing Peter for this answer, Christ says: "flesh and blood hath not revealed it unto thee, but my Father which is in heaven" (16:17). The second text is the narrative of the judgment on Jesus: "the high priest . . . said unto him, I adjure thee by the living God, that thou tell us whether thou be the Christ, the Son of God. Jesus saith unto him, Thou hast said [the Gospel of Mark has: 'I am']: nevertheless I say unto you, Hereafter shall ye see the Son of man sitting on the right hand of power, and coming in the clouds of heaven" (Matt. 26:63-64; see also Mark 14:61-62; Luke 22:66-70). (This contains an implicit and authentic exegesis of Daniel 7:13 in the sense of fully equating the Son of God with the Son of Man, the God-Man.)

This specific identification of the Son of God and the Son of Man,[39] which is implicitly understood over the full extent of the Synoptic Gospels, is the object of an express revelation in the Gospel of John. First of all, in the mysterious conversation with Nicodemus, the Lord refers to Himself as the only begotten Son sent into the world by the Father, but He also re-

---

39. Specifically, it is expressed in the genealogies of Christ in the Gospels of Matthew and Luke. The first of these genealogies ("the generation of Jesus Christ, the son of David, the son of Abraham" [Matt. 1:1]) refers to the Son of Man, while the second refers to the Son of God ("the son of Adam, which was the son of God" [Luke 3:38]).

fers to Himself as the Son of Man. Furthermore, He speaks not of His earthly humanity but of the pre-eternal Divine-Humanity, of Him "that came down from heaven, even the Son of man which is in heaven" (John 3:13). No exegetical intricacies or discoloring acids can destroy the fundamental meaning of these words, which become even more significant in the context: "If I have told you earthly things, and ye believe not, how shall ye believe, if I tell you of heavenly things? And no man hath ascended up to heaven, but he that came down from heaven, even the Son of man which is in heaven. And as Moses lifted up the serpent in the wilderness, even so must the Son of man be lifted up: That whosoever believeth in him should not perish, but have eternal life. For God so loved the world, that he gave his only begotten Son, that whosoever believeth in him should not perish, but have everlasting life" (3:12-16). Here we have not only the direct and total identification of the Son of Man and the Son of God but also the elevation of this identity to the heavenly Divine-Humanity.

We have a similar identification in Christ's discourse about the resurrection and the judgment in the fifth chapter of John. Here it is said about the Son that "as the Father hath life in himself; so hath he given to the Son to have life in himself; and hath given him authority to execute judgment also, because he is the Son of man" (5:26-27). Christ's discourse on the Eucharist in chapter 6 has a similar character: "Labour not for the meat which perisheth, but for that meat which endureth unto everlasting life, which the Son of man shall give unto you: for him hath God the Father sealed" (6:27). "I am the living bread which came down from heaven: if any man eat of this bread, he shall live for ever: and the bread that I will give is my flesh, which I will give for the life of the world" (6:51). "Except ye eat the flesh of the Son of man, and drink his blood, ye have no life in you" (6:53). This identification of the Son of God and the Son of Man is corroborated by the doctrine of the heavenly Divine-Humanity, which is expounded in the conversation with Nicodemus: "What and if ye shall see the Son of man ascend up where he was before?" (6:62). One finds the same identification in the eighth chapter, in the conversation with the Jews, where Jesus says: "When ye have lifted up the Son of man, then shall ye know that I am he, and that I do nothing of myself; but as my Father hath taught me, I speak these things" (8:28). Finally, in the Last Discourse (13:31) and before the meeting with the Greeks (12:23), the "Son of Man" has the same meaning in the context as the Son of God, the God-Man.[40]

---

40. The preexistence of the Son of Man in heaven and His being sent into the world, so decisively expressed in John (16:27-28), is tacitly understood also in the Synop-

The Lamb of God

Thus, on the basis of these comparisons of the Gospel texts, it becomes clear that "Son of Man" and "Son of God" are names that are identically applied by Christ to Himself, and that this is His own teaching about Himself. Sometimes this usage caused perplexity among the Jews (John 12:34), and sometimes such an equating of man with God was received by them as blasphemy (10:31-33). These were the main grounds for demanding that He be condemned to death (see 19:7).

It is an irrefutable truth that the Son of God identified Himself with the Son of Man. We must not exclude this identification from the Gospel or weaken it by various reinterpretations; rather, we must understand it in all its dogmatic significance. This means, first of all, that Jesus is not only the Son of God *without a relation* to humanity, and that He is not only the Son of Man *without a relation* to His Divinity. And He is not God *and* Man in alternation or in some other sense or relation. Rather, *He is the God-Man* who exists pre-eternally in heaven (the Son of Man come down from heaven [John 3:13]) and, in His Incarnation, on earth. His consciousness of self is one Divine-Human consciousness of self, which is revealed identically to itself in the two natures, according to the Chalcedonian dogma. This divine-humanity of Christ's consciousness has its foundation not only *post factum* of the Incarnation and the descent from heaven but also *ante factum*, in heaven. That is what made possible the reception of man's nature by the hypostasis of the Logos, that is to say, the Incarnation.

In Christ, the Face of God appears in the Human Face, which, as the true Image of God, is transparent for and as if adequate to the former. The living mystery of Christ's person consists in this Divine-Humanity of His Face. At times the divinity in Him is concealed behind the humiliation of the human image; at other times it shines forth with invincible force, which makes His enemies or those who are indifferent to Him recoil in perplexity: He passes through the midst of an angry mob (Luke 4:28-30; John 10:39); He makes a triumphal entry into Jerusalem before the face of His enemies (Matt. 21:8-9; Luke 19:36-40), and He casts out the merchants from the temple (Matt. 21:12; Mark 11:15; Luke 19:45) with "a scourge of small cords" (John 2:15). The band of men come to arrest Him retreats and falls to the ground before Him, who is unarmed (John 18:6). It is said about Him that "He taught ... as one having authority" (Matt. 7:29; Mark 1:22). The servants of the Pharisees sent to arrest Him attest: "Never man

---

tics, where it is said that the Son of Man "came" to serve, to give His life, to seek and to save that which is lost, to call sinners, and so forth (see Matt. 20:28; Luke 19:10; Mark 2:17; Matt. 9:13; Luke 5:32; Luke 4:43; Mark 1:38).

spake like this man" (John 7:46). He attributes to Himself the power to forgive sins (Matt. 9:6; Mark 2:10; Luke 5:24). He has the power to command the unclean spirits (Luke 4:36), and He gives this power to His disciples, the power to heal and to work miracles (Luke 9:1). At times His Divine Face becomes unbearably frightening for sinful men ("When Simon Peter saw it, he fell down at Jesus' knees, saying, Depart from me; for I am a sinful man, O Lord" [Luke 5:8]), and who could bear Him! Could we look into the divine abyss of the human eyes of Him who said: "I and my Father are one" (John 10:30) or "before Abraham was, I am" (John 8:58)? Could we lift our eyes upon Him who said: "Talitha cumi" (Mark 5:41) or "Lazarus, come forth" (John 11:43)? Can we bear to look at His Face, terrible in its wrath, when He says to all of us: "woe unto you, scribes and Pharisees, hypocrites" (Matt. 23)? Christ's Face is terrifying and unbearable for man when God appears in it.

Nevertheless, Christ's is the Divine-Human Face, the Human image of the Divine Spirit.[41] He usually conceals Himself behind this humiliation of His human image, and it is then that the words of the prophet Isaiah are applicable to Him: "He shall not strive, nor cry; neither shall any man hear his voice in the streets. A bruised reed shall he not break, and smoking flax shall he not quench" (Matt. 12:19-20, from Isa. 42:2-3). Living with Him, one could fail to notice Him; looking at Him, one could fail to see Him. He did not compel people to see Him with signs or with lightning bolts from the sky. He allowed people to disdain Him, to subject Him to humiliations, being spat upon and beaten, and finally to crucify Him. About Him the indifferent Pilate could indifferently say: "What is truth?" (John 18:38). He could say this before the face of the Truth in a Divine-Human form, and he could have Him, the God-Man, brought out to the people with the derisive and indifferent "Behold the Man!" (John 19:5). Looking at Him, Pilate did not see Him, like those Jews who cried: "Crucify Him, crucify Him!" (John 19:6) The humiliation that concealed even the human image of the God-Man was so profound and so alien to external human grandeur that the prophetic words of the Old Testament evangelist Isaiah could be applied to Him: "He shall grow up before him as a tender plant, and as a root out of a dry ground: he hath no form nor comeliness; and when we shall see him, there is no beauty that we should

---

41. This is the basis for the possibility of representing Christ on icons. By the way, the icon of Christ is not a representation of the living God-Man with the unbearable countenance of His Divinity but only a symbolic representation of His human face, a representation sanctified by the Church. See my book *The Icon and the Veneration of Icons*.

The Lamb of God

desire him. He is despised and rejected of men; a man of sorrows, and acquainted with grief: and we hid as it were our faces from him" (Isa. 53:2-3); "his visage was so marred more than any man, and his form more than the sons of men" (52:14).

On the basis of this text the opinion was promulgated that corporeal beauty was alien to the visage of Christ,[42] or even that He was purposely disfigured. According to this opinion, the state of humiliation to which human blindness corresponds is transferred to the image of Christ. Since He was sinless, the perfect man, and thus even the sole true man ("Behold the Man!"), the Second Adam possessed, to be sure, all the perfection of the beauty of the human image, which was created by God as the image of the incarnate Christ. This image was revealed in the glorified Christ after the Resurrection (He was recognized in this image, although not immediately, by Mary Magdalene and the disciples). This is the absolute human image, abiding in heaven at the right hand of the Father. This image is absolute on earth too, for the Face of the New Adam — the First Man and the All-Man — is the All-Face of all humanity in which every human face finds itself, its ray or reflection. Christ possesses the *fullness* of humanity and thus the fullness of the beauty of humanity, in conformity with the reposing upon Him of the Holy Spirit, the hypostasis of Beauty. He received this human visage from His Mother, the "New Eve," who in turn united in Herself the fullness of the humanity of the old Adam with all the personal sinlessness that was accessible to him in all the beauty of this sinlessness, in conformity with the fact that the Holy Spirit, the hypostasis of Beauty, made His abode in Her. As a son resembles his mother (and since there was no human father, the whole force of human heredity here was concentrated in the Mother), He received from Her, together with the fullness of the human essence, also His natural beauty, which became in Him the receptacle of the image of Divine beauty, of the God-Man. Therefore, together with the *personal* sinlessness of the Virgin Mary and the *absolute* sinlessness of the God-Man, we must recognize that She possesses the supreme beauty of the creaturely human image, the beauty of the "New Eve," and that He possesses the supreme beauty of the Divine-Human image, and consequently abso-

---

42. That was the opinion of Justin the Philosopher, Clement of Alexandria, Tertullian, Cyril of Alexandria, and Basil the Great. At a later date, the contrary opinion was triumphant, based on Psalm 45:2 ("Thou art fairer than the children of men"). This opinion was shared by Jerome, Augustine, John Chrysostom, and others. See the discussion in A. Michel, "Jésus-Christ," in *Dict. de théol. cath.*, vol. 7/1.1153.

Emmanuel, the God-Man

lute human beauty. But when Christ was in His state of humiliation, this beauty remained hidden for the world and inaccessible for human vision. This beauty was not outwardly blinding and astonishing but existed only for those who could see. In this Image we cannot admit a single negative feature proper to genuine disfiguration, for disfiguration is distortion and limitation, but these are incompatible with the perfection of the human nature revealed in Him.

And so, God lived on earth among people in the form of a man, concealed in His humiliation. God was the God-Man, and every act of His life was divine-human. For man, the personal I's consciousness of self is *conditioned* by the psycho-corporeal life. Likewise, in the God-Man, the life of His divine I was conditioned by His psycho-corporeal human life and passed in this life, although it never merged with and was never identified with this life. This *real conditionedness* of the life of the Divine I by the psychosomatic life of humanity expresses the kenosis of Divinity in Christ: this Divinity was arrested, as it were, in its absoluteness and independence from created things. It preserved its power and revealed itself only in His Divine Spirit, but here too only in conformity with and in proportion to the measure of His human growth in relation to the soul and body. In His Incarnation, Christ thus accepted and made His own all the needs, infirmities, and limitations of the life of the human body quickened by the soul. He had bodily needs and was thus dependent on them in His life. He knew hunger and thirst, fatigue and the need for sleep, during which, as is the case for all human beings, His daytime consciousness was extinguished, becoming submerged in the subconscious.[43] He could experience bodily sufferings (although sicknesses were foreign to Him), and they afflicted Him, unto the torments on the cross. Moreover, and most importantly, this was not for the sake of appearance; rather, it was an authentic part of the content of His life, of His personal Divine-Human consciousness of self. It was not appearance or make-believe when He hungered in the desert, thirsted at Jacob's well and on the cross, experienced fatigue, slept on the boat, and so on. He experienced the emotions of love, anger, sorrow, joy, and so on, which at times were expressed directly in His words: "O faithless and perverse generation, how long shall I be with you? how long shall I suffer you?" (Matt. 17:17; Mark 9:19; Luke 9:41). "I am come to send fire on the earth; and what will I, if it be already kindled? But I have a baptism to be baptized with; and how am I straitened till it be accom-

---

43. There is no indication in the Gospels that He saw heavenly dreams, although there is no direct denial of this.

The Lamb of God

plished" (Luke 12:49-50). "My soul is exceeding sorrowful, even unto death" (Matt. 26:38). "My God, my God, why hast thou forsaken me?" (27:46); and so on. All this represents the sacred human authenticity of the Divine-Human life.

The God-Man assumed this psycho-corporeal concreteness not only on the individual but also on the historical and social scale. Christ was not man in general but possessed the concrete historical traits of a Jew of the beginning of our era: He spoke the language of His people, lived in a specific geographic, natural, and historical milieu, and (which is especially noteworthy) did not differ from other Jews in His human visage (the woman of Samaria refers to Him as a Jew [John 4:9]). This historical concreteness of His manifestation does not diminish His real all-humanity in its universal depth; on the contrary, it presupposes it. But in this too He was a man who loved His people, considered Himself to be sent to them, and wept because of their obstinacy. He also loved the Holy Land with its nature, as well as the Holy City, His friends, and the entire modest surroundings, just as He loved the lilies of the valleys and the grasses of the fields. Human life was accessible to Him in all its sinless fullness, and through this fullness His divine-human consciousness grew and was revealed in His human life. This awakening and deepening of His consciousness is a mystery that we cannot understand on the basis of our experience but that is disclosed before us in His life and words.

All we can do is seek analogies with our own consciousness of self, which is revealed to us in and through our life in its divine depths and sources. This consciousness contains the consciousness of our own divine sonhood; in it, we seek and find God. A gracious, divine life begins in our natural life: "born, not of blood, nor of the will of the flesh, nor of the will of man, but of God" (John 1:13). This life in us is destined to ascend from glory to glory, while our knowledge in part becomes perfect ("even as also I am known" [1 Cor. 13:12]), so that "God will be all in all" (see 1 Cor. 15:28). This analogy of the sons of men with the Son of Man who is the Son of God is only a formal one, although it is based on the authentic image of God in man, the image of Christ's divine-humanity. Based on this, however, we can approach and ascend the holy mountain Sinai; we can gain access to the unfathomable consciousness of the God-Man as it is revealed to us in the Gospel. That which is revealed (or not revealed) in man only in the depths of his spirit shines forth here as the consciousness of authentic divine sonhood, of total concord and union with the Father. This consciousness always remains *divine-human,* however; it is never separated from the human consciousness, being contained in it, uniting itself

Emmanuel, the God-Man

with it, and permeating it. The God-Man, who was conscious of Himself as united with the Father in the depths of His personal consciousness of self, remained a co-man with respect to us — our brother — until the end of His earthly life; all that was revealed of Divinity in Him was revealed in human life without going beyond its limits, and this was expressed in human words addressed to men. The divinity was human and the humanity was divine; the two were commensurate and united in one divine-human life. This is precisely what the Gospel portrait of the God-Man signifies. And concerning the humanity of the God-Man, concerning this unfathomable convergence of the Divine and the human to the point of their living identification, can there be a stronger and more indisputable testimony than the following words of the Lord (preserved not by John but by Matthew): "Come unto me, all ye that labor and are heavy laden, and I will give you rest. Take my yoke upon you, and learn of me; for I am meek and lowly in heart: and ye shall find rest unto your souls. For my yoke is easy, and my burden is light" (Matt. 11:28-30).

The Gospels are doctrinal books, not "historical" ones. The history enters into the doctrine, into the teaching of the faith, and is subordinated to its goals. This makes it difficult, and sometimes impossible, to use them solely as historical books, to extract the "historical figure" of Christ from the "myth" or doctrine. This does not mean that they do not contain authentic history or that the facts they report are not historical events; it is that these facts are *not* arranged in a historical scheme of genesis, sequential appearance, development, and "evolution." The Gospels are expressly designed for the teaching of the faith; they are given to the Church as the revelation and testimony of faith in Christ, the Son of God, and outside this general dogmatic and artistic framework they fall apart into fragments that cannot be gathered into a "history." Their aim is not to show the genesis and development of the divine consciousness in the God-Man; on the contrary, they presuppose this consciousness and take it as their point of departure. They only show it from various points of view, in relation to different events of the God-Man's life; and although these events are given a certain external coherence and arranged in a certain chronological sequence, this chronology is intentionally made imprecise and only approximate. The historical character that the Gospel narratives possess is thus determined by the overall dogmatic architecture of the Gospels.[44] The Gospels approach the figure of the God-Man from dif-

---

44. The Gospels do not constitute the sole testimony on the basis of which *the dogmatic image of the Messiah* has been formed. The entire Old Testament is also the Old Tes-

ferent sides, focusing special attention first on one side and then on the other. These are not two different aspects of the same figure, nor two representations of different figures; this is one and the same figure, but with the predominant attention focused on one side or the other. The figure of Christ in the Synoptic Gospels is different from that in the Gospel of John: In the Synoptics, we primarily have the human image of the God-Man, whereas in John we primarily have His divine image. The Synoptics (Matthew and Luke) begin with the birth of Christ on earth, whereas John begins with the eternal being of the Logos. The Synoptics contain the preaching and describe the works of Christ, whereas John primarily reports Christ's teaching about Himself. In both cases, however, the divine-human unity is preserved; both represent the Man who is the bearer of Divinity and God who speaks through the Man. The Gospels attest to the great mystery of piety, to the manifestation of God in the flesh, and they tell about this in such a manner that God does not stop being Man, and Man is not reduced to ashes, not dissolved in Divinity. The constancy of humanity in the God-Man is the fundamental fact and the fundamental premise of the Gospel narration. In the God-Man, the divinity surpasses human possibilities but does not abolish the boundaries of the human essence and does not do violence to it; on the contrary, in its kenosis, the divinity in Christ limits itself to the measure of the human essence. The God-Man does *not* use His divine power to weaken and surpass the limits and infirmity of the human essence. Instead, He subordinates Himself to these limits; He does not provide the "signs" that are so often demanded from Him by the Jews.[45]

The Lord was born under conditions of extreme human infirmity, in the cold of a miserable manger, in abject poverty and humility. The angels were singing in the heavens, the shepherds were listening to them, and the magi were adoring Him, but He remained defenseless against Herod's persecution, from which He had to save Himself by fleeing to Egypt and awaiting there Herod's death before He could return (similarly, after

---

tament gospel, which is rich in prophecies and prefigurations of Christ and which expounds the life of His earthly ancestors, in short, the history of Christianity before Christ. Such a significance of the Old Testament is confirmed by the direct testimony of the Evangelists, by other New Testament writers in their insistent references to various Old Testament texts, and by the testimony of Christ's own words.

45. Some might cite as a counterexample the miracle of walking upon water. But Christ did not accomplish this miracle in order to dispense with a boat, advancing upon the water as he would upon land. He accomplished it in order to instruct His disciples. The case of the cursing of the fig tree is similar.

Emmanuel, the God-Man

John's arrest He flees the fury of another Herod [Matt. 4:12]). The apocryphal Gospels of the infancy have embellished the flight to Egypt and the Savior's early years with various miracles, but the Church has not recognized this legend and has left in shadow the Savior's years of infancy in their human humility. Christ's public ministry begins with His coming to John for baptism among a multitude of people, in order to fulfill all *human* truth, in which the truth of His Divine-Humanity has flashed like a bolt of lightning. Then He was "led up of the spirit into the wilderness" (Matt. 4:1) for the feat of fasting and prayer, which was accompanied by temptation. But all this was accomplished within the limits of the human essence, including hunger and those temptations by which Satan attempted to turn Him away from His path, although he also intended to turn away the One he supposed to be the "Son of God" from obedience to the Father. The beginning of Christ's ministry is preceded by the election and calling of the twelve (and later the seventy) apostles, as well as by preaching and miracles. His preaching impressed the people as being *prophetic*. This is, so to speak, a practical divine-humanity that the God-Man teaches men; but formally, this preaching preserves traces of prophetic preaching. It does not contain anything that surpasses the human understanding (which is why it is sometimes accepted even by those who do not recognize Christ's divine-humanity). Likewise, Jesus' prophecies, according to their *type*, are not different from those of the prophets, and they are expressed in the eschatological language and apocalyptic images proper to their epoch. These prophecies issued from the God-Man's messianic consciousness of self; they referred to Him Himself, but they were discourses pronounced for men in human language. In their essence, therefore, they did not surpass the limits of the human consciousness; they did not exceed the historical horizons of this consciousness.

In general, one can say that the Synoptics' image of the God-Man is predominantly the image of Christ the Messiah, the anointed of God, the Man upon whom the Father's favor reposed by virtue of the Holy Spirit. This image included human elevation and self-transcending in the Messiah, the God-Man. There are human prefigurings and precursors, as well as human ancestors, for Christ. He is predicted by the prophets, and in the Synoptics He turns toward us His human Face. This humanity of the Divine-Human Face is not diminished but is manifested in its greatest immediacy precisely at the end of His earthly path, at the hour of the passion, which corresponds to its authentic and not illusory character. Even when His divine consciousness attained its greatest profundity and greatest clarity, His humanity was not diminished but appeared to reach its peak. Before us, in all the authenticity and inseparability of the two natures, the true God-Man is present: God does not just cover His Divinity with humanity; He bears its burdens. True, this humanity manifests the divine light that permeates it, the divine light that, emanating from supratemporality, illuminates temporal events and abolishes the bounds of time. We have this primarily in John, but also sometimes in the Synoptics.

It would be tendentious and one-sided, however, to *oppose* the Synoptics' image of the God-Man in His humanity to the Gospel of John's image of the God-Man in His divinity. For the Synoptics' image of Christ is not the image of a man but the image of the God-Man, whose personal consciousness of self is determined by His Divine Sonhood. Christ's words that express the fullness of His consciousness of His Divine Sonhood (Matt. 11:27) are a natural bridge between the Synoptics' representation of Christ and His representation in the Gospel of John (with its two fundamental themes: "In the beginning was the Word" and "the Word was made flesh" [John 1:1, 14]). The latter is the Gospel of the Divine-Humanity, taken primarily from the Divine side. This naturally imparts an acute emphasis to its two fundamental themes: the testimony concerning the Divine Sonhood and the opposition and struggle between the God-Man and the world, between light and darkness — an antithesis that permeates the Gospel of John.

Although the Gospel of John contains the simulacrum of a chronological framework and historical narrative, a supratemporal spirit wafts from its pages, especially when it comes to the main thing — the representation of Christ. The first thing that merits attention in this Gospel is that here Christ's life has neither a beginning nor an end. The Gospel begins with the prologue about the Logos, and at the end the narration simply breaks off with the appearance of Christ to the apostles and concludes with the epilogue saying that "the world itself could not contain the books that should be written" about Christ (21:25). In this Gospel there is no Nativity (true, it is missing in Mark as well) and no earthly genealogy (which is also missing in Mark) but only a heavenly one, a logology; there is also no Ascension (which is also missing in Matthew). But there is a series of representations of Christ and a series of His discourses, which primarily and even almost exclusively contain the doctrine of Christ Himself as the Divine Son of the Divine Father. In this sense the Gospel of John chiefly contains the doctrine of the divine hypostasis of the God-Man and thus of His divine nature, which is inseparably linked with Him. The subject of this preaching, however, is not the Logos as the world-creating and world-maintaining Word (which is treated *only* in the prologue by the Evangelist himself) but the Logos as the Son in His relation to the Father. His divine consciousness is not immediate, for by humiliating Himself and assuming "the form of a servant," He removed from Himself His Divinity *for Himself,* although it continues to abide in Him. But He becomes progressively conscious of His Divinity, not through His own, direct hypostatic consciousness, but through the Father. It is only through His consciousness of His Sonhood, which remains His hypostatic consciousness, that He comes to know Himself in the Father and the Father in Himself. It is only through the Father that He comes to know His divine hypostasis, His Divine Sonhood. The Son's divine consciousness is therefore *mediated* by the knowledge of the Father being revealed in Him, that is, by *divine knowledge.* That is the most fundamental fact presented to us by the Fourth Gospel. Having become flesh, having humiliated Himself, the Logos acquires His Divinity only in union with the Father. For Him, the Divine Sonhood is the act of consciousness of self that determines all and triumphs over all. All human beings are sons of God, but no human being can be conscious of his divine sonhood in such a manner as to say: "I and my Father are one" (John 10:30).

Divine consciousness is the immediate life of Divinity, which cannot be other than itself and which does not know diminishment, origination, or becoming. In contrast, divine knowledge originates out of the depths of the creaturely consciousness, which must go out of itself, transcend itself; this is an act of faith and prayer — a *feat.* For this reason the Lord is called "the author and finisher of our faith" (Heb. 12:2). Faith is the transcending of one's creaturely being; prayer is the life of one's creaturely being in noncreatureliness, the going out of oneself. In His humanity, the God-Man received the creaturely nature and determined Himself by it while remaining Himself. Having become flesh, He established for Himself His relation to the Father as *to God.* His relation to the Father comes, so to speak, not out of His Divinity — which, for Himself, He removed from Himself (although of course it continued to abide in Him as an objective fact of His nature) — but out of the depths of His humanity. God is sought by the feat of faith, and it is only in response to faith that God reveals Himself, gives knowledge of Himself. God is acquired by prayer, which is the way of faith and the life of faith: "Out of the depths have I cried unto thee, O Lord. Lord, hear my voice: let thine ears be attentive to the voice of my supplications" (Ps. 130:1-2).

The Lord's feat of prayer to God was unceasing (and of course genuine), and from this prayer He drew the strength for preaching, for miracle-working, and for suffering. He did not pray to Himself, to His proper Divinity, which was naturally inherent to Him but kenotically weakened. He prayed to the Father, who for Him was, above all and before all, God. In God, He acquired His Father, and in Him He acquired Himself as the Son. To this one must add, in confirmation of this idea from the negative side, that during the days of His earthly ministry, the Lord not only did not solicit but even did not accept prayers addressed to Him as God. Such is precisely the meaning of His answer to the rich youth: "Why callest thou me good? there is none good but one, that is, God" (Matt. 19:17). In particular, after the confession of Peter, who recognized in Him Christ, the Son of the living God, nothing changes in His relation to the apostles: He remains the "Master" and does not accept divine adoration.

His prayer to the Father, through the feat of love and faith, was returned to Him as His own divine consciousness. It was returned to Him, however, not in Himself and from Himself as God, by whom all things were made and are preserved, but entirely and exclusively from the Father. It was returned to Him as the Son, obedient to the Father in all things and revealing the Father: The Divinity of the Son in the God-Man is the Divinity of the Father, which becomes the Divinity of the Son. Being the hypostatic God, the God-Man in His humiliation receives, as it were, deification from the Father through the Holy Spirit, who reposes upon Him. This deification differs, however, from that of the creature by the fact that the creature receives it as the supernatural, grace-bestowing principle of life, whereas the Son only returns to the heaven He voluntarily abandoned, to His proper natural consciousness of self. However, to the extent that a real return through the feat of faith, prayer, and the pleasing of God takes place here, to that extent a special deification of the God who has humbled Himself also takes place (see Acts 2:33, 36; Acts 5:31; Phil. 2:9). This is His sanctification: "whom the Father hath sanctified, and sent into the world" (John 10:36; cf. 17:18).

But this leads to a new and more general question (one that has already arisen in kenotic theology): the question of the interrelation between the Father and the Son. In the doctrine of the sending of the Son by the Father and of His filial obedience to the Father, do we not have a hidden subordinationism, which in the history of dogma is then made more acute in different variants of Arianism, ancient and modern? The Arians used in their own manner this general character of the relation of the Son to the Father, as well as certain texts and, first and foremost, Christ's words: "my Father is greater than I" (John 14:28). Pertinent here is the entire series of texts where the Son is represented as praying to the Father:

first of all, the prayer at Gethsemane (Matt. 26:39, 40, 53; Mark 14:36; cf. John 12:27-28; 18:11); the prayer on the cross (Luke 23:34); the prayer of John 14:16 ("I will pray the Father"); and the high-priestly prayer (John 17). Then there are Mark 13:32 (cf. Matt. 24:36; 20:23; 25:34 ["Come, ye blessed of my Father"]) and Luke 22:29 ("I appoint unto you a kingdom, as my Father hath appointed unto me"). The most essential testimony of the Gospels, which is more important than any particular text, is the fact that, over the course of His entire earthly ministry, Christ addresses the Father not only as the Father, with whom He abides in fullness of union, but also as His God ("to my God, and your God" [John 20:17]). This entire paradox, which one cannot fail to see in the Gospels, poses a difficult and serious problem for theology, and the christological difficulty (which is also the trinitarian difficulty) of this problem remains unresolved. Although Arianism was, in its epoch, rejected and anathematized by the Church, theologically it has by no means been fully overcome, which is attested by its continuing vitality in different forms, immediately after the First Ecumenical Council as well as later, even to the present day. In general, subordinationism has enjoyed a kind of illegal citizenship in theology, since it has been neither genuinely clarified nor condemned.

The fact is that Jesus, especially in the Gospel of John, confesses His total dependence on the Father, who *sends* Him into the world (see Matt. 10:40; 15:24; Mark 9:37; Luke 4:43; 9:48; John 3:17, 34; 4:34; 5:23-24, 30, 36-38; 6:29, 38-39, 44; 7:16, 18, 28-29; 8:26, 29, 42; 9:4; 10:36; 11:42; 12:44-45; 13:20; 14:24; 15:21; 16:5; 17:3, 8, 18, 21, 25). This sending of the Son by the Father is expressed in the fact that He came to do the Father's will (Matt. 26:42; John 5:30; 6:39; 15:10). Aside from this dependence, the Gospel of John attests to the fullness of His union with the Father: "the Father loveth the Son, and hath given all things into his hand" (3:35); "the Father . . . sheweth him all things that himself doeth: and he will shew him greater works than these, that ye may marvel" (5:20); "My Father worketh hitherto, and I work" (5:17); "as the Father raiseth up the dead, and quickeneth them; even so the Son quickeneth whom he will. For the Father judgeth no man, but hath committed all judgment unto the Son" (5:21-22); "I live by the Father" (6:57); "I am not alone, but I and the Father that sent me" (8:16); "He that sent me is with me: the Father hath not left me alone" (8:29); "as the Father knoweth me, even so know I the Father" (10:15); "I and my Father are one" (10:30); "the Father is in me, and I in him" (10:38; cf. 14:10-11); "no man cometh unto the Father, but by me" (14:6); "he that hath seen me hath seen the Father" (14:9); "the Father that dwelleth in me, he doeth the works" (14:10); "he that hateth me hateth my Father also"

(15:23); "all things that I have heard of my Father I have made known unto you" (15:15); "all things that the Father hath are mine" (16:15); "I came forth from the Father, and am come into the world: again, I leave the world, and go to the Father" (16:28); "I am not alone, because the Father is with me" (16:32); "as thou hast given him power over all flesh, that he should give eternal life to as many as thou hast given him. And this is life eternal, that they might know thee the only true God, and Jesus Christ, whom thou hast sent" (17:2-3); "all mine are thine, and thine are mine" (17:10); "that they all may be one; as thou, Father, art in me, and I in thee, that they also may be one in us . . . I in them, and thou in me" (17:21, 23). That is why Jesus demands that people believe in him, identifying this belief with belief in the Father: "He that believeth on me, believeth not on me, but on him that sent me" (12:44); "believe in God, believe also in me" (14:1). This is combined with the fact of the total *absence* in the Gospels of any saying of Christ in which He directly proclaims Himself to be God (as was proclaimed in Thomas's confession before the presence of the Resurrected Lord: "My Lord and my God" [John 20:28]). Christ Himself attests His Divinity only in connection with His relation to the Father and through the Father, in His Divine Sonhood: He is not God, but the Son of God, who Himself, in virtue of His proximity to the Father, lives by the Father's divine life, is filled with the Father's divine will, is God.

This fundamental antinomy and this obvious paradox of the Gospel doctrine of Christ is striking and cannot be missed. Not only can this antinomy not be smoothed over by a conciliatory apologetics, which in this case was sometimes employed in the polemic against Arianism, but it must be made even more acute in its real significance. In the Gospel we can find two sets of texts of equal power: One set of texts can be used to establish a distinction between the Father and the Son, which becomes a relative *inequality* between Christ and God; whereas the other set affirms Christ's *equality* with God, which proceeds from the perfect union of will, works, and life — in general, from their divine unity. If one does not go beyond the first term of this antinomy, one gets Arianism, or a multiform and multistage subordinationism in the trinitarian doctrine, which also extends to Christology. If one accepts only the second term of the antinomy, which is the dominant tradition, then one in effect weakens or rejects the opposite Gospel testimonies, and the real work of the Incarnation and the redemption inevitably receives a docetic coloration. Arianism was defeated at the Nicene Council, and in general in the "Nicene faith," by the affirmation of homoousianism in the doctrine of the Holy Trinity; the anathematization of Arianism should, of course, have been extended

Emmanuel, the God-Man

to all its consequences in the domain of Christology. Christological problems as such, however, were not an object of dogmatic examination at the First or the Second Ecumenical Council. In the fourth century the christological problem had not yet been posed in all its specificity, and in this domain one can say that Arianism was prohibited but not defeated and overcome. This also refers particularly to the *biblical* argumentation of Arianism, which essentially consisted in pointing out the existence of Gospel texts that speak of the dependence of the Son on the Father, texts that both Arians and anti-Arians interpreted incorrectly or at least one-sidedly with reference to the Logos and Christ.[46] The chief of these texts is: "my Father is greater than I" (John 14:28).[47] The Arians saw in this text a direct confirmation of the creatureliness of the Son.

This biblical antinomy or paradox can be interpreted in the light of the doctrine of *kenosis*. Jesus relates Himself to His Father both as to His Father and as to God, and He does so not in the capacity of God *and* Man but in the capacity of the God-Man, out of the depths and unity of His *Divine-Human* consciousness. Insofar as, in His descent from heaven and humiliation, He had removed from Himself His Divinity in His own life for Himself, He could in His earthly ministry relate Himself to the Father as to God, to whose will He had entrusted His entire life; apart from His Father's will He did not desire to have anything. He preaches and realizes the Kingdom of God, that is, the will of God the Father. All that He has, He receives from the Father; He does not have anything and does not desire to have anything that does not come from the Father. For Him who has removed from Himself His Divinity, the very descent from heaven and the Incarnation are not His proper act (unlike His supramundane self-humiliation, which He effected in harmonious union with the Father) but a sending from the Father. In His state of self-humiliation and self-emptying, His proper Divine hypostatic will is silenced in Him, as it were — this will that is proper to Him as the Second hypostasis, equal in honor and divinity to the Father and the Holy Spirit. He hears only the voice of the Father's will, to which He freely submits and to which He listens, not in the capacity of His own personal will, but precisely in the capacity of

---

46. See my book *The Burning Bush*, the patrological excursus.

47. In patristics, this text received two interpretations. The first is triadological — in relation to the Father as the begetting and unbegotten Principle (Athanasius, Gregory the Theologian, Cyril of Alexandria, John Chrysostom). The second is christological, from the point of view of the relation of Christ's human nature to God the Father (Athanasius, Basil the Great, Hilary, Cyril of Alexandria, and especially Augustine and Leo the Great).

The Lamb of God

the Father's will, commanding from on high: "I came down from heaven, not to do mine own will, but the will of him that sent me. And this is the Father's will . . ." (John 6:38-39). Having divinely abandoned His own will in the kenosis, the Son hypostatically does the Father's will, not in the capacity of His own divine will, which He had kenotically extinguished in Himself, but in the capacity of the will of the Father, who sent Him. The very idea of the *sending* is only the ultimate generalized expression of this fundamental idea of the *kenosis* of the Son, in virtue of which the Divine will and the Divine self-determination come to Him *from above,* from the Father, and are not present in Him as His proper hypostatically divine self-positing. The kenosis transforms the Son's divine consciousness of self into a *tabula rasa,* as it were, on which the will of the Father who "sent" Him writes its commands. These commands are written by the Father who, out of love for the world, did not spare His only begotten Son.

However, in this consciousness of self (insofar as in it the Divine Person is conscious of Himself with His proper nature), the Divine Sonhood, which represents the personal principle in the God-Man, is revealed. For the God-Man, *to be personally* is *to be the Son* of the Heavenly Father, to be conscious of Himself as the Father's Son. As a result, it is to receive from the Father His entire divine life, to acquire from Him His divine nature, and to know the depths of this nature by the Spirit of God. In short, it is to have all from the Father. Linked with His divine-human nature, His divine consciousness is not separated from this dual nature with its divine essence but also its creaturely, human limitations. His divine consciousness renders itself commensurate with these limitations; that is why, without ceasing to be the God-Man, He does not become God in His kenosis, although He has the divine hypostasis and the divine nature. There is an asymmetry of the natures here, a sacrifice of Divinity in the depths of Divinity itself. This is precisely what is expressed in this paradox, in this antinomy of the Divine-Human consciousness of self, which oscillates, as it were, between two modes of being: "My soul is exceeding sorrowful, even unto death" (Matt. 26:38) and "why hast thou forsaken me?" (27:46) at one pole and "All things that the Father hath are mine" (John 16:15) and "I and my Father are one" (10:30) at the other. On the one hand, there is the earthly ministry, whose course He Himself defines as follows: "Behold, we go up to Jerusalem; and the Son of man shall be delivered unto the chief priests, and unto the scribes; and they shall condemn him to death, and shall deliver him to the Gentiles: And they shall mock him, and shall scourge him, and shall spit upon him, and shall kill him: and the third day he shall rise again" (Mark 10:33-34). On the other hand, there is the manifestation of the heavenly glory on the Mount of the Transfiguration with the voice from heaven saying: "This is my beloved Son: hear him" (Mark 9:7). From the consciousness of the Divine Sonhood there issues His teaching about Himself as the way, the truth, and the life, as the one who resurrects and judges, with the exhortation to *believe* in Him together with the Father: "believe in God, believe also in me" (John 14:1).

It is direct divine consciousness that is expressed in this testimony of Christ about Himself, in His preaching about Himself, and in the concentration of His entire work upon Himself, upon His appearance, upon His revelation. But insofar as it is revealed during His earthly ministry, this divine consciousness is His *hypostatic* divine consciousness of Himself only as the Son of the Father; it is never His personal self-definition such as the one given in the Old Testament: "I am the LORD thy God." The personal consciousness of self, which does not know any degrees and which, once awakened, shines forth fully, does not correspond here to His divine being or self-revelation. It remains bound by the earthly fetters of a not-yet-glorified humanity. The Son of God and the Son of Man are one person and one living being, but when this one being appears before us in this bi-unity and the resulting complexity, then for us human beings this is perceived as the *alternating* manifestation of the two natures, a manifestation we are unable to unify since we are unable to penetrate into the depths of the mystery of the divine-human person. Nevertheless, the manifestation in Christ of the divine and human natures invariably remains *divine-human,* and the unity of the divine-human person is never interrupted by any alternation of the natures. This is one and the same Divine-Human I that is also the subject of all the psycho-corporeal states: fatigue, hunger, even sleep. This I is never extinguished;[48] it never stops being itself. It experiences human experiences but is never dominated by them to such a degree that the God-Man at any moment of His life effec-

---

48. In the kenotic literature there often arises the question of the character of Jesus' consciousness when He was asleep. This question can be resolved on the basis of the general kenotic principle according to which the personality manifests itself through the life of the human consciousness, connected with the psycho-corporeal life, and, to this extent, is psychologized and even somatized, so to speak. Consequently, the personality is subordinate to this extent to the state of sleep. The daytime consciousness is extinguished in sleep, whereas the life of the nighttime, sleeping consciousness, proceeding in the subconscious, represents a true enigma in man and, even more so, a mystery in the God-Man. The only indisputable thing is that sleep does not interrupt and does not fragment the personal consciousness but somehow enters into the life of the latter, although in a special manner. Thus, there is no special ontological problem here.

tively stops being the God-Man and is reduced to the level of man in his purely biological-somatic life. "Flesh" never gained dominion over the Divine Spirit; there is no evidence in the Gospels that it ever did. On the contrary, a highly significant testimony about just the opposite, about the dominion of the spirit over the flesh, is furnished by the conversation with the woman of Samaria (John 4): At first, Jesus experiences natural fatigue, thirst, and hunger, but these receive not a bodily but a spiritual satisfaction. When His disciples, having returned after buying food, beseeched Him: "Master, eat. . . . He said unto them, I have meat to eat that ye know not of" (4:31-32 and further).

B. Struggles and Temptations

Inexpressible by words but perceivable by the eyes of the spirit, there is a radiance of divine dignity, a cloud of glory, that surrounds the Lord in *all* the manifestations of His human nature. This does not diminish the authenticity of these manifestations, but they have no power over His spirit. They are received by Him only to be immediately seized by the spirit and made subject to it. This is not only the highest human genius that is accessible to man, and it is not only the highest human nobility, the purity of saintliness and sinlessness soaring above the earth. It is also all-conquering spirituality, spiritual vigilance ("the spirit indeed is willing, but the flesh is weak" [Matt. 26:41]), and unceasing ascesis — the victorious struggle of spirit against flesh, which is unceasingly overcome and spiritualized (this is an essential part of the Savior's redemptive feat). He restores in Himself the relation between spirit and body that is the norm for man: flesh does not dominate the spirit but is obedient to it. Because of Adam's fall, the abnormal became the norm: the spirit was made subject to the flesh. The human side of the God-Man's earthly ministry consisted in reversing the current of life, in restoring the norm, and this was accomplished not in virtue of divine omnipotence but by free human effort, by ascetic feat. This inner struggle never abated; on the contrary, it intensified as the end approached. We see the greatest intensity of this struggle in the agony at Gethsemane and in the suffering on the cross. This was not an unearned victory over human infirmity by God's power; this was a *human victory*, which alone was necessary and precious here, and which was accomplished in the God-Man. During the course of His entire earthly life, the divine-human consciousness of the God-Man was unceasingly engaged in this struggle of spirit against flesh, of holiness against the sinfulness of the world, which He came to save in the name of God's love for the world, taking upon Himself the sins of the world while at the same time overcoming it: "be of good cheer; I have overcome the world" (John 16:33). He struggled against the world, into which He had come "from heaven," being conscious of and attesting His foreignness to the world but also His connection with it: He was sent by the Father into the world "that the world through him might be saved" (3:17). He was sent to give His flesh "for the life of the world" (6:51), but at the same time He was conscious of His absolute oppositeness to the *sinful* world: "ye are from beneath; I am from above: ye are of this world; I am not of this world" (8:23); "they are not of the world, even as I am not of the world" (17:14). And in turn "the world knew him not. He came unto his own, and his own received him not" (1:10-11); "me [the world] hateth, because I testify of it, that the works thereof are evil" (7:7). "If the world hate you, ye know that it hated me before it hated you" (15:18; cf. 1 John 3:13); "my kingdom is not of this world" (18:36). But this hostility and struggle against the world take place for the sake of the salvation of the world, even as the struggle against the flesh takes place for the sake of the salvation of the flesh ("He is the saviour of the body" [Eph. 5:23]).

It is important to protect this idea from a monophysitic interpretation according to which, by His power, God in Christ gave Him the victory over the flesh and its infirmity, making any struggle in the true sense impossible: the clay cannot struggle against the potter. Such a mechanical interpretation, which abolishes the entire power of the redemptive feat, does not conform with the kenosis of the Son of God, who suppressed in Himself this power of His Divinity, although not its presence. He accomplished the kenotic feat of struggle with all the intensity of His human essence, illuminated and inspired by His Divinity. He stood defenseless and abandoned before the judgment of Pilate and of the high priests, although He could "pray to my Father [that he] give me more than twelve legions of angels" (Matt. 26:53). Christ's Divinity fortified His human power in this struggle; it did not replace it, however, but only inspired and confirmed Him in His way of the cross. Such too was the help from heaven: "there appeared an angel unto him from heaven, strengthening him" (Luke 22:43). But this did not lessen the struggle and the resulting sufferings or make them fictitious, just as His divinely filial prayer and unceasing feat of faith were not fictitious. "Behold, the hour cometh, yea, is now come, that ye shall be scattered, every man to his own, and shall leave me alone: and yet I am not alone, because the Father is with me" (John 16:32). The abandonment and the weakening caused by the intensity of the feat go even further, however, for from the cross there resounds the cry: "Eli, Eli, lama sabachthani? . . . My God, my God, why hast thou forsaken me?" (Matt. 27:46, with parallels).

Here we encounter the doctrine of the "Aphthartodocetics" or "Phantasiasts" (one of the branches of the monophysites, headed by Julian of Halicarnassus and Gaianos of Alexandria). Whereas Eutyches denied the consubstantiality of Christ's body with the human body, the Aphthartodocetics denied their identity with respect to state. According to this doctrine, Jesus' body, free of sin, corresponded to Adam's body before the Fall and was therefore free not only of all corruption but also of sinless passions (Leontius, *Contra Nest. et Eutych.*, PG 86.1325, 1329). If in the grave His body did not know decay (see Acts 2:31), this means that incorruptibility was inherent to Him from birth in virtue of His hypostatic union with the Logos. It does not mean, however, that His human needs and sufferings were only illusory; the Logos voluntarily, "economically," permitted them for Himself; His human needs and sufferings were not the result of a natural necessity. In this sense, Christ's entire earthly life is a permanent miracle. The logical accent falls here on the rejection of the *naturalness* of Christ's human life and, as a result, on the voluntary character of every act of this life (the "activists" considered even the Lord's body to be uncreated).

One of course cannot deny the general idea that the Logos assumed the human essence *voluntarily*. However, such an "occasionalistic" conception, according to which all acts of human life are expressly permitted by the divine will without being naturally conditioned, is incompatible with the idea of authentic divine incarnation, which loses here its ontological as well as soteriological meaning. Christ assumed flesh in order to live in it, not to act upon it from outside by a series of external impacts, as it were.[49] There is a radical imprecision, however, in this fundamental doc-

---

49. Professor V. V. Bolotov exhibits a certain lack of clarity and an indecisiveness on this subject: "It was not in virtue of physical compulsion but because of His own infinite mercy, voluntarily, that God the Word became incarnate and entered the sphere of influence of the given historical conditions, which, in the end, had to lead to His crucifixion. But the Church also recognizes that, at every moment of His earthly life, He had the power to remove Himself from the influence of this historical or natural causality: He could have refrained from fasting and then he would not have been hungry; He could have refrained from walking in the midday heat and then He would not have been fatigued to the point of enervation; He could have refrained from going to Jerusalem to His voluntary death; He could have come down from the cross, and so on. But at the same time, despite the voluntary character of His activities, we also recognize the natural

trine of the Aphthartodocetics concerning the relation of the "impassible" and "passible" natures in Christ. The question that was posed in this doctrine was clarified by St. John of Damascus, who distinguished the "corruptibility" proper to the human nature in its passive states from the corruptibility of the dead body: the former is proper to Christ in virtue of the authentic and salvific character of His in-humanization, whereas the latter is not proper to Him at all (see St. John of Damascus, *Critical Exposition of the Orthodox Faith*, book 3, ch. 28, c. 1100). However, a general question remains: What was the real difference between the human nature in Christ and that in men? This difference is externally manifested in the fact that the Lord's body in the grave did not know corruption, in contrast to the natural properties of the common human essence. The Aphthartodocetics justly felt that there was a special problem here: Incorruptible *in actu* in death, was Christ's body not incorruptible *in potentia* during His life? And in this case, how should one more precisely understand this incorruptibility? The human essence of the New Adam, free of original sin in virtue of the conception without seed from the Holy Spirit, *approaches* the essence of the first Adam before the Fall. It is an exaggeration to consider the New Adam's human essence to be free of the need for food and sleep, to be free of fatigue, and so on. It had not yet become a "spiritual body" but was only a "natural" and even an "earthy" body (see 1 Cor. 15:44-47). However, Christ's body did not know sicknesses, which are already the beginning of death; nor did it know natural mortality ("for God made not death" [Wisdom of Solomon 1:13]), although He did not yet possess active immortality. Before the Fall, Adam's body too was free of corruption, although it did not know the active victory over corruption. If the Lord's body were identical in all its properties with the body of the first Adam, in conformity with the doctrine of the Aphthartodocetics, it would really have differed from our body; and the salvation of man by Christ's assumption of our essence would have remained unrealized (a similar dogmatic misunderstanding characterizes the Roman Catholic doctrine of the "immaculate conception" of the Mother of God, which in effect breaks the connection between Christ and our humanity). Such a

---

necessity of these sufferings: Christ could have refrained from fasting, but after the forty-day fast He had to have been hungry; after having walked a certain distance under the midday sun, He had to have experienced fatigue; after having consented to being nailed to the cross, He had to have experienced horrible pain from the nailing of His hands. These two phenomena represent only two aspects of one and the same fact; they are analogous to sound and the vibration of the air, to light and the oscillation of the ether" (*Lectures on the History of the Ancient Church*, 4.346-47).

The Lamb of God

total identity does not exist, however; there is only an approximation, and it is essential to establish not only the similarities but also the differences.

First of all, it is impossible to separate Adam from the world, which is the peripheral body of man. The consequences of the Fall extended to the entire world and changed man's entire relation to nature ("cursed is the ground for thy sake" [Gen. 3:17]); this aggravated the infirmity of the human essence and its dependence on the natural world: its hunger, cold, thirst, and so on. The Lord came not into the Garden of Eden, into which the first Adam was placed, but into this world, the earth of anguish, where the creature is groaning and awaiting its liberation. He "appeared on earth and lived with men," thus burdening His flesh with the burden of the world's being. This is the first difference between His flesh and that of the first Adam. The second difference is that even though Christ, "made incarnate from the Holy Spirit and the Virgin Mary," was free of original sin, He took His flesh from His Mother, who was not free of original sin and thus carried within Herself its consequences as a diminished power of life. Was the Most Pure Mother of God subject to sicknesses during the course of Her life? We have no *direct* testimony relating to this. According to what the Church believes, Jesus' birth was accomplished without pain (thus, God's judgment on the proto-mother Eve was revoked: "in sorrow thou shalt bring forth children" [Gen. 3:16]). The superabundant grace of the Holy Spirit, reposing upon the Spirit-bearing Mother of God, removed bodily pain and sickness from Her, but it did not liberate Her from emotional sufferings, the greatest of which consisted in Her spiritual co-crucifixion with the Son at the foot of the cross (cf. *The Lamentation of the Mother of God* of Simeon Logothetes and various Stabat Maters). Nevertheless, the power of death, which usually manifests itself over the course of an entire human life in sicknesses, was not abolished in the Mother of God, for She knew natural death. She thereby attested that She was not separated from the human race (as follows from the Catholic dogma), but that she shared its mortal nature, which She also transmitted to Her Son. It was this mortality that He was destined to defeat. In Adam, mortality was not defeated by the positive power of immortality, although before the Fall it was absent in him or, more precisely, it remained only a potentiality of his creatureliness, which was actualized only after the Fall. This is what determines the relation of Christ's human essence to death. Being free of original sin, Christ, like Adam before the Fall, was not subject to death. He could not be touched by death's power, which is manifested in sicknesses of the body: His body was without sickness; it was not subject to suffering and infirmity. No longer proper to

Him was the blessed state of the body of Adam, who lived not in a world that had lost its order but in the garden of God. Although the New Adam could not die a *natural* death, He had yet to attain the victory over death as the positive force of immortality. Although He was nonmortal like the first Adam, by His human essence He was not immortal in the sense of absolute liberation from the power of death. Therefore, He *could* be subject to death, although not to a natural one but to a violent one. He tasted the death on the cross, although death turned out to be powerless to hold Him (see Acts 2:24). Consequently, the potentiality of death (although not in the form of sicknesses) was present in His humanity, taken from the Virgin; otherwise, He would not have been able to die, even by the violent death on the cross. Thus, even if His flesh was that of the first Adam, it was nevertheless weakened by the consequences of sin, by the infirmity of the human essence and of the entire world; and He had to defeat this infirmity: "He hath borne our griefs" (Isa. 53:4).

Thus, being sinless Himself, He took upon Himself the consequences of sin as the common infirmity of life in the world and in man. In this He did not separate Himself from humanity but fully assumed the human nature, including all the consequences of this assumption (contra the Aphthartodocetics). To be sure, this assumption of the human nature was voluntary, a feat of sacrificial love; but once it was accomplished, as "the descent from heaven," the life of the human nature in the God-Man attained its full force. He appears as the New Adam in His humanity. This humanity of His is free only of that with which the Incarnation is incompatible (i.e., of sin in all its forms and varieties, original and personal, natural and voluntary). But His humanity is not liberated from those *infirmities* that were the inevitable consequences of the Fall, including the possibility of knowing death. It is precisely these infirmities, generalized in death, that must be overcome if salvation is to be attained. In His sacrificial feat, the Son of Man does not separate Himself from the common human nature and from the common human fate. He makes them His own in order to become the Author of life, the New Adam. No Aphthartodoceticism, therefore, whether straightforward or subtle, must be allowed, for it diminishes the power of the salvific work and the authenticity of the Incarnation. In conclusion, we must say that Christ, in His humanity, cannot be directly identified with either the original Adam or the fallen Adam. Instead, He forms a living bridge between the two and raises them to a new and immortal human life. In connection with the authenticity of the in-humanization, it is important to examine the question of the *temptations* of Christ.

The Lamb of God

What does Satan's temptation of Christ in the wilderness represent, during which He saw in a vision or in inner contemplation three possible paths that were nondivine, that did not conform with the Father's will but that conformed with Satan's will? And first of all, to what degree was the temptation real for the God-Man Himself? Was He tempted? Was He accessible to temptation? For docetism or semi-docetism,[50] the temptation was clearly unreal, since it was excluded and rendered powerless in advance by the Divinity living in the God-Man (this conception would be legitimate if one ignored the kenosis of Divinity). But this rejection of the power of temptation and the opinion that it is illusory are clearly contradicted by the grave and severe words of the Epistle to the Hebrews affirming precisely the reality of the temptations: "Wherefore in all things it behoved him to be made like unto his brethren . . . for in that he himself hath suffered being tempted, he is able to succour them that are tempted" (2:17-18); "we have not an high priest which cannot be touched with the feeling of our infirmities; but was in all points tempted like as we are, yet without sin" (4:15). But the Epistle goes even further and says that, through His trials and temptations, Christ was "made perfect": "though he were a Son, yet learned he obedience . . . and being made perfect, he became the author of eternal salvation" (5:8-9; cf. 2:10; 7:28). The reality of the temptation was such that its conquest bore its own particular fruit: the one who conquered the temptation was "made perfect." A general preliminary question necessarily arises: *Could* Jesus have succumbed to sin even if in fact He did not succumb to it but overcame it *(potuit non peccare)*? Or was it the case that temptation had no power over Him *(non potuit peccare)*, and that the tempter had, so to speak, come to the wrong place, committing an *error in objecto*? In turn, the last term of this dilemma breaks up into two parts: Was the temptation powerless over the God-Man because God is not tempted? In this case, even if Christ permitted Satan to speak with Him and to unfold his temptations until he heard: "Get thee hence, Satan" from Christ (Matt. 4:10), did He do this only for the sake of edification and example, for the sake of appearance (just as supposedly it was for the sake of appearance that He prayed, etc.)? Or was the temptation powerless for the general reason that, at a certain

---

50. St. John of Damascus judges about this only in passing, noting: "The evil one attacked Christ from outside, not through His thoughts, as was the case with Adam, who also was attacked not through his thoughts but through the serpent. The Lord repelled the attack and dispelled it like smoke" (*Brief Exposition of the Orthodox Faith*, book 3, ch. 20, c. 1081).

Emmanuel, the God-Man

spiritual elevation and maturity, evil loses its power to seduce (thus, the holy angels are incapable of falling), and the very capacity to be tempted is overcome?

First of all, in examining *non potuit peccare*, the impossibility of being tempted by sin, one must exclude the first hypothesis, for it is essentially docetic: If the God-Man could treat the temptation only as God, (i.e., if He could treat it as something that did not exist), then the human essence in Him would not have had authentic being and would have been absorbed by Divinity (contrary to the inconfusability of the essences in Christ); or the flesh would have been only a transparent veil that let the light of divinity pass through it. The temptation would then not have taken place at all but would have been staged only for the sake of edification (which would have been a disgrace for the intelligent, though evil, spirit, who not only would have experienced inevitable failure here but also would have been relegated to playing a ridiculous and stupid role). The temptation *did* take place, however, according to the direct testimony of the Gospel. The first part of the dilemma therefore remains in force: the temptation could not have been crowned with success *(non potuit peccare)* precisely because of the holiness and spiritual power of the God-Man, which beat back all temptation. This proposition must be clarified more precisely, however, for it contains two different possibilities: The first is that, being powerless to seduce, the temptation was thus totally ineffective; the second is that, remaining powerless, the temptation was nonetheless effective, and therefore totally real in its consequences, although they turned out to be essentially opposite to what was intended. The first of these hypotheses coincides, in essence, with the docetic-monophysitic conception examined above, which of course must be rejected both in general (insofar as it abolishes the power of the Incarnation) and in particular (insofar as it introduces a theatrical illusoriness into the Savior's earthly life). To this docetic point of view it is necessary to oppose the kenotic point of view, which alone is capable of guaranteeing the reality of the humanity in Christ: The humanity is indeed the veil of the divinity, but it is a veil that really covers and conceals the divinity, not one that is totally transparent to and as if nonexistent for the divinity.

Therefore — and this is the main thing — the God-Man receives the temptation directly as such (otherwise there could be no temptation), but He receives it only in the measure of His humanity. To be sure, Christ's humanity is deified and overshadowed by the Holy Spirit; the Gospel even directly states: "then was Jesus led up of the Spirit into the wilderness to be tempted of the devil" (Matt. 4:1), immediately after the descent upon

Him of the Holy Spirit at His baptism. Although in the God-Man this humanity is not separated from the Divinity, it remains itself, and the temptation of the God-Man can be directed at it or, more precisely, by means of it. Furthermore, His humanity *needs* the temptation, and Jesus was *led by the Spirit* precisely to it. His humanity is capable of experiencing temptation, of hearing temptation in its depths, which is why the God-Man heard Satan (however we understand this image) and spoke with him, even if this temptation had no real effect on Him. Thus, in this case, *non potuit peccare* does not exclude but includes *potuit non peccare* (i.e., the real victory over the temptation, which one could not speak of with reference to Divinity, for whom the temptation does not exist). The temptation represents a *question* to which one answer or another is given; the two together, question and answer, constitute the temptation. To be sure, in no wise can we allow that Christ's answer to the tempter in the wilderness could be other than negative. One can say the same thing — *non potuit peccare* — about His final temptation, coming from the Jews: "if thou be the Son of God, come down from the cross" (Matt. 27:40). No trace of sin can attach itself to the purity, holiness, and devotion to God of the Son of Man: "Which of you can convict me of sin?" (John 8:46 [the King James Version has been modified to conform with the Russian Bible]).

The Gospel image of Christ, full of purity and holiness in every trait, is the greatest of miracles. The human imagination could never have invented this image. It was instead through the divinely inspired narrative of fishermen that the true Face of the Savior was revealed to us. But the evil spirit, blinded by envy and self-infatuation, could not discern this uniqueness of the "only one who is without sin" and approached Him in the hope of succeeding with his temptation, as the ancient serpent had succeeded in the case of the old Adam. Nevertheless, the New Adam too had to undergo the temptation of the old Adam. Herein lies an ontological necessity for the free being as such. Adam was created in the fullness of his humanity, but it was necessary for him not only to receive this fullness as a gift but also to disclose it through his own free and creative participation, for freedom is included in the fullness of humanity. The first Adam therefore remained in a state of immaturity as long as he was untempted, and in order to attain the perfect age he had to leave this untempted state through freedom. The trial of freedom was given to him by God Himself in the commandment of obedience. This commandment flowed from Adam's very nature, which had in itself the norm of the relation to God and the world; the substance of this commandment was that Adam should be himself, that he should remain ontologically faithful to himself, but now on the principle of freedom. However, besides the divine commandment directed at Adam's freedom, the deceitful temptation of the serpent became parasitically attached to his freedom. In both cases it was demanded of Adam that he determine himself actively and freely, that he leave the passivity of immaturity. Adam possessed the naïveté of the untried state, the childish ignorance of good and evil, but this naïveté was also a limitation. It was not the holiness of *non posse peccare* but only the freedom of indifference: *posse peccare et non peccare*. Creatureliness contains the possibility, although not the necessity, of the fall into sin, *posse peccare*; and this fall took place. This trial enriched our progenitors with the bitter experience of the knowledge of good and evil, of the power of sin and the difficulty of combating it. This trial did not strengthen man but weakened him, and the restoration of the original man constituted the task and work of the Second Adam. Christ became man, assimilating the fullness of the human essence not only in its nature but also in its freedom. This freedom was not abolished or paralyzed by His Divinity but only inspired by it. It preserved its power in the God-Man thanks to the fact that He "took upon him the form of a servant" (i.e., of man), and the form He took upon Himself was that of a man weakened by sin, although pure of sin. Thus He "was made in the likeness of men" (Phil. 2:7). This "likeness to men" necessarily includes human freedom, which is realized only in experience, in trials and temptations. The authenticity of the human nature therefore demands authenticity of feat, of struggle and temptations, and the God-Man's entire earthly life was filled with them. He had to struggle *unceasingly* against the inertia of the infirm flesh, not easily stirred by the vigilant spirit, and against the hostility of the sinful world with its temptations (which we would not dare to mention if the Gospels, attesting to the authenticity of the Incarnation, did not directly speak about them). Here His Divinity remained silent, consenting to the maximal trial of the humanity.

It is here that the question of the *power* of the temptation, and then of its *character*, arises. Creaturely freedom is marked by *instability*, inherent in both the human world and in the world of the immaterial spirits, which explains the fall of the angels as well as of man. The creature, created out of nothing, has two possibilities: to determine itself on the basis of being or to determine itself on the basis of nonbeing. In itself, however, this instability does not imply the necessity of the Fall. Adam could have resisted the temptation by remaining faithful to God's commandment, or he could have repented before being expelled from paradise. (This might have been possible for the fallen angels too before their definitive expulsion from heaven; see Revelation 12). Not being compulsory for the creature, this instability, this possibility of the Fall, can decrease and even be reduced to a potential state with the spiritual growth and increasing self-determination of the creature, acquired through freedom. Such is the state of the holy angels, who have overcome this instability in themselves, who by spiritual growth have abolished the possibility of the Fall: from *posse non peccare* they have ascended to the state of *non posse peccare*, but in such a way that the second and higher level does not abolish but presupposes and includes the lower level. In other words, this stability is not only a fact but also an act; it is a work of creaturely freedom, not a given. The nature of creatureliness here does not change and is not abolished; rather it is revealed in its power and fullness through freedom. The "sting in the flesh," the underground nothingness, exists;[51] but since it is always defeated, it remains powerless and ineffective, a zero (which nevertheless is a number, although a number with a purely potential value). A creaturely *stable instability* can thus exist, in the case of which the creaturely essence is preserved but grows beyond itself, becomes higher than itself; and in response to the feat of the creature, grace is of course bestowed, affirming creaturely stability now on the basis of divine stability. That is why we conceive a progressive series as irreversible; the "eternal life" of the future age is not subject to the possibility of new falls or different choices. This life is liberated from freedom as arbitrariness or *different* possibilities; it knows freedom only as an ontological path.

How can the aforesaid be applied to the humanity of Christ and to its temptations? Apollinarius delineated the problematic in all its acuteness when he posed the question of whether the fullness of the humanity in Christ implies instability as an inalienable property of His humanity, with this instability containing the threat of changeability. Frightened by this threat, Apollinarius abandoned the straight path and instead took the path that consisted in diminishing the fullness of the human essence in Christ in order to protect Him against instability. He thereby desired to insure that Christ was *atreptos* (without change). But Apollinarius had exaggerated the instability; he had bought the illusory insurance at too high a cost — the cost of doing violence to Christ's humanity and thus destroying the divine-human work. For Christ's humanity it is necessary to assure human (i.e., creaturely) freedom and thus the possibility of His being tempted, even if this possibility is included in the de facto overcoming of the instability. The former is the content and foundation of the feat,

---

51. A reference to Dostoevsky's *Notes from Underground*. — Trans.

whereas the latter is its accomplishment and power; but the feat itself consists in a real victory over a real temptation, which therefore is a trial (see James 1:2-4). Temptation proceeds from original creaturely infirmity, which is clothed in power and overcome by the latter only by means of trials in freedom.

Christ was really tempted. In other words, He really experienced the difficulties of His path, which He mastered. The first difficulty involved His human nature: it consisted in unceasingly having to overcome the disobedient and infirm flesh, which in its given state resists the spirit. A further difficulty was that of struggling against the hostility of the world, against human limitation, sinfulness, and malice, which did not cease until they were sated in His death on the cross. Finally, there was the struggle against the selfhood of the world that had fallen away from God, against the world that desires to live its own life, the life of the kingdom of this world. Having entered, with the descent from heaven, into the domain of the world's being, He received in His human essence the natural opacity and selfhood of this world, which, by a feat of freedom, He had to subject to God's will and steal away from the prince of this world. This element of the world rose in Christ's human nature as a tempting question, necessarily demanding a definitive, firm, and even authoritative answer; to evade this question, to render it nonexistent, would be to fall into a kind of Aphthartodocetism and diminish the work of the New Adam. This voice of the essence fallen away from God sounds in the temptations of Satan, who is the *personal* expression of creaturely selfhood in the spiritual world (at various times, by God's permission, he was also identified with fire, with tempest, and, in the temptation of Job, with leprosy).

The old Adam was tempted in paradise, in God's garden, into which the tempter had crept in the form of a serpent (i.e., in the form of a natural, animal being). The New Adam was tempted in the "wilderness," where He too found Himself in the company of "wild beasts" (Mark 1:13), isolated from people but in the presence of His own human essence, which was subjected to trial by prayer and fasting in its obedience to the spirit. This was the preliminary triumph of spirit over flesh, and it came not without struggle, for the Gospel says the temptation took place *not only* at the end of the period of isolation: "He was there in the wilderness forty days, tempted of Satan" (Mark 1:13; cf. Luke 4:2). Toward the end of this time ("when he had fasted forty days and forty nights, he was afterward an hungred" [Matt. 4:2]), the temptation had reached a certain intensity, and it is then that the prince of the world joined himself to the voice of the disobedient nature. All the temptations of the devil, which are spiritual

The Lamb of God

images or visions arising in the spirit from out of the depths of the human essence, are directed at creaturely, human freedom, which is disclosed as having at its disposition the power that is proper to man as the Son of God — "If thou be the Son of God" (Matt. 4:6). To be sure, the devil does not know the mysteries of the Divine-Humanity, but he knows human divine-sonhood, envy of which was one of the causes of his fall. And here he sees, or at least supposes, the supreme manifestation of this divine-sonhood: the manifestation of a certain Man-god. The general goal of these temptations is to awaken in the New Adam the same selfhood that is proper to Satan himself and that was awakened by him in the old Adam. The generalized aspect of this atheistic or even antitheistic selfhood is expressed by the three temptations, which are presented in ascending order (with variants, however, in Matthew and Luke): the temptation of power over nature for the satisfaction of the needs of the flesh ("economic materialism"), the temptation of the empty and soulless working of miracles for the sake of proud self-assertion, and finally, the temptation of power over the world, bought at the cost of the adoration of the prince of this world (Luke presents the two latter temptations, which are analogous, in reverse order). After the rejection of the temptations, that is, after the victory over the infirmity and selfhood of the human nature (although this is only a preliminary and initial victory, for the devil "departed from him for a season" [Luke 4:13]), the God-Man finds Himself in gracious communion with heaven: "angels came and ministered unto him" (Matt. 4:11; cf. John 1:51).

Was Jesus accessible to this temptation? Was it real for Him to such an extent that one can see in it an authentic trial that had to be experienced and overcome? Or was it only a docetic manifestation? It was absolutely real, for it was the voice of the human nature assumed by Christ (St. Gregory the Theologian's maxim is applicable here: "that which is not assumed, is not redeemed"). This was the first real victory of *deification* over the human nature. If we examine the character of the temptation, we will note that it did not include those impulses and desires of the flesh that, after the Fall, enslaved the human essence with animality and crippled it with passions. Such a temptation never came close to the God-Man. He remained above it, being liberated from the hereditary original sin; He was the New Adam, in whom was restored the integral virginity of the first man in his sophianicity.

In connection with this, however, a doubt can arise concerning at least the fullness, if not the authenticity, of the human essence in the

Emmanuel, the God-Man

God-Man: If He was free of that which, along with hunger, is the most agonizing thing for man, then is man wholly redeemed, and is the redemptive work fully accomplished? However, having assumed only the sinless "likeness of man," man's flesh, but not its sin, the God-Man thus could not receive into His nature that which is the center of the whole power of sin and which, at the same time, is unnatural for man, for it exists only within the limits of the life of sin and selfhood ("when they shall rise from the dead, they neither marry, nor are given in marriage" [Mark 12:25]). In this respect there is an essential difference between the functions of eating and sex. Eating is an ontological relation to the world; it is communion with the flesh of the world, a communion established by God in paradise and not abolished in the Heavenly Jerusalem (see Rev. 22:2), whereas sex and sexual conception, sexuality in general, entered the world with the Fall, as a principle of mortal and damaged life. Therefore, all that is connected with the proper life of sex as such does not belong to the nature of Adam received by the New Adam in its original state. To be sure, this nature was received by Him in the diminished state proper to fallen man. However, this reception extended only to "sinless passions," and the sexual life is not one of them. In this respect, Christ was *different* from the entire human race, for in Him the natural chastity and virginity of the race were restored. However, they were restored not naturally but by the grace of the Holy Spirit in the Most Holy Virgin and in the Forerunner of the Lord. It follows from this, as an opposite conclusion, that the existence of *sex* (but of course not the spiritual distinction between the male and female essences) is not essential for humanity and, as the "body of death," is even unnatural for humanity. Given this limitation, Christ took upon Himself the entire inertia of the human nature and the selfhood inherent in it in order, having overcome them, to crucify them. The old Adam had disobeyed and succumbed to temptation, whereas the New Adam follows the path of obedience to the end, which is precisely the victory over temptation. But if the victory is to be more than illusory and if the temptation is to be defeated, there must be something to defeat, that is, the temptation itself must be real.

Nevertheless, Satan manifested both blindness and the megalomania proper to him when he tried to tempt the Son of God (although he was not and could not be fully certain that this was the Son of God). This attempt was totally hopeless, and any probability of success, on which he evidently counted, was excluded in advance. Despite all the reality and power of the temptation, it was absolutely impossible for Satan to be victorious over Christ. Why? Is it not because the God-Man was protected from temptation by His Divinity? No, it did not protect Him in the capacity of a superior power, revoking the laws of the human essence. On the contrary, His Divinity permitted the temptation and did not interfere in the outcome of the struggle, leaving it for human freedom and diminishing itself to the measure of the human essence, as if hiding in it. But this human essence itself proved to be inaccessible to the temptation; it overcame its own natural instability. Before his fall, Adam was sinless and pure, but this does not mean that he was perfect; otherwise how could he have fallen so easily? The purity of untested virginity with its naïveté is different from the conscious purity of maturity, of moral perfection. Adam's experience, with all its fatal consequences, already lay in the past; this experience was known to the New Adam, who repulses the temptation not even by His own words but by the direct commandments of God (see Matt. 4:4, 7, 10). But aside from the general tested condition of the man, acquired through trials and temptations, Satan was also confronted here by supreme holiness and purity, as well as by an immeasurable genius and a fullness of the entire human essence that not only were not inferior to the genius and fullness of the first man whom he had deceived and seduced but were far superior to them, since they included the entire experience of the generations of the forefathers of the Savior as the *Son of Man*. Just as the angels, who have been tempted and have overcome the temptation, are no longer subject to the instability that can incline them to sin, so the human essence of the Savior, in His perfection, is free of all inclination to sin. In addition to these indirect deductions and theories, however, we have absolutely indisputable proof of this. In the God-Man, the humanity is united without separation and without confusion with His Divinity. His human will is in accord with and "follows" the Divine will. This is not an absorption or a coercion of the human essence by the divine essence but their harmonious participation in one life. Even in the most extreme state of kenosis, Christ's humanity is in continuous communion with His Divinity (according to the terminology of Catholic theology, it has a vision of the Divinity, *visio beatifica*); it is constantly nourished by the inspirations of Divinity and is deified by them. That is why, not even having need, in and of itself, of transcendental protection, Christ's humanity is thus protected from any possibility of temptation, without violating freedom (for "grace does not coerce").

But there is more. It is equally important that the hypostasis of the God-Man is the Logos, the Second Person of the Holy Trinity, even if diminished to the condition of becoming and in-humanization. Even in this diminished state, the Divine-Human hypostasis knows its Divine Sonhood

Emmanuel, the God-Man

and its Divinity. Satan's question, his hesitant attempt to tempt Christ, "if thou be the Son of God" (with the insane intention to subjugate even the God-Man), received an answer that signified Satan's defeat. Although *will*, insofar as it is an actual expression of *nature*, belongs to nature, nevertheless the *one who wills* is the one who realizes the volition. Although the human will in Christ, which was what was tempted in Him, also belongs to the human nature, nevertheless it was realized from the Divine hypostatic center, the Divine Person, although in a kenotically diminished state. In the union of the natures the human will became Divine-Human; it was in accord with the Divine will and "followed" it. To be sure, nothing sinful, no temptation, could approach the divine hypostasis of the Logos; *non posse peccare*, the absence of the tendency to sin (with which Apollinarius was so preoccupied), was fully assured, as follows from the definitions of the Fourth and the Sixth Ecumenical Councils. But this does not exclude the *accessibility* of Jesus' human essence to temptation *(posse non peccare)* or the reality of the temptation, even if it is ultimately impotent. The temptation was included in Christ's humiliation on His earthly kenotic path. Fated to fail but perfectly real, the temptation consisted in *conquering the difficulties* that arose on the path of obedience and humiliation. This conquest was not unearned, automatic, mechanical; it was the creative conquest — acquired at the cost of labor and suffering — of the creaturely essence of the flesh and its subordination to the spirit. And the experience of temptation, according to the testimony of the Apostle, was a *teleiōsis*, a "making perfect," for the Son of Man Himself. He was not imperfect in His divine nature, but in His kenosis, having subjected Himself to becoming, He followed in His human essence the path of obedience even unto the death on the cross; on this path He was *made perfect*, manifesting His divine power by His feat. The one thing is connected with the other, and Christ's redemptive work is divided into a series of separate acts on the path of perfection and victory over the world, until, in the presence of the cross, He could say about Himself: "Now is the Son of man glorified" (John 13:31) and "I have overcome the world" (16:33).

Analogous to the question of the reality of the temptations is the much-discussed question of the Savior's "ignorance," with a number of fathers leaning toward a de facto semi-doceticism (see above). The human essence, in the state in which it was assumed by the Lord (even if we completely disregard the fact that this essence was weakened by original sin), is conditioned by spatiality and temporality; that is, it is subject to becoming, both outwardly and inwardly. Although neither the one nor the other is proper to the Divine absolute spirit, the Lord, in His in-humanization, subordinated Himself to the limits of space and time by kenotically accepting becoming. He was born and lived in a definite place and in a definite epoch, and He never violated this spatiality and temporality of His earthly existence. I do not know to what extreme of doceticism one must go to think that this too was only for the sake of appearance, and that in reality Christ was present in different places at the same time and lived at different times (only theosophists who invent various reincarnations of Christ, His hidden life in India and so on, are guilty of such a lack of taste). A real attachment to some definite point of the world in its space and time is necessary to assure the reality of the Incarnation itself, by means of which "all power" over the world, in heaven and on earth, is acquired. Nevertheless, this condition does not constitute a *limitation*, which would truly be incompatible with Divinity. It is rather a self-constraint through *becoming*, in which all the links are interconnected in the unity of the whole. The Son of God, as the Son of Man, takes this becoming upon Himself. He does not and cannot lose anything of His own, but He is free to diminish Himself to the point of becoming, and He truly does so diminish Himself.

As a result, together with the spatiality and temporality of His being, He also accepts their limits, particularly with respect to knowledge, since omniscience and omni-spatiality are incompatible with the limitations and nonabsoluteness of the becoming being of the world. If one believes in the authenticity of the Incarnation, one must also believe in the self-diminution of Divinity, in the real kenosis of God, signifying His real entry into the domain of relative and becoming being, in which all things realize themselves only in development. Becoming, however, does not signify that all things flow and are fleeting, that all is vanity of vanities and illusion. On the contrary, all things flow out of the depths of being and flow into these same depths of being; in other words, becoming is a special form of the *fullness* of being. It is by no means the absence of this fullness. Just as His subordination to the conditions of space and time does not represent an inherent limitation, so Jesus' lack of knowledge is not an ignorance resulting from weakness of thought and intelligence. One can by no means say about an infant of genius, who is in a state of ignorance appropriate to his age, that he suffers from a limited intelligence or an incapacity to think. On the contrary, the entire power of thought and knowledge lives in him in a latent manner and appears in him progressively, arising out of ignorance, in the same way that light appears and shines forth in darkness. Given the authenticity of the diminution of God to the level of becoming, we must necessarily accept the reality of the progressive stages of development and growth, and in particular of knowledge, by which Divinity manifests itself to itself, diminished and as if extinguished for itself, although present in and by itself.

The whole power of the Incarnation is annulled if one denies "ignorance" *in this sense* in Jesus. There must be no concessions or compromises here, for having admitted docetism, if only at a single point, one leaves an opening through which the entire contents of the vessel will flow out. To be sure, in certain miraculous and extraordinary cases, the limits of spatiality and temporality are abolished or at least diminished: the prophets prophesied about future events, as if overcoming temporality; far from Bethany, the Lord announces that Lazarus is dead, and so on. However, these exceptions, which have an explanation, only confirm the general rule: The prophets were far from omniscient; and Jesus, having come to Bethany, inquires "Where have ye laid him?" (John 11:34), not with pretended ignorance (as some theologians think), but with authentic ignorance. This general idea must be extended to the entire earthly life of the Savior. The transcendental *depths* of His divine consciousness contain *all*, for He is the hypostatic Logos of all being; but in His Divine-Humanity, these depths were covered with a film of becoming with its fluctuating illumination. Christ knew in Himself His Divine Sonhood and thus confessed His Divinity, but He did not reveal — for Himself and for the world — this Divinity in its supratemporal and supraspatial absoluteness until the time came for this in His glorification.

This must also be extended to the question of the Son of Man's ignorance of the time of His Second Coming. On this subject some theologians in their apologetic zeal arrive at a meaning that directly contradicts Christ's own words. One of the possible meanings of Jesus' testimony about His ignorance of the time of the end of the world is that this time is determined not only by God's will but also by complementary human effort. This effort is yet to be accomplished and represents a variable, indeterminate quantity, the realm of human creative activity based on freedom. Here the Son of Man places Himself on the side of humanity, and in the name of humanity, in the face of the as yet unrealized and unknown future, in relation to which all prophecy is *conditional*, He speaks of His own ignorance, of the ignorance of the Son of Man. The fathers of the Church do not have a unanimous opinion on the subject of this "ignorance"; some are inclined to accept "economic" human ignorance (given Divine omniscience), whereas others reject all ignorance. The absence of a clear and distinct doctrine of kenosis makes it easy to understand this lack of unanimity.

C. The Filial Obedience

It is necessary to return once more to the question of how one should understand the meaning of the Lord's words: "my Father is greater than I" (John 14:28). In the *immanent* Trinity, this signifies, in conformity with the patristic interpretation, the "monarchy" of the Father, which is His personal property and does not contradict the equidivinity of the other hypostases, which differ from the Father in their personal properties. A fundamental difference also exists between the First hypostasis on the one hand and the Second and Third hypostases on the other: the First hypostasis is the revealed hypostasis, whereas the Second and the Third are the revealing hypostases. This is not a difference with regard to equidivinity, which is unchanged here. But it is nevertheless a *hierarchical* difference, which cannot be denied in the Holy Trinity. In human language, this difference is expressed as the *taxis*, the *order* of the hypostases. The recognition not only of personal but also of hierarchical differences within the Holy Trinity, differences that are pre-eternally overcome and removed by the reciprocal love within the one trihypostatic Subject, is not subordinationism (with its dark shadow, Arianism), which denies precisely the equidivinity of the hypostases. Nevertheless, there remain certain differences between the trinitarian hypostases that exclude the *abstract* equality of the persons in the capacity of three hypostatic centers within the limits of one trihypostatic Subject. However, the *equality* of the equidivine *persons* is preserved fully, and it logically (and ontologically) precedes the distinction between these three hypostases.

Hierarchism is inevitably introduced into the understanding of the Holy Trinity. This hierarchism is expressed, first of all, in the fact that the Father is "the Principle, the Proto-God, properly God, *ho Theos, autotheos*," whereas the other hypostases "originate" from Him: Being co-beginningless and equi-eternal with Him, the other hypostases *hierarchically* have their origin in Him and are coordinated with Him precisely in *this* manner. The Son reveals the Father as the Word; the Holy Spirit reveals mutually the Father and the Son; and both of them, the bihypostatic dyad, in revealing the Father, have their origin in Him and represent His revelation. The hierarchism of the Holy Trinity in this sense is recognized by the Church to the same degree that it rejects subordinationism. The concrete *difference* — alien to abstract equality or *indifference* — between the hypostases of the Holy Trinity can only be and necessarily must be hierachical in character. Given their equidivine and equihypostatic character, the hypostases have determinate, concretely coordinated interrelations, which are expressed in the *taxis*, or order: First, Second, Third. This is not an abstract enumeration, nor is it a subordination. Rather, it is a *hierarchical* trinitarian interrelation. In this interrelation, *each* of the hypostases is conditioned by each of the other two separately and by both of them in their active union. In this sense, there can be no question of a greater or lesser dependence of one on another: they are all equidependent. They all mutually reflect one another: the Father is the Father because the Son and the Holy Spirit exist; the Son is the Son because the Father and the Holy Spirit exist; the Holy Spirit exists in relation to the Father and to the Son. These interrelations are eternal, and therefore they do not pose the question of the equidivinity of the hypostases. The "origination" of the hypostases does not by any means signify *causal* origin, a common misconception of Catholic theology (by accepting causal origin, we would open the door to Arianism and subordinationism, and thus annul the triunity). "Origination" has only a hierarchical meaning here; that is, it corresponds to the difference between the hypostatic aspects of Divinity given their unity, inseparability, and mutual conditionedness. Dogmatically, this is expressed by their enumeration or numerical order. To be sure, this order, or *taxis,* is proper only to dogmatic speculation, not to the biblical word-usage. However, the Bible too knows the sequence: "in the name of the Father and the Son and the Holy Spirit" (although it is true that in the New Testament this usage is not always consistent).

This hierarchism of the "immanent" Holy Trinity is expressed by a fully determinate hierarchical interrelation in the "economic" Trinity, in the revelation of God in the world, in the manifestation of the equi-eternal hypostases in time. Outwardly, the hierarchism here inevitably appears as a certain subordinationism of the hypostases, with the Father at the head, who is the principle or the first will. This is already the case in the creation of the world, where the first principle is the will of the Father, who creates the world through the Son by the Holy Spirit; this holds also for the Divine Providence in relation to the world.[52] A special form of this hierarchical interrelation with the primacy of the Father is expressed in the *kenosis* of the Son. In the Incarnation, the Son removes from Himself His divine glory, empties Himself of His Divinity, extinguishes it in Himself, as it were. Therefore, the hierarchical place that is pre-eternally proper to Him in the Holy Trinity and, in particular, His relation to the Father, takes on externally "subordinationistic" traits. This

---

52. This hierarchism is preserved in the Holy Trinity also in relation to the redeemed humanity, because Jesus Christ is the intercessor before the Father (1 John 2:1; Heb. 8:6; 9:15; 12:24), as is the Holy Spirit (Rom 8:26; Gal. 4:6).

relation becomes one of voluntary and absolute obedience. By His will the Father takes the place in the Son of the Son's own Divinity, so to speak, which the Son, as it were, has abandoned. The Father becomes for the Son the Father and God, and the Son is *sent* into the world by the Father. To be sure, the will to Incarnation and the decision to kenotically abandon His Divinity is the proper work of the Son, in conformity with the will of the Father and accomplished by the Holy Spirit — both pre-eternally, "before" the creation of the world, and in the temporality of the world's being. By emptying Himself of His divinity, however, the Son already *hierarchically* abolishes, as it were, His equidivinity with the Father for the sake of His being sent into the world. Having emptied Himself of His divinity in virtue of this decision, the Son loses in the depths of the Holy Trinity His proper, hypostatic will. He *needs* to be sent by the Father; His "meat" is to accomplish the will of the One who sent Him. He and the Father become one, not only in the sense of their pre-eternal equidivinity and consubstantiality in the Holy Trinity, but also in the sense of the fullness of the kenotic dissolution of the Son in the Father. The Son does not go by His own will into the world but is sent by the Father (see John 17:18), just as the Father sends an archangel to announce the good news to the Virgin Mary. "My Father is greater than I" is said precisely in this *kenotic* sense. One should not shut one's eyes to the fact that this idea is expressed not only in this difficult text, which commentators have tried to neutralize by an artificial apologetic exegesis. This idea passes through all the Gospels, and it is expressed with a particular theological distinctness only in the Gospel of John. The Son does not have His own will but subordinates Himself to the Father's will; this distinctive *christological* subordinationism, which in no wise implies a trinitarian one, is clearly shown at the initial and concluding moments of Christ's earthly ministry: in His temptation in the wilderness and in the agony at Gethsemane, where "the prince of this world," who has "departed from him for a season" (Luke 4:13), again approaches Him. It is shown precisely in the prayer: "not as I will, but as thou wilt" (Matt. 26:39). The Son goes not by His own will to the cross but is sent by the Father. His torment on the cross is the Father's will, accepted by the Son as His own.

    The usual interpretation of John 14:28 ("my Father is greater than I") affirms that the Son speaks here in the name of His human nature (which introduces a "Nestorian" separation). But in fact these words are spoken from within the Divine *kenosis,* whose consequence was precisely the inhumanization. The assumption of the human essence is not the cause of the kenosis, in the diminution of the Son before the Father, but its consequence. Usually, this kenotic or christological subordinationism of the Son is underscored only in relation to the Father, and it is explained by the general "monarchy" of the Father in the Holy Trinity, on the one hand, and, on the other, by the in-humanization of the Son. But a certain christological subordinationism also exists not only in relation to the Father but also *in relation to the Holy Spirit.* Since there are no direct, pre-eternally hierarchical grounds for this in the interhypostatic relations of the Holy Trinity, the kenotic character of this subordinationism is manifested with a far greater reality here. To be sure, we do not have a text to attest it that is as clear as John 14:28, but to a certain degree the equally difficult text Matt. 12:32 (see also Luke 12:10 and Mark 3:29) approaches it in meaning: "whosoever speaketh a word against the Son of man, it shall be forgiven him: but whosoever speaketh against the Holy Spirit, it shall not be forgiven him, neither in this world, neither in the world to come." The rebellion against the Son of Man, in whom Divinity is *hidden,* is not the sin of direct rebellion against God, but the blasphemy against the Holy Spirit *is* the sin of direct rebellion.

The relation between Christ and the Holy Spirit can be expressed as follows: If the Son, sent by the Father, does the will of the Father, then the Holy Spirit is expressly given to Him by the Father in order to minister to Him and does not repose upon Him naturally — according to the order of the Divine procession of the Holy Spirit from the Father *through* the Son or *upon* the Son. At the same time as He removes the Glory from Himself and abandons His Divinity, the Son who humbles Himself also no longer knows, *for Himself,* this reposing of the Holy Spirit in which His Divinity is realized for Him. In this sense, the kenosis really signifies for the Son that in some sense He leaves the life of the Holy Trinity, although His naturally essential presence in the Trinity is preserved. Therefore, not only is the Son sent by the Father into the world, but the Holy Spirit is sent upon the Son by the Father in the days of the Son's earthly ministry, just as He is sent upon the Virgin Mary at the Annunciation and upon the apostles at Pentecost. Precisely speaking, this sending down of the Holy Spirit already begins at the Annunciation, where the Holy Spirit overshadows the Mother and thus the One who is to be born of Her.[53] Luke 2:40 attests to

---

53. This is expressed in the words of the archangel: "The Holy Spirit shall come upon thee, and the power of the Highest shall overshadow thee: therefore also that holy thing which shall be born of thee shall be called the Son of God" (Luke 1:35). Even if, following John of Damascus, one understands "the power of the Highest" to mean the

the reposing of God's grace upon the Infant. The hypostatic descent of the Spirit upon the Son (which, apart from the pre-eternal reposing, became possible in virtue of the kenosis) was accomplished — or, more precisely, was completed — at the baptism, when, for the One come down from heaven, once again "the heaven was opened, and the Holy Spirit descended . . . upon him" (Luke 3:21-22), "the Spirit of adoption" (Rom 8:15); and the Father's voice attested, at the same time, to the pre-eternal sonhood and to the adoption: "Thou art my beloved Son; in thee I am well pleased" (Luke 3:22).

This descent of the Holy Spirit upon Jesus and His reposing upon Him are manifested as a *leading* by the Spirit: in particular, immediately after the baptism, the Spirit "led" Jesus, who was "full of the Holy Spirit," into the wilderness for temptation (Luke 4:1); after His return, His first preaching in Nazareth was His testimony about Himself with the words of Isaiah: "the Spirit of the Lord is upon me" (Luke 4:18). According to His own testimony, He casts out "devils by the Spirit of God" (Matt. 12:28); and according to the testimony of the Forerunner, who saw the Spirit descending upon Him, He is the one who "baptizeth with the Holy Spirit" (John 1:33), the One to whom "God giveth not the Spirit by measure" (3:34). In other words, Christ is the Spirit-bearer Anointed by the Holy Spirit,[54] and it is only after the Resurrection that He Himself gives the Holy Spirit to His disciples; He promises to "pray the Father" (John 14:16) and to send down from the Father the Holy Spirit to His disciples after the Ascension. Thus, in the days of His earthly ministry, Jesus is the Spirit-bearer; He has upon Himself the anointment of the Holy Spirit, like the prophets, although in a different manner from them. In His kenosis, He resembles the prophets as One who receives the Spirit, although in His Divine-Humanity He differs from them immeasurably. He Himself grounds His ministry and His working of miracles on the fact that He has the Holy Spirit, as is attested by the Forerunner (John 1:33). Jesus thus places Himself in a subordinationistic relation not only to the

---

Logos, the idea of the sending down of the Holy Spirit upon the Son, who descends into the world in a state of kenosis, will still be sufficiently justified by the text. The expression, "she was found with child of the Holy Spirit" (Matt. 1:18; cf. 1:20), has the same meaning. This signifies precisely the reposing of the Holy Spirit upon the Mother and the Infant when the Infant was without separation from Her in Her womb.

54. Cf. St. John of Damascus: "about when [the Lord] was called Christ" (*Brief Exposition of the Orthodox Faith*, book 4, ch. 6, c. 1112). John cites here Cyril of Alexandria *(Ad Reginas)*: "Since the Word, having been made flesh, is anointed from God and the Father by the oil of joy, or the Spirit, He is therefore called Christ."

Emmanuel, the God-Man

Father but also to the Holy Spirit. This is of course not proper to the pre-eternal Logos in the "immanent" Trinity, but it becomes natural and even inevitable for Christ in His kenosis.

Even in the kenosis of the Son, however, insofar as it is manifested in relation to the Father and to the Holy Spirit, the inner hierarchy and, in particular, the monarchy of the Father are realized. The Father sends the Son into the world, reveals to the Son His will, gives Him power, and finally sends the Holy Spirit down upon Him (as well as upon the Virgin Mary). In a word, the Father is the determining principle in the entire ministry of the Son. The Holy Spirit, in contrast, is the accomplishing principle, which proceeds from the Father. By the Holy Spirit, Christ works miracles and preaches the good news, does the will of the Father, and is thereby Himself sanctified and deified in His humanity. In the Holy Spirit, the hypostatic love of the Father for the Son is accomplished not only pre-eternally but also in the Incarnation. In the descent of the Holy Spirit from heaven, one hears the voice of the Father saying: "This is my beloved Son, in whom I am well pleased" (Matt. 3:17; Mark 1:11; Luke 3:22; also at the Transfiguration: Matt. 17:5; Mark 9:7). In His turn, the Son too speaks of the Holy Spirit as proceeding from the Father; by praying to the Father, the Son will send the Holy Spirit down upon His disciples.

Thus, on the basis of eternal intratrinitarian relations, the economic Trinity, or, more precisely, the *christological* Trinity, is established in conformity with the kenosis of the Son and, as it were, His kenotic absence (not with respect to His hypostasis or His nature but with respect to His actual Divinity) in the Holy Trinity because of His descent from heaven. This self-emptying of Divinity in the Son is compensated by the Divinity of the Father and of the Holy Spirit, who, in conformity with their personal properties, deify the incarnate Logos and communicate their divine life to Him until the time when His kenosis will be concluded and replaced by His glorification and the restoration of His Divinity in the depths of the Holy Trinity, after His ascension to heaven.

Thanks to the kenosis of Divinity, the God-Man is conscious of His Divine Personality, of His Divine Sonhood, and of His divine life in the Father; He is conscious of Himself as the Son of God (although, in His state of humiliation, not yet as God). At the same time, however, He remains the Son of Man. He remains Man, who in His human consciousness also has the divine consciousness. In a word, He is the God-Man. And He announces His Divine Sonhood, His oneness with the Father, to His brothers, His co-men, as co-Man. This represents the most original, unrepeatable, and unique feature of His individuality compared with that of other men: being one of the sons of men, He speaks of Himself as being one with the Father, that is, with God, without thereby losing, diminishing, or denying His humanity. In speaking of His divinity to men, He does not proclaim Himself to be God but reveals Him — the Heavenly Father in His human life ("he that hath seen me hath seen the Father" [John 14:9]). It is impossible to express this divine-human life, with its unrepeatable originality, in human language, in terms of human psychology; and in general all attempts to represent Christ's "psychology" are spiritually tasteless and doomed to failure. There is no place here for "psychology" in the human sense, with its sinful limitations, even though the material in which Jesus' divine consciousness was revealed was the human psychical element, connected with corporeality. Thought inevitably returns here to the Apollinarian schema (which, as we know, is also the Chalcedonian schema): the Divine spirit living in animate human flesh. The difference is that Apollinarius understood this statically and mechanically, as the coercion of spirit over flesh, whereas it should be understood dynamically and kenotically, as authentic divine life, contained in the human essence in virtue of the kenosis.

The divine life in the God-Man is manifested as the triumph of the human essence, which turns out to be capable of obedience to the commands of the Divine Spirit of the Son, who does the will of the Father. This obedience is all-sided, both negative, in the sense of excluding and overcoming all that is illegitimate, and positive, in the sense of fulfilling God's commands *(oboedientia activa)* and suffering unto the death on the cross *(oboedientia passiva)*. In order to be complete, this triumph of the obedience of the flesh to the spirit, of the human essence and will to the divine essence and will, must be *exhaustive,* that is, nothing must remain untried and unexperienced in the experience of this obedience. All types of suffering — spiritual, psychical, and corporeal — must be experienced on the way of the cross in the struggle against the world in fulfillment of God's will. In the New Adam this suffering had not a limited and quantitative character but a universal and all-human character, and this *universality* of the night of Gethsemane and of the feat of the cross is the mystery of the God-Man. Furthermore, in order to be exhaustive, the feat of obedience had to take everything from the human essence of the God-Man and to leave nothing outside. However, that bad infinity of the indeterminate duration of life — which did not yet possess the power of positive immortality but possessed only the absence of the inevitability of death — also contains bad inexhaustibility. The New Adam possessed immortality in virtue of His human essence undamaged by sin, but this was not yet the victory over death. Death was not natural for the God-Man, but its very possibility was not defeated and excluded in His human essence. To be sure, in this respect He occupied a wholly exclusive position compared with all of humankind, for which death is inevitable. For Him it was completely otherwise: not being subject to death as necessity, He was the master of His life; He was in free possession of it: "No man taketh it [life] from me, but I lay it down of myself. I have power to lay it down, and I have power to take it again" (John 10:18). For the God-Man, therefore, death is a *sacrifice* pleasing to God: "Therefore doth my Father love me, because I lay down my life, that I might take it again. . . . This commandment have I received of my Father" (10:17-18). However, because of its lack of finality, it was precisely this bad infinity of de facto immortality that excluded the possibility of exhaustive obedience to God's will, since in virtue of it there always remained something not yet given. Also, and this is the most important thing, the supreme good would not have been given yet, and obedience would not have been experienced in relation to the supreme value, that is, in relation to life itself, which the Son of Man has the power to give and, consequently, not to give, for "no man takes it away from Me." Therefore, in order for obedience to become exhaustive, life itself must end, that is, it must be interrupted by death; life itself must be given for the sake of the obedience. Only then would this obedience and this trial be complete and exhaustive.[55]

This trial was given to the Son of Man to know: In response to His prayer, "if it be possible, let this cup pass from me" (Matt. 26:39), it did not pass from Him. The Father desired that the Son drink to the bottom the cup of death. The Son accepted this final obedience, which was the extreme of humiliation, as is said in the divine revelation about this self-humiliation: "He humbled himself, and became obedient unto death, even the death of the cross" (Phil. 2:8). In death, He voluntarily made the measure of the fallen humanity His own measure — *voluntarily* because death was not a natural necessity for Him but presupposed His consent to receive it, together with all men and instead of all men. Without this consent, death could not have overcome Him. We can find an indirect indication of this in Christ's words pronounced when Peter attempted to defend Him with a sword: "Thinkest thou that I cannot now pray to my Father,

---

55. "Skin for skin, yea, all that a man hath will he give for his life" (Job 2:4), says the ancient tempter before the face of God. And defeated in relation to Job, the same tempter attempts, in relation to the One whom Job prefigured, to repeat this temptation by the threat to take life away.

and he shall presently give me more than twelve legions of angels? But how then shall the Scriptures be fulfilled, that thus it must be?" (Matt. 26:53-54).

The Son's death is the direct will of the Father, and it is accepted by the Son's obedience. According to Philippians 2, this acceptance of death represents the extreme depths of the Son's kenosis, as well as the extreme depths of His humanity on His Divine-Human path. The slightest doubt concerning the authenticity of the death on the cross, the slightest hint of docetism here, leads to the denial of the entire work of the Incarnation. One must accept the full force of the fact that the God-Man suffered and tasted death not only in His humanity but also in His Divine-Humanity. One cannot separate, in opposition to Chalcedon, His humanity from His Divinity here, saying that He suffered not as God but only as man, since the death on the cross, just as His entire life, would then be only an appearance, in which His Divinity would not participate at all. On the contrary, the kenosis consists precisely in the fact that the Son diminished Himself in His Divinity and became the *subject*, the hypostasis, of the *Divine-Human* life, experiencing hypostatically all that His humanity experienced. His proper Divinity was therefore so diminished for itself, was so hidden in its own depths or potentiality, that it was no longer an obstacle for death and did not exclude its possibility. Unfathomably, His proper Divinity experienced death, without itself dying of course, but without resisting it. Since it was unnatural for the sinless New Adam, this death was even more terrible and agonizing than for the sons of the old Adam, who had been dying over the entire course of their mortal life. By contrast, it was realized exclusively by that act of violence done to life that was accomplished in the crucifixion. The cup of death was drunk, entire and undiluted, at Golgotha, and the horror of drinking it was already experienced at Gethsemane: "[He] began to be sore amazed, and to be very heavy; and saith unto them, My soul is exceeding sorrowful unto death" (Mark 14:33-34).

This is the *spiritual* agony of nonmortal life, which was *bodily* accomplished on the cross. It should be noted that the entire depth of His divine consciousness, His entire triumph, which is attested in the Last Discourse, the whole power of His union with the Father — in a word, His entire divine life — does not eliminate and does not diminish the suffering of death. The kenosis of Divinity — its diminution, passing here into extinction, as it were — is so deep that the abyss of death opens up for the God-Man, with the darkness of nonbeing and all the force of forsakenness by God. The yawning abyss of creaturely *nothing* in death opens up for the Creator Himself. The cry on the cross, "Eli, Eli, lama sabachthani? ... My

Emmanuel, the God-Man

God, my God, why hast thou forsaken me?" (Matt. 27:46), is the extreme limit of this self-emptying of Divinity in the suffering on the cross: He addresses here not the Father but God, for He is surrounded by the darkness of death, and the consciousness of His Divine Sonhood abandons Him. In the name of creation, the God-Man cries out to God — to God with whom He is one, to God who never forsakes Him — that He has forsaken Him. Like all men, He too remains alone in death. This cry of the dying God-Man bares the entire bottomless depth of the kenosis, the divine self-humiliation that is equaled only by the depths of God's love. As if to confirm that this is precisely the Son of God who in His Divine-Humanity is passing through the gates of death, His dying cry is replaced by the invocation to the Father that is the end of the kenosis: "Father, into thy hands I commend my spirit" (Luke 23:46), followed by His closing words, on the same subject: "it is finished" (John 19:30).

In the suffering on the cross we see to what degree the diminution of the Divinity is commensurate with the human measure. The Divinity is diminished to such a degree that it no longer resists death, and although it itself does not die, it co-dies, as it were, with His dying humanity. His divine hypostasis co-dies with Him and in Him, for it is the hypostasis of His humanity, inseparably united with His Divinity. Therefore, the God-Man dies in His integral unity in the whole complexity of His composition, but He dies *differently* in His two natures: His humanity dies, and as a result, His human hypostasis passes together with His humanity through the gates of death into the pre-ontic and non-ontic depths of creatureliness — this human hypostasis of His, which is the divine hypostasis of the Logos. But this hypostasis also brings down its divine nature to the extreme diminution of death. In *this sense,* death extends to the *entire* God-Man, not only to His humanity, but also to His Divinity, although *in different ways.* It is therefore absolutely impossible to exclude His Divinity from participation in death.

This idea must be extended further, however, beyond the Logos to the other hypostases of the Holy Trinity. Our attention is first arrested by the two cries of agony before death. The first cry concerns the forsakenness by God, signifying a certain distancing of the Father from the Son, with whom He remains in indissoluble personal unity. The Son calls to Him out of the depths of the creatureliness of His human essence. This forsakenness of the Son is an act of the Father that signifies the fact that He *assumes* the Son's death and thus participates in it, since for the Father the forsaking of the Son to death on the cross is not death, of course, but a certain image of spiritual co-dying in the sacrifice of love. Not less significant for this participation of the Father in the suffering of the Son on the cross is the final cry of the Son, commending His spirit into the hands of the Father. The Son returns into the bosom of the Father, but not to abide there eternally or to sit at the right hand of the Father in the glorious Ascension. That will come later. The incarnate Son is forcibly disincarnated, as it were, in death; and His Divine-Human spirit returns to His Father and His God, just as in the death of a man the dust returns to the earth, but "the spirit shall return unto God who gave it" (Eccles. 12:7). This is a special kenotic moment in the humiliation of the Son, in which the Father co-participates according to His own fashion. That is, He receives the spirit of the Son, who has abandoned His body, in order to watch over it during the three days before the Resurrection. In death, the spirits of all those sent to earth by God return to Him; here it is as if, among these spirits, the Father receives also the spirit of the Son who has tasted death. The Son's commending of Himself into the hands of the Father represents the most profound kenotic concealment of Divinity: It is a divine mystery, unfathomable by the human understanding, that the Father receives the Son in the devastation of death and watches over Him until the Resurrection. But pious thought can approach this mystery, for the Gospel attests to it.

The fact that the Son has been emptied of and forsaken by Divinity also signifies that He has been forsaken by the Holy Spirit, who ceaselessly reposes upon the God-Man; for the Holy Spirit is, above all, the palpable proximity of the Father, the abiding in the Father's love. The Holy Spirit is the hypostatic love of the Father for the Son and of the Son for the Father. The Holy Spirit is Their hypostatic union; thus Christ's saying, "I and my Father are one," tacitly implies: *in the Holy Spirit*. The abandonment by God, the distancing of the Father from the Son, necessarily signifies also the abandonment by the Holy Spirit, who descended upon the Son when He immersed Himself in the waters of the Jordan, symbolizing the death to come. The Holy Spirit returned, as it were, to the Father when the death of the God-Man was accomplished in all the intensity of the abandonment by God (and without this abandonment, death could not have been accomplished in the God-Man). Thus, this co-participation of the Holy Spirit in the kenosis of the Son, in His suffering on the cross, extends in its own fashion the kenosis of the Son to the Third hypostasis as well, for not manifesting oneself to the beloved is kenosis for hypostatic love. (We have the *human* image of this kenosis of the Spirit in the image of the Mother of God standing before the cross, with the sword piercing Her heart; moreover, the Son who is leaving Her commends Her into the care of the beloved disciple.) The Holy Spirit is Joy, and He is the Comforter; but in the torment and sorrow on the cross the Son remains without joy and comfort, which He finds only in obedience to the will of the Father and in prayer (see Heb. 5:7). Thus, if in the descent from heaven, in His Nativity, the Son abandons the heavenly glory that is in the Holy Trinity, then in His descent into the depths of the earth He is, as it were, even deprived of the trinitarian union, and His divine hypostasis ("My spirit") is commended into the bosom of the Father to be watched over.[56]

This is the significance of death on the pathways of the kenosis of the Son of God in the God-Man. But we also have a particular manifestation of the kenosis in His three-day presence in the grave. The One who in His hypostatic Divine Sonhood confessed about Himself that "I am the resurrection, and the life" (John 11:25) and that "as the Father hath life in himself, so hath He given to the Son to have life in Himself" (5:26), this One abides in the sleep of death. The abiding of the Son of God in the grave and the descent of the Creator of the world into nonbeing, from which He called the world to being, are a revelation of God's love not less astonishing than that manifested in the creation of the world. The death of the Savior was a disintegration of the human composition, just as it always is in the case of the death of a man. The three days in the grave signify the authenticity and fullness of death, in contrast to loss of consciousness. The Savior's soul was separated from His body, and His divine spirit was received by the Father: abiding in pre-eternal being in the supramundane or "immanent" Holy Trinity, "on the throne with the Father and the Spirit," but nevertheless in His kenotic humiliation being received by the Father as a spirit leaving its body, the Spirit of Christ at the same time remained unseparated from His soul (as is the case for every man in death) but also remained connected with His body.

The humiliation continues here as well. The only thing that is revealed to us about this is the preaching in hell (a doctrine accepted also by the *Symbolum Apostolicum*): "being put to death in the flesh, but quickened by the Spirit: by which also He went and preached unto the spirits in prison" (1 Pet. 3:18-19). The descent into hell of the God-Man, who was in a state of separation from the body, like all the souls of the deceased, is a further act of His kenosis, extending to His assimilation of the afterlife

---

56. The idea of the co-participation of the Holy Trinity in the redemptive sufferings (and thus in the kenosis of the Son) receives a confirmation in icons of the crucifixion (or of the body taken down from the cross) with the Father bending over the body and the Holy Spirit in the form of a dove.

The Lamb of God

state of the deceased, in order that He might continue to serve men even beyond the grave. In this afterlife state, Christ's holy soul communes with the supreme sphere of afterlife bliss: This is "paradise," to which He called the repentant thief. One should not forget, however, that this is only the "preliminary" bliss of souls separated from their bodies, *before* resurrection. As for Christ's body, it remains separated from His soul, but it is not entirely separated from the Divine Spirit, no longer being bound by spatiality. His body did not know corruption, being sanctified by the Divine Spirit who lived in His body and was not fully separated from it even after death. Furthermore, in virtue of its sinlessness and freedom from original sin, it was not subject to death. The power of death was limited in such a way that it could not destroy the dead body through corruption, though the soul had departed from it. The Son of Man had tasted death to the end, for a "corn of wheat" (John 12:24) fallen into the ground must die before it can bring forth fruit.

The *Triduum* — the three-day abiding in the grave, in the bosom of the earth, like Jonah's abiding in the belly of the whale — is a time of kenotic silence and concealment, the self-humiliation of the God-Man down to the state of a dead grain. It is the fullness of potentialization. This state of the repose of death, this "sabbath" of the Son of God, cannot be conceived as consisting of a series of discrete moments of time, in each of which it could have been interrupted by the will of the Divine Deceased. To be sure, this state too was included in the humiliation pre-eternally accepted by the Son: being accepted in its entirety, this humiliation was also accepted in each of its moments — both in the highest intensity of activity during the Lord's earthly ministry and in the sabbath of the repose of death. The Spirit of Christ was received by the Father, and it was the will of the Father that acted now. The Son had brought His humiliation to the extreme of self-devastation, to death, for in death, the personality with its freedom no longer exists, but only receptive passivity remains. Christ commended Himself into the hands of the Father when He gave up His spirit, and it is in His hands that He reposes in the grave. This brings us directly to the question of the resurrection of Christ in relation to His kenosis.

Christ rose from the dead, but He was raised by God the Father by the power of the Holy Spirit. That is a fundamental fact attested by Holy Scripture. Christ's resurrection was a raising that could be accomplished upon Him as a consequence of His victory over the world, over the flesh, over the prince of this world.[57] According to the testimony of the Apostle

---

57. See the chapter on the Resurrection of Christ in my work *On the Gospel Miracles*.

Emmanuel, the God-Man

Peter (as well as of the Apostle Paul), God *raised* Jesus (Acts 2:24). This means that, in relation to Christ, the Father remains God even in the Resurrection. As a result, this relation is not yet determined on the basis of equality in equidivinity; rather, it is determined on the basis of inequality in kenosis. After the Resurrection, Christ tells Mary Magdalene: "I ascend unto my Father . . . and to my God" (John 20:17). The resurrection-raising is an active-passive accomplishment, an act and an event, for in it the direct action of God upon Christ is united with the inner action of Divinity in Christ Himself. In His descent from heaven, the Son accepted for Himself birth, death, and resurrection. He commended Himself into the power of the Father as God for humanity and thus for Him as well in virtue of the unity of His Divine-Humanity.

The Resurrection does not yet conclude the path of the God-Man's earthly, kenotic ministry, although it passes, so to speak, into other dimensions, for after the Resurrection, Christ no longer lives with the disciples but only appears to them. This mysterious period of the forty days before the Ascension serves as the transition from the Resurrection to the Ascension. On the one hand, this transition is necessary for instructing the disciples and fortifying their faith, whereas on the other hand it has significance for the completion of the kenotic path, according to the words spoken by the Lord Himself to Mary Magdalene: "I am not yet ascended to my Father . . . I ascend unto my Father, and your Father; and to my God, and your God" (John 20:17). The content and form of this ascent are hidden from our eyes, as is in general the life of the Resurrected One on earth before the Ascension. We know this life only from His brief "appearances." But this life cannot be separated from the entire earthly, kenotic path, even if it comes at the end of this path; it cannot be separated from the path that extends from the descent from heaven to the return to heaven, to the Ascension.

But the most remarkable thing here is that this kenotic path includes not only the beginning but also the end, that is, the Ascension itself. This mysterious event of the Lord's life is not only an act but also a fact: It is said about Christ not only that He ascended *(anelēmphthē)* to heaven (Mark 16:19; Acts 1:2), but also that He was taken up *(hupsōtheis)* by the right hand of God (Acts 2:33). That is, the same relation that we observed in the Resurrection is repeated here: "the God of our Lord Jesus Christ, the Father of glory . . . according to the working of his mighty power, which he wrought in Christ, when he raised him from the dead, and set him at his own right hand in the heavenly places, far above all principality and power" (Eph. 1:17, 19-21; cf. Ps. 110). In addition, it is said about Him: "[He] sat on the right hand of God" (Mark 16:19; Heb. 10:12; 12:2; Col. 3:1); "[He] is gone into heaven, and is on the right hand of God" (1 Pet. 3:22; Rom. 8:34); and Stephen sees "the Son of Man standing on the right hand of God" (Acts 7:55-56).

In the shining of the glory, in the rays of the ascending sun, the human eye does not see and does not discern the accomplishments taking place in the heavens. However, these accomplishments, as well as their times and seasons, are indicated — as through a glass, darkly — by Revelation. Among the times so indicated is the *ten-day* period after the forty days between the Resurrection and the Ascension, the period before the descent of the Holy Spirit. It is only after this period that the heavens close, and we adore the Son together with the Father and the Holy Spirit with an equal adoration.

We have thus discerned the presence of kenosis in the God-Man, not only in those acts that refer to His earthly ministry, to His obedience and passion, but also in those acts that refer to His glorious resurrection and His glorification. The glorification is accomplished not by the Son Himself but by the Father *upon* the Son, although with the Son's direct participation. This is powerfully attested by the texts that refer to the glorification.

Above all, there is the fundamental kenotic text, Philippians 2. Having expounded the doctrine of the humiliation of Christ, who assumes the form of a servant and the likeness of men, the Apostle continues: "Wherefore God also hath highly exalted him, and given him a name which is above every name: That at the name of Jesus every knee should bow, of things in heaven, and things in earth, and things under the earth; and that every tongue should confess that Jesus Christ is Lord, to the glory of God the Father" (2:9-11). Here the restoration in Divinity, elevation that is a consequence of the humiliation, and the glorification of the Name of Christ above all names are the direct *work of the Father.* The cessation of the humiliation still presupposes, as a result, the continuation of the kenosis, which is overcome and concluded by the Lord Jesus Christ being clothed "in the glory" of God the Father. This is the restoration and the return of the glory of Divinity to the Son, the God-Man.

This general idea of the glorification of the Son by the Father is also expressed in the Son's own words: "It is my Father who glorifies me, of whom ye say, that he is your God" (John 8:54 [the King James Version has been modified to conform with the Russian Bible]). In this manner, Jesus replies to the Jews, opposing the glory that comes from the Father to human glory. Most crucially, the high-priestly prayer speaks of this directly:

"Father . . . glorify thy Son, that thy Son also may glorify thee" (John 17:1); and further we find this in the most general form, not admitting any doubts or limitations: "and now, O Father, glorify thou me with thine own self with the glory which I had with thee before the world was" (17:5). This is the prayer about being delivered from kenosis, about returning to heaven. To be sure, this glorification is not a one-sided act of the Father; it is conditioned by the God-Man's *readiness* for it. He testifies about Himself accordingly: "I have glorified thee on the earth: I have finished the work which thou gavest me to do" (17:4).

The interrelation between glorification and glorifiedness is also disclosed in the introductory words of the Last Discourse, which include all the fundamental facts of the glorification (i.e., the Resurrection, the Ascension, and the sending down of the Holy Spirit): "Now is the Son of man glorified, and God is glorified in him. If God be glorified in him, God shall also glorify him in himself, and shall straightway glorify him" (John 13:31-32). The glory that the Son, as God, had from all eternity ("before the world was") but voluntarily abandoned because of His love for creatures is now returned to Him by the Father. His immersion in kenosis is so deep and authentic that He must be resurrected, as it were, from this mystical death; He must be delivered from kenosis by the Father Himself in order to enter into His Glory as God sitting at the right hand of the Father. The image of the humble Lamb of God who takes upon Himself the sins of the world is replaced or completed by the image of the triumphant Lamb, for whom there is no longer any kenosis, for it has been overcome. This is the Christ of the Apocalypse, the sole New Testament book that manifests not the *kenotic* but the *glorified* image of the Lamb: "I . . . overcame, and am set down with my Father in his throne" (Rev. 3:21); "I am Alpha and Omega, the beginning and the ending, saith the Lord, which is, and which was, and which is to come, the Almighty" (1:8); "I am the first and the last: I am he that liveth, and was dead; and, behold, I am alive for evermore, Amen" (1:17-18).

Thus, in the course of the entire salvific work of Christ, from His descent from heaven to His return to heaven, the one concrete *Divine-Human* consciousness of the Son of God and the Son of Man remains proper to Him. This is not the alternation of the one and the other or the absorption of the one by the other but the real hypostatic unity of life in the hypostatic union of the two natures; this Divine-Humanity of Christ's consciousness is the miracle of miracles, the most miraculous thing in the whole Miracle of the Incarnation. This unity is *palpable* in the whole Gospel figure of the God-Man, but at the same time it remains absolutely inaccessible for us in its entirety. It remains transcendent for our human, *only* human consciousness. Nevertheless, this unity is revealed to and approaches our consciousness in certain aspects or states, such where the measure of the humanity as if veils, diminishes, or kenotically removes the divinity; and Christ then is present before us in His humanity. Such, for us, is the image of Christ in His earthly, prophetic ministry, but more than anything else it is the image of the suffering Christ: Behold the man! In contrast, in the glorified state, Christ's Divine-Human consciousness is shut off from us; it is concealed in the blinding light of the Resurrection. Our understanding must then satisfy itself solely with postulates and rational deductions, which are based on features observed by us or facts of the Divine-Human life and of the consciousness of the Resurrected Christ attested to by Revelation. However, this transcendence of Christ's Divine-Human consciousness has for us not an essential but only a temporal character. If in His earthly ministry the Lord called men "to learn from Him" and to "follow Him," then in His glorification He will raise all men and include all men in the life and the consciousness of the God-Man, in His Divine-Humanity, so that all of Christ's humankind will live by Christ's life and, consequently, by His divine consciousness. "Beloved, now are we the sons of God, and it doth not yet appear what we shall be: but we know that, when he shall appear, we shall be like him; for we shall see him as he is" (1 John 3:2).

CHAPTER 5

The Work of Christ

I. Christ's Prophetic Ministry

Christ speaks of the *work* for which He was sent to the earth: "I have glorified thee on the earth: I have finished the work which thou gavest me to do" (John 17:4). This work is not some separate act or fact of His life; rather, it encompasses His entire earthly ministry. It is therefore the *divine-human* work par excellence. That is, nourished by divine sources, it was also a human work; it was accomplished also through His human essence, in inseparable and inconfusable union with His divine essence. As a whole, this work constitutes the center of the entire life of humanity on earth; it is the chief and generalizing principle for the life of humanity. In its unity, this work is unfathomable and inexhaustible, for it constitutes the very foundation of the life of humanity in eternity, whereas our thought and knowledge always fragment their object, abstract from it its separate sides and thus inevitably take the part for the whole. In this sense, the theological doctrine of the *three* ministries of Christ is the product of such an inevitable abstracting or fragmentation of the unity of the whole. There are nevertheless sufficient biblical and theological grounds to use this distinction of three aspects for purposes of practical differentiation.

Christ's *prophetic* ministry situates Him, first of all, in the series of Jewish prophets or teachers of Israel, in conformity with Moses' prophecy: "The LORD thy God will raise up unto thee a Prophet from the midst of thee, of thy brethren, like unto me; unto him ye shall hearken" (Deut. 18:15). This is confirmed with regard to Christ in Acts 3:22-23, in the Apostle Peter's discourse to the people. Throughout all the Gospels, Jesus is called and venerated as a prophet by the people (see Matt. 21:11; Mark 6:15; Luke 7:16-17;

24:19; John 4:19; 6:14; 7:40); and He never objects to being called a prophet, the way He did when the youth called Him good (Matt. 19:16-17). Indeed, the Lord Himself speaks of Himself as a prophet, although in the third person: "A prophet is not without honor, save in his own country, and in his own house" (Matt. 13:57; cf. Luke 4:24). "I must walk today, and tomorrow, and the day following: for it cannot be that a prophet perish out of Jerusalem" (Luke 13:33). The Lord also did not reject the name "Master" (Rabbi), which was common for the prophets (see Matt. 8:19; 9:11; 12:38; 17:24; 22:16; Mark 5:35; 10:17 [it is significant here that, when called the "Good Master," Christ objects only to the first part, not the second part, of this appellation]; 10:51; Luke 7:40; 8:45; 19:39; John 1:38; 3:2; 11:28; 20:16). He even gives Himself this name: "Ye call me Master and Lord: and ye say well; for so I am. . . . I . . . your Lord and Master, have washed your feet" (John 13:13-14); "be not ye called Rabbi: for one is your Master, even Christ . . . neither be ye called masters: for one is your Master, even Christ" (Matt. 23:8, 10; cf. 26:18).

Christ says about Himself: "To this end was I born, and for this cause came I into the world, that I should bear witness unto the truth" (John 18:37). This bearing witness to the truth — whether it refers to the present, past, or future; to an individual human destiny or to the destiny of an entire nation or all of humanity; to the human soul or to the natural world — is the work of prophetic ministry, of true prophecy in contradistinction to prophecy that is false (see Lam. 2:14). The prophets proclaimed their word as God's word. Prophecy in Holy Scripture is primarily considered as the action of the Spirit of God in the Old Testament, which in the New Testament is manifested as the Holy Spirit, the Comforter, who "will guide you into all truth" (John 16:13).

In the mouths of the prophets, however, the *Word of God* became the *word of man*, which thus was intelligible to the sons of men. The prophet was the living intermediary between God and man: "I heard the voice of the Lord, saying, Whom shall I send, and who will go for us? Then said I, Here am I; send me" (Isa. 6:8). But he was not an oracle, a mechanical instrument for proclaiming visions incomprehensible to him. To be sure, the prophets themselves did not always fully and immediately understand their own prophecies, and especially their visions, but in any case they encompassed them in their *human* consciousness and proclaimed them in *human* language. Before being proclaimed to the people, the prophecies became the personal possession of the prophet and were thus stamped with his individuality. We know that both the prophets and the prophecies carry such an individual stamp; they express not only the personality of the prophet with its peculiarities but also his personal creative activity in its maximal intensity, which is needed to hear and to proclaim the word of God. The prophet experienced the highest degree of personal inspiration, which was also divine inspiration. The spirit heard by the prophet was not only his own spirit, revealed in its mysterious depths, which were inaccessible to the prophet in his normal state. This spirit also became permeated with and deified by the Spirit of God. At such a moment, the prophet perceived something that transcended him and his proper humanity. He clothed this perception in appropriate words in conformity with his powers and his individual style. The boundary between personal inspiration, which is not always good (and this leads to "false prophets" not only in the sense of intentional falsehood but also in the sense of subjectively sincere delusion), and divine inspiration is not an outer but an inner boundary; one needs the guidance of the Spirit of God, living in the Church, in order to distinguish between them.

And so, what constitutes human creative activity with regard to hearing and receiving prophecy? Sometimes this process is clearly revealed. We clearly see the human struggle and human sorrow of Jeremiah and other prophets when they inquire into the events they have witnessed. Prophets are men of intense thought and ardent heart, of sacrificial love and passionate faith. The prophet Daniel says about himself that, after his visions, he fainted and was sick for several days, that he was astonished by his vision and did not understand it (Dan. 8:27). His thought flitted about like a bird in a cage until he "understood by books the number of the years" and then "set [his] face unto the Lord God, to seek by prayer and supplications, with fasting, and sackcloth, and ashes" (9:2-3). In response to this sacrifice, Gabriel came to give him understanding (9:21-22). Likewise, in the following vision (Dan. 10), it was only after mourning and fasting for three weeks that Daniel again received a revelation. We can say, using the language of modern psychology, that revelation is preceded by the intense work of the spirit, which to a significant degree is carried out in the domain of the unconscious until some thought, word, or vision shines forth in the consciousness. The general conclusion is that the prophetic ministry, just as prophesying itself, does not by any means abolish the *humanity* of the prophet. On the contrary, it affirms his humanity in its maximal intensity, and it is this intensity that represents the subjective human condition for divine inspiration — the placing of the divine coal between open and parched lips (see Isa. 6:6-7).[1]

---

1. This subjective human aspect of the prophetic ministry is usually what is meant in those cases when the name of prophet is given to creative individuals in the domain of thought and word.

The Lamb of God

The question now arises: In what sense can one speak of Christ's prophetic ministry? In what sense does it resemble the prophetic ministry in general, and in what sense does it differ? If one begins by examining the externalities, one will remark that the word of divine truth proclaimed by the Truth Himself was at the same time a *human* word, inexhaustible in all its profundity but addressed to man and accessible to him. In this sense it does not differ from the word of the prophets. And insofar as it contains not just a promise of the future, not just its shadow, but proclaims the accomplishment itself, the word of Christ is more accessible than all other prophetic words. The Lord Himself places Himself among the prophets: "Ye have heard that it was said by them of old time [i.e., the prophets] . . . but I say unto you" (Matt. 5:21-22, 27-28, 33-34). He changes and completes the law, and at the same time He transcends it without revoking it. The Sermon on the Mount is preceded by the assurance that He has come not to destroy the law and the prophets but to fulfill them (5:17), and He gives a new confirmation of the inviolability of the law "till heaven and earth pass" (5:18). Furthermore, He completes and deepens the law, like the ancient prophets and especially like the greatest of them, Isaiah, with his doctrine of sacrifice (ch. 1), or Jeremiah, when he speaks of the new covenant with God (ch. 31) and of sacrifice (7:21-23), or Ezekiel (11:19-20; 36:26-27), and others.

With reference to the inner nature of Christ's prophetic ministry, a fundamental christological question arises: Was this ministry accomplished by the direct and immediate power of the Logos, as the word of the Word and about the Word, of the truth about the Truth? Or was Jesus a prophet like the other prophets? Was He inspired by the Holy Spirit, "who spoke by the prophets" (as the Creed says), and in this sense had need of a special overshadowing by the Holy Spirit? After all, the word of the Old Testament prophets was also the word of the Word, but nevertheless they were inspired by the Holy Spirit, who put the prophetic word into them, awakening it in the depths of their own spirit, producing it like fire from a stone out of their human essence; without this overshadowing there would have been no prophetic word. Was there such an overshadowing in the case of the prophet Jesus of Nazareth? According to the direct and irrefutable testimony of the Gospel, there *was*. The Gospel first speaks briefly of the grace of God reposing upon the Infant Jesus, and then it triumphantly proclaims the descent of the Holy Spirit upon Jesus at His baptism. It is only after this that His "public ministry" begins; Jesus becomes Christ, the Anointed. He is first led by the Spirit into the wilderness to be tempted by the devil (Matt. 4:1), after which He returns "in the

The Work of Christ

power of the Spirit into Galilee" (Luke 4:14); and "from that time Jesus began to preach" (Matt. 4:17). His first sermon in His native Nazareth was on Isaiah (61:1-2): "the Spirit of the Lord God is upon me," and He applied these words directly to Himself: "this day is this Scripture fulfilled" (Luke 4:21). The Evangelist applies another prophecy of Isaiah (42:1-4) to Him: "I will put my spirit upon him, and he shall shew judgment to the Gentiles" (Matt. 12:18).

But how should one understand this action of the Holy Spirit upon Jesus? It can be understood only in the light of the kenotic self-humiliation of the Lord. His divinity empties itself in immersing itself in the depths of the human essence; and His divinity shines forth in the human essence only to the extent that the latter encompasses the divinity's self-revelation, correspondingly being deified by it. The Holy Spirit reveals in Jesus His proper divine depths. As the Spirit of "adoption," the Holy Spirit *accomplishes* in Jesus that to which the Father attests: "this is my beloved Son." Just as in the human prophet the Holy Spirit discloses the depths of his human spirit and prophesies in those depths, so, in the God-Man Jesus, the Holy Spirit, sanctifying and deifying His humanity in order to enable its maximal interpenetration with the divine essence of the Logos, reveals Jesus' proper divinity, accomplishes in Him His divine-human unity. One can say that the action of the Holy Spirit in the God-Man is expressed in the essential "theandric" union and interpenetration of the two essences (a kind of *communicatio idiomatum*). The Holy Spirit is this very union. One should not forget that the Incarnation itself, the conception and birth of Jesus, was accomplished "from the Holy Spirit and the Virgin Mary." The descent of the Holy Spirit upon the Mother of God was the bridge upon which the incarnate Logos came down from heaven into the world; and His entire life in the Incarnation, in the union of His divine essence with His human essence in His kenosis, was accomplished by the Holy Spirit.

In His prophetic ministry in particular, insofar as the Divine-Humanity was manifested in it, the Holy Spirit was the active and accomplishing principle. The distinguishing feature of the action of the Holy Spirit in Jesus is that, in Him, the Holy Spirit reveals Him Himself, the divine Logos, "the way, the truth, and the life"; and the Truth announces itself through the God-Man for men in human language. For there is no other truth that could form the content of prophetic preaching besides that which is the Truth Himself, that is, the Logos. The Holy Spirit Himself proclaims to men this sole Truth: "He shall glorify me: for he shall receive of mine, and shall shew it unto you" (John 16:14); "He shall . . . bring all things to your remembrance, whatsoever I have said unto you" (14:26). Moved by the Holy Spirit, the God-Man in His prophetic ministry reveals not the new, revealed thing communicated by the Holy Spirit, as in the case of all the other prophets; instead, He reveals Himself, His own word. Just as in the "immanent" Holy Trinity the Holy Spirit reveals (accomplishes) the Son for the Father and the Father for the Son, so in the God-Man He does the same thing, revealing the beloved Son to the Father and the Father to the Son. That is why the Son, in His self-revelation in the God-Man, is identified, as it were, with the Father, the power of this identification being the Holy Spirit: "he that hath seen me hath seen the Father" (John 14:9); "I and my Father are one" (10:30). This living unity, this "one," is the Holy Spirit, which is why the Son's preaching about Himself is not only a preaching about the Father but also, in a concealed manner, a preaching about the Holy Spirit and therefore about the Holy Trinity. Thus, in His prophetic ministry, Jesus acts as Christ, the anointed by the Holy Spirit, "who speaks by the prophets."

The content of the Lord's prophetic preaching cannot be exhaustively communicated or fully characterized. All attempts to communicate it are incomplete and insufficient, and all characterization of it is inadequate, for man is not given the power to fully measure the words of the God-Man, although he is given the task of unceasingly measuring them. Christ Himself is the subject of His own preaching; all the particular themes of His preaching radiate out from this center. Those who do not wish to see this "Christocentrism" of His preaching, those who, like the moralizing rationalists, transform it into an anonymous "doctrine" — these cannot understand the "Gospel of the Kingdom." Christ's preaching begins with the news of the approach of the Kingdom of God, as does the preaching of the Forerunner, who prepares it. And the Kingdom of God is the Holy Spirit, who unites the Divine and the human in the God-Man. It is His divine Incarnation and His power in the personal life of man, in the world, in history, in the future age, "now and forever, and in the ages of ages." The Gospel teaching is concentrated precisely around this fact. In developing this fundamental idea, this teaching contains a religious morality in the capacity of a guide to the spiritual life, to the life of man in God and for God. God approached and revealed Himself to men in Christ in such a manner that it became possible to set as one's way, limit, and goal the supreme commandment: "Be ye . . . perfect, even as your Father which is in heaven is perfect" (Matt. 5:48). This approach of the Kingdom of God through the Incarnation also serves as the basis for another commandment, not less general: "seek ye first the kingdom of

God . . . and all these things shall be added unto you" (6:33). The given becomes that which is proposed as task; the preaching about the Kingdom of God is also the commandment about it.

The Sermon on the Mount, like the whole of the Gospel morality, has as its subject the relation of the soul to God, to heaven, to eternity, a relation in the light of which all earthly, relative, and transitory values fade and are abolished. These values are not annihilated but recede in their relativity, in the same way that a man who looks at the sky does not notice the horizon surrounding him, is oriented not toward the horizontal but toward the vertical. The necessary diagonal of the earthly and the heavenly, of the temporal and the eternal, is known by every man only in his own creative activity. If one sees in the Gospel words only a "doctrine" and does not notice the Teacher of this doctrine, these words are transformed into an abstract and lifeless morality, full of unrealizable demands, oriented toward utopian maximalism, and deprived of religious cohesion. To be sure, the Gospel morality appears to have such a center in the commandments of love for God and of love for one's neighbor, on which "hang all the law and the prophets" (Matt. 22:40). However, this is no longer the Old Testament commandment. It is a *new* commandment, which acquires true significance in connection with the revelation of God-Love, who is in the Holy Trinity and is revealed in Christ. Nevertheless, in this part, which can conditionally and imprecisely be called Gospel *morality*, Christ's preaching still resembles the prophetic preaching, while surpassing it. But Christ's preaching differs fundamentally from the prophetic preaching in that it is a teaching about Him Himself as the Son of the Father showing the Father, a teaching about the way, the truth, and the life. In contrast, the prophets testified only about the One who was to come, and they were of course very far from the idea of including a teaching about themselves in their preaching. When asked about himself, the greatest of the prophets, the prophet and forerunner John,[2] answered: "[I am] the friend of the bridegroom. . . . He must increase, but I must decrease" (John 3:29-30). The essence and chief content of Christ's prophetic ministry are not His words and discourses but He Himself, His living image as preserved in the Gospels. This image is our conscience into which every believing soul looks, listening to His words.

Christ's prophetic preaching about Himself can be viewed from three points of view: as a theological doctrine of God the Word, as an es-

---

2. See my book *The Friend of the Bridegroom: On the Orthodox Veneration of the Forerunner* (Paris, 1927) [published in 2003 by Eerdmans in Boris Jakim's translation].

chatology, and as an apocalypse. The theological doctrine is contained chiefly in the Lord's discourses in the Gospel of John, although one can find the fundamental ideas of this doctrine in the Synoptics as well. To what extent can one distinguish here Christ's prophetic preaching from the direct testimony of the hypostasis of the Logos about Himself? We could understand it in this latter sense if the Logos in the God-Man were not in a state of kenotic self-humiliation as a result of the inseparable and inconfusable union with the human essence. But precisely because of this union the depths of the proper consciousness of self of the Logos are revealed in the God-Man under the action of the Holy Spirit, and this revelation is thus a prophetic illumination. In this sense — but of course only in this sense — Christ's preaching about Himself must be seen as belonging to the prophetic ministry. But the unique content of this preaching and, above all, the Person of the Prophet infinitely surpass all the prophets and their preaching. The God-Man's preaching about Himself as the Logos, the Son of the Father, also approaches the prophetic preaching in that it is addressed to men, to the human consciousness, in that it is uttered in human language. In other words, what we have here is the application of the Chalcedonian dogma to the prophetic ministry, of this dogma according to which the self-revelation of the incarnate Logos, who in His humiliation took upon Himself the measure of humanity, must be realized without separation and without confusion, and consequently not only in the divine nature but also in the human nature.

Christ's preaching not only has a supremely elevated religious, moral, and theological content, but it also includes an apocalypse and an eschatology, that is, a revelation concerning the destiny of Christ's humankind in history, within the limits of this age and also beyond it. Christ reveals the *future* to His disciples, first directly from Himself and then by the Holy Spirit. He prophesies not only about "things which must shortly come to pass" (Rev. 1:1), that is, in history, but also about that which will take place after "the end of the age." In the Gospel we have the so-called Little Apocalypse (Matt. 24-25), as well as numerous scattered texts containing the Lord's prophetic sayings. To this we can append the Apocalypse of St. John, "the Revelation of Jesus Christ, which God gave unto him" (Rev. 1:1) and which in words and visions He reveals "unto His servants" through His beloved disciple.

A general question arises: How should one understand the character of these prophecies? Should one see them as belonging to the God-Man's "prophetic ministry," or should one understand them as direct words of God, proclaiming the determinations and will of God? The prophets

The Work of Christ

prophesied the future by the Spirit of God, and this constituted such an essential part of their ministry that, in the common usage, prophets are often identified with fortune-tellers or soothsayers. This view is one-sided, since there have been prophets, and very great ones like Elijah and Elisha, who did not predict the future at all, whereas others, like Moses and the forerunner of the Lord, John, the greatest of those born of women, did this only to a small degree in comparison with their overall ministry. Nevertheless, as a general rule, the prophets truly did "prophesy," that is, they predicted the future. The main subject of the prophesying was, of course, the coming Messiah, whose figure, before His coming, was described by the prophets in the so-called messianic prophecies, according to the testimony of the Lord Himself: "And beginning at Moses and all the prophets, he expounded unto them in all the Scriptures the things concerning himself" (Luke 24:27). But apart from this the prophets also prophesied about the destinies of nations and kingdoms, offering an apocalyptic scheme of history (as in Daniel) and eschatological visions of the end.

The question we must ask then is: How in general should one understand this foreknowledge of the future? First of all, we must absolutely exclude any interpretation that considers such prophesying to be an instrumental and mechanical or purely mediumistic pythonism, for the human individuality of the prophet is creatively manifested in his ministry. One thus needs to seek in humanity itself the foundations for the possibility of prophesying. A human being can attain a state of prescience in his mind and heart in proportion to the intensity of their relation to that at which they are directed. A human being is connected by invisible and usually intangible threads with the whole human race; the past is coiled within him and contains the future, insofar as the future is not only determined by freedom but is also governed by certain laws. One knows of various cases of the prevision of the future, concerning, of course, limited and particular events and possessing different degrees of clarity and precision. This intuitive seeing into the mist-shrouded distances and this sensitivity to that which is happening around one reach their maximal intensity and inspiredness in prophets, exclusively chosen and spiritually gifted persons. Their human inspiration, illuminated by the Holy Spirit, acquires the character of *divine inspiration* (i.e., of truth). Human seeking and questioning find their response no longer only in the proper depths of the human spirit, in the "subconscious," but also from above, from the Spirit of God. However, one cannot fail to see to what degree these prophecies bear the imprint of their human, individual origin, depending on the person and on the subject: Isaiah is distinguished from the other prophets as an "Old Testament evangelist," Daniel as an apocalyptist, Ezekiel as a seer of God, Jeremiah as a national prophet, and so on. It is especially important that these figurations of the future, these eschatological visions, are, as a general rule, far from being clear for the prophets themselves. These prophecies remain abstract and opaque. They are expressed by means of the apocalyptic and eschatological images common in the literature of that epoch, and they are therefore obscure and ambiguous, requiring interpretation. This is not something incidental; it is of essential importance: images of the future must not be concrete. Man does not need that. These images express only ontology, not concrete history. We can have a correct understanding of such prophetic visions, an understanding free of exaggeration, only if we do not forget that they have a *human* and thus a relative character.³

This human side of prophecies is also present in Christ's prophetic ministry. It is incorrect to understand these prophecies as divine determinations concerning the future directly announced by the Divinity of the Logos through the human essence; that is, it is incorrect to understand them as resulting from the omnipotent will of God. Such an interpretation would also contradict the Chalcedonian dogma concerning the inseparability and inconfusability of the two natures given the unity of the hypostasis, since this interpretation proposes a separation or alternation of the natures similar to what we have in the patristic conception of the miracles: Divinity works miracles, whereas humanity is a powerless receptacle. We find the same thing here: God prophesies, whereas man listens. This destroys the unity of the divine-human life in Christ, corresponding to the unity of the hypostasis, and it abolishes the kenosis of Divinity, which voluntarily diminishes itself to the measure of humanity and manifests itself only in union with humanity, to the extent humanity can receive it. Furthermore, the human nature, in separation from the divine

---

3. To this is added their *pragmatic* character, with which the *conventional* character of the prophecy is connected. In general, one must reject as crude and simplistic the notion that prophecy is achieved as a result of the ability of the prophet to see the future and to tell what he has seen. This is because it is possible to predict the future, which does not yet exist, not from this not-yet-realized future but only from the present, to the extent it is pregnant with the future. This future belongs not only to the present but also to human freedom, the unceasing participation of which inevitably renders prophecies of the future inaccurate and only conditionally true. The proper domain of prophecy refers therefore to those cases that reveal what God Himself desires to accomplish in the world. Therefore, among the prophecies, the messianic ones have a particularly essential significance, in that they speak of the coming Incarnation and redemption.

nature (from which God keep us!), would be incapable of receiving the word of the Divinity transcendent to it.

It is therefore necessary to recognize that the prophetic knowledge and prediction of the future that we have in the case of Christ is *similar*, although not identical, to that which we have in the case of the prophets. His prophesying originates in the depths of His sinless and universal human essence under the action of the Holy Spirit; furthermore, although the omniscience of the Logos was revealed and accomplished in this human knowledge, the measure of this knowledge during the days of Christ's earthly human ministry did *not* coincide with the omniscience and thus effectively limited it in the God-Man. His words about the future were prophetic words, clothed in the infallibility of the truth; they were not words of Divine omniscience inaccessible to man. This results in that providentially established limit to Jesus' prophetic knowledge which expressly distinguishes it from the omniscience of the Logos: These are His words about the Son's ignorance of the last day (Mark 13:32), words that are a *crux interpretum* and that are usually interpreted in the spirit of docetism with the effective rejection of the divine-humanity. However, Jesus failed to manifest omniscience not only in this case of fundamental importance but also in His everyday life. Omniscience would have transformed His divine-human life from a reality into an appearance and would have abolished His humanity. The Lord prophesied in certain particular chosen instances of intense prayer and inspiration; He did not apply His Divine power to escape the empirical realm and its limits. He asked: Who touched Me? Where did you lay him? In so asking He acknowledged that He was subject to all the force of empirical limitation, outside of which the human nature cannot exist in its concrete reality. The measure of His knowledge therefore was determined here by the measure of His human essence. To be sure, concretely this remains unfathomable for us as a mystery of the life of the God-Man, but the Gospel indicates these limits with perfect clarity.

Humanity, with its historical concreteness (and, as a consequence, its empirical limitations), is manifested in Jesus' prophecies in the fact that, in them, He reflects the world-view of His time, speaks in the language proper to His epoch, and uses images common in the prophetic and apocalyptic literature. Sometimes it is impossible to understand these images except by considering them in connection with the literary and historical tradition of that time (in particular, the most important texts of the "Little Apocalypse" have this character). The Savior's eschatological discourses therefore cannot be understood literally; they do not even lend themselves to a literal interpretation. They can be interpreted only according to their general meaning, which in this case, as in the case of many prophecies, represents precisely the unknown of the problem. This is the true word of the Truth but one that is clothed in a historical garment — in the imagery proper to the Palestinian-Judaic thought of the first century of our era. This form determines all that is relative in this imagery, at least to the extent that it requires an interpretation. To be sure, we must also postulate that the symbolism of Christ's prophetic discourses contains an inexhaustible and absolute meaning, which will be revealed in the fullness of times, and that, in this symbolism, the images are adequate to their content. But in its immediate concreteness this symbolism is addressed to Christ's contemporaries and bears the stamp of history.

Is Christ's prophetic ministry exhausted by His preaching? Or does it also include *works* that are proper to prophetic inspiration, that is, miracles or signs? In theology, the miracles are usually considered to belong to the domain of Christ's "royal ministry" and are viewed as manifestations of divine power over the world. Usually, they are understood only in relation to the Divine omnipotence. However, if we understand miracles in relation to the *Divine-Humanity*, we must first of all reject the interpretation according to which they result from God's omnipotence over the world, because the descent from heaven and the humiliation of Divinity in taking on the form of a servant (i.e., the in-humanization of Christ in general) are absolutely incompatible with the manifestation of this omnipotence in the days of Christ's earthly ministry. Such an interpretation would be tantamount to postulating a certain Divine coercion over the world or a new creative act.[4] Miracles are performed by the God-Man in the inseparable and inconfusable unity of His divine and human essences, by the power of faith and prayer, and by the Holy Spirit, as Christ Himself attests ("I cast out devils by the Spirit of God" [Matt. 12:28]). The divine essence manifests itself here only in harmony with the human essence and in conformity with the *measure* of humanity. Miracles had been performed by the prophets starting with Moses and Elijah, although the working of miracles did not constitute a necessary part of their ministry (John the Forerunner, the greatest of the prophets according to the testimony of the Gospel, did not work miracles). The character and content of the miracles of the prophets are, in general, the same as those of Christ's miracles, although they are miracles of a lower degree than His. Certainly, the prophets worked their miracles by the

---

4. I have already developed these ideas in my *On the Gospel Miracles* and do not consider it necessary to repeat here what I said in that work.

power of prayer and by the Spirit of God reposing upon them. This was their preaching, accomplished not by word but by deed; it was the attestation of God's power in them: Thus, it is said about Moses that he was "mighty in words and in deeds" (Acts 7:22), and the same expression is applied to Christ (Luke 24:19). There is no reason, as well as no possibility, to conceive of these miracles of the prophets in any other way; but also in the case of Christ there is no reason to consider the miracles as belonging to His "royal" ministry, understood (also erroneously: see below) in the sense of God's omnipotence, rather than as belonging to His prophetic ministry. Christ's miracles in the days of His earthly ministry do not manifest "royal" power over the world, for in descending into the world, He had abandoned such power and acquires it again only after His resurrection and glorification ("all power is given unto me in heaven and in earth" [Matt. 28:18]). Rather, they manifest prophetic power. This power is, of course, incomparably greater than that of the prophets, in conformity with the Divine Personality of the Miracle Worker and His miracle-working power. Nevertheless, Christ's miracles are not works of God accomplished *over* the world but the action of the God-Man *in* the world by God's power; typologically, therefore, they refer to the *prophetic* ministry. He said about Himself, "I cast out devils by the Spirit of God" (Matt. 12:28; or "with the finger of God" in Luke 11:20), and correspondingly in the prophets we read: "I am full of power by the spirit of the Lord" (Mic. 3:8) and "my spirit remaineth among you" (Hag. 2:5; cf. Ezek. 36:27; 37:14; Joel 2:28-29, etc.). God diminished Himself in the God-Man to the level of the prophetic ministry, and in response to this humiliation and self-emptying, the power of God descended upon Him and proceeded from Him.[5]

II. The High-Priestly Ministry of Christ

A. Christ as High Priest

In theology, the so-called high-priestly ministry is a generalizing concept expressing the significance of Christ's work that consists in the redemp-

---

5. "The power of the Lord was present to heal them [the sick]" (Luke 5:17). "And the whole multitude sought to touch him: for there went virtue out of him, and healed them all" (6:19). "Then he began to upbraid the cities wherein most of his mighty works were done.... If the mighty works, which were done in you, had been done in Tyre and Sidon, they would have repented long ago in sackcloth and ashes" (Matt. 11:20-21; Luke 10:13).

The Lamb of God

tion of the human race from sin by Christ's offering Himself, His life, His Body and Blood as redemptive sacrifice to God. Thus, the high-priestly ministry is usually considered exclusively from the point of view of *redemption* (i.e., from the point of view of the reconciliation of men with God through their liberation from sin), and the Incarnation is linked to sin. But in reality the high-priestly ministry is not limited solely to redemption from sin; its meaning extends further. That is, it establishes the universal *deification* of man's creaturely being; it lays the foundation for true divine-humanity. However, the relation between redemption and the deification or sanctification of the human essence, between these two aspects of Christ's high-priestly ministry, is such that the former precedes and conditions the latter. Redemption is the way to deification, and it is therefore natural to take redemption as the point of departure in the doctrine of the high-priestly ministry, which is what theologians usually do.

In order to speak with confidence and precision about the Lord's high-priestly ministry, one must of course take the biblical testimony as one's point of departure. Do we find testimony about this ministry in the Gospels? We do of course, but perhaps the form of this testimony is less direct than that concerning the prophetic ministry. Even this indirect testimony, however, clearly and convincingly indicates that Christ exercised a priestly function, namely the sacrificial one, and that He was therefore a high priest. The first and fundamental testimony, common to all three Synoptics (and also found in 1 Cor. 11:23-32), is the narrative of the Last Supper, in which the establishment of the Eucharist is portrayed with features exclusively proper to the offering of sacrifice. Here, Christ is both the sacrifice and the sacrificing priest: "offering and offered, receiving and distributed," as it is said in the priest's mystical Eucharistic prayer. Christ also pronounces the words concerning the sacrifice: "Take, eat: this is my body, which is broken for you" (1 Cor. 11:24); and "drink ye all of it; for this is my blood of the new testament, which is shed for many for the remission of sins" (Matt. 26:27-28). Parallel to this is the entire sixth chapter of John with its fundamental theme: "the bread that I will give is my flesh, which I will give for the life of the world" (6:51; cf. 6:53-56).

This institution by Christ of the Divine Eucharist imparts an oblational and sacrificial character to the Incarnation itself, as well as to Christ's entire work on earth.[6] Such a meaning can also be attributed to

---

6. We attribute a similar meaning to the images of the Apocalypse with their fundamental theme of the "slain Lamb," who has redeemed us by His blood and "hast made us unto our God kings and priests" (Rev. 5:9-10 and elsewhere). Cf. 1 Peter 1:19-20; and of

the "high-priestly" prayer (John 17), whose primary focus, however, is not redemption, but deification — the sanctification and glorification of humanity. And so, the Gospels show us the high-priestly ministry at work, but they do not contain a direct doctrine of this ministry, or at least not one that is articulated by the Lord. This ministry is also attested by numerous texts of the apostolic epistles, which speak of the redemption from sins by the blood of Jesus. We find a teaching about the high-priestly ministry in the Epistle to the Hebrews with its fundamental theme: the comprehension of the Old Testament on the basis of the New. Here, Christ's high-priesthood is considered in parallel with that of Aaron: "consider the Apostle and High Priest of our profession, Christ Jesus; who was faithful to him that appointed him, as also Moses was faithful in all his house" (3:1-2). He is "a great high priest that is passed into the heavens" (4:14), but He can be "touched with the feeling of our infirmities," for "in all points [He was] tempted like as we are, yet without sin" (4:15); "in the days of his flesh . . . he had offered up prayers and supplications with strong crying and tears unto him that was able to save him from death, and was heard in that he feared; though he were a Son, yet learned he obedience by the things which he suffered; and being made perfect, he became the author of eternal salvation unto all them that obey him; called of God an high priest after the order of Melchisedec" (5:7-10). It is impossible to more expressively link the two sides of the high-priestly ministry: kenotic humiliation as the foundation and path and "the passing into the heavens" as the completion and crowning.

Christ's priesthood is not that of the law, Aaron's; rather, it is a priesthood "after the order of Melchisedec," directly instituted by God, in virtue of His humiliation in His Incarnation. "Thou art a priest for ever after the order of Melchizedek" (Ps. 110:4) — this is repeated several times in the Epistle to the Hebrews. Christ offered Himself up in sacrifice just once (Heb. 7:27): not "by the blood of goats and calves, but by his own blood he entered in once into the holy place, having obtained eternal redemption for us" (9:12). And this is "the blood of Christ, who through the eternal Spirit offered himself without spot to God [in order to] purge [our] conscience from dead works" (9:14). He entered "into heaven itself, now to appear in the presence of God for us" (9:24) and "to put away sin by the sacrifice of himself" (9:26). "Christ was once offered to bear the sins of many; and unto them that look for him shall he appear the second

---

course the Forerunner's words in John 1:29: "Behold the Lamb of God, which taketh away the sin of the world."

time without sin unto salvation" (9:28). "After He had offered one sacrifice for sins . . . [He] sat down [forever] on the right hand of God" (10:12). We have "boldness to enter into the holiest by the blood of Jesus, by a new and living way, which he hath consecrated for us, through the veil, that is to say, his flesh" (10:19-20).

According to the general meaning of the teaching of the Epistle to the Hebrews, Christ as High Priest offers Himself to God the Father by the Holy Spirit, and thus with the participation of the entire Holy Trinity, in conformity with the character of each of the hypostases. This sacrifice-offering is expressed in obedience, in the experiencing of infirmities and temptations, and finally in the shedding of Christ's blood in His death on the cross; here He is not only the sacrifice, the slaughtered Lamb, but also the sacrificing Priest in the sense that the offering of sacrifice is His voluntary deed. He Himself offers Himself as sacrifice to His Father. However, He accomplishes this sacrifice-offering not by His own will but according to the Father's will, to which He fully subjects His own, filial, Divine-Human will. He makes the Father's will His own will. Thus, the High Priest is not only *fated* to become a sacrifice, but He also *wills* this fate. We have here not only the presence of the sacrificial victim but also the sacrificial state, not only the fact of the sacrifice but also the offering of sacrifice. And to the extent that the power of love is in general expressed in the sacrifice, God's love for the world is revealed in the high-priestly ministry: "In this was manifested the love of God toward us, because that God sent his only begotten Son into the world, that we might live through him" (1 John 4:9; cf. John 3:16). Going into the world, the Son says about Himself: "Lo, I come to do thy will, O God" (Heb. 10:7, 9; cf. Ps. 40:8).

The Incarnation itself, as the redemptive sacrifice of the reconciliation of the world with God, is already the Son's offering of Himself in sacrifice, that is, it is the acceptance of the high-priestly ministry. In coming into the world, Christ says: "Sacrifice and offering thou wouldest not, but a body hast thou prepared me" (Heb. 10:5). The assumption of the body, the Incarnation, is already the sacrifice of the love of the Lamb slaughtered before the creation of the world, just as the coming into the world is already the beginning of the high-priestly ministry. The entire earthly life of Christ, of the only one without sin in this world poisoned by sin, is truly a sacrificial suffering. It is a sacrificial suffering from the very beginning, the winter grotto with the humble crèche, to the very end, the crucifixion on Golgotha. He breathed the pestilential air of our fallen world. He lived with us, that is, in the midst of human sin and malice, constantly wounded and outraged by them. He was not of this world, but He lived in this world. In itself, this life — whatever the character of its particular events, from the luminous days of the Nazareth obscurity to the dark Jerusalem days — was one of constant suffering, never ameliorated but growing ever more intense, to the point where an open rupture with the world and with the Old Testament church became inevitable.

Nevertheless, because of the nonillusory character of His Incarnation, the earthly life of the Savior has different times and seasons, manifested in particular in relation to His works and thus in His various ministries. We distinguish thus, first of all, the time spent by the Lord in obscurity and the beginning of His public ministry. The demarcation here is the baptism of the Lord, with the descent upon Him of the Holy Spirit, who anointed Him for His ministry. This ministry is first manifested primarily as a prophetic one: "Jesus went about all Galilee, teaching in their synagogues, and preaching the gospel of the kingdom, and healing all manner of sickness and all manner of disease among the people. . . . And there followed him great multitudes of people from Galilee, and from Decapolis, and from Jerusalem, and from Judea, and from beyond Jordan" (Matt. 4:23, 25). Announcing that He is sent "to the lost sheep of the house of Israel," He also sends the twelve apostles to them for preaching and healing (10:6). He first acts within the limits of the Old Testament church, addressing it and attempting to make it believe in Him. Although He encounters resistance here, first muted but then increasingly evident and conscious, nevertheless a decisive break does not yet occur, and it thus still remains possible to do everything possible to convert Israel and at the same time to teach and instruct the chosen: first the twelve, and then the seventy apostles, together with others close to Christ.

The Gospel indicates the main periods in the life and ministry of Christ. There is a perfectly clear dividing line, a rupture, that separates the initial period of the prophetic ministry, with its as yet unexhausted possibilities, from the later period, where these possibilities appear to have been exhausted, and there is an inevitable break with the synagogue, having fatal consequences. At the same time, the first fruits of Christ's prophetic ministry ripen, especially the fruits of His interaction with the apostles. The growing exasperation of some of the apostles is accompanied by the achievement of a greater spiritual maturity by other apostles. This rupture is marked by the Transfiguration of the Lord, preceded by the conversation on the way to Caesarea Philippi, when Peter, in the name of all the apostles, confessed: "Thou art the Christ, the Son of the living God" (Matt. 16:16). After this confession, which the Lord commanded His

The Lamb of God

disciples to conceal for a time ("Then charged he his disciples that they should tell no man that he was Jesus the Christ" [16:20]), "from that time forth began Jesus to shew unto his disciples, how that he must go unto Jerusalem, and suffer many things of the elders and chief priests and scribes, and be killed, and be raised again the third day" (16:21); "and he spake that saying openly" (Mark 8:32). This was followed by Peter's protest, for which he was called "Satan" (Matt. 16:22-23), after which all the disciples were called to follow Christ, each with his own cross (16:24-27).

From this time on, Christ begins, as it were, to instruct the disciples concerning the idea of His coming suffering and death, getting them used to this idea, although it was difficult for them to assimilate.[7] Until this time, the Lord had not said anything about His coming passion, the condemnation to death, and the resurrection; but now He begins to prepare His disciples for this. To be sure, this was necessary above all for them, but at the same time it had become necessary also for Him, since the consciousness of the inevitability of this path had ripened in Him, together with the decision to break with the synagogue and take up the cross. To be sure, Christ came into the world as the Lamb of God, sacrificed before the creation of the world and taking upon Himself the sins of the world, in order, as the Son of Man, to be lifted up on the cross (see John 3:14); this pre-eternal sacrifice is the foundation of the cross of Golgotha for the salvation of the world. However, that which is established pre-eternally is revealed in time, as an event of the divine-human life, in which Christ's human essence, nonillusory and authentic, experienced its times and seasons and their accomplishments. In particular, this consciousness of the inevitability of the rupture and the decision to accept it with all its consequences (including the death on the cross) did not — according to the testimony of the Gospel — come to Christ all at once and from the very beginning in His earthly life. This consciousness arose in Him as a consequence of the entire experience of His life, together with the spiritual act of decision, as an inner sacrifice-offering, as *the will to the cross*. In its origin, this inner act is concealed from us; it is presented to us only after it has been accomplished. But in its preparation the Lord reveals Himself as

---

7. Thus, He once again discussed this subject with His disciples when they were descending the mountain after the Transfiguration (Mark 9:9-13) and after the healing of the possessed man during the stay in Galilee (Matt. 17:22-23; Mark 9:30-32; Luke 9:44-45). And He again discussed it when they were going up to Jerusalem; "and Jesus went before them: and they were amazed; and as they followed, they were afraid" (Mark 10:32; see also Matt. 20:18; Luke 18:31-34).

The Work of Christ

the sacrifice and the sacrificing priest at the Last Supper, and in the strict sense this is the beginning of His high-priestly ministry, which is already initially present in the Incarnation, as the self-emptying and sacrificial kenosis of Divinity. It was His spiritual act of decision that led Christ to set out on the path of His public, prophetic ministry, a path that led Him to John the Baptist so that, in a preliminary manner, He could "fulfill all truth" in the baptism.

His readiness for the sacrificial ministry then brings Him to Mount Tabor. There He meets the prophets Moses and Elijah, each of whom in his own way expresses the power of the Old Testament, and He speaks to them about "his exodus which he should accomplish at Jerusalem" (Luke 9:31 [the King James Version has been modified to conform with the Russian Bible]). The Transfiguration of the Lord is connected both outwardly and inwardly with what had occurred on the way to Caesarea Philippi. It is connected with it outwardly since it is posterior to it in time ("after six days" [Matt. 17:1]) and linked with it in the overall sequence of the Gospel narration (in all the Synoptics), and it is connected with it inwardly because these two events find themselves in a certain causal relationship. The link here is the difficult and ambiguous text that immediately follows Christ's exhortation to His disciples that they lift up their crosses. This exhortation is reinforced by the eschatological promise of a recompense after the coming of the Son of Man in His glory: "Verily I say unto you, There be some standing here, which shall not taste of death, till they see the Son of man coming in his kingdom" (Matt. 16:28; Mark 9:1: "the kingdom of God come with power"; Luke 9:27: "the kingdom of God"); and then there immediately follows the narrative about the Transfiguration of the Lord.

Even if one admits the possibility of *different* interpretations of this manifestation of the Kingdom of God (aside from the eschatological interpretation, there is the inwardly immanent or ecclesiological one), it is absolutely impossible to exclude the connection between these words and the Transfiguration. And if there is such a connection, what does it signify here? First of all, insofar as the Transfiguration, as the manifestation of the Lord in glory, is already the anticipation of His eternal and eschatological glorification (the glorification of the Lord "coming in His Kingdom" and in this sense of the kingdom "come with power") for "some," that is, for the three apostles on earth, the *Glory of God* already shines forth in the Transfiguration. It shines forth not only in Christ, transfigured in the image of His coming Glory, but also in this world, transfigured together with Him in certain of its parts: in Christ's garments and, of course, in the surrounding air, mountain, and land. What meaning can we attribute to this *anticipation* of Christ's Glory when the Glory was not yet proper to Him (for He Himself prays to the Father that the Father glorify Him with this Glory: John 17:5)? Is this a one-sided action of God's omnipotence, similar to the manifestation of God's Glory to Moses or Ezekiel, an action whose purpose is to educate the disciples and to prepare them for the passion ("in order that they come to understand the voluntary suffering when they see Thee crucified," as the kontakion of the Transfiguration says)? Even if there is an element of this, it clearly does not exhaust the immensity of this event. The Gospel tells of similar divine-human events that unfold not only in time, having a beginning, a middle, and an end, but also *above* time. Such is the Last Supper, at which Christ offers to His disciples His body in communion, "which is broken for us," *before* it was pierced with nails and a spear; as well as His blood, "which is shed for us," *before* it was shed for the remission of sins. Christ's sacrifice on Golgotha had not yet been accomplished in time, but it was already pre-accomplished in His decision, even as it had been pre-accomplished in the Divine Counsel, and it was already effective as if it had been accomplished. The same thing can be said about the Last Discourse, which begins ("now is the Son of man glorified" [John 13:31]) and ends ("that they may behold my glory, which thou hast given me" [17:24]) with Christ's testimony about glory and glorification. This, however, is on the very *eve* of the salvific passion, for the God-Man's decision already contains the accomplishment: the beginning merges with the end. Likewise, the Transfiguration of the Lord, as a manifestation of Glory, shows as already accomplished that which, in time, remains as yet unaccomplished and hidden in the Lord's decision concerning "the exodus at Jerusalem" (Luke 9:31) to undergo the salvific passion. Therefore, here too, we have in a single act the beginning and the end, the line of time woven into a single point. The Transfiguration thus acquires an eschatological meaning: it signifies the anticipation of the glorification of Christ, "coming in His Kingdom," of "the Kingdom of God come with power."

There is a feature, however, that essentially characterizes the Transfiguration not only as a testimony about glory but also as the very *being* of glory, for here Christ already shines with Glory. And this imparts to the Transfiguration a special meaning in Christ's ministry, with reference to His high-priestly ministry and thus with reference to the salvific passion. This is the same meaning that the baptism has for His prophetic ministry and in general for the beginning of His entire earthly ministry. The baptism was the descent of the Holy Spirit, anointing Christ for His prophetic ministry and in general for His entire earthly ministry. It was

Christ's personal Pentecost, in which the Holy Spirit, pre-eternally inseparable from His Divinity, hypostatically reposed upon His humanity. After Christ had received this Spirit of adoption, the voice of the Father attested from heaven: "This is my beloved Son, in whom I am well pleased" (Matt. 3:17). The Gospel account of the Transfiguration does not directly speak of the descent of the Holy Spirit, but it does indirectly attest to it in the appearance of the bright cloud that overshadowed Him. The cloud is the image of God's Glory, the symbol of the Holy Spirit (cf. Exod. 19:9; 34:5; Lev. 16:2; Deut. 33:26; 1 Kings 8:10; 2 Chron. 5:13). According to the Gospel account of the Transfiguration, "a bright cloud overshadowed them: and behold a voice out of the cloud, which said, This is my beloved Son, in whom I am well pleased" (Matt. 17:5). Here we have the testimony of the Father, identical to that at the baptism but now expressly repeated from "out of the cloud," which means a new bestowal of grace upon the Son, with the express aim of glorifying Him. The glorification is a work of voluntary suffering, of manifest obedience; and here, at this turning point of the Lord's earthly path, just before He sets out for Jerusalem to begin the Golgotha sacrifice, Glory is sent to Him by a new operation of the Holy Spirit, for "through the eternal Spirit [He] offered himself without spot to God" (Heb. 9:14). Furthermore, the Resurrection, the Ascension, and thus His entire glorification in general are accomplished by the Holy Spirit. Thus, if the theophany at the baptism is related to Christ's *entire* earthly ministry (in particular to the Transfiguration in the capacity of the accomplishing action of the Holy Spirit), the Transfiguration is related to the Golgotha sacrifice and is its mysterious anticipation. In this sense, if in the baptism, the general anointing of Jesus as Christ, He is directly anointed by the Holy Spirit as prophet, then the Transfiguration is the anointing of Jesus for the *high-priestly ministry*, that is, for the Golgotha sacrifice-offering, where He is both sacrifice and sacrificing priest. One can therefore say that, in a certain sense, in the Transfiguration Christ is made a "high priest forever after the order of Melchisedec" (Heb. 6:20). This priesthood of Melchisedec is characterized, first of all, by the fact that it is instituted directly by God and is not temporal but eternal[8] ("made like unto the Son of God [he] abideth a priest continually" [Heb. 7:3]). Second, this high-priesthood has force both on earth and in heaven,

---

8. It should be mentioned that both the Old Testament priesthood and the Old Testament ritual are defined as *eternal* institutions (see Exod. 12:14; 27:21; 28:43; 29:28; 40:15). But, clearly, they are so defined according to their inner meaning, not according to the duration of their existence, which is limited.

into which the High Priest Christ enters through a veil, that is, His flesh, with His blood; and He abides there eternally: "after the similitude of Melchisedec there ariseth another priest, who is made, not after the law of a carnal commandment, but after the power of an endless life" (7:15-16).

In the Transfiguration, heaven is united with earth; that which takes place in the Transfiguration takes place both for heaven ("the cloud") and for earth. Moses and Elijah speak of His entry into Jerusalem and of the earthly priesthood of Golgotha, and at the same time the voice from heaven attests to the eternal Divine-Sonhood of the Beloved Son: "For he received from God the Father honour and glory, when there came such a voice to him from the excellent glory, This is my beloved Son, in whom I am well pleased" (2 Pet. 1:17). And thus the high-priestly ministry *begins* — with the entry into Jerusalem with all its consequences. First of all, we have the definitive break with the synagogue. The prophetic ministry is included here in the high-priestly ministry in the sense that it is precisely the former that directly leads Christ to Golgotha. Christ abandons the idea of using preaching to convert and save the Jews, "the lost sheep of the house of Israel" (Matt. 10:6); on the contrary, His prophetic word becomes condemnatory, wrathful, irreconcilable. More and more frequently we find images of the rejection and condemnation of hard-hearted Israel; we find parables about the vineyard and the husbandmen of the vineyard and about the marriage feast in the speeches to the scribes and the Pharisees (Matt. 21–23) in response to their cunning questions. All of this acquires a generalized expression in the soul-rending cry of farewell: "O Jerusalem, Jerusalem, thou that killest the prophets, and stonest them which are sent unto thee, how often would I have gathered thy children together, even as a hen gathereth her chickens under her wings, and ye would not! Behold, your house is left unto you desolate" (Matt. 23:37-38). The prophetic ministry ends with a complete break. Henceforth, it fully merges with the high-priestly ministry. The foundation of the New Testament is laid, and the High Priest says: "This cup is the new testament in my blood, which is shed for you" (Luke 22:20). Henceforth the Prophet cedes His place to the High Priest, and the Transfiguration opens the way to the glorification. But this way leads through Jerusalem to Golgotha.

B. Redemption

The High Priest offers Himself in sacrifice to God, manifesting obedience "unto death, even the death of the cross" (Phil. 2:8), in His righteous life

The Work of Christ

and in His death on the cross. This sacrifice is defined in Scripture as "redemption" by blood, "propitiation," "justification," "reconciliation" (Rom. 3:21-29; 4:25; 5:7-10; 1 Cor. 6:20; 2 Cor. 5:15, 21; Eph. 1:7; Col. 1:14, 20; 1 Tim. 2:6; Heb. 9:12, 14, 26, 28; 10:12). "Ye are bought with a price" (1 Cor. 6:20; 7:23); Christ "died for all" (2 Cor. 5:15); "Christ hath redeemed us from the curse of the law" (Gal. 3:13); in Him "we have redemption through his blood" (Eph. 1:7); "when we were enemies ['by nature the children of wrath' (Eph. 2:3)], we were reconciled to God by the death of his Son" (Rom. 5:10); "He appeared to put away sin by the sacrifice of himself" (Heb. 9:26).

Many texts of this and similar content express the general idea that Christ offered the redemptive sacrifice in His blood and took upon Himself the sins of the world. This is a fact irrefutably attested by Scripture and just as irrefutably obvious for our immediate religious consciousness. In Christ we become reconciled with God. Christ is the intermediary for us; by faith in Him we recognize that we are justified before God. This fact is the point of departure for the theological doctrine of redemption, which begins with the following set of questions about the redemptive sacrifice: To whom is this sacrifice offered? How and why is it offered? What constitutes its power? Answers to these questions are offered by the various theological theories of redemption, which usually focus on one or another element of this fact and stylize it accordingly; because of this, an idea that in and of itself is true usually becomes one-sided.

In the patristic epoch, the primary focus was on the idea of ransom. The question posed by theologians was: To whom was the ransom offered: to the devil (the view of Origen, St. Gregory of Nyssa, and in a certain sense even St. John of Damascus) or to God (the view of St. Gregory the Theologian and others). From this particular question a transition was made to the doctrine of the *power* of the redemption, which is seen to consist in the victory over death in the Resurrection (St. Athanasius the Great), in the "medicine of immortality." The severe ascetic and juridical thought of the West, in the person of Anselm of Canterbury, posed the question of redemption as an act of justice, and in particular the question of the equivalence of sin and sacrifice. This juridical thought developed the classic theory of satisfaction, according to which only the death of the God-Man as God and also as Man could satisfy God's truth and reconcile fallen man with God (this is the theory that had the greatest influence both in Western and in Eastern theology). Further, the Post-Reformation epoch posed with particular acuteness the question of the very possibility of a sacrifice of "substitution," where one was sacrificed for all (see Socinus) in order to

The Lamb of God

satisfy God's truth. It also posed the question of the nature and power of this sacrifice as an example or image of compassionate love and thus of Divine Sonhood (the theoreticians of this view are Abelard, representatives of liberal German theology, and the Russian theologian Metropolitan Antonii), or finally as a redemptive sacrifice in the proper sense. It is necessary to pose the question of redemption in connection with the fundamental christological principles set forth in the present work.

The Logos is the demiurgic hypostasis, directed at the world in its creation, and the Logos is also the in-humanized hypostasis, God come into the world in order to save it. In creating the world out of nothing, with man at its head, in calling to life *creaturely* being with its changeability, God not only creates the world by His omnipotence and wisdom, but He also takes upon Himself the providential government of the world in its state of creaturely changeability, because of which, in its creaturely freedom, it can become tainted with evil and fall away from Him. In other words, God's pre-eternal counsel or plan concerning the *creation* of the world necessarily includes the counsel concerning its *salvation,* that is, concerning the unification of creation with God, or its deification, to which creation is predestined. Not only the fall that occurred but also the very changeability of the world and, in the final analysis, its *creatureliness* separate the world from God by an insurmountable distance, which can be overcome only by God, not by man.

This constitutes the general foundation for the Incarnation as the manifestation of God's love for the world. If the creation of the world is already a work of God's sacrificial love, in virtue of which the Absolute posits alongside itself relative being, then the Incarnation is God's sacrificial love that involves the humiliation of Divinity, condescending to the level of hypostatic union with man. But this sacrificial love of God for the world is the *pre-eternal* foundation of the Incarnation, which is thus the second and concluding act of the creation of the world. In this sense, the Logos is the Lamb of God sacrificed *before the creation of the world.* In creating the world, God takes responsibility for its salvation *upon Himself* and decides to supplement *with Himself* that which is lacking in creation: He decides to deify that which is created, to bestow eternity upon that which is becoming. The idea of the redemption is thus indissolubly linked with that of the creation, and in a certain sense they are *ontologically identical.* To admit some sort of occasionalism here, which would link the Incarnation exclusively with Adam's fall, is, at the very least, inappropriate in relation to God's eternity. According to such a supposition, one would arrive at the incongruous conclusion that, in having created the world, God first conducted the experiment, as it were, of leaving the world to its own devices, but then, after the fall of Adam, He changed His mind and reached a new decision, that is, He decided to become incarnate. Without mentioning the crude anthropomorphism of such a notion, one arrives at the conclusion that the cause of the Incarnation lies not even in *felix Adae culpa* (Adam's happy guilt), nor in Adam's fall, but simply in the devil, who succeeded in attaining his goal and seducing our progenitors. But one should not forget that, already in the pre-eternal Adam, God had foreseen the image of the New Adam, just as in Eve He had foreseen the image of the New Eve. It is therefore idle to ask whether the Incarnation would have taken place if Adam had not fallen, since this very category of possibility or indeterminacy is inapplicable to the proper ways of God, for which there can be no *either/or*.

The Incarnation is immanent to the very creation of the world, which has its head and center in man, the living image of God. That is why the redemption, which is included in the Incarnation, is thus, as a possibility, equally immanent to the creation of the world. Man is a creature of God; in virtue of his creatureliness he contains relativity or changeability, which includes the *possibility* of sin. This possibility is a constantly threatening reality that cannot be overcome by the powers of the creature alone. The Creator Himself takes it upon Himself to overcome this possibility: He takes it upon Himself to overcome not only sin but even creatureliness itself. With this He concludes His creation and thereby *justifies* the act of creation. If not for this divine action, creation would inevitably be imperfect in virtue of its origination out of nothing and thus in virtue of the limitedness and changeability of creaturely freedom. God cannot abandon the world — which, although it is perfect in the initial state of its creation ("it was good"), has in itself the inevitable ontological imperfection of creatureliness and the resulting incompleteness — to its own fate (as the Deists teach). A further task arises in connection with the creation of the world: the task of overcoming its creatureliness, of making the creation uncreated or supercreated, of deifying it. Such is true theodicy, which is precisely the Incarnation. Such is the *cost* of creation for God Himself, such is the *sacrifice* of God's love manifested in the creation of the world: "God so loved the world, that he gave his only begotten Son" (John 3:16). Christ's cross is inscribed in creation at its very origin, and in its initial act the world is already called to receive Divinity into its depths.

The Incarnation is the salvation of the world not only from its creaturely relativity or changeability, but also from sin. That is, the Incarnation is reconciliation and redemption. In fact, its first goal is to eliminate the evil consequences of the bad use of creaturely freedom, the consequences of the Fall, and to restore the fallen Adam. This goal must be the first, because until it is attained, man's communion with God cannot be restored, a communion that is crowned by man's deification. Precisely in this sense it is correct to say that Christ came into the world to save sinners from sin and that He is the Lamb of God who takes upon Himself the sins of the world, as the divinely inspired Isaiah attests with divine power, and together with him and after him the Forerunner of the Christ. The Incarnation, which ontologically includes the overcoming of the creatureliness of the creature in the Divine-Humanity, takes on the aspect of redemption, and Christ becomes the redemptive sacrifice. The God-Man experiences not only the general relativity but also the sinfulness of the creature — if not in Himself, then in the world and in humanity. In coming into the world, Christ enters the realm of sin-poisoned being. His redemptive suffering begins with His Incarnation. Absolutely without human sin, the God-Man experiences the sin surrounding Him as severe suffering. He has come to save the world, but it is alien to Him; and the hostility of the world to Christ gradually becomes so intense that the way out — in the form of the death on the cross — becomes clear and inevitable. From a specific moment of time, therefore, Christ begins to speak to His disciples about His coming suffering and death. But in what manner are these sufferings and this death fated to become those of the *cross*? How do they acquire the redemptive significance of the sacrifice on the cross for sin? This is connected with the God-Man's *inner acceptance* of His fate as the will of the Father and with the *Divine-Human* living-out of this fate. This is precisely what constitutes the high-priestly ministry of Christ, who offers Himself in sacrifice and manifests His obedience unto the death on the cross.

Having assumed the human essence in the Incarnation, the Lord shared the fate of this essence, except for sin. He bore upon Himself this fallen essence with its infirmities; and, sinless, He suffered not only from the assumption of this infirm essence, which was already a cross, but also from hostile sin (after all, it is said for a reason that "the Son of man is betrayed into the hands of sinners" [Matt. 26:45]) and from the prince of this world, acting through instruments obedient to him. Christ experienced sin as an unceasing suffering — from demons and from men: "O faithless and perverse generation, how long shall I be with you? how long shall I suffer you?" (Matt. 17:17; also Mark 9:19; Luke 9:41). Sometimes, although only in exceptional cases, words of wrath escaped His lips, words that were no longer only compassionate but also accusatory: "My house shall be called the house of prayer; but ye have made it a den of thieves"

The Work of Christ

(Matt. 21:13, with parallels); or concerning Herod: "tell that fox" (Luke 13:32); or finally the thunderous words addressed to the scribes and Pharisees: "Ye serpents, ye generation of vipers, how can ye escape the damnation of hell? . . . That upon you may come all the righteous blood shed upon the earth" (Matt. 23:33, 35). But this is also a cry of suffering and sorrow provoked by human hardness of heart. The Holy One, the only one without sin, bore upon Himself the sin of the world first of all as His *personal* suffering resulting from His collision with the world, for Christ had a human personality endowed with its particular destiny. He was a human individual (the fact that He was the God-Man does not change this).

Christ takes upon Himself the sin of the world and overcomes it by experiencing it in His life. This cannot be understood empirically, for what we have here is the metaempirical, metaphysical reality of a *whole* — specifically of the human race. Although, empirically, this whole exists in its parts, it precedes these parts (not temporally but ontologically). This whole of the human race — which was initially expressed in the universality of the original sin of Adam: "by one man sin entered into the world" (Rom. 5:12) — contains the integral of all human sins, not only natural but also personal. And in the depths of the in-humanization, which is the identification of the Son with the entire human race through the assimilation of the human essence, there lies the assimilation of sin and sins by their reception as His own. Humanity is united not only by the solidarity of good but also by the solidarity of sin: all human beings are guilty not only for themselves but also for all, with all, and in all things, although our knowledge does not encompass (in this age) this consciousness in its concreteness as it was encompassed by the consciousness of the New Adam. The in-humanization of the Logos is equivalent to His taking upon Himself of universal human sin through this identification with the human race, through this generic and not just individual assumption of the human essence. This assumption of the human essence therefore turns out to be the assumption of sin: "the Lamb of God who takes upon Himself the sins of the world" (cf. John 1:29); "he hath borne our griefs and carried our sorrows" (Isa. 53:4), and "the Lord hath laid on him the iniquity of us all" (53:6).

This self-identification of Christ with the human race, which is the basis of the dogma of the redemption, compels us to understand *literally,* not figuratively, Christ's words at the Last Judgment: "inasmuch as ye have done it unto one of the least of these my brethren, ye have done it unto me" (Matt. 25:40; and 25:45 expresses the same idea in a negative form). This identification, in virtue of which Christ's human nature is connected with

The Lamb of God

the nature of *all* human beings, thus extends Christ's human life to all of human history. The further question inevitably arises: Is this an external, empirical relation or an inner, metaempirical one? Clearly, this cannot be an external, empirical relation, since Christ lived an individual human life, defined and limited by space and time. And so it must be an inner relation, established by the general fact that Christ's in-humanization, in all its temporal moments or events, has a supratemporal, abiding significance. Christ's connection with the world and with humanity is not abolished by His departure from the world in the Ascension; rather, it is preserved, being extended to the past and to the future — in general to *all* time — supratemporally. This idea receives a general confirmation in the Church year, in which Christ's earthly life with its events is reproduced in a real and commemorative manner. Christ lives in His humankind; He suffers from its sufferings and sins, while at the same time abiding in glory at the right hand of the Father.[9] This is the ultimate antinomy for our reason (but it is not the only antinomy of this kind; consider, for example, the Eucharistic dogma). This antinomy indicates the limits to the knowledge of this age, in which we see as "through a glass, darkly" (1 Cor. 13:12).

The idea of the self-identification of Christ with all of humanity in His human essence should not be understood to mean that Christ's humanity replaces or evicts man's proper essence. Such a pan-Christism would contradict the *autonomy* of the human essence in its freedom. Christ's humanity does not replace our natural humanity, but co-lives, co-suffers, and is co-present with it by virtue of *identification*, which, however, presupposes for its existence the presence of two poles, two principles: on the one hand, the old Adam, this natural autonomous humanity; and, on the other hand, the New Adam, Christ's humanity. This is a *dynamic* identification of two principles, not a statics of unity in which there is no movement and therefore no identification. The identification of the *two*, of Christ's humanity and Adam's humanity, can have different degrees and different forms, in conformity with the manner in which we accomplish our salvation; but this identification is never replaced or absorbed by a simple unity. The creaturely essence preserves its autonomy irrespective of the degree of its deification, just as the fire engulfs but does not consume the Burning Bush; and although our humanity is *also* Christ's humanity, it always preserves its autonomy in Adam. After the Incarna-

---

9. These ideas have been developed in my essay "The Holy Grail," published in the journal *Put'* (The Way, Paris) (1932). [This essay is available in an English translation by Boris Jakim in *The Holy Grail and the Eucharist* (Hudson, N.Y., 1997). — Trans.]

tion, two centers appeared in humanity, divine and creaturely, which can coincide and be livingly identified but which cannot be abolished.[10]

This gives an indirect answer to the following question, which inevitably arises in the dogmatics of the redemption: Does not Christ's redemptive assumption of universal human sin abolish personal human freedom and thus personal human responsibility? Did Christ not accomplish His redemptive work in place of all human beings and for all their works? Is not freedom thus, in general, a human delusion that does not correspond to any reality? Without considering the doctrine of predestination (which is based on a misunderstanding that introduces time into Divinity, the temporal "pre" into the eternity of God[11]), let us indicate that the nature of the old Adam, with its autonomy and creaturely freedom, is not abolished by the Incarnation, which only introduces a new and second center into the nature of the old Adam. Human freedom is thus not abolished by the fact that the New Adam takes upon Himself or assumes the works of this freedom (i.e., sins); this assumption is precisely what constitutes the redemption. To be sure, real sin does not exist, and therefore cannot be assumed, before it is realized through freedom. It should be remembered, however, that creaturely freedom is not absolute freedom, which is proper only to God's omnipotence. Creaturely freedom exists only as a *modality* in relation to a reality that is given to it, and it is exhausted by this determinate form of realization of this reality. Creaturely freedom is effectively limited by the real possibilities that it cannot go beyond (except in an illusory fashion or in Luciferian pose). That is why human sins, as possibilities, can be known by God even before they are committed; and through this divine knowledge they can be redemptively assimilated and livingly overcome by the Lamb of God who takes upon Himself the sins of the world, that is, the works of rebellious and infirm creaturely freedom. This divine knowledge of these possibilities makes possible the *prevision* of future events, and this prevision does not revoke freedom, does not transform the actors into marionettes, but knows the *ways* of this freedom and the *possibilities* contained in it. This irrevocability and lawlike regularity can be accomplished freely in the sense of personal activity (this is the basis for predictions in the social sciences, in particular, the statistical study of "ensembles," with the laws governing them, which do not by any means revoke freedom).

---

10. On this basis, the communion with the Body and the Blood of Christ continues beyond the limits of this age, as the symbolism of the Apocalypse makes clear: the water of life flowing from the Lamb and "the tree of life" (Rev. 22:1-2).

11. See my essay "Judas Iscariot, the Traitor-Apostle," in *Put'* (1930).

The Lamb of God

It is this *knowledge* of the power and profundity of human sin in general with *all* its possibilities that constitutes the foundation of the redemptive self-identification of the Lamb of God with the fallen human race with all its sins in the past, the present, and the future. Thus, the redemption does not revoke creaturely freedom in its actual limits, not only because it is in general not a "predestination," but also because it presupposes human freedom, which is free to accept it or not accept it. Here, the duality of the centers of the one humanity, the old Adam and the New Adam, emerges with all the force of its reality. The redemption, covering the *entire* human race and accomplished in the New Adam, must be realized in freedom for each of the old Adam's children; the assimilation of the redemption is the proper work of each of them. The redemption thus becomes a work of human freedom and personal volition. Thus, in Holy Scripture, the testimony concerning the accomplished redemption links its realization with this volition: "he hath made him to be [the victim of] sin for us, who knew no sin; that we might be made the righteousness of God in him" (2 Cor. 5:21). Christ "died for all, that they which live should not henceforth live unto themselves, but unto him which died for them, and rose again" (5:15; cf. John 3:16). Thus, the redemption is *given* not as a compulsory or automatic act, but under the condition that it be received by faith and assimilated in freedom.

The redemption thus consists in the self-identification of the sinless New Adam with the sinful old Adam and in the New Adam's living-out the life of the old Adam with its sinfulness. This identification realizes the true unity of the two centers of man's nature; by a free act of His will Christ received into His sinless humanity the sinful humanity, centered in Adam. In virtue of this assimilation or identification, He presented Himself before God as one who bore upon Himself the sin of the entire old Adam; He presented Himself before God as sinful man and even as man bearing universal sin. This sin — which He took upon Himself not only ideally but also really, although He livingly experienced it in a sinless manner — became His burden, and it was now He who answered to God for human sin. He, the beloved Son in whom the Father was well pleased, was burdened with God's entire wrath directed at sin, which He bore: "it pleased the LORD to bruise him; he hath put him to grief" (Isa. 53:10). "To bear sin" is not just to attribute it to oneself ideally, while remaining apart from it; it is to experience its burden really, to suffer it to the end, to live it. God is not deceived, and He does not tolerate fakery. That is why, before the tribunal of God's Truth, redemption cannot be a mere appearance. Sin is just as real as the world and man, insofar as it is their state. To be sure, sin is not created by God; it is a product of creaturely freedom. But this freedom, in all its self-definitions, is real with all the reality of this world and of man; therefore, the sin that envelops the world and man is real. The difference is that the world and man, since they are created by God, are indestructible, whereas sin, which is a product of creaturely freedom, is destructible and must be destroyed. It must be lived-out and overcome, which is precisely what constitutes redemption.

Come down from heaven and sent into the world by the Father, the Son of God becomes, under the burden of the sin of the world, distant from the Father, who implacably commands Him to drink to the bottom the cup of His wrath directed at sin; and finally the Father abandons Him under this burden. This attests to the *authenticity* of the self-identification of the New Adam with the old Adam, which became objectively possible only in virtue of the Incarnation. "The Word was made flesh" (John 1:14), but this flesh is already sinful flesh, which, although it is free of *personal* sin in Him in virtue of His sinlessness, nevertheless remains in its sin. Through His humanity this sinful flesh becomes also His flesh. And in taking upon Himself the sin of the world, the Righteous One is equated, in the eyes of God, with sinners. He distances Himself from holiness in order to enter into sin, and He submerges Himself into this night of sin, the night of Gethsemane, into the sorrow unto death. The heart is dumbfounded by this sacrificial, salvific love, and the mind is stupefied by this mystery: suffering for the sins of the world as for His own, the God-Man takes sin upon Himself. How should one conceive this suffering, this assimilation of sins by the Logos? Can the God-Man, the "only one without sin," suffer from human sin? Can He, God, be abandoned by God? Can He die? However, this is precisely what constitutes the immediate goal of the coming into the world of the Logos, of His Incarnation. "Now is my soul troubled; and what shall I say? Father, save me from this hour: but for this cause came I unto this hour" (John 12:27).

If in itself the Incarnation is already the kenosis of Divinity, then Christ's redemptive sacrifice — His taking upon Himself of human sin and His suffering to the end the entire force of this sin as God's wrath and the distancing from God, where He even experiences an implacable and violent death as a capital punishment, as it were, for the sins of the world — represents the extreme limit to this general kenosis: "for this cause came I unto this hour." Divinity is incompatible with sin; it consumes sin with its fire. It becomes possible for the God-Man to take the sin of the world upon Himself only because He humiliates Himself by emptying Himself of His divinity (He "became obedient unto death" [Phil. 2:8]), by concealing His divinity, as it were. While preserving the entire power of its natural being, which can be neither abolished nor diminished, Divinity nevertheless potentializes itself, becomes as if inactive in the God-Man to the point of admitting the approach of sin, to the point of consenting, as it were, to the God-Man's taking upon Himself of sin: here too, the human will "follows" the divine. Hypostatizing His two natures, the divine hypostasis in the God-Man realizes in itself, in the redemption, only the *human* hypostasis, as it were, which becomes the subject of sin assimilated from the entire human essence and is burdened by it. In the capacity of the divine hypostasis hypostatizing the divine nature, the Logos possesses this nature bereft of "the kingdom, and the power, and the glory" (Matt. 6:13), as if deprived of its divinity in its kenosis. Here, on the cross, this deprivation of divinity reaches its extreme depth. Having become Christ's Divine-Human I, the Divine I of the Logos manifests itself in Christ Himself as the human I of the New Adam; and in its self-identification with the old Adam, the Divine I of the Logos takes upon itself the sins of the world, while at the same time remaining, of course, unchanged in its Divinity. The feat of redemption, as a sacrifice of love, has thus two aspects in the God-Man: (1) the sacrificial love of God, emptying Himself in His Divinity and, as it were, concealing Himself for Himself "in the form of a servant"; and (2) the sacrificial love of the Man who, while being absolutely free of personal sinfulness, takes upon Himself the sin of the entire world: this is His taking upon Himself by love of the burden of sin not committed by Him and alien to Him; this is the love of the God-Man for His fallen co-man. In the redemptive feat, His humanity becomes that which, in itself, it is not: It becomes sinlessly sinful; this is the love of the cross, symbolized by the intersection of two perpendicular lines.

In His obedience, the Son does in all things the will of the Father who sent Him into the world (see John 17:21, 23), and this will of the Father determines that He redemptively take upon Himself the sin of the world. The Father gives the cup to the Son, condemning Him to the death on the cross. The Father commands Him to overcome His human essence, which trembles before the burden of the world's sin. This agony is revealed, as is His entire life, in His prayer to the Father: "O my Father, if it be possible, let this cup pass from me: nevertheless, not as I will, but as thou wilt" (Matt. 26:39); "if this cup may not pass away from me, except I drink it, thy will be done" (26:42). (This is even more expressive in Mark 14:35-36: "And he went forward a little, and fell on the ground, and prayed that, if it were possible, the hour might pass from him. And he said, Abba, Father, all things are possible unto thee; take away this cup from me: nev-

The Work of Christ

ertheless, not what I will, but what thou wilt"; cf. Luke 22:42.) For the first and only time, it was as if this prayer of the Son was *not* heard, this prayer that rose from His trembling human essence, which had to accept the cross not by divine power but by human freedom. The will of the Father demanded obedience, which was manifested in all the intensity of the inner struggle. *Despite* the voice of the human essence, the New Adam had to subject this essence to the will of God; He had to manifest obedience to the end, and by this obedience to abolish Adam's disobedience.

This side of the redemptive sacrifice opens before us: the kenosis of the Divinity and the agony of the Humanity in the God-Man in connection with accepting the cup. The Father Himself gives it to His beloved Son. The Father Himself is not made incarnate, but it is He who sends the Son into the world; this sending is the sacrificial kenosis of the Father, although it is of course totally different from the kenosis of the Son. Begetting the Son and being well pleased in Him, the Father deprives Himself, as it were, of His Son by the act of sending Him into the world, culminating in His death on the cross. The Son is orphaned, and the Father is alone. The Begetter and the Begotten One abide in unchanging eternity as the mutual being of the Father and the Son. There is the Father who begets and the Son who is begotten. But in His kenosis the Son no longer lives in union with the Father, just as the Father no longer lives in union with the Son; for the Father *sent* the Son into the world, and the Son *was sent* by the Father to the cross. We have here "the Father's crucifying love and the Son's crucified love" (Metropolitan Filaret's audacious expression), and in this sense this is their *co-crucifixion*. But in the human crucifixion of the Son and the divine co-crucifixion of the Father, love itself is co-crucified, the hypostatic love of the Father and of the Son — the Holy Spirit, the joy of love uniting the Son with the Father (as it is said: "through the eternal Spirit [Christ] offered himself without spot to God" [Heb. 9:14]). This joy fades in the night of the Garden of Gethsemane and in the pitch blackness of the ninth hour. The Holy Spirit, who always reposes upon the Son, also appears to abandon Him. The hypostatic love of the Father and of the Son is co-offered in sacrifice for the sin of the world and thus co-participates in the suffering on the cross.[12] This love appears to become inactive in the night of the world. "It was night" (John 13:30), the

---

12. Certain Protestant kenotics (in particular, Gess) put forth the idea that, during the Incarnation, the Holy Spirit stops proceeding "and from the Son" *(filioque)*. This erroneous notion, associated with an erroneous dogma, expresses in a distorted manner the general idea that the Holy Spirit participates in the mystery of the redemption.

night in which the Son of God was crucified and died in order to become "the triumphant power of the cross" (as Metropolitan Filaret says) in the Resurrection. In the redemption we thus see the fullness of the revelation of God-Love in the Holy Trinity: the Lamb of God, sacrificed for the sin of the world; the Father, who receives this sacrifice; and the Holy Spirit, who accomplishes this sacrifice. The Son Himself, made incarnate and human, is the *High Priest*, who enters with His sacrificial blood into the Holy of Holies of the trinitarian Divinity. The sacrifice of the Son presupposes the co-sacrificial love of the entire Holy Trinity: "God so loved the world" (John 3:16), and love has no power without sacrifice.

How did the Redeemer accomplish this taking the sin of the world upon Himself? It has a passive aspect, the force of fact (a sort of *oboedientia passiva*), and an active aspect, the force of act (a sort of *oboedientia activa*). The Lord *suffers* the sorrow and the sins of the world, which remain foreign to Him. He suffers from sinners and experiences their hostility as His personal fate. But at the appointed time, which of course cannot be precisely pinpointed but which from a certain moment becomes perfectly clear, He takes the cross upon Himself. That is, He no longer suffers only from the sins of the world that besiege Him from outside; He now also *inwardly* assimilates these sins by a "compassionate love" (to use Metropolitan Antonii's expression) and by making them His own, as it were, He identifies His sinless human essence with the sinful essence of the old Adam. He, the Light of the world, submerges Himself in the darkness of sin, in the Gethsemane night of sorrow for sin.

This identification is a *voluntary* act of the God-Man, by virtue of which He becomes the Lamb of God who *takes* upon Himself the sin of the world. How this "taking" is accomplished is a mystery of the God-Man, the only one without sin, who makes Himself guilty and responsible for the sins of the world. But in the Gospel narrative we can discern the successive stages of this accomplishment: it is partly disclosed after the Transfiguration; it is attested at the Last Supper in the communion "for the remission of sins" (Matt. 26:28); and it becomes fully evident in the night of Gethsemane, when the Lord's soul became "exceeding sorrowful, even unto death" (Matt. 26:38), and He prayed until "His sweat was as it were great drops of blood falling down to the ground" (Luke 22:44). What was this prayer about? "Abba, Father, all things are possible unto thee; take away this cup from me: nevertheless, not what I will, but what thou wilt" (Mark 14:36). What does this prayer attest to? Aside from its general meaning — that is, aside from the fact that it expresses the agony of Christ's human essence in attestation of the authenticity, and not the docetic illusoriness, of His suffering — this prayer also expresses the *human* notion of *different* possibilities ("all things are possible unto thee"; "if it be possible").

This attests, first of all, to the depth of the kenosis, which in this case is accompanied by the fact that Christ was *ignorant*, so to speak, of the divine design with reference to Himself (just as He did not know the day and hour of the end of the world). In Jesus, the omniscience of the Logos is diminished, because of the kenosis, solely into obedience to the Father's will: "not what I will, but what thou wilt" (Mark 14:36). This also attests to a kenotic distancing from the Father so extreme that it could appear not to be proper to the One who said about Himself, "I and my Father are one" (John 10:30) and "the Son can do nothing of himself, but what he seeth the Father do" (John 5:19; and other texts). Here we have, as it were, a sundering into two of, and an opposition between, the will of the Father and that of the Son. It is the *sin of the world*, weighing upon Him and penetrating His human essence, that created this distance, this sundering, and this tremulous human prayer: "if it be possible." This prayer is for that which, in God's design, is impossible: to be delivered from what, in God's ways, is inevitable, since it is "for this cause" that the Son came into the world. In the prayer at Gethsemane we observe that the divine consciousness has receded deep inside Jesus, as it were, and that in conformity with this seeming fading of the light and the silencing of the voice of the divine essence, there rose the voice of the infirm and suffering human essence: "in the days of his flesh . . . he . . . offered up prayers and supplications with strong crying and tears unto him that was able to save him from death" (Heb. 5:7). (And what can these "days of flesh" signify if not this period of abandonment by God and its consequence: human infirmity?[13] What can they signify if not the days of His devastation, which reaches its peak in the night of Gethsemane and the suffering of Golgotha?)

But what does this prayer that the cup might pass from Him signify (Matt. 26:39, 42; Mark 14:36; Luke 22:42), this prayer offered "unto him that was able to save him from death" (Heb. 5:7)? This prayer attests that the willing acceptance of human sin has already been *accomplished* in the God-Man, and that this sin has been livingly experienced in all its force. This acceptance was included in God's plan for the world even before the world was created: "for this cause came I unto this hour" (John 12:27). But it is now the hour of the accomplishment of this acceptance, and the

---

13. Does not the Lord Himself say to His disciples: "the spirit indeed is willing, but the flesh is weak" (Matt. 26:41)?

The Lamb of God

black cloud of sin that enveloped the only one without sin was so dark that it covered the heavens and separated Him from the Father. The breath of sin was so deadly that its victim, the human essence, trembled convulsively in its exertion to liberate itself from this breath — "let this cup pass from me." This was not the will *against* the acceptance of sin; rather, this was the inevitable resistance of sinlessness to sin. Feeling the approach of spiritual death carried by this sin that distances one from God, the infirm and suffering human essence, "with strong crying and tears," calls "unto him that was able to save him from death" (Heb. 5:7), that is, from the death of sin, spiritual death. He "was heard for his piety" (5:7 [the King James Version has been modified to conform with the Russian Bible]), and an angel was sent to Him, "strengthening him" (Luke 22:43), when "being in agony he prayed more earnestly" (22:44). Help came from heaven, and the agony was resolved in *victory*. This is attested by the further events of this night and of the following day, when the tempter, through the Jews, makes his final and fruitless satanic attempt to revive the agony: "if thou be the Son of God, come down from the cross" (Matt. 27:40). But this attempt fails.

Did the Gethsemane agony have as its object not only the spiritual death, but also inexorable bodily death? There are no grounds to deny that voluntary acceptance of the bodily death was an element of the Gethsemane agony. But there are also no grounds to assert that it was the sole or even the main content of this agony, for in His prayer the Lord speaks in general of the cup (and earlier of the "baptism"), and not only of death. Even though this prayer can include death, its scope is greater than that. According to Metropolitan Antonii's excellent intuition in this matter (as well as according to the view of his predecessor, Metropolitan Filaret[14]), the universal human sin that weighed on Jesus and enveloped Him in its deadly breath was received by means of the cup and the "baptism," by compassionate love and by virtue of self-identification. Having taken sin upon Himself, the only begotten and beloved Son also took upon Himself God's anger at sin, God's hostility, and this led to a separation, as it were, with the Father. The torment of the only one without sin is caused by sin that became His own sin, as it were, having infected the Creator Himself through His creation. The burden was so heavy that, beneath it, His God-abandoned human essence suffered and became infirm. But only such suffering could overcome the power of sin; this was the price at which the

---

14. "The cup that His Father gives Him is the cup of all the impieties committed by us" (Filaret, *Orations and Discourses*, 1.150-51).

New Adam redeemed the disobedience of the old Adam. It would therefore be one-sided and incorrect not to include the night of Gethsemane in the redemptive sacrifice, this night in which the voluntary acceptance of the torment of the cross was accomplished. It would be incorrect to limit the power of this sacrifice to the Golgotha torment and the passion; it would also be incorrect to deny or to diminish the salvific power of the Golgotha torment and of the passion (which, among Western thinkers, Abelard and Socinus are inclined to do, as does the Russian theologian Metropolitan Antonii). But it is also necessary to forcefully affirm (as Metropolitan Antonii does) the salvific significance of the night of Gethsemane, which forms an indivisible whole with the day of Golgotha.

What is concealed in the darkness of the Gethsemane night? It is the love and only the love of the trinitarian God for the fallen creation: the love of the Son, suffering beneath the weight of sin and the anger of the Father that burdens Him because of this sin; the love of the Father, giving this cup of death to the beloved Son; and the love of the Holy Spirit, accomplishing this sacrifice of the God-Man's love for His fellow human beings, this sacrifice of the God-Man, who willingly grafts onto His sinless, immaculate human essence all the toxins of all the sins committed by humanity in order to weaken them and to blunt the sting of sin with His sufferings. In the night of Gethsemane, Christ suffered and fully lived out all the sins of all humanity and of every human being committed in the present, in the past, and in the future: That is the sweet and dread axiom of our faith. The sins of the essence of the old Adam are defeated and defanged in the essence of the New Adam; God's anger weighed upon them and was calmed. God's justice received satisfaction, the "ransom" was paid, and the reconciliation was accomplished — first in anticipation at Gethsemane, and then the "manuscript" of our sins was totally torn apart on the cross.

How was this exhaustive living-out of universal human sin possible in an individual human life, in a limited and even brief period of time? Here it is insufficient to refer to the fact that the Redeemer was not only man but also God and thus to the fact that upon the balance of justice there falls with its immeasurable weight not only His humanity with its sufferings but also His Divinity. The reverse is rather true: The Divinity in Christ is diminished to such a degree that it is left to His humanity to take upon itself and, in the state of forsakenness by God, to live out to the end the entire power, darkness, and torment of the world's sin: Christ is the Lamb of God who *takes* upon Himself the sin of the world. What does this "taking" mean? Clearly, it should not be understood as the empirical experiencing of all sins that have already been committed and that have not yet been committed in the course of our entire aeon, from the fall of Adam to the Last Judgment. It is a question here not of extensive or empirical experiencing but of some intensive quantity, which is and can be a real *equivalent* of the extensive quantity. This experiencing and this suffering include and concentrate in themselves the power of every sin and the power of all sins as a whole, in their integral. Clearly, it is a question here of a *special* form of the supernatural knowledge and the supernatural experiencing of universal human sinfulness on the part of the New Adam. In Him, every human being can find himself and his sin, as well as the power to be redeemed from it, if, by his freedom, through his essence of the old Adam, he desires to be included in this redemption, "to believe and be saved." The Creator alone knows and measures all the depths and all the possibilities of sin that creation can commit in its creaturely freedom — and He takes them upon Himself. In His supernatural knowledge and co-experiencing, the God-Man made the sin of the integral Adam *His own,* by suffering this sin to the end.

Is this possible? Is this conceivable? It is possible only for the One who, free of sin, was strengthened not only by the help of grace but also by union — without separation and without confusion — with the divine essence, and who had the Divine Logos as His hypostasis. This strengthening was not an external coercion upon the human nature (a *deus ex machina*), for His taking of sin upon Himself was accomplished in the depths of His human essence with the total preservation of creaturely freedom, which subjected itself to God's will. What happened was that the power of this humanity was immeasurably augmented through its deification, which was accomplished even before the definitive *glorification* of Christ. Only the deified humanity of the God-Man had the power to encompass and withstand the real experiencing of all human sin; and the divine essence and the divine will in Him consented fully to this. Thus, *only the God-Man* could take upon Himself all human sin (this would be absolutely impossible for any other human being, regardless of the degree of his holiness). However, this was accomplished by the power of His *human essence,* which accorded in all things with the divine essence: The New Adam in Christ, having His hypostasis in the eternal Logos, took upon Himself and experienced to the end the agony of the Gethsemane night; and consenting, His Divinity was silent, but His humanity was devastated by the suffering.

His taking upon Himself of all human sin was not accomplished in empirical multiplicity but, in its intensity and fullness, was equivalent to this multiplicity. This equivalence does not diminish the concreteness and the power of His experiencing of the sin. His experiencing of the sin was characterized by a sort of unique divine-human temporal intensity, thanks to which all the epochs with their sins could be experienced and redeemed in a few brief hours. In virtue of this concrete equivalence, there was no personal or historic sin that was not experienced and fully suffered by the God-Man as His own. This capacity for concentrated, intense experiencing manifests the depth of the God-Man's original human nature, unweakened by sin. It must be understood as the supreme capacity, although one that is still naturally human, as a capacity that is immeasurably intensified by the inspiration of Divinity living in it. Neither by thought nor by imagination can we come to a more precise understanding of this Gethsemane sorrow "unto death," of this bitterness of the poisoned cup of sin that the Son of Man drank to the bottom. But everyone who approaches Him with faith, love, and repentance will recognize and find in this sorrow his own sin experienced and redeemed by the sufferings of the God-Man.

There arises here a new question, even more vertiginous: Does this intense, so to speak *qualitative* assumption of quantity, this assimilation of all the sins of the present and of the future, correspond to a distinct, particular experiencing of the empirical sins that have already been committed in the past or that are yet to be committed in the future? In other words, does the redemption *continue* in time after having once been accomplished supratemporally and for all times on the cross? One cannot simply ignore this question, since the foundation for an affirmative answer is given in the Gospel image of the Last Judgment, where Christ takes His self-identification with the whole of humanity to the extreme. But in this case how should one understand this empirical and as if new burdening of Christ with our sins? There is nothing *ontologically* new here, because these sins, assumed and redeemed supratemporally, are in their entirety accomplished in an equivalent manner, *empirically,* in time, in which the content of the supratemporal is thus disclosed: unity in multiplicity and vice versa. We can dogmatically understand this, first of all, by analogy with the Church year, in which the various events of Christ's life — events that occurred just once in time and seemed to disappear in it, but that actually have a supratemporal significance — are "commemorated" (i.e., really take place).[15] Likewise, the redemptive sacrifice, accom-

---

15. This was already discussed in my essay "The Holy Grail." [See n. 9 above. — Trans.]

plished just once for eternity, is being accomplished empirically, so to speak, in the repeated liturgies. Therefore, the man who sins really tears open anew the bloody wounds of Christ, inflicted once on Golgotha; and this man receives remission of sins from Christ if he turns to Him for this remission (in baptism and in penitence). This extends also to the pre-Christian past, not empirically, because of the irreversibility of time, but in virtue of the unity and connectedness of the universal human life, as a result of which the past lives in the present and in the future. Beyond these general contours, however, the human eye can discern nothing in the mysterious darkness of the Gethsemane night.

The sin of the world, taken upon Himself as His own by the God-Man, was fully suffered by Him in the night of Gethsemane as, above all, something *alien*, horrible, and repugnant, which by its very approach caused inexpressible torment in the holy soul of the only one without sin. For God's love of man it was insufficient for God to become incarnate by assuming the human essence; this essence made it possible for Him to take upon Himself, with and through it, human sin and thus all the evil of the world. The tempter, who had once approached Him through His human essence in the wilderness but was defeated, had departed from Him only "for a season" (Luke 4:13). But now, thanks to the sin willingly taken upon Himself by Christ, the tempter approaches Him fully armed, as one having power over Him, although here he is again in error and is once again defeated: "the prince of this world cometh, and hath nothing in me" (John 14:30), nothing with which to accuse the God-Man and nothing with which to defeat Him. But he does have something with which to torment Him: his obedient instruments, whom he did not have then, in the wilderness. The very acceptance of the sin by the Sinless One was a suffering for Him; this identification of His humanity with the old Adam was accomplished at the cost of the cruelest torments for compassionate, self-renouncing, merciful love. But besides the acceptance of the sin, there was also the sin itself, which draws God's anger and which receives punishment as its inevitable consequence. This anger weighed on the God-Man, together with the sin He had taken upon Himself: see Isa. 53:4-8, 10. Christ endured the punishment for our sin. This punishment, just like the taking upon Himself of the sin, represented the *equivalent* of the punishment that would have been proper to humanity: the torments of hell. Certain commentators (especially among the Reformed) go so far as to assert that Christ suffered the genuine torments of hell *instead of* man. Such an assertion is, of course, erroneous. The torments of hell include not only the full suffering of sin through the punishment for it in the capacity of an inevitable consequence but also the state of the sin-corrupted soul of the sinner with its sinful passions, which do not find satisfaction, and with its powerlessness to achieve the good, a powerlessness that itself is a source of suffering. This is God's consuming love and, incapable of answering it, the ardent but impotent love for God; it is a fire in which the sinner burns and in which his sin is consumed to the point where he is totally reshaped in the purifying fire. This fire is not immeasurable, but has its measure, just as the immeasurable suffering of the Son of God had its human measure. Although the God-Man fully suffered the sins of the world, He Himself did not experience the suffering of *sinners*, for He is the only one without sin, and in this sense the torments of hell are inapplicable to Him. To be sure, in contrast to sinners, He endured personally, besides the sufferings due to sin, also the suffering due to the fact that He had taken sin upon Himself, but this is something wholly other than, even opposite to, the torments of sinners. Christ suffered here from the approach of the sin that was not proper to Him, while sinners are capable of suffering from the voluntary acceptance of sin and from the corruption resulting from it, as well as from the loss of the possibility of sinning beyond the limits of earthly life.

Christ's taking of sin upon Himself would have been docetic if it were not accompanied by all its consequences, that is, by God's anger and by His abandonment of Christ. God is merciful to the sinner, but hates sin; He forgives the former, but is implacable towards the latter. God's justice is as absolute as His love is limitless. Sin can and must be suffered to the end, rendered impotent, and destroyed; it is an illegitimate product of creaturely freedom and thus does not contain the power of being, for God did not create sin, just as He did not create death. But in this suffering of sin to the end, it is consumed by God's anger, which signifies torment or punishment for the subject or bearer of sin. With regard to sin, God does not have favorites when it comes to the application of His justice. If sin must be suffered to the end, it must be suffered to the end also by the God-Man, who took sin upon Himself. In this sense, it can truly be said that the God-Man fully suffers the *equivalent* of the punishment for universal human sin, that is, the equivalent of the torments of hell, although He suffers them differently from hell. There can be no question here of commensurability with respect to time, for, in general, the "eternal" torments are not measured by time; eternity is a quality, not a quantity. But the brief hours of the Savior's torments encompassed the entire "eternity" of torments with respect to their intensity. These torments were such that they were capable of abolishing and rendering impotent the sin of the world. This is precisely the redemption and the reconciliation with God. Once it is suffered to the end and redeemed, sin is no longer a barrier between God and the sinner; it is as if it does not exist. God's justice received the possibility of pardoning the sinner by a gift of grace *(gratia gratis data)*, and God's anger does not weigh on the sinner if he himself desires to *accept* this gift; for redemption is given for all, but the acceptance of redemption is left to human freedom and volition.

Certain authors (in particular, Socinus) have expressed doubts concerning the very possibility of redemption: How can the sin of one individual be pardoned in virtue of the sufferings experienced by another individual? The very manner in which this question is stated is marred by individualism and juridicism, however, for it considers only isolated individuals to whom the principle of formal justice is applied. However, such a difference between "mine" and "thine" is overcome by love, which knows not only the difference between I and thou but also their *identity*. That which is absurd for abstract justice becomes natural for love. And, above all, Christ is by no means "another" individual for every human being, for the New Adam includes in Himself every human individual. He is the universal man who includes every human being *naturally* in His essence and *compassionately* in His love. The sin He takes upon Himself by virtue of love is no longer a sin alien to Him; it is now His own sin, although not committed but only accepted by Him. Such is the power of *identification* that is manifested in the redemption. Personal in His hypostatic being, the God-Man is united with us in His humanity. That is why, in His salvific love, He can represent the sin of the entire world without violating Divine justice, for He has made this sin His own. Here we have not a *juridical* but an *ontological* relation, which is based on the real unity of the human essence, given its real multiplicity in the multi-unity of hypostatic centers. Christ assumed the *entire* human nature; He therefore can assume, in and through it, the entire sin of *all* human individuals, although personally He did not commit it. Thus, in His holy humanity, as well as in the universal human personality of the New Adam, every adamite can find and realize his justification and reconciliation with God. In virtue of His love, the Savior identifies Himself with every sinner who comes to Him, so that it can be said about each sinner: "not I, but Christ liveth in me" (Gal. 2:20).

By the power of His redemptive sacrifice, Christ the High Priest offers remission of sins to sinners who come to Him with faith, love, and repentance. Universal forgiveness of sins is acquired for all by the redemption, and it must be received with faith (see John 3:16-18). The objective accomplishment of salvation must be realized for every human being by his subjective acceptance (or nonacceptance) of the redemption on the basis of his *free,* personal self-determination (see Mark 16:16). But the subjective nonacceptance of redemption does not abolish its objective force. Through Christ's redemption from sin, every human being acquires in God his eternal, indestructible countenance, even if this countenance remains unmanifested in the particular human persona — in the "likeness." This human countenance, which is in the New Adam, is communicated to him in the sacrament of baptism as a new birth, and it is disclosed anew in the other sacraments of the Church. The connection between this objective principle of life and its subjectivity is established by means of freedom. Grace is a gift, and it is given freely; it does not coerce man (as *insuperabilis et indeclinabilis*), and it does not transform man into a thing, into an *object* of creation. Instead, it convinces, captivates, and regenerates. Salvation *exists* for *every* human being; it is acquired by Christ in His high-priestly ministry, whereas the path of the personal acquisition of salvation can be complex, broken, and contradictory. But in the end, God's love overcomes creaturely sin; and, in the fullness of time, "God will be all in all" (see 1 Cor. 15:28).

Thus, on the part of Divinity, redemption is love's sacrifice of itself for the salvation of the world: the countenance of love is veiled by the countenance of justice, in virtue of which sin must be suffered to the end in order that its bearer may be reconciled with God, even if this Bearer is the only one without sin, the Son of God. Inexorable and impartial, God's justice must be applied equally to all, even if its judgment falls upon God Himself, who, in the God-Man, assumed sin together with the human essence. For if pardon extends only to the sinner but not to the sin, then, in order to make it possible to pardon the sinner, God takes upon Himself the satisfaction of Divine justice for human sin. It is as if God, in the Holy Trinity, speaks once again in the Divine Counsel concerning man: Having created man, changeable in his creatureliness and now fallen, let Us re-create him, taking upon Ourselves the satisfaction of justice. This justice consists in the fact that the Author of man's being takes upon Himself the consequences of His act of creation — that is, the *possibility* of sin that has become a *reality.* God tells His creation: You are created by My hands. You are My work, and you would not exist if I did not will it. And, since I am responsible for you, I take upon Myself the responsibility for your guilt. I forgive you; I return your glory to you, for I take your sin upon Myself; I redeem it with My suffering. O the depths and abundance of God's love! God Himself takes upon Himself the sin of the world that has risen out of precreaturely nonbeing, redeeming it with the corresponding suffering of the God-Man. And the entire Holy Trinity, because of its inseparability, suffers with the Son of God from this sin: the Father suffers as the Just Judge who judges His Son and, in His Son, Himself as the Creator of the world; the Son suffers as the One who is judged and bears the condemnation; and the Holy Spirit suffers as God's love, offering sacrifice and suffering, as the sacrifice of love for the sake of love — of God's love for the world. All of this constitutes *the cup of Gethsemane*. This cup is received on the night of Gethsemane, but Christ continues to drink from it on Golgotha as well, where God's justice that weighs on the Son reaches its maximal power in His forsakenness and solitude on the cross in the face of death: "why hast thou forsaken me?" (Matt. 27:46). It is as if the inseparability of the Holy Trinity is disrupted; the Son is *alone*, and by this astonishing sacrifice of God, the "it is finished" (John 19:30) of the salvation of the world arrives. This is the *divine death*, for "my soul is exceeding sorrowful, even unto death" (Matt. 26:38), spiritual death, which is precisely forsakenness by God. The cup is drunk to the bottom, and the Son commends His Spirit into the Father's hands: The Divine Trinity is reunited into an inseparable unity.

But the redemption could not be limited to the assumption of sin and to spiritual death. It also had to include bodily death, in order to extend to man's *entire* pneumo-corporeal being: "He . . . became obedient unto death, even the death of the cross" (Phil. 2:8). The Redeemer tasted the *fullness* of death, not only spiritual death, the death of sin, and not only bodily death by crucifixion, but also the dual death: spiritual and bodily. And without this fullness, without the acceptance of the pneumo-corporeal death, the salvific "it is finished" would not have been possible.

This results, first of all, from the fullness of "obedience," that is, of *sacrifice*. When and by what could this sacrifice have been concluded, have exhausted itself? Could it have stopped midway? Or, having begun, could it have remained unfinished? Could the Son have accomplished the obedience to the end without giving all that He had to give, that is, life itself, after which there would have remained nothing to give, nothing that was not offered in sacrifice? The fullness of the sacrifice, its end, is only the death, the end of life, of the One who offers the sacrifice. Should the *spiritual* death, accepted by the Son for the sin of the world, have been extended into bad infinity as a night of Gethsemane without dawn? And should He always have been in the process of drinking the cup given to Him by the Father, without ever emptying it? Or could He have returned the cup to the Father without drinking it to the bottom? The torment, however, as an *equivalent* ransom for the sins of the world, should not be conceived as infinite and absolute, for the sin of the creature is limited and finite, and by no means absolute, just as creaturely being itself is relative and finite in all things. Nevertheless, the torment cannot be finite and limited, for the sin was committed against God, the absolute and infinite being (Anselm). Consequently, this torment is finite-infinite, that is, not having an inner end, being "eternal torment" by its ontological nature, it exhausts itself in death, which is thus the integral of bad infinity: The end of the torment arrives as the result of the end of the subject of the torments by His death. As the interruption of life, the death was immanently necessary, since it was implanted in the very nature of *spiritual death*, which, being "eternal," thus could not be temporally infinite (contrary to the usual conception according to which the "eternal torments" are considered to be infinite in time[16]).

Apart from all these considerations, however, the acceptance of *corporeal* death is necessary for the *fullness* of the redemption; without this death, the redemption would be unfinished. By his very essence, man is a pneumo-psycho-corporeal being, and the destructive and deadly power of sin could not be limited to the pneumo-psychical domain but inevitably had to extend also to the psycho-corporeal domain. Having become subject to spiritual death or sin, man also became subject to corporeal death, which was expressed in God's judgment over the fallen Adam: the disorganization of the life of the entire world (the cursing of the earth) and the inevitable death of man. This death is not only an external, coercive fact, not only an intrusion into life. It is also the concluding act of mortal life, the fruit of *mortality*, which extends to the whole course of life. Man starts to die beginning with his birth; the body of death bears a mortal illness, which sooner or later finishes its work, but which even before the end manifests its power in bodily sufferings and illnesses. The body is created

---

16. "Eternal torments," in the sense of temporal and bad infinity, would signify nothing else but ontological capital punishment with submergence in nonbeing. But nothing living, called to being by the Divine creative act, can be annulled in nonbeing. That is why the "eternal torments," in the capacity of the submergence in nonbeing, presuppose for their possibility a point of reference in being; that is, they are dialectically limited by being, whence the further dialectic of death develops. It is precisely the "eternal torments," the ontological dying of the subject, that are submerged in death, in nonbeing, (i.e., are annulled): death dies and life lives. But in order to be overcome, spiritual death or the eternal torments, whose equivalent is the Gethsemane agony, must be submerged in the death of nonbeing on the Golgotha cross, in order that, out of this death, new life may rise. Is it not to this dialectic of death that the obscure prophecy in Revelation 20:14 refers: "And death and hell were cast into the lake of fire. This is the second death"?

by God not as an instrument of suffering, but for the "glory," joy, and fullness of man; it became an instrument of suffering only as a result of sin. Predestined to live with the entire world and to rejoice in it, the body becomes the possibility for all kinds of sufferings and illnesses until the illness of illnesses, death, puts an end, in its integral, to the sufferings and illnesses by annihilating their subject, man. In virtue of the psycho-corporeal unity of man's being, the psychic and corporeal sufferings caused by sin cannot be separated from one another or opposed to one another. Therefore, one who participates in sin spiritually also becomes subject to it corporeally, that is, he becomes mortal. For this reason, the consequences of the Savior's assumption of human sin cannot be limited to the domain of spiritual experiences (the supposition that this is so constitutes the one-sidedness and thus the error of Metropolitan Antonii's theory) but must necessarily extend to corporeal life as well. Sin had to become the source of corporeal sufferings and death, for this power of death is proper to it. Together with sin, the Savior had to accept corporeal sufferings and to taste death, and He did this differently from every human being, who knows only his own sufferings and experiences only his own death. The New Adam, the Redeemer of the *entire* human race, had to experience corporeally the suffering of all human sufferings and to undergo the death of all deaths. He had to receive death, the universal and integral death, in order to defeat it, "trampling down death by death" (as the Paschal hymn says). Clearly, this must be conceived not as a quantitative equivalent but as a qualitative, intensive, integral equivalent, so that the torments experienced by Christ corporeally and in His corporeal death can, in their profundity and power, contain all the possible corporeal sufferings and the death of every human being.[17] This profundity and power of Christ's passion and death are confirmed by their voluntary character: "I lay down my life, that I might take it again. No man taketh it from me, but I lay it down of myself. I have power to lay it down, and I have power to take it again" (John 10:17-18). The Lord voluntarily accepts not only death but also *mortality;* and He accepts not only corporeal torments, but also "tormentability." In His passion and death on the cross, the New Adam descends down to the infirm being of the old Adam.[18]

---

17. This power of the sufferings and death of Christ finds a certain expression in works of art, for example in the *Crucifixion* of Matthias Grünewald.

18. A perplexing question can arise: Insofar as bodily sufferings are associated with personal sin and also with the common or original sin, can they be attributed to the only one without sin, even if only as an equivalent? The answer to this question is given in the

The Lord was born without sin, from the Holy Spirit and the Virgin Mary, and He was therefore free of original sin and from the sicknesses and mortality of the body. By His nature He was not subject to sicknesses and corporeal sufferings, since death had no power over Him. By His divine spirit, He was also the complete master of His body, which was therefore obedient to His commands. True, He admitted natural *infirmity* in the life of His body, an infirmity whose source was the general damaged state of creation because of original sin; for He lived on earth, which was accursed for man's sin, and the paradisiacal fruits of the tree of life, which would have replaced earthly food, did not grow for Him. On the contrary, man now got his "bread" by the sweat of his face (Gen. 3:19), and its quantities were therefore always limited, which led to the possibility of hunger, thirst, and bodily fatigue. Thus, the Lord *shared* with man this difficulty and insecurity of bodily life. He could experience hunger and thirst, fatigue and the need for sleep, although in particular cases He overcame them by the will of His spirit (which is clearly attested in the Gospel by the narrative of the devil's temptation with bread and by the narrative of the meeting with the woman of Samaria, as well as by the repeated mention of nights spent in prayer after days full of labor). He possessed a special power to pass unharmed through mobs of people who desired to strike Him with stones, to push Him off a cliff, and so on. There is no evidence in the Gospels that Jesus was ever subject to human sicknesses. In other words, voluntarily bearing the infirmity of the natural world and of the human essence, Jesus was not subject to sicknesses or the threat of death; mortality remained alien to His humanity.

This mortality could only have been *voluntarily* accepted or admitted by the human essence of the Savior, in whom the prince of this world himself had "nothing" (John 14:30); and the acceptance of mortality is the condition for the acceptance of death. Together with the spiritual acceptance of the sin of the world, at Gethsemane, Christ also bodily accepted the consequences of this sin, on Golgotha. Together with the spiritual torment of sin, Christ also bore its bodily consequences. This acceptance of mortality constitutes the invisible, although essential, condition of His passion, torments, and death on the cross. The words "my soul is exceed-

---

general doctrine according to which the Lord took upon Himself, for the sake of redemption, *all* sins and *all* sin with their weight and, consequently, with their consequences. It is therefore not legitimate to establish a distinction between that which can be included in the bodily suffering and death of Christ and that which must be excluded from them as improper.

ing sorrowful, even unto death" are pronounced not only about spiritual death but also about the mortality of the body. The sorrow that burdened Him due to the sins of the world also made His body accessible to death. Satan — who had in vain sought to kill Him, first with Herod's hands and then by means of the leaders of Israel, in whom he provoked rage at Jesus — now finds obedient instruments who are capable of accomplishing this deed: "When I was daily with you in the temple, ye stretched forth no hands against me: but this is your hour, and the power of darkness" (Luke 22:53). Christ, who previously had "passed by" the enemies who desired His death (John 8:59), now became accessible to them. The sin of the world taken upon Himself by Christ weighed not only on His "soul" but also on His corporeal being. "He hath poured out his soul unto death" (Isa. 53:12). The path from Gethsemane *necessarily* leads to Golgotha; and any attempt to separate or isolate them (such as the one made by Metropolitan Antonii) attests to an insufficient understanding of the connection between sin and death and makes illusory and inauthentic the entire terrible realism of the assumption of sin. Christ's words about the "exodus" at Jerusalem (see Luke 9:31 [Russian Bible]) thus invariably refer to the coming suffering and death.

However, Christ's suffering and death could only have been *coercive*, since they were not natural but voluntarily accepted: these were not sicknesses with natural death as their consequence but torture and murder (mocking, scourging, and crucifixion: see Matt. 20:19). This was the slaughter of the sacrificial lamb. The corporeal suffering and death accepted by the Savior in "obedience" to the Father, since they were an unnatural coercion over His essence, acquire a unique significance because of the power and intensity of the corporeal and spiritual sufferings in themselves (the abandonment and hostility, as well as the mocking, scourging, beatings, and horrible torments) and because of the natural characteristics of the Victim. The body that was being tormented was without spot and free of sicknesses; death was tasted by One who was immortal by His nature, and blood and water together with life poured out of the Most Holy Source of life. The bearing of the sin of the world was spiritually united with the bodily bearing of it in the passion and death on the cross.

The blind children of this world cannot understand the acceptance of death by the Son of God — Son of Man, God and Man, who empties Himself spiritually in the Holy Trinity and corporeally in the death on the cross. But this death is the *crowning* of the entire redemptive feat, its end and the beginning of the new life. The cup of Gethsemane is also the cup of death, the funeral baptism for the new life: "Know ye not, that so many of us as were baptized into Jesus Christ were baptized into his death?" (Rom. 6:3; also 6:4-10). That is why Scripture commonly refers to Christ's death, and in particular to His blood, as a certain substance of the redemptive sacrifice, as the "ransom" or "price" of our salvation. At the Last Supper Christ Himself speaks of the breaking of His body and the shedding of the blood of the New Testament "for the remission of sins" (Matt. 26:28). This is precisely the Golgotha sacrifice, in which is concentrated the entire fullness of the Divine emptying, of the salvific kenosis of the Son of God. The narrow interpretation of this sacrifice is thereby set aside, the interpretation according to which only the corporeal torments and the death on the cross have force here, or according to which, in general, the death is only an idea. This interpretation equates, or at least likens, Christ's death on the cross with the heroic deaths accepted and courageously borne by various men of action for their ideas. But Christ's passion and death are *not similar* to any human death, for His is a voluntary, unnatural death that, together with spiritual death, He took upon Himself because of the sin of the world. This is not just an external event or an evil chance that did not necessarily have to take place; nor was this merely the misfortune of an individual human being. No, it was the very essence, content, and power of the sacrificial life of the God-Man. It was love's sacrifice-offering. Only those who do not recognize God in the Righteous One of Golgotha are capable of blindly comparing this event — which caused the earth to shake, the sun to darken, and the whole universe to tremble — with the death of an individual man for his idea. The uniqueness of the Golgotha death is attested by the whole figure of the Victim, led "like a lamb to slaughter" (see Acts 8:32), humble and unbending, praying for His enemies and responding to mockery with meekness. The image of His sufferings and of His death crowns His preaching, the "prophetic ministry," which is essentially identical with and inseparable from His high-priestly ministry. The image of God crucified and dying on the cross for human beings, of His sufferings and death, is the response of the God of love to all the sufferings of the world that was created by Him — to Job's questioning moans and to all questionings. Into the creation of the world, God placed not only His omnipotence but also the Son's death on the cross. And this was the price He paid for creaturely freedom, for the sins, perversions, and destructions introduced by this freedom in the universe. But it is also by freedom, through His obedience unto death, that the Son restored man. The price for the freedom of man, the image of God in creation, is the death of God: "God so loved the world . . ." (John 3:16).

The Lamb of God

It is appropriate here to re-examine a question touched on above. It is the Son who is made incarnate, suffers, is crucified, and dies, but why does the Gospel speak here precisely of the love of His Father for the world, of the Father who sent His Son into the world, who "gave" the world His Son? Is the Father's participation in the redemption expressed only by this sending of the Son as an act of the Father's will? Or is the sending of the Son an act of sacrificial love for the Father as well, an act of spiritual co-crucifixion? But such is the case even in the case of human fatherhood, which exists in the image of the heavenly fatherhood: in his readiness to sacrifice Isaac, Abraham is an Old Testament image of the Father. And how should we conceive the Proto-Image, the Father, who sent His beloved Son because of His love for the world? Should we not simply and directly acknowledge the spiritual co-participation (i.e., without incarnation) of the Father in the Gethsemane sacrifice, and in this sense (but only in *this* sense) His spiritual co-crucifixion? To be sure, the suffering of the impassible God the Father is other than the suffering of the incarnate Son, but it is not a lesser suffering. In a certain sense, the suffering of the Father is *equivalent* to that of the Son, although this equivalence surpasses the human understanding, cannot be measured by a human measure. But can we conceive the reverse? Can we conceive that the Father sent the Son to suffer while He Himself remained dispassionate, that He sent the Son to suffer without co-suffering with Him?

We can say the same thing, although in another sense, about the Holy Spirit, the hypostatic love of the Father and of the Son, by virtue of which the Incarnation itself was accomplished. This love of the Father always reposed upon the Son, sharing His sufferings (just as His sufferings were shared by the Spirit-bearing Mother of God, standing at the foot of the cross), until it came time for the forsakenness by God, and the Holy Spirit too abandoned Him. The words "my God, why hast thou forsaken me?" (Matt. 27:46) can refer equally to the Father and to the Holy Spirit; or rather they can refer to both, since the Father's love reposed upon the Son in the Holy Spirit. The abandonment of the Son for the salvation of the world is the image of the spiritual co-crucifixion of the Love-Spirit with the Son, of the co-passion of the Third hypostasis, which co-passion, being different from the passion of the Son and that of the Father, cannot fail to be equivalent in its power to their passion. One should not think that, in the Holy Trinity, *only* the Son suffers for the sin of the world, whereas the other hypostases remain indifferent or participate only in an external manner, without co-passion. That would contradict the fundamental trinitarian dogma of God as trihypostatic love, the dogma of the consubstantial and inseparable Trinity, having one life in the three hypostases. The separation of one of the hypostases, the Second, out of the one life of the Holy Trinity and the interhypostatic love would contradict this unity; it would *sunder* the inseparability of the Holy Trinity. To be sure, in conformity with their personal properties, the different hypostases realize their life in the Holy Trinity in different ways — both in eternity and in relation to the world, creatively and providentially. Both the creation of the world and the Divine Providence are accomplished by the entire Holy Trinity, but with different actions of the particular hypostases. Analogously, however, the salvation of the world, its redemption, must also be understood as a joint act of the entire Holy Trinity; in this act, the effective redemption belongs to the Son who is made incarnate, whereas its crowning, its beginning and its end, belongs to the Father and the Holy Spirit. The entire Holy Trinity is spiritually co-crucified with the Son; and the cross of Christ, the tree of life, mysteriously contains "the image of the Holy Trinity" as Divine trihypostatic love. The suffering for the world is, in this sense, not only the kenosis of the Son but also — in another, special sense — the kenosis of the other hypostases, of the entire Holy Trinity.

However, can one speak of the co-passion or co-crucifixion of God with the God-Man for the salvation of the world? Is this not to anthropomorphize God and to disturb the repose of eternity with the intrusion of time and its accomplishments? The answer to this question is already given in the general doctrine of God and the world. The eternal and unchangeable, absolute and self-enclosed, self-sufficient being of God as the Absolute is antinomically united with the co-relative being of God for and with the world, which makes God's life connected with the world, in creation and providence as well as in redemption. And this revelation of the Absolute as the Creator and God includes the path to Golgotha, the suffering of God for and with the world. One cannot isolate this fact, attributing it to the Son alone and leaving the imperturbable repose of absoluteness for the other hypostases. No, the crucifixion of the Son takes place on earth, but it is co-experienced in heaven as well: the entire Holy Trinity is co-crucified with the Son — "God so loved the world." The dogma of the redemption, like all things in Christianity, must be understood in a *trinitarian* manner.[19]

---

19. It is worth remarking that the Divine Eucharist, which is the continuing high-priestly ministry of Christ and the continuing offering of the redemptive sacrifice, is also — according to the meaning of its prayers and operations — an action of the entire Holy Trinity. The majority of the priestly prayers (and this is in the most important part of the liturgy) are addressed to God the Father or to the entire Holy Trinity. In particular, the

Christ says about Himself with immense force, "he that hath seen me hath seen the Father" (John 14:9), and about the Holy Spirit He says, "I will pray the Father, and he shall give you another Comforter" (14:16; cf. 15:26). This is His identification of Himself and His work with the work of the Father and of the Holy Spirit. Here, one should not be afraid of "theopaschism," condemned by the Church in its antitrinitarian aspect. What the Church condemned was precisely the notion that it was not the Son alone who was crucified but the Father in His *fusion* with the Son — the "Son-Father." Such theopaschism represents a nondifferentiation or identification of the hypostases (modalism) and thus a negation of the Holy Trinity. The Church confesses that only the Son, the God-Man Jesus, suffered in the flesh, was crucified on the cross, and tasted death — in virtue of His assumption of the human essence; and in *this* sense neither the hypostasis of the Father nor the hypostasis of the Spirit suffers with Him. However, the nonparticipation of these hypostases in the work of the redemption directly contradicts the Church dogma of the Incarnation; and the rejection of this nonparticipation is by no means theopaschism in the bad sense, condemned and forbidden by the Church. When we speak of the spiritual "co-crucifixion" of the Father and of the Holy Spirit with the Son, we only express the Church doctrine of Their participation in the work of the redemption. God in His eternity, as the "immanent Trinity," is above the world; but the same Holy Trinity, as the Creator, finds itself in an "economic" interrelation with the world. In the redemption, we have the *complex* image of such an interrelation, where the hypostasis of the Son directly unites itself with the world and suffers in it, whereas the other hypostases, who do not have such a direct connection with the world, *spiritually* co-suffer with the Son in virtue of the unity of love.

C. The Death of Christ and His Descent into Hell

Christ's death was as authentic as His humanity: "Forasmuch then as the children are partakers of flesh and blood, he also himself likewise took

blessing of the Sacred Gifts is entirely an invocation addressed to the Father (beginning with the troparion of the third hour): "and make this bread the precious body of Thy Christ, and make what is in this chalice the precious blood of Thy Christ, by transmuting them by Thy Holy Spirit." This is also the case for all the further prayers, including "Our Father." This means that the liturgical mystery, just as the Golgotha sacrifice, is accomplished by the entire Holy Trinity. This is liturgical testimony about the trinitarian character of the redemption.

part of the same; that through death he might destroy him that had the power of death, that is, the devil" (Heb. 2:14). To be sure, this human death could not touch the Divine essence of the very Author of life, for God cannot die. But He could humble Himself and become "obedient unto death, even the death of the cross" (Phil. 2:8). In its Divine aspect, therefore, the death of the God-Man must be understood as *the extreme act of the kenosis of Divinity*, accepted together with the in-humanization. God could empty Himself, as if depotentializing Himself, in the Incarnation. He could humble Himself to the point of appropriating the scale of human life with its limitations, to the point of subjecting Himself to the laws of the infirm life of the body. But at its extreme limit, in order to exhaust all that is human, the kenosis must also include that act of life which consists in its interruption by death; it must include the end of life, or, more precisely, the "dormition" (there is no death as a positive principle of being, for God did not create it). Diminishing Himself to creaturely human life, God empties Himself unto death, through which He enters into the repose of the sabbath (see Heb. 4:3-4, 9-11).[20]

The Divine death is *voluntary* in the capacity of an act of "obedience" and kenosis, in the capacity of a dying in self-emptying or self-limitation. It is an act of the divine-human life, which also includes creaturely death. It *belongs* to the in-humanization, insofar as human life is mortal. But the Lord's death cannot be considered as the *end* of His earthly ministry or as His disincarnation and disinhumanization, as it were. On the contrary, it is the deepest point of His in-humanization. "For verily he took not on him the nature of angels; but he took on him the seed of Abraham. Wherefore in all things it behoved him to be made like unto his brethren" (Heb. 2:16-17). Christ, who in all things except sin was one with humanity, united Himself with humanity in death as well in order to defeat it, "trampling down death by death." Christ's death was the duel of death with Life, which defeated death, having taken into itself death's sting. But in order to accomplish this, Life had to experience all the impotence of creaturely life by tasting death. In this death, all the works of the earthly high-priestly ministry were "finished" (John 19:30), just as in creating the world, God finished His work in six days. And just as God rested from His

---

20. "Moses mysteriously prefigured this day when he said: 'and God blessed the seventh day.' For this is the blessed Sabbath. This is the day of repose when the only begotten Son of God rested from all His works, providentially in His flesh" (from the Matins of Holy Saturday). Cf. the magnificent antithetics of life and death in the praises and canon of Holy Saturday.

creation in order to providentially watch over the created world, so the Son of Man rested, like a corn of wheat in the heart of the earth, in order to save the world by His victory over death.[21]

God voluntarily subjected Himself to natural necessity, not desiring to surpass with His omnipotence the limits of the creaturely essence. After He became man, therefore, He did not negate human death for Himself. This death was not insurmountable and inevitable for Him, as it is for other men. He had the power to give His life by the voluntary feat of love and obedience; and for this reason His life is *sacrificial* and *redemptive*, for He Himself delivered His soul to death (see Isa. 53:12). According to His Divinity, the death of the God-Man was *voluntary* in virtue of His decision not to defend Himself against it by Divine power but rather to permit it and suffer it. In contrast, according to His humanity, His death was a *coercive* death, and it could only be such. Since He was free of original sin, Jesus was also free of death according to God's judgment, just as He was free of the rupture of life that was caused by sin and that leads to death by an inner necessity. In other words, His life was, in itself, not mortal, and therefore it was not subject to natural death. However, in living one life with mortal humankind, in the mortal world, Jesus was not protected against coercive death unless He wished to protect Himself against it in a divine manner, with "more than twelve legions of angels" (Matt. 26:53); but that did not, and could not, take place. But just as Adam's humanity before the Fall, Christ's humanity did not yet have the positive force of immortality. Given this situation, Jesus' death became inevitable, as a result of the hostility toward Him inspired by the prince of this world. But this coercive and in this sense unnatural death, which took place *in spite of* the fullness of life in Him, thus became more agonizing than any natural death. It became the death of all deaths. In it, Christ tasted not only His own death but also *mortality* itself. He died with all humankind; His death included every human death, and it was equivalent to all the deaths in humankind. Christ's death was universal and universally human, just as His sufferings, psychic and corporeal, dynamically included all human suffering. Herein lies the salvific and resurrect-

21. In this part of the present chapter, we need to consider once again, now in the light of the doctrine of Christ's high-priestly ministry, a number of questions that we had already touched upon in another connection, with reference to the doctrine of Christ's divine-human consciousness of self (at the end of the previous chapter). For this reason, certain repetitions are inevitable, but they are justified because the theological problems examined in the two chapters, as well as the points of view from which they are examined, are completely different.

The Work of Christ

ing power of Christ's death, as the victory over death, as the "death for every man" (Heb. 2:9).

In its consummation, Christ's death was similar to the death of every man. This death of every man consists in the disintegration of the complex human structure: the spirit together with the soul, losing the power to possess the body, is separated from it; and the body once again becomes dust and returns into the earth (see Gen. 3:19; Eccles. 12:7). In death, the line of demarcation passes where the human soul is united with the body and, through it, with the world; it does not pass where the soul is united with the spirit, which comes from God. The spirit does not die, although it loses the possibility of living the full human life in the body. The spirit finds itself in a state unnatural for it: that of the fleshless spirits, for whom, on the contrary, life in the body is not natural. The human spirit is not deprived of the possibility of continuing its life; it now receives revelations only from the spiritual world, not from the natural world. But here the spirit is not separated from the soul, which remains in the spirit as the potency of creaturely corporeal life. The soul borrows the power of life from the spirit, but it also contains the principle of death as the consequence of sin. In itself, the soul, as the animal principle, does not possess immortality. It receives immortality only in virtue of its connection with the spirit, which connection determines human individuality: In intelligent creation there is neither spirit independent of the creaturely soul (which is true for both the angelic world and the human world, for only God is a pure spirit) nor intelligent soul separated from spirit (for such a soul is proper only to animals). Although it is united with spirit, after death the soul becomes a mere potency of itself, for it is separated from natural life, its proper element. It becomes petrified, as it were, in the form that it assimilated for itself during life, and it remains in this state of potentiality until resurrection. By the form of its being, however, the soul also binds and determines the spirit, burdening the spirit or, on the contrary, leaving it free for its proper spiritual being. Death therefore contains a special experience of life, although in a state of unnatural disincarnation, an experience that is necessary, essential, and salvific for the life of sinful man. Death is the entry into the spiritual world. It is not only a punishment but also God's blessing on fallen humanity, for the afterlife of the soul is both initiation and catharsis, the mysterious night of life in which the soul matures for the immortal day. But the threshold to the afterlife of the soul is, properly speaking, death as dying, which Christ knew. Christ's death was accomplished when He "yielded up the ghost" (Matt. 27:50; cf. Mark 15:37; John 19:30), crying "with a loud voice . . . Fa-

The Lamb of God

ther, into thy hands I commend my spirit" (Luke 23:46; cf. Ps. 31:5). This attests precisely to the separation of the spirit and the body, which is then buried in the earth, since it has lost life and been transformed into earth — "returned into the earth."

However, this does not exhaust the testimony about Christ's death. At the Last Supper, He Himself speaks to His disciples of His death, referring to it as the breaking of His body and the shedding of His blood. Scripture more than once describes his death as the shedding of blood (this is done expressly in the Epistle to the Hebrews). The soul of animals is in the blood (see Lev. 17:11); this is the principle of corporeal life, and the shedding of blood is death in the capacity of the abandonment of the body by the soul. This particular significance of the shedding of blood in Christ's death is noted in John 19:34; here we see the indication that the spirit with the soul is separated from the body in Christ's death. We find a second indication in Acts 2:31: "His soul was not left in hell." In Christ's death, the Divine essence was *not separated* from the human essence, which is expressed in the uninterrupted union of the Divine spirit with the human soul.

After His death, the Lord entered the afterlife existence; this existence lasted for the mysterious period of "three days," the period of the fullness of death experienced by Christ. According to the testimony of Scripture, in the state of death, Christ's soul — abiding of course in inseparable union with the Divine Spirit — descended into hell (1 Pet. 3:18-19: "in prison"; *descendit ad inferna,* according to the Apostolic Creed). Hell is the "place" of the afterlife existence of all human souls before Christ, both in the Old Testament and in paganism. The so-called "preaching in hell," in which the Church believes, is the *appearance* of Christ to those who in earthly life could not see and know Him.[22] There is no justification to limit this appearance of Christ solely to the *limbus patrum* (that is, to the Old Testament saints), as Catholic theology does. One should rather extend the power of this preaching to all times and to all those who in earthly life did not and could not know Christ but met Him beyond the grave; for, even though they occurred in time, all the events of Christ's life have an omnitemporal, abiding significance. The "preaching in hell" is a symbolic designation of that mysterious abiding of Christ beyond our visible world (in the world "beyond the grave"), which constitutes the aspect

---

22. According to the Orthodox doctrine, St. John the Baptist is the Forerunner of Christ even beyond the grave: "You announced, also to those in hell, God who appeared in the flesh and who took upon Himself the sin of the world" (troparion).

of His salvific work and ministry that is unknown to us in this life. Being experientially inaccessible to us, this abiding is communicated to us by revelation in symbolically mythological images of "the descent into hell." In the present context this abiding must be understood as the afterlife state of Christ at the time of His death, a state that represents His continuing *high-priestly* ministry (not His *royal* ministry, as is commonly thought). His redemptive sacrifice thus manifests all its power not only in His life but also in His death, in His afterlife state.[23] Here too, the Son of God does not cease being the Son of Man, the God-Man: death does not separate the essences. His *ministry* continues beyond death in the afterlife world over the course of a definite period of time: three days (corresponding, perhaps, to the three years of His earthly ministry). In the afterlife state too, Christ preserves the inseparable and inconfusable union of the two natures in one divine hypostasis, in conformity with the testimony of the Church: "In the grave by Your flesh, in hell by Your soul like God, in paradise with the thief, and on the throne, You, O Christ, are with the Father and the Spirit" (from an Easter hymn). This hymn does not separate Christ's humanity from His divinity. Christ's abiding in "hell," that is, in the afterlife state, implies different possibilities for the souls of the deceased: the possibility of hell and the possibility of paradise, depending on the spiritual state of the deceased. That is why the thief, who descends into hell (sheol) together with Christ, abides there as if in "paradise," having been delivered from his sins on the cross.

What was Christ's abiding in the grave? Christ tasted true death, and His dead body was buried in the grave, like that of every deceased. However, both the Old Testament and the New Testament attest that this body was not touched by corruption, in clear contrast to every human death, which is accompanied by corruption. Does this not diminish the reality of His death? Could it be that what we call His death was only a lethargy resembling death, a cataleptic state? Was Christ's death death? Yes, it was, and fully so. This follows from the fact that His soul was separated from His body and descended into hell. This does not happen in the case of deathlike lethargy or catalepsy. Despite a temporary loss of consciousness, on this side of being the soul with its subconscious depths remains united with the body, which therefore does not decompose, although the soul is in a state of passivity resembling sleep. The incorruptibility of Christ's

---

23. "You descended to earth in order to save Adam, but You did not find him on earth; and so You descended to hell in order to search for him" (Praise at the Matins of Holy Saturday).

body does not alter the reality of His death, although it does attest to His death's unique character. This uniqueness is expressed, first of all, in the fact that Christ's death, despite all its authenticity and fullness, was not accompanied and could not be accompanied by the definitive separation between the Divine Spirit and Christ's body (although the soul could no longer be the intermediary).

The spirit in man communicates with the body *not* without mediation but through the intermediary of the soul, which is directed at the body and at the spirit: the soul is the active principle of the body and the receptacle of the spirit. The soul transmits the energy of the spirit to the body, and the spirit masters the body by means of the soul to the extent the soul itself is obedient to the commands of the spirit. Through the soul, the spirit establishes forever its connection with the body, at least with some grain of the body, this grain being an initial atom in the natural world (however more precisely we might define it). But this connection can be of varying power, which is revealed only in resurrection; for this reason death itself, in relation to the separation of spirit and body, has, so to speak, a varying intensity and fullness. A person with a developed spiritual life retains, even in death, a connection with his individual body, which remains the special place of his presence, despite the fact that he now abides in the afterlife world, that is, in a state of disincarnation. This is the spirit's actual memory of the body, and vice versa.

When this connection is manifest and palpable, we speak of holy relics (the *Trebnik* [*Book of Needs*] calls the bodies of all the deceased "relics").[24] However, the holy relics are not characterized by physical incorruptibility, at least as a general rule; even the so-called incorruptible relics are subject – though only slowly and partially – to decomposition in obedience to the law of the human essence. In contrast, the Savior's body, totally sanctified and deified by the Divine Spirit, preserved an immediate connection with Him even after it was separated from His soul in death; in this sense His body is the absolute Relic, and the foundation of all the holy relics is the Lord in the grave. In contradistinction to all the other holy relics, which are relatively "incorruptible," the Savior's dead body did not "know corruption" but remained truly incorruptible; death was powerless to touch with destruction the most pure body.

This takes us back, however, to the question of whether Christ's death was authentic, whether it was similar to every human death if it was so essentially different in this corporeal incorruptibility. This difference

---

24. See my essay "On Holy Relics" (in manuscript).

has its own particular basis, which is not annulled by the authenticity of the death. For Christ, His death was not an inner necessity implanted in a mortal life, for His life was by no means mortal, even as Adam's life before the Fall was not mortal, although it was not yet actually immortal, just like the Savior's human essence before the Resurrection. Death, expressed in decomposition and the return to the earth (the reverse path to that of man's creation), corresponds precisely to man's *mortality*, which originated under the influence of the deadly principle of sin. But Christ's body could not follow to the end this reverse path of the return of man to the earth, despite the authenticity of its separation from the spirit in His death. This was because Christ's *natural* humanity was not mortal, and His death was *voluntary* and, in a certain sense, *unnatural*, since it was murder by crucifixion. For this reason, His death was limited in its action; it could not fully accomplish its work, and even in the grave His body remained uncorrupted and in union with the spirit. His body did not become earth returned to the earth; it remained the incorruptible body of Christ.[25] Thus, even though it was an authentic death, the death of the only one without sin was nevertheless unique of its kind, just as His holiness was unique. Here we already see the beginning of the reverse movement, the beginning of the victory over death. Nevertheless, Christ's three-day abiding in the grave is still a continuing sacrifice that He, as High Priest, offers for the sin of the world.

D. The Glorification of Christ

1. The Resurrection of Christ

Christ's Resurrection must also be understood in relation to His high-priestly ministry. Prior to the passion, Christ speaks of His glorification: "Now is the Son of man glorified" (John 13:31). But in the high-priestly prayer He prays to the Father to glorify Him with the glory He had before the creation of the world; that is, He prays for *the end of the kenosis*, since this has already brought forth its fruits of salvation. Between the passion

---

25. The Church believes that, in virtue of the incorruptibility of Christ's body, the body of the Most Holy Mother of God also remained incorruptible in Her Dormition until She was raised from the dead. This was because Her body, being the receptacle of Divinity, was sanctified by the Divine Maternity and shared the properties of Christ's body, including incorruptibility.

and the glorification a cause-and-effect (or condition-and-effect) relationship is established: The glorification of the God-Man by divine glory becomes possible in virtue of His accomplished humiliation. This relationship is firmly established also in Philippians 2:9-11, which first speaks of the humiliation of the Lord in His in-humanization and His obedience unto the death of the cross, and then, as a consequence, of His glorification: "wherefore God also hath highly exalted him, and given him a name which is above every name ... that every tongue should confess that Jesus Christ is Lord, to the glory of God the Father." It should also be remembered that this glory is not *taken* by the Son but is *given* by the Father; the glorification is a work of the Father accomplished upon the Son through the Holy Spirit. The Lamb of God, predestined before the creation of the world to be sacrificed, came into the world "in these last times"; and God "raised him up from the dead, and gave him glory" (1 Pet. 1:20-21). This glorification consists of a series of accomplishments: the Resurrection, the Ascension, the sitting at the right hand of the Father, and, finally, the sending down of the Holy Spirit. Following this, Christ abides in heaven as God, together with His humanity. This is the vision of the first martyr Stephen: "being full of the Holy Spirit, [he] looked up stedfastly into heaven, and saw the glory of God, and Jesus standing on the right hand of God, and said, Behold, I see the heavens opened, and the Son of man standing on the right hand of God" (Acts 7:55-56).

  The Glory of God is Divinity itself, the Divine life in Sophia, the Wisdom of God. The glorification of Christ is, first of all, the cessation of the kenosis and the return of the fullness of the Divine life or the Glory to the Logos, this Glory that He removed from Himself in His "descent from heaven" and salvific kenosis. But this is not a mere abandonment or cessation of the kenosis; rather, it is its crowning, consisting in the deification and divine glorification of Christ's human essence, the "sitting at the right hand of the Father" (i.e., the identification in glory): "I have finished the work which thou gavest me to do. And now, O Father, glorify thou me with thine own self with the glory which I had with thee before the world was" (John 17:4-5), that is, before the hypostatic acceptance of the kenosis, which is essentially linked precisely to the creation. To the state of kenosis corresponds the fact that the Son, who abandoned His natural Divinity, His power or Glory, when He descended from heaven, now receives this Glory anew not by His own power (although He "thought it not robbery to be equal with God" [Phil. 2:6]) but *from* the Father, of course by the Holy Spirit. And just as the humiliation of the Son was in conformity with His humanity, so the degrees of His glorification are in conformity with the measure of the glorification of His humanity. The Son does not glorify Himself in humanity by virtue of His omnipotence; rather, He receives glorification from the Father. Adam's path to the glory of God was interrupted by his fall, in which "all have sinned, and come short of the glory of God" (Rom. 3:23). But the New Adam follows this path by a new obedience, and through Him, God calls us "unto his eternal glory by Christ Jesus" (1 Pet. 5:10).

In Jesus' humanity, sin is totally overcome. It is not only defeated in His earthly life but is nailed to the cross in His death. In Him, "the middle wall of partition" (Eph. 2:14) between God and man has been removed, and a path has been opened to new life in glory, which henceforth can be not only *given*, but also *received* as a worthy gift. Christ's sinless humanity, which had preserved the original purity of the image of God ("natural grace"), was sanctified by union with His Divinity, in the free harmonization of the two wills, Divine and human, in the unity of the hypostatic life of the two natures, inseparable and inconfusable. Accomplished to the end, unto the death on the cross, this harmonization of the two wills in the fulfillment of the Father's will in the God-Man had as its natural consequence the glorification of the God-Man in the two essences, with the perfect deification of Christ's humanity.

The Chalcedonian dogma of the two natures, inseparable and inconfusable, retains its validity with reference to Christ's glorification, which does not signify the absorption or dissolution of His humanity in Divinity. On the contrary, His human nature is preserved even when He sits at the right hand of the Father, but it is deified here to such an extreme degree that it is capable of becoming an inseparable part of the divine life of the God-Man and, in Him, an inseparable part of the life of the Holy Trinity. In heaven too, the Son of God is the Son of Man. This glorification, just like the kenosis and the redemption, is a work of the entire Holy Trinity, a work initiated by the will of the Father, who glorifies the Son, the God-Man, by the Holy Spirit. The reposing of the Spirit upon the Son — in the capacity of the Father's love, pre-eternal in the "immanent" Trinity and accomplishing in the "economic" Trinity — is, properly speaking, the glorification, the Divine life and glory. The separate acts of the glorification of the God-Man are not accomplished by Him upon Himself, self-hypostatically, beginning with the Resurrection. Rather, they are *trinitarian* acts, the action of the consubstantial and indivisible Trinity. The glorification is the crowning and also the consequence of the high-priestly ministry. The Father receives as agreeable the sacrifice of the Son, offered by Him in the name of humanity; and in virtue of this sacrifice, as the High Priest, He ascends with the blood of the sacrifice into the Holy of Holies, into the heart of heaven. Thus, the glorification belongs precisely to the high-priestly ministry; it is not the first act of the "royal ministry" (as is usually thought). The glorification is an action accomplished by God *upon* the God-Man; *it is not the God-Man's self-glorification.* Thus, in one of its aspects, the glorification still refers to the kenosis; it effectively belongs to the high-priestly "ministry," however paradoxical such a combination of notions might appear: kenotic glorification, glory in humiliation.

On the path of the glorification, there first appears the resurrection, the victory over death: "God resurrected Him, having loosed the pains of death: because it was not possible that he should be holden of it" (Acts 2:24 [the King James Version has been modified to conform with the Russian Bible]). It is attested, however, that Christ resurrected Himself from the dead, as He had predicted more than once. There is no contradiction here; on the contrary, one can and must harmonize His resurrection of Himself and His being raised by God. In the first case, we have the very *fact* of the resurrection, irrespective of how it is accomplished, and here it is indicated that the resurrection is the work of Christ Himself, which He accomplishes by His feat. "From that time forth began Jesus to shew unto his disciples, how that he must go unto Jerusalem, and suffer many things of the elders and chief priests and scribes, and be killed, and be resurrected again the third day" (Matt. 16:21 [the King James Version has been modified to conform with the Russian Bible]). In His way of the cross, in His "high-priestly ministry," the God-Man accomplished everything that can and must be accomplished on the part of the human essence in order for it to become worthy of and capable of resurrection and in order for it to become impossible for death to hold Him. However, in His state of humiliation, the Son of God does not raise Himself, for He kenotically removed His divine power from Himself. The Father raises Him by the Holy Spirit (see Rom. 4:24). By the action of His omnipotence — that is, by a new creative act in which the Son participates in the will of the Father by obedience and the Holy Spirit participates by the giving of life — God gives to Christ's soul the power to be united with His body, to awaken Him from His sleep of death; and this is precisely what the resurrection consists in.

Christ's resurrection must therefore also necessarily be understood as His raising, considering this precisely in the context of His kenotic and, in this case, high-priestly ministry, a ministry that does not end with this, although it has acquired new possibilities. But Christ's resurrection could not be accomplished *only as His raising from the dead*. That is, in and of itself, man's creaturely essence — not only in the state to which it was reduced after the Fall but even in the form in which it had been created by God — would not have been capable of encompassing the power of the raising. The human essence would simply have been destroyed, since the raising would have represented a new creation for it, abolishing and replacing the former creation. Before the resurrection to immortal life, man's nature must yet be elevated, not only in the negative sense, through the liberation from sin, but also in the positive sense, through its inner deification. It was on this path of inner deification, accomplished by divine action through human freedom, that the original Adam was placed; his freedom was tested against God's commandment, but he failed. Then the redemption from sin and the participation of human freedom in deification were accomplished through the union of the human nature with the divine nature in the unity of Christ's hypostasis. It was impossible for death to hold Him (see Acts 2:24), not only because the essence of the sinless Righteous One that it ravished did not belong to it, but also because His humanity, sanctified in Him in all its life and in all its being, was deified and acquired the *potency* of actual immortality. It was this actual immortality that was given to His humanity by the power of the divine raising.

Christ's resurrection was a creative action accomplished by the Father through the Holy Spirit upon the God-Man, but it was also the proper work of the Son; in this sense it was a *divine-human* act. The Father glorifies[26] and the Son receives glorification. Before the Fall, Adam had potential immortality *(posse non mori)* and potential glory, which he — and all men because of him — lost as a result of the Fall (see Rom. 3:23). Although by his creation, Adam received the image of God and the glory of God by a gift of the Holy Spirit, this for him was only a preliminary state, which he had to affirm and manifest by his freedom. But he did the opposite in committing the original sin, as a result of which he lost his glory and was deprived of immortality. That is why none of the raisings of the sons of Adam was a resurrection in the sense of a victory over death; Enoch and Elijah did not taste death, but they were not immortal.[27] Immortality, like glory, could not be an act accomplished *upon* man without

---

26. "Christ was raised up from the dead by the glory of the Father" (Rom. 6:4), and that is why "Christ also received us to the glory of God" (15:7).

27. According to one interpretation, accepted by the Eastern Church, they will be those "two witnesses" (Rev. 11:3-7) who will come at the last times and receive death from the beast.

at the same time being an act *in* man himself, who by his freedom spiritually masters his psycho-corporeal being. Christ accomplished this mastery in His humanity. He fully — both in His life and in His death — vanquished the creaturely infirmity of His human essence and offered it as a sacrifice of obedience to the Father's will. Thus, by His high-priestly ministry, by the sacrifice of His life, Christ acquired immortality: He earned and merited it. Nevertheless, it still had to be *given* to Him. Immortality, bestowed upon man not in the mortal but in the immortal or *spiritual* body, can only be an interaction, an act of synergism, between God and man. God bestows immortal life upon man when he becomes capable of and worthy of receiving it; but he is such only in the God-Man. "But now is Christ risen from the dead, and become the firstfruits of them that slept. For since by man came death, by man came also the resurrection of the dead. For as in Adam all die, even so in Christ shall all be made alive" (1 Cor. 15:20-22; cf. Rom. 6:4-9). Resurrection is a new creation of man in which man himself participates; it is the second and concluding act of the creation. Viewed from the divine side, Christ's resurrection is a *raising* in which the Father gives to the Son through the Holy Spirit "life in himself" (John 5:26); for the Son Himself, as the Divine-Human hypostasis, in His kenosis removed from Himself His proper Divine power of raising and receives it only by the will of the Father. Viewed from the human side, or more precisely from the Divine-Human side, it is a *resurrection,* for by His sacrificial, high-priestly ministry Christ gains power over His human essence, gives life to it. His death, together with His afterlife state, the descent into hell, becomes part of this ministry and concludes this sacrifice. His death is the final act of His earthly life, the final sacrifice and the final victory over death: "trampling down death by death." In Christ, no foundation remains for death; its power is exhausted, and He is resurrected from the dead.

The resurrection, as such, is thus not yet "proof of the true God" (to use Vladimir Solovyov's expression), who raises Himself by the power of Divine omnipotence. But it is a necessary event in the life of the God-Man, the worthy and essential conclusion of this life. Just as the divine essence and the human essence were united in Christ without separation and without confusion, so in the resurrection we have the synergism or harmony of the two essences; we have their inseparable and inconfusable, Chalcedonian union or, more generally, the harmonious participation of the Creator and creation, of God and man, in one act of raising-resurrection. St. Augustine said that God could create man without man, but that He cannot save man without man. Modifying this well-known formula, one can say that God could create man for undying life but that He cannot raise fallen man to immortal life without his participation, that is, without his inner victory over death, a victory that is the foundation of immortality.

Christ's resurrection is precisely the *victory* over death, and not merely an awakening from it (Rom. 6:9). His resurrection is not the restoration of mortal life but the elevation to the new immortal life in the spiritual and glorified body. This spiritual body is identical to the earthly body that was not found in the grave, but it is also *not* identical to it, differs from it. The Gospel narratives about the resurrection characterize only negatively the relation between the earthly body and the resurrected body; specifically, these narratives attest, directly or indirectly, that the sepulchre was empty and that there was no body in it.[28] This establishes a certain identity of continuity between the earthly body and the resurrected body of the Lord, but no identity of state can be established. On the contrary, as we can conclude from the Apostle Paul's general doctrine of resurrection, "It is sown a natural body; it is raised a spiritual body. There is a natural body, and there is a spiritual body. And so it is written, The first man Adam was made a living soul [Gen. 2:7]; the last Adam was made a quickening spirit. Howbeit that was not first which is spiritual, but that which is natural; and afterward that which is spiritual" (1 Cor. 15:44-46). Christ's resurrected body was thus no longer earthly but supraearthly: it was a body that could *appear* on earth according to its own volition but without being bound by the laws of earth. Thus, this body was not a *physical* body, although it had not lost the earthly nature, with which it preserved a certain metaempirical connection. In virtue of this connection the Lord abided on earth for forty days after His Resurrection, but His body was glorified.

Aside from the "appearances," Christ's resurrected body remained inaccessible to the disciples and beyond human perception. The Lord Himself rendered His resurrected body accessible to human perception. He returned it, as it were, to this world of sense perception, making it accessible to vision and even to touch: "a spirit hath not flesh and bones, as ye see me have" (Luke 24:39). These words of the Lord attest that the connection between His corporeality and this world was preserved during the forty days from the Resurrection to the Ascension. This was expressed in the possibility of His *appearing* in the flesh, even if this flesh was glorified — a possibility that was excluded after the Ascension. This poses the question of the

---

28. See Matt. 28:6; Mark 16:6; John 20:5-7.

spatiality of His resurrected body. In its appearances, it was necessarily subject to the laws of earthly spatiality, although in some of its properties it differed from earthly bodies (for example, it had the ability to pass through closed doors, to appear to the eyes of the disciples, and to disappear, which in *this* sense indicates a certain immateriality of the resurrected body). The possibility of the appearances of the Resurrected Christ and, in general, His presence within the limits of this world until the Ascension make it necessary to acknowledge that a certain spatiality was proper to the Lord's resurrected body, although this spatiality was *other* than that of the earthly material world (just as, in its own way, the spatiality of the angels is other than that of the material world, although the angels are nevertheless subject to the limits of spatiality). This new spatiality of the resurrected body, unfathomable to us, was nevertheless capable of intersecting our own spatiality at certain points, making possible the appearances of the Resurrected Lord to the disciples. Insofar as it still belonged to this world, we must not conceive the body of the Resurrected Christ as absolutely extracorporeal, because that would mean that it was extramundane — but it becomes such only after the Ascension. Christ still remained in the world, although in a new manner, so that "the descent from heaven" into the world had not ceased even after the Resurrection.

Also, even in the Resurrection, Christ's glorification was not definitive, just as His earthly ministry was not yet exhausted and completed. Both the glorification and the earthly ministry continue after the Resurrection in those mysterious forty days during which the Lord abides on earth. The forty days symbolize the *fullness* of the preparatory work: the forty years Israel spent in the desert before arriving at the Promised Land, the forty days Moses spent on Mount Sinai with his vision of the glory of God and the reception of the law, the forty days Christ spent in the desert before beginning His public ministry, and the forty days He spent on earth after the Resurrection, when He had "not yet ascended" to His Father but was only in the process of ascending "unto my Father, and your Father; and to my God, and your God" (John 20:17). For Him these forty days signify a certain mysterious *ascent,* clearly unfathomable for us in this age, an ascent not only to His Father, but also to God; that is, they signify a divine-human act. This attests that, even with the Resurrection, His divine-human path had not reached its end and that His glorification had therefore not been completed. Consequently, His glorification was not a momentary act, but a prolonged and continuing one. As long as the glorification remained unfinished, so did Christ's earthly ministry.

If His forty-day presence on earth is, for Him, an ascent to the Father, then in its other aspect it represents a new establishment of His connection with the earth, with this world. What we have in mind here is the completion of His prophetic ministry, insofar as He opened His disciples' "understanding, that they might understand the Scriptures" (Luke 24:45), "speaking of the things pertaining to the kingdom of God" (Acts 1:3). He also manifested Himself to His disciples in His resurrected body, thus attesting to the fact that He had preserved His connection with the world, a connection that included the ability to be touched and to partake of food[29] (although the former physical accessibility of His body by means of touch had — as in the case of Mary Magdalene — become impossible). This presence of the Resurrected Christ on earth to conclude His work was the continuation of His sacrificial and high-priestly ministry, as well as of His prophetic ministry, the two ministries being inseparably linked. Christ had not yet received power in heaven and on earth, although this power was included in His glorification, in the same way that the glorification is given to Him together with His passion on the cross: "Now is the Son of man glorified" (John 13:31). It was given, but not yet taken, not yet received, for this reception had to be preceded by a particular path, although no longer that of the ministry of the cross. The Resurrected Christ still had to suffer from the insufficient faith and ardor of His disciples (Matt. 28:17; Mark 16:13; Luke 24:11, 25), overcoming these deficiencies by preaching and by signs. The preaching of the Resurrected Lord is a necessary part of His ministry as a whole. This essentially includes all His *appearances* to the disciples, which were possible only as long as the Lord remained on earth — until the Ascension. He no longer lived on earth in some definite place, as in the days of His earthly life, although He was not yet in heaven. It would be more accurate to say that He abided *above* the earth, while still remaining in the world. The bound of His death and resurrection lay between the world and Him. Although it belonged to this world metaphysically, the *state* of His spiritual body was such that it could not be contained by the world and become accessible to human perception except by the special volition of the Resurrected Christ. Only then did it receive the capability of becoming accessible to human sense per-

---

29. See Luke 24:37-43. This text directly confirms the reality of the connection of Christ's glorified and spiritual body with this world. Being metaempirical, this connection can, by Christ's will, receive actualization — in the Eucharistic transmutation of the bread and wine into the Body and Blood of Christ. See my essay "The Eucharistic Dogma." [This essay is available in an English translation by Boris Jakim in *The Holy Grail and the Eucharist* (Hudson, N.Y., 1997). — Trans.]

ception. Christ's appearances were not just appearances of the spirit, as were, for example, all the angelophanies. Instead, He assures His disciples of the contrary (Luke 24:39). These were *bodily* appearances ("he was seen of above five hundred brethren at once" [1 Cor. 15:6]). His body preserved its individual traits: pierced hands, feet, and sides. The presence of the Resurrected Christ in the world before His Ascension represents a bridge between the present state of the world, where man has a natural body, and the glorified state of the world, after the universal transformation and transfiguration of the creature, where man will have a spiritual body. This presence of Christ was the appearance of the spiritual body on earth, which could bear this body without knowing it. If Christ had left this world immediately after His resurrection, then even the empty sepulchre could not have served to establish that it was precisely the resurrection of the body that had occurred and not a simple departure of Christ from this world with the abolition of the body (although in an extraordinary manner), as is the case with every death. Or is it possible to think that the disappearance of the body (not to mention the invention of the Jews that the body was stolen) signifies that it was "taken up into heaven," which is believed about the body of Moses, on the model of Elijah and Enoch? But this presence of the Resurrected Christ on earth and His appearances to the unraised humanity in the unglorified world were essential for His salvific work, because they concretely demonstrated the ontological identity of this world and the natural unity of man with His resurrected and glorified corporeality, with His spiritual body.

2. The Ascension of Christ

This significance of the Resurrected Christ's forty-day presence on earth — which attests to the accomplished *union* of earth and heaven, of the humiliated creature and the glorified creature — is indirectly disclosed in the distinctive (and antinomic, so to speak) Gospel narrative of the Lord's *final* appearance. The four evangelists conclude their narratives about this forty-day presence in different, and even contradictory, ways. Whereas Mark and Luke (both in his Gospel and in The Acts of the Apostles) end their narratives with Christ's Ascension to heaven and the final dispersion of the disciples, Matthew ends his narrative with Christ's appearance to the disciples and the promise: "I am with you alway, even unto the end of the world" (Matt. 28:20); while John's narrative, with the Lord's final mysterious words that John will "tarry till I come" (John 21:23), takes us up into the heavenly heights and there becomes silent. In any event, John

The Work of Christ

does not include a narrative about the Ascension (although Christ speaks about it in the Last Discourse). This Gospel antinomy, whose two terms are nonetheless equivalent, cannot be explained by referring to the literary schemes and other characteristics of the various Gospels. The antinomy attests that there remains an *identity* between Christ's abiding in the world and His state in the Resurrection and the Ascension. This identity is expressed by the simultaneous affirmation of His abiding in the world and of His Ascension to heaven: Christ is both there and here, both outside the world and in the world. Humankind does not lose Christ even in His Ascension, even as the ascended Christ does not terminate His connection with humankind: "I will not leave you comfortless: I will come to you. Yet a little while, and the world seeth me no more; but ye shall see me" (John 14:18-19). This *unity* of Christ, abiding on earth and sitting at the right hand of the Father, is attested with full clarity in the sacrament of the divine Eucharist, which is the mysterious bridge, living and ceaselessly crossed, between earth and heaven, the connection between the incarnate Christ, descended from heaven, and the Christ who ascended to heaven.[30] The one thing does not exclude the other; the two complement each other in a marvelous and salvific manner. The Christ who sits at the right hand of the Father also abides in the flesh on earth on innumerable altars.

What does Christ's Ascension signify? The Gospels tell about it briefly and symbolically: "he was received up into heaven, and sat on the right hand of God" (Mark 16:19); "he was parted from them, and carried up into heaven" (Luke 24:51). It is described in somewhat greater detail in Acts 1:9-11, where a new feature is added: "a cloud received him out of their sight," with the subsequent appearance of the angels. First of all, there arises a preliminary question analogous to the one we posed concerning the Resurrection: Did Christ raise *Himself* to heaven? That is the usual opinion of those who see here a manifestation of the "royal ministry." Or was He raised by the Father, of course through the Holy Spirit? We have a

---

30. The Church expresses the clear antinomicity of this idea in the kontakion of the Ascension: "Having accomplished providence upon us and having united us on earth with the heavenly, You ascended to heaven, Christ, our God; but You have not departed from us at all, but remain inseparably with us, and You proclaim to those who love You: 'I am with you and no one can do anything against you.'" The fact that Christ has not departed from the world, which this kontakion proclaims, is also proved by very deed, that is, by Christ's appearance after the Ascension to the Apostle Paul, who (and this is the most important thing in this case) speaks of this appearance among several appearances of Christ after the Ascension: "After that, he was seen of James; then of all the apostles. And last of all he was seen of me also . . . the least of the apostles" (1 Cor. 15:7-9).

direct and unambiguous answer in Scripture, in the Apostle Peter's discourse after Pentecost: Jesus was raised "by the right hand of God" (Acts 2:33), that is, by the Father through the Holy Spirit. Thus, we have here the same relation as in the case of the Resurrection: Christ raised Himself, but He was also raised. His Ascension refers also to His glorification by the Father, where His being taken into the cloud expresses the overshadowing by glory, according to the symbolism of both the Old and the New Testament (e.g., in the Transfiguration). That is why the Church sings: "Raise Thyself in glory, Christ, our God" (from the hymn of the Ascension). As the return of the Son to heaven, the Ascension was the work of the Father, who had sent Him into the world. Thus, it still belongs to the *kenosis*, which is still continuing, but which has nearly reached its end. The Ascension is accomplished *upon* the God-Man; His human essence has received the power of ascension from God by a certain act of continuing glorification: "the Father of glory . . . what is the exceeding greatness of his power to us-ward who believe, according to the working of his mighty power, which he wrought in Christ, when he raised him from the dead, and set him at his own right hand in the heavenly places" (Eph. 1:17, 19-20). The Ascension is accomplished not by the proper divine nature of the Logos, not by the omnipotent power of His Divinity, which remains, although in the kenotic self-diminution that is nearing its end. It is accomplished "by the right hand of God."[31] It is not the Divinity of Christ that is subject to Ascension, for Ascension does not exist for His Divinity, since He naturally and pre-eternally abides in heaven in the unity of the Holy Trinity. It is precisely His humanity that is subject to the Ascension, His humanity that finds itself in the most intimate union with the Divinity in the God-Man. As a creature, the humanity is, by itself, not capable of "ascending" to heaven, that is, to Divinity; it can only be raised to heaven. The humanity is the sacrifice that Christ, as the High Priest, offers to the Father. This sacrifice is received by the Father, and "after he had offered one sacrifice for sins, he forever sat down on the right hand of God" (Heb. 10:12 [the King James Version has been modified to conform with the Russian Bible]). He entered "into heaven itself, now to appear in the presence of God for us" (9:24). And if, according to the direct testimony of the Epistle to the Hebrews, Christ enters (ascends to) heaven as the High Priest, His Ascension must be considered to belong to His high-priestly ministry, not His royal ministry. The Ascension and the sitting at the right hand of the

---

31. This idea receives a plastic expression in certain ancient representations of the Ascension, where, by His hand, the Father raises the Son to heaven.

The Work of Christ

Father are one triumphant act of glorification; that which is said about the former pertains *a fortiori* to the latter:[32] Just as the Son was sent from heaven by the Father in kenotic and filial obedience, so He was returned or raised to heaven, and placed at the right hand of the Father by the Father Himself — all this following the order of the christological "subordinationism." From the grave to the Resurrection and from the Resurrection to the Ascension the path is the same: to the Father's glorification of the Son.

But just as the raising of Christ was at the same time His resurrection of Himself, and could not be other, so His Ascension, accomplished by the power of the Father, was also His elevation of Himself. For the Ascension too could not have been accomplished by a unilateral creative act of the divine omnipotence. It was an act of interaction (synergism) between God the Father and the God-Man, who in His humanity had already attained the capacity — and thus the necessity — for the Ascension. In the Gospels, the Ascension is not only a *fact* but also an *act:* "I go to prepare a place for you" (John 14:2; cf. 16:17); "I came forth from the Father, and am come into the world: again, I leave the world, and go to the Father" (16:28); "it is expedient for you that I go away" (16:7); "now come I to thee" (17:13). Just as death could not hold Him, so the world now cannot hold Him; He rises above the world, for "now I am no more in the world" (17:11). There was a time when "I was with them [the disciples] in the world" (17:12), but now "the hour [of glorification] is come" (17:1). This "hour" has not only an external but also an inner character. Christ said, "I have finished the work which thou gavest me to do. And now, O Father, glorify thou me" (17:4-5). This prayer — for the cessation of the kenosis and the return into the bosom of the Father, into the Glory of God — is already the accomplished Ascension in the God-Man Himself. There is an unrestrainable movement here through the death to the Resurrection and through the Resurrection to the Ascension.

The accomplishment of the Father's work on earth makes the Ascension the proper work of the God-Man, who came to earth not to abide there indefinitely but to fulfill a specific mission. After He fulfilled it, it became inwardly necessary and inevitable that He leave the world. Christ returns to the Father voluntarily, and in this the Divine essence and will are united with the human essence and will. The *actively* guiding will in this case can only be the Divine will, in contrast to what we have in the

---

32. Cf. Ephesians 2:6: "[God] hath raised us up together, and made us sit together in heavenly places in Christ Jesus."

passion, where the actively guiding will could only be the human will, with the tacit consent of the Divine will. For the human nature in itself, it is not natural to desire ascension to heaven, although this is perfectly natural for the divine nature. But in Christ the human nature attains such a fullness of deification that it itself becomes capable of desiring that which the divine nature desires. Existing in the world, the creaturely nature desires for itself supracreaturely and supramundane being; it desires divine being. The abyss lying between supracreaturely being and creaturely being, between divine being and human being, between the Proto-Image and the Image, is surmounted in the God-Man. He thereby manifests the will to Ascension; that is, He is not only elevated, but He elevates Himself. The Son of Man ascends to "where he was before" (John 6:62). The God-Man becomes God.

And so, what does Christ's Ascension to heaven (and His sitting at the right hand of the Father, which is identical to the Ascension) signify? Outwardly, the Ascension is characterized by the fact that the Lord solemnly climbed the Mount of Olives together with His disciples, blessed them, commanding them to await the promised descent of the Holy Spirit, and ascended to heaven. The Lord disappeared from the sight of the apostles. Even earlier, however, in the course of the forty days, each time when He appeared, He once again disappeared from their sight. But the Ascension marks a bound here in the sense that, after it, Christ no longer appeared to them (with the exception of the appearance to the Apostle Paul on the road to Damascus). His accomplished Ascension to heaven was specially announced to the apostles by the angels who appeared to them, and these angels also brought to them the promise of a new return of Christ to earth: He "shall so come in like manner as ye have seen him go into heaven" (Acts 1:11). To be sure, the Ascension to heaven is not Christ's departure into the astronomical space of the stars and galaxies, and in general it is not a departure to some other *place,* for "heaven" is not a place, and in any case it is not *another* place in relation to the earth. The Ascension signifies not a physical but a *metaphysical* departure from the world, analogous to Christ's metaphysical descent from heaven to earth, which resulted in His physical presence on the earth. Heaven is divine, supramundane, and supracreaturely being; it is the Holy Trinity itself *in its Glory,* and it is the Divine Sophia. To this, to His Glory, the Son of God who had descended to earth returns. And this return into the bosom of the Holy Trinity also signifies the sitting of Christ at the right hand of the Father; this position at the right hand of the Father preeternally belongs to the Son and is returned to Him in His Ascension.

The Work of Christ

What is the relation of Christ's Ascension to His Incarnation? Since it is His departure from this world into the transcendent, is it not also His disincarnation and dishumanization, the reverse of what took place in His "descent from heaven"? Such an interpretation, however, would abolish the salvific proclamation: "the Word was made flesh" (John 1:14). It would be a blasphemous heresy. The dogma of the Ascension contains precisely the idea that, in ascending to heaven, Christ's glorified human essence entered the very depths of the Holy Trinity: The God-Man occupied His place at the right hand of the Father in all the power not only of His divine nature (which in fact did not leave the bosom of the Father) but also of His human essence, composed of soul and body, of animated and spiritualized corporeality.

But in this case the following question arises: In what sense can the human psycho-corporeal essence be present in heaven, at the right hand of the Father, and what does the expression "at the right hand of the Father [*dextera Patris*]" mean? It goes without saying that "in saying that Christ corporeally occupied His seat at the right hand of God the Father, we do not understand the right side of the Father in a spatial sense. For in what sense can the Unlimited have a spatially right side? . . . By the right side of the Father we mean the glory and honor in which the Son of God, as God and consubstantial with the Father, abides before the ages and in which, having become incarnate after His descent to earth, He occupies His seat corporeally after the glorification of His flesh."[33] This thesis of St. John of Damascus, which expresses the general doctrine of the Church, does not, however, contain an answer to the question that interests us; or, rather, it does not even notice the question (just as it was not noticed by Catholic scholastic theology, medieval or modern). The corporeality of Christ on earth, even after the Resurrection, has its "flesh" and, consequently, its spatiality: "handle me, and see; for a spirit hath not flesh and bones, as ye see me have" (Luke 24:39). It differs from His earthly corporeality before the Resurrection by its state, that is, by a particular fineness. Despite this difference, however, the Lord *appears* to His disciples in a tangible and spatial form. With reference to the resurrected body, one can speak of a spatiality and of a corporeality that differ from our earthly spatiality and corporeality. Nevertheless, the resurrected and glorified body is still an animated *body*, although it is, to use the Apostle Paul's expression, a spiritual body, in contrast to the natural body (1 Cor. 15:44), since it is obedient to and transparent for the spirit. This spiritual body nevertheless remains a *body*; that

---

33. St. John of Damascus, *Brief Exposition of the Orthodox Faith*, book 4, ch. 2, c. 1104.

is, it belongs to our world with its spatiality. But how can this body, even if it is spiritual, abide in the Holy Trinity, "at the right hand of the Father," if God is Spirit and therefore no spatial definitions can be applied to Him? We are confronted here by an antinomy: on the one hand, disincarnation is inconceivable, but on the other hand, there is no place for the body of flesh, even if glorified, in the kingdom of the pure absolute Spirit, which Divinity is. A body can only be spatial, but no spatiality is compatible with spiritual being. If we attempt to evade this aporia by referring to the spirituality of the glorified body, we must remember that even this *spirituality* of the body still does not signify the revocation or total abolition of corporeality and thus of spatiality. It signifies only a special form of its being such as we have in the body of the Resurrected Lord. We arrive at a *contradictio in adjecto*, at a contradictory definition: a spiritual body understood as a *noncorporeal* body, or simply as a *nonbody*. To escape the antinomy in this manner by a logical contradiction is, of course, the worst possible means of overcoming it.[34] Is there any other escape from this impasse?

In the Ascension, the Lord truly departed from the world, but at the same time He preserved His connection with the world. It is precisely in virtue of this connection that the Ascension is not a disincarnation. On the contrary, it is only a *temporary* departure of the Lord from the world, after which He "shall . . . come in like manner as ye have seen him go into heaven" (Acts 1:11); that is, He will once again assume the corporeal human form, while, of course, at the same time remaining at the right hand of the Father.[35] But at the same time the Ascension, as His departure from

---

34. The question of the significance of *dextera Patris*, the sitting at the right hand of the Father, as well as that of the spatiality and in general of the corporeality of the body of the ascended Christ, was discussed in the Reformation in connection with the Eucharistic disputes associated with Luther's theory of the so-called *ubiquitas* of Christ's body. Luther explained the *praesentia realis* in the Eucharistic elements by the fact that the deified and glorified body of Christ receives the divine property of omnipresence. It is present in the whole world dynamically. *Dextera Patris* is not a "particular place" but the "universal power of God," which at the same time can be "nowhere and everywhere." Calvin and Zwingli argue against Luther's "ubiquism"; they support the medieval opinion that *dextera Patris* has a local character; for them, it is a particular place and, moreover, an extramundane one, and this local character excludes the *praesentia realis*. One need not bother to refute this primitive and crude notion.

35. A similar significance is possessed by the transmutation of the Sacred Gifts, that is, by the inclusion of the Eucharistic elements of bread and wine into the Body and Blood of Christ for communion. It is possible only by virtue of this connection of Christ with the world, which is a consequence of the Incarnation. (See my essay "The Eucharistic Dogma.")

the world, is a new change in Christ's corporeality compared with the Resurrection. It is equivalent to the abandonment of the earthly body, the flesh, for which there is no place in the Divine kingdom of the Spirit. This is least of all a separation from the body such as took place in death, defeated forever by the Lord. At the same time, it is not some *new state* of the glorified body in virtue of which it could enter into the depths of the Holy Trinity. This is because no spiritualization of the body can make it into a spirit; and to admit a substitution of the sort that we have in Luther, according to which the ascended body simply becomes a spirit, is, in any case, to fall into an ontological misunderstanding. The Lord's earthly glorified body belongs to the world, although it abides in a state in which it is inaccessible to man.

If, after the Resurrection, Christ's body was in a supra-earthly state, while preserving the ability to appear to the disciples, then after the Ascension it abides in a supramundane, although not extramundane, state. The supramundane state is not yet heaven; it is directed toward the world and is its limit and peak. There is erected here, so to speak, a ladder between earth and heaven that has been climbed down and up and has forever united heaven and earth. This corporeality, which exists supramundanely in the world, *belongs* inalienably to the Lord, and He will manifest it by His return to the earth. This corporeality is present in the world while at the same time being *connected* with His Divine Spirit, as a body obedient and perfectly transparent for His Spirit.

In trying to understand the Ascension, our thought is confronted by an antinomy: On the one hand, it is necessary to accept that the body of the Ascension belongs to the world and thus abides in it, but on the other hand, it is necessary to accept that it also belongs to the ascended Christ, who sits at the right hand of the Father. In essence, this antinomy is hinted at in the Gospel narrative about the Ascension, as we have pointed out above: The narrative in Mark and Luke ends with the Ascension, but in Matthew and to some extent in John it ends with Christ's promise that He will abide with us forever on earth (this also includes, of course, the Eucharistic presence, *praesentia realis*). Ascending with His body into the supramundane heaven, to the limits of the world, the Lord raises beyond its limits, into the extramundane "heaven," His *ideal image* or truly *spiritual body*, which expresses the whole ineffaceable power of the accomplished incarnation. This ascended "spiritual" body is no longer the body in the sense of the earthly incarnation; it is the ideal form or image of the body, its energy, by which the body was formed in the Incarnation and which lives and acts in the world through this body of incarnation. The Ascension, as the passage beyond the very *limits* of the world, unites the world and heaven, belonging to *both* at the same time. This heavenly spiritual "body" is truly *spirit* (as Luther correctly felt, although he did not consistently and clearly develop his notion). This is the very power of the Incarnation, the connection with the creaturely world, as a special "qualification" of the Divine Spirit of the Logos.

What does this "qualification" consist in? This can be clarified only by means of the fundamental concepts of sophiology. God has the Divine Sophia as the Divine, uncreated world, as the Divine All in unity, the All-unity; and the Holy Trinity is immediately directed toward the Divine Sophia by the Second hypostasis, by the Word by whom all things were made. In a certain sense, this all-unity can also be called the spiritual body of Divinity in the capacity of the Glory of Divinity. In its foundation or at its limit, in its entelechy, the creaturely world, or the creaturely Sophia, is this very same Sophia, although posited by the act of creation in the extradivine aseity of the world's being. In Christ, in His Divine-Humanity, the total sophianization of creation and, in this sense, the identification of the creaturely Sophia and the noncreaturely Sophia are attained. Therefore, the ascended Christ has Sophia as His spiritual body, or Glory, in a two-fold manner: not only as the Logos in eternal precreaturely or extracreaturely being but also as the God-Man in relation to creation, the heavenly image of Sophia being identified in Him with the creaturely image of Sophia through the Incarnation. Thus, the "spiritual body" in which Christ abides at the right hand of the Father is nothing other than this *connection of identification* of the Divine Sophia and the creaturely Sophia. And so, the spiritual body is the creaturely Image of the eternal Proto-Image in their identity, and this spiritual image can be realized in the flesh of the world; its spiritual reality can become a reality for the world as well. It is this spirituality of the ascended body of Christ, the energetic perfection of this body, that makes possible its *mysterious* abiding in the world. The ascended body is the Church, and it is the Eucharistic body of the Lord. The Lord is *spiritually* present on earth in His Church, which is His true "omnipresence." He returns to earth in the Divine Eucharist; He clothes Himself in His glorified body, and He mysteriously includes the Eucharistic elements, the Sacred Gifts, in this glorified body for spiritual and corporeal communion. That is what the Ascension means. In the Ascension, it is not Christ's flesh, belonging to this world, that is introduced into the depths of the Holy Trinity but the entire energy of the Incarnation, His spiritual image, the truly spiritual body. One can say that this is the *Body of the body,* as the ideal image of the Divine

The Work of Christ

Sophia in union with the creaturely Sophia. It is the connection and identity of the Divine Sophia and the creaturely Sophia.

The Ascension does not conclude and does not exhaust the work of the Incarnation.[36] The ascended God-Man who is sitting at the right hand of the Father in glory *returns* into the world, and the Heavenly Jerusalem, the City of God, descends from heaven to earth. The Lord is the Lord of creation not only from above, in the capacity of God, Creator, and Providence, but also inwardly, as the God-Man, in virtue of His inseparability with the earth. This inner connection is His life in the Church and the "royal ministry," which continues in the world (see below). Therefore, the Ascension in the sense of Christ's departure from the world is *not* definitive; and after His return into the world, "we [shall] ever be with the Lord" (1 Thess. 4:17). To be sure, this does not abolish the power of the Ascension as "the sitting at the right hand of the Father," as the glorification of the God-Man and, in Him, of His humanity. His abiding in heaven becomes fully compatible with His abiding in the human world, now forever: "Behold, the tabernacle of God is with men, and he will dwell with them [forever] . . . and God himself shall be with them" (Rev. 21:3); "the throne of God and of the Lamb shall be in it . . . and they shall see his face" (22:3-4). But in the Ascension, Christ does not definitively depart the world even

---

36. In order to correctly understand Christ's Ascension, it also necessary to correctly understand the Mother of God's Ascension. To be sure, the two are different. The Mother of God's Ascension does not by any means signify Her departure from the world into the realm of Divine being. It is rather Her abiding in Her raised and glorified body, which is transcendent for our perception, just as the body of the Resurrected Christ was inaccessible to human perception (apart from His *appearances*) even though it remained in the world. The body of the Mother of God, which was raised from the dead and ascended, signifies the total glorification of creaturely being prior to the universal transfiguration of the world. It is an anticipation of the universal transfiguration. The life of the Mother of God is directed toward God and is *graciously* united with Divine being, abiding in the state of total deification. However, She does not enter the interior of the Holy Trinity. The Mother of God is "glorified" by the Father, through the Son, by the Holy Spirit, who reposes upon Her; but here She nonetheless belongs to the creaturely world, although She is its highest peak, directly illuminated by the Divine Sun. Therefore, in connection with the ascension of the Mother of God, one cannot say that She left Her earthly body and abides in a "spiritual body," as in its ideal form. On the contrary, the Mother of God *retains* Her flesh, although in a glorified state, inaccessible to us. To the extent that it providentially becomes accessible to us, one can speak of the descent of the Mother of God to earth and of Her appearances. One can establish here a certain analogy with the state of the Resurrected Christ, who made His glorified corporeality accessible to man in His appearances.

during His elevation into heaven. On the contrary, He remains united with the world, not only eucharistically, through the mysterious partaking of His Body and Blood in communion, but also by the power of Christ acting in the world. This is His mystical, even if not sacramental, presence in the world; this is His invisible and spiritual presence in the world, His participation in human life, by which He fulfills His promise to abide with us always — now, and forever, and in the ages of ages. This is not the Lutheran, pantheistic omnipresence, but authentic dynamic pan-Christism, so to speak. It is the life of Christ in human beings and the life of human beings in Christ, and the closeness to us and inner intimacy of this life surpass all other closeness and intimacy. Not only does Christ act in the Church by *grace*, by the power of the Holy Spirit, who manifests Christ to us, but He also participates in all human life (according to the discourse on the Last Judgment) in virtue of His Incarnation, His divine-humanity. That is, He already effectively and, in *this* sense, naturally participates in it, for His human nature contains all humanity. For this invisible presence in the world, the ascended Christ has the path of inhumanization, the path that He Himself forged. The Lord Himself says about His Ascension that "I will not leave you comfortless: I will come to you. Yet a little while, and the world seeth me no more; but ye see me: because I live, ye shall live also" (John 14:18-19).

In the Ascension, we have the maximal revelation of the relation between God and Man, the principle of which was established in the creation of the world and of man in the image of God. We are filled with "astonishment," both philosophical and religious, when we ask ourselves how God could have left His eternity to go into the relative creaturely being of the world and of man — how He could have revealed Himself in relativity. Here we remain dumbfounded by the fact that this creaturely, temporal being was included in God's absolute being, by the fact that heaven opened up to receive the human essence, creaturely and relative, and thus identified itself with this essence. Something happens that is inconceivable metaphysically: the substantial difference between divine and creaturely being is overcome by the power of Divine love, which humbles itself to the point of going out of itself to creation and embracing it: The Absolute becomes God, united with creation in man through the God-Man. God is the Son of God, the Son of Man. Divinity has expanded in itself, as it were, introducing into its depths the creation, which has been called into being by Divine love. In God, His Divinity has become Divine-Humanity, which in the Son of Man communes with creaturely being. The dualism between God and creation is overcome, and the mono-

The Work of Christ

dualism of Divine-Humanity is established. In the heavenly God-Man, in the light of His Divinity, there is no longer a distinction between His uncreated divine essence and His created human essence. He is the one Son of God, the "Alpha and Omega, the beginning and the ending . . . which is, and which was, and which is to come, the Almighty" (Rev. 1:8).

In connection with the Ascension and the sitting of the God-Man at the right hand of the Father, there arises before us with extreme acuteness the general problem that we had already encountered when we were examining the doctrine of the creation of the world: Does God, absolute, unchangeable, and eternal, change in His being by becoming the Creator and establishing the world alongside Himself, by making Himself correlative to the world? Here, because of the Ascension and the sitting of the God-Man at the right hand of the Father, because of the appearance of the creaturely human essence in the Holy Trinity, does not the Holy Trinity itself change? Thought is confronted here by an obvious antinomy: both yes and no. *No,* because God's being is absolute and eternal, and temporal being and change do not exist for Him and in Him. *Yes,* because it is impossible to deny a certain absolute reality of the world created by God and thus the authenticity of Christ's humanity. Because of the Ascension to heaven of Christ's body in His Divine-Humanity in eternity, *aeternitas,* there arises another eternity, having a creaturely principle, *aeviternitas:* This is Christ's humanity, which, inseparable from the Divinity itself, is present in God's eternity in the God-Man who sits at the right hand of the Father. The supramundane God has united Himself with the world; He has become God *and* the world. This "and" is the union of the two natures in one Divine hypostasis, divine and human, without separation and without confusion, in one life.

The Chalcedonian dogma retains its validity in heaven as well. The two natures co-participate in the sitting at the right hand of the Father, for God and man are seated there in the one God-Man, the Son of God and the Son of Man in the one Son, God and creation in the one hypostasis of the Logos. There is no God without the world, and there is no world outside of God: the world is in God. Despite all this, the supramundane and eternal Holy Trinity remains in the immobile all-blessedness of its being. This apparent contradiction is resolved not by the opposition of abstract unchangeability to illusory change but by the general antinomic interrelation between God in Himself, or the Absolute, and God the Creator of the world, with which He has united His own being.

Here, the Ascension and the sitting at the right hand of the Father are only an unfolding of this general interrelation of God and the world.

Unchangeability is proper only to the Absolute, for whom there does not exist any interrelation with creation, or any interrelation at all. In the relation of God to the world, however, there is complete *interrelation;* and the mode of becoming that is proper to the world is shared, in the Divine condescension, by God: The creation of the world, the providential government of the world, the Incarnation, the Ascension, the sending down of the Holy Spirit, and so on, are all acts of the mutual becoming of God for the world and of the world for God. This fundamental theological antinomy cannot be elucidated any further; it must be accepted as an axiom (see the first chapter of the present work). In the relation between God and the world we cannot conceive a changeability of God such that something new (i.e., a true change) could arise for God Himself through the becoming of the world; this is guaranteed by the sophianicity of creation. God's eternity contains the images of all of creaturely being in its fullness as the Divine Sophia. In particular, the pre-eternal Divine-Humanity of the Son contains the whole fullness of Divine-Human being in its pathways from the Incarnation to the Ascension and His Second Coming into the world. In His eternal being, the pre-eternal God-Man possesses all the images of His humanity supratemporally and essentially, although they are manifested for creaturely humanity only in time. In this sense, one can say that the *place* for the sitting at the right hand of the Father is pre-eternally prepared and occupied by the Son, and it is only for this reason that the Ascension is realized also in time, in the Incarnation: We have here an ontological identity of the supratemporal and the temporal. That which is new in time (and all things are new in time) exists in its unchangeability from all eternity. Therefore, neither the Ascension nor the sitting at the right hand of the Father produces any change in the Divine Eternity; at the same time they are accomplishments that are realized in the divine-human process of the relations of God to the world.

The significance of the Ascension is not exhausted by the glorification of the Lord; for besides the accomplished Ascension there is also the Ascension that is *in the process of being accomplished:* this is the glorification of the creaturely, not yet glorified, earthly humanity, which, however, is naturally identical to that of Christ. In this sense the Ascension is *continuing;* it is the beginning and the end, the foundation and the goal: God has "raised us up together, and made us sit together in heavenly places in Christ Jesus" (Eph. 2:6). Through Christ, we "have access by one Spirit unto the Father" (2:18). This corresponds to the revelation of the power of the Ascension that we have in Christ's Last Discourse according to the Gospel of John: "In my Father's house are many mansions: if it were not so, I would have told you. I go to prepare a place for you. And if I go and prepare a place for you, I will come again, and receive you unto myself; that where I am, there ye may be also" (14:2-3). This refers to that final glorification when "God will be all in all." This glorification is beyond the limits of what is visible to us from "the kingdom of grace" in which we are found, and it is separated from us by the universal resurrection, accompanied by the end of this world and all that lies beyond it. However, we should remember that the ascension of humanity has already been *preaccomplished* in the person of the Most Holy Mother of God: The Church believes that, raised from the dead by Her Son, She has already entered the "mansion" prepared for Her.

Holy Scripture reveals that Christ's ministry and, consequently, His kenosis continue for a certain period of time also in heaven. Here it is necessary to speak of *time* even with reference to heaven. Christ's high-priestly ministry ends only with the definitive accomplishment of our salvation through the sending down of the Holy Spirit at Pentecost. Yet another ten days pass, according to the earthly calculation of time, a period that is totally unfathomable and mysterious in relation to the Son Himself but is known to us from its consequences — the sending down of the Holy Spirit: "I will pray the Father, and he shall give you another Comforter, that he may abide with you for ever" (John 14:16), "whom the Father will send in my name" (14:26). And further: "when the Comforter is come, whom I will send unto you from the Father, even the Spirit of truth, which proceedeth from the Father, he shall testify of me" (15:26); "I tell you the truth; It is expedient for you that I go away: for if I go not away, the Comforter will not come unto you; but if I depart, I will send him unto you" (16:7); "being by the right hand of God exalted, and having received of the Father the promise of the Holy Spirit, he hath shed forth . . ." (Acts 2:33). A clear causal connection is established here between the Ascension and Pentecost, and this relation is defined from two sides: "I will pray the Father" and "I will send unto you from the Father."[37]

The relation of the Son to the Father remains kenotic: Offering the sacrifice of His humanity, the High Priest intercedes before the Father for the sake of the *accomplishment* of His work on earth by the action of the Holy Spirit, whom the Father sends through the Son. As a result, there is

---

37. We will not examine here the general question of the procession of the Holy Spirit, leaving such an examination for our volume on pneumatology. [Bulgakov is referring to the second part of the present trilogy, *The Comforter*, available in Boris Jakim's translation (Eerdmans, 2004). — Trans.]

an aspect of the salvific work of Christ's in-humanization that corresponds to the action of the Third hypostasis; nevertheless, the sending down of the Spirit is realized by the Father with the direct participation of ("through") the Second hypostasis. The Holy Spirit cannot be sent or descend into the world *without* or *apart from* the Son as the God-Man: In His redemptive high-priestly ministry, the Son prepares the path for the Spirit into the world; He prepares a "place" for the Spirit's descent. This is the Church, Christ's humanity, His body. The Holy Spirit teaches the Church Christ's truth; He "reminds" it of this truth: "he shall take of mine, and shall shew it unto you" (John 16:15).

Thus, the sending down of the Holy Spirit is the final and concluding work of Christ's ministry, for which Christ prays to the Father in His high-priestly intercession for the world. This promise of the Holy Spirit concludes, according to Acts 1:4-8, the earthly presence of Christ on earth: "And, being assembled together with them, [He] commanded them that they should not depart from Jerusalem, but wait for the [fulfillment of the] promise of the Father, which, saith he, ye have heard of me" (1:4) (cf. "I send the promise of my Father upon you: but tarry ye in the city of Jerusalem, until ye be endued with power from on high" [Luke 24:49]); "ye shall be baptized with the Holy Spirit not many days hence" (Acts 1:5); "ye shall receive power, after that the Holy Spirit is come upon you" (1:8).

The Holy Spirit, always reposing upon Christ, overshadows Him after the Resurrection on the way to the Ascension. This is expressively indicated in Acts 1:2, where we are told that He gave His commandments through the Holy Spirit (cf. John 20:22: "he breathed on them, and saith unto them, Receive ye the Holy Spirit"). This is not Pentecost, which is realized through the sending down of the Spirit from the Father. Rather, this is testimony about the abiding of the Holy Spirit upon the Son in His Resurrection and in His continuing glorification. It is the preparation for Pentecost. Reposing upon Christ Himself, the Holy Spirit pours forth upon His earthly humanity in the person of the apostles, and this concludes Christ's work on earth. Henceforth, it is the Holy Spirit who reveals Christ and who acts in Christ's power, whereas Christ Himself abides in His divine glory. There cannot be a more expressive confirmation of this than the first testimony of the Church about itself, uttered by the Apostle Peter after the descent of the Holy Spirit. How is this discourse constructed? It begins, following the words of the prophet Joel, with a testimony about the accomplished descent of the Holy Spirit, but then it immediately passes to a preaching about Christ, about His death on the cross, His resurrection, and His glorification (Acts 2:14-26). We observe the same thing in all the further discourses: "Therefore let all the house of Israel know assuredly, that God hath made that same Jesus, whom ye have crucified, both Lord and Christ" (2:36). This is the first proclamation on earth by the Holy Spirit of the accomplished restoration of the Son of God–Son of Man in the Glory of His Divinity; henceforth He appears as God in His Glory. (Thus, Stephen, "being full of the Holy Spirit, looked up stedfastly into heaven, and saw the glory of God, and Jesus standing on the right hand of God" [7:55]; Saul too saw Him in "the glory of . . . light" [22:11].)

The salvation of the world has been accomplished. The path from heaven to earth and from earth to heaven has been taken and completed, and this path remains open forever in the descent of the Holy Spirit, who exists both in heaven and on earth. The high-priestly ministry is concluded. God is reconciled with fallen humanity, and man communes with the divine life in the God-Man, who abides at the right hand of the Father. Heaven has received Christ "until the times of restitution [*apokatastaseōs*] of all things" (Acts 3:21). "But this man, after he had offered one sacrifice for sins for ever, sat down on the right hand of God; from henceforth expecting till his enemies be made his footstool" (Heb. 10:12-13).

Christ's high-priestly ministry has been completed. "I have glorified thee on the earth: I have finished the work which thou gavest me to do. And now, O Father, glorify thou me" (John 17:4-5). However, this completion concerns only Him who has passed from humiliation to glory; this work is not yet concluded and exhausted for the world. On the contrary, the high-priestly ministry is an *eternal* ministry; it abides and continues forever. Christ is the High Priest *forever*, "after the order of Melchisedec" (Heb. 5:6): "This man, because he continueth ever, hath an unchangeable priesthood. Wherefore he is able also to save them to the uttermost that come unto God by him, seeing he ever liveth to make intercession for them" (7:24-25) as "the Son, who is consecrated for evermore" (7:28). Just as the Golgotha sacrifice, unique and accomplished just once, *has power* in all Eucharistic sacrifices, so Christ's intercession as the High Priest has power for all times and for all human beings. Man's reconciliation and reunification with God must be understood not as an act that occurred just once but as an act that continues for all times. It must be understood as an act that has the depth and power of eternity. It is in this sense that Scripture says: "wherefore he is able also to save them to the uttermost that come unto God by him, seeing he ever liveth to make intercession for them" (7:24-25); "it is Christ that died, yea rather, that is risen again, who is even at the right hand of God, who also maketh intercession for us"

(Rom. 8:34); "we have an advocate [comforter-paraclete] with the Father, Jesus Christ the righteous" (1 John 2:1).

He is the advocate-paraclete and also the intercessor or mediator. His high priesthood is no longer a ministry in *humiliation*; it now exists as high-priestly dignity and power. It remains, in essence, identical with the Incarnation, for it is precisely as the God-Man, who has united in Himself the two essences without separation and without confusion, that Christ is the eternal High Priest. He leads the creature to God; He introduces the creature into the life of the Holy Trinity. He is not only the reconciler of the *sinful* creature with God, but He is also the mediator between *creatureliness* itself and Divinity. In His high priesthood, He surmounts the ontological abyss separating the Creator and the creature. And this mediation will not cease in the ages of ages; it will continue even beyond the limits of this world. The Eucharistic sacrifice for the remission of sins will become the offering of love and the sacrifice of praise offered by man to God in the God-Man; at the same time it will become the divine food of the world, that tree of life whose prototype was present already in paradise and whose true image we have in the city of God descending from heaven (Rev. 21:2). In this sense, the Eucharist possesses the same power of eternity as Christ's High Priesthood. Divine-Humanity, the union of the Creator with creation, is realized in the Eucharist.[38]

Christ's Ascension signifies not the return of the Logos into the depths of the Holy Trinity, which He did not leave even in the state of kenosis,[39] but the completion of the kenosis. The kenosis was precisely "the descent from heaven" for the purpose of in-humanization, whereas the Ascension is the completion of the kenosis of in-humanization; it is a completion that is based on the latter (i.e., it is a return to heaven *in the flesh*). In the eternal and supramundane being of the Holy Trinity, where there can be no events and where there is no place for time, no change could occur. In Himself, God is "forever and the same, Thou and Thy Only Begotten Son and Thy Holy Spirit" (Preface, Liturgy of St. John Chrysostom). But in the life of the Holy Trinity *with the world and in rela-*

---

38. The Catholic theologian J. Pohle (*Die kath. Dogm.*, II, 202), on the contrary, considers it absolutely indisputable that, with the last mass celebrated on earth, Christ's priestly intercession in heaven will cease. This erroneous opinion is connected with the one-sided understanding of the Incarnation exclusively as redemption. What one fails to see here is the autonomous significance of the divine-humanity as such.

39. We encounter the contrary affirmation in certain extreme kenotic theories, for example, in Gess, who hypothesizes that, during the Lord's earthly kenosis, He was absent from the Holy Trinity.

tion to the world, we have a series of accomplishments, as we read in the same prayer: "Thou hast led us from nothingness to being; and Thou hast regenerated us, who are fallen. Thou hast even raised us to heaven and given us Thy kingdom to come." Through the Ascension, Christ's humanity appears in heaven, in the depths of the divine life of the Holy Trinity. Initially deified in the Incarnation and undergoing continuous deification in the course of Christ's entire earthly ministry,[40] His humanity now becomes perfectly and definitively deified to the point of fully receiving *the glory of God.* With the completion of the kenosis, not only does the Son of God receive from the Father the glory that belonged to Him before the creation of the world, but the Son of Man is also glorified in the God-Man. And this glorification of His *humanity* is not the return of the glory; creation receives it here for the first time. The God-Man's earthly humanity follows His Ascension to heaven, first the Most Holy Mother of God, and then the entire Church (Eph. 2:6) in the age to come. This is the deification of humanity.[41]

The Father saves and deifies the world through the Son, the God-Man; and it is through the Son that He sends the Holy Spirit into the world. The Holy Trinity is directed toward the world and is united with it through the God-Man in His Divine-Humanity, upon which the Holy Spirit reposes. The Divine-Humanity is therefore not only a fact but also an act; it is not only an event that occurred just once but also an abiding accomplishment, a continuing work of God and of man. The history of the world and of man has become a divine-human process. The Logos is now no longer only the demiurgic hypostasis by which God directs Himself toward the world in its creation but is also the *historical* hypostasis, the mediating Intercessor, who leads the world by the Holy Spirit to salvation. It is from this that Christ's promise gets its full significance: "I am with you alway, even unto the end of the world" (Matt. 28:20); for in the Ascension, the Incarnation itself receives its full power of eternity. The history of the Incarnation (if it is permissible to use such an expression) continues in heaven even after the Ascension, for this history includes new

---

40. That is why the following series of events is included in the general context of the mysterious priestly prayer in the liturgy of St. John Chrysostom: "remembering ... all that was done for us: the cross, the sepulchre, the resurrection after three days, the ascension to heaven, the sitting at the right hand, the second and glorious coming."

41. The Apocalypse vision of the heavenly Jerusalem also conforms with this: "I saw no temple therein: for the Lord God Almighty and the Lamb are the temple of it. And the city had no need of the sun, neither of the moon, to shine in it: for the glory of God did lighten it, and the Lamb is the light thereof" (Rev. 21:22-23).

events that have not yet occurred. Indubitably, among such events we can name the second and glorious coming, the parousia, as well as various events indicated in the book of Revelation (and also the appearances of Christ to the Apostle Paul, to Stephen, and to other righteous men of the Church). Here we touch upon a highly important truth, a truth that has not received a clear and authoritative dogmatic expression, although it possesses full power in the life of the Church. Even in His Ascension, Christ has preserved in all its power His connection with this world and, having ascended to heaven, He abides in the world and does not abandon it.[42] First of all, and most evidently, He does not abandon it thanks to the Divine Eucharist, which He established for that purpose: "this do in remembrance of me" (Luke 22:19), that is, not only in subjective and psychological remembrance, but also in objective and real remembrance, as the completion or reproduction of that which had taken place on earth. The Lord descends from heaven without abandoning it in order to be present on earth in the Eucharistic elements, the Sacred Gifts, which contain His *praesentia realis*. (In their practice of the adoration of the Sacred Gifts, the Catholics even want to extend this real presence of Christ on earth to an opposition to or, at least, to a certain limitation of the power of the Ascension.) The Divine Eucharist is thus the divine ladder between heaven and earth on which the ascended Lord descends into the world, and to that extent the Ascension is truly overcome in the Eucharist (although only within certain limits).

But alongside the Eucharist, the divine bread descending from heaven, there remains on earth the blood and water that flowed out of Jesus' side on the cross: This is the Holy Grail,[43] Christ's earthly humanity, which was separated from His resurrected and glorified humanity, but which also remains united with it. Outwardly, this flowing out of blood and water from Jesus' side manifests the fact that the ascended Christ abides on earth with His humanity. This fact must be generalized and will receive its correct dogmatic interpretation on the basis of the general postulate of our faith in the Incarnation: Not only does the entire Incarnation, the entire earthly life of the God-Man, represent a series of events

---

42. This ability not to abandon the earth even after leaving it by the ascension to heaven is attributed by the Church even to the Most Holy Mother of God: "In Your Dormition, You did not leave the world, O Mother of God" (troparion of the Dormition).

43. The dogmatic significance of this fact is clarified in my essay "The Holy Grail." [See n. 9 above. – Trans.]

with temporal significance, a series of events occurring in time, but it also receives a supratemporal significance or (if we attempt to express this idea in the language of time) a *continuing* significance in virtue of the divine-human character of these events. These events are taken out of time into eternity, but they are nevertheless directed at time. This truth acquires a religiously self-evident character in the liturgical life of the Church. The feasts of the Lord and of the Mother of God, as well as the entire Church year, with its quotidian commemorations, Holy Week, and daily Gospel readings — all this has such an eternal and temporal significance of remembrance and also the significance of accomplishments that have taken place just once in the temporal chain but that have acquired power for all times in eternity. Every feast is, on the one hand, a repetition of the event in our memory and, on the other hand, a certain identification with the event. We immerse ourselves here in the event itself and coexperience it. To be sure, the Eucharistic *sacrifice* presents us with the clearest evidence of this difference in the case of identity or this identity in the case of difference. The dogmatic doctrine is powerless to explain this sacrifice, at the same time both one and multiple, both repeated and not repeated. On the one hand, it is necessary to explain the *reality* of the sacrifice-offering on each altar and in each liturgy, and on the other hand, it is necessary to harmonize this multiplicity of sacrifices with the uniqueness and identity of the one Golgotha sacrifice.

Rational thought, which remains confined within the frame of space and time, confronts an insurmountable contradiction in this identity of what is different and this unity of what is multiple; this rational difficulty is one of the reasons why the doctrine of the Eucharistic sacrifice is rejected in Protestantism. This contradiction is removed only when the limits of space and time are abolished, which takes place in relation to the events of the Divine life: in the state of the God-Man's kenosis, these events occurred in time and in space, in conformity with the authenticity of the Incarnation; but in the state of the glorification of the God-Man, they receive the power of eternity. With reference to the life of this world, this power is manifested as freedom from the limitations of time and space. It is only in the light of this supratemporal-temporal significance, in virtue of which the rays of the one eternal sun penetrate into the apertures of time and illuminate and sanctify events at these points of time, that one can understand the dogmatic paradox that all the Eucharistic sacrifices are really the Golgotha sacrifice, even as all the commemorative Church celebrations of some Gospel event are that very event. The wounds on Christ's hands and feet were visible on His resurrected body, and they will be visible on the glorified body of the Lord when He comes to judge the world. These wounds contain a symbolic representation of the entire earthly life of the Savior in that which is central to this life: the feat of the cross, which includes and extends to His entire earthly life. Thus, Christ's Ascension and His sitting at the right hand of the Father must not be understood as the end or the cessation of His earthly work and of His connection with the earthly world. Rather, they should be understood precisely with reference to this connection, as one of the events in the entire series of the accomplishments of the Divine economy (it is not by accident that this event is included among the major feasts). The Christ who sits in Glory at the right hand of the Father is the same Christ who institutes the Last Supper and personally offers communion to His disciples. And He has continued to do this from that time forward, as the Church attests in its liturgical prayer.[44]

From all these facts of dogmatic significance, one can draw further conclusions concerning the relation between Christ's earthly abiding and His heavenly abiding, between His kenosis and His Ascension. Does not the abiding reality of the events of Christ's earthly life for the Church attest that the continuing reality of His kenosis as ministry remains compatible even with His glorified state? For Christ Himself in His glorified state, the kenosis has come to an end and become part of the past, so to speak; but in its relation to the life of the world, the kenosis can preserve its power: Christ suffers and is crucified in the world, for, in Him, the Golgotha sacrifice is being offered, "till he come" (1 Cor. 11:26). In His glorified humanity, the Lord sits at the right hand of the Father; but in His earthly humanity, for which He is the New Adam, in His body (that is, the Church, which finds itself in a militant state), Christ abides not only in a glorified state but also in a state of kenosis. This kenosis refers now not to the humiliation of Christ's Divinity but to His humanity; however, it refers not to Jesus' personal Humanity, which is also glorified in heaven, but to His earthly humanity, which is united with His Humanity as the New Adam. Christ, for Himself personally, has come to the end of His kenosis; but the kenosis is not yet completed for His humanity, which has not yet

---

44. "Listen to us, Lord Jesus Christ, our God, from Your holy habitation and from the throne of Your kingdom, and come to sanctify us; You who reside on high with the Father and who abide here invisibly with us, give to us with Your mighty hand Your most pure body and Your precious blood, to us and to all people" (prayer before communion). Related to this is also the identification of the priest with Christ: "You are the one who offers and is offered, who receives and is received, O Christ, our God" (prayer before the Cherubic Hymn).

experienced the "last time," which is to arrive after His First Coming and to continue until His Second Coming.[45] Having ascended to heaven, the God-Man, who sits at the right hand of the Father, lives in His humanity as in His body, the Church; and according to the testimony of the Gospel (in the discourse about the Last Judgment), He even lives in every human being.

If His earthly life extends to all times, His humanity expands to include all humanity. This refers not only to His redemptive suffering for the sins of all men, which He took upon Himself on earth, but in general to His participation in the destiny of humanity and the destiny of the world, in all of history, until its very end, as the book of Revelation shows. This participation is revealed in two aspects: as co-suffering with those who suffer and as the unceasing battle, together with the militant church, against the forces of hell. Both aspects must be understood in all their reality in order not to diminish the power of the words of Christ Himself and of those who bore witness about Him. And this reality, in its own way, is just as great as the mysterious omnitemporal reality of His completed earthly life.

We are compelled to conclude that Christ's earthly work, and not only His work but also His suffering in His *earthly* humanity, did not end even after the Ascension. This work has two aspects: First, Christ's already finished earthly life with its prophetic and high-priestly ministries is being mysteriously finished in the Church; and, as a result, the life of humanity in the Church includes the finished life of Christ. Second, Christ co-participates in the proper life of humanity: He co-suffers with humanity, being crucified with it and in it. He thirsts, is hungry, is cast into prison, is persecuted and insulted. That which, once and for all ages, He experienced and redeemed as human *sin*, He co-experiences as the *suffering* of humanity. To be sure, there is no possible rational or logical way to harmonize these apparently contradictory and mutually exclusive ideas: Christ in heaven, sitting in Glory at the right hand of the Father in glorified humanity, and Christ suffering on earth. However, this is not more difficult to accept than a fact already affirmed and confessed by the Church — the fact that the Church is the body of Christ and that He lives in this body not only in an accomplishment to come but here and now, in the militant Church, that He lives in it mysteriously, in virtue of His re-

---

45. The New Testament doctrine of the "last times" (1 Pet. 1:5; 1 John 2:18; 1 Cor. 10:11; Heb. 1:2, etc.) refers, above all, to the epoch after Christ irrespective of its duration; and therefore it has not a chronological but an ontological significance.

demptive feat. Thus, Christ's abiding in heaven is compatible with His life in the Church; to be sure, this life must be understood not as a passive and indifferent abiding, but as an unceasing activity, full of power, love, and compassion. There thus arises a new christological aporia consisting in the fact that Christ's work, the completion of which He Himself testifies about to the Father, continues in the world and, consequently, is not finished. Thus, there exists a suffering that has not yet been experienced, although it has all been experienced to the end on the cross; and there exists a ministry that has not yet been accomplished, although the High Priest has already entered with the sacrifice into the Holy of Holies. The consideration that this idea formally contradicts Christ's own words, "it is finished," can be removed exegetically by pointing out that, in general, these words attest to His accomplishment of that redemptive work for which He was sent into the world. But, in itself, this accomplished work can contain, as a consequence, further accomplishments. This accomplished work is the basis for new tasks, which it reveals. Although this accomplished work is already a decisive victory ("be of good cheer; I have overcome the world" [John 16:33]), this victory has been won only in the heart of the world; on its surface, however, sorrows, temptations, and woes still await the world. The time of the world has not yet ended; it continues. And the *assimilation* of the victory and of its fruits requires still further achievements, exertions, and struggles; it requires a special *ministry*. The prophetic and high-priestly ministry, as such, is completed in the sense that the victory has been won. But this marks the beginning of a further ministry of Christ on earth, even though the Ascension has been accomplished. This is no longer the prophetic and high-priestly ministry. This is His *royal ministry*.

III. The Royal Ministry of Christ

A. *Christ the King*

This question is one of the least clarified questions in Christology, and its treatment is often marked by incoherence and contradiction. Some theologians (in particular, the Russian theologian Metropolitan Makarii) primarily attribute Christ's miracles to the royal ministry; but the miracles in fact do not belong to it at all, and must rather be attributed to the prophetic ministry. Other theologians attribute the Resurrection, the descent into hell, the Ascension, and in general the entire glorification of Christ

The Work of Christ

to the royal ministry; but as we have already seen, these events belong to the high-priestly ministry. And so, as a result of this error, the royal ministry is usually considered not as a *ministry* at all but only as a manifestation of the Divine omnipotence, as an action of the heavenly King and God, and not of the God-Man who has removed His Divine glory from Himself.

Because of this, the very formulation of the problem is marked by obscurity and confusion. Scripture does in fact call God the King, who has His Kingdom ("for thine is the Kingdom, and the Power, and the Glory of the Father, of the Son, and of the Holy Spirit, now and forever, and in the ages of ages," we hear the priest repeatedly intone). "Sing praises to God, sing praises: sing praises unto our King, sing praises. For God is the King of all the earth" (Ps. 47:6-7). The Lord is "the King of Israel" (Isa. 44:6); "your Holy One, the creator of Israel, your King" (43:15); the "King of nations" (Jer. 10:7); "an everlasting king" (10:10); "the King of heaven" (Dan. 4:37). But this eternal Kingdom of God, which is also God's power and glory, belongs to God's eternity and expresses the general and fundamental relation of the Creator and Provider to creation.

This kingdom is also truly the foundation of the God-Man's royal power, which, however, is *acquired* by Him and realized only as the crowning of His earthly ministry: "All power is given unto me in heaven and in earth" (Matt. 28:18). The foundation for this *gift* is His entire earthly ministry, namely, the prophetic and high-priestly ministry. This relation is clearly demonstrated in Ephesians 1:19-22: "the working of his mighty power, which [God] wrought in Christ, when he raised him from the dead, and set him at his own right hand in the heavenly places, far above all principality, and power, and might, and dominion, and every name that is named, not only in this world, but also in that which is to come: and hath put all things under his feet, and gave him to be the head over all things to the church." In the royal ministry, therefore, it is necessary to distinguish, on the one hand, its preparation or, rather, its anticipation in Christ's earthly ministry, and on the other hand, its accomplishment in His glorification. This ministry is not simultaneous with the prophetic and high-priestly ministry but is accomplished after it.

Christ was born into the world as *King* on the throne of David, as the Son of David, the Son of Abraham (Matt. 1:1). Such was the promise of the archangel at the Annunciation: "The Lord God shall give unto him the throne of his father David: and he shall reign over the house of Jacob for ever; and of his kingdom there shall be no end" (Luke 1:32-33). Essentially the same promise was given by God to David together with the promise concerning the birth of his son, Solomon: "I will establish the throne of his kingdom for ever ... and thine house and thy kingdom shall be established for ever before thee: thy throne shall be established for ever" (2 Sam. 7:13, 16; cf. Ps. 132:11-14). With reference to Christ, this prophecy is confirmed in the Apostle Peter's discourse on the day of Pentecost (Acts 2:30). In conformity with this, Christ is born into the world as the "King of the Jews" (Matt. 2:2), to whom the wise men bring royal gifts; and this was also the message of the inscription that was nailed to His cross.

This promise concerning the enthronement of the descendant of David or in general the messianic King and concerning His eternal Kingdom is a thread that runs through the Old Testament prophecies: We find this promise in the Psalms and in the prophetic books, especially Isaiah (e.g., 9:7). Particularly noteworthy is the prophecy in Ezekiel: "I will take the children of Israel from among the heathen ... and bring them into their own land: and I will make them one nation ... and one king shall be king to them all. ... And David my servant shall be king over them; and they all shall have one shepherd ... my servant David shall be their prince for ever" (37:21-25). Also see Micah 5:2; Zechariah 9:9; 14:9; Jeremiah 23:5 ("Behold, the days come, saith the LORD, that I will raise unto David a righteous Branch, and a King shall reign and prosper, and shall execute judgment and justice in the earth"); Daniel 7:14 ("there was given him [the Son of Man] dominion, and glory, and a kingdom, that all people, nations, and languages, should serve him: his dominion is an everlasting dominion, which shall not pass away, and his kingdom that which shall not be destroyed"); and Psalms 2; 20; 21; 45; 72; 110. We can also mention the prophecies concerning the messianic reign: Isaiah 9; 11; 32; 35; Daniel 2:34-44; Psalms 2; 29; 45; 72; 89; 110. The people repeatedly call Jesus the Son of David, the royal descendant of the theocratic King: Matthew 9:27; 12:23; 15:22; 20:30-31; 21:9; Mark 10:47; Luke 18:38-39.

To be sure, there was a glaring contradiction between the title of King and the humble lot of the One who had no place to lay His head. Moreover, Judea had lost its political autonomy long ago, and among the people the title "Son of David" had been transformed into a memory or a dream. Nevertheless, the Lord never renounced this title, even though He had many opportunities to do so. On the contrary, when He was asked by Pilate, "Art thou a king then?" Jesus answered in the affirmative: "Thou sayest that I am a king" (John 18:37; cf. Matt. 27:11; Mark 15:2; Luke 23:3). It is true that, here, He adds that "My kingdom is not of this world: if my kingdom were of this world, then would my servants fight ... but now is my kingdom not from hence" (John 18:36). For His disciples He expressly opposed his ministry to the magnificence of earthly power: "the Son of

The Work of Christ

man came not to be ministered unto, but to minister, and to give his life a ransom for many" (Matt. 20:28).

There is only one event where the Lord manifested His royal magnificence in the days of His earthly ministry: this is His *royal entry* into Jerusalem, which the Church celebrates as a major feast and thus considers to be one of the fundamental and most significant events of Christ's life. But the independent meaning of this entry and all its importance remain obscured, as it were, between the event of the raising of Lazarus and the imminent passion.[46] This triumphal entry of the meek King into the Holy City, however, has a prefigurative significance in relation to the coming Kingdom of Christ; and this is completely analogous to the prefigurative significance of the Transfiguration of the Lord in relation to His glorification, the entry into Glory. And just as the rays of His Glory shone forth here on earth on Mount Tabor, so the coming of His Kingdom was also shown on earth in the Holy City. The glorification of Christ that is included in His voluntary passion ("Now is the Son of man glorified" [John 13:31]) is prefigured and prerevealed in these two events. The first, the Transfiguration, is the beginning, the departure to Jerusalem, whereas the second is the entry into the city for the fulfillment of the passion, which leads to His glory and kingdom. Thus, according to the Gospel, the Lord's entry into Jerusalem represents the *sole* external manifestation on earth of Christ's "royal ministry," which He concealed in His kenosis.

The entry has an expressly premeditated character. Christ, who earlier had declined royal honors and had immediately departed alone to the mountain when He "perceived that they would come and take him by force, to make him a king" (John 6:15), now *arranges* His royal entry for Himself. He sends two disciples into a nearby village to bring back "an ass, and a colt the foal of an ass" (Matt. 21:5), for His entry into Jerusalem. The Lord was clearly applying to Himself the prophecy of Zechariah (9:9; cf. Isa. 62:11): "Rejoice greatly, O daughter of Zion; shout, O daughter of Jerusalem: behold, thy King cometh unto thee: he is just, and having salvation; lowly, and riding upon an ass, and upon a colt the foal of an ass." This event is presented in the light of this prophecy not only in Matthew

---

46. Even in the proper troparion of the feast, we read: "affirming before Your passion the universal resurrection, You raised Lazarus from the dead, O Christ, our God! Thus, we too, like adolescents, bearing the sign of victory, cry out to You, the vanquisher of death: Hosanna in the highest! Blessed is he that cometh in the name of the Lord!" In this passage, the raising of Lazarus is compared with the future victory over death in the resurrection, but there is no mention of the event celebrated by the feast. It is left in dogmatic shadow.

21:4-5, but also in John 12:15-16, where, moreover, it is noted that: "These things understood not his disciples at the first: but when Jesus was glorified, then remembered they that these things were written of him, and that they had done these things unto him." The Lord's triumphal entry was accompanied by a multitude of people, who had gathered because of the astonishing news of the miracle of the raising of Lazarus, and who desired to see both the One who had raised Lazarus from the dead and the one who had been raised (see John 12:9, 17-18). The impression made by this procession was such that "all the city was moved, saying, Who is this?" (Matt. 21:10). Sharpened by their hostility and their fear, the perspicacity of the Pharisees told them: "behold, the [whole] world is gone after him" (John 12:19). In this purely Jewish procession the Gospel of John also includes the participation of the Greeks, evidently of the proselytes who had come for the feast: They too desire to see Jesus, which in fact takes place when He solemnly testifies about Himself and the people hear the voice from heaven, announcing His glorification (John 12:20-31).

The people greeted Jesus as a king, as "the Son of David" (i.e., the King of the Jews): "Hosanna to the son of David" (Matt. 21:9). True, in answer to the question, "Who is this?" they said amongst themselves: "This is Jesus the prophet of Nazareth of Galilee" (21:10-11). However, this was only their manner of designating the person who had previously been known to them as a prophet, but now was greeted by them as the King. This is precisely what one learns from the exclamations of the people when they greet Him. It is instructive to compare these exclamations as they are recorded in the different Gospels:

> **Mark 11:9-10**: "Hosanna; Blessed is he that cometh in the name of the Lord: Blessed be the kingdom of our father David, that cometh in the name of the Lord: Hosanna in the highest."
>
> **Matthew 21:9**: "Hosanna to the son of David: Blessed is he that cometh in the name of the Lord; Hosanna in the highest."
>
> **Luke 19:38**: "Blessed be the King that cometh in the name of the Lord: peace in heaven, and glory in the highest." (This is an evident echo of the song of the angels glorifying the birth of the Savior, Christ the Lord, in the city of David: Luke 2:11-14.)

"Blessed is he that cometh in the name of the Lord" is a direct application of the messianic Psalm (118:26), which apparently had been sung liturgically on the eve of Passover. The same goes for the use of palms in the procession around the altar; the people used to wave them while exclaiming, "Hosanna! Save us now!" Here (in place of or apart from its direct liturgical application), the people applied this messianic text to the Messiah Himself, who accepted such an application. Furthermore, He even applied it to Himself, both before and after the event considered. *Before* this event, He applied this text prophetically in His sorrowful address to Jerusalem: "Behold, your house is left unto you desolate: and verily I say unto you, Ye shall not see me, until the time come when ye shall say, Blessed is he that cometh in the name of the Lord" (Luke 13:35). *After* this event, He applied this text at the end of the condemnatory discourse in Matthew 23:38-39. The first application can, in any case, be considered to concern the royal entry into Jerusalem, whereas the second can be considered to concern only the coming, apocalyptic entry, within the limits of earthly history. That is, the second application concerns the one-thousand-year kingdom or the eschatological appearance of Christ the King in His Glory. In any case, however one interprets the text and conceives the relation between Luke 13:35 and Matthew 23:38-39, it remains unquestionable that the text applied to the Lord's triumphal entry into Jerusalem also concerned the coming, glorious entry. The first event becomes transparent for the second. The first event is the earthly, historical precursor of the second, and this also confirms the apocalyptically eschatological and mystical significance of the second event.

The people greeted Jesus with honors due to a king; they spread garments for Him to walk on (see 2 Kings 9:13 and 1 Mac. 13:51). And they exclaimed "Hosanna!" — which here signified not only a prayer for blessing but also the welcome that was addressed to the Son of David, that is, to the Messiah (this identification was customarily professed by the Scribes: Mark 12:35). But the most important thing for us here is that these exclamations represented a greeting directly addressed to the King and the Kingdom: "Blessed be the kingdom of our father David, that cometh in the name of the Lord."[47] "Blessed be the King that cometh in the name of the Lord."

This was the entry of the King and the multitude's greeting of the King. The Lord was greeted as one who, in the name of God, was to restore "the throne of his father David" (Luke 1:32). The Lord did not reject this greeting; He accepted it. And when the chief priests and the scribes heard

---

[47]. The expression "coming," *hē erchomenē*, usually has the nuance of future time, but here, in this context ("Blessed is he that cometh in the name of the Lord," which indisputably refers to Christ who is entering the city), it also receives the nuance of present time, although in conjunction with the sense of future time.

even from the mouths of children the same shout of welcome, "Hosanna to the son of David," "they were sore displeased, and said unto him, Hearest thou what these say?" (Matt. 21:15-16). The Lord answered by referring to Psalm 8:2, and He added: "if these should hold their peace, the stones would immediately cry out" (Luke 19:40). This was already a direct challenge to the leaders of the Jewish people, and for these leaders there remained the final and decisive choice: to follow Christ or to come out against Him. But there was no doubt as to what they would choose: This is clearly demonstrated by the fact that "when he [Christ] was come near, he beheld the city, and wept over it, saying, If thou hadst known, even thou, at least in this thy day, the things which belong unto thy peace . . ." (Luke 19:41-44). The future fate of Jerusalem was already clear.[48]

Having entered the Holy City, which this day had received Him as its King, the Lord wasted no time in abandoning it. He did this after having manifested His vocation of messianic and theocratic King by purifying the Temple, that is, by chasing out the merchants (Matt. 21:12-13; Luke 19:45-46; in Mark 11:15-17, this was on the following day), as well as by a number of healings (Matt. 21:14-15). This purification of the Temple, especially in this context, was also a manifestation of messianic authority.

However, this royal glory did not last long, just as the light of Tabor had quickly faded. After the royal glory faded, the week of Christ's passion began. The Lord's entry into Jerusalem was only a symbolic anticipation of future accomplishments lying beyond the passion and the resurrection. However, the entire *fullness* of the theophany manifested in Christ would not have been realized if the rays of His glory had not shone forth on earth in the Transfiguration and if the appearance of His Kingdom had not been manifested in His royal entry. His entry was a prophecy about that which is to come; it has an apocalyptic and eschatological significance, and this significance can be fully understood only by putting it in the general context of the doctrine of Christ's royal ministry.

Christ's enthronement on earth as King is connected with His Incarnation. He was already born as the "King of the Jews," whom the magi sought in order to venerate Him ("Where is he that is born King of the Jews?" [Matt. 2:2]). And since the fullness of His ministry in the Incarnation is realized in His death on the cross, it is precisely on the cross that we have the inscription bearing this name, "King of the Jews," just as the

---

48. Therefore, one cannot consider a total invention the Jews' accusation against Jesus before the Roman authorities, namely, that He said He was "Christ a King" (Luke 23:2) — "whosoever maketh himself a king speaketh against Caesar" (John 19:12).

way of the cross begins with the triumphal entry of the King of the Jews. The Incarnation is already the beginning of the coming of Christ's Kingdom, which includes, but is not identical with, the Kingdom of Heaven or of God. The preaching of the "Gospel of the Kingdom" therefore opens with the same good news announced by the Forerunner and by Christ: "the Kingdom of God is at hand." The Kingdom of Heaven (= the Kingdom of God) simultaneously has immanent, transcendent, and historical aspects. In its immanent aspect, it is spiritual and religious; it is the life in God: "Blessed are the poor in spirit: for theirs is the kingdom of heaven" (Matt. 5:3). This Kingdom is taken "by force" (11:12), and its crowning is "righteousness, and peace, and joy in the Holy Spirit" (Rom. 14:17). In its transcendent aspect, the Kingdom of God arrives through God's action in the world and upon the world: "inherit the kingdom prepared for you from the foundation of the world" (Matt. 25:34). It also has a historical and apocalyptic aspect: It is the one-thousand-year reign of the saints with Christ, His coming in glory. The concept of the Kingdom of God is many-sided; it does not even fit within the frame of Christology but spills over into pneumatology (as well as into general triadology). However, the coming of the Kingdom of God into the world begins with and is essentially connected with Christ's *enthronement*, which we must now examine in detail. We must first distinguish two forms of His enthronement or His royal ministry (which are the same thing): *before* and *after* His glorification in the Resurrection and the Ascension.

B. The Form of Christ's Enthronement

In the days of His earthly ministry, Christ's reign was limited to His *spiritual* power over men, whatever the form in which it was manifested: words or deeds, teaching or miracle-working. In other words, His reign merged with His prophetic ministry, with the manifestation of His power (Matt. 11:20-23; 13:54; Luke 4:36; 5:17, etc). This direct action upon souls is a kingdom not of this world, a kingdom that does not need and even renounces the sword, just as in general it renounces all earthly power (Luke 22:25-27; John 18:36). The irresistible nature of the figure of Christ and of His words is that unique power by which He is enthroned in souls; and only by this power was He, the meek King, enthroned in the Holy City during those brief hours when He was the King in Jerusalem. He renounced the *other* power, however, the power of this world, which power was for Him the final temptation from the prince of this world, who acted through the instruments obedient to him: "If he be the King of Israel, let him now come down from the cross, and we will believe him" (Matt. 27:42; cf. Mark 15:32; Luke 23:37). But He remained defenseless in the hands of His enemies, drinking the cup given to Him by the Father.

This obedience was His victory over the world, His enthronement over the world, which was attested by the inscription on the cross: "King of the Jews." This refers not to the reign of God in the world and over the world as the Almighty, the Creator of heaven and earth, but to the Divine-Human reign instituted on the earth by the feat of the God-Man. This is the fulfillment of the promise concerning the theocratic Kingdom of the Messiah given in the prophecies and prefigurations of the Old Testament. This is the Kingdom of God *in* the world, not *over* the world, although it comes from on high, not from this world. This is the power and the truth of the Incarnation, in which heaven and earth, the Divine and the Human, are united. God is enthroned in a *new* way over the world: in man and through man in the God-Man. In this enthronement, just as in the resurrection, we have a two-fold act: By His obedience to the Father, the God-Man defeats the world and becomes *worthy* of having power over this world, which power He had removed from Himself in His kenosis. God the Father now gives Him this power, not just as to His only begotten Son, who pre-eternally has the kingdom, the power, and the glory in the Holy Trinity, but as to the God-Man, who has humbled Himself and taken upon Himself the form of a servant. Just as God the Father raises Christ from the dead while at the same time Christ is resurrected by His own power, so the Son is given power by the Father while at the same time taking it. "All power is given unto me in heaven and in earth" (Matt. 28:18), proclaims the Resurrected One; and this communication of power is identical with the resurrection. It is the resurrection itself: "Giving thanks unto the Father . . . who hath delivered us from the power of darkness, and hath translated us into the kingdom of his dear Son" (Col. 1:12-13). But the "one like unto the Son of man" (Rev. 1:13), that is, Christ, testifies about Himself: "To him that overcometh will I grant to sit with me in my throne, even as I also overcame, and am set down with my Father in his throne" (3:21). And the voices around the throne of God testify: "Worthy is the Lamb that was slain to receive power, and riches, and wisdom, and strength, and honour, and glory, and blessing" (5:12). (Phil. 2:9-10 should also be mentioned in the context.) Power over creation is given by the Father to Christ, and it is also taken and assimilated by Christ as the *consequence* of His high-priestly ministry.

However, this power that is given to Christ must still be actualized

The Work of Christ

by Him, like the prophetic and high-priestly ministries. The difference is that these ministries are accomplished by Christ in the days of His earthly service (although the high-priestly ministry spills over beyond the limits of the latter). The royal ministry, however, begins and is accomplished only after Christ's departure from the world, that is, after the Ascension. This feature imparts to the royal ministry an especially mystical character. Christ is the King in the world, but He does not reign in it in the fullness of the Kingdom of God. He is still *being enthroned* in the world. His royal ministry in the world *continues* even now, in contrast to the other ministries, which have ended and are active only in their fruits. Christ's Kingdom in the world still remains a kingdom not of this world, although, in the fullness of time, it will completely overcome the world. It will "come into" the world.

This definitive coming of Christ's Kingdom lies at the very bound of this world, and it thus acquires a transcendentally *eschatological* character. The coming of the kingdom begins with the Second Coming of Christ. Christ returns into the world as King: "Then shall the King say unto them" (Matt. 25:34), sitting "upon the throne of his glory" (25:31). This eschatological accomplishment has a *historical* or (which is the same thing) apocalyptic anticipation or preparation. The enthronement is accomplished in the battle for the kingdom, in the war of the prince of this world, of the forces of the Antichrist, against the power of Christ. Such a war would be impossible as far as the power of God as the Creator over creation is concerned. However, here it is a question precisely of the Kingdom of Christ the God-Man in the world; and He acts here not by Divine omnipotence and not by the power of this world, "not by might, nor by power, but by my spirit" (Zech. 4:6). (Correspondingly, it is said in 2 Thess. 2:8 that "the Lord shall consume [the Wicked] with the spirit of his mouth, and shall destroy [him] with the brightness of his coming," that is, by spiritual power.) The enthronement of Christ in the world is a tragedy of the antagonism and separation of light and darkness; this is the fundamental theme of both the Gospel of John and the book of Revelation, uniting the two books despite all their differences.

This enthronement is clearly prefigured in Holy Scripture. The basic text here is, of course, 1 Cor. 15:24-28: "Then cometh the end, when he shall have delivered up the kingdom to God, even the Father; when he shall have put down all rule and all authority and power. For he must reign, till he hath put all enemies under his feet. The last enemy that shall be destroyed is death. For he hath put all things under his feet. But when he saith all things are put under him, it is manifest that he is excepted, which did put all things under him. And when all things shall be subdued unto him, then shall the Son also himself be subject unto him that put all things under him, that God may be all in all." This text, a true *crux interpretum,* represents a micro-apocalypse of history and eschatology. It becomes intelligible if we take as our starting point the fundamental premise concerning Christ's royal ministry, namely, that His enthronement takes place during the course of history as a whole, crowned by eschatology. At the extreme bound of history, the Kingdom of Christ is abolished, to be replaced by the Kingdom of the Father and thus of the entire Holy Trinity. This is the Kingdom of Heaven (of God), where there will no longer be a boundary between God and the world that has fallen away from Him and opposes Him. In this kingdom, "God will be all in all."[49] On the basis of this text, one can affirm the *continuing* ministry of the God-Man in the world even *after* the Ascension, notwithstanding His sitting at the right hand of the Father. Consequently, this ministry remains *unfinished.* As a result, Christ's ministry goes beyond the limits of His personal glorification, which thus remains incomplete, and the state of creation remains limited, until God becomes all in all and the final enemy, death, is abolished and all things are made subject by the God-Man to the Father's will. In other words, the glorification remains unfinished as long as Christ's enthronement continues, as long as the Kingdom of Christ has not finished its work and has not been replaced by the Kingdom of God.

Christ's continuing royal ministry is *based* on His already accomplished high-priestly ministry: "this man, after he had offered one sacrifice for sins for ever, sat down on the right hand of God; from henceforth expecting till his enemies be made his footstool" (Heb. 10:12-13). Compare this with Hebrews 2:8-9, an interpretation of Psalm 8:4-6, concerning the son of man, who is identified here with the Son of Man: "in that he put all in subjection under him, he left nothing that is not put under him. But now we see not yet all things put under him. But we see Jesus . . . for the suffering of death, crowned with glory and honour."

This general idea of Christ's continuing enthronement,[50] of His

---

49. Only a *christological* interpretation, applied to the not-yet-finished royal ministry of the God-Man, excludes the trinitarian-subordinationistic interpretation of 1 Cor. 15:22-28, which otherwise becomes inevitable.

50. One can see Old Testament prefigurations of this continuing enthronement in the theocratic reigns of David and Solomon, the first of which is full of battles and victories over enemies, whereas the second shows the kingdom in all its glory, wisdom, and power (to be sure, in the best epoch of this reign).

The Work of Christ

royal ministry, which is being accomplished *in history,* is disclosed in the book of Revelation as the apocalypse, that is, as the revelation of the hidden, inner content of history. In the heavenly vision of the One who sits on the throne and who holds in his right hand a book, in this vision of the historical destiny of the Church and, with her, of the historical destiny of humanity and the entire world, "no man in heaven, nor in earth, neither under the earth, was able to open the book, neither to look thereon" (Rev. 5:3). But as one of the elders said, "Behold, the Lion of the tribe of Judah, the Root of David, hath prevailed to open the book, and to loose the seven seals thereof" (5:5). "In the midst of the throne . . . stood a Lamb as it had been slain, having seven horns and seven eyes, which are the seven Spirits of God sent forth into all the earth" (5:6). And when the Lamb took the book, all fell down before Him, and one heard voices saying, "Worthy is the Lamb that was slain to receive power, and riches, and wisdom, and strength, and honour, and glory, and blessing" (5:12). This is echoed by the voices of "every creature which is in heaven, and on the earth, and under the earth, and such as are in the sea, and all that are in them" (5:13). This is the enthronement of the Lamb on earth, or the beginning of His royal ministry.

The Kingdom of the Lamb is not only His personal dignity and ministry. It is also the royalty that He communicates to His people; it is the special royal dignity and charisma of the people of God, of the "royal priesthood" (1 Pet. 2:9), of the co-reign with Him in His Kingdom (see Rev. 20:4-6 concerning the reign with Christ in the first resurrection and in the one-thousand-year reign, as well as Rev. 22:5 concerning the reign in the heavenly Jerusalem). In the same way, Christ's High Priesthood extends to the "holy nation" (1 Pet. 2:9), the "kingdom of priests" (Exod. 19:6), the "Priests of the LORD" (Isa. 61:6), the "spiritual house, an holy priesthood" (1 Pet. 2:5) — having "made us kings and priests unto God and his Father" (Rev. 1:6). (It is characteristic that the royal and priestly dignities are united and identified, as it were, in conformity with the union of the two ministries in Christ.) Correspondingly, in Revelation 5:10, Christ's enthronement also includes those redeemed by His blood: "[Thou] hast made us unto our God kings and priests: and we shall reign on the earth."

With the loosing of the seals, earthly history begins. This history takes place simultaneously in the spiritual world and in the human world, under Christ's royal government. After the seven seals (Rev. 6-8) and the seven trumpets (Rev. 8-10), there follows (10:1) the appearance of "another mighty angel" (*ischuron,* "the Holy Mighty One," the Son), who swears that "there should be time no longer" (10:6) but that "the mystery of God

The Lamb of God

should be finished, as he hath declared to his servants the prophets" (10:7). In this appearance of "another angel," it is difficult not to perceive, if not Christ Himself (see his description in 10:1-3), then at least His express messenger, bearing the imprint of His image. The seventh angel already announces the ongoing enthronement of Christ; he announces the advent of the new, concluding epoch, although history does not end at once (11:18). "And the seventh angel sounded; and there were great voices in heaven, saying, The kingdoms of this world are become the kingdoms of our Lord, and of his Christ; and he shall reign for ever and ever" (11:15). And the elders, worshipping God, say: "We give thee thanks, O Lord God Almighty, which art, and wast, and art to come; because thou hast taken to thee thy great power, and hast reigned" (11:17). Here the enthronement is spoken of as a *new* event being accomplished in history; the expressions used to describe it are imprecise, but they resemble those used in 1 Cor. 15 and speak of the kingdom that "will have no end." Chapter 12 of Revelation describes the appearance of the woman clothed in the sun, as well as the war in heaven of Michael and the angels against the dragon and his minions, who were cast down to earth. And again a loud voice from heaven proclaims: "Now is come salvation, and strength, and the kingdom of our God, and the power of his Christ: for the accuser of our brethren is cast down" (12:10). But even after this, history *continues*, unveiled in the further chapters with their symbolism of the beasts (Rev. 13),[51] the earthly visions alternating with heavenly ones (Rev. 14). The final accomplishments are preceded by the song of Moses, the friend of God, the founder of the Old Testament theocracy, a song sung by the seven angels: "Great and marvelous are thy works, Lord God Almighty; just and true are thy ways, thou King of saints. Who shall not fear thee, O Lord, and glorify thy name for thou only art holy: for all nations shall come and worship before thee; for thy judgments are made manifest" (15:3-4). After the seven vials and the appearance of the whore of Babylon, the beasts and kings with the eighth beast at the head will "make war with the Lamb, and the Lamb shall overcome them: for he is Lord of lords, and King of kings" (17:14; cf. 1 Tim. 6:15). This war is accompanied by terrible catastrophes. Afterward, one again hears voices of praise: "Alleluia: for the Lord God om-

---

51. We refrain here from the task of interpreting the Apocalypse in all the complexity of its literary architecture with the alternation of symbols and visions, especially since all that can be offered are hypotheses. We do no more than note certain symbols whose meaning is indisputable, and which retain their validity despite different interpretations of individual visions.

nipotent reigneth. Let us be glad and rejoice, and give honour to him: for the marriage of the Lamb is come, and his wife hath made herself ready" (19:6-7). Then the appearance of the One sitting on the white horse is described, the One who "was clothed with a vesture dipped in blood: and his name is called The Word of God. . . . And he hath on his vesture and on his thigh a name written, KING OF KINGS, AND LORD OF LORDS" (19:13, 16). After this battle and the binding of Satan, there follows the first resurrection: "they lived and reigned with Christ a thousand years" (20:4); "they shall be priests of God and of Christ, and shall reign with him a thousand years" (20:6). Then the nations deceived by the liberated Satan, Gog and Magog, come forth for battle, but here history passes into eschatology — the judgment and the universal resurrection (20:11-15). And at the bounds of the future age the descent from heaven of the new Jerusalem takes place, in which God will dwell with men (Rev. 21–22). This mystical book ends with a new testimony of Christ about Himself: "I am the root and the offspring of David" (22:16), that is, the *King*. To this the Church responds with the invocation: "Even so, come, Lord Jesus" (22:20).

The images of the Apocalypse clearly reveal the fundamental idea indicated in the New Testament concerning the royal ministry of the Lord Jesus Christ: namely, that this ministry takes place in *history*, and that it takes place not only as the inner manifestation of the power of the accomplished redemption but also as the new and effective action of the "Lamb as it had been slain" (Rev. 5:6). This enthronement of the Lamb is realized in the war of the Lamb against the forces opposed to Him — first in their confused interaction and then in the final separation of the forces of good and the forces of evil. Only as its final result does this tragic accomplishment include the triumph of the new city descending from heaven onto the new earth under the new heaven. This tragedy fills *all* of history from the Ascension of the Lord to heaven until the very end of history. Christ's enthronement is accomplished by a long and intense battle, and this enthronement represents His continuing ministry, which does not end until the end of history. It represents His royal ministry on earth. Here, according to the mystical images of Revelation, Christ redescends from heaven to earth for this battle, and those who serve Him and do His work participate in it. On the one hand, there are those "that were slain for the word of God, and for the testimony which they held" (Rev. 6:9); they lament about themselves: "How long, O Lord, holy and true, dost thou not judge and avenge our blood on them that dwell on the earth?" (6:10). On the other hand, these very same, together with those who did not worship the beast, participate in the first resurrection and reign upon the earth (20:4-5). Since the battle continues with growing intensity until the very end of history, it follows that Christ's royal ministry too is continuing and is not yet finished. The entire Apocalypse (i.e., the revelation of the true content of history) is in fact this continuing enthronement.

That which Revelation portrays primarily in the historical aspect is portrayed *in its essence* (i.e., primarily eschatologically) in the "Little Apocalypse" of the Gospels, that is, in Christ's discourse about the end of the world, as well as in certain texts of the apostolic epistles. To be sure, the imagery used in the Little Apocalypse differs from that of the book of Revelation, and its representations are on another plane. Revelation refers to that "which must shortly come to pass" (1:1), that is, to the future, as far as its *content* is concerned. The goal of the Little Apocalypse, in contrast, is to exhort, to warn of the sorrows and trials that — instead of the expected messianic kingdom — await the faithful, beginning with the fall of Jerusalem, which symbolically merges with the end of the world: "be ye . . . ready" (Matt. 24:44); "take heed that no man deceive you" (24:4).

However, a more careful analysis even of the Little Apocalypse in the Gospels (Matt. 24-25; Mark 13; Luke 21) shows that here too we truly have an apocalypse (although under a stark eschatological illumination), that is, a revelation of history in certain of its aspects, from a certain angle. In conformity with its main task, the exhortation of Christians to courage, vigilance, and patience in their trials, this Little Apocalypse shows, above all, the entire tragic character of history. This is done in response to the tacit question, repeatedly posed by the disciples, concerning the messianic kingdom as the earthly triumph of the followers of the Messiah. The mother of Zebedee's sons (Matt. 20:20-21), as well as they themselves (Mark 10:35-37), ask Christ that He grant that they may sit at His right hand and at His left hand "in thy kingdom." This, of course, signifies the messianic kingdom according to the customary Jewish notions of the time. The Lord's answer is that, "Ye shall drink indeed of my cup, and be baptized with the baptism that I am baptized with: but to sit on my right hand, and on my left, is not mine to give, but it shall be given to them for whom it is prepared of my Father" (Matt. 20:23). Even after the Resurrection, before the Ascension, the disciples are still capable of asking Him: "Lord, wilt thou at this time restore again the kingdom to Israel?" (Acts 1:6).

The Lord reveals to the four disciples closest to Him that it is not the kingdom and the glory, not repose and idleness that await them, but the most painful and difficult trials. The history of the Church, within the framework of general history, is not an idyll, and not the repose of an attained kingdom, but tragedy, struggle, and division; that is, it is that

The Work of Christ

which is shown in the Revelation of St. John. In accordance with the general goal, however, attention here is drawn primarily to the somber hues. Nevertheless, the Little Apocalypse does speak of the preaching of the Gospel to all nations; that is, it speaks of the universal triumph of the Church as the condition preceding the coming of the end. In response to the disciples' tacit question concerning the kingdom that has already come, the Lord in His prophecy tells them that the tragedy of the enthronement, of the institution of His reign, is *only beginning*. That is the main and fundamental meaning of the eschatological discourses, which are difficult to understand in their details also in part because they are expounded in the apocalyptic language of the time, using prophetic eschatological images from the Old Testament (see Isa. 13:9-22; 24:10-21; 34:4; Joel 2:30-31; also Acts 2:19-20). Furthermore, these discourses are characterized by the confusion of different planes, a confusion that is natural in prophecies and to some extent is intentional. It is as if we are viewing a series of parallel mountain ranges receding into the distance but merging into a single strange image.

Nevertheless, one can identify the basic ideas contained in these discourses. First of all, our attention is drawn to the union and even fusion (in the disciples' questions) of two events: the destruction of the Temple in Jerusalem with the taking of the city and "the end of the world" with the coming of Christ (Matt. 24:3). This union is rooted in the consciousness proper to the Old Testament church: The end of the Temple and of Jerusalem merges in this consciousness with the end of the world and is its prefiguration, as it were. Historically, however, this event is in actuality only the threshold of a new historical epoch. But the Lord does not object to this confusion; on the contrary, in responding at the same time to both questions, He speaks of both the one and the other, simultaneously and in alternation (see Matt. 24:4-14 and 24:15-22; and again 24:23 and further). Along with that which refers directly to Jerusalem and the Temple (Matt. 24:15-22; Mark 13:14-20; Luke 21:20-24), there is also a characteristic transition to Christian history: "Jerusalem shall be trodden down of the Gentiles, until the times of the Gentiles be fulfilled" (Luke 21:24). That is, Christ indicates the time of the universal triumph of Christianity, which will deliver the decisive blow to the false Judaic messianic apologetics. Here the Savior warns of the three tragic trials that man will be subject to in history before the end ("for all these things must come to pass, but the end is not yet" [Matt. 24:6]). The end will come only after the "gospel of the kingdom shall be preached in all the world for a witness unto all nations" (24:14). These trials comprise temptations from false teachings, various counterfeits of Christianity, the spreading of lawlessness and lovelessness, and terrible convulsions in the spiritual world, which are described in the language of Old Testament prophetic symbolism (24:29).

Furthermore, one hears about the appearance of the sign of the Son of Man, and then about Him Himself, "coming in the clouds of heaven with power and great glory" (24:30); and "with a great sound of a trumpet," the angels sent by Him "shall gather together his elect" (24:31). But is this the end? Exegetically, one can doubt it, for the discourse then appears to touch upon history that is still continuing: from the image of the fig tree with its spreading branches we learn only that "summer is nigh: So likewise ye, when ye shall see all these things, know that it is near, even at the doors" (24:32-33). "And when these things begin to come to pass, then look up, and lift up your heads; for your redemption draweth nigh.... So likewise ye, when ye see these things come to pass, know ye that the kingdom of God is nigh at hand" (Luke 21:28, 31). "Nigh at hand," but that means that it has not yet come, and history appears to continue even *after* the appearance in heaven of the sign of the Son of Man and of Him Himself. In this case, does this not beg to be compared with the spiritual event that in Revelation 20 is symbolized as the "first resurrection"? To be sure, the resemblance between the two events is not obvious, if only because of the obscurity of these prophetic texts; however, the resemblance is not without foundation: History continues *after* both of these events, at least according to the direct testimony of the Gospel. The difficulty of the text is exacerbated by the following words: "Verily I say unto you, This generation shall not pass away, till all be fulfilled. Heaven and earth shall pass away: but my words shall not pass away" (Luke 21:32-33; Mark 13:30-31). To what do these words refer? Do they refer to the destruction of Jerusalem and of the Temple, which did in fact take place forty years later, during the lifetime of the given generation? Or do they refer to what is contained in chapter 23 and concerns not only a single generation but the entire human race? In both cases it is a question of events that are still within the limits of history, *before the end*.

Christ does not directly predict the end as an event within the limits of historical time, he only indicates it in a general way. This is clear from what follows in His discourse: "of that day and hour knoweth no man, no, not the angels of heaven [neither the Son: Mark 13:32], but my Father only" (Matt. 24:36; cf. Acts 1:7) Whatever *christological* interpretation one may offer for this ignorance of the Son, it remains unquestionable that this attests to a certain *impossibility of prophesying* about the end. It attests that this subject surpasses the capacities of human knowledge, and that, inevitably, there can be no direct prophecy about the end as an event, even in this eschatological discourse. This impossibility can be interpreted in different ways. It can signify the fact that the human empirical consciousness cannot encompass that which is transcendent to it; it can signify that this knowledge is unnecessary for this consciousness; or it can signify (and this is the most important possibility) that the very coming of the end depends *also* upon human participation and activity accomplished on the basis of human freedom, which should not be paralyzed or even affected by this knowledge that is beyond its capacities and unnecessary for it (just as a person finds himself in ignorance as far as his own death is concerned). Therefore, the transcendent consummation of the end appears, empirically, to be just as unexpected as the coming of the deluge in the days of Noah, or the rain of fire in the days of Lot (see Matt. 24:37-39; cf. Luke 17:26-30), so that it is possible that "scoffers" may appear, who express disbelief in His very coming (2 Pet. 3:3-4). And from this, precisely from the fact that the end remains *unknown* as a kind of *transcensus*, although it is certain, one draws a general conclusion: "Watch therefore: for ye know not what hour your Lord doth come" (Matt. 24:42; cf. 24:44; 25:13). And then there follows the confirmation by parable of the same idea: Matt. 24:45-51 (the parable of the faithful and unfaithful servants), 25:1-12 (the parable of the ten virgins), and 25:14-30 (the parable of the talents, which contains a summons precisely to earthly, historical work, to the multiplication of one's talents). All this is concluded by the representation in parable of the Last Judgment, not with reference to the time of its coming but with reference to its content. The parallel to the eschatological chapters of Matthew (in Mark 13) follows, in general, the same plan and has the same content, with the addition of certain details that have the practical aim of exhortation: These include the persecutions and the help of the Holy Spirit (Mark 13:11-13), with the general exhortatory conclusion: "Watch ye therefore" (13:35). In general, we find the same thing in Luke 21:5-36, with particular emphasis on the persecutions and God's help with regard to them (21:12-19).

Various apostolic epistles add certain particular details to the Gospel apocalypse. Let us first mention 2 Thess. 2:3-12, which speaks of the wicked one as a personal manifestation of theomachy and anti-Christianity. Certain other texts also concern the presence of men of disbelief, sin, and vice "in the last days" (2 Tim. 3:1-9; 1 Tim. 4:1-3; 2 Pet. 3:3-4). These texts, applied by the authors in part to phenomena of the contemporary life, also have, above all, an exhortatory significance: they represent warnings and appeals to remain firm and to confess the faith. Particularly noteworthy here are 1 Corinthians 15:22-24 and 1 Thessalonians 4:14-17. The first of these texts speaks of the universal resurrection of the dead: "in Christ shall all be made alive. But every man in his own order: Christ the firstfruits; afterward they that are Christ's at his coming. Then cometh the end." In this imperfectly clear and mysterious text, it appears possible to distinguish *two* resurrections: first, "they that are Christ's at his coming" are resurrected, and this, evidently, is followed by the universal resurrection of the dead. But the text is silent as to whether these resurrections are fused in time into a single act, or whether two acts and perhaps even two events are distinguished here, analogous to the first and second resurrections in Revelation, with the former being associated with the coming of the Lord, which, just as in the Little Apocalypse of the Gospels, does not yet mean the end of history.

Likewise, 1 Thessalonians speaks of the meeting in the air of the Lord who is descending from heaven and of the abiding with Him: "we which are alive and remain unto the coming of the Lord shall not go before them which are asleep. For the Lord himself shall descend from heaven with a shout, with the voice of the archangel, and with the trump of God: and the dead in Christ shall rise first: Then we which are alive and remain shall be caught up together with them in the clouds to meet the Lord in the air: and so shall we ever be with the Lord" (1 Thess. 4:15-17 [the King James Version has been modified to conform with the Russian Bible]). This text also speaks of "those who are Christ's" ("the dead in Christ") as those to whom is attributed the meeting with Christ in the air through rapture in the clouds. In this way, they are separated from out of the whole of humanity, which is still awaiting its resurrection. But a question arises here: Does this not indicate the same distinction that we have in Revelation between the first and the second resurrection? Is it not the case that two different apocalyptic planes are distinguished here, which, when viewed from a particular angle, merge into one, universal resurrection of the dead?

The reign of Christ is thus His *divine-human* ministry. This is not God's power over creation, not His power that transcendentally and supramundanely governs the world. It is not "providence." It is rather the God-Man's ministry that is immanent to the world, where the God-Man — having in His Incarnation removed from Himself His divine power over the world and having received it from the Father after the Resurrection in virtue of His salvific feat — actualizes this power in subjecting to Himself the world and His enemies in order to offer the kingdom to the Father by His continuing *ministry*, precisely the *royal* ministry, through the ongoing enthronement. The latter is accomplished not by virtue of the Divine omnipotence but through the inner overcoming of the world, through the struggle against enemy powers, through victory by persuasion. According to Holy Scripture, this enthronement of Christ is accomplished in a two-fold manner: through Christ's humanity, or the Church, and by Christ Himself personally. In this latter case, it is also accomplished in a two-fold manner: through the action of Christ in history and through His last coming, which will be followed by the end of the world.

Christ makes His humanity participate in His royal ministry, making us the "royal priesthood," "kings and priests." Reigning in us, He reigns in the world, establishing His Kingdom through us. This reign in and through us is, first of all, the action of His word in our souls; it is the work of "prophetic ministry," spiritual power, the kingdom not of this world, the active preaching of the Gospel that is directly indicated by Christ in His commandment to the disciples in connection with His acceptance of power: "All power is given unto me in heaven and in earth. Go ye therefore, and teach all nations, baptizing them in the name of the Father, and of the Son, and of the Holy Spirit" (Matt. 28:18-19). The preaching of the Gospel to the entire universe, "for a witness unto all nations" (24:14), is the precondition of this reign, of this enthronement. But this conquest of souls, where they become adherents of the Gospel of the Kingdom, must be expressed, and cannot fail to be expressed, in life and in works. According to the words of the Apostle, "other foundation can no man lay than that is laid, which is Jesus Christ. Now if any man build upon this foundation gold, silver, precious stones, wood, hay, stubble; every man's work shall be made manifest: for the day shall declare it, because it shall be revealed by fire; and the fire shall try every man's work of what sort it is. If any man's work abide which he hath built thereupon, he shall receive a reward. If any man's work shall be burned, he shall suffer loss: but he himself shall be saved; yet so as from fire" (1 Cor. 3:11-15 [the King James Version has been slightly modified to conform with the Russian Bible]).

This trial by fire is, in the figurative language of the Apostle, the criterion of the last, universal accomplishment, which reveals itself as the work of all humanity at the Last Judgment. There is no justification, however, to examine this work only in the light of personal destiny, in the light of personal recompense or "reward." It also has an objective, suprapersonal, all-human, historical significance: "the work will abide," but those whose work is burned will "suffer loss," and if they themselves are saved, it will be as if from fire, and they will be deprived of participation in the common work of humanity; they will be outcasts, as it were.

The Apostle's words in 2 Cor. 5:1-4 have a similar meaning. This text speaks of a heavenly dwelling, of a "house not made with hands"; that is, it speaks of the sophianic glory of our divine proto-image, of our heavenly dwelling in which we desire to be clothed. Here too, however, we face the danger that even "being clothed" we shall "be found naked," for "we that are in this tabernacle do groan, being burdened: not for that we would be unclothed, but clothed upon, that mortality might be swallowed up of life." A direct and positive correlation is established here between the "earthly house" and heavenly glory, in which mortality is not abolished but is swallowed up by life, is raised to heavenly glory. Therefore, "we must all appear before the judgment seat of Christ; that every one may receive the things done in his body, according to that he hath done, whether it be good or bad" (5:10). Having called us in Christ to His Kingdom, God gave us superabundant grace "in all wisdom and prudence; having made known unto us the mystery of his will, according to his good pleasure which he hath purposed in himself: that in the dispensation of the fullness of times he might gather together in one all things in Christ, both which are in heaven, and which are on earth" (Eph. 1:8-10; cf. 4:10). From Christ the Head, the whole body, "by joints and bands having nourishment ministered, and knit together, increaseth with the increase of God" (Col. 2:19).

In the general perspective of the royal ministry it is absolutely impossible to understand human "works" (i.e., the co-reign with Christ, the co-participation in His royal ministry) only in the transcendental and eschatological sense, in the sense of the foundation for "recompense" or in general for the personal destiny of this or that soul. This co-participation necessarily also has a historical and apocalyptic significance, in the capacity of God's *work* on earth and in history through human beings. Christ speaks of works that will be *greater* than those He Himself accomplished (to be sure, those works which He accomplished during the days of His earthly ministry). He speaks of works to which His followers are called by the Holy Spirit. This indicates the universal participation of humanity in the works of God. The prophecies are silent about what these works will be at the ultimate limit, about what the *common task* of humanity is. This is entrusted to creative human inspiration in history, for human beings will be instructed by the Holy Spirit. God has left human beings in ignorance as to the measure of their participation in His work; however, Scripture indicates what the final and general task and victory of this reign of Christ will be: "The last enemy that shall be destroyed is death" (1 Cor. 15:26; cf. 15:53-56). "But thanks be to God, which giveth us the victory

The Work of Christ

through our Lord Jesus Christ" (15:57). And it pleased the Lord to allow us to participate in this victory, whatever our part in it may be.

After the Incarnation, the entire humanity of the human race is Christ's, and all that is good in this humanity belongs to Christ. He acts in humankind not only by the effect of His teaching and His Image, not only by the power of persuasion, but also by His immediate power, by producing a certain inner change, for He who has been baptized in Christ has put on Christ (Gal. 3:27), and Christ lives in him (2:20): "If any man be in Christ, he is a new creature" (2 Cor. 5:17; cf. Gal. 6:15). Christ lives in His humankind, being enthroned in and through it in His royal ministry. In proportion to this enthronement, the Ascension is overcome in the sense of the *removal* of Christ from the world; instead, in accordance with His promise, He is present in the world "always, now and forever." It is overcome, on the one hand, by the presence of Christ in the world in the blood and water that flowed out of His side: This is the Holy Grail.[52] On the other hand, it is overcome in the Holy Eucharist, through which Christ communes with those who take communion.

This mysterious presence of Christ in the world and in humankind also corresponds to the mysterious unity of His humanity with our own, a unity that is based on the fact that Christ assumed the human essence not partially and individually but in its integral universality, as the New Adam. Therefore, not only those who know Him in this life but also those who do not know Him, and — strange to say — even those who deny Him, commune with Him and are subject to Him. The history of humankind after Christ is not only the history of Christian humankind but also the history of Christ's humankind. Christ's power, actualized by the Holy Spirit, unifies all of human history and makes it the apocalypse, or revelation, of Christ. And the works of this humankind, disparate and contradictory, are included, in their synthesis, in the work of Christ. According to the parable of the Last Judgment, Christ lives with every human being and with humankind as a whole, which will be judged as a whole (in the capacity of "all nations") in its entire common work, in conformity with the personal participation in it of every human being. This co-being with Christ (by the action of the Holy Spirit, who overshadows Him) does not abolish personal human freedom; it does not make man a blind instrument. By His inner power, however, Christ's humankind integrates its works into the common work, forging through these works a path to the transfiguration of the world or to the end of this age. This integration of the subjective and as if

---

52. See my essay "The Holy Grail."

autonomous human works into one whole, into *history*, is in general always the action of Divine Providence. But this integration changes palpably after the Incarnation; it is now accomplished, not only from outside, as if transcendentally, *upon* man, but also inwardly and immanently, in man himself. It is accomplished as the action of Christ living in humankind. The principle that unites *all* of humanity — a principle that is in part known and in part unknown, and in general not fully knowable — is not only the natural unity of humanity in Adam, which by itself already establishes the unity of its history with its laws and its goal-directedness. It is also the divine-human unity of humanity in the New Adam, in Christ. He bestows upon humanity a new nature, as it were, making it a "new creature." The action of Christ is not exhausted by the *personal* Christianity and the *personal* life in Christ of every individual human being; it also includes the *natural* life of humanity. *All* of humanity has changed with respect to its destiny; it has become other than itself as a result of the Incarnation, for Christ is the King of all humanity, and He has the power to judge it for its works. The discourse by way of parable about the Last Judgment (where the Judge attests that Christ lives in every man and can in some way be known to and accessible to every man judged by Christ) confirms the general idea that all of human history after Christ, with its broken and strange dialectic, is essentially a *Christian history*, connected with the Church of Christ, which is its inner entelechy. It is precisely this that is attested by the book of Revelation, which portrays the fates of the nations as one interconnected body (in the same way that the Old Testament history of the prophets does: see Isaiah, Jeremiah, Daniel, et al.).

But do we not thereby transform Christ's power into a *natural* power, as it were? Is this not a kind of naturalism? That is the legitimate doubt that comes to mind. However, strictly speaking, what does this "natural" power represent? Does it represent a physical or a metaphysical principle? Does it represent a power contained in the *mechanism* of the world, or does it represent a specially qualified, new *energy* of life, even if it realizes itself through the action of natural forces? In this sense, what, for example, does the power of the universal resurrection represent, this power that, according to Scripture, is directly based on the power of Christ's resurrection? ("For as in Adam all die, even so in Christ shall all be made alive" [1 Cor. 15:22].) Resurrection extends to *all* human beings, irrespective of the *personal* relation to Christ of each of them: it extends to those who knew Him in earthly life and to those who did not know Him, to those who believed in Him and to those who did not believe in Him. According to the meaning of the apostolic doctrine of the universal resurrection, they will be raised not by the power of a new creative act of God's omnipotence but by the power of their *inner connection* with Christ, the "firstfruits" of the dead; in this case, however, this inner connection has not a *personal* but a *natural* character. For *all* will be raised, simply in virtue of the fact of their humanity, which, having become Christ's, received from Him also the power of resurrection.

But if all natural humanity will be raised in Christ (and this does not provoke any doubts with regard to the naturalism that is also contained in a certain sense in this idea), why can it not be connected with Him in its historical life? For life, death, and resurrection are interconnected; and from this interconnection it is not possible to isolate resurrection as an external act that has no inner foundation for itself in all human life connected with Christ, as an act that appears as a *deus ex machina* and expressly surpasses the human essence. To be sure, resurrection is accomplished by God's power acting in man, "with the trump of God" (1 Thess. 4:16), but it acts to reveal and realize that principle of immortality that *already lives* in man through his natural communion with Christ in His inhumanization.

Christ's immortality is therefore, in a certain sense, the *law* for human beings in their resurrection; and in a certain sense we must extend this idea to all human natural life. This idea is included in the more general idea that eschatology, the end of the world and the resurrection, does not arrive as a *deus ex machina*[53] but is prepared by *history,* which, as the apocalypse, is in a certain sense included in eschatology but also transcends it. Eschatology presupposes *discontinuity, transcensus,* which is what the idea of the *end* consists in. However, according to both the Gospel apocalypse and the Revelation of John, the world must ripen for the end, and history will end inwardly, having accomplished its work. But this work is not only, so to speak, the algebraic sum of an infinite series of separate personal works in their random chaoticity; it is also a positive integral in the natural regularity of an ordered series. This regularity is Christ, "by whom are all things, and we by him" (1 Cor. 8:6). In other words, in the history of humanity after the Incarnation — with all the intensity of the battle between light and darkness, between Christianity and antiChristianity, with all the acuteness of the dialectical antithetics of this

---

53. Although in the Gospels the coming of Christ is likened to the deluge, this analogy is valid only in the sense that His coming will be unexpected for those who cannot see the blossoming of the fig tree and the approach of the last times, even if they cannot be known precisely.

battle — the work of Christ is being done. Those are in error who, focusing their attention solely on the separate moments of the historical tragedy, on its soul-rending contradictions, see its entire result only in the appearance of the Antichrist, in universal decline and corruption, and in general reduce this result not to zero but to a negative quantity. In any case, the Apocalypse not only contains images of tragic antagonism; it also contains the victory and enthronement of Christ on earth after the first resurrection, as well as the descent of the heavenly city at the end. History is eschatologically overcome only when a certain transcendent moment arrives, a moment that represents the action of God *upon* the world. This is precisely the moment of the universal resurrection and the transfiguration of the world: "Behold, I make all things new" (Rev. 21:5), a new heaven and a new earth (Rev. 21:2; 2 Pet. 3:13), with the new Jerusalem, descending from heaven. To be sure, this new creature, whose renewal is the overshadowing of the Comforter Spirit, is already in a certain sense the supraworld and suprahistory, to which the life of this age and of this world *transcends*. And this life is truly new: "it doth not yet appear what we shall be" (1 John 3:2). However, this *transcensus* and this overshadowing presuppose, as their object (or receptacle), this world, and this earth, and this history, although in their transfigured state; and in this sense there is a direct connection between them.

The world must ripen for its end, and Christ's work in this world, however we understand it, must end within the limits of the world. In the New Testament prophecies (both in the Gospel apocalypse and in the Revelation of John) the boundary between history and suprahistory, or the end, between apocalypse and eschatology, is almost imperceptible, since, in the perspective view, the two appear to merge into one. Nevertheless, this boundary does exist, so that the new arises from the old, like a new birth, with new life. Therefore, the historical apocalypse should not swallow up or abolish eschatology; nor should eschatology swallow up or abolish history: the two condition each other, and it is wrong to separate them. The *parousia*, the second and glorious coming of Christ, is situated at the very boundary of the eschatological *transcensus*: it belongs equally to the historical apocalypse and to eschatology, as "the life of the future age."

We do not inject a false determinism when we say that history has a law that governs it, namely, the enthronement or royal ministry of Christ in His humanity. Such determinism would be incompatible with the creature's personal freedom and responsibility, limited as they are. However, it is necessary to render its due to the determinism that, in the final analysis, is true; we mean *sophianic* determinism, which is based on the natural properties of being that are given to the creature. When He became incarnate, Christ became the law of being for natural humanity; He became its supreme inner natural reality, although one that was concealed, still submerged in the old Adam, in the old natural and human world. This reality of Christ's humanity does not depend on its free and personal acceptance or nonacceptance by every human individual. Every human individual is truly free to accept it or not accept it, being called to this choice; but one cannot make this reality nonexistent or create one's own nature for oneself. This is because freedom is only a *mode* of being, not its content: in itself, *nothing* is emptiness that, for itself, does not even have independent nonbeing. It acquires nonbeing only from natural being. This higher naturalness of Christ's creation remains unknown outside of Christianity; but this naturalness does not thereby become unreal, even though, beyond the visible limits of the Church, we cannot empirically feel and know the world and humanity as the body of Christ. We know only that all things that lie beyond these limits are also *included* in the sphere of the Church's influence, in the history of the Church. Here the free self-determination of man is accomplished, as it were, in crepuscular obscurity, not in relation to Christ Himself, but nonetheless in relation to the principle of Christ — in relation to goodness, conscience, Divinity.[54] After Christ, the entire history of humanity takes a new direction, in virtue of this dynamic pan-Christism. As far as the elect (i.e., Christians) are concerned, this self-determination is accomplished in full consciousness and with full responsibility; and this is attested at Christ's judgment.

If we pose the question of the accomplishment of Christ's royal ministry in connection with the dogma of the Ascension, it is revealed to us from a new point of view that the Ascension, in the capacity of the continuing definitive glorification of the God-Man, does not by any means signify that He has completely departed the world and has terminated all connection with it. In Christ's royal ministry, which continues beyond the Ascension, this indissoluble connection with the world is manifested in its own manner and in different aspects. First of all, it is manifested as *spiritual* power in the capacity of the continuing action of Christ's prophetic ministry, through His teaching and, chiefly, through His holy image, which is imprinted in men's hearts and calls men to follow Him. Sec-

---

54. Peter tells Cornelius: "God hath shewed me that I should not call any man common or unclean. . . . God is no respecter of persons: but in every nation he that feareth him, and worketh righteousness, is accepted with him" (Acts 10:28, 34-35).

ond, it is manifested as *Eucharistic* power, the mysterious connection of the glorified Christ with man in communion and the unceasing sanctification of the elements of the world through the presence in them of the Sacred Gifts, the Body and Blood of Christ. Third, this connection is also a *natural* and *human* one, realized through the pouring forth of blood and water from Christ's side, through which, in His earthly state, He invisibly abides with His humankind, co-suffering with it and never abandoning it on its earthly path. Fourthly and finally, it is manifested as an *energetic* connection. Having assumed in His humanity the entire old Adam, Christ is the immanent law of humankind, not only in the order of free grace, but also in the order of nature. Christ *leads* His humankind, despite its antagonism and resistance, which are a manifestation of the freedom of the fallen man. This *dynamic* presence of Christ in humankind extends its influence beyond the limits of Christian humankind. It extends its influence to all men, to those who know Him and to those who do not know Him: "he must reign, till he hath put all enemies under his feet" (1 Cor. 15:25). Christ's action in the world merges here with the general action of Divine Providence, which guides the world and watches over it. This is a necessary postulate of Christology.

The personal work of salvation is thus interwoven into the general work of humankind; and these threads of subjective freedom and objective givenness combine to form the variegated and intricately worked fabric of history. It is impossible for man to consider, assess, integrate, and connect all the actions of human freedom or individuality in history, with its supramundane roots at the boundary of time and with its empirical destinies — only Divine Providence can do that. However, we are familiar with the fundamental elements of this process, as well as its teleology, its inner entelechy. By the power of Christ, human history moves toward its end, which is universal resurrection and the transfiguration of the creature. In this world, all things that are necessary for its transition to the being of the other world are being accomplished. The common work of historical humanity is the enthronement of Christ in the world, after which the Son will give His Kingdom to the Father. This leads to the general eschatological conclusion related to the *time* of the Second Coming. The God-Man said that even He was ignorant of this time, since, by His humanity, He too was included in the historical process, whose flow incorporates the participation of human freedom and prepares the ripening of the fig tree of the world for the approach of the end. Like His First Coming into the world, His Second Coming is not a unilateral but a bilateral act. For the Second Coming to be accomplished, the time for the end of the world must arrive through the work of the world itself. Among other conditions, this time is determined by human freedom; and depending on this freedom, it can be shorter or longer, although it arrives according to the will of the Heavenly Father, who establishes the times and seasons of the accomplishments. In this sense, the Second Coming is not only a Divine work but also a human one, which is to be accomplished on the pathways of history. Such is the importance, seriousness, and significance of human history after Christ on the pathways of His enthronement, which is being accomplished in us and through us. History is not an empty corridor that we must come to the end of in order to escape from this world into the other world. It belongs to the work of Christ in His Incarnation. It is the apocalypse that is moving toward eschatological consummation. It is the divine-human work on earth.

This lays the foundation for an apocalyptic-eschatological, immanent-transcendent, religious evaluation of the common work of humanity in the world. Being in essence Christ's work, man's creative activity in history must reveal and manifest the entire profundity and power of humanity. It must reveal in man the image of God. Consequently, all *worthy* human creative activity, "culture," is called to transfiguration in the Kingdom of God as the self-revelation of true humanity, even if in its immediate form it was tried by fire. The humanization of the world, with man's domination of it in the name of God, to which he was called at his creation, refers to the manifestation of man's royal ministry in virtue of his participation in that of Christ, irrespective of how far man's aspirations might go on this pathway, even including his active participation in the universal resurrection, in accordance with N. F. Fedorov's "project."[55] The only thing we must reject decisively here is any interpretation of this project according to which the human-engineered resurrection fully supplants the work of God, history absorbs and abolishes eschatology, and resurrection stops being resurrection and becomes merely a reproduction of human *likenesses,* of "robots." Such an interpretation must be rejected because what is essential for man is the union of *personal* spirit with ani-

---

55. The "project" of the eccentric Russian philosopher Nikolai Fedorov (1828-1903) was expounded in his main work, *The Philosophy of the Common Task*. According to this project, it is man's task to aid God in the work of resurrection by developing technological means to raise from the dead all the human beings who have ever died. This "active Christianity" is the common task of humanity, and Fedorov considers that its commencement will already begin to overcome the poisonous "unbrotherly" state that has dominated humanity throughout history. With the abolition of death, the ultimate goal is the transfiguration of humanity and, then, of the entire universe. — Trans.

mate body. The mechanical resurrectors plan to resurrect only the latter, but after death, the human spirit remains in the hands of God. Therefore, a resurrection that is only *immanent* is impossible; it is religious nonsense. Resurrection cannot be accomplished without a Divine act — the return of the human spirit into the body, with the creative restoration of the capacity of the soul to quicken the body. However, in no wise does this mean that, in resurrection, everything from beginning to end must be the work of God without any participation of man. On the contrary, resurrection too must become a divine-human work in which Christ's humanity too, living in the Church, will, in His Name, realize all that is accessible to man on the path to universal resurrection. This crowns the earthly work of humanity. Even if this idea does not have eschatological *necessity,* in any case it expresses one of the historical possibilities on the pathways of the maturation of the human race in its progress beyond the limits of history, in the battle against the last enemy, death, also by human powers. But these possibilities are not given to man but only proposed to him as a task and entrusted to his creative freedom. One therefore cannot dogmatize about these possibilities; one can only theoretically "preview" them, defining their place in the understanding of the end.[56]

However, Holy Scripture attests that, even before the end, Christ will appear mysteriously in the world and in history; and this appearance will also pertain to His enthronement. We have such a testimony in the prophecy concerning the *first* resurrection (Revelation 20), in which only the elect participate: "they lived and reigned with Christ" (20:4). This is related here as a certain event among other events in history. The text attests, in any case, to some special and exclusive closeness to Christ of those who have come back to life. To negate this event by a spiritualistic interpretation that does violence to the text (following St. Augustine and Tichonius) is neither theologically nor exegetically permissible. Such an exegesis would be a false reading of Scripture in the name of a prejudiced and one-sided theological doctrine. At the same time, history does not yet provide data that would enable us to concretely grasp and understand this prophecy, which contains the indubitable promise that, on the pathways of Christ's enthronement in history, there will be an entire epoch

---

56. In accordance with the plan of the present work, questions of eschatology will be treated in depth in a later volume. In the present work, eschatology is only touched upon in passing, with reference to Christology. [Eschatology is treated in depth in the final part of this trilogy, *The Bride of the Lamb,* available in Boris Jakim's translation (Eerdmans, 2002). — Trans.]

when Christ's presence on earth will be expressly tangible for the elect, and He will personally participate in the historical accomplishment. In other words, this will be a *divine-human* process: "they . . . reigned with Christ a thousand years" (Rev. 20:4).

In addition to the thousand-year reign, this personal participation of Christ in history is also expressed in the mysterious appearance of Christ for the final battle against the forces of anti-Christianity, against the beast and the false prophet, which is described in Revelation 19:11-21. The vision begins with the appearance in the opened heaven of the One sitting upon a white horse, followed by armies of heaven also upon white horses. This is followed by a description of the battle with the beast and the kings of the earth and their armies, evidently on earth. The mysterious meaning of this image does not yield to direct interpretation, but it is indisputable that this appearance corresponds to some earthly event, that it takes place not only in heaven but also in history. (Was the appearance of Christ in heaven to the Apostle Paul not similar to this? Even though this appearance to Paul was heavenly, that is, transcendental, it also belonged to history and even to personal biography.)

The enthronement of Christ on earth for His one-thousand-year reign will become perfectly evident, as evident as His enthronement was during His royal entry into Jerusalem. The curve of history, with upward and downward fluctuations, goes upward at this point and meets heaven; but then it falls sharply downward in the final revolt of Gog and Magog, beyond which one can see the end and the interruption of the curve, the *transcensus*. This prophecy — contrary to the prevailing doctrine, which it would be erroneous to consider as the dogmatic definition of the Church — refers to the as-yet-unactualized future, so that it is impossible to conceive it concretely. According to the content of this prophecy, one can in any case establish that, during the "first resurrection," the wall separating the world of the living from the world of the dead disappears, as it were, precisely for the souls who have come back to life and who reign with Christ for a thousand years. It is through these souls that Christ Himself reigns on earth. This event, connected also with the enchainment of Satan for a thousand years, represents an important step on the path of Christ's enthronement; and in general it belongs to His royal ministry.

But this does not exhaust the personal and direct participation of Christ in the earthly history of His enthronement. An analysis of the eschatological texts convinces us that they are marked by a certain obscurity as far as Christ's Second Coming, the parousia, is concerned. Specifically, it is unclear if the parousia is already the *end*, or only one of the concluding events within the limits of history.[57] There also remains the question whether the parousia is connected at least with the event that Revelation describes as the first resurrection. In this case, the Last Judgment merges with the parousia only in the general eschatological perspective, but the two events are not the same. This type of merging is common in apocalyptics. If one in fact understands this event as the appearance of Christ in history, one must see it as one of His most decisive actions on the path to enthronement in the world. If one primarily understands it eschatologically, as the coming of the end, then in this case His appearance as "King" represents, at the same time, the final link in the historical chain. It represents His true enthronement, which, immediately, is already also the "judgment."

This concludes His royal ministry, as well as His glorification. Until this happens, however, Christ's earthly ministry and, thus, His kenosis in this ministry continue uninterrupted. Power has been *given,* but it has not yet been definitively received (just as glorification was given before the passion: "Now is the Son of man glorified" [John 13:31]). Risen, ascended, and sitting at the right hand of the Father in the glory of God, Christ nevertheless continues His earthly ministry. Christ's earthly enthronement is the path through history to His reign, which "will have no end." The Lord abides invisibly with us on earth. His Ascension and His sitting at the right hand of the Father have not taken Him from us, from our earthly pain, from our suffering, from our struggle, our agony. Residing in the glory of the Holy Trinity, as God in heaven, He remains mysteriously united with the world. He remains with us, as co-man, as God-Man, in the continuing enthronement, which is being accomplished "in tribulation, and in the kingdom and patience of Jesus Christ" (Rev. 1:9), with the participation of the faithful. Christ's humiliation went through many stages before it was overcome by the glorification. In essence, His humiliation is already overcome, but it continues to be experienced in that which constitutes the consequence of this overcoming, in the enthronement of Christ

---

57. Likewise, the meaning of 2 Thess. 2:8 is unclear: "And then shall that Wicked be revealed, whom the Lord shall consume with the spirit of his mouth, and shall destroy with the brightness of his coming." According to the scheme of the Apocalypse, the defeat of the "beast" will occur not before the end of the world but only before the thousand-year reign and the first resurrection, whereas before the end of the world the revolt of Gog and Magog will occur. In the present case, however, nothing prevents one from interpreting this prophecy "spiritually," that is, nothing prevents one from seeing in the "Wicked" the bearer of the spirit of impiety, who will be defeated by the spirit of Christ in "the brightness of his coming," that is, by Christ's power acting in the world.

on earth, which still finds itself under the burden of the sin of the old Adam. Even until the present day, Christ continues to *receive* the power given to Him together with humanity; and even until the present day, He continues to accomplish His royal ministry. True God, reigning in us and over us on earth, He is being enthroned for His eternal Kingdom, about which we always pray to the Father:

Thy Kingdom come!

And we call out to the Son:

Even so, come, Lord Jesus!

APPENDIX

The Lamb of God: On Divine-Humanity, Part 1

Summary prepared by Sergius Bulgakov

The fundamental idea governing the Christology of the author of *The Lamb of God* is Divine-Humanity, that is, the perfect union of Divinity and Humanity in Christ, and then in general of God and the world. In this sense, his task is to develop a Chalcedonian theology. In its general tendency, this work is thus directed both against pantheism and against Protestant transcendentalism. The problem treated in this work is the christological one: How is the Divine Incarnation *possible*? What does it presuppose for itself, and what does it contain in itself?

The author begins with an extensive patrological introduction. He finds that the christological problem was first posed by Apollinarius of Laodicea. Following him, the schools of Alexandria (St. Cyril) and Antioch (Theodore of Mopsuestia, Nestorius, Theodoret, and others, including, in a certain sense, Pope Leo the Great) dialectically express, as thesis and antithesis, the doctrine of the unity and duality of the natures in Christ. This antithetics is overcome by the *synthesis* of the Chalcedonian dogma of the duality of the natures in one hypostasis.

However, here we have only a dogmatic, not a theological, synthesis; until the present day, a theological synthesis is still being sought by theological thought. It is still the "unknown quantity," as it were. The attempt to find such a synthesis by Leontius of Byzantium in his doctrine of the "in-hypostatization" of the two natures by the Logos is only a formal

---

This is the first translation of this summary, first published in the Russian theological journal *Put'*, no. 41 (1933): 101-5. Throughout this summary, Bulgakov refers to himself in the third person (as "the author"). — Trans.

scholastic theory with the imprint of Aristotelism and cannot satisfy modern thought. St. John of Damascus does not introduce any new theological ideas into Christology but only summarizes the views of his predecessors. The monothelitic and dithelitic disputes, as well as the definition of the Sixth Ecumenical Council, move in the plane of the earlier theology and do not advance the christological doctrine. They only give a more concrete expression to the Chalcedonian formula, not only in relation to the duality of the natures, but also in relation to the duality of the wills, while theologically leaving the question insufficiently clear, despite the labors of St. Maximus Confessor. With this, creative thought in the domain of Christology breaks off, and the desired theological synthesis in the doctrine of Christ remains something for the future — and in particular for our epoch — to achieve.

The fundamental question of Christology is: How can one understand the union of the two natures, Divine and human, in the one hypostasis of the Logos not only from the negative side, as it is defined in the Chalcedonian dogma (with its four negatives: inconfusably, unchangeably, indivisibly, inseparably), but also from the positive side? We know what the Chalcedonian "no" is, but what is its "yes"?

In developing his Christology, the author positively and openly relies on sophiology, the doctrine of the eternal and the creaturely Divine Wisdom.

The Holy Trinity has its nature or ousia, which is not only the inexhaustible depth of life, but also the self-revelation of Divinity. This nature or ousia is not a hypostasis, but belongs to the trinitarian hypostasis, is hypostatized, with the Logos being the hypostasis that is immediately directed toward Sophia. The ideal All of the Logos is accomplished and thus hypostatized by the Holy Spirit, and these two hypostases reveal the Father. In this way, in the ousia as Sophia, the consubstantial and inseparable life of the Holy Trinity is realized. Sophia is *ens realissimum* as the divine world, possessing the eternity of God. She is the Glory of God as Divine bliss in the trihypostatic love of God for His own Divinity.

Together with this, Sophia is the pre-eternal humanity, as the Proto-Image, in the image of which man is created; and the Logos is, in this sense, the heavenly Man even apart from His Incarnation. The Divine Wisdom, being the eternal Proto-Image of the creaturely world in God, is the essential foundation and content of creation, being submerged in becoming. The Divine world and the creaturely world are correlated with one other as the eternal Sophia and the creaturely Sophia. Being identical in their foundation, the Divine world and the creaturely world are different in their mode of being. The former is pre-eternally existent in God, whereas the latter, as having arisen "out of nothing," is a becoming world, although Sophia is the foundation and the entelechy for it too. The creaturely world has its center in man, who is created in the image of the Divine Logos. Man has an uncreated spirit, which has come out of God and which has been called by God to hypostatic being; he also has his nature, which is the world as the creaturely Sophia, in his psycho-corporeal organism. In the Creator and in creation, Sophia is the bridge that unites God and man; and it is this *unity* of Sophia that constitutes the Chalcedonian "yes," the foundation of the Incarnation.

In Christ, as the uncreated hypostatic spirit, the Second hypostasis itself, the Logos, is present; His two natures are the Divine Sophia and the creaturely Sophia, the heavenly and the earthly humanity — one and the same principle in two forms, divine fullness and creaturely becoming. Therefore, the two natures may be positively correlated through the communication of properties *(communicatio idiomatum)* in the deification of the creaturely essence by the Divine essence. Sophia, as the *divine-humanity,* is precisely the ontological foundation of the Divine Incarnation that makes it understandable as "the Word was made flesh" (John 1:14). This is also what gives meaning to the identification of the two names — the Son of God and the Son of Man — by which Christ is called in the Gospels of the God-Man.

The union of the two natures in the one life of the one Person can be understood only on the basis of the principle of the self-diminution (kenosis) of the Divine essence in the God-Man to the human measure. This kenosis, however, should be understood not as the abandonment by the Logos of His Divinity (as this is usually interpreted in kenotic theories) but as His abandonment of the Divine Glory, of the fullness of the sophianic life, with His submergence in becoming. Christ follows this path of humiliation until His human essence becomes capable of receiving glorification. The in-humanization of the Logos — with the acceptance of the measure of the human essence as the abandonment of the fullness of the Divine life and glory, "the descent from heaven" — is expressed in the fact that, for Him, the limit of the human is also His own limit. Therefore, the authenticity of His human development, and of His ignorance and prayer, is accepted. And the working of miracles is viewed not as a manifestation of Divine power over the world but only as the acts of a spirit-bearing miracle-worker, by analogy with human miracle-working.

In the light of this general idea of the descent of the divine self-consciousness to the human measure, the author examines the Gospel image of Christ with His divine-human self-consciousness. The characteristics of this divine-humanity are also defined in the doctrine of Christ's three ministries.

In particular, the *prophetic* ministry emphasizes His humanity, in virtue of which the Divine truth humanly proclaims itself not from its own Divine Person, as God, but according to the type of the prophets, while, of course, surpassing them; Christ proclaims the Divine truth not as God but as "rabbi" and "master," as the God-Man, manifesting His Divinity in man and through man. The prophetic ministry includes all of Christ's *works*, in particular miracle-working, which were proper also to other prophets; but the main content of His prophetic preaching is He Himself and His divine-human image.

In the *high-priestly* ministry of the sacrificial obedience of love for the Father and for human beings, the main role is played by redemption, understood ontologically as well. The Divine Incarnation is not only a means to redemption from sin but also the elevation of man to divine-humanity, to which he was summoned when he was created. However, being a creaturely being, the creaturely Sophia, man is separated from the Creator by an insurmountable abyss, which becomes even deeper as a consequence of sin, resulting from the perverse character of the creature. And, in creating man, God-Love pre-eternally takes upon Himself the Creator's responsibility for the restoration of the creature, perverse in its freedom. By the sacrifice of the pre-eternally slaughtered Lamb, He redeems this natural creatureliness and the perverse sinfulness, elevating man to the divine-humanity to which he was summoned. Here, redemption is revealed not as a work of the Second hypostasis alone but as a joint act of the entire Holy Trinity. In virtue of the unity of His human nature with the common human nature, the God-Man is identified with the old Adam; and by means of His compassionate love, He makes Adam's sin His own. He takes upon Himself the anger of the Father, which weighs upon Adam and which results in abandonment by God and death. This partaking of the deadly cup of sin takes place spiritually at Gethsemane and bodily on Golgotha, and it culminates in death. Bodily and spiritually, Christ suffers through the equivalent, as it were, of all human sins, of all the torments of hell for these sins; as a result he nullifies the power of sin, makes it nonexistent, so to speak, and reconciles with God those human beings who by their freedom desire to gain this reconciliation, this salvation. God glorifies Christ for this sacrificial obedience, by which He restores man and becomes worthy and capable of receiving glorification. The latter is expressed in the Resurrection and the Ascension, which are accomplished by the Father by the power of the Holy Spirit but also by the divine-human power of Christ Himself. Therefore, the glorification belongs to the high-priestly ministry and presupposes the not-yet-concluded kenosis, which is finally overcome only in the sitting at the right hand of the Father.

What can we say about the *royal* ministry? In contrast to the other two ministries, it has not yet been completed but is a continuing ministry that will not end until the Reign of Christ is realized in the world and He gives His Kingdom to the Father. Christ's royal dignity is manifested symbolically in His royal entry into Jerusalem. This dignity is realized by Christ's power in the world through His faithful servants, and the Apocalypse contains symbols of this enthronement in the world, which is destined to be manifested even before the visible end of the world, before the end of this age.

The further parts of this book on Divine-Humanity will be devoted to the doctrine of the Holy Spirit, and to ecclesiology and eschatology.[1]

---

1. Bulgakov is referring to part 2 of this trilogy (*The Comforter* [Eerdmans, 2004]) and part 3 (*The Bride of the Lamb* [Eerdmans, 2002]). — Trans.

Index

Adam, 9-10, 12, 79, 113, 138, 145, 149-151, 172, 177, 179, 181-182, 188-189, 200-201, 204-206, 217, 243, 271, 286, 289-291, 299-300, 312, 344-354, 357-358, 360, 365-366, 379, 381, 383, 432, 436, 441; and creaturely Sophia, 146; and freedom, 294-295; temptation of, 295, 297
Abelard, 344, 357
Agatho, Pope, 83
Agnoetae, 253
Alexandria, school of, 19, 33, 42, 49, 51, 57, 62, 208
Angels, 79, 127, 149, 163
Animals, 141
Annunciation, 179, 193n, 200, 247, 266, 307, 411
Anselm of Canterbury, 343, 365
Antioch, school of, 5, 7, 18, 19, 20, 22, 28, 31, 33-35, 39, 41-42, 45, 47-48, 50-51, 55-57, 62, 85, 208, 217, 256
Anti-Sophia (fallen Sophia, Achamoth), 154; and beauty, 155-156, 187, 199
Antonii, Metropolitan, 344, 354, 356, 357, 366, 368
Aphthartodocetics (Phantasiasts), 288-289
Apocalypse, 328-329, 331, 334n, 349n, 405n, 406, 420-428, 432-434, 439
Apocatastasis, 151-152

Apollinarianism, 21, 32-33, 39, 49, 59, 71, 74, 80, 189n, 194, 208
Apollinarius of Laodicea, 2, 5, 8, 12, 13-14, 19, 20, 22, 26-27, 28, 31, 34, 36, 37, 39-40, 50, 71, 74, 183, 208-209, 256, 296, 301, 310; and Arius, 18; and Chalcedonian dogma, 10-11, 30n; and composition of the God-Man, 7; and conception of divine-humanity, 3-4, 16; and deification, 15; and "man from heaven," 9, 16-17; origin of Christology, 4
Apophatic theology, 112, 121n
Arianism, 216, 280-281, 283, 304-305
Aristotle, 64-67, 75, 104
Arius, 18, 220
Ascension, 133, 192, 202, 219, 227, 314, 317-319, 348, 385-402, 404-406, 408-410, 417, 419, 420, 424, 435, 440
Assumption of human nature (human essence), 205, 242, 288-289, 306, 346-347, 360
Athanasius, 3, 8, 14, 52, 343
Augustine, 53, 384, 438

Beauty, 155-156; in Christ, 272-273
Becoming, 197; of world, 134, 160
Berdiaev, Nikolai: *Destiny of Man,* 133n
Boehme, 97, 134
Boethius, 63, 71

449

Index

Bulgakov, Sergius: biography, x-xi

Cain, 204
Calvinism, 159
Chalcedon, Council of, 33, 44, 45, 47, 50-51, 53, 57-58, 61-62, 69, 87, 182, 194-196, 224, 241
Chalcedonian Creed, viii, 250
Chalcedon, Definition of, 51, 56-64, 84-85, 87, 182-184, 194-196, 202, 206-207, 209-211, 235-236, 238-239, 244-245, 248-249, 259, 270, 328, 330, 381, 399
Chalcedonian doctrine, xi, 7, 10, 12-13, 17, 30n, 32, 34, 36-37, 38, 44, 48, 50-51, 61-62, 68, 75, 208, 310; and kenosis, 239
Christ, xiv, 4, 9, 16, 21, 36, 40, 72, 75, 81, 108, 114, 138, 168, 174, 180, 193, 198, 200, 202, 232, 270-271; Ascension, 133, 192, 202, 219, 227, 314, 317-319, 348, 385-402, 404-406, 408-410, 417, 435, 440; baptism of, 264, 308, 337; body of, 289-290, 367, 385-388, 393-396; crucifixion, 31; death of, 372-379; divine consciousness, xi, 233-234, 236, 240-241, 250-251, 262-263, 265-266, 275, 277, 279-280, 284-285, 355; and Divine-Humanity, ix, xiii, xv; Divine Infant, 176, 202, 232, 234, 241, 247, 253-254, 262; divine nature (divine essence) of, viii, 5-7, 10-11, 13, 18, 28, 35, 41, 49-50, 53-54, 73, 77, 189, 193-194, 197, 199, 201, 216, 224-225, 230, 238, 241, 243, 247, 253, 255, 257-258, 261, 300, 352, 358; divine will, 81-82, 84, 244-245, 301; Emmanuel, 233, 239, 255-256; forsakenness of, 313-314, 355-357, 364; form of a servant, 42, 46, 215-217, 224, 230, 279, 296, 318; and freedom, 295; genealogy, 180; glorification, xii, 217, 238-239, 242, 253, 309, 318-320, 339-341, 358, 379-383, 386, 390-391, 393, 397, 400, 402-403, 405, 407-408, 410, 413, 417, 420, 435, 440; God-Man, dogma of, 182, 187-189, 196, 210, 221, 235; growth and development of, 241-242, 247, 253-254, 262-263, 303; relation with Holy Spirit, 307-309; human consciousness, 229, 233, 241, 262, 265; human nature (human essence) of, viii, 5-8, 10-11, 17, 14-15, 18, 27, 28, 33-35, 41, 49-50, 53-54, 68-69, 71, 73, 77, 184-186, 188-189, 193-194, 196, 199, 201, 203-207, 217, 235, 239, 241-243, 252, 255-258, 286, 289-291, 293, 295, 297-301, 306, 310, 347-348, 352-356, 358, 360; human will, 78-80, 82, 84, 86, 301; ignorance of, 253, 301-303, 355; and image of God, 139, 146; Jesus, 37-38, 73, 198, 207, 230, 241, 246-247, 249, 262; as King, 411-412, 415-419, 440; as Messiah, 277; and Mother of God, 115; and nature, 156; obedience to Father, 306-307, 310-312, 342, 352-353, 355, 364, 368, 373, 380, 391, 418; passion of, 31, 366, 369; person of, 34, 203-204; resurrection, 133, 237, 251, 255, 308, 316-320, 343, 354, 379, 382-391, 393, 395, 402; and Sophia, 203; struggle of, 286-287, 297, 300; suffering of, 259, 273-274, 284, 286-288, 310, 312-314, 338, 346, 348, 351, 355-356, 358, 360-362, 366, 368-369, 372, 374, 409; temptation of, 291-294, 296-301, 308, 360; unity of, 24, 28-30, 50, 52, 55-56, 58, 61, 81, 86, 207, 221; victory over death, 310-312, 374, 382, 385
Christianity, xv, 193
Christology, viii, xi, 1, 4, 7-8, 11-13, 15, 17-18, 19, 39, 46, 48, 52, 55-57, 67, 70, 73-74, 87-88, 185, 192, 200, 207-209, 221, 259, 282-283; Antiochene, 34; Apollinarius' problematic, 3; and Definition of Chalcedon, 59, 64; and interpretation of Divine-Humanity, 23; Protestant, 206; royal ministry, 410
Church, 198, 207, 401, 409; and Ascension, 296-297; as Body of Christ, 205; and Mother of God, 202
Communicatio idiomatum (communication of properties, perichoresis), 28, 44, 71, 74, 209-210, 248, 256, 258-259, 261, 325

450

Index

Consciousness: Christ's divine consciousness, 229, 233-234, 236, 240-242, 250-251, 263, 265-266, 270, 277-279, 284-285, 313, 319-320, 355; Christ's human consciousness, 229, 233, 241-242, 262, 265, 270

Consciousness of self: in man, 231, 236, 262, 273-274

Creation of world, 119-121, 123-126, 130, 148, 158, 171, 197, 227, 344-345; as kenosis, 223; Six Days, 127-129, 133, 136, 157; and Third hypostasis, 129

Cross, 243, 257-258, 260-261, 273, 281, 286-288, 312-314, 338, 346, 352-354, 357, 364, 368-369, 373, 382, 402, 410, 416; and Holy Trinity, 371

Crucifixion, 31, 336, 353-354, 364, 371

Cyril of Alexandria, 8, 14, 15, 18, 19, 33, 34, 36, 37, 39-41, 45, 47-48, 50-51, 52, 55-56, 60, 73-74, 194, 208, 211, 218-219, 237, 256; Acacius, epistle to, 30-31; anti-Nestorianism, 22-23, 26, 29, 42; and Apollinarianism, 21-22; Chalcedon epistles, 57-59; christological definitions, 21, 23-26, 58; doctrine of Incarnation, 27; doctrine of Theotokos, 32n; and monophysitism, 28; polemic against Theodoret, 29-30; problem of Christ's passion, 31; terminological imprecision, 20, 32

Deification (theosis), 15, 38, 73, 138, 163, 198, 209-210, 225, 230, 242, 245, 249-250, 253, 280, 298, 334-335, 346, 358, 383; of Christ's human essence, 252, 256, 392; of humanity, 405; of world, 171

Deism, 158-159, 163

Descent from heaven, 214, 219, 224, 229, 253, 317, 386, 404

Descent into hell, 315, 376-377, 410

Diodore of Tarsus, 5, 18, 33, 36

Diophysitism, 35, 39, 53, 57, 74, 87

Dioscorus, 53, 57

Divine-Humanity, ix, xi, xiii-xv, 3-4, 16-17, 23, 28, 30, 41, 48-49, 69, 72-74, 83, 86, 94, 114-117, 136, 166, 173-174, 181, 183, 187-189, 202, 209-210, 233-234, 237-239, 241-242, 251, 253, 259, 269-270, 277-278, 303, 313, 317, 319-320, 331, 346, 396, 398, 400, 405; of Emmanuel, 256; and Eucharist, 404; name of Jesus, 247; origin of, viii

Divine-human (or theandric) energy, 72-73, 75, 80, 83-84, 86, 209, 248, 261

Divine Infant, 175, 202, 232, 234, 241, 247, 253-254, 262

Divine Maternity, 179

Divine Personality, 95-97, 102-103, 105

Divine Sonhood, 143-144, 233, 264-267, 278-279, 282, 285, 303, 309, 315, 342, 344

Divine world, 101, 103-104, 106-107, 111-113, 117, 126, 131, 162, 173, 174, 187, 197; and humanity, 136

Docetism, 4, 30, 33, 219, 236, 237, 254, 256, 292, 302-303

Dogmatics, 1-2

Dostoevsky, Fyodor: *Notes from Underground*, 296n

Dyothelitism (dogma of two wills and energies), 73-77, 80-87, 210, 224, 244-246

Ebionism, 219

Ebionites, 4, 257

Ecclesiastes, 132, 152

Ecumenical councils, 1, 12, 18, 46, 57, 194, 220, 283

Emmanuel, 233, 239, 255-256

Ephesus, Council of, 22, 41, 47, 51-53, 58

Eternal torments, 365

Eternity: and man, 135; and temporality, 131-133, 135, 139n

Enthronement of Christ, 416-420, 428-429, 438-440; and Apocalypse, 421-424

Eucharist, 269, 334, 348, 371n, 387n, 389, 394n, 395-396, 398, 403, 406-407, 436; and Divine-Humanity, 404

Eutyches, 27, 28, 51-53, 57, 288

Eutychianism, 25, 32, 51, 57

Eve, 149-151, 179, 200-201, 345

Faith, 279
Fall, 6, 145-146, 149, 151, 169-171, 181, 200-201, 204, 286, 290-291, 295-296, 298, 300, 344-346, 358, 379, 381; and the Incarnation, 172, 175, 177; and nature, 152-154
Father, God the, 56, 108, 110, 114-116, 139-140, 175-177, 217, 229, 260, 264-266, 268-269, 279, 285, 304-305, 309-310, 314, 317-319, 346, 356, 401, 405, 441; begetting the Son, 98-100, 111, 129, 225-226, 353; obedience of Christ, 306-307; prayer to, 218, 254-255, 279-281; revelation of, 166-167, 197, 225; sending of the Son, 281-284, 351, 353, 370, 402; sitting at right hand of, 389-395, 397, 399-400, 408-409, 440
Feasts, 407-408
Fedorov, Nikolai, 437
Female principle, 115, 140
Feofan, Bishop, 215n, 216
Fichte, 90-91, 96
Filaret, Metropolitan, 353-354, 356
Filioque: and kenosis, 226n
Flavian, Archbishop, 51-53
Flesh, 213-214, 229, 252; of Christ, 236, 257, 259, 286-287; weakness of, 243
Florensky, Pavel, x
Form of a servant, 215-217, 224, 230, 279, 295, 318. *See also* kenosis
Freedom, 142-143, 147, 161-162, 349-351, 370, 383, 436-437; of Adam, 294-295, 346; of Christ, 295, 300; of God, 222-223; of the Lord, 215; and Mother of God, 179

Gaianos of Alexandria, 288
Gethsemane, 240, 242-243, 254, 281, 286, 306, 310, 312, 353-355, 360, 364, 367-368; the agony, 356-359
Glorification, xii, 111, 227, 401, 409; of Christ, 217, 238-239, 242, 253, 309, 318-320, 339-341, 358, 379-383, 386, 390-391, 393, 397, 400, 402-403, 405, 407-408, 410, 413, 417, 420, 435, 440; of Mother of God, 202
Glory, 111, 154, 165n, 217, 224, 227, 236, 251, 286, 339-340, 380, 392, 396-397, 405, 409; and Sophia, 107-110, 117, 153, 167-168
Gnapheus, Peter, 260
God: as Absolute, 121-122, 128-130, 135, 157-159, 191, 222, 245, 260, 371; as Creator, 121, 124, 126-130, 135, 159-160, 163-164, 171, 182, 191-192, 213-214, 217, 222-223, 227, 242, 256, 345, 356, 358, 371, 384, 404; interaction with world, 160-161; and temporality, 157-158, 161
God-Man, dogma of, 182, 187-189, 196, 210, 221, 235, 278
Golgotha, 79, 232, 242-243, 254, 260, 312, 336, 340-342, 355, 357, 360, 364, 367-369, 371, 403, 407
Gospels: doctrine of Christ, 282-283; figure of Christ, 275-278
Grace, 161-163, 168, 178, 362-363, 398
Gregory of Nyssa, 8, 12, 13, 183, 343
Gregory the Theologian, 13, 24, 298, 343

Hartmann, Eduard von, 148
Hegel, 97, 108n, 120, 134
High-priestly ministry, xi, 333-336, 339-342, 346, 354, 362-363, 377, 381, 384, 387, 390, 401-404, 409-411, 418-421; and glorification, 382; and resurrection, 379
Hilary of Poitiers, 211; notion of kenosis, 219
Hinduism, 89, 134
Holy Grail, 406
Holy Spirit, 100-101, 110, 114-116, 128, 139, 165, 167, 175, 178, 190, 205, 213-214, 225-226, 229, 260, 283, 293, 304-305, 318, 329, 331, 340, 353, 370, 380, 398, 403, 405, 430-431; and Ascension, 389-390; and baptism of Christ, 264, 337; relation with Christ, 307-309; and creation of the world, 129; and the Incarnation, 176-177; kenosis of, 129-130, 314-315; overshadowing of Virgin Mary, 178-179, 200-201, 307; Pentecost, 401; and Transfiguration, 341; and resurrection, 402
Holy Trinity, 76, 95, 97-99, 103, 105-108,

Index

123, 128, 138, 166-167, 174, 175, 181, 186, 188-189, 193, 207, 221, 228-229, 241, 264, 282, 300, 306-307, 354, 363-364, 368, 370-371, 390, 393, 396, 399, 404-405, 420, 440; economic, 190-192, 222-223, 227, 305, 309, 381; hierarchism of, 304-305; and high-priestly ministry, 336; immanent, 190-191, 222, 227, 260, 304-305, 309, 315, 326, 372, 381; and Incarnation, 192; and kenosis, 226-227; and prophetic ministry of Christ, 324-326; and Sophia, 110-111, 136; *taxis* of, 190
Homoousianism, 282
Humanity (man), 137, 144-145, 173; of Christ, 180, 185-186, 188-189, 200, 202, 204-205, 207, 217, 230, 235, 239-240, 252, 254, 256-257, 262, 270-271, 273-279, 291, 293-295-296, 299-300, 310, 312-313, 320, 348, 354-355, 358, 367, 374, 379, 381, 405, 409; consciousness of self, 231, 236, 262; creative activity of, 437-438; as creaturely Sophia, 174, 187, 230; and Divine world, 136; and the Fall, 146, 149-150, 152-153; glorification of, 400; as god-man, 138, 230; image of God, 139-140, 146, 150-151, 164-165, 230; likeness of God, 147; and nature, 151-156; sophianicity of, 150; and spiritual being, 230-231
Humiliation of the Lord, 214-215, 217-220, 223-224, 231, 237, 240, 249, 255, 257, 259, 263, 271, 273, 279-280, 283, 301, 314-316, 318, 325, 328, 351, 380, 382, 403, 440. *See also* kenosis

Icons, 88, 246; of Christ, 271n; of crucifixion, 315n
Ignorance: of Christ, 253, 301-303, 355; of Second Coming, 303
Immaculate Conception, 178n, 206, 289
Image of God, 34, 88, 91, 111-112, 135, 138-141, 146, 150-151, 163-165, 174, 185, 187, 199, 230, 233, 235, 238, 249, 270; and creation, 143; and likeness, 147-149; and natural world, 144; in Sophia, 144
Immortality, 384-385, 433

Impassibility, 258-261
Incarnation, ix, xi, 4, 8-9, 16-17, 21, 25, 26-27, 48, 79, 88, 133, 140, 149, 168-170, 173, 175, 180, 184-186, 189, 193, 196-201, 206, 208, 213, 215, 223, 232, 236, 240, 242, 247, 256-257, 260, 270, 282-283, 288, 293, 302-303, 312, 325-326, 334, 336-337, 344-346, 348-349, 372, 395, 397, 398, 406-407, 431, 437; and Ascension, 393, 405; and enthronement, 416; and the Fall, 172, 177; and the Holy Spirit, 176; and the Holy Trinity, 192; and kenosis, 211, 219, 254, 351; ontological foundations, 171; and salvation, 172; and Sophia, 203; and Virgin Mary, 178, 202
In-humanization, 175, 185, 232, 240, 289, 300, 306-307, 347-348, 373, 380, 402, 404, 433
In-hypostatization, 7, 64-71, 183-186
Irenaeus, 3, 8
Islam, 159

Jansenism, 159
Jesus, 37-38, 73, 198, 207, 230, 241, 249, 252, 254, 260, 262, 265; divine consciousness in, 262, 264; name of, 246-247; personal consciousness, 264; as prophet, 250; prayer, 254
Joachim of Fiore, 97
John of Antioch, 22, 47, 58
John of Damascus, viii, 7, 15, 64, 66n, 71-74, 82, 87, 103, 184, 209, 245n, 256, 258-259, 261n, 289, 292, 343, 393; and notion of deification, 210; and theandric principle, 248
John the Forerunner, 299, 308, 326, 329, 332, 346, 376n
Joseph, 180, 247
Julian of Halicarnassus, 288

Kant, x, 93, 123, 161
Kataphatic theology, 112, 112n
Kenosis, xi-xii, 31, 45-46, 54, 99, 128, 134, 143, 147, 177, 211, 215-217, 219, 221, 223-225, 228, 231-232, 235-238, 240, 242, 244, 247n, 249, 251, 253-255, 257, 259,

453

262-265, 273, 280, 283-284, 287, 300-303, 305-307, 309-310, 312-313, 316-320, 325, 328, 353, 355, 373, 379, 381, 401, 404, 407, 413, 418, 440; and Ascension, 408; bibliography, 220; and Chalcedonian dogma, 239; of the Father, 129; and Filioque, 226n; and glorification, 382; of Holy Spirit, 129-130, 314-315; of Holy Trinity, 371; and the Incarnation, 211, 219, 254; and sleep of Jesus, 285; and Sophia, 220

Kingdom of God (of Heaven), 326, 339-340, 387, 411, 417, 420

Lamb of God, 99, 113, 168, 177, 227, 263, 319, 335n, 346, 349-350, 357, 397; and Divine-Humanity, 115; enthronement of, 421, 423; sacrifice of, 129, 169, 171, 336, 338, 344, 354, 368-369, 380; and Sophia, 111

Last Discourse, 319, 389, 400-401

Last Judgment, 347, 358, 359, 398, 409, 427, 429, 431-432, 440

Last Supper, 339-340, 354, 376, 408

Lazarus, 252-253, 254

Leibniz, 78, 91

Leo the Great, 45, 73, 239; Tome, 43-44, 51, 53-60

Leontiev, Konstantin, 155

Leontius of Byzantium, 7, 63, 72-74; and in-hypostatization, 64-71

Lermontov, Mikhail, 155n

Likeness of God, 147-149, 363

Logos, 16-17, 27, 28, 35, 68, 81, 113-115, 140, 166-167, 174, 176-177, 180, 182, 184-186, 188-189, 191, 193, 196-203, 218, 224-229, 232, 234-236, 242, 245, 250, 254-255, 262, 276, 288, 300, 301, 324, 328, 330, 331, 344, 352, 355, 358, 380, 390, 404; in Gospel of John, 278-279; inhumanization of, 175, 347; as Jesus, 198; and Sophia, 108, 110, 136, 138

Love: in divine life, 104-106, 352, 371; of Father and Son, 99-100, 353, 357, 370; God's love for man, 357, 360; God's love for the world, 120, 122, 129-130,

134, 171-172, 260, 265-266, 344, 352, 363, 370, 398

Luther, Martin, 232n, 251n, 396

Macarius of Antioch, 83, 86

Makarii, Metropolitan, 410

Male principle, 115, 140

Marcian, Emperor, 59

Mariology, 200

Maximus the Confessor, viii, 75, 78, 245n; divine-human energy, 80; and dyothelitism, 81-82; logology, 126n; and monothelitic dispute, 76-77

Melchisedec, 255, 335, 341-342

Miracles, 237, 240, 410; and prophetic ministry, 332-333

Molinism, 159

Monophysitism, 7, 8, 14, 20, 27, 28, 32, 33, 52, 55-57, 62-63, 64, 71, 73, 74, 75, 77, 80, 87, 208, 210, 218, 219, 236, 248, 256

Monothelites, 86

Monothelitism, 74-77, 82-84, 87, 246

Mother of God (Virgin Mary), 4, 14, 16, 52, 68, 115, 140, 176-177, 193, 199, 206, 271, 289-290, 299, 314, 325, 401, 405; ascension of, 397n, 406n; and creaturely Sophia, 200-203, 205-206; dormition, 379n; and Incarnation, 178-179; in Nicene Creed, 214; and Old Testament church, 178; Overshadowing of, 179, 181, 200-201, 307; Protestantism's attitude, 200; sophianicity of, 201; Theotokos, 22-23, 32n, 39, 40-41, 200, 202, 205; veneration of, 202, 206; virginal conception, 180-181, 201

Nature, 151-155; as fallen Sophia, 156

Natures of Christ, viii, 5-6, 15, 16-17, 19, 52-55, 59-60, 71, 74-75, 77, 81, 85, 87, 196, 200, 202, 209-210, 234, 238-239, 246, 249, 251, 253, 278, 285; glorification at right hand of Father, 399; union of, 7, 18, 21, 25-26, 28, 33, 35, 37-38, 43, 58, 72, 183, 193-195, 198-199,

207-208, 211, 217, 219, 235-236, 243-244, 248, 252, 256, 258-259, 261-262
Nestorianism, 5, 20, 22, 57, 59, 63, 64, 68, 71, 194
Nestorius, 18, 22, 24, 26-29, 32n, 33, 39, 50, 57, 74-75; *The Bazaar of Heracleides*, 40n, 42-44, 47, 51, 54-55; kenosis, 45-46; prosopon, notion of, 41-47, 55; terminological problem of Theotokos, 40-41;
Nicaeno-Constantinopolitan Creed, Nicene Council, 3, 282
Nicene Creed, 18, 170, 172, 214
Nothing, 124-125, 127, 147-148
Novatian, 53

Obedience of Christ, 306-307, 310-312, 342, 352-353, 355, 364, 368, 373, 380, 391, 418
Old Testament church, 166-167, 199; and Virgin Mary, 178
Origen, 16, 343
Original sin, 150, 177-178, 181, 199, 200, 205, 243, 298, 301, 347, 383
Ousia, Divine, 102-105

Palamas, Gregory, 116, 122n
Paganism, 164-165
Pantheism, 121, 134
Panentheism, 121
Passion, 260-261, 340, 366, 369, 416
Patripassianism, 260
Paul, Apostle, 144, 165, 187, 215, 392, 439; on resurrection, 385
Paul of Samosata, 4, 36, 219
Pentecost, 200, 307, 390; and Ascension, 401
Peter, Apostle, 165, 390, 402; confession of, 266, 268, 280
Philippians 2:6-8: 214-217, 295, 312, 318
Plato: *ekmageion*, 127; *Phaedo*, 144; *Timaeus*, 125
Porrée, Gilbert de la, 97
Prayer: high-priestly, 318-319, 335, 379; of Son to the Father, 218, 254-255, 279-281, 352-356, 379
Predestination, 349

Prophecy, 321-323, 329-331; of Christ, 277, 331-332; of Daniel, 323
Prophetic ministry, xi, 250, 321-322, 324-328, 330, 337, 340, 387, 409-411, 417, 419, 429, 435; and Israel, 342; and miracles, 332-333
Prosopon, 41-43
Protestantism: Christology, 206; Eucharistic sacrifice, 407; and Mother of God, 200-201
Providence, 149, 160, 162, 175, 190, 193, 222, 227-228, 257, 371, 432, 436
Pseudo-Dionysius, viii, 125; divine-human (or theandric) energy, 72-73, 75, 80, 83-84, 86, 209
Pyrrho, 75, 77

Redemption, 169-170, 180, 206, 242, 282, 333-334, 343-347, 349-350, 352-354, 357, 359, 362-365, 368, 371-372, 374, 377, 381, 383, 424
Relics, 378
Renouvier, Charles, 148
Resurrection, 133, 237, 251, 255, 308, 316-320, 343, 354, 382-391, 393, 395, 402, 410, 416-418, 432, 439; and high-priestly ministry, 379; universal, 433-434, 438
Royal ministry, xi, 377, 389-390, 410-411, 430, 437, 441; and Ascension, 435; enthronement, 416-423, 428-429, 434, 438-440; entry into Jerusalem, 413-417
Royal priesthood, 429

Sacrifice: of Lamb of God, 129, 336, 338, 344; redemptive, 343-344, 353-354, 357, 359, 362, 369, 374, 377
Salvation, xiii, 151, 169-170, 362-363, 371, 403, 405, 436; and the Incarnation, 172
Schelling, 97, 120, 134
Schopenhauer, 78, 119, 148
Second Coming, 253, 303, 400, 406, 409, 419, 434, 436-437, 439-440
Severus, 14
Sermon on the Mount, 324, 327

Seventh Ecumenical Council, 211, 246; veneration of icons, 88
Sex, 299
Sixth Ecumenical Council, 83, 85, 87-88, 195, 199, 210, 224, 244, 248, 301
Sobornost: and divine love, 104
Socinus, 343, 357, 362
Solovyov, Vladimir, viii, x, 384; *Lectures on Divine Humanity*, 114n
Son of God, 43, 54-55, 113-114, 116, 139, 143, 166, 168, 175-177, 179-182, 190, 217, 221, 229, 233-234, 243, 252, 257, 260, 264-270, 274-275, 280-282, 285, 298-299, 302, 304-305, 351, 354, 363-364, 372, 381, 441; begottenness, 97-100, 111, 129, 225-226, 353; His coming into the world, 169; and Sophia, 111
Son of Man, 43, 113, 151, 179-180, 182, 187, 221, 233-234, 252-253, 269, 285, 300, 302-303, 311, 316, 338-339, 359, 374, 377, 381, 398-399, 426; Daniel's vision, 168, 267; meaning of, 267-268, 270; and sons of men, 274
Sophia, creaturely, ix, xi, 126, 131, 144, 146, 148, 153, 159-161, 163, 165n, 173-174, 187, 197, 199, 220, 230, 396-397; and Christ, 203, 225; and Mother of God, 200-203, 205-206
Sophia, Divine, ix, xi, 117, 119, 126-127, 131, 144-145, 154, 159-160, 163, 165, 171, 176, 197-199, 206, 220, 228, 230, 238, 380, 392, 396-397, 400; and Christ, 203; as Divine eternity, 133; as Divine-Humanity, 187; and Divine Spirit, 174; as Divine world, 103, 106-108, 112-113, 136, 139; as Glory, 107-110, 112, 153, 167-168, 224; as God's nature, 102-105, 108; and Holy Trinity, 110-111; as humanity, 113-114; icon of, 108n; and Logos, 108, 136, 138; love for God, 105-106; and nature, 151, 153; Old Testament revelation of, 167-168; as pan-organism of ideas, 113; and sacrifice of the Lamb, 111; and the Son, 111; as Wisdom of God, 107-109
Sophianicity, 145, 174, 197, 199, 220, 400; of world, 117, 153, 161, 164; and man, 150, 173, 298; of Mother of God, 201, 203, 205
Sophianization, 147, 200, 396; of man, 225
Sophronius, 75
Spatiality, 132n
Spinoza, 161
Spirit, creaturely, 91-93
Spirit, personal, 89-91
Struggle: of Christ, 286-287, 297
Subordinationism, 304-307, 391
Suffering: of God, 257-261, 372

Tareev, Mikhail, 216n
Temporality (time): and eternity, 131-133, 135, 139n, 233; and God's life, 134-135, 157, 161, 197-198; and humanity, 232-233
Temptation: of Adam, 295, 297; of Christ, 291-294, 296-301, 308, 360
Tertullian, 53, 138
Theodore of Mopsuestia, 5, 18, 33, 34, 38-41, 44; notion of goodwill, 37; notion of inhabitation, 36
Theodoret, 18, 22, 26, 29-31, 33, 50-51, 74; *Eranistes*, 48-49; and Nestorius, 47
Theopaschism, 257, 260, 372
Tiamat, 125
Tichonius, 438
Transfiguration, 240, 254, 266, 285, 337, 339-340, 342, 354, 413; and the Holy Spirit, 341
Triduum (three days in the grave), 315-316; descent into hell, 315, 376-377
Trinitarian terminology, 3-4

Virginal conception, 180-181, 201
Vrubel', Mikhail, 155n

World: becoming of, 134, 160; God's love for, 120, 122, 129-130, 134, 171-172; and grace, 161; and the Incarnation, 172; indestructibility of, 148-149; and Sophia, 160; sophianicity of, 161; structure of, 163

Zenkovsky, V. V., 153

www.ingramcontent.com/pod-product-compliance
Lightning Source LLC
Chambersburg PA
CBHW021845300426
44115CB00005B/26